AND BOOK TRAINING PACKAG

ExamSim

Experience realistic, simulated exams on your own computer with Osborne's interactive ExamSim software. This computer-based test engine offers both standard and adaptive test modes, knowledge-based and product simulation questions like those found on the real exams, and review tools that help you study more efficiently. Intuitive controls allow you to move easily through the program: mark difficult or unanswered questions for further review and skip ahead, then assess your performance at the end.

Knowledge-based questions present challenging material in a multiple-choice format. Answer treatments not only explain why the correct options are right, they also tell you why the incorrect answers were wrong.

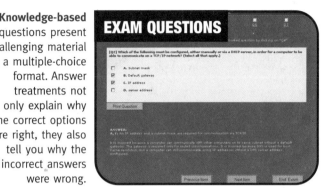

Additional CD-ROM Features

- Complete hyperlinked e-book for easy information access and self-paced study

- **DriveTime** audio tracks offer concise review of key exam topics for in the car or on the go!

System Requirements:

A PC running Internet Explorer version 5 or higher

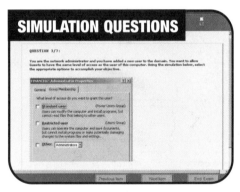

Realistic Windows 2000 product **simulation questions** test the skills you need to pass the exam—these questions look and feel like the simulation questions on the actual exam!

Detailed **Score Reports** provide score analysis and history to chart your progress and focus your study time.

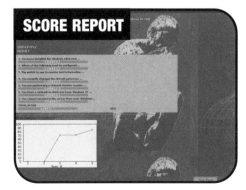

MCSE Windows 2000 Professional Study Guide

(Exam 70-210)

MICROSOFT CERTIFIED SYSTEMS ENGINEER

MCSE Windows® 2000 Professional Study Guide

(Exam 70-210)

Syngress Media, Inc.

Osborne McGraw-Hill

Berkeley New York St. Louis San Francisco Auckland Bogotá Hamburg London Madrid Mexico City
Milan Montreal New Delhi Panama City Paris São Paulo Singapore Sydney Tokyo Toronto

Osborne McGraw-Hill
2600 Tenth Street
Berkeley, California 94710
U.S.A.

For information on translations or book distributors outside the U.S.A., or to arrange
bulk purchase discounts for sales promotions, premiums, or fund-raisers, please contact
Osborne/**McGraw-Hill** at the above address.

MCSE Windows 2000 Professional Study Guide (Exam 70-210)

1234567890 PBT PBT 0198765432109

Book P/N 0-07-212387-7   and   CD P/N 0-07-212388-5
parts of
ISBN 0-07-212389-3

Publisher	**Editorial Assistant**	**Indexer**
Brandon A. Nordin	Tara Davis	Karin Arrigoni
Vice President and	**VP, Worldwide Business**	**Computer Designers**
Associate Publisher	**Development**	Lauren McCarthy
Scott Rogers	**Global Knowledge**	E. A. Pauw
	Richard Kristof	Dick Schwartz
Editorial Director		
Gareth Hancock	**Series Editors**	**Illustrators**
	Dr. Thomas W. Shinder	Robert Hansen
Associate Acquisitions Editor	Debra Littlejohn Shinder	Michael Mueller
Timothy Green		Beth Young
	Technical Editor	
Editorial Management	James Truscott	**Series Design**
Syngress Media, Inc.		Roberta Steele
	Copy Editor	
Project Editors	Beth Roberts	**Cover Design**
LeeAnn Pickrell		Greg Scott
Mark A. Listewnik	**Proofreader**	
	Linda Medoff	

This book was composed with Corel VENTURA ™ Publisher.

From Global Knowledge

At Global Knowledge we strive to support the multiplicity of learning styles required by our students to achieve success as technical professionals. In this series of books, it is our intention to offer the reader a valuable tool for successful completion of the MCSE Windows 2000 Certification Exams.

As the world's largest IT training company, Global Knowledge is uniquely positioned to offer these books. The expertise gained each year from providing instructor-led training to hundreds of thousands of students worldwide has been captured in book form to enhance your learning experience. We hope that the quality of these books demonstrates our commitment to your lifelong learning success. Whether you choose to learn through the written word, computer-based training, Web delivery, or instructor-led training, Global Knowledge is committed to providing you the very best in each of those categories. For those of you who know Global Knowledge, or those of you who have just found us for the first time, our goal is to be your lifelong competency partner.

Thank you for the opportunity to serve you. We look forward to serving your needs again in the future.

Warmest regards,

Duncan Anderson
President and Chief Operating Officer, Global Knowledge

The Global Knowledge Advantage

Global Knowledge has a global delivery system for its products and services. The company has 28 subsidiaries, and offers its programs through a total of 60+ locations. No other vendor can provide consistent services across a geographic area this large. Global Knowledge is the largest independent information technology education provider, offering programs on a variety of platforms. This enables our multi-platform and multi-national customers to obtain all of their programs from a single vendor. The company has developed the unique Competus™ Framework software tool and methodology which can quickly reconfigure courseware to the proficiency level of a student on an interactive basis. Combined with self-paced and on-line programs, this technology can reduce the time required for training by prescribing content in only the deficient skills areas. The company has fully automated every aspect of the education process, from registration and follow-up, to "just-in-time" production of courseware. Global Knowledge Network through its Enterprise Services Consultancy, can customize programs and products to suit the needs of an individual customer.

Global Knowledge Classroom Education Programs

The backbone of our delivery options is classroom-based education. Our modern, well-equipped facilities staffed with the finest instructors offer programs in a wide variety of information technology topics, many of which lead to professional certifications.

Custom Learning Solutions

This delivery option has been created for companies and governments that value customized learning solutions. For them, our consultancy-based approach of developing targeted education solutions is most effective at helping them meet specific objectives.

Self-Paced and Multimedia Products

This delivery option offers self-paced program titles in interactive CD-ROM, videotape and audio tape programs. In addition, we offer custom development of interactive multimedia courseware to customers and partners. Call us at 1-888-427-4228.

Electronic Delivery of Training

Our network-based training service delivers efficient competency-based, interactive training via the World Wide Web and organizational intranets. This leading-edge delivery option provides a custom learning path and "just-in-time" training for maximum convenience to students.

ARG

American Research Group (ARG), a wholly-owned subsidiary of Global Knowledge, one of the largest worldwide training partners of Cisco Systems, offers a wide range of internetworking, LAN/WAN, Bay Networks, FORE Systems, IBM, and UNIX courses. ARG offers hands on network training in both instructor-led classes and self-paced PC-based training.

Global Knowledge Courses Available

Network Fundamentals
- Understanding Computer Networks
- Telecommunications Fundamentals I
- Telecommunications Fundamentals II
- Understanding Networking Fundamentals
- Implementing Computer Telephony Integration
- Introduction to Voice Over IP
- Introduction to Wide Area Networking
- Cabling Voice and Data Networks
- Introduction to LAN/WAN protocols
- Virtual Private Networks
- ATM Essentials

Network Security & Management
- Troubleshooting TCP/IP Networks
- Network Management
- Network Troubleshooting
- IP Address Management
- Network Security Administration
- Web Security
- Implementing UNIX Security
- Managing Cisco Network Security
- Windows NT 4.0 Security

IT Professional Skills
- Project Management for IT Professionals
- Advanced Project Management for IT Professionals
- Survival Skills for the New IT Manager
- Making IT Teams Work

LAN/WAN Internetworking
- Frame Relay Internetworking
- Implementing T1/T3 Services
- Understanding Digital Subscriber Line (xDSL)
- Internetworking with Routers and Switches
- Advanced Routing and Switching
- Multi-Layer Switching and Wire-Speed Routing
- Internetworking with TCP/IP
- ATM Internetworking
- OSPF Design and Configuration
- Border Gateway Protocol (BGP) Configuration

Authorized Vendor Training
Cisco Systems
- Introduction to Cisco Router Configuration
- Advanced Cisco Router Configuration
- Installation and Maintenance of Cisco Routers
- Cisco Internetwork Troubleshooting
- Cisco Internetwork Design
- Cisco Routers and LAN Switches
- Catalyst 5000 Series Configuration
- Cisco LAN Switch Configuration
- Managing Cisco Switched Internetworks
- Configuring, Monitoring, and Troubleshooting Dial-Up Services
- Cisco AS5200 Installation and Configuration
- Cisco Campus ATM Solutions

Bay Networks
- Bay Networks Accelerated Router Configuration
- Bay Networks Advanced IP Routing
- Bay Networks Hub Connectivity
- Bay Networks Accelar 1xxx Installation and Basic Configuration
- Bay Networks Centillion Switching

FORE Systems
- FORE ATM Enterprise Core Products
- FORE ATM Enterprise Edge Products
- FORE ATM Theory
- FORE LAN Certification

Operating Systems & Programming
Microsoft
- Introduction to Windows NT
- Microsoft Networking Essentials
- Windows NT 4.0 Workstation
- Windows NT 4.0 Server
- Advanced Windows NT 4.0 Server
- Windows NT Networking with TCP/IP
- Introduction to Microsoft Web Tools
- Windows NT Troubleshooting
- Windows Registry Configuration

UNIX
- UNIX Level I
- UNIX Level II
- Essentials of UNIX and NT Integration

Programming
- Introduction to JavaScript
- Java Programming
- PERL Programming
- Advanced PERL with CGI for the Web

Web Site Management & Development
- Building a Web Site
- Web Site Management and Performance
- Web Development Fundamentals

High Speed Networking
- Essentials of Wide Area Networking
- Integrating ISDN
- Fiber Optic Network Design
- Fiber Optic Network Installation
- Migrating to High Performance Ethernet

DIGITAL UNIX
- UNIX Utilities and Commands
- DIGITAL UNIX v4.0 System Administration
- DIGITAL UNIX v4.0 (TCP/IP) Network Management
- AdvFS, LSM, and RAID Configuration and Management
- DIGITAL UNIX TruCluster Software Configuration and Management
- UNIX Shell Programming Featuring Kornshell
- DIGITAL UNIX v4.0 Security Management
- DIGITAL UNIX v4.0 Performance Management
- DIGITAL UNIX v4.0 Intervals Overview

DIGITAL OpenVMS
- OpenVMS Skills for Users
- OpenVMS System and Network Node Management I
- OpenVMS System and Network Node Management II
- OpenVMS System and Network Node Management III
- OpenVMS System and Network Node Operations
- OpenVMS for Programmers
- OpenVMS System Troubleshooting for Systems Managers
- Configuring and Managing Complex VMScluster Systems
- Utilizing OpenVMS Features from C
- OpenVMS Performance Management
- Managing DEC TCP/IP Services for OpenVMS
- Programming in C

Hardware Courses
- AlphaServer 1000/1000A Installation, Configuration and Maintenance
- AlphaServer 2100 Server Maintenance
- AlphaServer 4100, Troubleshooting Techniques and Problem Solving

Syngress Media

Syngress Media creates books and software for Information Technology professionals seeking skill enhancement and career advancement. Its products are designed to comply with vendor and industry standard course curricula and are optimized for certification exam preparation. You can contact Syngress via the Web at www.syngress.com.

Contributors

Pawan K. Bhardwaj (MCSE, MCP+I, CCNA) has spent 13 years in the IT industry working at various systems and network-support levels. He has been involved in designing and implementing LAN and WAN solutions for several small and medium sized companies. He also taught MCSE classes for a year in India before coming to the U.S.

He is currently working as a Windows NT Consultant with a turnkey solution provider in New Jersey. He can be reached at pawan_bhardwaj@hotmail.com.

Paul J. Edwards is the president and sole full-time employee of NetSys, a Milford, Connecticut-based network consulting practice. Currently, he spends most of his time tutoring students in Windows NT and Windows 2000. He achieved his MCSE and CCNA certifications through self-study and hands-on experience. He did his undergraduate work in accounting and worked as a credit manager for over 15 years. He states that being a father of three children and husband to a most loving and supportive wife is one of the keys to his success. He may be reached at pedwards@flaghouse.com.

Alfred Gattenby (MCSE+I, CNE, MCPSB, MCT, A+, CCNA) has worked for the U.S. Navy full time for the past 13 years. Al specializes in Exchange Server roll outs, Terminal Server projects, and integrating technologies. Recently, he participated in a ground up installation for the Navy's newest hospital in Portsmouth, Virginia, and in the migration of over 5,000 Navy e-mail accounts from a Unix-based mail platform to Exchange.

Al lives and works in Virginia Beach, Virginia, where you can find him training sailors for FCTCLANT, Damneck, Virginia. He teaches two courses, Information System Administration and Advanced Network Analyst.

Chris Thi Nguyen is a research analyst with Killer Apps, Inc. and Assistant News Editor for *Windows 2000 Magazine*. His specialty areas are user interfaces, knowledge management applications, collaboration applications, and emergent networking technologies. He has written for *Windows 2000 Magazine* on real-time community applications, Total Cost of Ownership studies, and new network-based storage solutions. He received a bachelor's degree in Philosophy from Harvard University.

Chris is currently writing technology white papers for a variety of enterprises.

Erik Sojka (MCSE) is a system administrator and trainer currently working for a major software company. He has a B.S. in Information Science and Technology from Drexel University.

Barrie Sosinsky is currently the Research Editor for *Windows 2000 Magazine*, and served as News Editor from 1998-1999. His Industry Trends column appears in the *Windows 2000 Magazine*, and he is a frequent contributor to the Windows 2000 Magazine Web site (www.win2000mag.com) where a body of his news and analysis may be found. In total, he has written over 300 magazine articles for a variety of publications on topics as diverse as operating systems, hardware, application software, databases, collaboration and groupware, and the Internet. His consulting company, Sosinsky and Associates (Medfield, Massachusetts) does industry research for companies such as EMC, Data Return and Anysoft.

Barrie is a long-time book author who has been lead author on over 25 book titles and a contributor to more than a dozen others. His last book was *Teach Yourself Windows 2000 in 24 Hours* from Sams Publishing (Macmillan). Other books have included *The Windows NT 4 Answer Book* (Wiley), *The Warp Book* (Prima), *The BackOffice Bible* (IDG), *Building Visual FoxPro 5 Applications* (IDG), *The Web Page Recipe Book* (PTR), and others.

His company specializes in custom software (database and Web related), training, and technical documentation. He can be contacted at barries@killerapps.com.

Cameron Wakefield (MCSD, MCP) is a Senior Software Engineer and has passed ten Microsoft Certification exams. He works at Computer Science Innovations, Inc. (www.csihq.com) in Melbourne, Florida, where he develops custom software solutions ranging from Satellite Communications to data-mining applications. His development work spans a broad spectrum including Visual C++, Visual Basic, COM, ADO, ASP, Delphi, CORBA, UNIX and others. He does some work through his own business, developing software for a Brazilian Hematology company and developing Business-to-Business Web applications. He also teaches Microsoft Certification courses for Herzing College (AATP) where he teaches in the MCSE and MCSD programs. His formal education was in Computer Science with a minor in Math at Rollins College. He lives in Rockledge, Florida, with his wife Lorraine and daughter Rachel. He also plays racquetball competitively in central Florida. He can be contacted at cwakefield@csihq.com.

Technical Editors

James Truscott (MCSE, MCP+I) is an instructor in the MCSE program at Eastfield College and the Dallas County Community College District. He is also Senior Instructor for the Cowell Corporation and is teaching the Windows 2000 track for CLC Corporation in Dallas, Texas.

He also serves as Webmaster for Cowell Corporation in Richardson, Texas, and does consulting services for several Dallas-based businesses. His passion for computers started back in the 1960 when he was a programmer for Bell Telephone. One of his current projects includes developing Web sites for his students.

D. Lynn White (MCPS, MCSE, MCT, MCP+Internet, CTT) is president of Independent Network Consultants, Inc. Lynn has more than 15 years of programming and networking experience. She has been a system manager in the mainframe environment as well as a software developer for a process control company. She is a technical author, editor, trainer and consultant in the field of networking and computer-related technologies. Lynn has been presenting mainframe, Microsoft official curriculum, and other operating systems and networking courses in and outside the United States for more than 13 years. Lynn is the Series Editor for Osborne/McGraw-Hill for both the Network+ and A+ Series. Her latest certification is the CTT (Certified Technical Trainer) by the Chauncey Group International. Lynn would like to extend thanks to her family and friends for always being there for her over the years.

Series Editors

Debra Littlejohn Shinder (MCSE, MCP+I, MCT) is an instructor in the AATP program at Eastfield College, Dallas County Community College District, where she has taught since 1992. She is Webmaster for the cities of Seagoville and Sunnyvale, Texas, as well as the family Web site at www.shinder.net. She and her husband, Dr. Thomas W. Shinder, provide consulting and technical support services to Dallas area organizations. She is also the proud mom of a daughter, Kristen, who is currently serving in the U.S. Navy in Italy, and a son, Kris, who is a high school chess champion. Deb has been a writer for most her life and has published numerous articles in both technical and non-technical fields. She can be contacted at mailto:deb@shinder.net.

Thomas W. Shinder, M.D. (MCSE, MCP+I, MCT) is a technology trainer and consultant in the Dallas-Ft. Worth metroplex. Dr. Shinder has consulted with major firms, including Xerox, Lucent Technologies, and FINA Oil, assisting in the development and implementation of IP-based communications strategies. Dr. Shinder attended medical school at the University of Illinois in Chicago and trained in neurology at the Oregon Health Sciences Center in Portland, Oregon. His fascination with interneuronal communication ultimately melded with his interest in internetworking and led him to focus on systems engineering. Tom works passionately with his beloved wife, Debra Shinder, to design elegant and cost-efficient solutions for small and medium-sized businesses based on Windows NT/2000 platforms.

ACKNOWLEDGMENTS

W e would like to thank the following people:

- Richard Kristof of Global Knowledge for championing the series and providing access to some great people and information.
- All the incredibly hard-working folks at Osborne/McGraw-Hill: Brandon Nordin, Scott Rogers, Gareth Hancock, and Tim Green for their help in launching a great series and being solid team players. In addition, Tara Davis and LeeAnn Pickrell for their help in fine-tuning the book.
- Monica Kilwine at Microsoft Corporation, for being patient and diligent in answering all our questions.

CONTENTS AT A GLANCE

XV

CONTENTS

11 Implementing, Managing, and Troubleshooting Network Protocols and Services **587**

PREFACE

This book's primary objective is to help you prepare for the MCSE "Installing, Configuring, and Administering Windows 2000 Professional" exam under the new Windows 2000 certification track. As the Microsoft program transitions from Windows NT 4.0, it will become increasingly important that current and aspiring IT professionals have multiple resources available to assist them in increasing their knowledge and building their skills.

At the time of publication, all the exam objectives have been posted on the Microsoft Web site and the beta exam process has been completed. Microsoft has announced its commitment to measuring real-world skills. This book is designed with that premise in mind; its authors have practical experience in the field, using the Windows 2000 operating systems in hands-on situations and have followed the development of the product since early beta versions.

Because the focus of the exams is on application and understanding, as opposed to memorization of facts, no book by itself can fully prepare you to obtain a passing score. It is essential that you work with the software to enhance your proficiency. Toward that end, this book includes many practical step-by-step exercises in each chapter that are designed to give you hands-on practice as well as guide you in truly learning Microsoft Windows 2000 Professional, not just learning *about* it.

In This Book

This book is organized in such a way as to serve as an in-depth review for the MCSE "Installing, Configuring, and Administering Microsoft Windows 2000 Professional" exam for both experienced Windows NT professionals and newcomers to Microsoft networking technologies. Each chapter covers a major aspect of the exam, with an emphasis on the "why" as well as the "how to" of working with and supporting Windows 2000 as a network administrator or engineer.

About the CD

The CD-ROM contains the CertTrainer software. CertTrainer comes complete with ExamSim, Skill Assessment tests, CertCam movie clips, the e-book (electronic version of the book), and Drive Time. CertTrainer is easy to install on any Windows 98/NT/2000 computer and must be installed to access these features. You may, however, browse the e-book directly from the CD without installation. For more information on the CD-ROM, please see Appendix A.

In Every Chapter

We've created a set of chapter components that call your attention to important items, reinforce important points, and provide helpful exam-taking hints. Take a look at what you'll find in every chapter:

■ Every chapter begins with the **Certification Objectives**—what you need to know in order to pass the section on the exam dealing with the chapter topic. The Objective headings identify the objectives within the chapter, so you'll always know an objective when you see it!

■ **Exam Watch** notes call attention to information about, and potential pitfalls in, the exam. These helpful hints are written by authors who have taken the exams and received their certification—who better to tell you what to worry about? They know what you're about to go through!

■ **Practice Exercises** are interspersed throughout the chapters. These are step-by-step exercises that allow you to get the hands-on experience you need in order to pass the exams. They help you master skills that are likely to be an area of focus on the exam. Don't just read through the exercises; they are hands-on practice that you should be comfortable completing. Learning by doing is an effective way to increase your competency with a product. The practical exercises will be very helpful for any simulation exercises you may encounter on the MCSE "Installing, Configuring, and Administering Microsoft Windows 2000 Professional" exam.

■ The **CertCam** icon that appears in many of the exercises indicates that the exercise is presented in .avi format on the accompanying CD-ROM. These .avi clips walk you step-by-step through various system configurations and are narrated by Thomas W. Shinder, M.D., MCSE.

on the
! o b

- **On the Job** notes describe the issues that come up most often in real-world settings. They provide a valuable perspective on certification- and product-related topics. They point out common mistakes and address questions that have arisen from on the job discussions and experience.

- **From the Classroom** sidebars describe the issues that come up most often in the training classroom setting. These sidebars highlight some of the most common and confusing problems that students encounter when taking a live Windows 2000 training course. You can get a leg up on those difficult to understand subjects by focusing extra attention on these sidebars.

- **Scenario and Solutions** sections lay out potential problems and solutions in a quick-to-read format:

SCENARIO & SOLUTION

Is Active Directory scalable?	Yes! Unlike the Windows NT security database, which is limited to approximately 40,000 objects, Active Directory supports literally millions of objects.
Is Active Directory compatible with other LDAP directory services?	Yes! Active Directory can share information with other directory services that support LDAP versions 2 and 3, such as Novell's NDS.

- The **Certification Summary** is a succinct review of the chapter and a restatement of salient points regarding the exam.

✓ - The **Two-Minute Drill** at the end of every chapter is a checklist of the main points of the chapter. It can be used for last-minute review.

Q&A - The **Self Test** offers questions similar to those found on the certification exams. The answers to these questions, as well as explanations of the answers, can be found at the end of each chapter. By taking the Self Test after completing each chapter, you'll reinforce what you've learned from that chapter while becoming familiar with the structure of the exam questions.

- The **Lab Question** at the end of the Self Test section offers a unique and challenging question format that requires the reader to understand multiple chapter concepts to answer correctly. These questions are more complex, and more comprehensive than the other questions, as they test your ability to take all the knowledge you have gained from reading the chapter and apply it to complicated, real-world situations. These questions are aimed to be more difficult than what you will find on the exam. If you can answer these questions, you have proven that you know the subject!

The Global Knowledge Web Site

Check out the Web site. Global Knowledge invites you to become an active member of the Access Global Web site. This site is an online mall and an information repository that you'll find invaluable. You can access many types of products to assist you in your preparation for the exams, and you'll be able to participate in forums, online discussions, and threaded discussions. No other book brings you unlimited access to such a resource. You'll find more information about this site in Appendix B.

Some Pointers

Once you've finished reading this book, set aside some time to do a thorough review. You might want to return to the book several times and make use of all the methods it offers for reviewing the material:

1. *Re-read all the Two-Minute Drills,* or have someone quiz you. You also can use the drills as a way to do a quick cram before the exam. You might want to make some flash cards out of 3 x 5 index cards that have the Two-Minute Drill material on them.

2. *Re-read all the Exam Watch notes.* Remember that these notes are written by authors who have taken the exam and passed. They know what you should expect—and what you should be on the lookout for.

3. *Review all the S&S sections* for quick problem-solving.

4. *Re-take the Self Tests.* Taking the tests right after you've read the chapter is a good idea, because the questions help reinforce what you've just learned. However, it's an even better idea to go back later and do all the questions in the book in one sitting. Pretend that you're taking the live exam. (When you go through the questions the first time, you should mark your answers on a separate piece of paper. That way, you can run through the questions as many times as you need to until you feel comfortable with the material.)

5. *Complete the Exercises.* Did you do the exercises when you read through each chapter? If not, do them! These exercises are designed to cover exam topics, and there's no better way to get to know this material than by practicing. Be sure you understand why you are performing each step in each exercise. If there is something you are not clear on, re-read that section in the chapter.

INTRODUCTION

This book is designed to help you pass the MCSE "Installing, Configuring, and Administering Microsoft Windows 2000 Professional" exam. At the time this book was written, the exam objectives were posted on the Microsoft Web site, and the beta exams had been completed. We wrote this book to give you a complete and incisive review of all the important topics that are targeted for the exam. The information contained here will provide you with the required foundation of knowledge that will not only allow you to succeed in passing the MCSE "Installing, Configuring, and Administering Microsoft Windows 2000 Professional" exam, but will also make you a better Microsoft Certified Systems Engineer.

The following table details the exams required for the Windows 2000 Certification track; however, the nature of the Information Technology industry is changing rapidly, and the requirements and specifications for certification can change just as quickly without notice. Microsoft expects you to regularly visit their Web site at www.microsoft.com/mcp/certstep/mcse.htm to get the most up to date information on the entire MCSE program.

Core Exams		
Candidates Who Have *Not* Already Passed Windows NT 4.0 Exams All Four of the Following Core Exams Are Required:	OR	Candidates Who Have Passed Three Windows NT 4.0 Exams (Exams 70-067, 70-068, and 70-073) Instead of the 4 Core Exams on Left, You May Take:
Exam 70-210: Installing, Configuring and Administering Microsoft® Windows® 2000 Professional		Exam 70-240: Microsoft® Windows® 2000 Accelerated Exam for MCPs Certified on Microsoft® Windows NT® 4.0. The accelerated exam will be available until December 31, 2001. It covers the core competencies of exams 70-210, 70-215, 70-216, and 70-217.

Core Exams
Exam 70-215: Installing, Configuring and Administering Microsoft® Windows® 2000 Server
Exam 70-216: Implementing and Administering a Microsoft® Windows® 2000 Network Infrastructure
Exam 70-217: Implementing and Administering a Microsoft® Windows® 2000 Directory Services Infrastructure
PLUS – All Candidates – 1 of the Following Core Exams Required:
*****Exam 70-219**: Designing a Microsoft® Windows® 2000 Directory Services Infrastructure
*****Exam 70-220**: Designing Security for a Microsoft® Windows® 2000 Network
*****Exam 70-221**: Designing a Microsoft® Windows® 2000 Network Infrastructure
PLUS – All Candidates – 2 Elective Exams Required:
Any current MCSE electives when the Windows 2000 exams listed above are released in their live versions. **Electives scheduled for retirement will not be considered current.** Selected third-party certifications that focus on interoperability will be accepted as an alternative to one elective exam.
*****Exam 70-219**: Designing a Microsoft® Windows® 2000 Directory Services Infrastructure
*****Exam 70-220**: Designing Security for a Microsoft® Windows® 2000 Network
*****Exam 70-221**: Designing a Microsoft® Windows® 2000 Network Infrastructure
*****Exam 70-222**: Upgrading from Microsoft® Windows® NT 4.0 to Microsoft® Windows® 2000
** Note that some of the Windows 2000 core exams can be used as elective exams as well. An exam that is used to meet the design requirement cannot also count as an elective. Each exam can only be counted once in the Windows 2000 Certification.

Let's look at two scenarios. The first applies to the person who has already taken the Windows NT 4.0 Server (70-067), Windows NT 4.0 Workstation (70-073), and Windows NT 4.0 Server in the Enterprise (70-068) exams. The second scenario covers the situation of the person who has not completed those Windows NT 4.0 exams and would like to concentrate *only* on Windows 2000.

In the first scenario, you have the option of taking all four Windows 2000 core exams, or you can take the Windows 2000 Accelerated Exam for MCPs if you have already passed exams 70-067, 70-068, and 70-073. (Note that you must have passed those specific exams to qualify for the Accelerated Exam; if you have fulfilled your NT 4.0 MCSE requirements by passing the Windows 95 or Windows 98 exam as your client operating system option and did not take the NT Workstation Exam, you don't qualify.)

After completing the core requirements, either by passing the four core exams or the one Accelerated exam, you must pass a design exam. The design exams include Designing a Microsoft Windows 2000 Directory Services Infrastructure (70-219), Designing Security for Microsoft Windows 2000 Network (70-220), and Designing a Microsoft Windows 2000 Network Infrastructure (70-221). One design exam is *required*.

You also must pass two exams from the list of electives. However, you cannot use the design exam that you took as an elective. Each exam can only count once toward certification. This includes any of the MCSE electives that are current when the Windows 2000 exams are released. In summary, you would take a total of at least two more exams, the upgrade exam and the design exam. Any additional exams would be dependent on which electives the candidate may have already completed.

In the second scenario, if you have not completed, and do not plan to complete the Core Windows NT 4.0 exams, you must pass the four core Windows 2000 exams, one design exam, and two elective exams. Again, no exam can be counted twice. In this case, you must pass a total of seven exams to obtain the Windows 2000 MCSE certification.

How to Take a Microsoft Certification Exam

If you have taken a Microsoft Certification exam before, we have some good news and some bad news. The good news is that the new testing formats will be a true measure of your ability and knowledge. Microsoft has "raised the bar" for its Windows 2000 certification exams. If you are an expert in the Windows 2000 operating system, and can troubleshoot and engineer efficient, cost effective solutions using Windows 2000, you will have no difficulty with the new exams.

The bad news is that if you have used resources such as "brain-dumps," boot-camps, or exam specific practice tests as your only method of test preparation, you will undoubtedly fail your Windows 2000 exams. The new Windows 2000 MCSE exams will test your knowledge, and your ability to apply that knowledge in more sophisticated and accurate ways than was expected for the MCSE exams for Windows NT 4.0.

In the Windows 2000 exams, Microsoft will use a variety of testing formats which include product simulations, adaptive testing, drag-and-drop matching, and possibly even "fill in the blank" questions (also called "free response" questions). The test-taking process will measure the examinee's fundamental knowledge of the Windows 2000 operating system rather than the ability to memorize a few facts and then answer a few simple multiple-choice questions.

In addition, the "pool" of questions for each exam will significantly increase. The greater number of questions combined with the adaptive testing techniques will enhance the validity and security of the certification process.

We will begin by looking at the purpose, focus, and structure of Microsoft certification tests, and examine the effect that these factors have on the kinds of questions you will face on your certification exams. We will define the structure of exam questions and investigate some common formats. Next, we will present a strategy for answering these questions. Finally, we will give some specific guidelines on what you should do on the day of your test.

Why Vendor Certification?

The Microsoft Certified Professional program, like the certification programs from Cisco, Novell, Oracle, and other software vendors, is maintained for the ultimate purpose of increasing the corporation's profits. A successful vendor certification program accomplishes this goal by helping to create a pool of experts in a company's software and by "branding" these experts so companies using the software can identify them.

We know that vendor certification has become increasingly popular in the last few years because it helps employers find qualified workers and because it helps software vendors like Microsoft sell their products. But why vendor certification rather than a more traditional approach like a college degree in computer science?

A college education is a broadening and enriching experience, but a degree in computer science does not prepare students for most jobs in the IT industry.

A common truism in our business states, "If you are out of the IT industry for three years and want to return, you have to start over." The problem, of course, is *timeliness*; if a first-year student learns about a specific computer program, it probably will no longer be in wide use when he or she graduates. Although some colleges are trying to integrate Microsoft certification into their curriculum, the problem is not really a flaw in higher education, but a characteristic of the IT industry. Computer software is changing so rapidly that a four-year college just can't keep up.

A marked characteristic of the Microsoft certification program is an emphasis on performing specific job tasks rather than merely gathering knowledge. It may come as a shock, but most potential employers do not care how much you know about the theory of operating systems, networking, or database design. As one IT manager put it, "I don't really care what my employees know about the theory of our network. We don't need someone to sit at a desk and think about it. We need people who can actually do something to make it work better."

You should not think that this attitude is some kind of anti-intellectual revolt against "book learning." Knowledge is a necessary prerequisite, but it is not enough. More than one company has hired a computer science graduate as a network administrator, only to learn that the new employee has no idea how to add users, assign permissions, or perform the other day-to-day tasks necessary to maintain a network. This brings us to the second major characteristic of Microsoft certification that affects the questions you must be prepared to answer. In addition to timeliness, Microsoft certification is also job-task oriented.

The timeliness of Microsoft's certification program is obvious and is inherent in the fact that you will be tested on current versions of software in wide use today. The job task orientation of Microsoft certification is almost as obvious, but testing real-world job skills using a computer-based test is not easy.

Computerized Testing

Considering the popularity of Microsoft certification, and the fact that certification candidates are spread around the world, the only practical way to administer tests for the certification program is through Sylvan Prometric or Vue testing centers, which operate internationally. Sylvan Prometric and Vue provide proctor testing services for Microsoft, Oracle, Novell, Lotus, and the A+ computer technician certification. Although the IT industry accounts for much of Sylvan's revenue, the company provides services for a number of other businesses and organizations, such as FAA pre-flight pilot tests. Historically, several hundred questions were developed for a new Microsoft certification exam. The Windows 2000 MCSE exam pool is expected to contain hundreds of new questions. Microsoft is aware that many new MCSE candidates have been able to access information on test questions via the Internet or other resources. The company is very concerned about maintaining the MCSE as a "premium" certification. The significant increase in the number of test questions, together with stronger enforcement of the NDA (Non-disclosure agreement) will ensure that a higher standard for certification is attained.

Microsoft treats the test-building process very seriously. Test questions are first reviewed by a number of subject matter experts for technical accuracy and then are presented in a beta test. Taking the beta test may require several hours, due to the large number of questions. After a few weeks, Microsoft Certification uses the statistical feedback from Sylvan to check the performance of the beta questions. The beta test group for the Windows 2000 certification series included MCTs, MCSEs, and members of Microsoft's rapid deployment partners groups. Because the exams will be normalized based on this population, you can be sure that the passing scores will be difficult to achieve without detailed product knowledge.

Questions are discarded if most test takers get them right (too easy) or wrong (too difficult), and a number of other statistical measures are taken of each question. Although the scope of our discussion precludes a rigorous treatment of question analysis, you should be aware that Microsoft and other vendors spend a great deal of time and effort making sure their exam questions are valid.

The questions that survive statistical analysis form the pool of questions for the final certification exam.

Test Structure

The questions in a Microsoft form test will not be equally weighted. From what we can tell at the present time, different questions are given a value based on the level of difficulty. You will get more credit for getting a difficult question correct, than if you got an easy one correct. Because the questions are weighted differently, and because the exams will likely use the adapter method of testing, your score will not bear any relationship to how many questions you answered correctly.

Microsoft has implemented *adaptive* testing. When an adaptive test begins, the candidate is first given a level three question. If it is answered correctly, a question from the next higher level is presented, and an incorrect response results in a question from the next lower level. When 15 to 20 questions have been answered in this manner, the scoring algorithm is able to predict, with a high degree of statistical certainty, whether the candidate would pass or fail if all the questions in the form were answered. When the required degree of certainty is attained, the test ends and the candidate receives a pass/fail grade.

Adaptive testing has some definite advantages for everyone involved in the certification process. Adaptive tests allow Sylvan Prometric or Vue to deliver more tests with the same resources, as certification candidates often are in and out in 30 minutes or less. For candidates, the "fatigue factor" is reduced due to the shortened testing time. For Microsoft, adaptive testing means that fewer test questions are exposed to each candidate, and this can enhance the security, and therefore the overall validity, of certification tests.

One possible problem you may have with adaptive testing is that you are not allowed to mark and revisit questions. Since the adaptive algorithm is interactive, and all questions but the first are selected on the basis of your response to the previous question, it is not possible to skip a particular question or change an answer.

Question Types

Computerized test questions can be presented in a number of ways. Some of the possible formats are used on Microsoft certification exam and some are not.

True/False

We are all familiar with True/False questions, but because of the inherent 50 percent chance of guessing the correct answer, you will not see questions of this type on Microsoft certification exams.

Multiple Choice

The majority of Microsoft certification questions are in the multiple-choice format, with either a single correct answer or multiple correct answers. One interesting variation on multiple-choice questions with multiple correct answers is whether or not the candidate is told how many answers are correct.

Example:

1. Which two files can be altered to configure the MS-DOS environment? (Choose two.)

Or

1. Which files can be altered to configure the MS-DOS environment? (Choose all that apply.)

You may see both variations on Microsoft certification exams, but the trend seems to be toward the first type, where candidates are told explicitly how many answers are correct. Questions of the "choose all that apply" variety are more difficult and can be merely confusing.

Graphical Questions

One or more graphical elements are sometimes used as exhibits to help present or clarify an exam question. These elements may take the form of a network diagram, pictures of networking components, or screen shots from the software on which you are being tested. It is often easier to present the concepts required for a complex performance-based scenario with a graphic than with words.

Test questions known as *hotspots* actually incorporate graphics as part of the answer. These questions ask the certification candidate to click on a location or graphical element to answer the question. For example, you might be shown the diagram of a network and asked to click on an appropriate location for a router. The answer is correct if the candidate clicks within the *hotspot* that defines the correct location.

Free Response Questions

Another kind of question you sometimes see on Microsoft certification exams requires a *free response* or type-in answer. An example of this type of question might present a TCP/IP network scenario and ask the candidate to calculate and enter the correct subnet mask in dotted decimal notation.

Simulation Questions

Simulation questions provide a method for Microsoft to test how familiar the test taker is with the actual product interface and the candidate's ability to quickly implement a task using the interface. These questions will present an actual Windows 2000 interface that you must work with to solve a problem or implement a solution. If you are familiar with the product, you will be able to answer these questions quickly, and they will be the easiest questions on the exam. However, if you are not accustomed to working with Windows 2000, these questions will be difficult for you to answer. This is why actual hands-on practice with Windows 2000 is so important!

Knowledge-Based and Performance-Based Questions

Microsoft Certification develops a blueprint for each Microsoft certification exam with input from subject matter experts. This blueprint defines the content areas and objectives for each test, and each test question is created to test a specific objective. The basic information from the examination blueprint can be found on Microsoft's Web site in the Exam Prep Guide for each test.

Psychometricians (psychologists who specialize in designing and analyzing tests) categorize test questions as knowledge-based or performance-based. As the names imply, knowledge-based questions are designed to test knowledge, while performance-based questions are designed to test performance.

Some objectives demand a knowledge-based question. For example, objectives that use verbs like *list* and *identify* tend to test only what you know, not what you can do.

Example:

Objective: Identify the MS-DOS configuration files.

  1. Which two files can be altered to configure the MS-DOS environment? (Choose two.)

     A. COMMAND.COM

     B. AUTOEXEC.BAT

     C. IO.SYS

     D. CONFIG.SYS
        Correct answers: B, D

Other objectives use action verbs like *install, configure,* and *troubleshoot* to define job tasks. These objectives can often be tested with either a knowledge-based question or a performance-based question.

Example:

Objective: Configure an MS-DOS installation appropriately using the PATH statement in AUTOEXEC.BAT.

The following is a *knowledge-based* question:

1. What is the correct syntax to set a path to the D: directory in AUTOEXEC.BAT?

   A. SET PATH EQUAL TO D:

   B. PATH D:

   C. SETPATH D:

   D. D:EQUALS PATH
      Correct answer: B

The following is a *performance-based* question:

1. Your company uses several DOS accounting applications that access a group of common utility programs. What is the best strategy for configuring the computers in the accounting department so that the accounting applications will always be able to access the utility programs?

   A. Store all the utilities on a single floppy disk and make a copy of the disk for each computer in the accounting department.

   B. Copy all the utilities to a directory on the C: drive of each computer in the accounting department and add a PATH statement pointing to this directory in the AUTOEXEC.BAT files.

   C. Copy all the utilities to all application directories on each computer in the accounting department.

   D. Place all the utilities in the C: directory on each computer because the C: directory is automatically included in the PATH statement when AUTOEXEC.BAT is executed.
      Correct answer: B

Even in this simple example, the superiority of the performance-based question is obvious. Whereas the knowledge-based question asks for a single fact, the performance-based question presents a real-life situation and requires that you make a decision based on this scenario. Thus, performance-based questions give more bang (validity) for the test author's buck (individual question).

Testing Job Performance

We have said that Microsoft certification focuses on timeliness and the ability to perform job tasks. We have also introduced the concept of performance-based questions, but even performance-based multiple-choice questions do not really measure performance. Another strategy is needed to test job skills.

Given unlimited resources, it is not difficult to test job skills. In an ideal world, Microsoft would fly MCP candidates to Redmond, place them in a controlled environment with a team of experts, and ask them to plan, install, maintain, and troubleshoot a Windows network. In a few days at most, the experts could reach a valid decision as to whether each candidate should or should not be granted MCDBA or MCSE status. Needless to say, this is not likely to happen.

Closer to reality, another way to test performance is by using the actual software and creating a testing program to present tasks and automatically grade a candidate's performance when the tasks are completed. This *cooperative* approach would be practical in some testing situations, but the same test that is presented to MCP candidates in Boston must also be available in Bahrain and Botswana. The most workable solution for measuring performance in today's testing environment is a *simulation* program. When the program is launched during a test, the candidate sees a simulation of the actual software that looks, and behaves, just like the real thing. When the testing software presents a task, the simulation program is launched and the candidate performs the required task. The testing software then grades the candidate's performance on the required task and moves to the next question. Microsoft has introduced simulation questions on the certification exam for Internet Information Server 4.0. Simulation questions provide many advantages over other testing methodologies, and simulations are expected to become increasingly important in the Microsoft certification program. For example, studies have shown that there is a very high correlation between the ability to perform simulated tasks on a computer-based test and the ability to perform the actual job tasks. Thus, simulations enhance the validity of the certification process.

Another truly wonderful benefit of simulations is in the area of test security. It is just not possible to cheat on a simulation question. In fact, you will be told exactly what tasks you are expected to perform on the test. How can a certification candidate cheat? By learning to perform the tasks? What a concept!

Study Strategies

There are appropriate ways to study for the different types of questions you will see on a Microsoft certification exam.

Knowledge-Based Questions

Knowledge-based questions require that you memorize facts. There are hundreds of facts inherent in every content area of every Microsoft certification exam. There are several keys to memorizing facts:

- **Repetition** The more times your brain is exposed to a fact, the more likely you are to remember it.

- **Association** Connecting facts within a logical framework makes them easier to remember.

- **Motor association** It is often easier to remember something if you write it down or perform some other physical act, like clicking on a practice test answer.

We have said that the emphasis of Microsoft certification is job performance, and that there are very few knowledge-based questions on Microsoft certification exams. Why should you waste a lot of time learning filenames, IP address formulas, and other minutiae? Read on.

Performance-Based Questions

Most of the questions you will face on a Microsoft certification exam are performance-based scenario questions. We have discussed the superiority of these questions over simple knowledge-based questions, but you should remember that the job-task orientation of Microsoft certification extends the knowledge you need to pass the exams; it does not replace this knowledge. Therefore, the first step in preparing for scenario questions is to absorb as many facts relating to the exam content areas as you can. In other words, go back to the previous section and follow the steps to prepare for an exam composed of knowledge-based questions.

The second step is to familiarize yourself with the format of the questions you are likely to see on the exam. You can do this by answering the questions in this study guide, by using Microsoft assessment tests, or by using practice tests on the included CD-ROM. The day of your test is not the time to be surprised by the construction of Microsoft exam questions.

At best, performance-based scenario questions really do test certification candidates at a higher cognitive level than knowledge-based questions. At worst, these questions can test your reading comprehension and test-taking ability rather than your ability to use Microsoft products. Be sure to get in the habit of reading the question carefully to determine what is being asked.

The third step in preparing for Microsoft scenario questions is to adopt the following attitude: Multiple-choice questions aren't really performance-based. It is all a cruel lie. These scenario questions are just knowledge-based questions with a story wrapped around them.

To answer a scenario question, you have to sift through the story to the underlying facts of the situation and apply your knowledge to determine the correct answer. This may sound silly at first, but the process we go through in solving real-life problems is quite similar. The key concept is that every scenario question (and every real-life problem) has a fact at its center, and if we can identify that fact, we can answer the question.

Simulations

Simulation questions really do measure your ability to perform job tasks. You must be able to perform the specified tasks. There are two ways to prepare for simulation questions:

1. Get experience with the actual software. If you have the resources, this is a great way to prepare for simulation questions.

2. Use the practice test on this book's accompanying CD-ROM, as it contains questions similar to those you will find on the Microsoft exam. This approach has the added advantage of grading your efforts. You can find additional practice tests at www.syngress.com and www.osborne. com.

Signing Up

Signing up to take a Microsoft certification exam is easy. Sylvan Prometric or Vue operators in each country can schedule tests at any testing center. There are, however, a few things you should know:

1. If you call Sylvan Prometric or Vue during a busy time, get a cup of coffee first, because you may be in for a long wait. The exam providers do an excellent job, but everyone in the world seems to want to sign up for a test on Monday morning.

2. You will need your social security number or some other unique identifier to sign up for a test, so have it at hand.

3. Pay for your test by credit card if at all possible. This makes things easier, and you can even schedule tests for the same day you call if space is available at your local testing center.

4. Know the number and title of the test you want to take before you call. This is not essential, and the Sylvan operators will help you if they can. Having this information in advance, however, speeds up and improves the accuracy of the registration process.

Taking the Test

Teachers have always told you not to try to cram for exams because it does no good. If you are faced with a knowledge-based test requiring only that you regurgitate facts, cramming can mean the difference between passing and failing. This is not the case, however, with Microsoft certification exams. If you don't know it the night before, don't bother to stay up and cram.

Instead, create a schedule and stick to it. Plan your study time carefully, and do not schedule your test until you think you are ready to succeed. Follow these guidelines on the day of your exam:

1. Get a good night's sleep. The scenario questions you will face on a Microsoft certification exam require a clear head.

2. Remember to take two forms of identification—at least one with a picture. A driver's license with your picture and social security or credit card is acceptable.

3. Leave home in time to arrive at your testing center a few minutes early. It is not a good idea to feel rushed as you begin your exam.

4. Do not spend too much time on any one question. You cannot mark and revisit questions on an adaptive test, so you must do your best on each question as you go.

5. If you do not know the answer to a question, try to eliminate the obviously wrong answers and guess from the rest. If you can eliminate two out of four options, you have a 50 percent chance of guessing the correct answer.

6. For scenario questions, follow the steps we outlined earlier. Read the question carefully and try to identify the facts at the center of the story.

Finally, we would advise anyone attempting to earn Microsoft MCDBA and MCSE certification to adopt a philosophical attitude. The Windows 2000 MCSE will be the most difficult MCSE ever to be offered. The questions will be at a higher cognitive level than seen on all previous MCSE exams. Therefore, even if you are the kind of person who never fails a test, you are likely to fail at least one Windows 2000 Certification test somewhere along the way. Do not get discouraged. Microsoft wants to ensure the value of your certification. Moreover, it will attempt to so by keeping the standard as high as possible. If Microsoft certification were easy to obtain, more people would have it, and it would not be so respected and so valuable to your future in the IT industry.

1

Introduction to Installing, Configuring, and Administering Windows 2000 Professional

CERTIFICATION OBJECTIVES

W elcome to Windows 2000 and the first of Microsoft's core topics for the Windows 2000 Microsoft Certified Systems Engineer (MCSE) certification track. For many MCSE candidates, Exam 70-210, "Installing, Configuring and Administering Windows 2000 Professional," will be the first Windows 2000 exam to study for and take.

The Windows 2000 operating system introduces major changes to Microsoft networking. Although Windows 2000 is built on the NT kernel, the differences between NT 4.0 and the new operating system are significant—so much so that Microsoft has recently begun referring to the transition as a *migration,* rather than an upgrade (in fact, the name of Exam 70-222 was changed from "Upgrading from Microsoft Windows NT 4.0 to Windows 2000" to "Migrating from Microsoft Windows NT 4.0 to Windows 2000"). The terminology matters, because a migration implies changing to a whole new operating system and a whole new way of doing things—and this is exactly what learning Windows 2000 involves.

It may not seem so at first glance, especially for users of Windows 2000 Professional. The interface, though it has a different look and feel from NT Workstation "out of the box," will be familiar in appearance to those who have used Windows 98, as well as those who have installed Internet Explorer 4.0's Active Desktop on their Workstation machines. Under the hood, however, you will find big differences.

A subtle, but noticeable—and welcome—change is the stability of the new desktop operating system. You will also find that hardware support has been increased significantly over that of NT Workstation, and at last you aren't forced to choose between Plug and Play support *or* a secure, stable client operating system.

Microsoft created Windows 2000 Professional to work in conjunction with the Windows 2000 Server family, and knowing the intricacies of the operating system is essential to performing the duties of an administrator. Unlike the NT 4.0 certification track, in which you could choose to test on Windows 95 or 98 instead of NT Workstation, the Windows 2000 certification requires that you master Professional to obtain the MCSE.

Prior knowledge of NT Workstation provides a good foundation for studying for this exam, but it's not enough. Professional includes numerous features you will not have encountered in using NT, and many of the old, familiar tasks are accomplished in new ways. Don't expect Exam 70-210 to be a "no-brainer" just because you're a long-time user of NT; Windows 2000 Professional is much more than just a pretty interface.

This book will help prepare you not only to pass Microsoft Certification Exam 70-210, "Installing, Configuring, and Administering Windows 2000 Professional," but will also prepare you for the exciting experience of applying your knowledge and skills in the real world, as you use and support this innovative new desktop operating system.

CERTIFICATION OBJECTIVE 1.01

What Is Installing, Configuring, and Administering Windows 2000 Professional?

Microsoft Exam 70-210 covers a lot of ground. Those three words—*installing, configuring,* and *administering*—sum up just about everything you can do with a computer operating system, with the exception of writing the code for it in the first place (fortunately, you *don't* have to demonstrate your ability to do *that* in order to pass this exam).

What is "Installing, Configuring, and Administering Windows 2000 Professional?" In order to answer that question, let's break the exam topic down into its component parts. First, and most basic, what do we really mean by *installation?* To the uninitiated, installing a program—even an operating system—seems simple enough: you put the CD into the drive and type **setup**, or with autorun, you don't even have to do that. A few clicks of the mouse, wait while some files are copied, and you're ready to roll. Well, maybe. In actuality, installation issues can be the source of the most frustrating troubleshooting sessions you'll ever experience.

Although the Windows 2000 installation process is designed to go smoothly, and is a vast improvement over the installation routines of many other operating systems, it is important to *plan* the deployment of a new operating system carefully, whether you're upgrading one stand-alone computer or performing an automated unattended installation to hundreds of computers across a network. We will look at installation a little more closely in the next section.

But first, let's move to the second word in this exam title: *configuring.* The American Heritage Dictionary defines the verb *configure* as "to arrange, set up, or shape with a view to specific applications or uses." Configuration of an operating system, then, involves specifying settings that will govern how the system behaves.

We will discuss some elements of operating system configuration in the section entitled "Configuration Issues."

The last activity listed is *administration*. What do we really mean when we refer to *administering* Windows 2000 Professional? The word *administer* is generally used as a synonym for *manage*, which in turn means "to exert control." One of the many enhancements to Windows 2000—both the Professional and Server incarnations— is the ability Microsoft has given administrators to apply the degree of control desired, in a flexible and granular manner. We will look at some of the ways you can do that in the section entitled "Administration Issues."

Installation Issues

Installing Windows 2000 Professional is a straightforward task—*if* you have properly prepared for the installation. Before you rip open the shiny new holographically enhanced CD, take a moment to evaluate the hardware, consider the installation options, and go through the installation "Scenario & Solution" included at the end of this section.

Proper preparation can make the difference between a quick and easy transition to the new operating system and a lengthy troubleshooting nightmare.

Planning for Installation

Prior to installation, you should perform the following preparatory tasks:

- Evaluate the hardware to ensure that it meets minimum system requirements.
- Determine whether you will upgrade or perform a fresh installation.
- Consider your options for partitioning your hard disk(s).
- Decide which file system(s) to deploy on each partition.
- Ensure that you are in compliance with the licensing agreement.

exam
ⓦatch

If you are upgrading your current operating system to Windows 2000 Professional, Microsoft recommends that you back up your current files before upgrading, in case you need to restore the current operating system.

It is much easier to go through the setup and configuration process smoothly if you already have the information at hand that you will be asked for by the Setup program. For example, if you will be joining the computer to a domain, you should have the domain name and be sure that a computer account has been created in the domain, or that you have the proper administrative credentials to create one.

Evaluating the Hardware

It is important to first determine whether there are any hardware issues that will prevent you from running Windows 2000 Professional on the computer. This involves two steps:

1. Check the minimum system requirements (shown in Table 1-1) and ensure that your computer meets or exceeds them.

2. Check the Hardware Compatibility List (HCL) and determine whether your hardware devices are listed.

The published system requirements for Windows 2000 have changed several times during the beta phases prior to release of the operating system. The hardware requirements you should be familiar with for exam purposes are shown in Table 1-1.

Note that in some instances, Microsoft designates both "minimum supported" and "minimum recommended"; in these cases, the operating system will not install if it detected less than the minimum supported specification. However, for acceptable performance, you should ensure that the system meets the "minimum recommended" specification.

TABLE 1-1	Hardware Component or Device	Minimum Requirements
Minimum System Requirements for Installing Windows 2000 Professional	Processor	Pentium, Pentium II or III, or equivalent (includes AMD K-6, K-6 II or III, K-7 Athlon)
	Random Access Memory (RAM)	32MB minimum supported 64MB minimum recommended
	Free hard disk space	650MB minimum supported 2GB minimum recommended
	Video display adapter	VGA resolution or higher
	Networking components	Network interface card (NIC) if Windows 2000 Professional will be connected to a network
	Other	CD-ROM drive unless installing over the network, Keyboard, pointing device

The Hardware Compatibility List (HCL)   The Hardware Compatibility List is published by Microsoft for each of its operating systems, and is updated on a monthly basis. There is a copy of the HCL on the Windows 2000 Professional CD, located in the Support folder and named Hcl.txt. This copy is dated 12/07/99. An updated copy of the HCL can be found on Microsoft's Web site. Go to www.microsoft.com and do a site search for "hardware compatibility list."

If your hardware components are listed on the HCL, this means they have been tested and found to work with Windows 2000. If your system components are *not* on the list, this does not necessarily mean they *won't* work with Windows 2000, but you have no assurance that they will.

Upgrade or New Installation?

The next question to consider is whether to upgrade your existing client operating system—Windows 95, 98, or NT Workstation—to Windows 2000 or perform a fresh installation. An upgrade will retain some of the operating system settings; however, a fresh installation often presents fewer problems. A fresh installation will require that you reinstall all application programs, reconfigure your desktop settings, and so forth, from scratch.

Upgrading Existing Operating Systems   Windows 2000 Professional supports upgrade paths from the operating systems shown in Table 1-2.

Microsoft provides a Compatibility tool, which can be downloaded from their Web site (search the Downloads section for chkupgrd.exe). You can run this utility at the command line to generate a report that specifies which of the computer's components are and aren't compatible with Windows 2000. The report is created as a text file that can be saved and opened in Notepad or any other text editor.

TABLE I-2	Existing Operating System	Upgrade Path
Upgrading Existing Client Operating Systems	Windows 95	Upgrade directly to Windows 2000 Professional.
	Windows 98	Upgrade directly to Windows 2000 Professional.
	Windows NT 3.51 and 4.0	Upgrade directly to Windows 2000 Professional.
	Windows NT 3.1. and 3.5	Upgrade to NT 3.51 or 4.0, and then upgrade to Windows 2000 Professional.
	Windows 3.*x* and Windows for Workgroups 3.11	No upgrade path—install Windows 2000 Professional and reinstall all applications.

on the
ⓘob

Windows 95 and 98 computers are often used as clients in Microsoft domain networks. However, unlike Windows NT (and Windows 2000 Professional) clients, they cannot actually join the domain; that is, the computer itself does not have a machine account in the domain, but a user who has a user account in the domain can log on to the domain from the Windows 9x machine. Consequently, if you upgrade a Windows 9x computer to Windows 2000 Professional, you will have to create a computer account for it in the domain. On the other hand, if you upgrade a Windows NT computer to Windows 2000, there will already be a machine account for it in the domain.

Fresh Installation with Dual Boot Configuration   If you wish to be able to boot into your existing operating system after you install Windows 2000, you will need to install a fresh copy of Windows 2000 to a different partition. (It is possible to install to a different directory in the same partition, but this is not recommended, as it can cause file overwrite problems.)

When you install Windows 2000 Professional in this manner alongside another Microsoft operating system, the Boot menu will allow you to select the operating system to which you wish to boot each time you start the computer. See Figure 1-1 for an example of the Windows 2000 Professional Boot menu.

FIGURE 1-1

The Windows 2000 Boot menu allows you to select operating systems in a dual (or multiple) boot configuration

```
Please select the operating system to start:


    Microsoft Windows 2000 Professional
    Microsoft Windows 2000 Advanced Server
    Microsoft NT 4.0 Workstation
    Microsoft Windows 95

Use ↑ and ↓ to move the highlight to your choice.
Press Enter to choose.
Seconds until highlighted choice will be started automatically: 0




For troubleshooting and advanced startup options for Windows 2000, press F8
```

The previously installed Microsoft operating systems will be automatically added to the Boot menu. If you wish to dual or multiboot Windows 2000 with a non-Microsoft operating system such as Linux/UNIX, OS/2, or NetWare, it is best to use a third-party boot manager program such as System Commander or Boot Magic to create a Boot menu that will let you select from the various installed operating systems.

Fresh Installation to Clean Disk   The second way to do a fresh installation of Windows 2000 Professional is to format the hard disk—wiping out all previous operating systems, applications, and data—and install to a clean hard disk. This method is the most time-consuming because it requires you to reinstall and reconfigure all programs and restore data from backup. However, it reduces the chances of conflicts caused by old .dll files and other remnants of previous operating systems and applications.

If you choose to install to a clean disk, you should use a utility such as fdisk or a third-party application such as Partition Magic to delete the partition(s) on the disk and create new partitions. See the next section for the factors you should consider in creating a partitioning scheme.

Considering Disk and File System Options

If you are performing a fresh installation to a clean disk, you must determine how to partition the disk(s) prior to installing Windows 2000. If you are installing alongside an existing operating system, you can use the Windows 2000 Setup to create a new partition from free space, or you can install to an already-existing partition.

During Setup, you should only create and size the partition on which you intend to install Windows 2000 Professional. After the installation, you can use the Disk Management tool to make any further changes or create new partitions on the disk.

Creating Partitions on an Unpartitioned Disk   If your disk is brand new, or if you have deleted all the partitions on the disk, you will need to create at least one partition in which to install Windows 2000 Professional. You can create partitions in one of several ways:

- You can use the fdisk utility from an MS-DOS boot disk; however, you will be limited to the 2GB partition size supported by MS-DOS.

- You can use a third-party program such as Partition Magic, which runs from a bootable floppy (see www.powerquest.com for more information).
- You can use the Windows 2000 Setup program to create and size the installation partition.

The partition to which Windows 2000 Professional will be installed must be a minimum of about 650MB. Microsoft recommends that the installation partition be 1GB or larger.

on the Job

A 1GB installation partition will suffice in a classroom/lab environment; but in the "real world," more is better—at least when it comes to partition sizes. It is likely that in the future you will need to install service packs, operating system tools, and updates that need to reside on the same partition as your operating system files. In addition, both the built-in disk defragmenter utility and third-party disk maintenance tools like Diskeeper need a certain amount of free space for the defragmentation process. Finally, some applications will not work properly unless installed to the default partition. Realistically, 2 to 4GB is preferable for the installation partition, as it gives you "room to grow." Remember that you cannot create a partition over 2GB with DOS utilities.

Installing to an Existing Partition or Free Space on a Partitioned Disk
If you already have a partitioned disk that has 650MB or more of unused space on a FAT, FAT32, or NTFS partition, you can install Windows 2000 to that partition. Or, if you have 650MB or more of unpartitioned (free) space on the disk in addition to existing partitions, you can create a partition in the free space and install Windows 2000 Professional into the new partition.

exam Watch

If you're performing a new installation, Windows 2000 Setup automatically selects an appropriate disk partition—unless you click Advanced Options during Setup and specify otherwise.

Choosing a File System   Windows NT supported only two file systems: FAT16 (often referred to simply as FAT) and NTFS. Windows 2000 will run on any of three choices:

- **FAT16**   Compatible with MS-DOS, Windows 3.*x*, Windows 9*x*, NT, and many non-Microsoft operating systems

- **FAT32** Compatible with Windows 95b (OEM version) and Windows 98; offers advantages in support of large hard disks
- **NTFS 5** The Windows 2000 version of the NT file system; compatible with Windows 2000 and Windows NT 4.0 with service pack 4 or above installed

In order to take advantage of all of Windows 2000's new features, you will need to format or convert your disk partitions to NTFS. However, if you run other operating systems on the same computer (dual or multiboot), you may wish to run Windows 2000 on a FAT or FAT32 partition for compatibility reasons.

SCENARIO & SOLUTION

If I want to install Windows 2000 to an existing partition, what file system must it be formatted in?	You can install Windows 2000 to a FAT, FAT32, or NTFS partition. By default, the existing file system will be kept intact.
What are the advantages of converting the existing partition to NTFS?	Converting the partition to NTFS will allow you to use file-level encryption and compression, assign file-level access permissions, create dynamic disks, and benefit from all Windows 2000 disk management features.
What are the disadvantages of converting the existing partition to NTFS?	If you are dual or multibooting with another operating system, such as MS-DOS, or Windows 95 or 98, files on NTFS formatted partitions will not be available when you are booted into those operating systems. Windows NT 4.0 with service pack 4 or above installed *can* access Windows 2000 NTFS files.
If I convert my partition to NTFS, will I lose the data on the partition?	No, the data is preserved when you *convert* the partition to NTFS. If you *format* the partition in NTFS, however, all data will be lost.
What if I don't convert to NTFS during Setup, but decide I want to use the NTFS file system later?	You can convert a FAT or FAT32 partition to NTFS at any time, using the command-line Convert utility.
Can I convert back to FAT or FAT32 from NTFS?	No, conversion is a one-way process. To go back to FAT or FAT32, you must back up all your data, reformat the partition (erasing all data), and restore the files from backup.

Addressing Licensing Issues   Before you deploy Windows 2000 Professional in a networked environment, it is important that you understand licensing requirements.

Each client computer on which you install Windows 2000 Professional requires a software license to run the operating system on that computer. In addition, if the clients will connect to a Windows 2000 server, you also must purchase a CAL (Client Access License).

CALs come in two varieties: Per Seat and Per Server.

■ **Per Seat licensing**   A separate CAL is needed for each client computer. The client can use that CAL to connect to any server on the network.

■ **Per Server licensing**   Each server is assigned a specified number of CALs. Each CAL allows one client connection. You can only have as many clients connected to the server simultaneously as the number of CALs you have for that server.

on the
job

Per Seat licensing is preferable (less expensive) in an organization that has many servers to which clients need to connect. Per Server licensing may save you money if there is only one server, especially if clients do not all connect at the same time (such as when network users work in shifts). Anonymous connections through IIS to Web services, Telnet, and FTP do not require licenses.

Using the Setup Program

You can start the Windows 2000 setup process in one of several ways:

■ From inside an existing operating system such as Windows 9*x* or Windows NT, insert the Windows 2000 Professional CD. If autorun is enabled, the CD will start automatically. If autorun is disabled, use Windows Explorer to navigate to your CD drive, and double-click the Setup icon. Either way, the CD "splash screen" will appear, giving you the choices shown in Figure 1-2.

■ Use the Windows 2000 setup boot disks (see the upcoming "From the Classroom "sidebar for instructions on creating the boot disks).

■ Boot from the Windows 2000 CD if you have a CD-ROM drive that is bootable (you may have to enter your computer's BIOS/CMOS setup to change the boot device order).

The Windows 2000 Professional CD options: install the operating system, install add-on components, or browse the CD

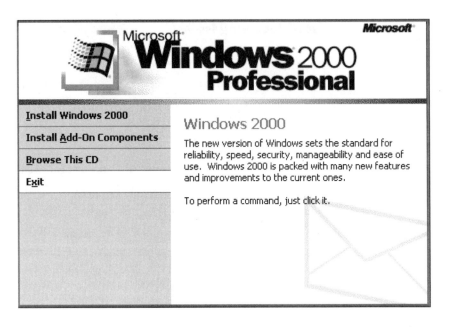

FROM THE CLASSROOM

Creating Four Bootable Setup Disks

To create the four setup disks used to install Windows 2000 Professional on a clean disk when your CD-ROM drive is not bootable, you should boot into your current operating system, open a command prompt, and change drives to the letter representing your CD-ROM drive (type the drive letter followed by a colon and press ENTER). Change to the Bootdisk folder (type **cd bootdisk**, and press ENTER), and type the command **makeboot a:** (there should be a 1.44MB blank formatted floppy disk in drive A:). Windows 2000 will run a script to create the four bootable setup disks. Follow the instructions on the screen to complete the process. When all four disks have been created, type **exit** and press ENTER to close the command prompt.

—*Debra Littlejohn Shinder, MCSE, MCP+I, MCT*

The Setup Process   Microsoft divides the installation process into four steps:

1. Setup program (using the setup boot disks)
2. Setup Wizard (graphical interface, information gathering)
3. Networking components installation (detecting NIC, installing networking software, and configuring protocols)
4. Finishing setup (installing Start menu items, registering components, saving the configuration, removing temporary files)

The Setup program is text based, and involves creating and formatting the partition on which Windows 2000 will be installed and copying setup files to the disk. The computer will restart after the files are copied and the Setup Wizard, shown in Figure 1-3, will start.

The wizard walks you through a series of dialog boxes in which you provide necessary information such as the regional settings choices, user and organization names, computer name, administrator account password, dialing information, and date and time settings.

FIGURE 1-3

The Windows 2000 Setup Wizard is the graphical portion of the installation

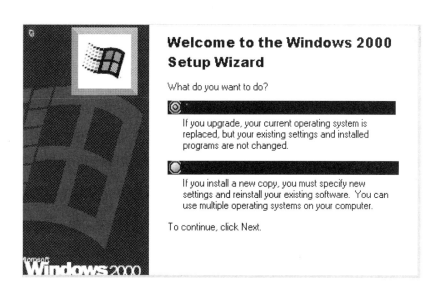

Welcome to the Windows 2000 Setup Wizard

What do you want to do?

If you upgrade, your current operating system is replaced, but your existing settings and installed programs are not changed.

If you install a new copy, you must specify new settings and reinstall your existing software. You can use multiple operating systems on your computer.

To continue, click Next.

The network interface card is then detected, and networking components are then installed. These include

- Client for Microsoft Networks
- File and Printer Sharing for Microsoft Networks
- TCP/IP protocol stack
- Other protocols and network client software that is desired

During this phase, you will be asked to specify whether the computer will join a workgroup or domain, and the name of the workgroup or domain to join.

exam
Ⓦatch

In order for a Windows 2000 Professional computer to join a domain, there must be a computer account created for it in the domain by a domain administrator. This can be done on the domain controller prior to the Professional computer joining the domain, or it can be done from the Professional computer in the process of setting up networking components, if you have administrative privileges to create a computer account in the domain.

In the last step, more files will be copied and, based on the choices you made during setup, your Start menu items will be installed, components will be registered (initialization information added to the Registry), the configuration will be saved, and the temporary files that were copied to the disk for use in installation will be removed. After the final step, the computer will restart and you can run Windows 2000 Professional for the first time.

on the
Ⓙob

Before you begin the installation, you should read the file Read1st.txt, which is on the Windows 2000 Professional CD. This file contains late-breaking information that was unavailable when this book and Windows 2000 Help files were written, including important preinstallation notes.

Unattended Installations

In a large organization, when you want to deploy Windows 2000 Professional to many computers simultaneously, it would be extremely time-consuming to have to visit each machine and go through all the steps to install the operating system. Thus, Microsoft has provided the ability to perform unattended installation over the network, using a *distribution server*. This is a server on which the Windows 2000 installation files reside.

When the operating system is installed over the network, there is no need for the client machine to have a CD-ROM drive.

Running the Setup in unattended mode requires the construction of an *answer file,* which contains the information you would normally have to key in during the setup process. Thus, no user intervention is required. To invoke unattended setup mode, you use the /unattend switch to run winnt32.exe from inside Windows 9*x* or NT.

This book contains an entire chapter devoted to performing unattended installations of Windows 2000 Professional. For detailed information on creating the answer file and deploying the operating system to multiple computers over the network, see Chapter 3.

Configuration Issues

Once Windows 2000 Professional has been installed on the computer, modifications can be made to the appearance and behavior of the operating system using various configuration components. These include

- **The Microsoft Management Console**   The MMC is the common interface used for administrative tasks.

- **The Windows 2000 Control Panel**   Many configuration settings and modifications can be made via the Control Panel applets. The Control Panel provides a graphical interface for editing certain Registry settings and Active Directory information.

- **The Registry**   In some cases, in order to make the desired changes, you will have to modify the Registry directly using a provided registry editing tool.

- **The Administrative Tools**   Predefined MMCs are provided that contain utilities for managing various components of the operating system.

Using the MMC

The Microsoft Management Console provides a consistent, familiar interface regardless of what administrative task is being performed. The MMC is a framework that hosts *snap-ins,* which are modular components designed for performing one or more administrative functions (such as the Computer Management snap-in, shown in Figure 1-4).

FIGURE 1-4

The Microsoft
Management
Console
displaying the
Computer
Management
snap-in

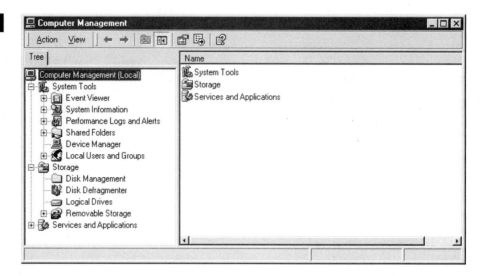

As you can see, the console shows a hierarchical tree in the left panel.
Double-clicking any of the tools shown there will display details in the right panel.
The MMC is handy for centralizing administration, and you can delegate authority
and create custom MMCs that contain only those administrative tools that are
needed by the users to whom authority is delegated.

exam
ⓦatch

*Custom consoles are saved in the Administrative Tools folder with a .msc
extension. You can save a custom console in either author mode (which
allows full access to all MMC functionality) or user mode, which can be
configured to restrict users' access.*

Windows 2000 Control Panel

The Control Panel in Windows 2000 functions similarly to the Control Panel in
Windows 9x and NT, except that "under the hood" there are now two locations
where information is stored, modified by the Control Panel applets. The Control
Panel in previous operating systems was a graphical interface for editing Registry
information. The Windows 2000 Control Panel provides applets that edit the
Registry and modify information stored in the Active Directory. The applets
available in the Control Panel may vary, depending on the services you have
installed. Figure 1-5 shows a typical Windows 2000 Professional computer's
Control Panel.

FIGURE 1-5 The Windows 2000 Professional Control Panel

As you can see, the Control Panel provides a means for configuring and modifying settings for various components, including:

- **Accessibility Options** Customizes features designed to provide better accessibility for the disabled.

- **Add/Remove Hardware** Guides you in the process of installing, removing, and troubleshooting hardware.

- **Add/Remove Programs** Installs and removes application programs and Windows components.

- **Administrative Tools** A collection of utilities for configuration and management of the computer.

- **Date/Time** Allows you to set the date, time, and time zone.

- **Display** Lets you customize the desktop appearance and modify display settings; used to set wallpaper, fonts, colors, screen resolution, and so on.

- **Folder Options** Allows you to change the appearance of folders, change file associations, and configure offline folders.

- **Fonts**   Used to install, delete, and manage fonts.

- **Internet Options**   Lets you configure options for your Web browser.

- **Keyboard and Mouse**   These applets allow you to set options for your keyboard and pointing device, including customizing cursors.

- **Network and Dial-up Connections**   Used to configure new network connections and the properties of the protocols, user preferences, and other settings.

- **Printers**   Allows you to install, delete, configure, and manage both local and network printers.

- **Regional Options**   Customizes settings for display of time, language, and other region-specific settings.

- **Scheduled Tasks**   Used to set up tasks to run automatically at specified dates and times.

- **Sounds and Multimedia**   Lets you set system sounds for specified events and configure sound devices.

- **System**   Provides system information and allows you to modify environment settings, network identification information, performance options, and startup and recovery information.

- **Users and Passwords**   Manages local user accounts.

Microsoft always recommends, if possible, you use the Control Panel interface to make changes rather than editing the Registry directly. Unfortunately, that's not always possible, which brings us to the next component.

The Windows 2000 Registry

The Registry is the hierarchical database that stores operating system and application configuration information. It was introduced in Windows 9x and NT, and replaced much of the functionality of the old initialization, system, and command files used in the early versions of Windows (.ini, .sys, and .com extensions).

Registry Data   The types of data that make up the Registry include

- Hardware information
- Driver information

- Application initialization information
- Network protocol information
- Operating system configuration information

The Registry data is organized into five *subtrees* (groups of keys, subkeys, and entries stored in a hive file in the <systemroot>\System32\Config directory), which correspond to five Registry keys as follows:

- **HKEY_LOCAL_MACHINE**   Stores information about the hardware, software, system devices, and security information for the local computer

- **HKEY_USERS**   Holds information and settings for the environments of all users of the computer

- **HKEY_CURRENT_USER**   Has information about the user who is currently logged on

- **HKEY_CLASSES_ROOT**   Contains information used for software configuration and object linking and embedding (OLE), as well as file association information

- **HKEY_CURRENT_CONFIG**   Holds data about the current hardware profile that is in use

Editing the Registry   Some Windows 2000 configuration settings can be changed only by editing the Registry. For example, to enable large TCP window support, you must make a change in the appropriate Registry key. Windows 2000 provides two registry editing tools (as did Windows NT 4.0): regedit.exe and regedt32.exe. These utilities are similar, but have subtle differences. regedt32 allows you to change security settings, and has a read-only mode that is safer to use to prevent accidental changes that could cause serious problems. regedit has better search functionality.

on the
()ob

Editing the Registry is a task that should not be undertaken casually. Mistakes in editing the Registry can result in systemwide problems or even render your computer unbootable. Microsoft recommends that you always back up the Registry before making any changes.

Figure 1-6 shows the Registry of a Windows 2000 Professional computer, viewed via the regedt32 utility.

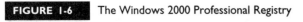 FIGURE 1-6   The Windows 2000 Professional Registry

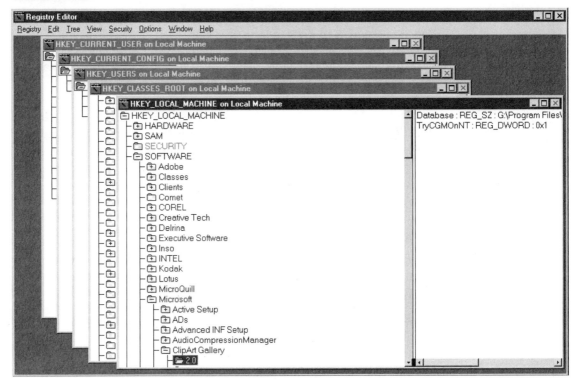

Registry changes are saved immediately and automatically as you make them, and take effect immediately.

Using the Administrative Tools

Windows 2000 provides a set of administrative tools, located in the Control Panel applet by that name, which allow you to use predefined MMCs to accomplish various management tasks. The Administrative Tools menu will contain different items, depending on the services you have installed. Some of the Windows 2000 Professional Administrative Tools include the applets shown in Figure 1-7.

These include the Component Services, Computer Management, ODBC settings, the Event Viewer, the Local Security Policy settings, Performance (the System Monitor), the Services applet, and the Telnet Server Administration tools.

FIGURE 1-7

The Windows
2000 Professional
Administrative
Tools

If you are an administrator, you can install the Server Administration tools on your Windows 2000 Professional Workstation. These include the Active Directory Users and Computers, Active Directory Sites and Services, DNS, WINS, and so forth, and this will allow you to perform domain administration tasks from your desktop.

Common Configuration Tasks

Let's take a look at some common configuration tasks and how they are performed on your Windows 2000 Professional computer. One important aspect of configuring Windows 2000 is setting up the networking components to connect to your network. This includes installing and configuring the protocol(s), if not installed during the setup process.

Protocol Configuration   *Protocols* are sets of rules that computers use to communicate. Protocols usually work together in *stacks,* so called because in a layered networking model, they operate at different layers or levels. Windows 2000 uses the TCP/IP protocol stack for many functions, including logon, file and print services, and replication of Active Directory information. TCP/IP is, of course, also the protocol stack of the global Internet, and is necessary for Internet connectivity. Thus, it is the default protocol of Windows 2000.

Other protocols supported by Windows 2000 include NetBEUI (used for communicating on small, nonrouted Microsoft networks), NWLink (Microsoft's implementation of Novell's IPX/SPX protocol stack, required for connecting to NetWare servers prior to version 5), and DLC (a nonroutable protocol used for connecting to IBM mainframes and some network-connected laser printers).

NetBEUI is a simple protocol that requires no special configuration. However, TCP/IP and NWLink both have configuration properties that can be set and modified. Experienced Windows NT administrators who are faced with changing protocol settings in Windows 2000 for the first time may find themselves temporarily at a loss—the procedure for doing so is one of the many subtle changes between the old operating system and the new.

Let's look at how the properties for TCP/IP and NWLink are configured.

SCENARIO & SOLUTION

Which protocol is the fastest?	NetBEUI, because of its simplicity and low overhead, is the fastest of the three network/transport protocols. TCP/IP is slowest, and NWLink falls somewhere in between.
Which protocol is the most difficult to configure?	Manual configuration of TCP/IP is the most complex, due to the need to assign a correct IP address and calculate a subnet mask that defines the network and host portions of the IP address. If the network is routed, a default gateway must be specified. Finally, you may need to designate DNS and WINS servers.
If it's so difficult to configure TCP/IP and it's the slowest protocol stack, why use it?	TCP/IP is the default protocol of Windows 2000, and the protocol of the global Internet, because it works on almost any computer platform and operating system and is flexible and highly routable, making it most suitable for large internetworks like the Internet.
What is NWLink good for?	NWLink is Microsoft's implementation of Novell's IPX/SPX protocol stack, and is required to connect to older NetWare servers (prior to version 5). NWLink is also a routable protocol that is faster and easier to configure than TCP/IP, and thus suitable for certain Microsoft networks where TCP/IP's complexity is not needed and there is no need to access the Internet.

CERTIFICATION OBJECTIVE 1.02

Configuring TCP/IP Properties

In Chapter 11, we will walk you through the process of configuring TCP/IP in a step-by-step fashion, addressing the options applicable to different network infrastructures.

The TCP/IP Properties sheet is accessed by selecting Start | Settings | Network And Dial-Up Connections and choosing the Local Area Connection (or other connection whose TCP/IP properties you wish to configure). The status box will be displayed; and if you click Properties, you will see a dialog box similar to the one shown in Figure 1-8.

By double-clicking the protocol you want to configure—in this case, the Internet Protocol, TCP/IP—you will be able to make changes to the protocol's configuration properties.

The TCP/IP Properties sheet is shown in Figure 1-9.

FIGURE 1-8

The Local Area
Connection
Properties sheet

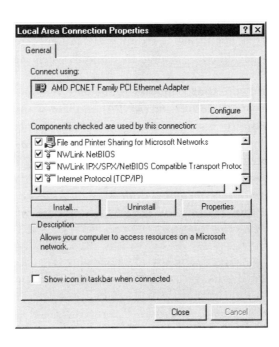

FIGURE 1-9

The TCP/IP
Properties
configuration
sheet

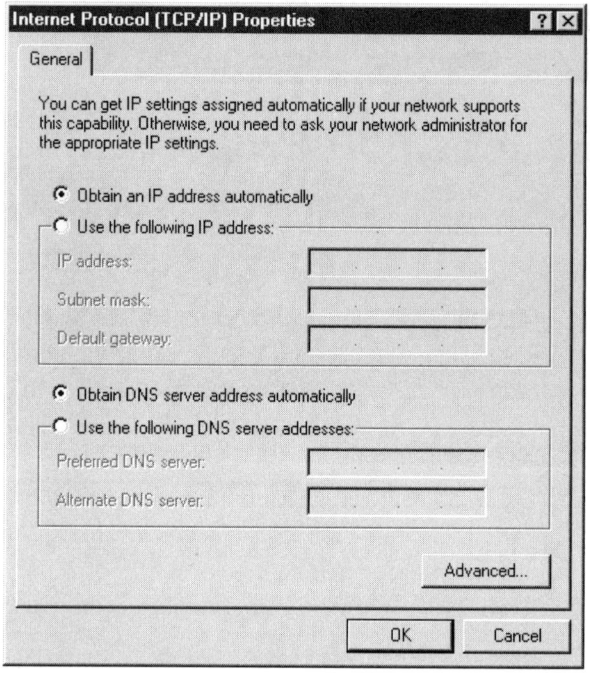

In the Properties sheet shown, the Windows 2000 Professional computer is configured to obtain an IP address and other TCP/IP information from a DHCP server. The Dynamic Host Configuration Protocol (DHCP) is used to automatically assign addressing settings dynamically when the computer comes online.

exam
Watch

Be aware that Windows 2000—like Windows 98—by default has Automatic Private IP Addressing (APIPA) enabled. This is a feature that allows a computer configured to be a DHCP client to assign itself an IP address for temporary use if there is no DHCP server available when it comes onto the network. The APIPA address range is 169.254.0.0 through 169.254.255.255; these addresses are reserved for APIPA and are not routable on the Internet. Computers obtaining addresses via APIPA can communicate only with other computers using the 169.254.x.x address range. APIPA can be disabled by editing the Registry.

By selecting the Use The Following IP Address radio button, you can assign a *static* IP address (one that remains the same) and configure the subnet mask and default gateway, as well as DNS server addresses. The Advanced tab allows you more options, such as assigning multiple IP addresses or multiple gateways to this network adapter.

exam
ⓦatch

The Domain Name System (DNS) method of name resolution was optional with Windows NT, but is an integral part of a Windows 2000 network because DNS is used by the Active Directory.

CERTIFICATION OBJECTIVE 1.03

Configuring NWLink Properties

The NWLink IPX/SPX/NetBIOS–compatible protocol is used to connect to NetWare servers; all NetWare versions prior to version 5 required IPX/SPX to communicate. NetWare 5 is capable of running TCP/IP only.

on the
ⓙob

Although usually thought of as the "NetWare protocol stack," NWLink (IPX/SPX) can also be used on a pure Microsoft network in situations in which there is no need to connect to the Internet, and the need for a routable protocol precludes using NetBEUI.

NWLink is installed and configured through the Network And Dial-Up Connections | Local Area Connection property box, as shown previously in the TCP/IP section. By double-clicking NWLink IPX/SPX/NetBIOS Compatible Transport Protocol in the list, you can display the NWLink configuration Properties sheet shown in Figure 1-10.

Configuring NWLink is less complex than manually configuring TCP/IP. You need to enter an internal network number (in many cases, the default 00000000 will work) and either set the frame type to Auto Detect or enter a frame type that matches that of the NetWare server. Frame types supported are

- Ethernet 802.2
- Ethernet 803.3
- Ethernet II
- Ethernet SNAP

The NWLink
IPX/SPX/
NetBIOS
Compatible
Transport
Protocol
Properties
sheet

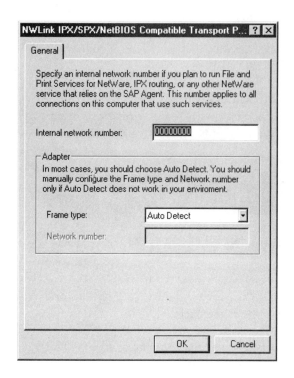

exam
ⓦatch

The standard frame type for NetWare 2.x and 3.11 servers is 802.3.
NetWare 3.12 and later versions use a default frame type of 802.2.

When you set a specific frame type (instead of using Auto Detect), you will need
to enter a network number (sometimes referred to as the external network number,
to distinguish it from the internal network number that identifies the computer on
the network for internal routing). The external network number must be unique
for that segment; computers on the same segment that use the same frame type
must also use the same network number, in order to be able to communicate with
one another.

Hardware Configuration and Management   Configuring hardware in
Windows 2000 is in many cases much easier than the same task in Windows NT,
primarily due to the new support for Plug and Play. Remember, though, that this

only applies to devices that are Plug and Play compatible, and the computer's BIOS must also support PnP.

The Add/Remove Hardware Wizard, shown in Figure 1-11, provides a step-by-step guide to installing, removing, and troubleshooting hardware peripherals.

Chapter 7 goes into great detail on how to configure various hardware devices and their device drivers, including

- DVD and CD-ROM drives, hard disks, and removable media devices
- Display adapters and monitors
- Mobile/portable computer hardware; APM and PCMCIA (PC Card) devices
- Input/output devices such as keyboards, pointing devices, printers, scanners, digital cameras, and smart cards.
- Modems
- Infrared, wireless and Universal Serial Bus (USB) devices
- Multiprocessor systems
- Network Interface Adapters

FIGURE 1-11

The Add/Remove Hardware Wizard simplifies the installation and configuration of legacy Plug and Play devices when needed

There are some devices that Windows 2000 cannot detect; in these cases, you will have to manually install and configure the hardware. This may require you to determine what hardware resources are available. To do this in Windows 2000 Professional, perform the following sequence: Start | Settings | Control Panel | System | Hardware, and select the Device Manager tab.

On the View menu, select Resources by type. Figure 1-12 shows the IRQs in use on the system.

When you have determined what resources are available, you can install the hardware device manually, using the Add/Remove Hardware Wizard. You can also change the resources being used by a device by selecting to list devices by type in the View menu, and then right-clicking on the device name and selecting Properties from the shortcut menu. This will bring up the device's Properties sheet, and you can choose the Resources tab and click Change Setting to modify the IRQ, I/O, and memory ranges being used.

FIGURE 1-12

Using Device Manager to view the available resources

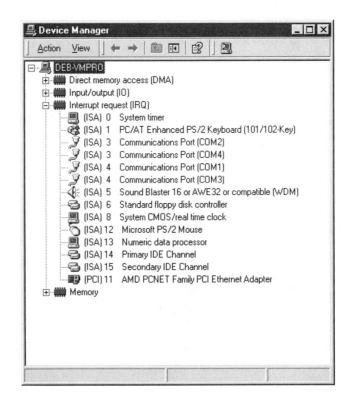

Configuring Remote Access Services   Windows 2000 Professional makes it easy to set up a remote access connection, and for the exam, you will need to be able to configure both dial-up and virtual private networking (VPN) connections. Remote Access Services (RAS) allows you to connect to either a remote access server or the Internet (through an ISP or online service) over a dial-up connection.

You use the Start | Settings | Network And Dial-Up Connections feature to create a new connection, and you can then use Internet Connection Sharing (ICS) to share that connection with other computers on your network. Chapter 11 will provide step-by-step instruction in how to create a dial-up connection and connect to a dial-up server, as well as how to make and use a VPN connection. The Network Connection Wizard guides you through the process.

To share a connection, you right-click on the connection name in the Network And Dial-Up Connections folder, select Properties, and then select the Sharing tab. You will see the dialog box displayed in Figure 1-13.

FIGURE 1-13

Sharing a
connection with
other computers
on the LAN

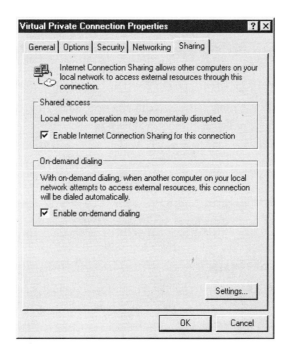

Internet Connection Sharing (ICS) is provided with both Windows 2000 Professional and Server. Windows 2000 Server also supports Network Address Translation (NAT), which is configured through Routing and Remote Access (RRAS) and allows for more flexibility and modification of default configuration settings. ICS can be thought of as "NAT lite"—it uses the same address translation technology, but is a much simpler version of NAT that is useful for connecting a few computers on a small LAN to the Internet or a remote server through a single phone line and account. The NAT protocol provided in Windows 2000 Server allows you to change the IP address range of the DHCP allocator, and can be used when there are DNS and DHCP servers on the network (ICS should not be used in those circumstances).

Security Configuration   The last of the Windows 2000 configuration issues covered by this exam is security. Windows 2000 gives the administrator far more flexibility and many options for controlling access and securing confidential data than were available in NT. Security features in Windows 2000 include

- **EFS (Encrypting File System)**   Allows you to encrypt data on NTFS partitions at the file level without the need for third-party software, so that other users will not be able to read the data even if they have NTFS permissions to the file or folder.
- **Local Group Policy settings**   Windows 2000 Professional's local group policies allow you to enable auditing of security events, manage account policies, and control user rights.
- **Windows 2000 authentication**   Windows 2000 can use various authentication methods depending on the network environment. NTLM can be used when Windows 2000 Professional is used as a client in an NT domain, and Kerberos is used in a Windows 2000 domain tree, providing support for two-way transitive trusts between domains.

Administration Issues

Administration issues that you must be familiar with for Exam 70-210 include

- Using Active Directory
- Group Policy Administration
- Management of Shared Resources

■ Assigning Access Permissions

■ Auditing

■ Performance Monitoring and Troubleshooting

■ Data/Disk Management

Let's take a brief look at each of these topics now. They will be covered in more detail in the chapters to follow.

Using Active Directory

One of the most exciting new features in Windows 2000 is the Active Directory, Microsoft's new, improved, sophisticated *directory services* technology. The Active Directory is implemented on Windows 2000 domain controllers, and the directory can be accessed from Windows 2000 Professional as an Active Directory client.

on the **Job** *Windows 95 and 98 can also function as Active Directory clients, with the add-on client software that is provided on the Windows 2000 Server CD. The client software will allow Windows 9x clients to utilize the benefits of the Distributed File System (Dfs) and search the Active Directory for resources. Note that the Active Desktop must be enabled on the 9x computer (which necessitates installing Internet Explorer 4.01 on Windows 95 machines) in order to run the Directory Client Setup Wizard.*

Overview of Active Directory What is a directory service, anyway? A *directory,* in this context, is a database that contains information about objects and their attributes. An analogy would be a telephone directory; the "objects" it contains are names, and the attributes of each object include the telephone number and address associated with that name. Directories utilized by network operating systems can, of course, be much more complex. The *directory service* is the component that organizes the objects into a logical and accessible structure, and provides for a means of searching and locating objects within the directory. The directory service includes the entire directory *and* the method of storing it on the network.

The Active Directory arranges objects—including computer information, user and group information, shared folders, printers, and other resources—in a hierarchical structure, in which domains can be joined into *trees* (groups of domains that share a contiguous namespace), and trees can be joined into *forests* (groups of domain trees that share a common schema, configuration, and global catalog). Active Directory also allows you to place objects into *container objects* called *organizational units (OUs)* and assign administrative authority on a more granular level than was possible in "flat" NT domains. See the later section on terminology, "What You Should Already Know," for definitions of these terms; all of these concepts will be addressed in great detail in the core Exams 70-215, "Implementing and Administering Windows 2000 Server," and 70-217, "Implementing and Administering Windows 2000 Directory Services Infrastructure."

The Active Directory simplifies administrative tasks and offers more flexibility and levels of control, at the same time making it easy for users to locate and access resources without knowing the physical location of those resources on the network.

The Windows 2000 Active Directory is compatible with industry standards such as LDAP (the Lightweight Directory Access Protocol), and thus can interact with other LDAP directory services such as Novell's NDS (Novell Directory Services).

Users, Groups, and Computers   As with Windows NT, Windows 2000 networks provide both local and domain user accounts. Local accounts allow users to log on at the particular computer, while domain accounts allow logging on to the Windows 2000 domain and using resources throughout the network. Information about domain accounts is stored in the Active Directory on Windows 2000 Server domain controllers. Also like NT, users can be placed into *groups* to make it easier to manage large numbers of users. Unlike NT, there are two types of groups in a Windows 2000 domain: *security groups,* to which access permissions can be assigned and which are similar to the groups you may be familiar with from working with NT; and a new type, *distribution groups,* which are used by applications for nonsecurity purposes.

On a Windows 2000 Professional computer, you can create a local user account or a local group by using the Computer Management MMC. Domain user accounts and groups are created on domain controllers (or Windows 2000 Professional workstations running the server tools) using the Active Directory Users and Computers administrative tool.

Windows 2000 also includes built-in system groups. You do not assign users to these groups; their membership is based on user characteristics. Examples of system groups include

■ **The Everyone group**   Encompasses all users

- **Authenticated users group**   Includes all users with valid user accounts (does not include anonymous users)

- **Creator-owner**   The user who originally created or has taken ownership of a resource

- **Network**   Includes users who are connecting to a shared resource over the network

- **Interactive**   The user account physically logged on to the computer

- **Anonymous**   Users who were not authenticated by Windows 2000 logon authentication

- **Dialup**   Users connected over a dial-up connection

A computer account must be created in a domain for each Windows 2000 computer that wishes to join the domain. Only domain administrators can create computer accounts. Computer accounts are managed through the Active Directory Users and Computers MMC on a domain controller.

Publishing Resources to the Directory   Resources—such as folders and printers, which are available to be shared on the network—can be *published* to the Active Directory. The resources that are published to the Directory can be easily located by users, who can query the Directory based on the resource's properties (for example, to locate all color printers). You can search by specified advanced criteria to locate

- Users, contacts, and groups
- Computers
- Printers
- Shared folders
- Organizational units
- Customized specification

Figure 1-14 shows the Active Directory query box.

You can query
the Active
Directory
to locate any
resource that
is published in
the Directory.

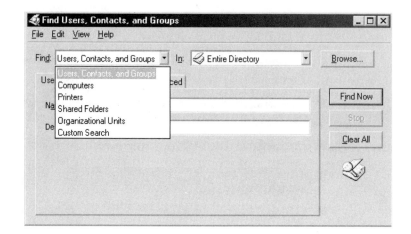

Group Policy Administration

Windows 2000 uses *Group Policy* and the local security policy to control the desktop environment, assign user rights, and set audit policies. In a Windows 2000 domain, administrators can use the Group Policy MMC snap-in to specify logon/logoff and startup/shutdown scripts, deploy software, configure security, and redirect folders to a network location.

Group policy administration is an important topic in Exam 70-217, "Implementing and Administering a Windows 2000 Directory Services Infrastructure." For Exam 70-210, you need to be familiar with the Windows 2000 Professional local policy settings. Figure 1-15 shows the Group Policy MMC for the local computer policies.

Creating a Group Policy MMC in Windows 2000 Professional   You can create a custom MMC for managing local group policy on a Windows 2000 computer by following these steps:

1. Type **mmc** at the command prompt or in the Start | Run box. This will open an empty MMC console.

2. On the Console menu, select Add/Remove Snap-In.

3. In the Add/Remove Snap-In dialog box, click Add.

4. In the Add Standalone Snap-In dialog box, select Group Policy.

5. Accept the default group policy object, Local Computer Policy, by clicking Finish. Click Close, and then OK.

FIGURE 1-15

Windows 2000
Professional
local computer
policy MMC

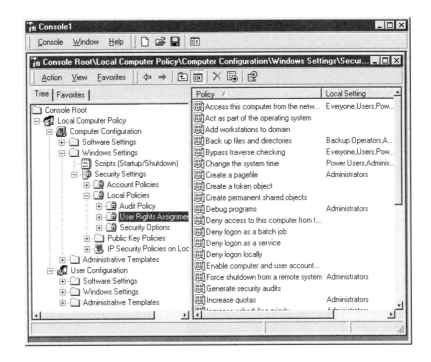

6. The MMC will now display the Local Computer Policy settings, as shown
previously in Figure 1-15.

Group policy is addressed in detail in Chapter 12, "Implementing, Monitoring,
and Troubleshooting Security."

Using the Local Security Settings Tool   A subset of the group policy
settings, local security settings, can be accessed and administered using the Local
Security Settings utility, found in the Control Panel's Administrative Tools menu.
The Local Security settings include

- ■ **Account Policies**   Password policies and account lockout policies
- ■ **Local Policies**   Audit policies, user rights assignment, and security options
- ■ **Public Key Policies**   Configure encrypted data recovery agents and trusted
certificate authorities.
- ■ **IP Security (IPSec) Policies**   Configure network IP security on the local
machine

Managing Shared Resources

A *shared resource* is a device, data, or program that is made available to network users. These can include folders, files, printers, and even Internet connections. Chapter 4 will walk you, in detail, through the process of sharing resources and connecting to shared resources on a Windows 2000 network, including shared folders, printers, and Internet connections.

Shared Folders   Sharing folders so that other users can access their contents across the network is easy in Windows 2000, as easy as right-clicking the folder name in Windows Explorer, selecting the Sharing tab, and choosing Share This Folder. An entire drive and all the folders on that drive can be shared in the same way.

exam
ⓦatch   *The name of the folder will be the default name of the share, but you can change the share name by typing in a different one. This does not change the name of the folder itself.*

You can limit the number of users allowed to connect to the shared folder or drive simultaneously. You may wish to do this to reduce the load placed on your computer when it acts as a server; the more users connected, the bigger the performance hit you'll experience.

Shared Printers   The process for sharing a printer attached to your local computer is similar to that for sharing a folder or drive. If the users who will access your printer will do so from machines that don't run the Windows 2000 operating system, you will need to install drivers for the other operating system(s).

exam
ⓦatch   *When you install a printer on a Windows 2000 Professional computer, it is not shared by default. When you install a printer on a Windows 2000 Server computer, it is shared by default.*

If your computer is a member of a Windows 2000 domain, you can publish the printer to the Active Directory to make it easier for other users to locate.

FROM THE CLASSROOM

File and Print Sharing

In order to share folders or printers, File And Printer Sharing For Microsoft Networks must be enabled. This is the service that allows other computers on the network to access your resources, and is the equivalent of the Server Service on NT 4.0 computers. You can configure the service, which is installed by default, by right-clicking the desired connection (for example, the local area connection) and selecting Properties. File And Printer Sharing For Microsoft Networks will be listed on the General tab.

—Debra Littlejohn Shinder, MCSE, MCP+I, MCT

Connection Sharing A dial-up or VPN connection can be shared with other computers on the LAN, using Internet Connect Sharing (ICS). How to share a connection, and the specifics of using a shared connection, will be addressed in detail in Chapter 11.

Assigning Access Permissions

One of the most common tasks in administering a network is managing the assignment of access permissions. Windows 2000 allows you to control access to objects in several ways. Shared resources are protected by share permissions, which are assigned to the share and apply only when the resource is being accessed across the network. Resources located on NTFS formatted partitions can further be protected by NTFS file-level permissions, which apply both to across-the-network access and to users accessing the resource from the local machine. Permissions can also be assigned to Active Directory objects, in a Windows 2000 domain environment.

Although permissions work much as they did in Windows NT 4.0, you will find that you can assign permissions on a far more granular basis.

Permissions can be explicitly assigned or inherited from a parent object. Windows 2000 allows you to control the inheritance behavior. Understanding the different types of permissions, how they interact, and how inheritance works will be important in passing the Windows 2000 Professional certification exam. These topics are covered in both Chapters 4 and 5.

Auditing

Windows 2000 gives you the ability to audit security-related events, to track access to objects, use of user rights, and detect attempted and successful access (authorized and unauthorized) to the network.

Auditing is not enabled by default, but once enabled, a security log is generated that provides information you specify in regard to specific activities that are performed on the computer.

Monitoring and Troubleshooting

A network administrator is tasked with ensuring the continued performance of the network and the computers on the network. Practicing preventative maintenance requires the ability to monitor various performance-related issues.

Windows 2000 includes the Performance tool, accessed via the Administrative Tools menu. The System Monitor is part of this utility, and allows you to collect and view data about current memory, disk, processor, and other system activity. The second part of the Performance tool is the Logs and Alerts function, which allows you to specify notification when a particular counter's value goes above or below the threshold you define.

Data Management

In Windows 2000, you have a great deal of flexibility in managing disks and data. The Disk Management component of the Computer Management snap-in gives you the ability to configure hard disks as either basic or dynamic storage. With dynamic storage, you are able to divide disks into *volumes,* instead of the traditional primary and extended partitions. Windows 2000 allows you to create spanned and striped volumes on a dynamic disk.

SCENARIO & SOLUTION	
What is a simple volume?	A simple volume is a volume created on a dynamic disk that is not fault tolerant, and includes space from only one physical disk.
What is a spanned volume?	A spanned volume is similar to a volume set in NT 4.0. It contains space from multiple disks (up to 32), and provides a way to combine small "chunks" of disk space into one unit, seen by the operating system as a single volume. It is not fault tolerant.
What is a striped volume?	Like a stripe set in NT 4.0, a striped volume combines free space from up to 32 physical disks into one volume by writing data across the disks in stripes. This increases performance but does not provide fault tolerance.

exam
ⓦatch

Windows 2000 Server allows you to create fault-tolerant volumes—mirrored volumes and RAID 5 volumes—on dynamic disks; however, Windows 2000 Professional does not support disk fault tolerance.

Another advantage of dynamic disks is the ability to resize volumes without losing data and without restarting the operating system.

Using Disk Quotas   Windows NT administrators often wished there was a way to restrict the amount of disk space that could be allocated to a particular user. Unfortunately, to accomplish this in NT, it was necessary to buy third-party add-on software. Windows 2000 provides *disk quotas*, a new feature that allows you to track and control disk usage for individual users or groups.

Disk quotas can be enabled only on NTFS formatted volumes, and only by an administrator.

Data Compression   Windows 2000 offers the capability of compressing data on a file-level basis, as long as the files and folders are located on an NTFS formatted partition or volume. Compression saves disk space; however, NTFS compression cannot be used in conjunction with file encryption.

Data Encryption   Unlike Windows NT 4.0, Windows 2000 provides the Encrypting File System (EFS) that allows you to encrypt and decrypt data on a file-by-file basis, as long as it is stored on an NTFS formatted partition or volume. EFS is based on *public key cryptography.*

Windows 2000 also provides a recovery function that can be used by administrators to recover encrypted data if necessary.

The cipher.exe utility allows you to encrypt files at the command line, or EFS can be implemented via the Windows Explorer.

EFS only encrypts data that is stored on disk; it does not encrypt data sent over the network. Windows 2000 provides IPSec and PPTP encryption for security when transmitting data across the network.

on the

Job

EFS uses 56-bit encryption by default. This is because of legal restrictions on exporting encryption technologies with stronger security. You can order a 128-bit encryption package called CryptoPAK from Microsoft (available only in North America) for stronger security.

Data Backup   A backup and disaster protection plan is an essential part of a network administrator's duties, and Windows 2000 provides a built-in Backup utility that can be used to back up data to tape or file, or to create an Emergency Repair Disk (ERD) that can be used to repair a computer with damaged system files.

The Backup utility can be accessed from the System Tools menu (Start | Programs | Accessories | System Tools) or by typing **ntbackup** at the command line.

The Windows 2000 Backup utility allows you to schedule regular backups, and includes both the Backup Wizard and the Restore Wizard to guide you through the processes of backing up and restoring data (see Figure 1-16).

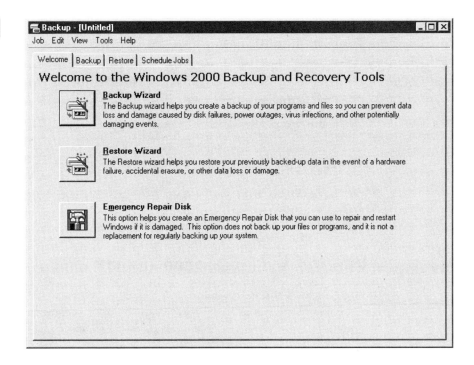

FIGURE 1-16

The Windows
2000 Backup
utility

CERTIFICATION OBJECTIVE 1.04

Overview of Exam 70-210

For a complete list of the learning objectives for Exam 70-210, see the Microsoft Web site at www.microsoft.com/mcp/exam/stat/SP70-210.htm. The objectives are somewhat broad, and you'll note that they are performance based. This does not mean that you don't need to know any of the theory behind the concepts being tested. It does mean that *only* knowing the theory, without having ever put it into practice by working with the operating system, will make it difficult or even impossible for you to pass the exam.

The objectives are divided into logical categories that include all the general topics discussed earlier—more specifically,

- Installation issues, both attended and unattended
- Resource management
- Hardware and device driver issues
- Performance monitoring and optimization
- The Desktop environment
- Network protocols and services
- Security

Correlation Between Windows 2000 and NT 4.0 Exams

It might be tempting to try to draw a correlation between the NT 4.0 core exams and the new Windows 2000 core exams. In so doing, you might conclude that Exam 70-210, the Windows 2000 Professional exam is a replacement for the old NT Workstation exam (70-073). However, the Windows 2000 Professional exam requires more in-depth knowledge of basic networking concepts, along with the essentials of installing, using, and troubleshooting the operating system.

Target Audience

Microsoft's stated "target audience" for this exam is somewhat different from the intended audience for the Networking Essentials exam (70-058), for which Microsoft lists no prerequisites on the exam preparation Web page. There has been a lot of talk, with the advent of the Windows 2000 certification track, about Microsoft's desire to "raise the bar" and restore the MCSE to the status of a "premium" certification. This is reflected in the suggested prerequisites.

Experienced Networking Professionals

According to the Microsoft Web site and documentation, exam candidates are presumed to be networking personnel operating in medium-to-very-large computing environments with a minimum of a year's experience in administering and implementing Windows networking components and supporting 200 or more users in five or more physical locations. It is also presumed that the exam taker is familiar with typical network services and applications, such as file and print sharing, databases, messaging services, proxy and/or firewalls, dial-in remote access servers, Web hosting, and desktop management and control.

What If You're New to Networking?

The preceding does not mean that if you don't have on-the-job experience as a network administrator, you won't be able to pass the Windows 2000 exams. It does mean that if you don't meet the description of the exam's "target audience," you will need to study harder and, in particular, you will need to get more hands-on practice in working with the products.

This book contains a large number of practical exercises that walk you through the steps of procedures common to working network professionals. In order to really understand the concepts and skills covered by the exam, it is essential that you do more than read through the exercises—you must work through them on a Windows 2000 computer. This can be done on a relatively simple home network, and we highly recommend that you consider setting up a two- or three-system lab if you don't have access to a network on the job or in a classroom situation. The cost of doing so is an investment that can quickly pay for itself in terms of time saved in obtaining the certification.

Exam Objectives

Let's take a look at what's included in each of the broad exam objectives mentioned earlier.

Installing Windows 2000 Professional

This objective involves performance of both attended and unattended installations of Windows 2000 Professional. You should be familiar with the use of Remote Installation Services (RIS), and how to use the System Preparation tool. You need to be able to create answer files for an unattended install, using the Setup Manager.

Additionally, you should be well acquainted with issues involved in upgrading to Windows 2000 from previous versions of Windows, including Windows NT 4.0 and Windows 95 and 98. You'll be required to know how to apply update packs to installed software applications, and how to prepare a computer to meet upgrade requirements. You must also know how to deploy service packs, and understand the basics of troubleshooting a failed installation.

Implementing and Conducting Administration of Resources

For this objective, it is important to be very familiar with the process of monitoring, managing, and troubleshooting file and folder access in Windows 2000. You must be able to configure and troubleshoot file compression, know how to control access to files and folders using share and NTFS permissions, and be able to optimize access.

You should be well versed in creating and removing shared folders, and know how to manage and troubleshoot Web server resources. Be sure you know how to connect to both local and network print devices, can manage printers and print jobs, and know how to control access to printers using permissions. You should be able to connect to a printer over the Internet, as well as to a local print device.

This objective also requires that you understand configuration and management of file systems. You must be capable of converting from one file system to another, and know how to configure file systems using FAT16, FAT32, and NTFS.

Implementing, Managing, and Troubleshooting Hardware Devices and Drivers

This seemingly simple objective covers a lot of ground. You will be expected to know how to implement, manage, and troubleshoot disks and storage devices—including hard disks and the configuration of volumes, CD-ROM and DVD devices, and removable media such as tape drives.

In addition, you need to be able to implement and manage display devices, including multiple-monitor configurations. You should be able to install, configure, and troubleshoot display adapters, and be familiar with common video problems and their solutions.

Implementation, management, and troubleshooting of mobile computer hardware are other important aspects of this objective. Be sure you know how to configure the Advanced Power Management (APM) feature, as well as how to configure and work with PCMCIA (PC card) services and devices.

Be very well acquainted with the intricacies of installing, using, and troubleshooting input and output devices. These include keyboards, pointing devices, scanners, printers, multimedia devices, smart card readers, and digital cameras. Know how to install and manage modems and other communications devices such as ISDN terminal adapters. Be able to install, configure, and manage infrared (IrDA) devices and wireless communications devices, and know how to work with Universal Serial Bus (USB) devices.

This objective also requires that you have mastered installing and updating hardware device drivers, both for Plug and Play devices and those that must be installed manually. Pay special attention to configuration and troubleshooting of network interface cards (NICs), and be aware of the procedures for monitoring and configuring multiple processing units.

Monitoring and Optimizing System Performance and Reliability

Performance monitoring is the focus of this next exam objective. In this regard, you should be able to manage and troubleshoot driver signing, which is a new feature in Windows 2000. Know how to use and address problems with the Task Scheduler, and practice managing and troubleshooting the offline files feature, including synchronization.

You should be able to optimize and troubleshoot the Windows 2000 Professional desktop environment and system performance. This includes memory performance, processor utilization, disk performance, network performance, and application performance. You should be familiar with using the System Monitor and other built-in tools to help you accomplish these tasks.

Ensure that you understand the concept of hardware profiles, and how and when to use them. Also be sure you know how to use the Windows Backup utility to back up data to tape or file, and how to recover user and system data. You should be acquainted with the Safe Mode feature, and know how to troubleshoot system restoration using it. Finally, you will need to know how to install and use the Recovery Console in Windows 2000 Professional.

Configuring and Troubleshooting the Desktop Environment

Another very important exam objective, this one deals with controlling the desktop environment, which involves configuring and managing user profiles, enabling multilanguage/multilocation support, and configuring local settings.

You must also know how to use Windows Installer Packages to deploy software, how to configure and troubleshoot desktop settings, the configuration and troubleshooting of fax support, and how to manage the accessibility services provided in Windows 2000.

Implementing, Managing, and Troubleshooting Network Protocols and Services

Windows 2000 is built around networking, and this objective requires that you be able to configure networking protocols on a Windows 2000 Professional computer, establish dial-up networking connections, understand and use virtual private networking (VPN), and be familiar with configuration and troubleshooting issues for Internet Connection Sharing (ICS).

Be intimately familiar with the procedure for configuring TCP/IP properties, including manual IP address assignment, the function of the subnet mask and default gateway, and using the Dynamic Host Configuration Protocol (DHCP) and Automatic Private IP Addressing (APIPA) to obtain TCP/IP information.

You should also be able to use TCP/IP utilities such as IPCONFIG to verify settings and gather configuration information, and know how to connect to shared resources on a Microsoft network, via My Network Places and Windows Explorer, by mapping network drives, and through the UNC path.

Implementing, Monitoring, and Troubleshooting Security

The last exam objective for 70-210 deals with security issues. Security is a big topic in Windows 2000, and is addressed specifically in elective Exam 70-220, "Designing Security for a Windows 2000 Network."

For the Windows 2000 Professional exam, you will need to be acquainted with these specific security issues:

- Data encryption using EFS (the Encrypting File System)
- Using local Group Policy to provide security
- Configuring, managing, and troubleshooting local user accounts and account settings, and how to create and administer local users and groups
- Assigning and troubleshooting user rights
- Auditing issues
- User authentication issues
- Configuring and troubleshooting domain user accounts

In essence, you should be comfortable with implementing, configuring, managing, and troubleshooting a security configuration on Windows 2000 Professional computers that are members of a Windows 2000 domain.

What We'll Cover in This Book

Each of the exam topics covered in the 70-210 list of objectives will be addressed in this book. However, we will go beyond the basic "how to" aspect, even though the certification objectives are written almost exclusively as performance-based statements. We know that in order to really understand what you're doing, you need to know the theory behind it. If you have many long years of on-the-job experience working with NT, *and* have worked a great deal with extra add-on software and third-party products, you may already be familiar with the concepts behind these task-oriented objectives. Otherwise, it will benefit you to read the explanatory text carefully and perform the exercises in each chapter.

Knowledge

In the beginning of each chapter, we will try to provide you with a foundation of knowledge upon which conceptual comprehension and practices skills can be built. This includes definitions of new terms, explanations of processes, and discussions of relationships between components.

Topic Tie-Ins

We will cross-reference subjects that appear elsewhere in the book, that tie in to the topic of the chapter and/or that will aid you in understanding the material to be presented in the chapter.

Concepts

In addition to basic knowledge-based information such as definitions and relationships, we will provide an overview of the concepts behind the skills-based exercises. For example, encrypting data using EFS involves a skill set. Understanding the *concept* of encryption—using a secure defined algorithm to scramble data so that it will not be readable by unauthorized persons—is not absolutely necessary in order to perform the task, but will certainly be helpful to you in making configuration decisions.

Inasmuch as possible, the authors will attempt to make all abstract concepts as easy to understand as possible, using analogies and graphical illustrations.

Practical Skills

The heart of Windows 2000 exam preparation is development of practical skills— the ability not just to know about the operating system, but also to use it to perform common network administration tasks. The exams are performance based, as is obvious from the wording of the exam objectives, almost all of which use action verbs such as configure, install, monitor, troubleshoot, manage, create, remove, implement, and the like.

More so than with the NT exams, it is imperative that you do the practical exercises in each chapter, that you experiment with various settings and options, and that you get hands-on experience in performing the tasks about which you read.

Many of the exam questions will be relatively simple for those who have worked with the product, and almost impossible to answer for those who haven't gone through the processes themselves. In this book, we attempt to simulate the Windows 2000 working environment as much as possible by liberal use of screenshots and detailed descriptions of what to expect in response to particular actions or commands; however, there is no substitute for *doing it yourself.*

Chapter-by-Chapter Overview

The material in this book is broken into chapters based on logical topic divisions and with an eye toward presenting material in "manageable chunks." You may notice that some exam objectives have been spread across more than one chapter; while in other cases, a chapter may span multiple objectives. This is because some of the topics are relatively straightforward and simple to explain and master, while others are so complex that they must be broken down into several component parts and require background information in order to give a real understanding.

Let's look briefly at the layout of the book and what we'll address in each chapter.

Chapter 2: Performing an Attended Installation of Windows 2000 Professional

Chapter 2 begins at the beginning, taking you through the installation process in detail. The installation issues we touched upon briefly in this chapter will be expanded and extrapolated into practical exercises. Various installation scenarios will be addressed, and common installation problems will be discussed and resolved. You'll learn to install from a CD or over the network from a network share.

Chapter 3: Performing an Unattended Installation of Windows 2000 Professional

Chapter 3 continues the installation topic, building on the relatively simple process of installing Windows 2000 Professional to a single computer that you mastered in Chapter 2 and moving on to complex enterprisewide deployment of a Windows 2000 Professional rollout to multiple computers simultaneously, using the unattended install features such as scripting support and Remote Installation Services (RIS). In this chapter, you learn all about the utilities provided to prepare for such a rollout, including SysPrep and RIPrep.

Chapter 4: Implementing and Conducting Administration of Resources

Once you've learned all about installing the operating system, you will be ready to tackle Chapter 4, which plunges you directly into the processes involved in managing resources on your newly installed Windows 2000 Professional machine. This chapter starts with controlling file and folder access, and introduces you to file compression and access optimization.

You'll learn how to create, manage, and remove shared folders, and how to assign permissions to restrict access. You'll find out how permissions work in Windows 2000, including inheritance behavior, and how inheritance can be blocked or forced.

You will learn how to connect to shares on Windows-based machines on your network, and also how to connect to a NetWare server and access its resources. This chapter also discusses accessing and using an FTP server, and wraps up by discussing Microsoft's Internet Information Server (IIS), which provides access to Web resources, and how it is installed, configured, and managed.

Chapter 5: Implementing Printing and File Systems

Chapter 5 will take you into the tasks of connecting to and using printers. You will learn to connect to local and network printers, and how to manage printers and print jobs. You'll also find out how to control access to printers using permissions, how to connect to an Internet printer, and how to locate a printer in the Active Directory and connect to it.

This chapter will also cover the basics of configuring and managing file systems. You will start with a review of the characteristics of the FAT, FAT32, and NTFS file systems and criteria for choosing which file system to use in a particular situation. You will learn how to convert a partition from one file system to another, using Windows 2000's convert.exe utility, and then we will discuss how to configure file systems.

Chapter 6: Implementing, Managing, and Troubleshooting Disks and Displays

Chapter 6 addresses the configuration and management of disks and display devices, two of the most important hardware components on your Windows 2000 Professional computer. You will learn about various disk device types, and how to install and manage them. First, we will look at CD-ROM drives, and then we will discuss the newer technology, DVD.

We'll talk about hard disks and how they are configured in Windows 2000. We'll look at the new disk management features of the new operating system, including the ability to work with either traditional basic disks or convert them to a new type, dynamic disks, which allow you to resize volumes without losing data and provide the means to create fault-tolerant volumes such as mirrored and RAID 5 volumes. We'll discuss the characteristics, advantages, and disadvantages of each.

Then you will learn about using removable media, such as tape devices commonly used for backup. You'll find out about new, high-performance technologies like fibre channel, and we will discuss the 1394 interface (FireWire) and the popular new Universal Serial Bus interface (USB), all of which offer faster transfer of data than was possible with old serial or parallel connections.

When we turn to the topic of display devices, you will learn how to install a video adapter, and how to troubleshoot common problems that occur relating to display adapters and monitors. Topics include using the VGA startup mode to diagnose and repair video-related problems. You'll also find out how to take advantage of Windows 2000's support for multiple displays, and how to configure your Windows 2000 Professional computer to use up to 10 monitors in a multiple display arrangement.

Chapter 7: Implementing, Managing, and Troubleshooting Hardware Devices and Drivers

In Chapter 7, you will explore methods for managing and troubleshooting a large number of hardware devices and their device drivers. Windows 2000's hardware support and Plug and Play capabilities make it far more "hardware friendly" than NT, and a wide variety of devices can be used. The first section will focus on hardware associated with mobile/portable computers, including Advanced Power Management (APM)—a feature long awaited by laptop users running NT—and how to configure and use PCMCIA (PC card) services.

The next part of the chapter addresses the use and synchronization of offline files, an exciting new feature in Windows 2000 that allows users to continue working with network files and programs even when disconnected from the network.

Input and output devices—such as keyboards, pointing devices, scanners, printers, and even the new "smart card" readers—are discussed in the next section. Special attention is given to configuring and using multimedia devices and digital cameras. How to set up, configure, and troubleshoot modems (necessity in this Internet-connected era) is covered thoroughly, and you will learn the basics of Windows 2000's Telephony Application Programming Interface (TAPI) and how it works with communications programs and network services.

New connectivity types, such as infrared (IrDA), wireless, and Universal Serial Bus (USB), will be addressed, and you will learn how to install, configure, and manage these interfaces and devices in Windows 2000.

An essential element of hardware management is working with device drivers, and you will learn about installing and updating drivers. Windows 2000 Professional, like NT 4.0 Workstation, supports multiple processing (two processors), and we also cover special issues and problems that occur with multiprocessing units. Finally, we will look at how to make various types of network interface cards (NICs) work in your network environment, and we'll talk about configuring and troubleshooting network adapters to pin down hardware-related connectivity problems.

SCENARIO & SOLUTION

What is WDM, and what does it have to do with Windows 2000's increased hardware support?	The Win32 Driver Model (WDM) provides a standard for device drivers that will work across Windows platforms (specifically Windows 98 and 2000), so that you can use the same drivers with the consumer and business versions of the Windows operating system.
What are the power options included in Windows 2000?	Power options are dependent on the particular hardware, but include Standby mode (which turns off the monitor and hard disks to save power) and Hibernation (which turns off the monitor and disks, saves everything that is in memory to disk, turns off the computer, and then restores the desktop to the state in which you left it when the computer is turned on).
What type of multiprocessing does Windows 2000 support?	SMP (Symmetric Multiprocessing), in which all processors are treated as equals, and any thread can be run on any available processor. Windows 2000 also supports processor affinity, in which a process or thread can specify which set of processors it should run on (APIs must be defined in the application).

Chapter 8: Monitoring and Optimizing System Performance and Reliability

In Chapter 8, system performance and reliability are the focus, and you will learn about another new feature in Windows 2000: driver signing, options for which include ignoring device drivers that are not digitally signed, displaying a warning when it detects device drivers that are not digitally signed (the default), or preventing you from installing device drivers without digital signatures.

The second topic addressed in this chapter is the Task Scheduler, which allows you to schedule any script, program, or document to run at a time that is convenient for you. Task Scheduler starts each time you start Windows 2000, and it runs in the background. You can use the Scheduled Task Wizard, accessed via Control Panel, to set up specified tasks to run daily, weekly, or monthly, and customize how tasks run at the scheduled times.

Next, we address how to configure and troubleshoot desktop performance issues in Windows 2000. These include memory performance, processor utilization, disk performance, network performance, and application performance. Administrators have flexibility and control over optimization of different resources, and this section will tell you how to get the most out of your Windows 2000 Professional computer.

Next we look at hardware profiles, which are sets of instructions that tell Windows 2000 which devices to start when you start your computer, or what settings to use for each device. Hardware profiles can be devised to make it easy to use portable computers in different environments, and you will learn how to configure and manage them via the Hardware tab in the System applet in the Control Panel.

The last part of this chapter takes you through the concepts and processes related to recovering systems and user data in the event of system failure, disk failure, or other catastrophes that threaten loss of vital data. You will learn about the Windows Backup utility, how to use Safe Mode and other startup options for troubleshooting and repair activities, and what you can do with the Recovery Console (a command-line interface that provides a limited set of administrative commands that are useful for repairing a computer, starting and stopping services, reading and writing data on a local drive, repairing a master boot record (MBR), and formatting drives).

Chapter 9: Configuring and Troubleshooting the Desktop Environment

Chapter 9 introduces you to configuration, control, and troubleshooting of the Windows 2000 Professional desktop environment. This involves creating and managing user profiles, which define customized desktop environments including individual display settings, network and printer connections, and other specified settings. You'll also learn how to configure roaming profiles, which follow users regardless of what computer they log on to.

You will learn how to restrict users from changing their desktop settings, how to control what icons appear on users' desktops, and how to restrict the Start menu to only those items you wish to appear.

Another topic addressed in this chapter is configuration and troubleshooting of facsimile (fax) support in Windows 2000. You will learn how the Windows 2000 Fax feature, which supports classes 1, 2, and 2.0 fax devices, interacts with the fax modem, and how to use the supported Fax commands that are available in the Start | Programs | Accessories | Communications | Fax menu if you have a fax modem or other fax device installed and configured.

The chapter wraps up with an overview of the accessibility services, such as

- **Magnifier**, which enlarges part of the screen for better viewing
- **Narrator**, which reads the screen text using speech synthesis
- **On-screen keyboard**, which allows for the use of a pointing device to type onscreen
- **Control Panel Accessibility Options**, including StickyKeys, FilterKeys, ToggleKeys, SoundSentry, ShowSounds, High Contrast, MouseKeys, and SerialKeys.
- The **Accessibility Wizard**, which helps set up the previously listed programs and options based on an individual's customized needs.

Chapter 10: Configuring Multilanguage Support and Using Windows Installer

Chapter 10 addresses Windows 2000's support for multilanguage and multi-location support. In this chapter, you will learn a little about UNICODE, which is a 16-bit character encoding standard developed by the Unicode Consortium between 1988 and 1991 that uses two bytes to represent each character and enables almost all of the written languages of the world to be represented using a single character set. With multiple languages installed on your computer, you can compose documents that contain more than one language.

In this context, we will also discuss the Right-To-Left (RTL) Orientation API that can be used to support languages such as Hebrew and Arabic. You will learn how to enable and configure multilanguage support and how to configure your local settings. We will also discuss how to avoid using "illegal" characters in computer names, account names, and passwords in a multilanguage system.

This chapter also introduces you to the Windows Installer components:

- The installer service
- The msiexec.exe program, which reads the package files and applies transforms
- The installation package files (.msi files), which contain a relational database that stores the instructions and information needed to install a program
- Transforms, which are files with an .mst extension, used to manipulate the installation process

Chapter 11: Implementing, Managing, and Troubleshooting Network Protocols and Services

In Chapter 11, you will learn some very important concepts and procedures, including configuration and troubleshooting issues associated with the TCP/IP protocol. Here you will go through the process of configuring a DHCP client, assigning an IP address, and configuring your Windows 2000 Professional computer to use a DNS server for name resolution. Also addressed is IP Security (IPSec), a new feature included in Windows 2000, which provides for encryption of data as it travels between two computers, protecting it from modification and interpretation if anyone were to see it on the network. You will learn how to use IPSec policies on a Windows 2000 Professional workstation.

Dial-up networking is another big issue, and this chapter takes you through the process of connecting to a dial-up server using the built-in dial-up networking components. You will learn to make, configure, use, and troubleshoot dial-up connections.

You will also learn how to establish virtual private networking (VPN) connections over the Internet to connect securely to a private network. You learn about the options available for doing so, specifically the two tunneling protocols supported by Windows 2000:

- PPTP (Point to Point Tunneling Protocol)
- L2TP (Layer 2 Tunneling Protocol, which offers better security through the use of IPSec)

Windows 2000 Professional can function as a dial-up server, hosting one inbound remote access connection at a time. You will learn how to use the Network Connection Wizard to configure incoming connections, specify users who will be allowed to access the computer via dialup, and set callback security options.

You will learn about connection as a remote client to a dial-up server, and how and when to use the link protocols, PPP and SLIP, for remote connections. We will then go on to discuss how to connect to the Internet (through an Internet Service Provider) using dial-up networking.

Internet Connection Sharing (ICS), a form of Network Address Translation, is another new feature in Windows 2000 Professional (and Windows 98SE) that we will examine in this chapter. You'll find out how to set up a shared connection so that other computers on your local area network can access Internet resources through the ICS host machine that is connected to the Internet over a modem, ISDN, or DSL terminal.

The chapter ends with a look at using the File and Print Sharing service for Microsoft Networks (the equivalent of the Server Service in Windows NT) and how it can be optimized.

Chapter 12: Implementing, Monitoring, and Troubleshooting Security and User Accounts

In Chapter 12, we look at a topic of growing importance: network security issues. You will learn about some of the new security features included in Windows 2000, and how to implement, monitor, and troubleshoot them to ensure protection of your sensitive data. Specifically, we will talk about the Encrypting File System (EFS), which can be used to protect data on the computer's hard disk. We will also examine Windows 2000 certificate services, and you will learn how to set up certificates, using certificate authorities (CAs), and using the cipher.exe utility at the command line to encrypt and decrypt data.

This chapter also discusses group policy and its role in securing your network, and you will practice using the Group Policy Editor to configure user and computer settings and apply group policies to local users. Troubleshooting group policy will be included in this section, as well.

CERTIFICATION OBJECTIVE 1.06

What You Should Already Know

Because Microsoft's target audience for the Windows 2000 exams is those who have experience working with medium to large multisite, multidomain NT networks, there is a presumption that you will have mastered the knowledge, concepts, and terminology presented in the Windows NT 4.0 certification exams.

If you do not have extensive real-world networking experience and you have not already attained the Windows NT MCSE, you should take extra time to ensure that you are familiar with Microsoft networking concepts, Windows 2000 concepts, and the terminology that is peculiar to Microsoft operating systems.

Microsoft Operating System Basics

Windows 2000 is the culmination of Microsoft's many years of designing, marketing, testing, and improving on the original "Windows" operating system concept.

The job of a network administrator shares some characteristics with that of a physician (certainly a key element in the success of both involves having plenty of patience/patients). You can think of the network operating system as your patient—it is often up to you to bring it into the world (installation), nurture it and see that it grows in a healthy way (configuration and maintenance), practice preventative medicine (monitoring and optimization), and diagnose and treat its illnesses (troubleshooting).

In order to take care of a patient properly, a doctor needs to know as much about the patient as possible, and that includes not only the background of the patient but that of his family and ancestors. Likewise, you will better understand Windows 2000 if you know a little about its predecessors. So let's take a look at the "family history" of Windows.

A (Very) Brief History of Windows

Microsoft's first operating system, MS-DOS, was text based like other operating systems of the time (and like some operating systems, such as UNIX, today). The idea of a graphical user interface was developed by Xerox at the Palo Alto Research Center (PARC) and first implemented in the Xerox Alto and Star computers in the late 1970s and early 1980s. Apple Computer picked up on the idea and designed the Lisa, and then the Macintosh; the latter was released in 1984. A year later, Microsoft released the first version of Windows, its entry into the GUI race. It was not an overnight success.

Windows 3.x   Popular wisdom says the third time is a charm, and for Microsoft, the old saying seems to hold true. It was not until the release of Windows version 3 in 1990 that the operating system began to draw support, both from third-party software developers and from personal computer users. There were good reasons for this: The first two versions were not much like the Windows we know and love (well, *some* of us love it) today. The Program Manager interface and familiar icons weren't included; prior to version 3, Windows was not much more than a menu system that made DOS a little easier to use.

Windows 3 changed everything. It was a 16-bit operating system with a user interface that resembled the look and feel of IBM's (at that time not yet released) OS/2, with 3-D buttons and the ability to run multiple programs simultaneously, using a method called *cooperative multitasking*. Windows 3 also provided *virtual memory*, the ability to use hard disk space to "fool" the applications into behaving as if they had more RAM than was physically installed in the machine.

Version 3.1 was released in 1992, and offered better stability and a large number of third-party applications that ran on it. With the release soon after of Windows for Workgroups 3.11, which added networking support, Windows was well on the way to becoming the dominant desktop operating system that it is today.

We must note, however, that Windows up through version 3.11 actually was *not* an operating system; rather, it was a GUI shell that ran on top of MS-DOS.

Windows 9x   In August of 1995, Microsoft released its long-awaited upgrade of Windows, Windows 95. For the first time, Windows could be installed on a machine that didn't already have MS-DOS installed. There were many improvements made—the new Windows offered 32-bit functionality (although still retaining some 16-bit code for backward compatibility with old applications), *preemptive multitasking* (a more efficient way to run multiple programs in which the operating system controls use of the processor, and the crash of one application does not bring down the others that are currently running), and support for filenames longer than the DOS-based eight-character (with three-character extension) limit.

Windows NT   As successful as the consumer versions of Windows proved to be, it was not nearly as well received in the business world. Companies needed reliability and security, two areas in which Windows 3.*x* and 9*x* did not particularly excel. Enter Microsoft's corporate networking solution: Windows NT.

The NT kernel (the core or nucleus of the operating system, which provides basic services for all other parts of the operating system) is built on a completely different architecture from consumer Windows. In fact, NT was based on the 32-bit preemptive multitasking operating system that originated as a joint project of Microsoft and IBM before their parting of the ways, OS/2. NT provided the stability and security features that the "other Windows" lacked, albeit at a price, and not only a monetary one; NT was much pickier in terms of hardware support, did not run all of the programs that ran on Windows 9*x* (especially DOS programs that accessed the hardware directly), and required more resources—especially memory—to run properly.

However, as NT 3.*x* matured into NT 4.0, the server version became a viable option to UNIX and NetWare, and the Workstation version became a desktop standard in business environments when high reliability and security were important issues.

Windows 2000   Microsoft's latest incarnation of the corporate operating system was originally called NT 5, but the name was changed to Windows 2000 between the second and third beta versions—perhaps to underscore the fact that this is truly a *new* version of the operating system, not merely an upgrade to NT. The NT kernel is still there; but so many features have been added and so many of the ways of doing things have changed, that it soon becomes evident we are dealing with a product related to—but by no means the same as—the operating system from which it evolved.

Operating System Architectures

You will find similarities and differences when you compare the NT 4.0 and Windows 2000 operating system architectures. In both cases, the architectural structure is modular, and there are two modes: *user* and *kernel*. Kernel mode is sometimes referred to as protected mode; this is the layer that has access to system data and hardware, as well as direct access to memory.

The Windows 2000 kernel mode components include

- The Executive, which performs the majority of input and output, and object management (excluding keyboard and screen I/O)
- The Device Drivers
- The Microkernel, which manages the microprocessor
- The Hardware Abstraction Layer (HAL)

User mode contains the environmental subsystems, which allow Windows 2000 to run applications written for other operating systems, such as 16-bit Windows applications or MS-DOS programs. It also includes the *integral subsystems,* made up of the security subsystem and the workstation and server services.

Microsoft Networking

This exam will presume that you have some familiarity with basic Microsoft networking concepts. If you have no networking experience or knowledge, we recommend that you study one of the many introductory networking texts, such as the Windows NT 4.0 MCSE study guides for Networking Essentials.

It is important to understand the differences between two basic types of local area networks (LANs), which in Microsoft terminology are called workgroups and domains.

Peer-to-Peer Networks (Workgroups)

A *workgroup* is also referred to as a peer-to-peer network, because all the computers connected together and communicating with one another are "created equal." That is, there is no central computer that manages security and controls access to the network. Windows 2000 Professional computers can be configured to function as part of a workgroup. In a workgroup, each computer user must manage his or her own administrative tasks, and any computer can act as a server (sharing its resources with others on the network) or as a client (accessing the resources of others).

Workgroups are less secure than server-based networks, and more difficult to manage as the number of computers grows, so this setup is not recommended for networks of more than ten computers. Note that a workgroup can have a dedicated file server, but does not have a *logon authentication server* (referred to in Microsoft parlance as a *domain controller*).

Server-Based Networks (Domains)

Microsoft calls server-based networks *domains*. A domain is a group of computers and users that log on to a central server called a *domain controller*. This server, also called a logon authentication server, contains security information for user and computer accounts that allow access to the entire domain. Domains provide for greater security and centralization of administration, and are recommended for all but the smallest networks.

In Windows 2000, domains are organized into *domain trees,* and these trees can be joined in *forests.* The domains within a tree or forest enjoy implicit trust relationships with one another, meaning users with accounts in one domain can access resources in another domain (provided they have the necessary permissions).

Operating System and Networking Terminology

For those who are beginning their study of Windows 2000 with little exposure to real-life networking and network operating systems, one of the most important (and perhaps most tedious) tasks is to "learn the language" of Microsoft operating systems and computer networking. At times, as you read through the study material, you may feel as if you're floating in a sea of acronyms and unfamiliar words.

In this book, our policy is to spell out all acronyms in full the first time they appear, and to define new terms within the text whenever possible. However, what's a well-known term to a networking professional may be "new" to you; and in a book this size, trying to flip back through the pages to find the first occurrence of a word could be a time-consuming process.

We suggest that you make liberal use of the Glossary. If you run across a word or term whose meaning you're not sure of, and that's not obvious from the context, don't just skim over it and hope it will be clarified later. Taking the time to look it up may seem to slow down your study, but in actuality it's one of the best ways to ensure that you remember the meaning later.

"Double Meanings"

Don't despair if you find that definitions are not always absolutely consistent from one source to the next. Within the computer industry and even within the more narrowly defined networking world, there are many subspecialty areas that have their own brand of jargon.

For example, you will see the word *server* used to describe a powerful computer that runs a special Server operating system such as Windows 2000 Server or Advanced Server. You will, however, also see the word *server* used to refer to *any* computer that allows other computers to access its resources, such as files, folders, and printers, over the network—thus, in this sense, a computer running Windows 2000 Professional can be a server.

It is always very important to keep the context in mind when determining the meaning of a new term or acronym. If the discussion pertains to Web pages, ASP probably means *Active Server Page.* On the other hand, the same abbreviation can stand for *Application Service Provider,* a company that offers individuals or companies access over the Internet to applications that would otherwise have to be located in the person's or company's own computers. Similarly, DLC can stand for either *Data Link Control* or *Digital Loop Carrier.*

Terms to Know

This is by no means a comprehensive list of the terms you should be familiar with before you begin to seriously study the Windows 2000 Professional operating system, but ensure that you at least know the basic meaning of the following:

- **Application** A program designed to perform a specific function directly for the user or for another application program; for example, word processors, database programs, graphics/drawing programs, Web browsers, e-mail programs.

- **Audit** The process of tracking network activity.

- **Boot** The process of loading an operating system into the computer's memory (RAM) so that applications can be run on it.

- **Client** A computer or program that accesses the resources of another computer or program across the network.

- **Device** A computer subsystem; for example, disk drives, printers, ports.

- **Driver** Software that allows the operating system to communicate with a device.

- **Encryption** Scrambling of data to make it unreadable so an unauthorized person cannot decipher it.

- **Group** An account that contains other accounts (called group members).

- **IRQ (interrupt request)** An electronic signal that is sent to the computer's processor requiring the processor's attention.

- **LAN** Local area network, a network that is confined to a limited geographic area.

- **Modem** A communication device that *modulates* and *demodulates* a signal, converting it from digital to analog for transfer over telephone lines, and back again.

- **Network** Two or more computers connected together by cable or wireless media for the purpose of sharing data, hardware peripherals, and other resources.

- **Object** A named set of attributes that represent a resource.

- **Paging file** A file on the hard disk (or spanning multiple disks) that stores some of the program code that is normally in the computer's RAM. This is called *virtual memory,* and allows the programs to function as if the computer had more memory than is physically installed.

- **Plug and Play**   The ability of the computer operating system to detect and automatically configure devices.

- **Printer**   The software interface between the operating system and a print device.

- **Print device**   The physical hardware component that produces printed documents.

- **Protocol**   A set of rules and procedures used by computers and computer components to communicate with one another.

- **RAID**   Redundant Array of Independent (or Inexpensive) Disks.

- **Resource**   A part of a computer system that can be shared.

- **Server**   A computer that shares its resources with other computers on the network.

- **Share**   A resource that can be accessed by other computers on the network.

- **TCP/IP**   Transmission Control Protocol/Internet Protocol, the protocol stack of the Internet, and the default network transport protocol of Windows 2000.

- **Trust relationship**   A connection among domains in which users who have accounts in and log on to one domain can then access resources in other domains, provided they have proper access permissions.

- **User account**   The information that defines a particular user on a network, including the username, password, group memberships, and rights and permissions assigned to the user.

CERTIFICATION SUMMARY

This chapter provided a brief introduction to the concepts and procedures that will be covered in this book, and an overview of how these topics relate to the objectives of Exam 70-210, "Installing, Configuring, and Administering Windows 2000 Professional." We looked at the components that make up the exam title and discussed specific issues related to installation, configuration, and administration.

We reviewed each exam objective briefly, and provided a few helpful hints for dealing with the question formats that you might expect to encounter on the Microsoft Windows 2000 Professional exam. We also gave you a brief chapter-by-chapter summary to let you know what's coming up, in more detail, in the rest of the book.

Finally, we looked at what you should already know before beginning to prepare for this exam, based on Microsoft's stated target audience. We covered some basic information about the history of the Windows operating system family, Microsoft networking concepts, and how to "learn the language" and decipher the jargon often associated with computer networking.

This chapter was designed to be the "first course" that will whet your appetite for more in-depth information about the many facets of Windows 2000 Professional. Now you're ready for the meat and potatoes, and the remaining chapters should provide plenty of material for you to sink your teeth into. Read, learn, and enjoy!

✓ TWO-MINUTE DRILL

What Is Installing, Configuring, and Administering Windows 2000 Professional?

❑ Proper preparation can make the difference between a quick-and-easy transition to the new operating system and a lengthy troubleshooting nightmare.

❑ Once Windows 2000 Professional has been installed on the computer, modifications can be made to the appearance and behavior of the operating system using various configuration components.

❑ The Microsoft Management Console provides a consistent, familiar interface regardless of what administrative task is being performed.

❑ Configuring hardware in Windows 2000 is in many cases much easier than the same task in Windows NT, primarily due to the new support for Plug and Play.

❑ One of the most exciting new features in Windows 2000 is the Active Directory, Microsoft's new, improved, sophisticated *directory services* technology.

❑ Windows 2000 uses *Group Policy* and the local security policy to control the desktop environment, assign user rights, and set audit policies.

Overview of Exam 70-210

❑ According to the Microsoft Web site and documentation, exam candidates are presumed to be networking personnel operating in medium-to-very-large computing environments with a minimum of a year's experience in administering and implementing Windows networking.

❑ To pass Exam 70-210, you must be very familiar with all aspects of conducting both attended and unattended installations of Windows 2000 Professional.

❑ You should be able to install, configure, and troubleshoot hardware devices of various types, and monitor and optimize performance and reliability.

❑ You will need to know how to configure and manage the desktop environment, including implementation of user profiles, enabling and using multilanguage/multilocation features, and using Windows Installer components to deploy applications.

❑ Exam 70-210 requires that you be able to install and troubleshoot network protocols and services, particularly TCP/IP and related services such as DNS, DHCP, and APIPA, and be familiar with VPNs and ICS.

❑ You will need to be well versed in Windows 2000 security features, particularly EFS, group policy, and user rights and access permissions.

What We'll Cover in This Book

❑ The heart of Windows 2000 exam preparation is development of practical skills—the ability not just to know about the operating system, but also to use it to perform common network administration tasks.

❑ You will learn to use the unattended install features such as scripting support and Remote Installation Services (RIS), and you will learn about the utilities provided to prepare for a full-scale rollout of Windows 2000 Professional—including SysPrep and RIPrep.

❑ This book will provide you with the characteristics of the FAT, FAT32, and NTFS file systems, and criteria for choosing which file system to use in a particular situation. You will learn how to convert a partition from one file system to another, using Windows 2000's convert.exe utility.

❑ An essential element of hardware management is working with device drivers, and you will learn about installing and updating drivers.

❑ You can use the Scheduled Task Wizard, accessed via the Control Panel, to set up specified tasks to run daily, weekly, or monthly, and customize how tasks run at the scheduled times.

❑ UNICODE is a 16-bit character encoding standard developed by the Unicode Consortium between 1988 and 1991 that uses two bytes to represent each character and enables almost all of the written languages of the world to be represented using a single character set.

❑ Windows 2000 Professional can function as a dial-up server, hosting one inbound remote access connection at a time.

❑ The Encrypting File System (EFS) can be used to protect data on the computer's hard disk.

❑ Local user accounts grant access to the particular machine, and domain user accounts allow a user to log on to the Windows 2000 domain and access resources across the network.

What You Should Already Know

❑ Windows 2000 is the culmination of Microsoft's many years of designing, marketing, testing, and improving on the original "Windows" operating system concept.

❑ In both Windows NT 4.0 and Windows 2000, the architectural structure is modular, and there are two modes: *user* and *kernel.*

❑ In a workgroup, each computer user must manage his or her own administrative tasks, and any computer can act as a server (sharing its resources with others on the network) or as a client (accessing the resources of others).

❑ Microsoft calls server-based networks *domain*s. A domain is a group of computers and users that log on to a central server called a *domain controller.*

❑ For those who are beginning their study of Windows 2000 with little exposure to real-life networking and network operating systems, one of the most important (and perhaps most tedious) tasks is to "learn the language" of Microsoft operating systems and computer networking.

SELF TEST

The following questions will help you measure your understanding of the material presented in this chapter. Read all of the choices carefully, as there may be more than one correct answer. Choose all correct answers for each question.

1. Which of the following can be directly upgraded to Windows 2000 Professional with no interim steps? (Select all that apply.)

   A. Windows for Workgroups 3.11

   B. Windows 95

   C. Windows 98

   D. Windows NT 3.5

2. Which of the following networking components are installed by default when you install Windows 2000 Professional? (Select all that apply.)

   A. TCP/IP protocol stack

   B. NWLink IPX/SPX compatible protocol

   C. Client for Microsoft Networks

   D. Data Link Control protocol

3. Which of the following is the Registry hive in which information about object linking and embedding and file associations is contained?

   A. HKEY_CLASSES_ROOT

   B. HKEY_LOCAL_MACHINE

   C. HKEY_CURRENT_CONFIG

   D. HKEY_CURRENT_USER

4. Which of the following is the feature included in Windows 2000 Professional that allows you to connect several computers to the Internet through one phone line, modem, and ISP account with a single public IP address?

   A. NAT

   B. ICS

   C. Proxy

   D. Default gateway

5. Which of the following is used in performing an unattended installation of Windows 2000 Professional? (Select all that apply.)

A. RIS

B. RRAS

C. .msi files

D. Setup Manager

6. Which of the following is used to gather information about the performance of hard disks, memory, the processor, and the network?

A. Computer Resource Manager

B. Accessibility Wizard

C. Group Policy

D. System Monitor

7. Which of the following is a TCP/IP command-line utility used to gather configuration information about your system?

A. MMC

B. IPCONFIG

C. SYSINFO

D. ATTRIB

8. Which of the following is used to encrypt data on the hard disk?

A. IPSec

B. Dfs

C. EFS

D. RIP

9. Which of the following Windows 2000 Professional components provides access to Web resources and allows you to publish and manage Web sites on an intranet or on the Internet?

A. Peer Web services

B. Domain Name Services

C. Windows Internet Name Services

D. Internet Information Services

10. Which of the following can be accomplished with the convert.exe utility? (Select all that apply.)

    A. A FAT partition can be converted to NTFS without losing data.

    B. A FAT32 partition can be converted to NTFS without losing data.

    C. An NTFS partition can be converted to FAT32 without losing data.

    D. A FAT32 partition can be converted to FAT16 without losing data.

11. Which of the following Windows 2000 features allows users to keep working with network resources even when disconnected from the network, and then automatically synchronizes the data when the user reconnects to the network?

    A. My Network Places

    B. Offline Files

    C. Briefcase

    D. Roaming user profiles

12. Which of the following is the function of the WDM?

    A. It is the Windows Domain Manager, used to administer Windows 2000 domains.

    B. It is the Web Data Model, which defines the format of HTTP-coded documents.

    C. It is the Win32 Driver Model, which allows the same device drivers to be used across Windows 98 and Windows 2000 platforms.

    D. It is the Wavetable Device Mode, which should be configured if you have a soundcard that supports .midi files.

13. Where was the idea of a graphical user interface (GUI) first originated?

    A. By Apple Computer, in the Macintosh

    B. By Xerox, in the Alto

    C. By Microsoft, in Windows

    D. By Sun, in the SPARC Workstation

14. Which components of the Windows 2000 architecture are parts of the kernel mode? (Select all that apply.)

    A. The Hardware Abstraction Layer

    B. The environmental subsystem

C. The Executive

D. The security subsystem

15. Which of the following is true of a peer-to-peer network? (Select all that apply.)

A. It is more secure than a server-based network.

B. It is also referred to as a workgroup.

C. It is recommended for networks with ten or fewer computers.

D. It is organized into trees and forests.

SELF TEST ANSWERS

1. ☑ **B, C.** You can directly upgrade both Windows 95 and Windows 98 to Windows 2000.
   ☒ **A** is incorrect because there is no upgrade path for Windows 3.*x* and Windows for Workgroups; you must perform a fresh installation of Windows 2000 Professional and reinstall all applications. **D** is incorrect because in order to upgrade from Windows 3.5 to Windows 2000, you must first go through the interim step of upgrading to NT 3.51 or 4.0, and then upgrade to Windows 2000.

2. ☑ **A, C.** By default, the TCP/IP protocol stack, Client for Microsoft Networks, and File and Printer Sharing for Microsoft Networks are installed. Other protocols and network components can be installed as desired.
   ☒ **B** is incorrect because NWLink IPX/SPX is an optional component, which is not installed by default, and that is most often used to connect to NetWare networks. **D** is incorrect because the Data Link Control (DLC) protocol, traditionally used to connect to IBM mainframes and HP network-connected printers, is not installed by default.

3. ☑ **A.** HKEY_CLASSES_ROOT holds information about OLE and file associations.
   ☒ **B** is incorrect because HKEY_LOCAL_MACHINE contains information about the hardware and software on the system. **C** is incorrect because HKEY_CURRENT_CONFIG contains data about the current hardware profile in use. **D** is incorrect because HKEY_CURRENT_USER contains information about the user whose account is currently logged on.

4. ☑ **B.** Internet Connection Sharing (ICS) is built into Windows 2000 Professional and allows you to connect computers on a LAN to the Internet through a single public IP address and one phone line, modem, and ISP account.
   ☒ **A** is incorrect because, although ICS is in fact a limited form of Network Address Translation (NAT) technology, in Microsoft terms NAT is the more full-featured protocol included in Windows 2000 Server, but not available in Windows 2000 Professional. **C** is incorrect because although MS Proxy Server allows you to share an Internet connection, it is a separate product and is not included in Windows 2000 Professional. **D** is incorrect because although the ICS host is sometimes referred to as a gateway, the default gateway refers to the IP address of a router.

5. ☑ **A, D.** The Remote Installation Service is used for performing an unattended installation over the network, and the Setup Manager can be used to create an answer to be used in the unattended installation process.

☒ **B** is incorrect because RRAS is the Routing and Remote Access Service, which is used after installation to configure routing protocols and manage remote access connections. **C** is incorrect because .msi files are components of the Windows Installer system used to deploy application software.

6. ☑ **D.** The System Monitor is a component of the Performance tool, and is used to gather information about system components.
☒ **A** is incorrect because there is no such thing as the Computer Resource Manager. **B** is incorrect because the Accessibility Wizard is used to implement features that make Windows 2000 easier to use for disabled persons. **C** is incorrect because Group Policy is used to control the user and computer environment, not to collect system information.

7. ☑ **B.** IPCONFIG will display the IP address, subnet mask, and default gateway being used by the system. Using the /ALL switch will display more detailed configuration information.
☒ **A** is incorrect because all the MMC snap-ins can be used to gather configuration information; they are not command-line utilities. **C** is incorrect because SYSINFO does not exist. **D** is incorrect because ATTRIB is a DOS command-line utility used to show and change file attributes.

8. ☑ **C.** EFS, the Encrypting File System, is a new feature included in Windows 2000 that allows you to encrypt data on the hard disk so it will not be readable by unauthorized persons.
☒ **A** is incorrect because IPSec is used to encrypt data that travels across the network. **B** is incorrect because Dfs is the Distributed File System, which makes it easier to organize and locate files on the network, but does not encrypt them. **D** is incorrect because RIP is the Routing Information Protocol used for dynamically exchanging routing information between routers.

9. ☑ **D.** Internet Information Services (IIS) version 5 is included with Windows 2000 Professional and Server.
☒ **A** is incorrect because peer Web services was the name of the Web server software included in Windows NT 4.0 Workstation. **B** is incorrect because the Domain Name *System* (DNS) is used for host name resolution, not publishing Web pages. **C** is incorrect because the Windows Internet Name Services (WINS) is used for NetBIOS name resolution, not publishing Web pages.

10. ☑ **A, B.** You can convert a FAT or FAT32 partition to NTFS without losing data, using the convert.exe command.
☒ **C** and **D** are incorrect because you cannot convert NTFS back to FAT or FAT32, and you cannot convert between the two versions of FAT using the convert command.

11. ☑   **B.** The Offline Files feature is designed to allow for seamless continuation of working with network resources when disconnected from the network, and then synchronizing the data when the user reconnects.
    ☒   **A** is incorrect because My Network Places merely displays the network browse list, showing available network resources. **C** is incorrect because the Briefcase is designed for synchronizing files transferred from one computer to another, such as a laptop and desktop computer. **D** is incorrect because roaming user profiles allow users' desktop settings, Start menus, and other preferences to follow them from one computer to another.

12. ☑   **C.** The Win32 Driver Model (WDM) is designed to allow the use of the same device drivers for both the Windows 98 and Windows 2000 operating systems.
    ☒   **A, B,** and **D** are incorrect because there are no such features in Windows 2000 as the Windows Domain Manager, Web Data Model, or Wavetable Device Mode.

13. ☑   **B.** The first commercial GUI interface was developed and implemented by Xerox at the Palo Alto Research Center (PARC) and used in the Alto and Star computers.
    ☒   **A** is incorrect because although the Apple Lisa implemented the GUI, it did so after Xerox's initial implementation. **C** is incorrect because Microsoft's first GUI, Windows, was released after the Apple Lisa. **D** is incorrect because Sun did not originate the GUI concept in the SPARC workstation.

14. ☑   **A, C.** The Hardware Abstraction Layer (HAL) and the Executive, which performs most I/O functions, are both part of the kernel mode of the architecture.
    ☒   **B** and **D** are incorrect because the environment subsystem and the security subsystem are part of the user mode of the architecture.

15. ☑   **B, C.** A peer-to-peer network, also called a workgroup, is recommended for small networks of ten or fewer computers.
    ☒   **A** is incorrect because a server-based network is more secure than a workgroup, due to the centralized security database. **D** is incorrect because trees and forests are concepts that are used in Windows 2000 domain (server-based) networks to provide trust relationships between domains.

2

Performing an Attended Installation of Windows 2000 Professional

I n this chapter, we will discuss how to perform an attended installation of Windows 2000 Professional. In Windows 2000, installation has been made easier than Windows NT 4.0, and some additional features have been added. Before actually starting the installation process, you should plan ahead.

Prepare for the installation before you start. You need to determine if your computer meets the minimum hardware requirements. You will need to decide how to partition your hard drive and what file system to use. During installation, you have to decide whether to join a domain or a workgroup. Also during installation, you need to choose which optional components to install and how to configure the computer to operate on the network.

You can perform an attended installation of Windows 2000 Professional from a CD-ROM, or across the network from a distribution server. When installing over the network, there are many options to customize the installation process. It is important to understand these options. There are several ways to upgrade your workstation, and you will need to choose the best method for your enterprise.

Periodically, Microsoft releases fixes to its operating systems known as *service packs*. Service packs contain bug and security fixes. Normally, you want to have your computers running the latest service pack that is available. However, you should test the service packs for your environment prior to deploying them.

On occasion, the installation of Windows 2000 Professional will fail. When it does, you need to be prepared to solve the problems. You should know the common problems that can occur, and understand that Setup creates log files that can be used to help with troubleshooting.

CERTIFICATION OBJECTIVE 2.01

Performing an Attended Installation of Windows 2000 Professional

There are many choices you will have to make when performing an attended installation of Windows 2000 Professional. By preparing for installation ahead of time, you will be prepared to make these choices. You should make sure that you meet the hardware requirements; determine how to partition the hard disk; select the file system to use, and whether to join a domain or workgroup, and which components to install. For attended installation, you can install from the CD-ROM or across the network.

Windows 2000 Professional Hardware Requirements

There is some preparation you need to do before installing Windows 2000 Professional. There are some options that you will be required to choose from during installation, and things will go more smoothly if you determine which choices to make ahead of time. You will need to ensure that your computer has the minimum required hardware, determine how to partition your hard disk, choose a file system, and determine whether to join a domain or a workgroup.

Before starting installation, make sure that your hardware meets the minimum requirements and that it is compatible with Windows 2000. See the following list for the minimum requirements for running Windows 2000 Professional.

- 133-MHz Pentium or higher CPU.
- Windows 2000 Professional supports up to two processors.
- 64MB of RAM is the required minimum.
- To install Windows 2000 Professional, the Setup process needs approximately 1GB of free space. You need a minimum of 650MB of free space, with 2GB recommended on the partition on which Windows 2000 Professional is going to be installed. Once Setup is complete, the temporary files will be deleted, and Windows 2000 Professional will require less free space. You might need more than the minimum space required depending on your configuration and options. See the following list for cases where more disk space is needed.
    - You will need additional space for each additional component you install.
    - If you use the FAT file system, you will need an additional 100–200MB of free space.
    - If you install across the network, you will need as much as 100–200MB of additional free space for additional driver files required for the network installation.

exam
W a t c h

There are usually some questions pertaining to the hardware requirements. Make sure you know what they are and how to determine if an existing computer meets the requirements.

Keep in mind that your computer will be severely limited by using the bare minimum hardware requirements. You should always perform some analysis and testing to determine what hardware is needed for your computer. You will need to take into account the applications that will be run and how much network traffic your workstation will use.

You also need to make sure your hardware and BIOS are compatible with Windows 2000 Professional. Before installation, verify that all of your hardware is on the Hardware Compatibility List (HCL). The HCL is a listing of all the hardware that has passed the Hardware Compatibility Tests (HCTs) and the devices that are supported by Windows 2000 Professional. The testing is performed by Windows Hardware Quality Labs (WHQLs) and by hardware vendors to prove compatibility with Windows 2000 Professional. If your hardware is not on the HCL, your computer may not work correctly after installing Windows 2000 Professional. The HCL can be found on the Windows 2000 Professional CD-ROM in the Support directory, or you can access the latest version of the HCL on the Microsoft Web site. Ensuring your BIOS is compatible with Windows 2000 is also very important.

If your computer is not compatible, you might not be able to use the advanced Power Management or Plug and Play features of Windows 2000 Professional, or your computer may not work correctly. If your hardware is not found on the HCL, contact the hardware vendor to see if they have any updates to make the hardware compliant with Windows 2000. To help with determining the compatibility, you can use the Windows 2000 Compatibility Tool to generate a hardware and software compatibility report. This tool is run during Setup, but you should run it before running Setup so you can fix any potential problems ahead of time. There are two ways to use the Compatibility Tool. First, you can run **Winnt32 /checkupgradeonly**. This will start Setup to generate a compatibility report without starting installation of Windows 2000. This will generate a report named Winnt32.log in the *<systemroot>* folder. Second, you can run the Windows 2000 Readiness Analyzer. This will generate the report without running Setup. This tool can be downloaded from Microsoft at www.microsoft.com/ windows2000/upgrade/compat. The Readiness analyzer will not work if you have a dual-boot configuration with Windows 95, Windows 98, and Windows NT. The report will provide a listing of the hardware and software that is incompatible with Windows 2000.

on the **Job**

Windows 2000 has updated the serial port configuration. If your BIOS is not updated, your COM ports may not function.

Partitioning the Hard Disk

When performing a new installation, you need to decide how to configure your hard disk. The hard disk contains one or more partitions. Each partition is a logical drive and is assigned a drive letter, such as C: or D:. Each partition can use a different file system, such as FAT, FAT32, and NTFS. You can create partitions prior to installation, during the setup process, or after Windows 2000 Professional is installed. During setup, you should only create and size the partition on which you are installing the operating system. You can use the Disk Management tool to configure other partitions after installation. The partition on which you installed the Windows 2000 Professional operating system files is called the boot partition. It contains all the files needed when running Windows 2000 Professional. When the computer boots up, the active partition (normally the C:\ drive) is searched for the files needed to load Windows 2000 Professional (Ntldr, Ntdetect.com, Boot.ini). These files load the Windows 2000 Professional operating system from the system partition. If Windows 2000 Professional is installed on the boot partition, then this partition is both the system and boot partition.

exam **Watch**   *The partition on which Windows 2000 is installed is called the "boot partition."*

One important fact to remember is that if you delete an existing partition, you cannot access the information that was previously stored on that partition. Before deleting a partition, if there is any data that you need on that partition, make sure you back up the data. Actually, it is recommended that you back up all of your data before changing your partition configuration.

When creating a partition on which to install Windows 2000 Professional, you need to make sure the partition is large enough for the operating system, applications, and data that will be stored on the partition. To install Windows 2000 Professional, Setup needs at least 1GB of free disk space, with 650MB of free space on the partition on which Windows 2000 Professional will be installed. Also keep in mind that if you are going to configure your computer for multiple operating systems, you need to install Windows 2000 Professional on its own partition. This prevents Setup from overwriting files needed by other operating systems.

Choosing a File System

Once you have decided how to partition your hard disk and which partition to install Windows 2000 Professional on, you need to decide which file system to use for the partition. Windows 2000 supports the following file systems: NTFS, FAT, and FAT32. In most configurations, the NTFS file system is the best choice. The only reason to use FAT or FAT32 is for a dual-boot configuration where you have more than one operating system that can be run on a computer. During setup, you can convert an existing FAT or FAT32 partition to the new NTFS. This allows you to keep your existing data on the partition. If you do not need to keep the existing data on the partition, it is recommended to format the drive with NTFS rather than converting it. This will erase all existing data on the partition, but the partition will have less fragmentation, and thus better performance.

exam
ⓦatch

The only reason to use the FAT or FAT32 file system is for dual-booting configurations. If you are not configuring your computer for dual-booting capability, you should use NTFS.

NTFS   The NTFS file system provides the following features:

- ■ **Security at the file and folder level**   This allows you to control access down to the file level.

- ■ **Disk compression**   This allows you to compress folders, subfolders, and files to increase the amount of file storage, but will slow access to the files.

- ■ **Disk quotas**   This allows you to limit the amount of disk space used by each user.

- ■ **File encryption**   Folders, subfolders, and files can be encrypted and decrypted automatically by the operating system.

- ■ **Active Directory**   This allows domain-based security. (While Active Directory is technically not a feature of NTFS, it is important to note here that you have to be using NTFS to use Active Directory on the files and folders.)

With Windows 2000 using NTFS, you can use remote storage, dynamic volumes, and mount volumes to folders. These features will be discussed later in the book. Partitions that use the NTFS file system can only be accessed by Windows NT and Windows 2000. However, if you use any of the new NTFS features provided by Windows 2000, you will not be able to access it from Windows NT. For example, if a file is encrypted in Windows 2000, the file will not be available for reading in NT. NTFS is the best choice when security is an issue.

on the job

You can use important features such as Active Directory and domain-based security only by choosing NTFS as your file system.

FAT and FAT32   The FAT (or FAT16) file system allows access from multiple operating systems, including Windows 2000, Windows NT, Windows 95/98, MS-DOS, Linux, and OS/2. It is a less-efficient file system with fewer features than NTFS, and does not offer any built-in security. FAT32 enhances the FAT file system by allowing larger partition sizes and smaller cluster sizes. FAT partitions were limited to 4GB. With hard disks commonly larger than 8GB, FAT32 was introduced in Windows 98 to extend the partition sizes. FAT32 is compatible with Windows 95b (OSR2), Windows 98, and Windows 2000. Windows NT cannot use FAT32 partitions.

on the job

Many people make the mistake of thinking FAT partitions were limited to 2GB. It is possible to install NT 4 onto a 4 Gig FAT partition. When you are installing NT 4, it will ask you, "where do you want me to install?" it. At that point you can take, for example, two 2GB partitions, and delete one, which will then make a 4GB partition. Then you can format it as FAT, and install NT there.

How do you choose which file system to use on partitions? It depends on how your workstation will be configured. Microsoft recommends the NTFS partition with single-boot operating system for computers running Windows 2000. Also, NTFS is the only file system that supports the new Active Directory introduced with Windows 2000. If you want to dual-boot with Windows 2000 and Windows 95/98, then you will need to choose the FAT or FAT32 file system on the first partition. Some new features have been added to NTFS by Windows 2000. For example, if you used the new encryption feature on a file, that file would not be readable when you booted up into Windows NT. When configuring a computer for dual-booting between Windows 2000 and Windows NT 4.0, Microsoft recommends using a FAT partition (not FAT32, because Windows NT 4.0 does not recognize FAT32). This ensures that when the computer is booted up into Windows NT 4.0, it will have access to all of the files on the computer.

Multiboot Configurations   With many versions of the Windows operating system now available, some users will need to have multiple operating systems installed on the same computer. The user can choose which operating system to load. During installation, you can upgrade an existing Windows operating system to Windows 2000; but when you do, you cannot load the pre-existing operating system. When configuring your computer for multiboot operations, consider the following points:

- To upgrade an existing Windows operating system to Windows 2000, you must install Windows 2000 in the same directory. To dual-boot with the existing Windows operating system and Windows 2000, you must install Windows 2000 in a different directory so it doesn't overwrite the existing files. (Microsoft also recommends that you install to a different partition.)

- When dual-booting Windows 2000 with MS-DOS or Windows 95/98, install Windows 2000 last, because older operating systems overwrite the Master Boot Record and you won't be able to boot into Windows 2000.

- You cannot install Windows 2000 in a compressed drive that is not compressed with NTFS.

- All applications must be reinstalled on Windows 2000 when you do not upgrade from the existing operating system. To save disk space, you can install most applications to the same directory in which they are currently installed.

- With Windows NT 4.0 Service Pack 4 and earlier, NT4 is able to read data on NTFS partitions, but it cannot read files encrypted in Windows 2000.

SCENARIO & SOLUTION

What type of file system should I use if I am dual-booting between MS-DOS and Windows 2000?	FAT is the only file system that MS-DOS recognizes.
What type of file system should I use if I am dual-booting between Windows 98 and Windows 2000?	FAT and FAT32 are the only file systems that you can use with Windows 98. FAT32 is a better choice if your partition is greater than 2GB.
What type of file system should I use if I am dual-booting between Windows NT4 and Windows 2000?	FAT or NTFS. Windows NT 4 does not recognize FAT32. You should be concerned about the new NTFS 5, since some features in the new version of NTFS won't function correctly in version 4, such as file and folder encryption.
What type of file system should I use if I am dual-booting between Windows 95 and Windows 2000?	FAT or FAT32 are the only file systems that you can use with Windows 95. FAT32 is only available on Windows 95 OSR2 (also called Windows 95B). FAT32 is a better choice if you are running OSR2.*x* and your partition is greater than 2GB.

Domain or Workgroup Membership

A *domain* is a grouping of accounts and network resources that are grouped together using a single domain name and security boundary. All user accounts, permissions, and other network details are all stored in a centralized database on the domain controllers. A single login gives users access to all resources they have permissions for. Domains are recommended for all networks with more than ten computers, or networks that are expected to grow to larger than ten computers in the near future. There are a few requirements to join a domain. You will need to know the domain name. You must have a computer account for the computer you are installing Windows 2000 Professional on. This account can be created either by the administrator before installing Windows 2000 Professional or during setup with the username and password of an account with the permissions to create a computer account. You will also need at least one domain controller and Domain Name Server (DNS) online when you install Windows 2000 Professional.

A *workgroup* is a logical grouping of resources on a network. It is generally used in peer-to-peer networks. This means that each computer is responsible for access to its resources. Each computer has its own account database and is administered separately. Security is not shared between computers, and administration is more difficult than in a centralized domain. A workgroup is only intended as a convenience to help find resources. When browsing the network, the resources in your same workgroup are found first. It does not provide any security. In a workgroup, you might have to remember a different password for every resource you want to access. To join a workgroup during installation, all you need is a workgroup name. This can be the name of an existing workgroup or a new one. You must join a workgroup or a domain during installation, but you can change these memberships later as needed.

Windows 2000 Professional Application Compatibility

In addition to determining that your hardware is compatible with Windows 2000, you should also verify that your software is compatible with Windows 2000. Most applications that were compatible with Windows NT 3.51 and 4.0 will be compatible with Windows 2000. Since Windows 95 and 98 were compatible with MS-DOS applications, some applications that ran on Windows 95 and 98 will not be compatible with Windows 2000. This is especially true for older programs that accessed the hardware directly. Windows 2000 does not allow the hardware to be accessed directly; it must be accessed through the operating system. This was also true in Windows NT. Prior to upgrading to Windows 2000, you should remove the following types of applications:

- Any third-party Plug and Play tools. These are no longer needed, since Windows 2000 is now Plug and Play compatible.

- All third-party network protocols and client software. However, you can look on the CD-ROM in the i386\winntupg folder to see if there is an update for your networking software. If there is, then you can leave your software installed.

- You should remove antivirus software and any third-party disk quota software because of the changes to NTFS. It needs to be compatible with NTFS 5.

- If you have any third-party power management software, you should remove it, because Windows 2000 has changed its power management support.

Installing from the Windows 2000 CD-ROM

When installing Windows 2000 Professional from a CD-ROM, you will need to boot the computer from either the CD-ROM or from floppy disks. During installation, you will use some setup wizards to guide you through the process. This process is similar to the installation of Windows NT 4.0. The installation of Windows 2000 Professional has four basic steps:

1. Running the setup program.
2. Running the Setup Wizard.
3. Installing networking.
4. Completing installation.

You have several options to start the installation. On the Windows 2000 Professional CD-ROM, you can run Setup.exe to launch the installation. Setup will then run either Winnt.exe or Winnt32.exe, depending on which operating system you are currently running. If you are running MS-DOS or Windows 3.x, Setup will run Winnt.exe. If you are running Windows 95/98 or Windows NT, Setup will run Winnt32.exe. You can also run Winnt.exe or Winnt32.exe directly. The Winnt.exe and Winnt32.exe files are located in the I386 directory on the CD-ROM. You can also start installation by booting from the Windows 2000 Professional CD-ROM or from the Setup boot disks.

FROM THE CLASSROOM

On Installing Windows 2000

The installation process for Windows 2000 is much improved over Windows NT. Microsoft integrated some of the features used in the Windows 98 Setup program to enhance installation. Windows 2000 Setup Plug-and-Play technology allows your devices to automatically be detected and configured as in Windows 98. One of the most common Setup problems has to do with hardware problems. This is why checking your hardware for compatibility with Windows 2000 is one of the most important steps in the installation process. Specifically, many people find that their COM ports do not work after installing Windows 2000. Windows 2000 uses COM ports differently than it did in Windows NT. The fix for this is to upgrade the computer's BIOS with a version that is compatible with Windows 2000.

Other types of problems have to do with understanding the installation process, and the settings and options that are available and how to choose them. Another question often asked is why FAT32 cannot be selected for a partition's file system during Setup. This is not a problem, per se, but a feature. Setup will choose between FAT (sometimes called FAT16) and FAT32 for you based on the partition's size. If a partition is smaller than 2GB, then it automatically uses FAT. If the partition is larger than or equal to 2GB, then it uses the FAT32 file system.

When entering the computer name, some users complain that the name originally contained an underscore (_) that was replaced by a dash (-). This is also a feature, not a problem. Active Directory is based on DNS, and some DNS servers do not allow the underscore character (Microsoft DNS servers do). If you wish, you can change the name to use the underscore after installation. Setup does allow you to enter other characters that are not compliant with DNS, and you are given a warning when you do. It is recommended that you do not use any characters that are not compliant with DNS in a Windows 2000 network (including those that were previously allowed under NetBIOS naming conventions) because of the move to DNS for name resolution.

These are just a few of the problems that may arise during Setup. Remember to check your hardware and software for compatibility and make sure you understand the Setup processes. Determine ahead of time the options you will choose. It is also important to understand the differences between Windows 2000 and Windows NT.

—Cameron Wakefield, MCSD, MCP

Step 1: Run the Setup Program

The first step for installing Windows 2000 Professional is the text-mode portion of Setup, which is very similar to the Windows NT 4.0 text-mode portion of Setup. This portion of Setup copies the minimum version of Windows 2000 Professional to memory to begin the setup. You will have the option to run Setup, repair an existing Windows 2000 Professional installation, or exit Setup. Then you will have to agree to the terms of the license agreement in order to continue with Setup. The next step is to select a partition on which to install Windows 2000 Professional. You can choose an existing partition, create a new partition from free space, and even delete a partition to create free space. When deleting partitions, keep in mind that you will lose all the data on that partition. After you have selected a partition to install to, you will have to decide whether to use the FAT or NTFS file system. Then Setup will copy files to the hard disk and reboot the computer. Exercise 2-1 walks you through the steps for this phase of Setup.

EXERCISE 2-1

Starting the Installation

Let's get started installing Windows 2000 and perform the text-mode portion of Setup.

1. To start installation from the CD-ROM, you can boot from the Windows 2000 Professional CD-ROM. Place the CD-ROM in the drive and reboot the computer. Make sure your BIOS is set up to boot from the CD-ROM drive. When you boot from the CD-ROM, Setup will copy the minimum version of Windows 2000 Professional to memory and start the text-mode portion of Setup. If you have any Small Computer System Interface (SCSI) or Redundant Array of Independent Disks (RAID) devices on the computer, press F6 to install the drivers for these devices.

2. You will come to the Welcome To Setup screen. You have three options from which to choose:

   ■ You can run Windows 2000 Setup. Press ENTER for this option.

   ■ Repair an existing Windows 2000 installation. Press R for this option.

   ■ Exit Setup without installing Windows 2000. Press F3 for this option.

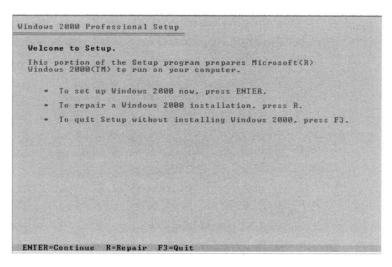

3. If the hard disk contains an operating system that is not compatible with Windows 2000, a screen will appear, notifying you that you could lose data if you continue with Setup. You have two options at this point:

   ■ Continue Setup. Press C for this option.

   ■ Quit Setup. Press F3.

4. Now you will have to read the license agreement and then choose to agree or to not agree with it. If you do not agree to the terms, then you will not be able to continue with Setup. You can use PAGE DOWN to read the entire agreement. To accept the conditions of the agreement, press F8. If you do not accept the terms of the agreement, press the ESC key Setup will quit.

5. The next screen will show you the existing free space and/or existing partitions on the hard disk. You will have three options:

   ■ To set up Windows 2000 Professional on the selected partition, press ENTER.

   ■ To create a new partition in the unpartitioned space, press C. When you select this option, you will have the option of how large to make that partition, or to go back to the previous screen without creating a new partition. Either accept the default size of all remaining free space or type in the size you want for the new partition. Then press ENTER to create the partition, or ESC to cancel creating the partition.

■ To delete the selected partition, press D. Be careful deleting any partitions; any files stored on that partition will be lost.

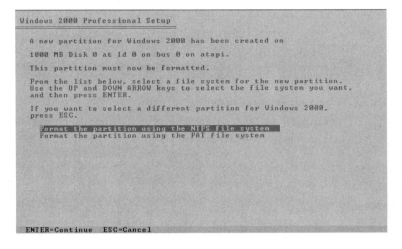

```
Windows 2000 Professional Setup

    The following list shows the existing partitions and
    unpartitioned space on this computer.

    Use the UP and DOWN ARROW keys to select an item in the list.
        • To set up Windows 2000 on the selected item, press ENTER.
        • To create a partition in the unpartitioned space, press C.
        • To delete the selected partition, press D.

    1000 MB Disk 0 at Id 0 on bus 0 on atapi
        Unpartitioned space                    999 MB




    ENTER=Install   C=Create Partition   F3=Quit
```

6. After you press ENTER to install Windows 2000 Professional on the selected partition, you will come to the screen for formatting the partition. You can choose from NTFS or FAT—NTFS is the default. (Note: If the partition size is larger than 2GB, then it will automatically use the FAT32 file system.) Choose the file system to format the partition, and press ENTER. Since you are installing Windows 2000 Professional, you should always choose NTFS.

```
Windows 2000 Professional Setup

    A new partition for Windows 2000 has been created on

    1000 MB Disk 0 at Id 0 on bus 0 on atapi.

    This partition must now be formatted.

    From the list below, select a file system for the new partition.
    Use the UP and DOWN ARROW keys to select the file system you want,
    and then press ENTER.

    If you want to select a different partition for Windows 2000,
    press ESC.

        Format the partition using the NTFS file system
        Format the partition using the FAT file system




    ENTER=Continue   ESC=Cancel
```

7. A screen will appear, showing the progress of formatting the partition. When the formatting is complete, it will organize the hard disk and then start copying files to the Windows 2000 Professional installation folder automatically without user interaction.

8. Setup will then initialize your Windows 2000 configuration and copy the necessary files to the hard disk for the next phase of setup.

9. The last step for this phase is to reboot your computer. A screen will appear, telling you to remove any floppy disks from your drive, and to press ENTER to restart the computer. If you don't respond in 15 seconds, it will automatically restart the computer.

10. When the computer boots up, there will be a progress bar at the bottom that says "Starting Windows . . . ." You can press F8 for troubleshooting options. When the computer boots up, you will be in the Setup Wizard phase of the Windows 2000 Professional installation.

Step 2: Run the Setup Wizard

The second step for installing Windows 2000 Professional uses the Setup Wizard. This begins the Windows or GUI portion of Setup. You will have to provide some information for setting up Windows 2000 Professional. Setup will perform some initial hardware detection and allow you to customize your keyboard and locale configuration. Then you will need to enter name and company information. This allows you to personalize the software on the computer. You will need a product key in order to continue with Setup. The product key can be found on the Windows 2000 Professional CD-ROM case. A unique computer name needs to be entered, as well as a password for the Administrator account. The computer name is a NetBIOS name that can be up to 15 characters in length. Setup will automatically generate a 15-character computer name for you. You can either accept this or enter your own. The NetBIOS name must be different from other computer names, workgroup names, and domain names on the network. The Administrator account password can be up to 127 characters in length. Although it is strongly recommended not to do it, you can leave the password blank. Then you need to choose which optional components to install. Finally, you need to set up the date, time, and time zone for the computer. Exercise 2-2 walks you through the steps for this phase of Setup.

Running the Setup Wizard

Now we will perform the GUI portion of Setup and enter some information needed by the Setup program.

1. After completing the text-mode portion of the installation, your computer will reboot. After reboot, the first screen will welcome you to the Windows 2000 Setup Wizard. Click Next to continue.

2. The Setup Wizard will detect and configure some of the devices on your computer, such as the keyboard and mouse.

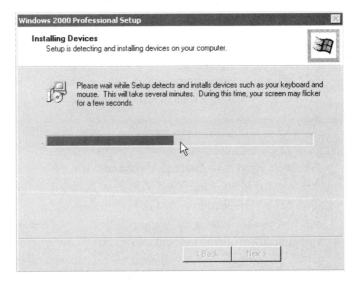

3. Now you will need to select your Regional settings. You can customize your locale and keyboard settings. Either customize the settings or accept the default, and click Next to continue.

4. This screen allows you to personalize your software by entering your name and organization information. After you have entered your information, click Next to continue.

5. Now you need to enter your product key. This key can be found on the Windows 2000 CD-ROM case. Enter the number, and click Next to continue.

6. This screen allows you to enter a name for your computer and the password for the Administrator account. The computer name will need to be unique

on the network. You will have to enter the Administrator password twice, as shown in the following illustration. When you have entered this information, click Next to continue.

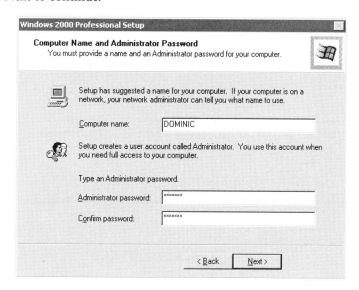

on the **job** *If you have a modem attached to your computer, Setup will prompt you to enter dialing information for your modem here.*

7. Now you need to decide which optional components of Windows 2000 Professional you would like to install.

8. Last, you can set the date, time, and time zone. Setup now moves into the network portion of Setup.

Step 3: Install Windows 2000 Networking

Now that Setup has finished gathering information about your computer, it is time to install the Windows 2000 networking components. You will need to decide which networking components to install. By default, Setup will install the following components:

■ Client for Microsoft Networks

- File and Print Sharing for Microsoft Networks
- TCP/IP with automatic addressing

You can install other components if you need them. In this phase, you will also join a domain or workgroup. If you join a domain, you will need to have a computer account on the domain. If you don't already have an account for your computer, you can add one from Setup (you will need administrative privileges for the domain to do so). Exercise 2-3 walks you through the steps for this phase of Setup.

EXERCISE 2-3

Installing the Networking Components

1. The Network Settings screen allows you to either choose the typical settings or customize the settings (see the following illustration). The Typical settings option will install Client for Microsoft Networks, File and Print Sharing for Microsoft Networks, and TCP/IP with automatic addressing. The Customize settings option allows you to install and configure the networking components to your requirements, such as specifying TCP/IP addresses and choosing other components to install.

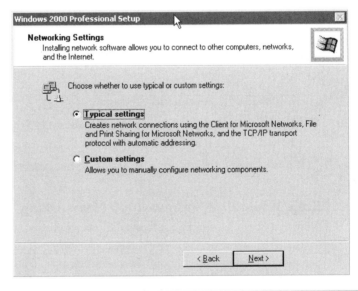

2. The Workgroup Or Computer Domain screen allows you to choose between joining either a workgroup or a domain. To join a workgroup, select No, and enter the workgroup name. To join a domain, select Yes, and enter the name of the domain you want to join.

3. The Join Computer To Domain dialog box allows you to enter the username and password of an account that has the proper permissions to join the computer to the domain.

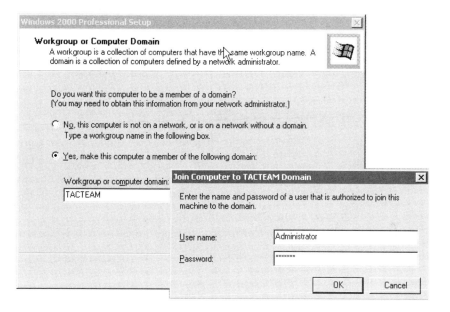

4. The networking components will now be installed. The networking portion of Setup is now complete.

Step 4: Complete the Setup Program

Setup has a few more tasks left to complete the installation of Windows 2000 Professional. It will finish copying files to the hard disk and save the configuration you have chosen to hard disk. Then it will remove the temporary files and restart the computer. Exercise 2-4 walks you through the steps for this phase of setup.

Completing the Setup Program

1. Setup will now complete the installation. It will set up the Start menu shortcuts and register components.

2. Setup will then finish copying files to the computer, such as accessories and bitmaps.

3. Then Setup will apply and save to hard disk the configuration settings you entered earlier.

4. Finally, Setup will remove the temporary setup files, and restart the computer.

5. Windows 2000 Professional is now installed on your computer.

Installing from a Network Server Share

Installing Windows 2000 Professional over the network is similar to installing it from the CD-ROM, except that the source location is different and the process will be slower since the files have to be transferred across the network. When installing Windows 2000 Professional on multiple computers, installing over the network is easier and more efficient than installing each one separately from a CD-ROM. The installation can be performed on identical computers or computers with different configurations. The Setup program will be run from a shared folder on the network. The Setup program will then copy the needed files to the client computer to start installation. The installation can be customized by using different Setup options available from command-line switches.

Distribution Server

The first requirement for network installation is a distribution server that contains the installation files. The distribution server can be any computer on the network to which the clients have access. To set up the distribution server, create a shared folder to hold the setup files. For Intel-based installations, copy the i386 directory from the Windows 2000 Professional CD-ROM to the shared folder.

Second, the computer on which Windows 2000 Professional is to be installed needs to have a 650MB (or more as necessary) partition. In Windows NT 4.0, network installations required a FAT partition. In Windows 2000, you can perform a network installation to either a FAT or NTFS partition.

Third, the client computer that you are installing to needs a networking software client that allows it to connect to the distribution server. If the client has an existing operating system with a network client, you can connect to the distribution server and start the installation from it. Otherwise, you need to create a boot disk that includes a network client that can connect to the distribution server.

Exercise 2-5 shows the basic steps for installing Windows 2000 Professional using a network installation.

Modifying Setup Using WINNT.EXE

You can customize the network installation process for Windows 2000 Professional by changing how the Setup program runs. This can be accomplished by using command-line switches when running the Winnt.exe program. The Winnt.exe program is used for network installations that use an MS-DOS network client.

Enumerate the Switches   The options available for customizing Setup are listed in Table 2-1, which lists the available options for running Winnt.exe. Notice that there aren't any switches for creating Setup disks. To create the Setup disks, you

---

EXERCISE 2-5

Network Installation of Windows 2000 Professional

Let's look at the basic steps used to install Windows 2000 over the network.

1. Boot from the network client on the target computer.

2. Connect to the shared folder on the distribution server.

3. Run Winnt.exe from the shared folder on the distribution server. Setup starts and creates a temporary folder named Win_nt.~bs on the system partition, and copies the Setup boot files to the folder.

4. Setup then creates a temporary folder named Win_nt.~ls, and copies the installation files from the distribution folder to this folder. Setup does not create the Setup floppy disks as it did in Windows NT 4.0.

5. You will then be prompted to restart the computer. When the computer restarts, you can proceed with the installation as described earlier.

6. Setup restarts the client computer and starts the Windows 2000 installation

TABLE 2-1	The Winnt.exe Switches

Switch	Description
/a	Enables the accessibility option.
/e[:*command*]	Executes a command before the final phase of Setup.
/I:[:*inf_file*]	The filename of the Setup information file (without the path). The default file name is Dosnet.inf.
/r[:*folder*]	Creates an additional folder within the system root folder (where the Windows 2000 system files are located).
/rx[:*folder*]	Also creates an additional folder within the system root folder, but Setup deletes the files after installation is completed.
/s[:*sourcepath*]	Specifies the location of the Windows 2000 installation files. It must contain the full path using the drive letter (e.g., f:\path) or UNC (\\server\shared_folder\path).
/t[:*tempdrive*]	The drive that contains the temporary setup files. If you do not use this switch, Setup will decide for you by using the partition with the most available space.
/u[:*answer_file*]	Performs an unattended installation by using an optional answer file. When using the unattended installation option, you are required to use the /s switch.
/udf:id[,*UDF_file*]	Indicates an identifier (*id*) that Setup uses to specify how a Uniqueness Database File (UDF) modifies an answer file (see the /u entry). The UDF overrides values in the answer file, and the identifier determines which values in the UDF file are used. For example, /udf:RAS_user,Our_company.udf overrides settings specified for the identifier RAS_user in the Our_company.udf file. If no *UDF_file* is specified, Setup prompts the user to insert a disk that contains the $Unique$.udf file.

must use the Makeboot.exe program located on the Bootdisk folder of the Windows 2000 Professional installation CD-ROM. To create the Setup disks using floppy drive A: go to the Makeboot folder on the installation CD-ROM, double-click the folder, and then double-click the file Makeboot.exe. Be sure that you have a formatted floppy in the A: drive. The Setup disks will be created on four floppy disks.

Modifying Setup Using Winnt32.exe

The Winnt32.exe program is used to customize the process for upgrading existing installations. The Winnt32.exe program is used for installing Windows 2000 from a computer that is currently running Windows 95/98 or Windows NT. As with the Winnt.exe program, you can use command-line switches to customize the setup process. The options available for Winnt32.exe are listed in Table 2-2.

TABLE 2-2   The Winnt32.exe Switches

Switch	Description
/copydir[:*folder_name*]	Creates an additional folder within the system root folder (where the Windows 2000 system files are located).
/copysource[:*folder_name*]	Also creates an additional folder within the system root folder, but Setup deletes the files after installation is completed.
/cmd[:*command_line*]	Executes a command before the final phase of Setup.
/cmdcons	Installs additional files to the hard disk that are necessary to load a command-line interface for repair and recovery purposes.
/debug[*level*][:*file_name*]	Creates a debug log at the level specified. By default, it creates C:\Winnt32.log at level 2 (the warning level).
/s[:*source_path*]	Specifies the location of the Windows 2000 installation files. It must contain the full path using the drive letter (e.g., f:\path) or UNC (\\server\ shared_folder\path). To simultaneously copy files from multiple paths, use a separate **/s** switch for each source path.
/syspart[:*drive_letter*]	Copies Setup start files to a hard disk and marks the partition as active. You can then install the hard disk in another computer. When you start that computer, Setup starts at the next phase. Use of this switch requires the **/tempdrive** switch.
/tempdrive[:*drive_letter*]	Places temporary files on the specified drive and installs Windows 2000 on that drive.
/unattend[*number*] [:*answer_file*]	Performs an unattended installation. The answer file provides the custom specifications to Setup. If you do not specify an answer file, all user settings are taken from the previous installation.
/udf:id[,*UDF_file*]	Indicates an identifier (*id*) that Setup uses to specify how a Uniqueness Database File (UDF) modifies an answer file (see the /u entry in Table 2-1). The UDF overrides values in the answer file, and the identifier determines which values in the UDF file are used. For example, /udf:RAS_user,Our_company.udf overrides settings specified for the identifier RAS_user in the Our_company.udf file. If no *UDF_file* is specified, Setup prompts the user to insert a disk that contains the $Unique$.udf file.

e x a m
ⓦa t c h   *It is important to know the difference between command-line switches for Winnt.exe and Winnt32.exe. Most of the switches have similar functionality with a different syntax. Ensure that you know the different syntaxes for each.*

SCENARIO & SOLUTION

To specify which drive to use to store the temporary files during setup, which Winnt command-line switch should you use?	The /t switch allows you to specify the drive to use to store the temporary files during Setup.
To specify an unattended installation of Windows 2000 Server and the answer file to use, which Winnt command-line switch should you use?	The /u[:*answer_file*] performs an unattended installation using the specified answer file.

CERTIFICATION OBJECTIVE 2.02

Upgrading to Windows 2000 Professional

When you have existing Windows computers on your network, you have to decide whether to upgrade them or install Windows 2000 Professional as a new installation for dual-booting. In this section, we are going to talk about upgrading an existing Windows computer to Windows 2000 Professional. When you upgrade an existing operating system, you install it in the same partition and folder in which the existing operating system is installed. When you select to perform an upgrade, Windows 2000 will automatically install in the same folder as the existing operating system. When upgrading from Windows, you can upgrade from the following versions: Windows NT 3.51 and 4.0 Workstation, Windows 95, and Windows 98. If you are running Windows NT 3.1 or 3.5, you must first upgrade to Windows NT 3.51 or 4.0, and then upgrade to Windows 2000.

exam
ⓦatch

If your existing computer is running a version of Windows NT earlier than 3.51, then you cannot upgrade it directly to Windows 2000 Professional. You must first upgrade it to Windows NT 3.51 or Windows NT 4.0 Workstation.

The upgrade process is generally the same as a clean installation, except that you must install to the same directory as the current operating system. You must also be running the operating system you want to upgrade. Prior to upgrading, you should check your current configuration, in case some of your configuration is not automatically upgraded. You should check your existing network settings such as TCP/IP, DNS, and WINS. It is a good idea to write down these settings in case you have to manually reenter them.

You can upgrade Windows NT 3.51 or 4.0 Workstation from any service pack that has been released. You don't have to upgrade to the latest service pack first.

Networking Requirements

When determining the network requirements for Windows 2000, some areas to consider are the network protocol requirements and name resolution. When using TCP/IP as the network protocol, you should decide whether to provide automatic or manual assignment of IP addresses. For name resolution, you need to determine your DNS requirements and whether you need to use WINS.

TCP/IP Requirements

The TCP/IP network protocol is the protocol used across the Internet. The Windows 2000 Setup program makes it easier to configure TCP/IP. Each Windows 2000 Professional workstation should be given an IP address. This IP address can be assigned dynamically through a DHCP Server or manually by assigning a static IP address. If there are a small number of computers on a workgroup (i.e., five or less), then you can allow the computers to assisgn themselves addresses to the computer using Automatic Private IP Addressing (APIPA). For larger networks, especially networks with more than one subnet, you should dynamically assign IP addresses using DHCP. The DHCP server must be assigned a static IP address so other computers can locate it, and the DHCP server will assign other computers an IP address dynamically.

In Exercise 2-6, we will look at your current TCP/IP configuration so that you can use the same information in your Windows 2000 installation. This exercise is performed using Windows NT 4.0. However, most of the exercise will also work on Windows 95/98.

DNS Services

Now that your workstation has an IP address, we need to discuss name resolution. Since an IP address is a group of numbers (e.g., 192.168.1.1), you need to provide a way for users to use names to access computers rather than IP addresses. Name resolution allows users to use a name that is easier to remember than an IP address to access a computer on the network or Internet. One of the types of name resolution is the Domain Name System (DNS). DNS maps a domain name to an IP address. Windows 2000 uses DNS as the primary name resolution method. DNS services are required for Internet e-mail, Web browsing, and support for clients running Windows 2000 and Active Directory Services.

CertCam 2-6

Determining Current TCP/IP Configuration

Note that this exercise should be performed on the pre-existing operating system prior to installing Windows 2000.

1. On the desktop, right-click on the Network Neighborhood icon and select Properties from the context menu to bring up the Network dialog box.

2. By default, the Identification tab will be displayed. This tab shows your current computer name and domain name. Click the Protocols tab. The Protocols screen is shown here.

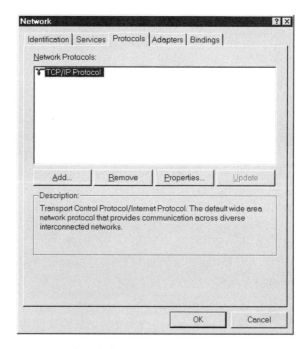

3. Select TCP/IP Protocol and click Properties. This will bring up the Microsoft TCP/IP Properties dialog box.

4. By default, the IP Address tab will be selected, as shown here.

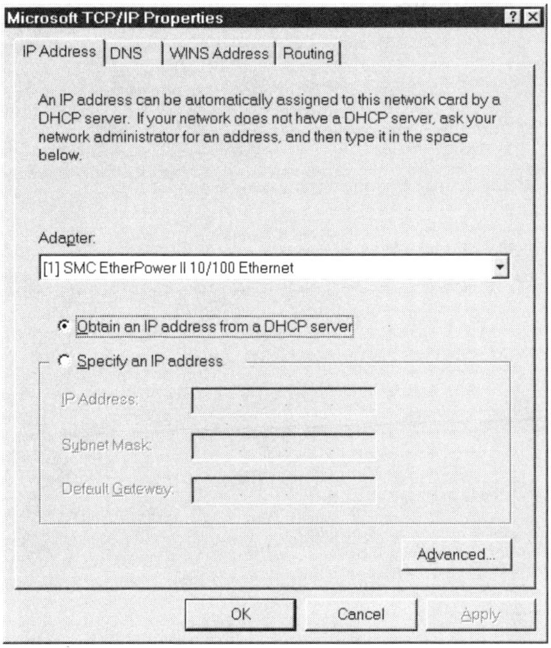

5. Notice that the option for Obtain An IP Address From A DHCP Server is selected. This means it is configured for automatic IP addressing using

DHCP. With the Specify An IP Address Selection, you can manually configure your IP address as shown here.

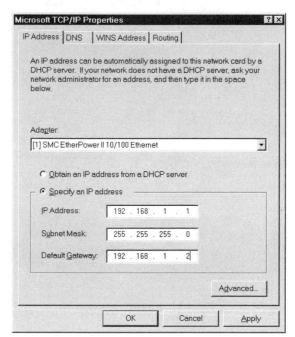

6. Click the DNS tab. This will display your DNS settings, as shown in the following illustration. Since I am using DHCP, most of the settings are left

blank. If your computer is manually configured, you should document the current settings.

7. Click the WINS Address tab. This will display your WINS configuration, as shown here. You should document your current WINS settings.

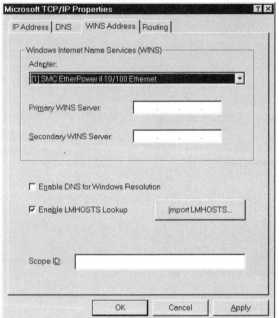

8. Once you have documented your current TCP/IP configuration, click OK to close the dialog box.

WINS Services

If your network will be supporting clients that are running Windows NT or Windows 95/98, then you should use the Windows Internet Name Service (WINS) to support them. WINS is used to map NetBIOS computer names to IP addresses. This allows users to access other computers on the network by their computer names. WINS servers should be assigned a static IP address. This allows clients to be able to find the WINS server by its IP address. It cannot find the WINS server by name, because it needs to know where the WINS server is to translate the name into an IP address.

Upgrading with a Compact Disc

To upgrade an existing version of Windows to Windows 2000 Professional, insert the Windows 2000 Professional CD-ROM in the CD-ROM drive; and if Autorun is on, it will automatically start Setup. Or, you can run Winnt32.exe from the I386 folder on the CD-ROM. You cannot upgrade using the boot disks or when booting from the CD-ROM. You must upgrade by starting Setup from Winnt32 or using Autorun on the CD-ROM. When you start using Autorun, you will see the window shown in Figure 2-1.

When you click Yes to upgrade to Windows 2000 Professional, it will check to see if you can upgrade. For example, if you are running Windows 3.1, you cannot upgrade to Windows 2000 Professional. If you try, you will get the message box notifying you that you cannot upgrade from the existing operating system. If you click on OK, it will bring you to the Setup screen—but the only option available will be to perform a clean install (Figure 2-2).

If your computer can be upgraded, you can choose the upgrade option and run Setup to upgrade your computer to Windows 2000 Professional.

Upgrading from a Network Distribution

Upgrading to Windows 2000 Professional is basically the same as from the CD-ROM, except you will start the installation by running the Winnt32.exe program from a distribution server. You will still have the same limitations and requirements as with the CD-ROM installation, plus you will have to be able to access the shared folder where the Setup files are located.

Upgrading Using unattend.txt

You can also upgrade to Windows 2000 Professional with an unattended installation. Instead of prompting the user, Setup will retrieve answers to the questions from an answer file called unattend.txt. You can use the Winnt.exe and Winnt32.exe programs to perform an unattended installation of Windows 2000

FIGURE 2-1	
Upgrading to Windows 2000 Professional	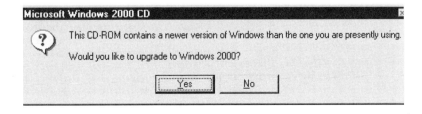

FIGURE 2-2

Upgrade or clean
install option
screen

Professional. Following is an example of using the Winnt.exe program. The example assumes the X:\ drive is mapped to the distribution folder. The /s switch specifies the location of the source files, the X:\i386 folder in the example. The /u switch specifies an unattended installation using the X:\unattend.txt file as the answer file. The /t switch specifies the drive where the source files will be copied to.

```
Winnt /s:X:\i386 /u:Z:\unattend.txt /t:c
```

The syntax for using the Winnt32.exe program to perform an unattended installation is shown next. The /s switch is used to specify where the source files are located; the X:\i386 folder is used in the example. The Winnt32.exe program uses the /unattend switch rather than the /u switch to specify an unattended installation. The number after the /unattend switch specifies how long to wait to reboot the computer after copying the source files. The number is ignored when run from Windows 95 or 98. The Winnt32.exe program uses the /tempdrive switch rather than the /t switch to specify the drive to store the temporary files.

```
Winnt32 /s:X:\i386 /unattend 10:X:\unattend.txt /tempdrive:C
```

Applying Update Packs to Installed Software Applications

Update packs (also called upgrade packs) are used to update applications to make them compatible with Windows 2000. During the upgrade process to Windows 2000 Professional, you will be given the opportunity to apply any update packs. The software vendor provides these update packs. You should contact your software vendors for your software's compatibility with Windows 2000 and see if they have any update packs available. These update packs can move registry keys, and update files to resolve incompatibility problems. This is performed by a migration DLL that is used by Setup to update an application.

CERTIFICATION OBJECTIVE 2.03

Deploying Service Packs

Periodically, Microsoft releases service packs for its operating systems. A service pack typically contains bug fixes, security fixes, system administration tools, drivers, and additional components. Microsoft recommends installing the latest service packs as they are released. Also, new in Windows 2000, you do not have to reinstall components after installing a service pack as you did in Windows NT. You can also see what service pack is currently installed on the computer by running the winver utility program. It opens the About Windows dialog box, which will display the version of Windows you are running and the version of the service pack.

To install a service pack, you use the Update.exe program. When a service pack is applied, Windows 2000 tracks which service pack was installed and which files were added and/or replaced. This way, when a component or service is added or removed, if any of the required files were included in the service pack, the operating system will automatically retrieve those files from the service pack. This prevents you from having to reinstall the service pack.

Testing Service Packs

Prior to deploying them to the enterprise, you should perform some testing first. Some applications have problems running after new service packs are installed. To test new service packs, you should create test environments for each computer

CertCam 2-7

Determining the Version of Windows 2000 and Service Pack Level

Let's walk though a check of your version of Windows 2000.

1. From the Start menu, click Run.

2. When the Run dialog box comes up, enter **winver** for the program to run, and click OK, as shown here.

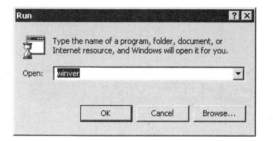

3. The About Windows dialog box will appear as shown in the following illustration. It shows the version of Windows (5.0) as well as the build number. Since no service packs are available, the service pack installed isn't displayed.

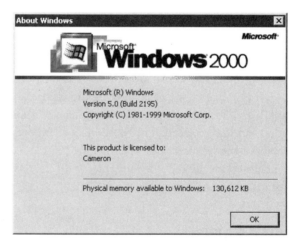

4. Click OK to close the dialog box.

configuration in your enterprise. Make sure the test computers have the same hardware, are running the same software, and are performing the same operations as the computers in the enterprise. This allows you to find potential errors prior to deploying a service pack throughout your enterprise.

Integrating Service Packs with Distribution Images

You can include service packs with a distribution image. This is called service pack *slipstreaming*. Using slipstreaming, you can install Windows 2000 with the service pack already applied to the installation files on a CD-ROM or distribution folder. You will not have to apply the service pack after installation of Windows 2000 Professional. To apply a service pack to distribution files, you use the Update.exe file with the /slip switch. This will overwrite the existing distribution files with the service pack files.

CERTIFICATION OBJECTIVE 2.04

Troubleshooting Failed Installations

Once in a while, you will have some problems when trying to install Windows 2000 Professional. Problems can also occur after installation is complete and you are restarting the computer for the first time. You need to be able to solve these problems when they occur.

Resolving Common Problems

If the CD-ROM you are installing from has errors on it, you will not be able to install from it—you will have to get another CD-ROM. If you don't have an additional copy, contact Microsoft or your vendor. Windows 2000 Professional does not support some CD-ROM drives. If this is the case, you will have to either replace the CD-ROM drive with a drive that is supported, or choose a different installation method such as a network installation. When you install Windows 2000 Professional, you have to ensure that you have enough free disk space. If you don't, the Setup program can create a new partition if there is any space on the hard disk.

If not, you can delete and create partitions as needed, so that you can create a partition large enough to install Windows 2000 Professional on. You can also add another hard disk or delete some applications that are not being used to free up some space.

When installing Windows 2000 Professional, you can sometimes get an error when trying to locate the domain controller. Check that you entered the correct domain name and that a domain controller is running on the network. Also verify that the DNS server is running. If you cannot locate a domain controller, join a workgroup; and then later, after installation, when you can locate a domain controller, join the domain.

Sometimes problems show up after installation is complete and you are starting Windows 2000 Professional for the first time. If Windows 2000 Professional fails to start, verify that all of the hardware is on the HCL, and that all of the hardware is being detected. Sometimes a dependency service will fail to start. If this occurs, verify that the correct network adapter is being installed, and check the configuration settings (e.g., transceiver setting). Also verify that you have installed the correct protocol and that the computer name is unique on the network.

Setup Logs

During the GUI phase of Setup, log files are created. These log files are located in the directory in which Windows 2000 is being installed. The following are four of the log files that are created:

- **Setupact.log**   The Action log file contains details about the files that are copied during Setup.

- **Setuperr.log**   The Error log file contains details about errors that occurred during Setup.

- **Setupapi.log**   This log file contains details about the device driver files that were copied during Setup, and can be used to facilitate troubleshooting device installations. This file contains errors and warnings, along with a timestamp for each issue.

- **Setuplog.txt**   This log file contains details about the device driver files that were copied during Setup.

Let's take a look at what is in your Setup Logs in Exercise 2-8.

EXERCISE 2-8

Looking at the Setup Logs

To look at the Setup Logs, perform the following steps:

1. Open My Computer.

2. Open up the C: drive. (If you installed Windows 2000 Professional on a different drive, then open up that drive. The rest of the exercise will assume drive C:. Just replace drive C: with the appropriate drive as necessary.)

3. Open the Winnt folder. (Again, this exercise assumes you used Winnt as the installation folder name. You can replace it if you installed to another folder name.)

4. Open the Setupact.log file for review. See the following for an example of the first few lines of the log file. When you double-click the log files, the log file will be opened up in Notepad by default.

```
GUI mode Setup has started.
C:\WINNT\Driver Cache\i386\driver.cab was copied to
C:\WINNT\System32\storprop.dll.
C:\$WIN_NT$.~LS\i386\SPOOLSV.EX_ was copied to
C:\WINNT\System32\SPOOLSV.EXE.
```

5. Close Setupact.log.

6. Open the Setupapi.log file for review. The following is an example of the first few lines of the log file.

```
[2000/02/21 13:25:25 324.12]
Munged cmdline: setup -newsetup
EXE name: C:\WINNT\system32\setup.exe
Installing Device Class: {6BDD1FC1-810F-11D0-BEC7-08002BE2092F} 1394.
Class install completed with no errors.
[2000/02/21 13:25:26 324.15]
Installing Device Class: {72631e54-78a4-11d0-bcf7-00aa00b7b32a} Battery.
Class install completed with no errors.
[2000/02/21 13:25:26 324.20]
Installing Device Class: {4D36E965-E325-11CE-BFC1-08002BE10318} CDROM.
Class install completed with no errors.
```

7. Close the Setupapi.log.

8. Open the Setuperr.log file for review. If there weren't any errors during Setup, then this file will be empty.

9. Close Setuperr.log.

10. Open the Setuplog.txt file for review. The following is an example of the first few lines of the log file.

```
13:24:58.559 syssetup.c @ 1214 Setup: (non-critical error):
 Failed load of ismif32.dll.
13:24:59.510 ctls.c @ 807 SETUP: Enter RegisterOleControls
13:24:59.520 ctls.c @ 860 SETUP: back from OleInitialize
13:24:59.520 ctls.c @ 879 SETUP: filename for file to register is rsabase.dll
13:24:59.520 ctls.c @ 433 SETUP: loading dll...
13:24:59.560 ctls.c @ 504 SETUP: ...dll loaded
13:24:59.560 ctls.c @ 533 SETUP: registering...
13:24:59.560 ctls.c @ 581 SETUP: ...registered
```

11. Close Setuplog.txt.

SCENARIO & SOLUTION

You have a distribution server that clients use to upgrade to Windows 2000 from. After they upgrade, they install a service pack from another network location. What can you do to simplify this process?	Service packs can be integrated or slipstreamed into a distribution image using the Service Pack Update.exe program. This will install the service pack files during Setup.
You are trying to install Windows 2000 with a dual-boot configuration. The partition you want to install to is not big enough, but you have 2GB of unpartitioned disk space. What can you do to make the partition large enough?	During Setup, you can delete the partition that is not large enough and then create it again, using the unpartitioned space of the hard disk to increase the size. Note that the operating system(s) cannot be on the partition you are going to delete.

CERTIFICATION SUMMARY

Installing Windows 2000 Professional is easier than it was in Windows NT 4.0. Some of the administrative overhead that was required in Windows NT 4.0 has been removed. Before starting the installation process, there is some preparation you should do first. You should check the computer for meeting the minimum hardware requirements. Check that all of the hardware is on the Hardware Compatibility List (HCL). You must decide how to partition the hard disk and which file system to use. You should decide whether to join a workgroup or a domain. Also, decide whether to configure the computer for single or multiboot operations.

Windows 2000 is most commonly installed from the CD-ROM. The CD-ROM installation has four basic stages: running the Setup program, running the Setup Wizard, installing networking, and completing installation. Phase 1, running the Setup program, is the text-mode portion of Setup. You will choose the partition for installing to, and choose which file system to use. Then Setup will copy files to the hard disk and reboot the computer. Phase 2, running the Setup Wizard, will configure the licensing mode. You can choose Per Seat or Per Server. If you choose Per Server, you must enter the maximum number of concurrent connections. You must enter a unique computer name and password for the Administrator account. Then you choose the optional components to install. Phase 3, installing networking, configures the computer to use the network. It installs the protocols and networking services. If you join a domain, your computer must have an account on the domain. Phase 4, completing installation, finishes copying files to the hard disk, saves the settings to hard disk, removes temporary files, and restarts the computer.

Installing Windows 2000 Professional from the network is very similar to installing from the CD-ROM, except the source is located in a different place. When installing Windows 2000 to a large amount of computers, installing over the network is more efficient. For network installations, a distribution server must be used. A distribution server is a computer on the network that can be accessed by the client computers. It needs a shared folder that contains the /i386 folder from the Windows 2000 Server CD-ROM. You can customize the installation using command-line switches.

There are a variety of methods you can use when upgrading your Windows computer to Windows 2000 Professional. You can use the Windows 2000

Professional CD-ROM, install across the network, and even perform unattended installations. One crucial aspect of upgrading is verifying that your hardware is compatible with Windows 2000. You should check the HCL for compatibility.

Windows 2000 has made using service packs easier. You can use slipstreaming to integrate service packs with a Windows 2000 distribution image. Another new feature is that you don't have to reinstall a service pack after adding components or installing applications; Windows 2000 automatically uses the existing service pack files.

On the rare occasion that a Windows 2000 installation should fail, you should understand the common causes of failure and how to solve the problems. In the event of more complicated failures, you can use the Setup log files to assist you in troubleshooting.

✓ TWO-MINUTE DRILL

Performing an Attended Installation of Windows 2000 Professional

❑ Before you start the Windows 2000 installation, you must do some preparation.

❑ You should check your existing hardware against the Hardware Compatibility List (HCL).

❑ Microsoft provides the HCL for all hardware that is supported by Windows 2000.

❑ The hard disk can be partitioned before, during, or after installation.

❑ Windows 2000 can be installed on a FAT, FAT32, or NTFS partition. NTFS is recommended for single-boot configurations. For dual-booting with Windows 95/98, you may choose the FAT or FAT32 file system.

❑ NTFS provides enhancements over FAT, such as security, encryption, compression, and the Active Directory.

❑ You can perform an attended installation of Windows 2000 Professional from a CD-ROM or across the network.

❑ You can upgrade existing Windows operating systems to Windows 2000, or install it separately for single- or multiboot configurations.

❑ There are many command-line switches available to customize the Setup program.

❑ To create the Setup floppy disks, you must use the Makeboot.exe program.

❑ When a large number of installations are required, you may choose to install Windows 2000 Professional over the network.

❑ You must have a valid Product Key in order to install Windows 2000 Professional.

❑ During Setup, you must provide a unique name for the computer.

❑ To install Windows 2000 Professional over the network, you need to set up a distribution server.

❑ To set up the distribution server, copy the /i386 folder from the CD-ROM to the shared folder on the distribution server.

❑ In Windows 2000, you can perform a network installation to a client with a FAT or NTFS partition. In Windows NT 4.0, you could only perform a network install to a client with a FAT partition.

❑ The client you are installing across the network to must have network client software that allows it to connect to the distribution server.

❑ You can customize the network installation process by using the command-line switches for Winnt.exe and Winnt32.exe.

Upgrading to Windows 2000 Professional

❑ Only Windows NT 3.51 and 4.0 Workstations, Windows 95, and Windows 98 can be upgraded to Windows 2000 Professional.

❑ You can upgrade using the CD-ROM, from a network distribution server or unattended.

❑ Make sure the computer meets the minimum hardware requirements.

❑ Make sure that all of the hardware and software is compatible with Windows 2000.

Deploying Service Packs

❑ Microsoft periodically releases updates to Windows operating systems.

❑ These updates contain bug and security fixes called service packs.

❑ Service packs are installed using the Update.exe program.

❑ You don't have to reinstall service packs after adding or deleting components or services.

❑ You should test your service pack for software compatibility prior to deploying it.

❑ You can include a service pack in a distribution image.

❑ You can deploy service packs using group policies.

Troubleshooting Failed Installations

❏ If the installation CD-ROM is damaged, you will have to replace it.

❏ Ensure there is enough free disk space prior to installation.

❏ Make sure the domain controller is online and available.

❏ Verify that the DNS server is running.

❏ The Setupact.log contains details about the files that are copied during Setup.

❏ The Setuperr.log contains details about errors that occurred during Setup.

❏ The Setupapi.log contains details about the device driver files that were copied during Setup.

❏ The Setuplog.txt contains details about the device driver files that were copied during Setup.

SELF TEST

The following questions will help you measure your understanding of the material presented in this chapter. Read all of the choices carefully, as there may be more than one correct answer. Choose all correct answers for each question.

Performing an Attended Installation of Windows 2000 Professional

1. Which of the following is NOT a minimum hardware requirement for Windows 2000 Professional?

   A. 133-MHz Pentium CPU

   B. At least two CPUs

   C. 128MB RAM

   D. 650MB partition

2. You are preparing to install Windows 2000 Professional on your computer. You check your hardware on the HCL, and your network card is not on the list. What should you do?

   A. Install Windows 2000 Professional and see if it works.

   B. Check the hardware vendor's Web site.

   C. Use the Windows 98 driver that came with the card.

   D. Do not install Windows 2000 until you get a network card on the HCL.

3. Which of the following file systems does Windows 2000 support? (Select all that apply.)

   A. FAT

   B. FAT32

   C. HPFS

   D. NTFS

4. You are installing Windows 2000 Professional and Windows 98 on the same computer with a dual-boot configuration. After installing Windows 2000, you realize that all of the applications you installed on Windows 98 are not available on Windows 2000. Which of the following should you do?

   A. Create shortcuts to the executables for the applications.

   B. Import the application settings in the Windows 98 Registry to the Windows 2000 Registry.

C. Reinstall all of the applications.

D. Export the Windows 2000 Registry to the Windows 98 Registry.

5. You want to install Windows 2000 Professional on a computer that currently is running Windows 98. You want to be able to run both operating systems with a dual-boot configuration. Currently, the computer has a hard disk with one 4GB partition. Which file system should you choose when installing Windows 2000?

A. FAT

B. FAT32

C. NTFS

D. You must install the NTFS upgrade to Windows 98 and then convert the partition to NTFS.

6. You are an administrator installing Windows 2000 Professional on a computer, and you just remembered that you forgot to add the computer account to the domain. The Windows 2000 domain controller is in another building, and you don't want to walk over there to add it to the domain. What should you do?

A. You must walk over to the domain controller to create a computer account.

B. Enter your administrator account's username and password when prompted.

C. Nothing. Windows 2000 Professional is automatically added to the domain by the Setup program.

D. Add the computer to a workgroup with the same name as the domain, and the domain controller will automatically add it to the domain when it sees it on the network.

7. During installation of Windows 2000 Professional, you want to install WordPad. Which of the following components includes the WordPad program?

A. Windows Media Services

B. Management and Monitoring Tools

C. Accessories and Utilities

D. Office programs

8. During installation of Windows 2000 Professional, you are prompted to enter a name for your computer. Which of the following is a requirement for the computer name?

A. You must use your name for the computer name.

B. The computer name must be unique on the network.

    C. The computer name must be the same as the domain name.

    D. The computer name must be the same as the workgroup name.

9. During installation of Windows 2000 Professional, you choose the Typical option for Network components to install. Which of the following will NOT be installed?

    A. Client for Microsoft Networks

    B. File and Print Sharing for Microsoft Networks

    C. NetBEUI

    D. TCP/IP

10. You are performing a Windows 2000 Professional installation over the network with the Winnt.exe. Which switch should you use to specify the source of the installation files?

    A. /a

    B. /r

    C. /rx

    D. /s

11. You seem to be having trouble when running the Windows 2000 Professional Setup program. You decide to try to debug the installation. Which switch can you use with the Winnt32.exe program to accomplish this?

    A. /d

    B. /debug

    C. /log

    D. /troubleshoot

12. What is the default filename used for the setup information file with Winnt32.exe command-line switch /I?

    A. Setup.inf

    B. Info.inf

    C. Setupinfo.inf

    D. Dosnet.inf

Upgrading to Windows 2000 Professional

13. Which versions of Windows can be upgraded to Windows 2000 Professional?

    A. Only Windows 95 and Windows 98.

    B. Only Windows NT 4.0 Workstations and Windows 98.

    C. Only Windows NT 3.51 and 4.0 Workstations and Windows 98.

    D. Windows NT 3.51 and 4.0 Workstations, Windows 95, and Windows 98 can be upgraded to Windows 2000 Professional.

Deploying Service Packs

14. Which of the following are NOT generally included in a Windows 2000 Professional service pack?

    A. Drivers

    B. New components

    C. Microsoft Office fixes

    D. Bug fixes

15. Which of the following methods CANNOT be used to deploy service packs in Windows 2000?

    A. Using the Update.exe program

    B. Including the service pack in a distribution image

    C. Using the SPInstall.exe program

    D. Using group policies

16. You have a computer running Windows 2000 that keeps hanging and requires a reboot often. You know there has been a service pack released to fix the problem, but you are not sure what service pack the computer currently has. Which of the following programs can be used to find out which service pack has been installed on the computer?

    A. SPVer.exe

    B. Ver.exe

    C. Winver.exe

    D. Update.exe /ver

17. You are going to be installing Windows 2000 on some new computers. However, a new service pack was just released. You want to include the service pack as part of the distribution image. Which of the following command-line switches is used to integrate the service pack with a distribution image?

   A. /slip

   B. /s

   C. /integrate

   D. /copy

Troubleshooting Failed Installations

18. During the installation of Windows 2000 Professional, you are trying to join a domain and you receive an error that Setup cannot locate a domain controller. Which of the following do you NOT need to check?

   A. Check that you entered the correct domain name.

   B. Verify that a domain controller is available.

   C. Verify that a WINS server is running.

   D. Verify that a DNS server is running.

19. You installed Windows 2000 on a new computer to the default location on the C: drive. You are encountering some strange errors, and it was recommended to review the Setup log files. In which directory would these log files be found?

   A. C:\

   B. C:\Winnt

   C. C:\Winnt\System

   D. C:\Winnt\Log

20. Which of the following is NOT a log file created by Windows 2000 Setup?

   A. Setupact.log

   B. Setup.log

   C. Setuperr.log

   D. SetupLog.txt

21. You installed Windows 2000 Professional on a computer. You are having some trouble with one of the devices on your computer. Which of the following Setup files should you use for troubleshooting to find errors that might have occurred while installing this device?

  A. Setupact.log

  B. Setuperr.log

  C. Setupapi.log

  D. SetupDeviceErr.log

LAB QUESTION

You are tasked with starting a network for a new company. You want to use Windows 2000 for all of your computers. You have to give a presentation to management explaining the issues involved with installing Windows 2000 Professional on the network. The following is a list of topics to cover in the presentation. Write about the areas of concern of each of the topics listed.

1. System Requirements

2. Hardware Compatibility

3. Optional Device Inventory

4. Mass Storage Devices

5. BIOS

6. Important Files to Review

7. What File System to Use

8. Planning Disk Partitions

9. Networking: TCP/IP, IP Addresses, and Name Resolution

10. Deciding Between Workgroups and Domains

SELF TEST ANSWERS

Performing an Attended Installation of Windows 2000 Professional

1. ☑ **B.** In order to install Windows 2000 Server, only one CPU is required.
   ☒ **A** is incorrect because a 133-MHz Pentium CPU is the minimum requirement for the CPU. **C** is incorrect because 128MB of RAM is the minimum requirement for memory. **D** is incorrect because a 650MB partition is the minimum requirement for disk space.

2. ☑ **D.** If your network card is not on the Hardware Compatibility List (HCL), then it has not been tested and proven to be compatible with Windows 2000 Server. If it is not on the HCL, your computer may not operate correctly.
   ☒ **A** is incorrect because you should not install Windows 2000 if any of your hardware is not on the HCL. **B** is incorrect because even if the vendor says it is compatible, you cannot be completely sure unless it is on the HCL. **C** is incorrect because most drivers designed for Windows 98 will not work correctly on Windows 2000. You should never use drivers not specifically designed for Windows 2000.   ,

3. ☑ **A, B, D.** Windows 2000 supports the FAT, FAT32, and NTFS file systems.
   ☒ **C** is incorrect because Windows 2000 does not support the High Performance File System (HPFS).

4. ☑ **C.** If you install Windows 2000 to a separate directory than the existing operating system, you will then have to reinstall all of the applications.
   ☒ **A** is incorrect because creating a shortcut does not configure the application. Most applications require some Registry settings and system files copied to the system directory. **B** is incorrect because you can't import Registry settings from Windows 98 to Windows 2000. The two Registries are not compatible with each other. **D** is incorrect because you cannot export the Windows 2000 Registry to Windows 98. Even if you could, it would not configure the Windows 2000 Registry with the settings for the applications.

5. ☑ **B.** Windows 98 can only use the FAT and FAT32 file systems. Since the partition is larger than 2GB, Microsoft recommends using the FAT32 file system. In order to dual-boot with Windows 98 and Windows 2000, you should use FAT32. Windows 98 cannot use the NTFS file system.
   ☒ **A** is incorrect because FAT is not recommended for use on partitions larger than 2GB; Microsoft recommends using FAT32 for partitions larger than 2GB. **C** is incorrect because Windows 98 cannot use NTFS; if you convert the partition to NTFS, Windows 98 will no

longer be functional. **D** is incorrect because there is no such thing as a Windows 98 NTFS upgrade; Windows 98 cannot use NTFS.

6. ☑ **B.** You can create a computer account in a domain during Setup if you have a valid username and password for an administrator account.
☒ **A** is incorrect because you can create the computer from the computer you are running Setup on; you don't have to do it from a domain controller. **C** is incorrect because no computer accounts are automatically added to a domain controller; an administrator must create the account. **D** is incorrect because a domain controller does not automatically add computer accounts to the domain; an administrator must add it to the domain.

7. ☑ **C.** WordPad program is part of the Accessories and Utilities optional component. To select WordPad, click Details and select WordPad.
☒ **A** is incorrect because the Windows Media component provides multimedia support, allowing you to deliver content using Advanced Streaming Format over an intranet or the Internet. **B** is incorrect because the Management and Monitoring Tools provides tools for communications administration, monitoring, and management, including programs that support development of customized client dialers for remote users and implementation of phone books that can be automatically updated from a central server. **D** is incorrect because Office Programs is not an optional component.

8. ☑ **B.** Each computer on the network must have a unique computer name.
☒ **A** is incorrect because you are not limited to using your name as a computer name. A computer name should be descriptive, but it is not required to be. **C** is incorrect because if all computers in a domain used the domain name as their computer name, then the computer names would not be unique. **D** is incorrect because if all computers on a network used the workgroup names as their computer names, then the computer names would not be unique.

9. ☑ **C.** The only network protocol installed by default is TCP/IP. NetBEUI is not installed.
☒ **A, B,** and **D** are incorrect because the default network components that are installed are Client for Microsoft Networks, File and Print Sharing for Microsoft Networks, and TCP/IP.

10. ☑ **D.** The /s switch specifies the location of the Windows 2000 installation files.
☒ **A** is incorrect because the /a switch enables the accessibility option. **B** is incorrect because the /r switch creates an additional folder within the system root folder (where the Windows 2000 system files are located). **C** is incorrect because the /rx switch creates an additional folder within the system root folder, but Setup deletes the files after installation is completed.

11. ☑ **B.** The /debug switch allows you to turn debugging on. You can also set the level of debugging and the filename to hold the debug log. By default, it uses the file C:\Winnt32.log at level 2 (the warning level).

☒   A, C, and D are incorrect because they are not valid command-line switches for the Winnt.exe program.

12. ☑   D. If you do not specify a setup information filename with the /I switch, it will use the file Dosnet.inf by default.
    ☒   A, B, and C are incorrect because the correct filename is Dosnet.inf.

Upgrading to Windows 2000 Professional

13. ☑   D. It is all the listed Windows operating systems.
    ☒   A, B and C all can be upgraded to Windows 2000 Professional, but not all the possible operating systems are listed in these choices.

Deploying Service Packs

14. ☑   C. An operating system service pack does not contain fixes for Microsoft Office; Microsoft Office has its own service packs.
    ☒   A, B, and D are incorrect because operating system service packs can contain drivers, new components, and bug fixes.

15. ☑   C. There is no such thing as an SPInstall.exe program to install service packs. The Upgrade.exe program is used to install service packs.
    ☒   A is incorrect because the Upgrade.exe program can be used to install service packs. B is incorrect because you can integrate service packs into distribution images. D is incorrect because group policies can be used to deploy service packs.

16. ☑   C. The Winver.exe program will display a dialog box that lists the version of Windows that is currently running, the build number for the operating system, and the service pack that is installed.
    ☒   A and B are incorrect because there is no such thing as a Windows file called SPVer.exe and Ver.exe. D is incorrect because the Update.exe program does not take a /ver switch to show the current service pack level.

17. ☑   A. The Update.exe program uses the /slip switch to specify that you want to integrate a service pack with an existing distribution image.
    ☒   B, C, and D are incorrect because these are not valid switches for the Upgrade.exe program; the /slip switch is used.

Troubleshooting Failed Installations

18. ☑ **C.** You do not need the WINS service to locate a domain controller. Windows 2000 only uses DNS for name resolution.

☒ **A** is incorrect because you do need to enter the correct domain name in order to join a domain. **B** is incorrect because you do need to verify that a domain controller is online and running in order to join a domain. **D** is incorrect because you do need to verify that there is a DNS server online and available to locate a domain controller.

19. ☑ **B.** The Setup log files are created in the system root folder, which is the directory where you installed Windows 2000.

☒ **A, C,** and **D** are incorrect because the log files are located in the system root folder, not the partition's root or the System or the Log directory of the System Root.

20. ☑ **B.** Setup does not create a log file called Setup.log.

☒ **A** is incorrect because Setup creates the Setupact.log file. **C** is incorrect because Setup does create the Setuperr.log file. **D** is incorrect because Setup does create the SetupLog.txt file.

21. ☑ **C.** The Setupapi.log file contains details about device driver files that were copied, as well as errors and warnings that have occurred during Setup.

☒ **A** is incorrect because the Setupact.log file is used to log details about the files that are copied during Setup. **B** is incorrect because the Setuperr.log contains details about general errors that occur during Setup, not device driver installation errors. **D** is incorrect because a SetupDeviceErr.log file is not created by Setup.

LAB ANSWER

1. System Requirements

   You have to ensure that the computers on which you are going to install Windows 2000 Professional have the adequate resources. Not only does the computer have to meet the minimum requirements, but it also must be able to handle the load that will be placed on it. Some of the components to look at are the CPU, RAM, hard disk controller, hard disk space, and the network card. You also want to ensure the computer has a CD-ROM drive and/or DVD drive, and a floppy disk drive.

2. **Hardware Compatibility**

   You should make sure that the computers on which you are installing Windows 2000 Professional are compatible with Windows 2000 Professional. During Setup, your hardware will be checked for compatibility, and any conflicts will be reported. However, you should check your hardware against the HCL before running Setup to prevent problems during installation. You should also make sure that the device drivers for your hardware are designed for Windows 2000.

3. **Optional Device Inventory**

   Windows 2000 now supports Plug and Play, so your devices will be detected, configured, and installed automatically. If any of your hardware is not Plug and Play compatible, then you need to take some extra steps to prevent conflicts. Take an inventory of all the devices in the computer. Take note of the IRQ and memory address each device uses. This can help prevent conflicts that cannot be resolved during Setup. For instance, if two devices use the same IRQ, and one of the devices does not use Plug and Play, you can either remove one of the adapters before installation and install it after setup, or modify the IRQ setting of one of the devices before setup using the jumpers if available. See Table 2-3 for some information to gather.

4. **Mass Storage Devices**

   If you are going to be using a mass storage device (e.g., SCSI or RAID) for your hard disk, you need to make sure the hard disk controller is on the HCL. If it is not on the HCL, check the vendor for an updated driver designed for Windows 2000 Professional that has been tested for compatibility. If there is one available, put it on a floppy disk and have it available during Setup.

5. **BIOS**

   The basic input/output system (BIOS) of a computer is software that the operating system can use to communicate with the hardware devices. The current BIOS standard is called the Advanced Configuration and Power Interface (ACPI). Windows 2000 supports this standard, as well as the older Advanced Power Management (APM) standard. You need to make sure that the BIOS is compatible with Windows 2000. Check the HCL and check with the vendor to see if there is a BIOS upgrade for Windows 2000.

6. **Important Files to Review**

   On the Windows 2000 Professional CD-ROM, there are some files in the root directory that you should read prior to installation. The file Read1st.txt contains notes that can be critical to

TABLE 2-3	Video	Adapter or chipset type, and how many video adapters
What to Check If Your Hardware Is Not Plug and Play	Network	IRQ, I/O address, DMA (if used) connector type (for example, BNC or twisted pair), and bus type
	SCSI controller	Adapter model or chipset, IRQ, and bus type
	Mouse	Mouse type and port (COM1, COM2, bus, or PS/2), or USB
	I/O port	IRQ, I/O address, and DMA (if used) for each I/O port
	Sound adapter	IRQ, I/O address, and DMA
	Universal serial bus (USB)	Devices and hubs attached
	PC Card	What adapters are inserted, and in which slots
	Plug and Play	Whether enabled or disabled in BIOS
	BIOS settings	BIOS revision and date
	External modem	COM port connections (COM1, COM2, and so on)
	Internal modem	COM port connections; for nonstandard configurations, IRQ and I/0 address
	Advanced Configuration and Power Interface (ACPI); Power Options	Enabled or disabled; current setting
	PCI	What PCI adapters are inserted, and in which slots

the success of installation. The file Readme.doc contains information about the usage of hardware, networking, applications, and printing.

7. **What File System to Use**

   Windows 2000 supports the FAT, FAT32, and NTFS file systems. Since you are installing Windows 2000 Professional, it is recommended that you use the NTFS file system. NTFS is a more powerful file system than FAT and FAT32. NTFS supports the Active Directory, as well as built-in domain-based security and other features not available in FAT and FAT32. Since this is a new installation, you should not configure the computers for multiboot; therefore, there isn't any good reason to choose FAT or FAT32.

8. **Planning Disk Partitions**

   Since this will be a new installation, you should plan how you will partition your disk prior to starting installation. You need to determine the size of the partition you will be installing

Windows 2000 Professional on. There aren't any hard-and-fast rules, but you should make the partition big enough for the operating system, applications that will be installed on this partition, and any other files that will be stored on it. Setup requires at least 1GB of free space with 650MB of free space on the partition it is installing to, but you should provide a much larger partition. With hard disks so cheap in price, it is not uncommon for 10GB partitions to be used. This allows space for a variety of items, including optional components, user accounts, Active Directory information, logs, future service packs, the pagefile used by the operating system, and other items.

During Setup, create and size only the partition on which you want to install Windows 2000. After Windows 2000 is installed, you can use Disk Management to manage new and existing disks and volumes. This includes creating new partitions from unpartitioned space; deleting, renaming, and reformatting existing partitions; adding and removing hard disks; and upgrading and reverting hard disks between basic and dynamic formats. Setup examines the hard disk to determine its existing configuration, and then offers the following options:

- If the hard disk is unpartitioned, you can create and size the Windows 2000 partition.

- If the hard disk is partitioned but has enough unpartitioned disk space, you can create the Windows 2000 partition by using the unpartitioned space.

- If the hard disk has an existing partition that is large enough, you can install Windows 2000 on that partition, with or without reformatting the partition first. Reformatting a partition erases all data on the partition. If you don't reformat the partition, but you do install Windows 2000 where there was already an operating system, that operating system will be overwritten, and you will have to reinstall any applications you want to use with Windows 2000.

- If the hard disk has an existing partition, you can delete it to create more unpartitioned disk space for the Windows 2000 partition. Deleting an existing partition also erases any data on that partition.

9. **Networking: TCP/IP, IP Addresses, and Name Resolution**

To set up TCP/IP on your computers, each computer needs to have an IP address. This can be provided automatically by DHCP or assigned manually. Because these addresses are numbers and can be hard to remember, you will also have to provide users with names that can be resolved to IP addresses by DNS and WINS.

When using TCP/IP, it requires that an IP address be provided for each computer. The following list describes the methods you can use to provide an IP address:

- For a limited number of servers (five or fewer) on a small private network, you can use the Windows 2000 Server feature called Automatic Private IP Addressing (APIPA) to automatically assign IP addresses for you.

- If your network has more than one subnet, choose one server on which to install and configure the Dynamic Host Configuration Protocol (DHCP) component. It must itself be assigned a static IP address (so other computers can locate it). In this situation, in order to support clients, you might also need one or more servers with the DNS component and/or the Windows Internet Name Service (WINS) component.

- If a particular server will be directly providing access to users on the Internet, you must assign that server a static IP address.

To make it easier for users, you can allow users to use names instead of IP addresses. DNS or WINS can translate these names to IP addresses. DNS is a hierarchical naming system used for locating computers on the Internet and private TCP/IP networks. DNS is required for Internet e-mail, Web browsing, and Active Directory. DNS is also required in domains with clients running Windows 2000. DNS is installed automatically when you create a domain controller unless the Windows 2000 software detects that a DNS server already exists for that domain.

10. **Deciding Between Workgroups and Domains**

A domain is a grouping of accounts and network resources that are grouped together using a single domain name and security boundary. All user accounts, permissions, and other network details are stored in a centralized database on the primary domain controller and replicated to the backup domain controllers. A single login gives the user access to all resources for which they have permissions. Domains are recommended for all networks with more than ten computers or for networks expected to grow to larger than ten computers in the near future. There are a few requirements to join a domain. You will need to know the domain name. You must have a computer account for the computer on which you are installing Windows 2000 Professional. This account can be created either by the administrator before installing Windows 2000 Professional or during Setup with the username and password of an account with the permissions to create a computer account. You will also need at least one domain controller and Domain Name Server (DNS) online when you install Windows 2000 Professional.

A workgroup is a logical grouping of resources on a network. It is generally used in peer-to-peer networks. This means that each computer is responsible for access to its resources. Each computer has its own account database and is administered separately. Security is not shared between computers, and administration is more difficult than in a centralized domain. Workgroups are only intended as a convenience to help find resources. When browsing the network, the resources in your same workgroup are found first. It does not provide any security. In a workgroup, you might have to remember a different password for every resource you want to access. To join a workgroup during installation, all you need is a workgroup name. This can be the name of an existing workgroup or a new one. You must join a workgroup or a domain during installation, but you can change these memberships later as needed.

3

Performing an Unattended Installation of Windows 2000

I n the previous chapter, you learned how to perform an attended installation of Windows 2000 Professional. Since attended installation takes a considerable time and you have to answer a lot of setup questions, it is not a desired method of installation when you have hundreds or thousands of computers. This is where unattended setup comes to the rescue for network administrators. This chapter walks you through the various tools and methods that can be used to automate and customize the deployment of Windows 2000 Professional.

You might be familiar with the unattended installation of Windows NT Workstation 4.0 using the Setup Manager. While the improved Setup Manager still remains an excellent choice for generating custom answer files in Windows 2000 for unattended installations, we now have other deployment tools such as the System Preparation tool (Sysprep) and the Remote Installation Service (RIS). We will learn how the automated and customized installations can be performed on computers with similar or different hardware configurations using these tools.

CERTIFICATION OBJECTIVE 3.01

Disk Duplication Methods

The deployment of a new operating system is one of the most challenging and time-consuming tasks that a network administrator has to perform. The disk duplication methods are particularly useful when you need to deploy Windows 2000 Professional on a large number of computers. This is also known as *disk imaging* or *cloning*. These tools make the rollout fast and easy. The installations using disk duplication become more easy and efficient when all the computers have identical hardware. The disk duplication tools that we will be discussing here are the System Preparation (Sysprep) and Remote Installation Preparation (RIPrep).

Which Duplication Tool to Use, and When

Given that we have two excellent disk duplicating or imaging tools, it becomes necessary to decide on what tool to use and where. The first condition is that both Sysprep and RIPrep tools are meant for clean installations and cannot be used for upgrading the computers from any previous operating system. While images created using Sysprep can be distributed with any third-party utilities, RIPrep requires that you distribute the image using the Remote Installation Service only. Both methods have their own merits and demerits, and some basic requirements that must be met.

Where to Find Sysprep and RIPrep?

Before we can use any of the tools, we need to find out where these tools are located in the Windows 2000 Professional CD. The RIPrep tool comes with Windows 2000 Server. You will find the Sysprep tool and the Setup Manager in the Deploy.cab file of the Support\Tools folder on your Windows 2000 Professional CD. Writing installation scripts or answer files using the Setup Manager is discussed later in this chapter in the section "The Scripted Method." In Exercise 3-1, we will learn how to extract these files.

EXERCISE 3-1

Extracting the Windows 2000 Professional Deployment Tools

You can extract the Windows 2000 Professional Deployment Tools by performing the following steps:

1. Select a computer where you want to extract the deployment tools. Log on as administrator.

2. Insert the Windows 2000 Professional compact disk in the CD-ROM drive. Close the window that pops up immediately after inserting the CD.

3. Open Windows Explorer and create a folder named Deptool on the C: drive. We will use this folder to keep the files extracted from the Support\Tools folder on the CD-ROM.

4. Considering that D is the drive letter for your CD-ROM, double-click the Deploy.cab folder located in the D:\Support\Tools folder. You can see this in the following illustration.

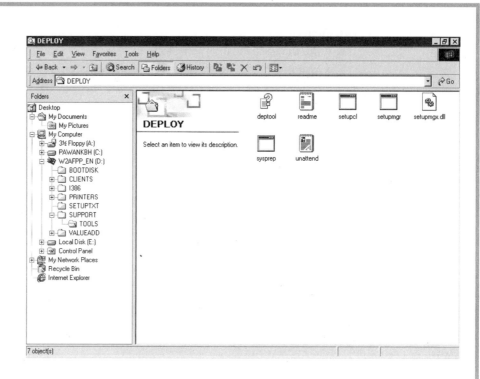

5. From the File menu, click Edit | Select All. All the files are selected. Right-click any of the files and click Extract.

6. In the Browse For Folder window, select the Deptool folder on the C: drive. Click Deptool and then click OK.

7. The file extraction takes only a few seconds. Check the contents of the Deptool folder in the Windows Explorer. You will notice that seven files have been copied to this folder.

SCENARIO & SOLUTION

I have a large number of computers running Windows 98 in my office. Can I use any disk duplication method to upgrade these computers to Windows 2000 Professional?	No. The disk duplication tools can be used only for clean installations. In case you wish to upgrade, use the scripted method.
Most of the computers in my office were supplied by the same vendor and have identical hardware. Which imaging tool is best for me?	Use Sysprep. Sysprep is the best tool to copy the image of a computer to other computers that have identical hardware configurations.
I wish to use the Sysprep utility for imaging my computer, but I cannot find this file. Where can I locate this file?	The Sysprep.exe file is located in the \Support\Tools\Deploy.cab file on the Windows 2000 CD-ROM. Double-click the Deploy.cab file to extract all files to your hard drive.

Sysprep

Sysprep provides an excellent means of saving installation time and reducing installation costs. It is also helpful in standardizing the desktop environment throughout the organization. Since one Sysprep image cannot be used on computers that have different hardware and software applications, you can create multiple images when you have more than one standard. It is still the best option when the number of computers is in hundreds or thousands and you wish to implement uniform policies in the organization.

After configuring one computer with the operating system and all the applications, Sysprep is run to create an image of the hard disk. This computer serves as the master or model computer that will have the complete setup of the operating system, application software, and any service packs. The image is called the *master image* and is copied to a CD or put on a network share for distribution to many computers. Any third-party disk-imaging tool can then be used to replicate the image to other identical computers. Some of the image-copying tools are DriveImage from PowerQuest and Norton Ghost from Symantec.

exam
Ⓦatch

The Sysprep tool can be used only for clean installations. It cannot be used for upgrading a previous operating system.

Requirements for Running Sysprep

As we observed earlier, the Sysprep tool is an ideal imaging solution for computers that have identical hardware configurations. The following points describe in detail the various requirements that must be met in order to use Sysprep.

- The master computer on which the image is to be created must be identical to all the computers that will receive the image. The administrator can use disk duplication to conduct a fast, easy deployment on systems that aren't identical using the same image on different hardware configurations (so long as they are compatible with the copied images). For example, you cannot use the image created on a single-processor unit on a computer with two processors. The Hardware Abstraction Layer (HAL) must be similar.

- The master and the destination computers must have identical hard drives and controllers. The hard drive capacity required on the destination computers has to be at least equal to the hard drive capacity on the master computer. For example, Sysprep will not help if the master computer has an IDE hard drive and the destination computer has a SCSI hard drive, even if the capacity of both hard drives is the same.

- There is an exception for Plug and Play devices. These Plug and Play devices need not necessarily be identical. Examples of such are video cards, network adapters, sound cards, and modems. The Sysprep master image automatically runs a full Plug and Play device detection on the destination computer.

- The Sysprep tool only creates the master image. You will need some third-party utility to distribute the master image. There is no limit on the number of master images that you can create. For example, if your company has five different hardware configurations, you can create five master images.

- You need to have administrative privileges on the master computer on which you wish to run Sysprep. It is also advisable that you test the applications thoroughly and apply all necessary service packs before creating a master image.

- The most important and mandatory requirement for running Sysprep is that you must have a volume licensing agreement.

exam
ⓦatch

Be aware that Sysprep cannot be used in environments in which every other desktop has its own custom configuration.

Components of Sysprep

The Sysprep utility has the four components associated with it: sysprep.exe, sysprep.inf, setupcl.exe, and the Mini-Setup Wizard. The following sections describe the function of each of these components.

Sysprep.exe   This is the main Sysprep executable file. This command has the following syntax:

```
Sysprep.exe [/quiet] [/nosidgen] [/pnp] [/reboot]
```

- **/quiet**   This option runs SysPrep in a quiet mode and does not generate any messages on the screen.
- **/nosidgen**   Runs SysPrep without generating any security ID. This allows the user to customize the computer. This is particularly useful when you do not wish to clone the master computer on which SysPrep is being run.
- **/pnp**   This option forces a full Plug and Play detection on the destination computer.
- **/reboot**   This forces a reboot of the master computer after the image has been created.

Sysprep.inf   Sysprep.inf is an answer file that must be used when you wish to automate the Mini-Setup Wizard. This file needs to be placed in the %Systemroot/%sysprep folder. When the Mini-Setup Wizard is run on the computer on which the image is being distributed, it takes answers from the Sysprep.inf file without prompting the user for any input.

Setupcl.exe   The function of this file is to run the Mini-Setup Wizard and to regenerate the security IDs on the master and destination computers. The Mini-Setup Wizard starts on the master computer when it is booted for the first time after running Sysprep.

Mini-Setup Wizard   The purpose of this wizard is to add some user-specific parameters on the destination computer. These parameters include the following information:

- End-user license agreement (EULA)
- Product key (serial number)

- Username, company name, and administrator password
- Network configuration
- Domain or workgroup name
- Date and time zone selection

The preceding information in the Mini-Setup Wizard can be automated using the Sysprep.inf file. The syntax and structure of the Sysprep.inf file is similar to the answer file created by Setup Manager. You may also use the Setup Manager to create an answer file for the Mini-Setup Wizard.

exam
ⓦatch
Using Sysprep.inf gives you an option to provide answers to all or some of the user input required by the Mini-Setup Wizard. The user is prompted for any answers that are not included in the Sysprep.inf file.

The Sysprep Process—Creating a Master Image

Let's look at the process of creating a master image using Sysprep to better understand the various steps involved.

1. Select a computer that has hardware identical to all or many of the other computers. Install Windows 2000 Professional on this computer. For a description of how to install Windows 2000 Professional, refer to Chapter 2. It is recommended that you do not make the computer a member of any domain. Also, keep the local administrator password blank.

2. When the Windows 2000 Professional setup is complete, log on to the computer as administrator. Make necessary changes to the Windows configuration that you wish to standardize throughout your organization. Install any custom or business applications on this computer. Apply service packs, if any.

3. Test all the components of the operating system and the applications on the master computer for reliability. When you have finished, delete any unwanted files, such as setup and audit logs.

4. Prepare the master image by running the Sysprep utility. Exercise 3-2 describes how to run Sysprep. When the image has been created, the system either shuts down automatically or prompts you that it is safe to shut down. When you restart the computer, a Mini-Setup Wizard starts running on the master computer. This happens because the Sysprep process takes off the security ID of the computer, and this needs to be restored.

5. The next step is image distribution. This can be accomplished by using any third-party utility. When the destination computer is started for the first time, a Mini-Setup Wizard is run. Sysprep adds this wizard to the master image.

EXERCISE 3-2

Running Sysprep from Windows Explorer

Perform the following steps to run Sysprep from Windows Explorer.

1. Log on to the master computer as an administrator.

2. Open Windows Explorer and click the Deptool folder that we created in Exercise 3-1, which contains the Sysprep.exe and setupmgr.exe files.

3. Double-click the Sysprep.exe file. A message appears on the screen saying that some of the security parameters of your computer might change. Click OK.

4. The computer starts shutting down.

You are done! This creates a master image of the computer.

Running Sysprep from the Command Prompt

This method of running Sysprep gives you the option of using any or all of the optional switches associated with Sysprep. In this exercise, we will use the /reboot switch.

1. Log on to the master computer as an administrator.

2. Select Start | Run, and type **cmd**. The DOS prompt window opens.

3. Change to the system root by typing **cd **. Create a directory named Sysprep by typing **md Sysprep**.

4. Change to the Sysprep folder by typing **cd Sysprep**.

5. Copy the sysprep.exe and the setupcl.exe files from the Deptool folder to this folder. Use the following two commands:

```
copy c:\deptools\sysprep.exe
copy c:\deptools\setupcl.exe
```

6. Run Sysprep from the c:\Sysprep directory by typing the following command:

```
Sysprep /reboot
```

7. A warning message appears on the screen, as shown in the following illustration, saying that the execution of Sysprep may change some security settings of this computer. Click OK.

8. Since we used the /reboot option with Sysprep.exe, the master computer prepares the image and restarts automatically.

on the job *It is best to perform the Sysprep installation when you have a large number of computers that need a clean installation. Usually this is not the case. You may have computers that are already running some other operating system and applications. Even in the networked environments in which users have their home and data folders on the servers, data is still stored locally. Be sure to ask the users about the importance of their data, and make tape backups before you go ahead with your plans for a mass deployment using any of the tools.*

RIPrep and Remote Installation Services

The Remote Installation Services (RIS) is a part of the Windows 2000 Server operating system. It is installed as an optional service on the Windows 2000 Server and facilitates installation of Windows 2000 Professional remotely on a large number of computers with similar or dissimilar hardware configurations. This not only reduces the installation time, but also helps keep deployment costs low. The Remote Installation Preparation (RIPrep) utility is used to create a master image of a fully configured client computer running Windows 2000 Professional. This image that is independent of the client hardware is uploaded to the RIS server for distribution to other client computers.

While RIS is an excellent utility provided by Microsoft, it requires careful study and planning before it can be used. RIS needs services like Active Directory, DNS, and DHCP to be running on the network. The client computers need to have either one of the 25 supported network adapters or a PXE-based Boot ROM that supports booting from the network.

To better understand the Remote Installation process, consider that a client computer boots using either the Remote Boot Disk prepared by an RIS server or a compatible Boot ROM on the network interface card (NIC). While a BootP message is displayed on the client, it connects to the DHCP server that is preconfigured to allocate an IP address to this client. The Boot Information

Negotiation Layer (BINL) extensions on the DHCP server redirect the client computer to the RIS server on the network. A Client Installation Wizard is downloaded to the client. This utility prompts the user to log on. Upon successful logon, the RIS server contacts the Active Directory to determine what options of the Client Installation Wizard (CIW) are to be displayed to the user. It also checks with the Active Directory to find out what images the user is authorized to select. Active Directory makes use of TFTP (Trivial File Transfer Protocol) to transfer the first few required files to the client. The DNS server plays its role in locating the Active Directory server on the network. Once the user selects an image, the setup starts running on the client computer. The sequence of protocol activities is DHCP, BINL, and TFTP.

The image that is to be distributed to the client can be prepared by any of the disk duplication methods. RIPrep is one such wizard that is more or less similar to the system preparation tool. The difference is that RIPrep removes the security ID from the master computer and all the hardware-specific settings. This makes the image independent of the hardware configuration. The RIS, as a whole, is a great utility aimed at reducing deployment time, administrative efforts, and costs.

exam
Ⓦatch

The Remote Installation Service can be used only to distribute Windows 2000 Professional operating system images. You cannot use it to deploy any version of Windows 2000 Server or any other operating system.

Components of the Remote Installation Service

Primarily there are five different parts of the RIS service:

- Remote Installation Services on the server running the Windows 2000 Server operating system. The RISetup.exe file is run from the Start menu.
- Administration of Remote Installation Services.
- Client Installation Wizard—The executable file is OSChosser.exe.
- Remote Installation Preparation Wizard—The RIPrep.exe is the executable for this wizard and has to be run from the RIS server.
- Remote Installation Boot Disk—This disk is used to boot the client and connect to the RIS server to get an initial IP address from the DHCP server. This further starts the Client Installation Wizard.

e x a m
ⓦa t c h

The RIS can be used to duplicate only a single hard drive and a single partition, usually the C: drive.

Establishing an RIS Server

Now that you are familiar with the RIS service and its various components, let's move ahead and learn how to set up the RIS server. First, we need to know the requirements that must be met in order to set up the RIS server.

The RIS services need the following network services running on the RIS server or elsewhere on the network.

Domain Name Service   The RIS is dependent on the Domain Name Service (DNS) for locating the directory services and the machine accounts for the client computers.

Dynamic Host Configuration Protocol   The DHCP services are used to provide initial IP addresses to the client computers when they start up. An IP address is necessary to continue participating in a TCP/IP network.

Active Directory Services   This service provides the means for locating the RIS servers and the client computers on the network. The RIS server must have access to the Active Directory.

The hard drive requirements for installing RIS services are as follows:

- The volume chosen to hold the images must be formatted with NTFS.
- The partition on which you install RIS cannot be the partition on which the Windows 2000 Server operating system files are installed.
- The RIS server must have enough free hard drive space to hold at least one Windows 2000 Professional image. This space is roughly 800MB to 1GB.
- This volume must be shared on the network.

Exercise 3-4 shows how the Remote Installation Service is installed on a Windows 2000 Server.

EXERCISE 3-4

Installing the Remote Installation Service

Select the Windows 2000 Server (in case you have many servers running on the network) and log on as an administrator.

Insert the Windows 2000 Server CD-ROM in the CD-ROM drive. Close the dialog box that pops up after inserting the CD-ROM.

1. Click Start | Settings | Control Panel. The Control Panel window opens.

2. Click Add/Remove Programs. The Add/Remove Programs window opens.

3. Click the Windows Components tab. It takes a while for this window to open.

4. Select the Remote Installation Service check box. Click Next.

5. At this point, the Remote Installation Services are installed. Click Finish to complete the installation.

6. A dialog box appears saying that the Systems Settings have changed and that you must restart your computer. Remove the Windows 2000 Server CD from the CD-ROM drive.

7. Click Yes.

on the *job*

In Exercise 3-4, we simply clicked Yes to reboot the server. In practice, you must be very careful while rebooting any server that is live on the network. In case you are performing this exercise on a live server or you are not the network administrator, you must ask the network administrator whether it is safe to reboot the server. At the minimum, you must send a message to all the connected users that the server will be rebooted in the next five minutes or so and that they must save their work.

Once the RIS service has been installed on a Windows 2000 Server, it needs to be configured. In Exercise 3-5, we will learn how to configure this service.

EXERCISE 3-5

Configuring the Remote Installation Service

Execute the following steps to configure the Remote Installation Service:

1. Click Start | Run, type **RISetup.exe**, and press ENTER. This starts the Remote Installation Services Setup Wizard. A welcome screen appears.

2. In the Remote Installation Folder Location window you are prompted to enter the path of the volume that will hold the remote installation images. Enter the correct path of the folder, as shown in the following illustration. You may also click Browse to locate the folder. Click Next.

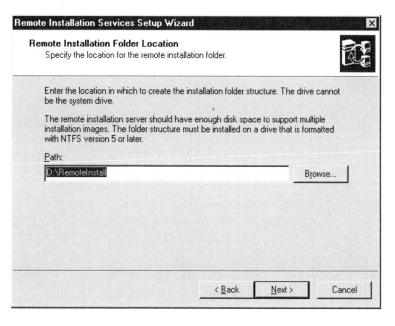

3. The Initial Settings window opens, as in the following illustration. In this window, you can specify how this RIS server will respond to the clients. By default, the RIS server will not respond to the clients until it is configured to do so. Here you may choose for the RIS server to respond or not to respond to the unknown clients requesting the RIS service. For the purpose of this exercise, select the Respond To Client Computers Requesting Service check box. Click Next.

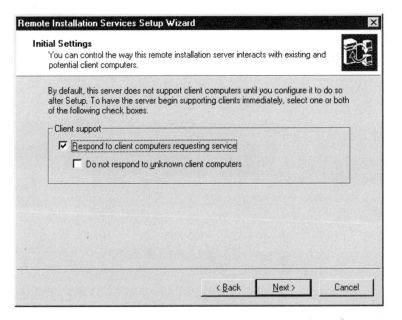

4. The Installation Source Files Location window appears. As shown in the following illustration, you are prompted to specify the location of Windows 2000 Professional files. These files are located in the i386 folder of the CD-ROM drive. Check for the correct drive letter of the CD-ROM drive and type in the path. If you are unsure about the CD-ROM drive letter, you may click Browse to locate the correct path. We are using F:\i386 in this exercise. Make sure that the Windows 2000 Professional CD-ROM is inserted in the CD-ROM drive.

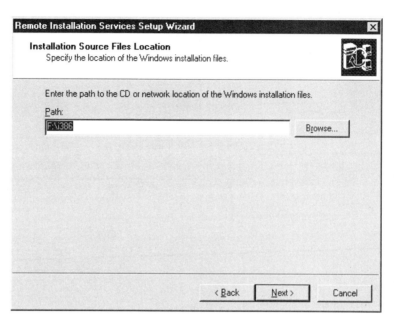

5. The next window prompts you to enter the name of the folder in which the Windows 2000 Professional image(s) are to be stored. The default folder name is win2000.pro. This folder resides under the folder we selected in step 2, earlier in this exercise.

6. The Friendly Description And Help Text window is the next to appear on the screen. You may give a description to the image so that the users may identify the image when the Client Installation Wizard runs. The default-friendly description of the image is "Microsoft Windows 2000 Professional" (shown in the following illustration), and the default help text is "Automatically installs Windows Professional without prompting the user for input." You may type in any custom friendly description and help text that suits the requirements of your organization. This is particularly useful when you have more than one image meant for various departments in your company. If there is only one image, it is best to keep the defaults.

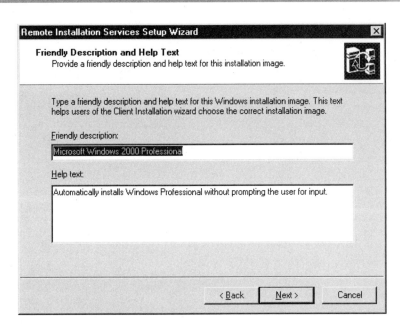

7. The next illustration shows the next window that appears in the RIS Configuration Wizard. It shows the various settings that you have chosen. If you see anything incorrect, you may click Back and make necessary corrections. Otherwise, click Finish.

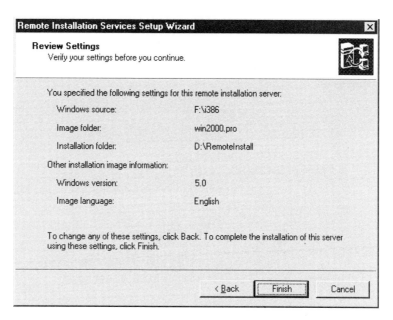

8. It takes a while for the wizard to install the settings of the RIS service that you have selected. When finished, a window appears that shows each of the services. The following tasks are shown as they are completed:

- A remote installation folder is created.

- The necessary files needed by the service are copied in the folder just created.

- The Windows installation files are copied to the win2000.pro folder.

- The screen files for the Client Installation Wizard are updated.

- An unattended Setup answer file is created.

- The Remote Installation Services are created.

- The registry of the RIS server is updated with new and/or modified entries.

- A Single-Instance-Store Volume is created.

- The required Remote Installation Services are started.

9. This finishes the initial configuration for the RIS services. A check mark appears before each of the tasks when complete. You are prompted to click Done. Why wait? Click it and you are done! The server does not reboot after this configuration.

Single-Instance-Store Volume You just read that the Remote Installation Service creates a single-instance-store volume. What is this for? Well, when you have more than one image on the RIS server, each holding Windows 2000 Professional files, there will definitely be duplicate copies of hundreds of files. This may consume a significant hard drive space on the RIS server. To overcome this problem, Microsoft introduced a new feature called the Single-Instance-Store. This helps in deleting all the duplicate files, thus saving on hard drive space.

Authorizing the RIS Server

The next step in establishing the RIS server is to authorize it in the Active Directory in order for the RIS server to serve the client computers. If this step is skipped, the RIS clients will not be able to get a response from the RIS server. In Exercise 3-6, we will authorize the RIS server in the Active Directory to respond to the requesting RIS clients and provide IP addresses. This authorization is done from the DHCP Manager MMC snap-in on a server that is running the DHCP service. By default, this service is disabled.

EXERCISE 3-6

Authorizing the RIS Server

Let us now walk through the process of authorizing the RIS Server.

1. Log on to the server as a domain administrator where the DHCP services
    are running. This may or may not be the same server as the RIS server.

2. Click Start | Programs | Administrative Tools | DHCP.

3. The DHCP Manager window opens, as shown in the following illustration.
    Right-click DHCP in the left pane and click Add Server.

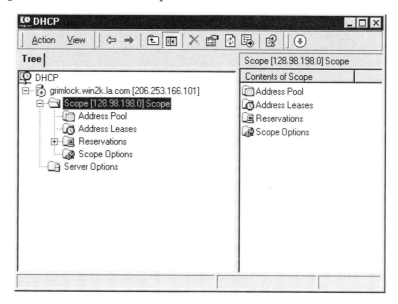

4. The Add Server dialog box appears. Type in the IP address of the RIS server
    and click OK.

5. Right-click again on DHCP and click Manage Authorize Servers.

6. Select the RIS server and click Authorize. Click OK.

exam
ⓦatch   *In order to authorize the RIS server in the Active Directory,
you must have domain administrator rights.*

Restricting Client Installation Options with Group Policy

When you have a large network with hundreds of computers and many images, you need to restrict access to the options that are presented to the users when the Client Installation Wizard runs. We can actually restrict the clients from choosing an incorrect installation option by applying a group policy for the RIS server. This is accomplished from the Active Directory Users and Computers MMC snap-in.

EXERCISE 3-7

Restricting Client Installation Options

The following is the method to restrict client installation options.

1. Log on to the RIS server as domain administrator.

2. Click Start | Programs | Administrative Tools | Active Directory | Users and Computers.

3. Select the container for the RIS policy settings. By default, these are set within the Default Domain Policy Object.

4. In the left pane, right-click the domain name and click Properties. Click the Group Policy tab in the Properties window.

5. Click the Default Domain Policy and click Edit. Double-click the User Configuration. Double-click the Windows Settings.

6. Click the Remote Installation Services. An icon for Choice Options appears in the right pane.

7. Double-click the Choice Options. The following three options are displayed:

   ■ **Allow**   This option allows the users to choose an installation option.

   ■ **Don't Care**   In this option, the predefined group policy is applied to all users.

   ■ **Deny**   This does not allow the users to access a particular installation option.

8. After making a selection, close all the windows. Close the Active Directory window as well.

Restricting the Operating System Image Options

The next step is to specify which client or user will use which image. This is an important step to ensure that the user installs a correct operating system image. If this is not done, the client may choose a wrong image, and all the efforts for saving time on unattended installations would be wasted. By applying user or group security policies, we can specify which image the user can see and install. You may either choose to show all the images to the user, or you can restrict the user from seeing any of the images available on the RIS server that are not meant for him.

EXERCISE 3-8

Restricting the Operating System Image Options

Perform the following steps to restrict the image options.

1. Log on to the RIS server as a domain administrator.

2. Click Start | Programs | Accessories | Windows Explorer.

3. Locate the win2000.pro folder and double-click it to expand. Double-click the i386 folder.

4. Right-click the Templates subfolder and click Properties. The Properties window for the templates opens.

5. Click the Security tab. This is where you can select a user or group of users and set permissions on it. Select the Everyone group in the upper part of the dialog box, and click Remove.

6. To add a particular user or group that will have access to this image, click Add. Select the user or the group, and click OK. It is recommended that you set permissions for groups rather than individual users.

7. To add another group that will have access to this image, repeat step 6. Click OK to exit. Close all windows.

on the
 job

To ensure that the users pick up a correct image, the following steps are recommended:
1. *Determine the client requirements and make groups of users with identical requirements.*
2. *Prepare images based on the group requirements.*
3. *Set permissions on images based on the user groups. Do not allow all user groups access to all images.*

Client Requirements for Remote Installation

The client computers requesting the Remote Installation Service are required to have one of the following configurations:

- The client computer must have a network adapter that is supported by Remote Installation Service and a Remote Installation Boot disk. This is discussed later in this chapter.

- The client computer meets the Net PC specification. The network adapter should be set as the primary boot device.

- The client computer has a network adapter with a PXE-based Boot ROM. The BIOS must be configured for booting from Boot ROM.

The Client Installation Wizard

It's time now to turn to the client side. When a client computer boots using either the Remote Installation Boot disk or the PXE-based Boot ROM, it tries to establish a connection to the RIS server. If the RIS server is preconfigured to service the RIS clients, it helps the client get an IP address from the DHCP service. The Client Installation Wizard is then downloaded from the RIS server. This wizard has four installation options. The options that are presented to the user depend on the group policy set in the Active Directory. A user may get all four options, or may not get any of the options starting an automatic setup. The four installation options are as follows:

- Automatic Setup

- Custom Setup

- Restart a Previous Setup Attempt

- Maintenance and Troubleshooting

Automatic Setup   Automatic Setup is the default option. This is also the easiest installation method. This allows the user to select the operating system image. No more questions are asked of the user. The various configuration parameters are predetermined.

Custom Setup   This flexible option allows the user to override the process of automatically naming a computer. This also allows the users to select a location in the Active Directory where the computer account will be created. This option requires significant administrative efforts, as almost every aspect of the installation can be customized.

Restart a Previous Setup Attempt   As the name suggests, this option enables the user to restart a failed setup attempt. The user is not prompted for any input that he has already entered. This option is particularly useful if for some reason the user loses connection to the RIS server during setup, or in case there is accidental shutdown of the client computer.

Maintenance and Troubleshooting   This option provides access to any third-party maintenance tools you may wish to use before the installation starts. Since this option is not meant for every user, the administrator can restrict access to this option in the group policy set in the Active Directory.

After making a selection from the preceding options, a list of available image options is displayed to the user. When a selection is made, the user is presented with a summary screen. The installation begins immediately after this.

exam
ⓦatch

If the domain administrator has authorized the user for only one image, the user is not prompted for image selection, and the installation starts as soon as the user selects the Automatic Setup option.

The Remote Installation Preparation Wizard

The Remote Installation Service supports two types of images: CD-ROM based and those prepared by using the Remote Installation Preparation (RIPrep) Wizard. The CD-ROM–based image is similar to installing Windows 2000 Professional from the setup CD-ROM. The only difference is that the installation files are stored on the RIS server. The RIPrep Wizard enables the network administrator to distribute a standard desktop configuration that includes the operating system and the applications to a large number of client computers. This not only helps in maintaining a uniform standard across the enterprise, but also cuts on the costs and time involved in a large-scale rollout of Windows 2000 Professional.

The limitation of the RIPrep is that it can replicate images only of a single disk with a single partition. However, the flip side is that the client computers need not have identical hardware configurations, with the only exception that the Hardware Abstraction Layer (HAL) must be the same. The RIPrep utility automatically detects the difference between the source and destination hardware configurations using the Plug and Play support.

How does RIPrep work? Well, first we need to install Windows 2000 Professional on a client computer that is chosen to act as a model. This installation is performed as a remote installation using an existing RIS server on the network. Next, all the required applications, as defined in the enterprise standards, are installed locally on this computer.

The operating system and the applications are tested in all respects for reliability. The RIPrep is then run on this computer to create an image of the operating system and the applications. This image is uploaded to the RIS server for further distribution to the clients that need a similar configuration.

Running the Remote Installation Preparation Wizard

Follow these steps to run the Remote Installation Preparation Wizard.

1. Select a client computer as a model and install the Windows 2000 Professional operating system from an existing RIS server on the network.

2. Install any applications on this computer that meet the requirements of your desktop standards. Configure the operating system and the applications. Test all aspects of the client computer for reliability.

3. Connect to the RIS server for running the RIPrep Wizard. Click Start | Run and type in the correct path of the RIPrep.exe file as follows:

   `\\RISserver_name\RemoteInstallshare_name\Admin\i386\RIPrep.exe`

4. The Remote Installation Preparation Wizard starts with a welcome screen. Click Next.

5. When prompted, type in the name of the RIS server on which the image is intended to be copied. By default, the same RIS server is chosen that is running the RIPrep Wizard. Click Next.

6. Next, you are prompted for the name of the directory in which the image is to be copied. Type in the name, and click Next.

7. The Friendly Description and Help Text prompts appear. In case you plan to create more than one image, it is recommended that you type in the correct name and description of the image. This is helpful for identifying an image when the other clients are presented with image selection options.

8. The next window displays a summary of the selections that you have made. In case you need to change any settings, click Back and review the settings.

9. If everything seems fine, click Next.

The image preparation and replication to the RIS server take a few minutes. Once the image is copied to the RIS server, any remote boot client can use the image for installation.

The Remote Installation Boot Disk

When the client computer starts up, it needs to contact the RIS server. There are two ways to accomplish this. One, the client must have a PXE-based Boot ROM on the network adapter. Second, the client must boot using a Remote Installation Boot disk. The Remote Installation Boot disk simulates the PXE boot process. This helps the client in getting an IP address from any DHCP server on the network. Once the client gets the IP address, it can communicate with other computers on the network. The Remote Installation Service includes a boot disk generator utility.

The boot disk generator utility RBGF.exe currently supports only 25 PCI-based network adapters. Since many of the popular adapters are supported, this eliminates the need for purchasing new adapters for hundreds of client computers. The RBGF.exe utility can be run from any of the following computers:

■ The RIS server

■ A client computer that has a connection to the RIS server

■ From any client connected to the RIS server on which the Windows 2000 Server Administrative Tools are installed

Creating a Remote Installation Boot Disk

These are the steps to create a Remote Installation Boot disk.

1. Ensure that the RIS server is up and running. Log on as an administrator.

2. Click Start | Run, and type in **RBGF.exe.** Click OK. If running this command from another computer, type in the following command and click OK:

   `\\RISServer_name\RemoteInstall\Admin\i386\RBGF.exe`

3. The Windows 2000 Remote Installation Boot Disk Generator window opens, as shown in the following illustration.

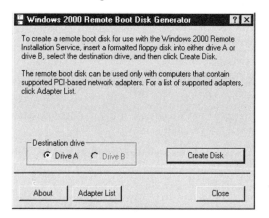

4. Check the path of the destination disk. It is usually the A: drive. Insert a blank formatted floppy disk in drive A:.

5. Click Adapter List to see a list of supported adapters. Make sure that the adapters you have are in the list.

6. Click Create Disk. This creates a Remote Installation Boot disk. Remove the disk and close the Windows 2000 Remote Boot Disk Generator window.

Troubles Using the Remote Installation Service

The Remote Installation Service is dependent on many other services running on the network. The complete RIS setup itself is not an easy operation for any network administrator. To have a fully functional RIS system, you must ensure the following:

- The RIS server is up and running.
- The DHCP server is authorized to service RIS clients in the Active Directory.
- An IP address scope has been created in the DHCP server for RIS clients and has been activated.
- If there is a router on the network between the RIS server and the clients, configure it to forward BootP broadcasts.

SCENARIO & SOLUTION

How do I know what kind of PCI adapters are supported by RIS service? Is there any special utility to check this?	The list of supported adapters can be viewed while running the RBGF.exe utility. In the Remote Boot Disk Generator window, click the Adapter List. This shows you a list of all supported adapters.
My office has nearly 250 computers and I wish to use RIS for deployment of Windows 2000 Professional. What permissions are needed if I want some of my colleagues to help me with the rollout.	Anyone who is involved in configuring the RIS service will need domain administrator rights. If your colleagues will do only the client installation, you need to give them permissions on the images they will use and sufficient rights so that they are able to create computer accounts in the domain.
I am planning to use RIS. What other servers or services are required for RIS to run smoothly?	The first requirement of RIS is the installation and configuration of RIS itself. Apart from this, you need to have Active Directory services, and DNS and DHCP servers running on the network. These services need not be running on the same Windows 2000 server.
I created five different images using the RIPrep utility for various departments. How do I make sure that wrong images are not installed on computers in these departments?	Make groups of users according to department, if you have not done this earlier. Give image access permissions to these groups based on their departments.

CERTIFICATION OBJECTIVE 3.02

The Scripted Method

This method for Windows 2000 Professional installation uses an answer file to specify various configuration parameters. This is used to eliminate user interaction during installation, thereby automating the installation process. Answers to most of the questions asked by the setup process are specified in the answer file. Besides this, the scripted method can be used for clean installations and upgrades.

Windows 2000 Professional CD-ROM includes a sample answer file unattend.txt located in the \i386 folder. This file can be edited and customized for individual installation needs. The Setup Manager Wizard can be used to quickly create a customized answer file. This minimizes the chances of committing syntax-related errors. Once the answer file is ready, the Windows 2000 Professional installation can be started in an unattended mode by using the winnt or winnt32 command with /u switch.

The following is the command syntax for unattended installation using a script file:

```
Winnt32 /b /s:d:\i386 /u:d:\i386\unattend.txt
```

The /b switch tells the setup that it is a floppyless install, /s specifies the source path for the installation files as d:\i386, and the /u switch tells that it is an unattended install and specifies the location of the answer file as d:\i386\unattend.txt.

Creating a Custom Answer File

The unattend.txt answer file included in the Windows 2000 Professional CD-ROM may not be suitable for all unattended installations. You can create custom answer files either by using the Notepad or by modifying the unattend.txt file. If you decide to use Notepad, be careful to follow the correct syntax. It is also not mandatory to name the answer file as unattend.txt. In case you wish to create several answer files, you may name the files that suit your requirements. The other option is to use the Setup Manager to create a customized answer file.

The following is an edited version of the unattend.txt file that comes with Windows 2000 Professional CD-ROM:

```
; This file contains information about how to automate the installation
; or upgrade of Windows 2000 Professional and Windows 2000 Server so the
; Setup program runs without requiring user input.
```

```
[Unattended]
Unattendmode = FullUnattended
OemPreinstall = NO
TargetPath = WINNT
Filesystem = LeaveAlone

[UserData]
FullName = "PBHARDWAJ"
OrgName = "First MCSE, Inc."
ComputerName = "TestComp"

[GuiUnattended]
; Sets the Timezone to the Pacific Northwest
; Sets the Admin Password to NULL
; Turn AutoLogon ON and login once
TimeZone = "004"
AdminPassword = pass
AutoLogon = No
AutoLogonCount = 15

[GuiRunOnce]
; List the programs that you want to launch when the machine is logged into for
the first time

[Display]
BitsPerPel = 8
XResolution = 800
YResolution = 600
VRefresh = 70

[Networking]
; When set to YES, setup will install default-networking components. The
components to be set are
; TCP/IP, File and Print Sharing, and the Client for Microsoft Networks.
InstallDefaultComponents = YES

[Identification]
JoinWorkgroup = Workgroup
; In order to join a domain, delete the line above and add the following lines
; JoinDomain = DomainName
; CreateComputerAccountInDomain = Yes
; DomainAdmin = Administrator
; DomainAdminPassword = AdminPassword
```

CERTIFICATION OBJECTIVE 3.03

Performing an Unattended Installation of Windows 2000 Professional

Unattended installations are the desired way to deploy Windows 2000 Professional when it is not feasible to install the operating system manually on a large number of computers. Windows 2000 can be installed in an unattended mode by creating custom script files. These script files provide answers to the setup questions that would otherwise have to be typed in by the person who is installing the operating system.

This section deals with creating custom answer files using Setup Manager. We will learn how to set up a network share for distribution of Windows 2000 Professional installation files, and how to use the Setup Manager to create customized installation scripts.

Setting Up a Network Share

A network share is a centralized shared folder on the network usually located on a file server where the installation files are stored. This folder also holds the necessary service packs or upgrades for the applications. Creation of a network share is a recommended method of distributing installation files for many reasons. Many of the computers on the network may not have a CD-ROM drive. In order to run the installation on a large number of computers simultaneously, it is necessary to have setup files on one or more of the file servers. The winnt32 setup command permits use of up to eight source file locations when you use the /s switch.

EXERCISE 3-11

Creating a Network Share

Perform the following steps to create a Network Share.

1. Log on to a server that has been selected to act as a distribution server.

2. In Windows Explorer, create a folder named Win2kPro.

3. Share the folder as Installs.

4. Insert the Windows 2000 Professional CD-ROM in the CD-ROM drive. Copy the entire i386 folder to the Installs folder.

5. Create another folder named OEM in the Win2Kpro folder. Copy any driver files you may need during setup. The Windows 2000 setup automatically copies the contents of this folder to a temporary folder during the text mode of setup.

SCENARIO & SOLUTION

If an answer file comes with Windows 2000 Professional, why can't I use it for all installations?	The answer file included with Windows 2000 Professional is basically to help the administrators understand its usage and the syntax and, in its most generalized form, uses many default parameters. Many setup parameters in this file may not suit your requirements. It has to be edited before you can use it.
Why do I need to create a network share when I can use the CD-ROM for installations?	You need a network share when you wish to install Windows 2000 Professional or any other operating system simultaneously on many computers. In case you have many computers running setup and notice that the server holding the network share is very slow, you may need to create more network shares.
I hate using Notepad or Wordpad and typing the tough syntax for editing or creating a custom answer file. Is there another option that can help me create an answer file?	Yes. Use Windows 2000 Setup Manager Wizard. This graphical tool helps you create custom answer files or scripts for many computers at a time without much effort.

Using Setup Manager

In Exercise 3-1 we extracted the Windows 2000 Professional deployment tools into a local folder on our hard drive. The Setup Manager Wizard is one of them. This method is fast and very easy to use. The Setup Manager has an easy-to-use graphical interface. This wizard makes it easy to specify the computer- and user-specific information in the answer files and can create a distribution folder.

The Setup Manager provides you with the option of either creating a fresh answer file or modifying an existing file. You may also choose to copy the configuration of the computer on which you are running the Setup Manager. Exercise 3-12 describes how to use the Setup Manager for creating one or more answer files. This exercise will create three files: unattend.txt, unattend.bat, and unattend.udf.

EXERCISE 3-12

Using Setup Manager to Create Answer Files

CertCam 3-12

Perform the following to utilize Setup Manager to create answer files.

1. Log on as administrator on a computer running the Windows 2000 Professional operating system. In Windows Explorer, change to the folder in which the deployment tools are located.

2. Double-click the setupmgr.exe file. The Windows 2000 Setup Manager welcome screen opens. Click Next to continue.

3. You are prompted to select the type of answer file. Click the Create A New Answer File radio button, as shown in the following illustration. This opens another screen and you are prompted to select an operating system.

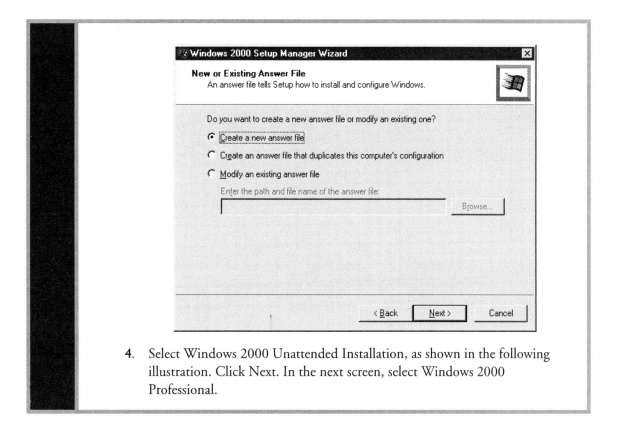

4. Select Windows 2000 Unattended Installation, as shown in the following illustration. Click Next. In the next screen, select Windows 2000 Professional.

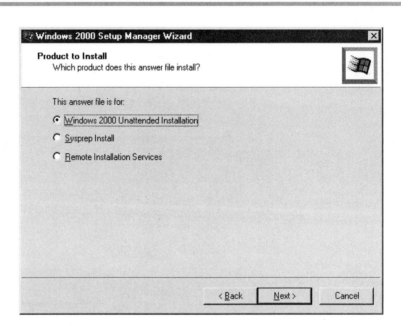

5. The User Interaction Level screen appears next. You are presented with the following five options:

- **Provide Defaults**   To accept or modify the default answers.

- **Fully Automated**   The setup is fully automated. The user is not allowed to change any answers.

- **Hide Pages**   The pages for which the answers are supplied by the script are not shown to the user.

- **Read Only**   The user can see the answers on any unhidden setup pages, but cannot change them.

- **GUI Attended**   In this case, only the text-mode phase of the setup is automated. The user must type in the answers in the graphics phase.

6. For the purpose of this exercise, we will select the Fully Automated option, as shown in the following illustration.

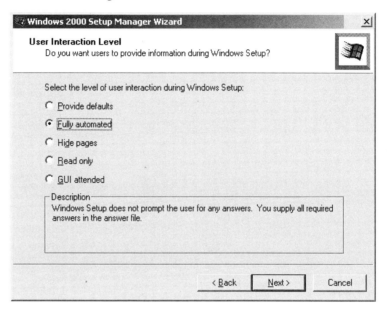

7. Click the I Accept The Terms Of The License Agreement button. Click Next. This brings up the Customize The Software screen.

8. Type in your name and the name of your organization. Click Next.

The next screen is for the Computer Names. You may select to create answer files for one computer or for many computers. In this exercise, we will create two answer files for use with two computers. Here you may either type in the names yourself or give the name of a text file that contains the various computer names. This is useful when you have a large number of computers that will use this answer file. The Setup Manager can also generate the computer names automatically.

9. Type **TestComp1** and click Add. Type **TestComp2** and click Add. As shown in the following illustration, these names are added in a separate box that shows the names of the computers to be installed. Click Next.

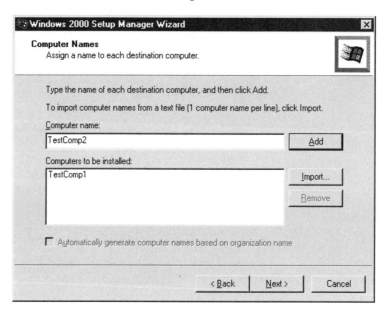

10. The next window is for supplying the Administrator Password. There are two options: Prompt The User To Supply A Password and Use The Following Administrator Password. You will notice in the next illustration that the first option is grayed out because we selected a Fully Automated installation earlier. Leave the password blank in this exercise.

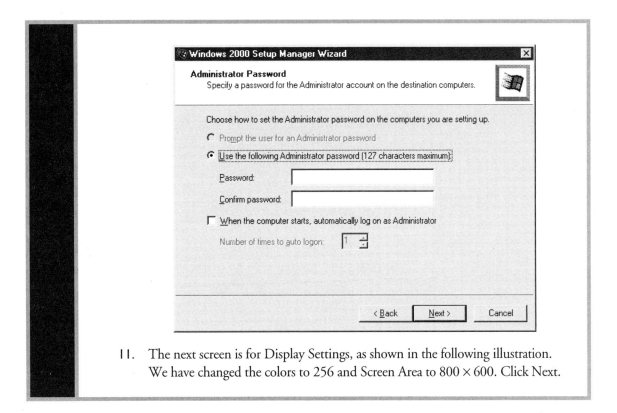

11. The next screen is for Display Settings, as shown in the following illustration. We have changed the colors to 256 and Screen Area to 800 × 600. Click Next.

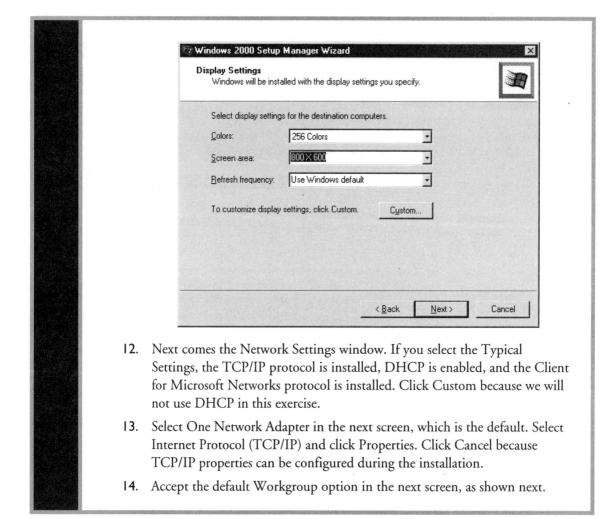

12. Next comes the Network Settings window. If you select the Typical Settings, the TCP/IP protocol is installed, DHCP is enabled, and the Client for Microsoft Networks protocol is installed. Click Custom because we will not use DHCP in this exercise.

13. Select One Network Adapter in the next screen, which is the default. Select Internet Protocol (TCP/IP) and click Properties. Click Cancel because TCP/IP properties can be configured during the installation.

14. Accept the default Workgroup option in the next screen, as shown next.

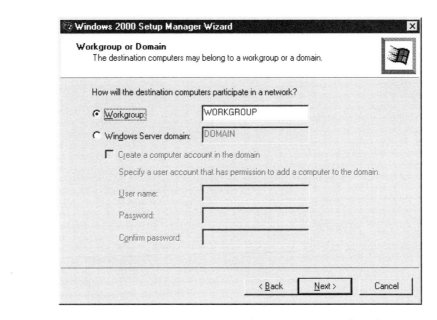

15. The next screen prompts you to select the Time Zone. Select the appropriate time zone and click Next.

16. The Additional Settings screen appears next. Select the defaults in the next few screens that prompt you for answers on Telephony, Regional Settings, Languages, and the Browser and Shell Settings. Click Next.

17. The following illustration shows the Installation Folder window. Type in the folder name in which you wish to install Windows 2000 Professional.

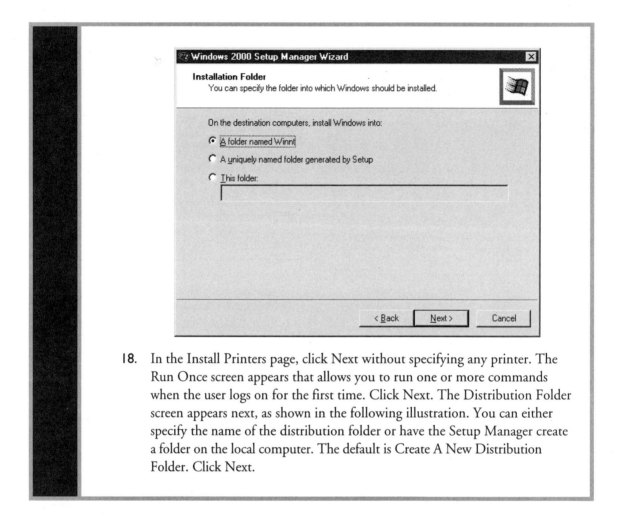

18. In the Install Printers page, click Next without specifying any printer. The Run Once screen appears that allows you to run one or more commands when the user logs on for the first time. Click Next. The Distribution Folder screen appears next, as shown in the following illustration. You can either specify the name of the distribution folder or have the Setup Manager create a folder on the local computer. The default is Create A New Distribution Folder. Click Next.

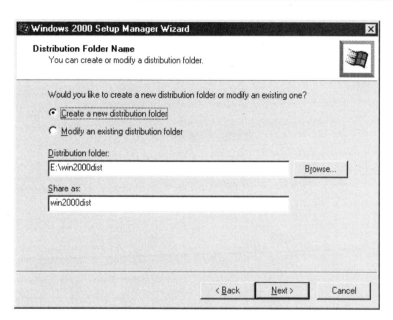

19. The next few screens prompt you for Additional Mass Storage Devices, Hardware Abstraction Layer, running any Additional Commands, and OEM Branding. Accept defaults and click Next.

20. The Answer File Name window is next, as shown in the following illustration. Type in the name of the folder in which you wish to save the answer file. Click Next. In the next screen, you are prompted to specify the location of the setup files. Click Next to accept the default location as CD-ROM drive.

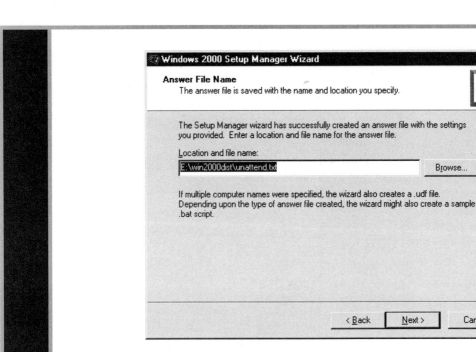

It takes a few minutes for the Setup Manager to copy the installation files from the CD-ROM to the distribution folder. When this is complete, the last window, Completing The Windows 2000 Setup Manager Wizard, appears as shown in the following illustration. Notice that Setup Manager has creates two files in the distribution folder: unattend.txt and unattend.bat.

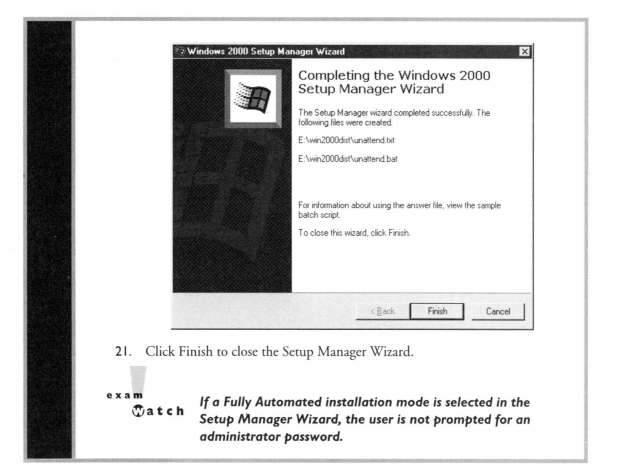

21. Click Finish to close the Setup Manager Wizard.

exam
ⓦatch   *If a Fully Automated installation mode is selected in the Setup Manager Wizard, the user is not prompted for an administrator password.*

Using an Unattend.txt Script

In Exercise 3-12, we created an unattended answer file named unattend.txt. Once the file is created, it is recommended that you print a copy of this file to check for any irregularities. If you find anything wrong, you may use Notepad or any text editor program to make necessary corrections in this file; otherwise, leave the file intact.

Note that the scripted method of installation can be used for clean installations as well as for upgrades. In order to use the answer file or the script file for automatic setup, we use it with winnt or winnt32. The following is the syntax for this setup command:

```
Winnt32 /b /s:d:\i386 /u:c:\install\unattend.txt
```

The various switches used in the preceding command are as follows:

- **/b**   Tells the setup that this is a floppyless installation. The user is not prompted to insert any floppy disks.

- **/s: d:\i386**   Specifies the location of the Windows 2000 Professional setup files, which in this case is the \i386 folder on the D: drive. Change it to the correct letter of your CD-ROM drive.

- **/u: c:\ install\unattend.txt**   Specifies that this is an unattended installation and the unattend.txt answer file is located in the \install folder on the C: drive.

Check the syntax of the command and press ENTER. You are done!

FROM THE CLASSROOM

Using Setup Manager for Unattended Installations

In practice, when you choose to use Setup Manager for unattended installations, there is a lot of planning that has to be done beforehand. Installation needs vary from one network environment to another. Here are some general guidelines that are helpful while using Setup Manager:

1. Know the present setup, including computer hardware and installed applications. Make a list of the computer names. Decide whether you need to upgrade or do a clean install.

2. Make a note of all network-related information, such as TCP/IP addressing scheme, name of the domain controller, DHCP server, and DNS server.

3. Arrange for any service packs or application upgrades to address any compatibility issues with Windows 2000 Professional.

4. Document each piece of information that you collect.

5. When you create scripts for unattended answer files, test one or two installations using your script files before applying them to mass setup. It is recommended that you take a hard copy of some scripts and check for any irregularities.

In practice, it is a bit difficult to have a complete automated installation process that does not ask for any user intervention. Setup Manager helps you automate it to an extent wherein very little user intervention is needed.

—*Pawan K. Bhardwaj MCSE, MCP+I, CCNA*

CERTIFICATION SUMMARY

Windows 2000 ships with many utilities that facilitate unattended installations of the operating system. The unattended installations make the rollout fast and reduce the cost in medium and large organizations. These are also helpful in standardizing the desktop environment throughout the organization. Disk duplication tools like the System Preparation tool (Sysprep) and the Remote Installation Preparation Wizard are used to prepare replicas of a completely configured Windows 2000 Professional computer. The Remote Installation Service (RIS) is included with Windows 2000 Server and is quite useful in delivery of the Windows 2000 Professional operating system. The Setup Manager Wizard is used to create custom answer files for unattended setup.

The system images prepared by Sysprep have to be distributed to other computers using some third-party imaging utilities. This utility also requires that all the destination computers have hardware identical to the master computer. When an image of the system is created using Sysprep, it rips off the master computer from its user-specific settings. A Mini-Setup Wizard that runs on the next reboot can help restore all these settings. It is recommended that the master computer be tested in all respects before running Sysprep to create an image.

The image prepared by the RIPrep utility is independent of the hardware of the destination computers. You do not need a third-party utility to distribute the prepared image; the RIS server handles the job of distribution. RIS service requires fully functional Active Directory services, DHCP services, and the DNS services running on the network. The client computers need to have a PXE-based Boot ROM, or must boot from the Remote Installation Boot disk prepared using the RBGF.exe utility. This Remote Installation Boot disk starts the Client Installation Wizard on the destination computers. The administrator can control access to the Client Installation Wizard options and the images that a user can select.

The unattended installations use an answer file that supplies answers to various questions prompted by the setup wizard. The sample answer file unattend.txt file can be edited using Notepad. The Setup Manager Wizard helps in creating customized answer files for one or many of the computers for fully automated installations. Once the answer file is ready, the installation can be started in an unattended mode using the winnt or winnt32 command with the /u switch and specifying the location of the installation files and the answer file. Unattended mode can be used either for a clean install or for an upgrade.

TWO-MINUTE DRILL

Disk Duplication Methods

❑ The disk duplication methods that come with the Windows 2000 operating system reduce the rollout, save costs incurred on deployment, and help standardize the desktop environment throughout the organization.

❑ The disk duplication methods can be used only for clean installs. These methods do not support upgrading from a previous operating system.

❑ System Preparation (Sysprep) is used to prepare an image of a computer fully configured with the operating system and the applications.

❑ Sysprep requires that the source master computer and all the destination computers have identical hardware, but Plug and Play devices are exempted from this condition. The image distribution job is handled by a third-party utility.

❑ The Remote Installation Service is included with the Windows 2000 Server operating system for remote installation of Windows 2000 Professional. This service is dependent on Active Directory service, DHCP service, and the DNS service running on the network.

❑ The RIS service can deliver images prepared by the Remote Installation Preparation (RIPrep) Wizard. The image is stored in the RIS server.

❑ The Client Installation Wizard runs on the RIS client computer when booted using a PXE-based Boot ROM or a Remote Installation Boot disk that is prepared using the RBGF.exe utility. This utility supports only 25 PCI-based network adapters.

The Scripted Method

❑ Windows 2000 Professional installation can be automated using scripted answer files that provide the answers to many or all of the setup questions.

❑ The unattend.txt is the default answer file that comes with Windows 2000. This file can be modified to suit individual installation needs using Notepad.

❑ The Setup Manager Wizard is used to create custom answer files that provide various configuration parameters. To start Setup Manager Wizard, run the setupmgr.exe file.

❑ The Setup Manager can create a new answer file or modify an existing file. It can also create an answer file that duplicates the configuration of the computer on which the wizard is being run.

❑ The Setup Manager can create answer files for one or all of the computers that need unattended installations. The installation can be fully automated, wherein the user is not prompted for any input.

Performing an Unattended Installation of Windows 2000 Professional

❑ The unattended installation of Windows 2000 Professional is done using the winnt or winnt32 command with the /u switch and specifying the location of the installation files and the answer file.

❑ The user wishing to do an unattended setup may modify the default answer file using Notepad, or create a custom answer file using the Setup Manager Wizard.

❑ The unattended installation method can be used either for a clean install or to upgrade a previously installed operating system.

❑ If a Fully Automated installation mode is selected in the Setup Manager Wizard, the user is not prompted for an administrator password.

SELF TEST

The following questions will help measure your understanding of the material presented in this chapter. Read all of the choices carefully, as there may be more than one correct answer. Choose all correct answers for each question.

Disk Duplication Methods

1. Which of the following tools are included with Windows 2000 Professional for large-scale deployment of the operating system? (Select all that apply.)

   A. Setup Manager

   B. Sysprep

   C. Remote Installation Services

   D. All of the above

2. Which of the following operating systems can be delivered using the Windows 2000 Remote Installation Services? (Select all that apply.)

   A. Windows NT 4.0 Workstation

   B. Windows 98

   C. Windows 2000 Professional

   D. All of the above

3. Which of the following options is used to install third-party maintenance utilities from the Client Installation Wizard?

   A. Automatic setup

   B. Custom setup

   C. Restart a previous setup attempt

   D. Maintenance and Troubleshooting

4. How many remote boot disks do you need for running RIS installation in case the client computers on your network do not have PXE-based boot ROMs?

   A. Only one for all supported network adapters

   B. As many as the number of client computers on the network

   C. As many as the number of types of supported network adapters you have on the client computers

   D. As many as the number of images you wish to prepare for your clients

5. You suspect that some of the computers in your office may not have network adapters supported by the Remote Installation Service. How can you find out what network adapters are not supported?

   A. Run the command makeboot a: and click the Check Adapters tab.

   B. Run winnt32 /ox.

   C. Run RBGF.exe and click the Adapter List tab.

   D. Refer to the Windows 2000 Server Resource Kit.

6. You wish to use the Remote Installation Services for preparing and distributing images of the client containing the operating system and application files. Which of the following computers can become RIS clients? (Select all that apply.)

   A. All kinds of Intel-based computers and laptops

   B. Computers with a single network adapter supported by RIS

   C. Computers with network adapters having PXE-based Boot ROM on them

   D. Net PCs with or without network adapters configured as the primary boot device

7. Your manager has read about Sysprep for imaging Windows 2000 computers and is very excited about this utility. He wants you to use this utility for all installations in the company, and asked you to find out the hardware requirements. What conditions must be met before you can use this utility?

   A. The source and the destination computers should have hardware that is identical in all respects.

   B. The source and the destination computers must have all hardware identical except the Plug and Play devices.

   C. The source and the destination computers must have the same HAL.

   D. The source and the destination computer must have at least the motherboard and the CPU identical.

8. Which of the following statements is true about the hard drive requirements on the RIS server volume that holds the images?

   A. This volume on the RIS server must be formatted with NTFS.

   B. The volume can be the same as the RIS server boot volume.

   C. The volume must have a minimum of 400MB free space.

   D. The RIS service is independent of any volume constraints.

9. After preparing one of the Windows 2000 Professional computers to transfer the image of the operating system and the applications using the RIPrep tool, you rebooted it as required by the procedure. What you see now is that the system is running the setup again. What could be the reason?

A. The RIPrep has to be run on the RIS server and you did it on the client by mistake.

B. The RIPrep deletes the current installation after making the image.

C. While running RIPrep, it takes off all the computer-specific configuration and security ID of the client, which has to be restored.

D. You must not have rebooted the client manually after running RIPrep.

10. While trying to boot from the RIS boot disk after preparing the RIS server, you find that it is not responding. The computer times out displaying an error message "No boot file received from DHCP, BINL or BootP." You know that the RIS server is online. What must you do to resolve the problem?

A. Restart the client computer.

B. Restart the RIS server.

C. Stop and restart the BINL service.

D. Restart the DHCP server.

11. Kristen wants to standardize and automate the Windows 2000 Professional installations using the RIPrep utility included with the Windows 2000 Server operating system. She prepared a prototype computer that is configured as follows:

CPU: 266 MHz; RAM: 128 MB; Hard Disk: 4GB (two partitions)

Drive C: is 1.5 GB, NTFS with Windows 2000 and Office 2000

Drive D: is 2.5 GB, NTFS with the custom business application used by the company

Can you recognize the problem she might face?

A. Drive C: is too small to run RIPrep. It must be at least 2GB.

B. Both partitions must be of equal size.

C. There should not be multiple partitions. The operating system and all applications have to be on a single partition.

D. The C: drive can have only the operating system on it. The applications must be installed on drive D:.

12. You are trying to use the Sysprep tool from the command prompt. Which option can you use with the Sysprep.exe command so that there are no messages displayed on the screen?

A. /nodisplay

B. /quiet

C. /q

D. /nosidgen

The Scripted Method

13. What does the Setup Manager included in the Windows 2000 Professional CD-ROM do? (Select all that apply.)

A. Helps in automating the Windows 2000 Professional installations

B. Creates scripts for multiple computers with similar or dissimilar hardware

C. Lowers the cost of operating system deployment

D. All of the above

14. You are creating custom answer files using the Setup Manager Wizard for automated installation of Windows 2000 Professional. You selected the Create A New Answer File option. What kind of answer files can you create?

A. Windows 2000 unattended installation

B. Remote Installation Services

C. Sysprep install

D. All of the above

15. A client computer has been powered on using a remote boot disk. This computer is supposed to contact a preconfigured RIS server for installation of Windows 2000 Professional. What is the correct sequence of activities taking place on initialization?

A. DHCP, BINL, and TFTP

B. BINL, DHCP, and TFTP

C. TFTP, BINL, and DHCP

D. TFTP, DHCP, and BINL

Performing an Unattended Installation of Windows 2000 Professional

16. Matt created some setup scripts using the Setup Manager and had selected the Fully Automated installation option. He wanted the users to choose their own passwords for the local administrator account. When one of the users started installation using the script, he did not see any option displayed to him. This happened to a few other users also. Can you tell Matt what could be the problem?

    A. Windows 2000 supports strong security. The users are allowed to specify or change administrator passwords.

    B. Even if the password option is not displayed, the users will still be able to select their administrator passwords at a later stage.

    C. With the Fully Automated installation option, the users are not prompted to type in the local administrator passwords.

    D. None of the above.

17. Your company has three departments named production, marketing, and accounts. These departments have 100, 80, and 65 client computers, respectively. All computers are currently running Windows NT 4.0 Workstation. The applications running on computers within a department are standardized. The hardware is standardized throughout the company with the exception of 12 servers. The servers have already been upgraded to Windows 2000. Here is what you have to do with the help of the departmental system administrators:

Required Result: Each departmental administrator should be able to work on a project independently.

Optional Desired Results: The computers in all departments must be upgraded to Windows 2000 Professional from the existing operating system.

The applications should also be installed along with the operating system according to the department.

Proposed Solution: Install RIS on one of the Windows 2000 Servers and authorize it to service the client computers. Prepare three different prototype computers, one for each department. Run RIPrep on each of the prototypes to copy the images to the RIS server. Give permissions to departmental administrators to install the images on client computers in their respective departments. Make remote boot disks and distribute them to departmental administrators so that they can work on the project at their own pace.

What results does the proposed solution produce?

A. The proposed solution does not produce the required result.

B. The proposed solution produces the required result, but none of the optional results.

C. The proposed solution produces the required result and only one of the optional results.

D. The proposed solution produces the required result and both of the optional results.

18. When do you need a customized answer file in unattended setup? (Select all that apply.)

A. When you want to have more control over the installation process

B. When you want to process custom upgrade packs

C. When you want additional PnP device drivers to be installed

D. When all of the computers in the network have different settings

E. All of the above

LAB QUESTION

You are the network administrator of a company called My Company, Inc. The company has six Windows 2000 servers that were upgraded from Windows NT 4.0 last month. There are seven departments within the company, and the total number of client computers is nearly 175 at a single location, all running Windows NT 4.0 Workstation on different hardware configurations. Your current project requires you to install Windows 2000 Professional and business applications on all 175 workstations. The software configuration is almost the same on all departmental computers except that the accounts department has some custom-built software for accounting. The management would not like to hire anyone from the outside to do the upgrade due to reasons of data security. You have decided to use the Remote Installation method to accomplish this.

The following are some steps that could help you perform a successful RIS-based deployment of Windows 2000 Professional. Can you find out whether some steps are missing or are incorrect?

1. Install Remote Installation Service on one of the servers using Control Panel | Add Remove Programs | Add Remove Windows Components.

2. Ensure that you have a DNS server running on the network.

3. Create a DHCP scope on the DHCP server and activate it.

4. Install Windows 2000 Professional on a computer using RIS.

5. Install all business and custom applications on this computer and test it.

6. Run RIPrep on the test computer to make an image of the system and copy it to the RIS server.

7. Make Remote Boot Disks for the clients using the RBGF.exe utility.

8. Boot the client computers using the Remote Installation Boot disk to run the client Installation Wizard.

9. When given a choice, select the image appropriate to the department.

SELF TEST ANSWERS

Disk Duplication Methods

1. ☑ **A, B.** The two tools included with Windows 2000 Professional for large-scale deployment are the Setup Manager Wizard and the Sysprep utility. The Setup Manager helps in creating customized answer files for unattended installation. The Sysprep tool is used to copy complete system images to computers with identical hardware.
    ☒ **C** is incorrect because the Remote Installation Service is a part of the Windows 2000 Server and is not included with Windows 2000 Professional.

2. ☑ **C.** Windows 2000 Professional. The Remote Installation Service is designed to deliver only the Windows 2000 Professional operating system or any images based on this OS.
    ☒ **A** and **B** are incorrect because the Remote Installation Service cannot distribute or even prepare images based on these operating systems.

3. ☑ **D.** When the Client Installation Wizard starts on a client computer, the user is given four setup options. The Maintenance and Troubleshooting options enable access to install third-party tools that may be helpful to the user.
    ☒ **A** is incorrect because the Automatic option is used for a fully automated setup. **B** is incorrect because the custom setup option cannot be selected to install any third-party utilities. This option enables the user to configure the operating system in a desired way. **C** is also incorrect because this option is used when a setup attempt has failed or aborted. When selected, the setup does not prompt the user for any answers that were previously provided.

4. ☑ **A.** You need only one remote boot disk for all the supported network adapters. The disk created using the Remote Boot Disk Generator (RBGF.exe) utility contains drivers for all supported network adapters. A list of adapters can be viewed by clicking the Adapter List tab on the Remote Boot Disk Generator screen.
    ☒ **B** is incorrect because creating multiple boot disks will create only duplicate disks, resulting in a waste of time and floppy disks. This is helpful only if you need to run the remote installation simultaneously on many client computers. **C** is incorrect because one disk contains drivers for all types of supported network adapters. **D** is incorrect because the number of boot disks has no relation to the number of images you wish to deliver.

5. ☑ **C.** A list of adapters supported by the Remote Installation Service can be viewed by clicking the Adapter List tab when running the RBGF.exe utility. Here you can find out which of the adapters are not supported by RIS.

☒ **A** is incorrect because this command is used for creating four setup boot disks in Windows 2000. **B** is incorrect because this is an invalid command. This command was used in Windows NT for creating setup disks. **D** is incorrect because you need not refer to the Resource Kit when an option is available online for verifying whether the network adapters are supported or not.

6. ☑ **B, C.** The client computers must have a supported adapter or an adapter that has a PXE-based Boot ROM configured as the primary boot device.
☒ **A** is incorrect because being an Intel-based computer only does not satisfy the requirements to become an RIS client. Laptop computers have PC Card modems and cannot be RIS clients. **D** is incorrect because if you have a Net PC, it must be configured to boot from the network.

7. ☑ **B, C.** In order to use the Sysprep tool, you must ensure that the source and the destination computers have identical hardware. The Plug and Play devices may or may not be identical, because the Sysprep image when copied to a destination computer enables Plug and Play detection.
☒ **A** is incorrect because the Plug and Play devices need not be identical. **D** is incorrect because identical HAL, the motherboard, and the CPU alone on the source and the destination computers will not satisfy the Sysprep requirements.

8. ☑ **A.** The Remote Installation Service requires NTFS on the RIS server volume that is used to store the images. The RIS images have NTFS security parameters set. The user is given the image options based on the NTFS access set by the administrator for that user.
☒ **B** and **C** are incorrect because the volume must be separate from the RIS server boot volume. Also, this volume must have enough space to hold at least one image that is nearly 800MB. **D** is incorrect because there are certain requirements for the RIS volume that must be met.

9. ☑ **C.** The RIPrep tool is run on the client computer that is fully configured with the operating system and applications. When you run this utility, it removes the user-specific settings from the client computer. On restart, it runs a Mini-Setup Wizard so that you can restore your earlier settings.
☒ **A** is incorrect because the RIPrep is always run on the fully configured client computer and not on the RIS server. The RIS server only stores the image. **B** is incorrect because RIPrep does not delete the current installation on the client. **D** is incorrect because the removal of user-specific settings from the client computer will not be affected, even if you choose to reboot the computer manually.

10. ☑ **C.** Stop and restart the BINL service. The possible cause of this timing out is that the BINL service on the RIS server is not responding. This happens after the computer has received an

IP address from the DHCP server. Stopping and restarting the BINL service on the RIS server will help resolve the problem.

☒ **A** is incorrect because restarting the client computer will not help, as the problem is not at the client end. **B** is not a good choice because if stopping and restarting only the BINL service can help resolve the problem, there is no need to restart the RIS server. **D** is incorrect because the DHCP server is not an issue, as the client already has the IP address.

11. ☑ **C.** There should not be multiple partitions. The operating system and all applications should be on a single partition . The RIPrep utility supports only one hard disk and a single partition. Kristen should have made a single partition in the model computer and installed both the operating system and the applications on that drive.

☒ **A, B,** and **D** are incorrect because RIPrep supports only one hard drive and a single partition.

12. ☑ **B.** In order to avoid displaying any messages on the screen while running the Sysprep utility, we specify the /quiet switch. This runs Sysprep in a quiet mode and no user interaction is required.

☒ **A** and **C** are incorrect because there are no such options with the Sysprep command. **D** is incorrect because the /nosidgen switch is used to avoid generation of security identifiers.

The Scripted Method

13. ☑ **D.** The Setup Manager is helpful in automating the Windows 2000 Professional deployment by creating answer files or scripts for multiple computers. This reduces the time taken and costs involved in the deployment.

14. ☑ **D.** The Setup Manager can create custom answer files for all of the given choices: Windows 2000 Professional, RIS install, and Sysprep install.

15. ☑ **A.** DHCP, BINL, and TFTP. When a computer is started using a remote boot disk, it first tries to contact the DHCP server for getting an IP address. After getting an IP address, the computer contacts the RIS server for getting the boot file. This is accomplished by the BINL service running on the RIS server. TFTP is then utilized to transfer the necessary boot files from the RIS server to the client computer.

☒ **B** and **C** are incorrect because BINL and TFTP do not initialize before the DHCP. DHCP must first provide an IP address to the Client. **D** is incorrect because TFTP works after the DHCP and BINL.

Performing an Unattended Installation of Windows 2000 Professional

16. ☑ C. The setup will not prompt the user for a local administrator password when the Fully Automated installation option is selected in Setup Manager. The purpose of a Fully Automated setup is defeated if the user is prompted for input every now and then during the setup. This is why no option is displayed.

☒ A is incorrect because security is not an issue here. It is, of course, true that Windows 2000 supports strong security. B is incorrect, although it seems correct. The user can change the password, but this is not what the question asks.

17. ☑ C. The proposed solution produces the required result and only one of the optional results. The departmental administrators will be able to run the Client Installation Wizard independently on the client computers in order to install the system images. RIPrep will create the images of the prototype computers that can be distributed to the clients in three departments. This satisfies the second of the optional desired results.

The first optional desired result cannot be produced with the proposed solution because the Remote Installation Service cannot be used to upgrade any existing operating system. The RIS utility is only for clean installs.

18. ☑ E. All the conditions listed need customized answer files. The unattend.txt answer file that comes with Windows 2000 cannot be used in any of the given situations. This file can be edited using a text editor or Notepad.

LAB ANSWER

The steps given seem to be perfect, but in fact, they are not. The following important steps are missing.

1. After installing Remote Installation Services on the Windows 2000 Server, it has to be configured. To configure RIS, run **RISetup.exe** from the command prompt. This is an important step in which the RIS server is configured to respond to the client computers requesting the RIS service. Without this configuration, the clients will not get any response from the RIS server when they start up using the Remote Installation Boot disk. A remote installation folder is also configured in this step.

2. Authorize the RIS server in the Active Directory. This has to be done from Start | Programs | Administrative Tools | DHCP.

3. The next important missing step is that you have to check whether the client computers have supported network adapters or not. Run the RGBF.exe utility and click the Adapter List tab to view a list of supported adapters.

4. We are still forgetting that there have to be two different images. The steps in the question mention that only one image is to be created. This is incorrect.

This procedure assumes that you have domain administrator rights and are the only one performing the remote installations. If you have some other persons who will help you in carrying out the deployment, you will need to give them rights so that they can create computer accounts in the domain.

4

Implementing and Conducting Administration of Resources

N TFS and Share permissions are a big part of The 2000 Professional exam and the NT 3.51 and 4.0 tests before it. This is the way it should be—as an administrator, you will be working with both on a regular basis. I am often asked by co-workers to lock down some important files locally on their PC; but to also make them available, or share them across the network. At first, this might seem counter-intuitive; but believe me, it is perfectly safe to share your important documents and files across your network as long as you use the right combination of Share permissions and NTFS permissions to secure them. This is a big point: information you share has to be secured, because there are thousands of hackers out there looking for what they consider to be a good time, namely, tampering with or reading your data.

Disk compression is also a featured objective on the exams you're studying for. Even today, when 20GB hard drives rule the land, there are lots of legacy systems or laptops that have, by 2000 Professional's standards, small drives. For these systems, compressing data still makes perfect sense.

CERTIFICATION OBJECTIVE 4.01

Monitoring, Managing, and Troubleshooting Access to Files and Folders

We will cover a lot of territory here. This is a large topic, and you will see several questions on your certification test that come straight from this material.

File Compression

Even in this age of huge hard drives, there are often times when it would be convenient to compress some data. Whether you are zipping data with a software package you've purchased or running a file system–based compression scheme, the idea is to maximize the amount of hard drive space you have available for other data. The first recommendation is to delete any unnecessary files on your drive (temp files, Internet cache, and so on), and then make backups of your data that can be removed. If you have 100MB of scanned images, try to put them on a CD-ROM or zip disk to free up room. You may surprise yourself and free up so much room that you no longer require compression. However, in many cases, you will still need to compress your data.

The good news is that Windows 2000 Professional supports file-level compression. You'll need to be running the NTFS file system, but other than that, compression is easy to set up.

exam
Watch

The only compression scheme supported under 2000 Professional is NTFS compression. Other compression schemes that compress the entire drive will not work under Windows 2000 Pro. Most notable in this category is Microsoft's own DriveSpace, for Windows 95/98.

on the
Job

Compression and encryption under 2000 Professional are mutually exclusive. You may not compress any encrypted files or folders. If you have marked a volume or folder with the compression attribute, any encrypted files or folders within it will not be compressed.

The compression algorithm used in NTFS compression is very robust. It reduces the size of a text-based file by around 50 percent, and executables by around 40 percent. It is possible to realize a 40–50 percent gain in the effective size of your volume or drive when it is compressed.

Enabling File Compression

Compression is activated or disabled in two ways: either by using a GUI (My Computer or Windows Explorer) or with a command-line utility, compact.exe. Exercise 7-1 will walk you through the process of enabling file compression.

CertCam 4-1

Enabling File Compression

1. From within My Computer or Windows Explorer, right-click a folder or file to be compressed.

2. From the context menu, select Properties.

3. A Properties sheet with several tabs will now appear. From the General Tab, Attributes, select the Advanced Attributes tab. If an Advanced Attributes tab is not visible, you are not working on an NTFS volume. To compress data, it must reside on an NTFS partition.

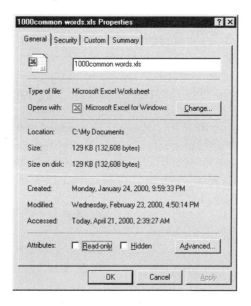

EXERCISE 4-1

4. The Advanced Attributes tab has two sections: Archive And Index Attributes in the top section, and Compress Or Encrypt Attributes in the bottom half. This last one is the one we're interested in.

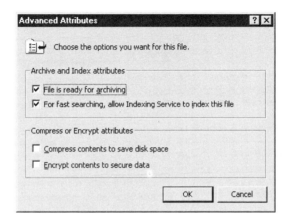

5. Enabling or disabling compression is simple. Select the check box for compression to enable compression for this file, and deselect it to disable compression.

6. After selecting or deselecting the Compress Contents To Save Disk Space check box, click Apply for the compression or decompression to take effect.

7. After either enabling or disabling compression, and depending upon the amount of data you've just compressed/decompressed, you'll notice that once you click Apply, your PC may become less responsive to foreground applications. This is normal; your machine has a lot of data to run its

compression algorithm against. This selection is available for individual files, folders, and even entire drives, as long as they reside on NTFS partitions. The following illustration shows the Properties sheet for the Excel document again after compression. Notice the size on disk: 53K versus the original 129K. This file was reduced to 40 percent of its original size.

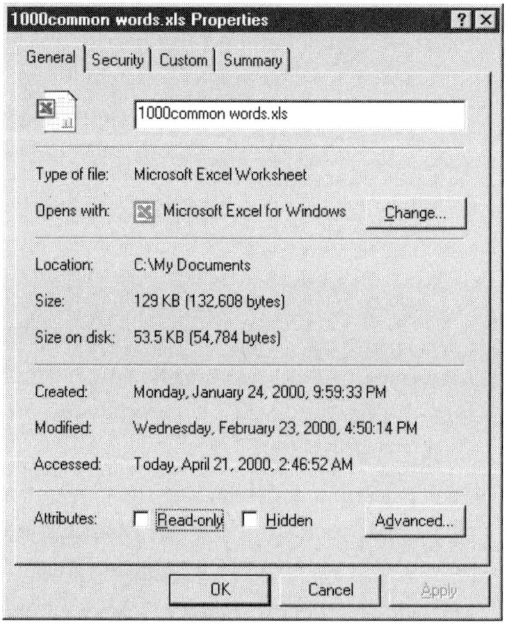

It is possible to compress almost any volume under Windows 2000 Professional, even your system and boot partitions. The only file that may not be compressed is Pagefile.sys, your swap file. The other exception is any files that are encrypted.

Compact.exe, the command-line utility, is also easy to work with. With it, you can compress, decompress, or view the compression attributes of a directory or file. To use it, go to Start | Programs | Accessories | Command Prompt.

Compact.exe may be used to automate compression routines, most typically in a batch file.

The syntax of the compact.exe and the most common switches are listed next.

compact [/c] [/u] [/s] [/f] [/I] [/a] *file/folder_name*

- **/c** Compresses the selected files. If working with a directory, it will be marked with a compression attribute so that data added afterward will be compressed.

- **/u** Uncompresses the selected files. If working with a directory, it will be marked with a cleared compression attribute so that data added later will not be compressed.

- **/s** Performs the compression operation on all data in a directory.

- **/f** Forces the compression operation on all selected files, even those previously compressed.

- **/I** Continues the compression operation even after errors have occurred.

- **/a** Displays files with the hidden or system attributes.

- *file/folder_name* Specifies the file or folder that you are working with.

By default, you cannot view or set the compression attribute on hidden or system files using compact.exe. To manipulate these files, first clear the attribute in question using Explorer or attrib.exe. After you have finished manipulating the compression, reset the original attributes to system or read only.

Impact of Compression on Performance

Although it is possible to compress any volume under Windows 2000 Professional, understand that you will see a decline in performance if the data you're working with is compressed. The application in which you are accessing the compressed data will have to uncompress the data to work with it, and then when you save it again, it will have to be compressed once more. This may not sound like a big deal—but if your entire Windows 2000 Boot partition is compressed, every system file that is used by the operation system (read "lots of files") will have to go through this same procedure. You will definitely see a difference in performance when your operating system is compressed!

One major difference between the compression routines used with Windows NT 4.0 and Windows 2000 is how a compressed file is handled when copied over the network. In Windows NT 4.0, the file was first decompressed on the source machine, and then transferred over the network. In Windows 2000, the file is left in its compressed state during the network transfer, and then decompressed on the target machine. Compressed files, therefore, move over the network quicker, and the end user may experience better response times with compressed files when accessing them over the network.

Rules for Compression Attributes

The compression attribute does not stay with a file or folder if it is copied. A copy operation inherits the attributes of the location it is copied to. If the new location is a folder that has the compression attribute set, the data you copied will retain its compression (or more correctly, it will lose its compression attribute, but gain a new compression attribute from its new location). If the destination location does not have the compression attribute set, the data will no longer be compressed. A move, on the other hand, will always retain the compression attribute regardless of where you move the data to, unless you move it to a different partition or an encrypted folder.

Exceptions to the Rules

Moving data across a partition is the same as a copy and delete operation. If a file that is compressed is copied to a new location, its compression attribute is lost, but it may be compressed again if the new location has a compression attribute set. The exception is when a compressed file is copied or moved to an encrypted folder. When a compressed file is copied or moved to an encrypted folder, it inherits the encryption attribute and loses the compression attribute. If you move or copy the encrypted file to a compressed folder, it will remain encrypted and will not be compressed.

Viewing Compression with Alternate Colors

If you're working with compressed data quite often, you may also wish to configure your Tools, Folder options to display compressed data in a different (alternate) color. This will allow you to tell easily what data is compressed when you view it from Windows Explorer or My Computer.

e x a m
ⓦatch

Microsoft wants you to know how to display compressed files/folders in an alternate color. The default color is blue (Figure 4-1).

FIGURE 4-1

Notice the top selection, Display Compressed Files And Folders With Alternate Color

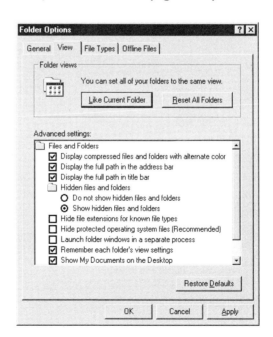

SCENARIO & SOLUTION	
What is the command-line utility that I would use in a batch file to automate compression routines?	Compact.exe.
If my compressed file is moved from a location on a partition to a different location on that same partition, what will happen to its compression attribute?	It will remain compressed.
If my compressed file is copied to a different partition, what will happen to its compression attribute?	The compression attribute will be lost.
Where do I configure alternate colors for compressed folders/files?	The View tab of the Folders Option Properties sheet; select Display Compressed Folders And Files With Alternate Color.

Using NTFS Permissions to Control Access to Files and Folders

Permissions, permissions, permissions. It would be very easy to get lost in a tangle of permissions with Windows 2000 Professional. An administrator can create as complicated or as simple a set of individual and group permissions as he or she wants. I prefer the KISS strategy myself (keep it simple, stupid). However, one of the beautiful things about this new operating system is the level of control you can affect on your files and folders permissions (security). An administrator can affect permissions locally on the hard drives and even on some removable media as well.

First, let's talk about why file and folder permissions are such a big deal. You can prevent people from seeing or editing your data by simply not sharing it on the network, right? Well, no, you really can't. Even if someone doesn't know your password, he or she can probably still boot your computer locally from a boot disk and then read your data locally. To protect your data from local attacks, you need to implement local security. "Local" meaning, in this context, on your PC, as opposed to implementing security over the network (those who attach to your machine remotely). The really beautiful thing is that NTFS permissions also apply to those who connect to your PC over the network!

NTFS permissions have been with us since NT 3.1 was first released and the NTFS file system made its debut. Now we have a new NTFS files system, NTFS 5.0, but our file and folder permissions are still similar. To implement file and folder permissions that will be applied locally, you *must* be using NTFS for the file system on the partition. There is no such thing as local security for the FAT file systems.

File Permissions

File permissions are configured from within the Properties sheet for the file in question. Let's go back to the Excel document we compressed earlier. Right-click it and select Properties (Figure 4-2).

Now select the Security tab (Figure 4-3).

File permissions include Full Control, Read & Execute, Modify, Read, and Write. Each of these permissions consists of a logical group of special permissions.

Table 4-1 lists each file permission, and which special permissions are associated with that permission.

Although file permissions are made up of individual special permissions, they are really still simple and easy to work with. If you assign the file permission Read to a user or group, you have actually given that user or group many different special permissions that have been grouped together to represent the permission Read. Those special permissions are List Folder/Read Data, Read Attributes, Read Extended Attributes, Read Permissions, and Synchronize.

FIGURE 4-2

The Properties sheet

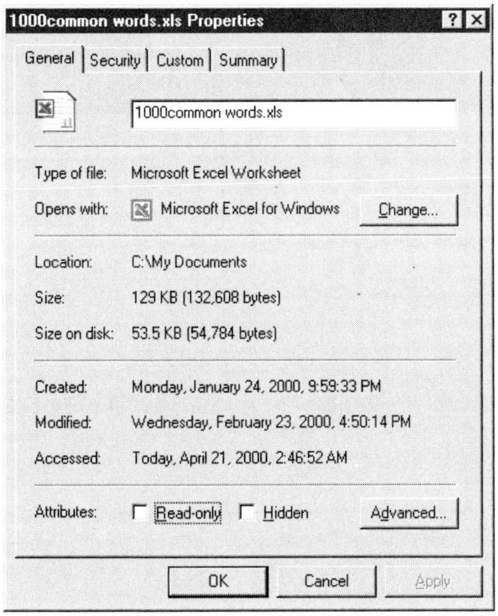

FIGURE 4-3

The Security tab of the Properties sheet

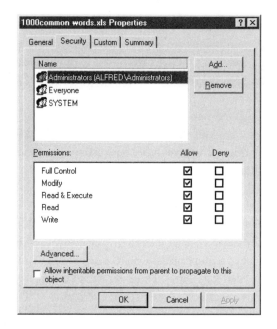

TABLE 4-1   NTFS Permissions and Special Permissions Cross-Referenced

Special Permission	Full Control	Modify	Read & Execute	Read	Write
Traverse Folder, Execute File	X	X	X		
List Folder, Read Data	X	X	X	X	
Special Permissions	Full Control	Modify	Read and Execute	Read	Write
Read Extended Attributes	X	X	X	X	
Read Attributes	X	X	X	X	

TABLE 4-1   NTFS Permissions and Special Permissions Cross-Referenced *(continued)*

Special Permission	Full Control	Modify	Read & Execute	Read	Write
Create Folders, Append Data	X	X			X
Create Files, Write Data	X	X			X
Write Attributes	X	X			X
Write Extended Attributes	X	X			X
Delete Subfolders and Files	X				
Delete	X	X			
Read Permissions	X	X	X	X	X
Take Ownership	X				
Change Permissions	X				
Synchronize	X	X	X	X	X

Folder Permissions

Folder permissions are very similar to file permissions; the one big difference is the necessity of adding permissions to browse through or list the folder's contents.

Again, with Explorer or My Computer, right-click the folder you wish to work with. Select Properties to bring up the Properties sheet for the folder, and select the Security tab (Figure 4-4).

You'll see the difference right away between file and folder permissions. There's a new permission listed for Folders: List Folder Contents. Folder permissions include Full Control, Modify, Read & Execute, List Folder Contents, Read, and Write.

Each of the folder permissions is actually a logical grouping of special permissions (just as file permissions actually consisted of a logical grouping of special permissions). Table 4-2 lists these special permissions.

FIGURE 4-4

The Security tab

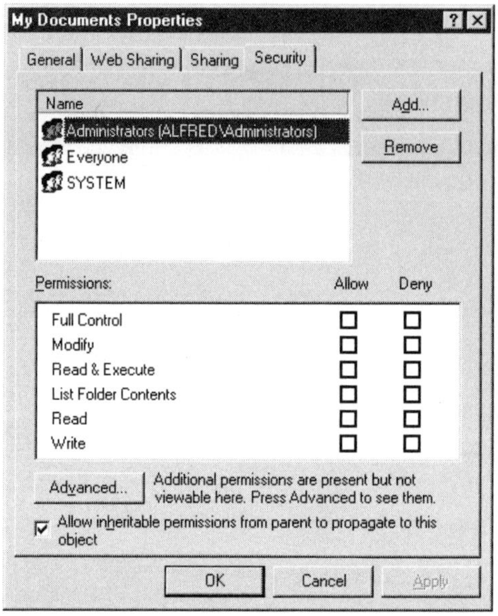

My Documents Properties

General | Web Sharing | Sharing | Security

Name

Administrators (ALFRED\Administrators)
Everyone
SYSTEM

Add...
Remove

Permissions:	Allow	Deny
Full Control	☐	☐
Modify	☐	☐
Read & Execute	☐	☐
List Folder Contents	☐	☐
Read	☐	☐
Write	☐	☐

Advanced... | Additional permissions are present but not viewable here. Press Advanced to see them.

☑ Allow inheritable permissions from parent to propagate to this object

OK   Cancel   Apply

TABLE 4-2 Folder Permissions and Their Special Permissions Cross-Referenced

Special Permissions	Full Control	Modify	Read & Execute	List Folder Contents	Read	Write
Traverse Folder, Execute File	X	X	X	X		
List Folder, Read Data	X	X	X	X	X	
Read Attributes	X	X	X	X	X	
Read Extended Attributes	X	X	X	X	X	
Create Folders, Append Data	X	X				X
Create Files, Write Data	X	X				X
Write Extended Attributes	X	X				X
Write Attributes	X	X				X

| TABLE 4-2 | Folder Permissions and Their Special Permissions Cross-Referenced *(continued)* | | | | | |

Special Permissions	Full Control	Modify	Read & Execute	List Folder Contents	Read	Write
Delete Subfolders and Files	X					
Delete	X	X				
Read Permissions	X	X	X	X	X	X
Change Permissions	X					
Synchronize	X	X	X	X	X	X
Take Ownership	X					

Let's take each of these permissions one at a time, and make sure we know what each allows or doesn't allow us to do. This is a recap of file and folder special permissions.

- **Traverse Folder, Execute File** Traverse Folder allows or denies browsing through folders to reach other files/folders.

- **List Folder, Read Data** List Folder allows or denies viewing file/subfolder names. Read Data allows or denies reading data in a file.

- **Read Attributes** Allows or denies viewing the attributes of a file/folder.

- **Read Extended Attributes** Allows or denies a user viewing the extended attributes of a file/folder. (Extended attributes are generated by programs and differ from system attributes.)

- **Create Files, Write Data** Create Files allows or denies creating files in a folder. Write Data allows or denies appending new data to a file and overwriting existing information.

- **Create Folders, Append Data** Create Folders allows or denies creating folders within a folder. Append Data allows or denies appending new data to a file without changing the existing content of that file.

- **Write Attributes** Allows or denies changing attributes of a file/folder.

- **Write Extended Attributes** Allows or denies changing extended attributes of a file/folder.

- ■ **Delete Subfolders and Files** Allows or denies deleting subfolders and files.
- ■ **Delete** Allows or denies deleting the file/folder.
- ■ **Read Permissions** Allows or denies reading permissions of the file/folder.
- ■ **Change Permissions** Allows or denies changing permissions for the file/folder.
- ■ **Take Ownership** Allows or denies taking ownership of the file or folder.
- ■ **Synchronize** Allows or denies different threads to synchronize with other threads.

on the job

The concept of Ownership for objects in Windows 2000 Professional is very important. When you create a file, folder, or other object, you're its owner. Every object has an owner, and you can easily tell who it is. If you create an embarrassing file and store it on an NTFS partition, an administrator (or just about anyone for that matter) can view the ownership of it and immediately tie it back to you.

Advanced Permissions

Okay, now we've seen all the special file and folder permissions and know that they are combined together to make standard permissions. This is convenient for us, as now we don't have to track or enter several types of special permissions to accomplish our job. Alas, we're still not finished with these two. There are also advanced permissions for both files and folders. To access the advanced permissions, you need to right-click your file/folder and select Properties to bring up the Properties page, and then select Security to bring up the Security Properties. Now you'll notice toward the bottom an Advanced tab. Go ahead and click it. Here is where you can control exactly what special permissions to assign to your file/folder, if you need to. Remember that the standard permissions already are made up of these special permissions. The odds are good that you'll never need to be this selective about what specific special permission you assign to a file/folder; however, it certainly is nice to know that you can be this selective if you need or want to (Figure 4-5).

The Advanced tab brings up the Access Control Settings for your file/folder.

Here you actually have a list of the users/groups that have security entries associated with this folder/file. Double-click one and you'll see a complete list of all the selectable special permissions (Figure 4-6).

There they all are, and you can simply go in and specifically allow or deny any special permissions you would like (Figure 4-7).

FIGURE 4-5

The Advanced
tab of the
Security
Properties sheet

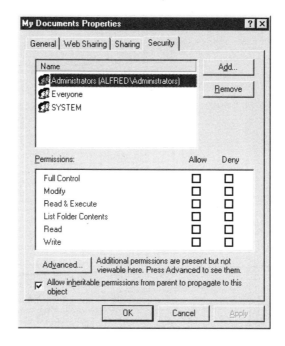

FIGURE 4-6

Advanced Access
Control Settings

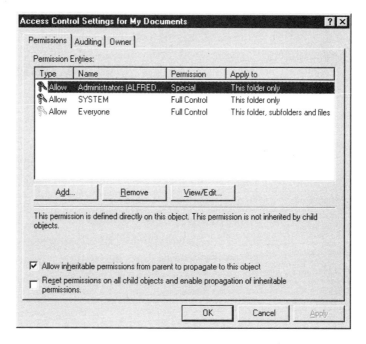

FIGURE 4-7

Special
permissions

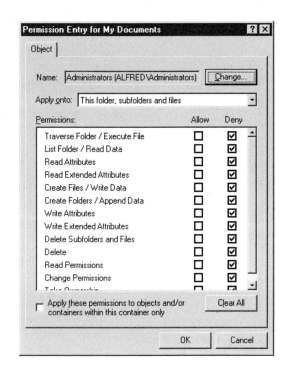

When you're working with permissions for a file, the only thing for which you're modifying the permissions is that file, and that file only. When you're working with a folder, however, the changes in permissions you make can impact that folder and any subfolders or files within it. You need to make a decision when you're working with folder permissions, and determine whether you want your changes to apply to only the folder you're working on, or all of its subfolders, and even all of the documents and data within all those subfolders. This is still easy to do. From within the Permission Entry Properties sheet, select the Apply Onto pull-down menu and make your selection for how these permission changes will be applied (Figure 4-8).

Permissions Inheritance

The file or folder you're working on can inherit permissions from parent objects. Let's say that you're configuring permissions on a folder in your C: drive named

Apply Onto
pull-down menu

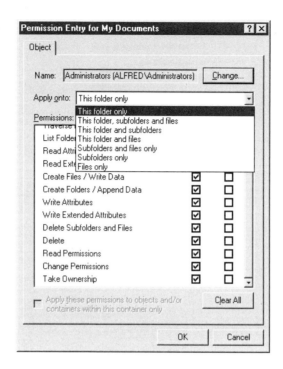

temp. C:\temp\. The parent object for this folder is the C: drive. If you make any changes to the permissions associated with the C: drive, they may or may not affect the permissions you've set for your temp folder. What determines whether your folder will inherit permissions from its parent object? Go back to the Access Control Setting Properties page for your folder, and toward the bottom, you'll see it: a check box that allows inherited permissions from parent objects. If you don't want any inherited permissions for your folder, deselect that check box. Be careful, however. When you clear that check box for a folder, your system will present you with a few choices in the form of a pop-up box (Figure 4-9).

You will need to determine if you wish to keep any inherited permissions, or if you want to remove any inherited permissions now. Think about this before making a selection. Important permissions may have been assigned to or inherited by this object that you need to keep (Figure 4-10).

FIGURE 4-9

Access Control
Settings

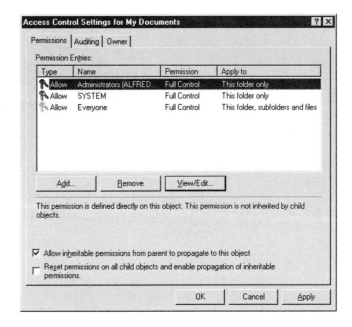

FIGURE 4-10

Security
Permissions
Propagation
pop-up menu

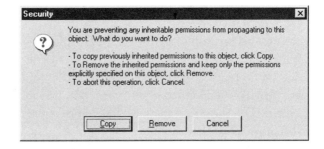

SCENARIO & SOLUTION

How do the file and folder permissions differ?	Folder permissions include the permission to list folder contents. Folder permissions may also apply to objects within the folder, and even to files located in the folder.
Where would you access the Advanced Permissions tab?	From the Properties sheet for your file/folder, select the Security tab, and then the Advanced tab.
Which permission allows or denies changing permissions of the file or folder, such as Full Control, Read, and Write?	Change.

Optimize Access to Files and Folders

Exam 70-210 requires that you know what file and folder permissions are, and that you can use them in the real world. This is where optimizing comes in. Expect to encounter scenario-based questions with users belonging to more than one group and having more than one set of permissions for a file/folder. You will be asked to resolve the permissions and determine the effective permissions for that user in relation to that resource.

There are the two rules to remember:

- A user's effective permission to a file/folder is the accumulation of all the permissions he or she has.

- The Deny permission overrides rule 1. No matter what permissions a user has from other group memberships, if that user or a group he or she belongs to has been specifically denied access, he or she will not be able to access the resource.

Let's say a user, jimbob, has Read permission for a file. A group jimbob belongs to, sales, has the Full Control permission. Jimbob has the Full Control permission on this file due to his group membership. Now, if jimbob belongs to yet another group, contract workers, and this group has been specifically denied access to this file, he has no access to this document.

Least-restrictive permission applies in all instances, except for Deny.

exam

ⓦatch

You will probably see one or more questions on your exam that are scenario-based permissions questions. These are easy "gimme" questions if you remember these two rules.

Other things to remember when preparing for Exam 70-210:

■ You can set file and folder permissions only on drives formatted to use NTFS.

■ To change permissions, you must be the owner or have been granted permission to do so by the owner.

■ Groups or users granted Full Control for a folder can delete files and subfolders within that folder, regardless of the permissions protecting the files and subfolders.

If the check boxes under Permissions are shaded, or if Remove is unavailable, then the file or folder has inherited permissions from the parent folder.

CERTIFICATION OBJECTIVE 4.02

Managing and Troubleshooting Access to Shared Folders

Share permissions are managed in much the same way as NTFS permissions. The main difference between the two is that Share permissions have no local significance—they only apply to users who attach to your PC over the network. If someone is logged on to your PC locally, the share will have no effect—unlike NTFS permissions, which always apply.

Create and Remove Shared Folders

We have networks, and we have computers. How do we share data between them? We create and manage *shares*. Folders, files, and printers are a few of the resources that may be shared with other users across your network.

Creating Shares

Creating shares is a straightforward process. You can share information regardless of the file system in use. Fat 16, Fat 32, NTFS, and even UDF (Universal Disk Format, used to read DVD volumes) and CDFS file systems may be shared.

To create a share, do the following:

■ From Windows Explorer or My Computer, right-click the folder or file to share. Select Properties, and then select the Sharing tab (Figure 4-11).

Initially, the file/folder will have the Do Not Share This Folder check box selected. To share it, select Share This Folder. Your system will fill in a default share name

The Sharing tab

for you, although if you desire a different share name you can change it. (You can always come back and change it later as well.) If you wish, you may provide a comment or description for your share to make it easier for people browsing through shares to identify the kind of share you've created. I like to include some information that will identify where this share is physically located (see Figure 4-14 later in the chapter). Everyone who sees this share will know it's on my computer, and it's where I store working documents.

Limiting Concurrent Connections

If you'd like to specify a maximum number of concurrent connections to this share, you may limit this as well by selecting a user limit. The maximum number that can ever connect to a share on a Windows 2000 Professional computer is ten. This is a hard-coded limit of the operating system. If you need to have more than ten connections to your share at once, you need to upgrade to one of the 2000 Server operating systems.

You may wish to limit the number of concurrent connections to fewer than ten, however, to reduce the performance hit on your machine when it is functioning as a server.

Using Permissions to Control Access to Shared Folders

Now that you have created a share, you need to secure it. The default Share permission is Full Control for the Everyone group. Remember that the Everyone group includes literally *everyone* who is accessing the computer. From the Properties sheet for your file/folder and the Sharing tab, select Permissions to modify Share permissions (Figure 4-12).

There are only three permissions associated with Shares: Full Control, Change, and Read. (Table 4-3 lists the Share permissions and their associated special actions.)

exam
ⓦatch

To share folders and drives, you must be a member of the Administrators, Server Operators, or Power Users group.

FIGURE 4-12

Share permissions

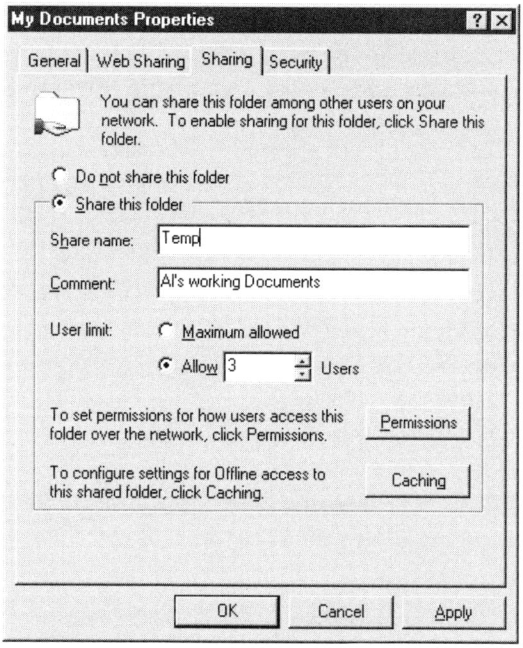

My Documents Properties

General | Web Sharing | Sharing | Security |

You can share this folder among other users on your
network. To enable sharing for this folder, click Share this
folder.

○ Do not share this folder
● Share this folder

Share name: Temp

Comment: Al's working Documents

User limit: ○ Maximum allowed
● Allow 3 Users

To set permissions for how users access this
folder over the network, click Permissions. [Permissions]

To configure settings for Offline access to
this shared folder, click Caching. [Caching]

[OK] [Cancel] [Apply]

TABLE 4-3 Special Actions and Share Permissions

Action	Full Control	Change	Read
Traversing to subfolders	X	X	X
Viewing file/subfolder names	X	X	X
Viewing data in files and running programs	X	X	X
Changing data in files	X	X	
Adding files/subfolders to the shared folder	X	X	
Deleting subfolders/files	X	X	
Taking ownership	X		
Changing permissions	X		

on the **Job**

Not all special action permissions are available for all file systems. The Full Control Share permission will only give you the special actions Changing Permissions and Taking Ownership if the share is on an NTFS partition.

One may use the Computer Management console (select Start | Programs | Administrative Tools | Computer Management) to view all your shares (even hidden administrative shares), and who has a session to your PC and even which file they specifically have open or are using (Figure 4-13).

With Windows 2000, all your local drives on your computer, such as drive C:, are automatically shared using a *drive letter*$, such as C$ or D$. These are administrative shares. They are not visible by browsing; in other words, they will not show up in My Network Places. These drives are not shown with the hand icon that indicates sharing in My Computer or Windows Explorer.

on the **Job**

You can hide any share from the Browse list and My Network Places by placing a dollar sign at the end of the share name.

FIGURE 4-13

The Management console

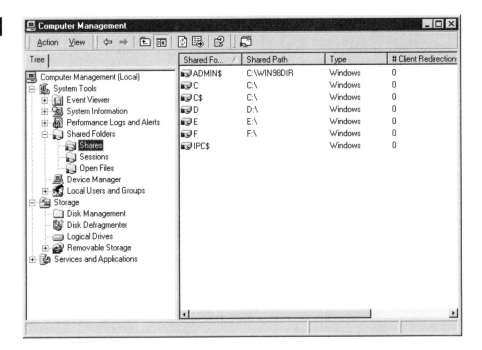

on the
() o b *These administrative shares are available over the network if you know the*
UNC path. Remember that hackers know all about administrative shares,
and will exploit them if they can.

To keep your drives secure, you should create a difficult password for the
Administrator account; this is the password that will allow access to an administrative
share. It is also a good idea to rename the Administrator account using the Local Users
and Groups snap-in. Make your passwords difficult to guess and long. It may only take
a few minutes for a hacker to run a password attack successfully on a four-character
password. However, if your password is 12 characters long, and has UPPER and lower
case characters and even special characters like ^&*, it may be impossible for a hacker
to figure out.

on the
() o b *If you are running Windows 2000 on a network that also has legacy*
computers running Windows95/98, you may want to use passwords shorter
than 14 characters. Windows 95/98 only supports passwords up to 14
characters in length.

You may also disable your Server service as an extra layer of security. This will
prevent you from sharing resources on your PC, but you can still connect to other
computers' shares from your PC; and it will now be impossible for someone to
establish a connection to your PC over the network. To stop this service, open your
management console and select Services and Applications | Services (Figure 4-14).

To stop sharing an administrative share temporarily, right-click it, click Sharing,
and then click "Do not share this folder." However, keep in mind that Windows
2000 will re-create the share when the system is restarted.

We also have rules for Share permissions and how they're applied. A user's
effective permission for a share is the accumulation of the permissions he or she has
been given due to group memberships and individual permissions. Again, we have
the same exception: the Deny permission overrides everything else.

Remember jimbob? If he as a user has full control of a share, and a group he
belongs to has Read, he has the accumulation of the permissions; that is, he has
Full Control plus Read (or effectively, Full Control). If he belongs to a group that
has been denied access, he is denied access no matter what other permissions he has.

FIGURE 4-14

The Server
service

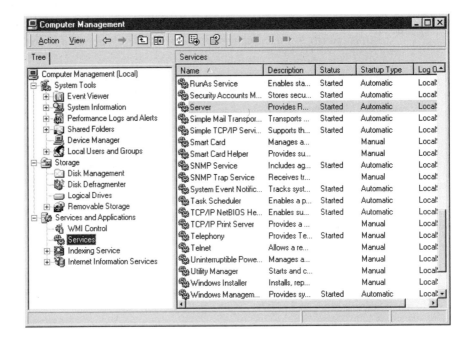

Caching

To make shared network files available offline (when you are no longer on the network, or the resource in question is no longer on the network), Offline Files stores a version of the files in a reserved portion of disk space on your computer in a cache. (Cache in this context is a local copy of a share's contents. A PC attaching to a share that allows caching will download and store locally a copy of some or all of the share's contents.) The computer can access this cache regardless of whether it is connected to the network. Not only does this make data available when your PC or the one accessing your data is offline, it speeds up network performance. Cached data does not need to be read over the network; it is cached locally, and it is the local copy that the user will access. There are three caching options to choose from when sharing files. To select one of the three options, do the following:

- Open Windows Explorer or My Computer, right-click a share, and select Sharing. On your Sharing Properties dialog box, click Caching (Figure 4-15). There are three settings from which to choose.

FIGURE 4-15

Manual Caching
For Documents

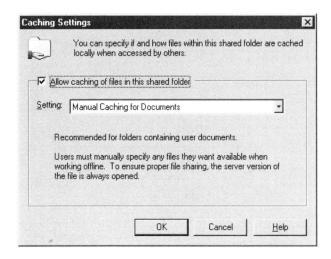

Manual Caching For Documents provides offline access to those files that someone specifically identified while browsing your share. This is the default caching option (Figure 4-16).

Automatic Caching For Documents caches every file that a user opens from your share and makes them available offline. This setting does not make every file in your share available offline, just those that have been opened or used by a user (Figure 4-17).

FIGURE 4-16

Automatic
Caching For
Documents

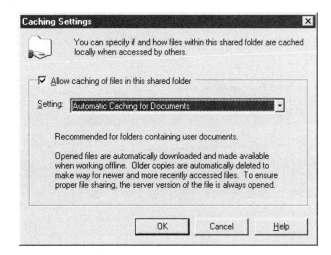

Automatic
Caching For
Programs

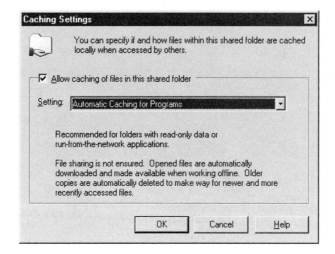

Automatic Caching For Programs provides offline access to shared folders containing files that are not changed. This is great for information that needs to be accessed, but never changes. It can greatly increase the responsiveness of your network.

To eliminate any problems with having many different versions of a document cached locally on different PCs, you may wish to set Read Only permissions on documents when Automatic Caching for Documents is enabled.

SCENARIO & SOLUTION

What are the three Share permissions?	Full Control, Change, and Read.
Which cache setting only saves offline copies of files that are specifically selected by a user?	Manual Caching For Documents.

Remember the rules for applying local NTFS permissions and Share permissions. For either permission, it is always the accumulation of all permissions granted, unless the Deny permission is invoked. Deny always overrides other permissions. Also note, we've talked about these permissions separately. When a Share permission and a local NTFS permission are both applied, they behave differently. When both are present, the user gets the MOST restrictive permission of the accumulation of each type. That is, if a user has the Share permission Read, and the NTFS permission Full Control, that user is limited by the most restrictive permission; in this case, the user has Read only.

Another example: Jimbob has the Share permission Full Control over the Documents share. The document he's interested in in this share is Resume.doc. For it, he has the NTFS permission Modify. He gets the most restrictive of the two different permissions; in this case, he has Modify, not Full Control.

CertCam 4-2

EXERCISE 4-2

Share and NTFS Permissions

Assume that you are an administrator for your organization. You need to determine if your existing Share and NTFS permissions are adequate.

Your primary considerations are:

1. Ensure that the Sales group has Full Control of the Sales Share.

2. Ensure that the Human Resource group has the ability to Read all data in the Sales share.

Your secondary considerations are:

1. The Contract Workers group should be denied access to the Sales share and all data within it.

2. The Clerical group should be able to take ownership of the Sales folder.

Your organization's existing Share and NTFS permissions for the shared Sales folder are listed in the following table.

Group	Share Permission	NTFS Permission
Human Resources	Full Control	Read
Clerical	Full Control	Change Permissions
Contract Workers	No Access	No Access
Sales	Full Control	Full Control

1. Does this fulfill

    A. All the Primary and all the secondary considerations.

    B. One of the primary considerations and all the secondary considerations.

    C. Two of the primary considerations and one of the secondary considerations.

    D. None of the primary or secondary considerations.

Please consider all that you've learned so far in this chapter while thinking about this question.

A is the correct answer. Of your primary considerations

1. **Ensure that the Sales group has Full Control of the Sales Share.** This first one is accomplished. The Sales group has been assigned Full Control of the Share and the NTFS permissions.

2. **Ensure that the Human Resources group has the ability to Read all data in the Sales share.** This one is also taken care of; the Human Resources group has the Full Control permission for the Share, and Read permission for the folder. They have effective Read permission, as it is the most restrictive permission of the Share and NTFS permissions.

Of the secondary considerations

1. **The Contract Workers group should be denied access to the Sales share and all data within it.** This is met as well; the Contract Workers have been given No Access to both the Share and the folder's NTFS permission.

2. **The Clerical group should be able to take ownership of the Sales folder.** This one is accomplished. The Clerical group has Full Control to the Share and Change permissions for the folder's NTFS permission. They will have the ability to take ownership if needed by granting themselves the ability to take ownership of the folder.

All of the primary considerations were met and all of the secondary considerations were met.

Connecting to a Windows Shared Folder

To connect to shares on other PCs, you have a couple of choices; one common method is to map a network drive with Windows Explorer.

To map a drive letter to a network share, perform the following steps:

1. Open Windows Explorer.

2. From the Tools menu, select Map Network Drive.

3. Select the drive letter you wish to use for the shared resource.

4. Type the server and share name of the resource as its UNC (Universal Naming Convention) path. The syntax is *servername**sharename*. You may also browse to locate the resource.

on the
job

To reconnect to the mapped drive every time you log on, ensure the Reconnect At Logon check box is selected.

It is also possible to map a network drive using the net use command from a command prompt. The syntax is as follows:

NET USE *drive_letter: \\computername\sharename*

You may also access a share via My Network Places by simply double-clicking it on the Desktop. This will display all the shared resources available to you that have been identified by the computer Browse service for your domain/workgroup and any others on your network.

Connecting to a NetWare Server

One of the things that makes Windows 2000 Professional adaptable and so powerful is its ability to connect to and work with many different kinds of computer networks. Windows 2000 Professional comes with Client services for NetWare (CSNW), and there is additional support with the 2000 Server products to act as a Gateway for 2000 Pro to operate in a Novell network (GSNW), allowing a smooth transition into a NetWare network.

exam
ⓦatch

2000 Professional's client services for NetWare only allow integration into a NetWare network running bindery security or NDS. This means that integration is limited to NetWare versions 3 and 4 only. Windows 2000 CSNW does work with NetWare 5.0 running IPX/SPX if the NetWare server is running on pure IP (you have to use the Novell client).

To connect to a NetWare volume by using My Network Places (note that this will work only if there is a NetWare server connected to your network),

1. Double-click My Network Places (it's located on the Desktop).

2. Double-click NetWare Network if visible; if not, double-click Entire, and then double-click NetWare or Compatible Network.

3. Double-click a tree or volume to see the contents. Now you can browse the contents to see other volumes and computers.

4. When you find the folder that you want to access, double-click the folder to expand it.

5. If you want a mapped network drive to this resource, select the Tools menu and then Map Network Drive.

6. You may also use the Net command from a command prompt to attach to a NetWare volume.

NET USE *drive_letter:* \\UNC_Name\NetWare_Name

e x a m
ⓦa t c h

To view or connect to NetWare resources, you must first install Client Service for NetWare on your 2000 Pro PC along with NWLink (Microsoft's implementation of Novell's IPX/SPX protocol), or you may implement Gateway Service for NetWare on a 2000 Server.

Connecting to an FTP Server

FTP (File Transfer Protocol) is one of those ideas that is legendary today. It has been with us for two decades now, which is more than a lifetime in computer years. Windows 2000 Professional has built-in command-line support for using FTP as a client. It may also be an FTP server if you've installed Internet Information Server (IIS). We'll be discussing FTP client from a command prompt, which is the subject of one of the objectives for Exam 70-210.

The syntax for FTP follows, along with its most common switches.

ftp [-v] [-n] [-i] [-d] [-g] [-s:*filename*] [-w:*windowsize*] [*computer*]

- **-v**   Verbose, limited information from the remote server is displayed.
- **-n**   Cancels autologin upon initial connection.
- **-I**   Turns off prompts during file transfers.
- **-d**   Displays all ftp commands passed between the client and server.
- **-g**   Permits the use of wildcard characters.
- **-s:***filename*   Specifies a text file containing commands.
- **-w:***windowsize*   Overrides the transfer buffer size (default is 4,096 bytes).
- *computer*   Specifies the computer name, domain name, or IP address of the computer you are connecting to.

IIS

Windows 2000 Pro includes Internet Information Server (IIS) version 5.0. Although it is not quite as robust or scalable as its counterpart on 2000 Server, it is a powerful Web server for workgroup or Web development use.

Installing and Configuring IIS

IIS (version 5.0) is not installed on 2000 Professional during a typical install. You can install IIS by using the Add/Remove Programs application in the Control Panel.

To install Internet Information Services,

1. Click Start | Settings | Control Panel, and start the Add/Remove Programs application.

2. Select Add/Remove Windows Components to select and install IIS.

on the **job**

If you upgraded to Windows 2000 from Windows 95/98 or an earlier version of NT, Internet Information Server (IIS) will be installed during the upgrade if Personal Web Services (Win 9x) or Peer Web Services (NT) was installed on the previous operating system.

You may test your install of IIS by opening a browser and entering **http://***localhost* for the URL.

Managing IIS

IIS 5.0 is managed from the Internet Information Services snap-in. It is very similar to the Internet Service Manager from IIS 4.0. To open the IIS snap-in, click Start | Settings | Control Panel. Double-click Administrative Tools, and then double-click Computer Management. Under the Server Applications And Services tab, expand Internet Information Services (Figure 4-18).

With your Web site selected, you can access the properties from the Action pull-down menu (Figure 4-19).

This Properties page is where you manage security, custom-error pages, how your site is tuned to perform, and much more.

FIGURE 4-18

Internet
Information
Service

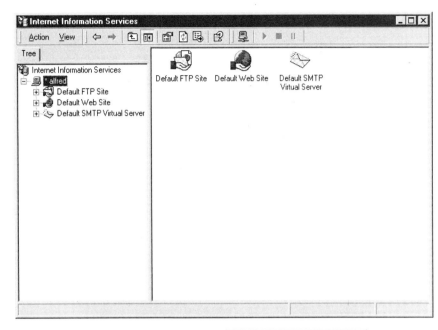

FIGURE 4-19

Your Web site
properties

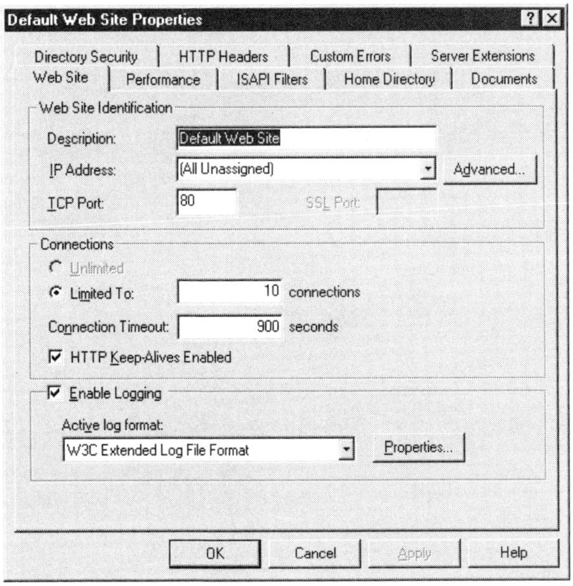

Troubleshooting Web Server Resources

For troubleshooting IIS 5.0, there are two tools included in Windows 2000 Professional, the snap-in and the command iisreset. We've already shown you the snap-in, so let's talk about iisreset.

The syntax is as follows:

iisreset *web_server_name*

Not only can you administer your PC's IIS 5.0, but you can also attach to a remote computer. The switches are listed in Table 4-4.

To stop and restart the Internet Services for a computer named workstation1,

iisreset workstation1 /restart

To display the status of the Internet Services for this same computer,

iisreset workstation1 /status

on the **job**

With the command-line utility iisreset, you can manage your Web site remotely as well.

TABLE 4-4		
iisreset Switches	/reboot	Forces a reboot of the computer
	/restart	Stops and then restarts all Internet services
	/start	Starts Internet services
	/stop	Stops Internet services
	/rebootonerror	Reboots the computer if an error is detected stopping, starting, or restarting the Internet services
	/noforce	Will skip terminating the Internet services if stopping them fails
	/status	Displays status of all Internet services
	/disable	Disables restarting Internet services
	/enable	Enables restarting of Internet services

FROM THE CLASSROOM

Share and NTFS Permissions

The interaction of Share and NTFS permissions can be confusing, especially for students who are new to network administration. There are a few rules to apply, but they aren't hard. Just apply these rules in order and you'll breeze through this portion of your certification exam(s).

1. All NTFS permissions are applied for a user based upon his or her permissions and the permissions of all the groups he or she has membership in. The effective permission (what the user has) is the accumulation of all the user's permissions and all of that user's groups' permissions.

2. NTFS permissions are always the accumulation of all the permissions, except when Deny comes into play. If a user has an individual permission or a group permission of Deny, it overrides all the other permissions.

3. Share permissions follow the same two rules. A user's permissions on a share

are the accumulation of his user permissions and groups' permissions.

4. Again, there is an exception: Deny overrides all other permissions.

5. The last rule to remember is that when NTFS permissions and Share permissions overlap (they often do), a user gets the MOST restrictive permission of the accumulation of each of the two. If a user has NTFS permissions of Read and Share permissions of Full Control, that user's effective permissions for the NTFS/Share combination is Read.

Always remember that shares have no local significance unless a user at the local machine is accessing the resource through the share. NTFS permissions, on the other hand, apply whether a user is logged on locally or attached remotely to a share over the network

—*Alfred Gattenby, MCSE+I, MCT, CNE, CCNA*

CERTIFICATION SUMMARY

For Exam 70-210, you will need to know the rules for file compression in Windows 2000. A move on the same partition retains compression attributes. A copy or a move to a different partition does not. Compressed data stays compressed if it is sent over the network; this is a big difference in compression between NT 4.0 and Windows 2000 Professional.

Keep the rules for permissions straight and you will do fine on this section of your exam. When a user belongs to multiple groups with different NTFS permissions, the effective permissions are always the accumulation of the different permissions, except that the Deny permissions overrides everything else. Resolving multiple Share permissions works the same way as resolving multiple NTFS permissions.

When NTFS and Share permissions are both applied (which occurs when a shared resource on an NTFS partition is accessed across the network or through the share), the resulting permission is the most restrictive of the two. A Share permission of Read and an NTFS permission of Full Control yield an effective permission of Read, because it is the more restrictive of the two.

Also remember that, generally, shares are only applied over the network, and do not apply to a user locally at the PC where the share is. However, if a user sitting at the local computer accesses the resource through the share (that is, through My Network Places or the Network part of Windows Explorer, or using the UNC path at the command line), then Share permissions *do* apply. Otherwise, Share permissions do not provide local security.

If you have IIS installed on Windows 2000 Professional, you can manage your Web site with two different utilities: the Internet Information Services snap-in and the command iisreset.

TWO-MINUTE DRILL

Monitoring, Managing, and Troubleshooting Access to Files and Folders

❑ The only form of compression you may use with 2000 Professional is NTFS compression. Other compression schemes are not supported.

❑ Compression and encryption are mutually exclusive. A compressed file cannot be encrypted, and an encrypted file may not be compressed. A file that is compressed may have an encryption attribute set, but it will lose its compression attribute.

❑ To modify compression from a command prompt, use Compact.exe. Compact.exe may be used in scripts or batch files to automate compression routines.

❑ NTFS permissions are the only form of local security for your hard drives. Unlike Share permissions, they always apply, whether a user is logged on locally or over a network.

❑ NTFS file permissions include Full Control, Modify, Read & Execute, Read, and Write.

❑ Each of these NTFS permissions consists of a logical group of special permissions. These special permissions may be modified.

❑ File and Folder permissions are the same, except that folders contain one new permission, List Folder Contents.

❑ A user's effective permission to a file/folder is the accumulation of all the permissions he has been allowed, either as a member of security groups or individually. As with Share permissions, a user's permission is the accumulation of the permissions he has through his individual account or his groups' permissions. There is an exception to this rule: Deny. Deny overrides all other permissions.

Managing and Troubleshooting Access to Shared Folders

❑ Folders, files, and printers are a few of the resources that may be shared with other users across your network. Resources on any file system may be shared, but all shared special actions are not available unless the share resides on an NTFS partition.

❑ The maximum number of users that may connect to a share on a Windows 2000 Professional computer is ten. This number may be lowered but never increased. If you want to limit the share to less than ten simultaneous users, you can do so. If you want more than ten simultaneous users, you need to upgrade to one of the 2000 Server operating systems.

❑ There are only three permissions associated with Shares: Full Control, Change, and Read.

❑ A user's effective permission to a share is the least-restrictive permission he or she has been allowed. The exception to this rule is Deny. If a user or a group a user belongs to has the Deny permission, it overrides all other permissions.

❑ Share permissions have no local effect unless the person who is logged in at the local machine is accessing the resource through the share. Shares only apply to users attaching to your PC over the network; however, this can include someone sitting at the local machine.

❑ When both Share and NTFS permissions are present, the user gets the MOST restrictive permission of the final accumulation of each of the two.

❑ IIS 5.0 is managed from the Internet Information Services snap-in or from the command prompt with iisreset.

SELF TEST

The following questions will help you measure your understanding of the material presented in this chapter. Read all of the choices carefully, as there may be more than one correct answer.

Monitoring, Managing, and Troubleshooting Access to Files and Folders

1. Which file system is required for compression?

   A. NTFS

   B. FAT 16 or FAT 32

   C. FAT 32

   D. Any file system

2. On an NTFS volume, you display the Properties sheet for a file and select the Advanced tab. What two attributes may you enable/disable from this sheet? (Select two answers.)

   A. Archive and Index attributes

   B. Full Control attributes

   C. Compress or Encrypt attributes

   D. Advanced permission attributes

3. What are two methods to manage compression? (Choose two answers.)

   A. Use Compress.exe

   B. Use Compact.exe

   C. Use Windows Explorer

   D. Use the Compression Manager snap-in

4. Which permission would User1 have on this document? User1 has the NTFS permission Read. A group User1 belongs to has the NTFS permission Full Control, and another group User1 belongs to has Execute permission.

   A. Read

   B. No Access

   C. Full Control

   D. Full Control of the folder and Read for the file

5. Which of the following is not an NTFS permission for a file?

    A. Full Control

    B. Execute

    C. Read

    D. List Folder Contents

6. Which of the following permissions would allow you to manage permissions for a file?

    A. Take Ownership

    B. Manage

    C. Read

    D. Synchronize

7. When you apply NTFS permissions to a folder, the default APPLY TO selection will force these NTFS changes onto what?

    A. That folder only

    B. That folder and all subfolders, but not the contents

    C. Only the contents of that folder

    D. That folder and the files within it

8. You have the user permission Read for a document, and you also belong to three groups that have the following permissions for this document: Group1 has Full Control, Group2 has Delete, and Group3 has been denied all permissions. What is your effective permission for this object?

    A. Delete

    B. Full Control

    C. No Access

    D. Read

9. An embarrassing file has been found on an NTFS network share. What is the fastest way to identify who created this file?

    A. View your security logs.

    B. Ask around the office.

    C. Track the document with an audit, and wait to see who uses it.

    D. View the Owner attribute from the Advanced Properties tab of the document.

Monitoring, Managing, and Troubleshooting Access to Shared Folders

10. Where would I specify the maximum number of connected users for a share?

    A. The Sharing tab, Permissions tab.

    B. The Sharing tab, Allow radio button, specify the number you want.

    C. It is not possible to specify a maximum number.

    D. The Security tab of the Properties sheet for the folder/file.

11. A user is sitting locally at a PC that has a working documents share for the department. This user has Deny permissions for the share. What is the user's effective permission while he or she is logged on locally to that PC?

    A. Full Control

    B. No Access

    C. Read

    D. Change

12. What is the default permission for a share?

    A. Everyone, Full Control.

    B. Everyone, No Access.

    C. Everyone, Read, and List.

    D. There are no default Share permissions.

13. What are the three Share permissions?

    A. Read, List, Full Control

    B. Full Control, Deny, No Access

    C. List, Full Control, Execute

    D. Full Control, Change, Read

14. What would be the correct command-line syntax to map a network drive as P: on the share management on a computer named office1?

    A. \\office 1 net use :p

    B. net use P: \\office1\management

    C. connect to P: office1 management

    D. net use P: \management\office1

15. Which of the following will occur to my 2000 Pro workstation if I terminate all the administrative shares and reboot?

    A. A Blue Screen will result.

    B. The missing administrative shares will prevent RPC communication, and you will not be able to log on to the domain.

    C. The administrative shares will re-create themselves normally the next time you reboot.

    D. You cannot terminate administrative shares.

16. Which of the following groups may not create shares?

    A. Administrators

    B. Server Operators

    C. Account Operators

    D. Power Users

17. What FTP switch permits the use of wildcard characters?

    A. -g

    B. -v

    C. -n

    D. -i

LAB QUESTION

Assume that you are administering a share for your organization. You are required to do the following.

Primary Considerations

1. Make shared data available to network users both online and offline.

2. The offline data should improve the performance of your network.

3. A large number of users should be able to access the data.

Secondary Considerations

1. The data should be protected from any access by the Sales group.

2. The HumanResources group requires complete access to the data.

You create a share on your 2000 Pro PC named HR. For this share, you have left the default Share permissions intact. Additionally, you have given the HumanResources group Full Control of the share. You also configure Automatic Caching Of Documents for the share.

You configure NTFS permissions for the folder, giving Human Resources Full Control, and you specifically deny access to the Sales group.

I. Does this fulfill

    A. All the primary and all the secondary considerations.

    B. Two of the primary considerations and all the secondary considerations.

    C. Two of the primary considerations and one of the secondary considerations.

    D. None of the primary or secondary considerations.

Please consider all that you've learned in this chapter while thinking about this question. You will see scenario-based requirements questions on some of your certification exams.

SELF TEST ANSWERS

Monitoring, Managing, and Troubleshooting Access to Files and Folders

1. ☑ **A.** Compression is an NTFS attribute; only NTFS volumes support compression.
   ☒ **B** and **C** are incorrect because although FAT 16 and FAT 32 are supported file systems for 2000 Pro, there are no supported compression schemes for these file systems. **D** is incorrect. Only the NTFS file system may be compressed on 2000 Pro.

2. ☑ **A, C.** The Advanced attributes tab deals with two attributes: Archive and Index in the top half, and Compress or Encrypt attributes in the bottom half.
   ☒ **B** and **D** are incorrect because there is no such thing as Full Control or Advanced Permissions attributes.

3. ☑ **B, C.** Compact.exe is the command-line program to manage compression. It is useful for batch processing of compression commands. One may also use Windows Explorer or My Computer to manage compression with a GUI.
   ☒ **A** and **D** are incorrect because there is no such thing as Compress.exe or the Compression Manager snap-in.

4. ☑ **C.** The user has Full Control for the file. Remember that for NTFS permission, the user gets the least-restrictive permission with the exception of Deny. Since there are no Deny permissions associated with this user or his group, he gets the least-restrictive permission—in this case, Full Control.
   ☒ **A, B,** and **D** are incorrect because they do not follow the rules for permissions.

5. ☑ **D.** List Folder Contents is an NTFS folder permission, not a file permission. File and folder permissions' big difference is the addition of List for folders, where files does not have List as a permission.
   ☒ **A, B,** and **C** are incorrect because they are permissions for a file.

6. ☑ **A.** Take Ownership allows you to take ownership of this file. The owner may then set any permissions he or she wishes. Manage, Read, and Synchronize will not allow you to change permissions.
   ☒ **B, C,** and **D** are incorrect because they allow only limited access to the file; with these permissions, it is not possible to modify permissions.

7. ☑ **A.** The default APPLY TO selection for a folder NTFS permission is to force the NTFS permissions on that folder only, not any of its contents. You may change this setting through the pull-down menu if you wish these changes to take effect on the contents and even on subfolders and their contents.

☒   **B, C,** and **D** are incorrect because they are not the default setting in the APPLY TO pull-down menu.

8.   ☑   **C.** Remember the rules for NTFS permissions: A user always gets the least-restrictive permission, except when one of those permissions is Deny. Deny trumps all other permissions. Since Group3 has been denied access, and this user is a member of Group3, this user is denied access.
☒   **A, B,** and **D** are incorrect because they do not follow the rules for permissions.

9.   ☑   **D.** Every object on an NTFS partition has an owner. It is very easy to identify who this is by viewing the Advanced properties of the Properties sheet for that object. The owner is the person who created or downloaded that document to the NTFS partition.
☒   **A, B,** and **C** are incorrect; they may work, but they are not the easiest way to find out whose document it is.

Monitoring, Managing, and Troubleshooting Access to Shared Folders

10.   ☑   **B.** The maximum number of users allowed per share with 2000 Pro is ten. You may limit this easily by entering a new value with the Allow radio button.
☒   **A** is incorrect; you may set the available permissions here, but not maximum users. **C** is incorrect because it is possible to specify a maximum number of users. **D** is also incorrect; the Security tab of the Properties sheet is used to configure NTFS permissions, not manage Share permissions.

11.   ☑   **A.** Shares only apply to users who are connecting over the network. A user logged on locally on the PC that has the share does not have any Share permissions applied to him or her. Even if that user has been denied access to the share by being given the Deny permission, he or she may access the share and do anything to it when logged on locally to the PC that has the share.
☒   **B, C,** and **D** are incorrect because the user is logged on locally; therefore, the share has no effect on this user.

12.   ☑   **A.** The default Share permission for all shares is Everyone, Full Control.
☒   **B, C,** and **D** are incorrect; they are not the default Share permission.

13.   ☑   **D.** There are only three Share permissions: Full Control, Change, and Read.
☒   **A, B,** and **C** are incorrect because they are not all Share permissions.

14.   ☑   **B.** The correct syntax for the net use command is net use *drive_letter:* *\\server_name\share_name.*
☒   **A, C,** and **D** are incorrect because they do not follow the correct syntax for net use.

15. ☑ **C.** Windows 2000 Pro re-creates an administrative share every time the machine reboots.
    ☒ **A** is incorrect. This will not cause a Blue Screen. **B** is incorrect. You will be able to log on normally. **D** is also incorrect. You may terminate administrative shares temporarily. The next time you reboot, they will be re-created.

16. ☑ **C.** The Account Operators group has several rights, but not the right or permission to create shares.
    ☒ **A, B,** and **D** are incorrect because these groups can create shares.

17. ☑ **A.** The -g switch permits the use of two wildcard characters (* and ?).
    ☒ **B** is incorrect; -v specifies verbose mode. **C** is incorrect; the -n switch cancels autologin upon initial connection. **D** is incorrect; the -i switch turns off prompts during file transfers.

LAB ANSWER

B is the correct answer. Your primary considerations are

1. **Make shared data available to network users both online and offline.** This first one is accomplished. The data is shared and configured for automatic caching for documents. It will be available online and offline.

2. **The offline data should improve the performance of your network.** This one is taken care of by the caching selection. Often-used documents will be cached locally, speeding up the performance of your network.

3. **A large number of users should be able to access the data.** This one is not taken care of. The share is on a 2000 Pro workstation. Remember that there is a hard-coded limit of ten users at one time for a share on 2000 Pro. To allow more concurrent sessions, you need to upgrade to 2000 Server.

Your secondary considerations are

1. **The data should be protected from any access by the Sales group.** The data is protected from access by the Sales group. Although the default Share permission of Everyone Full Control was left on the share, the folder was locked down against Sales access by NTFS permissions.

2. **The Human Resources group requires complete access to the data.** This one was accomplished. The Human Resources group has Full Control to the share, and Full Control for the NTFS permissions. They will have complete access to the data.

Two of the primary considerations were met, and all of the secondary considerations were met.

5

Implementing Printing and File Systems

CERTIFICATION OBJECTIVES

I n this chapter, we'll cover two basic topics in Windows 2000 Professional management: printers and file systems.

We'll look in depth at Professional's network printing abilities, including the new Internet printing features. We'll also look at Professional's integration of printers with Active Directory. We'll walk you through how you can define printers on your system, and take you on a brief tour of how a document goes from electronic form to printed form.

Then we'll take a look at file systems. We'll explain the general notion of a file system, and then get to know the two main file systems that you'll have to deal with: the old FAT and the new NTFS. We'll cover NTFS' special features—disk logging, intelligent disk writing, file attribution, and more—and discuss when you want to use NTFS and when you want to use FAT.

CERTIFICATION OBJECTIVE 5.01

Connecting to Local and Network Print Devices

The most significant changes in configuring and administrating Windows 2000 Professional's printing features come from Professional's bolstered network printing features.

In this section, we'll review basic print administration, walking you through printer installation and configuration, and examine Microsoft's relatively flexible printer management capabilities.

Basic Terms

Microsoft has made the printing process pretty transparent to the average user. However, there's a lot of complexity beneath the surface; you'll need to learn the following basic Microsoft terms in order to get a handle on all the pieces of Windows 2000 Professional's printing infrastructure.

- **Print Device**   What most people casually call a "printer" is called the *print device* in Windows 2000 to differentiate the logical printer from the physical device used to do the printing. The print device is the physical device that outputs data to paper; these range from old-school, dot-matrix printers to speedy laser printers.

- **Printer or Logical printer**   The logical printer is the software interface between the operating system and the actual, physical printer. You can define a logical printer as having a set of print properties, one of which is output to a particular printer or print device; and you can define another logical printer with a different set of properties that outputs to that same print device. When you use the Add Printer Wizard, you are creating a logical printer. The simple term *printer* causes a lot of confusion in the Windows world unless you differentiate between a print device and a logical printer.

- **Print job**   The print job is the source code that contains both the material to be printed and the instructions for printing. When you tell a word processor to print a document, it sends the document and instructions as a *print job* to the logical printer.

- **Printer driver**   The printer driver is the software that serves as the interface between the general print instructions generated by an application and contained in a print job, and the specific inputs required by a particular model of printer from a particular manufacturer. Each particular printer works best with its own specific printer driver, although you may find that generic print drivers or print drivers written for another manufacturer's printer may work satisfactorily. The latter is particularly true when the two printers or print devices are based on the same print engine that is repackaged by different original equipment manufacturers (OEMs). Since a driver is essentially a first-layer interface between an operating system and a printer, there is a different driver for each different combination of operating system and printer.

- **Print processor**   The print processor is a software component that works with the printer driver from a particular manufacturer to translate print jobs into instructions comprehensible to the particular model of print device.

- **Print spooler**   The print spooler is the application that holds print jobs in memory or on disk until it can be printed. This is the component associated with the "print queue" that you get when you double-click the printer icon that appears on your taskbar when you're printing. The print spooler is actually a collection of dynamic link libraries (DLLs). (The term *spool* is actually an acronym for "simultaneous print operations on line.") Print spoolers come in two varieties: local spoolers and network spoolers, called *network print providers*.

- **Print router**   The print router examines a print job to see if it's bound for a local or a network printer, and sends it to the correct spooler.

- **Print server**   The print server is the system that manages printers in a network printing setup.

- **Print monitor**   The print monitor is what actually communicates with the printer; the print monitor transmits data to the printer and, if the printer is connected to the print server with a bidirectional port, the print monitor can receive error reports and supply them to the operating system.

exam
ⓦatch

Microsoft distinguishes between two sorts of print monitors: language monitors and port monitors. A port monitor manages the actual I/O port that connects the computer to the print device; every print device needs a port monitor. Port monitors handle one-way communication from the computer to the print device. A language monitor is only necessary if the print device has bidirectional communications capability. The language monitor can pick up the error messages sent by the print device to the computer, and send them to the spooler.

on the
Ⓙob

What we've given you is the Microsoft standard definitions. Be forewarned; not everybody uses these definitions. Some of your co-workers may use "printer" to refer to the software component (what Microsoft calls the "logical printer") and use "printer" to refer to the hardware component (what Microsoft calls the "print device"). In fact, while, say, the help files associated with Windows 2000 use the "printer/logical printer" distinction, old-school Microsoft-authored architecture and theory use the "printer/print device" distinction. Confusing, eh? We certainly think so.

The Basics of the Printing Process

It'll help in managing printers to understand exactly how a document—say a Word 2000 .DOC file—becomes a set of printed pages.

When a user initiates a print request in Word, Word sends the document as a *print job* to the appropriate *print driver.* In the Microsoft world, applications send documents as a series of calls to an API called the *graphical device interface (GDI).* The driver takes the print job and translates it from GDI calls into model-specific instructions. The driver then sends the translated print job to the *print processor.* The *print processor* arranges the translated print job into routable form and sends the arranged, translated print job to the *print router.* The print router examines the print job, determines whether the print job is bound for a local or network printer, and then sends the print job to either a local spooler or the network spooler. The spooler holds the print jobs in a stack (typically first-in, first-out) and, as the printer becomes freed up, feeds each print job to the *print monitor.* The *print monitor* actually sends the data to the *print device,* and there the data is transformed into ink on paper.

Defining Printers

By this stage in Microsoft's development, printer calls are exceptionally well integrated into Windows-compatible applications. All you have to do in order to create a printer is inform the operating system that there is a print device by a manufacturer and supply the model.

This process of informing your operating system of a printer's existence is called "defining" the printer. You're essentially creating a printer name and then attaching a set of directions to an actual printer.

You can define a local printer—a printer directly connected to your computer. You can also define a networked printer—a printer that is already defined as a local printer on another computer on your local network.

The new printing feature for Windows 2000 is Internet printing. This means that you can define as a printer for your computer a local printer attached to a computer that you connect to through the Internet. This feature expands the realm of "network printing" beyond the local intranet to encompass the whole Web.

CertCam 5-1

Defining a Local Printer

Perform the following steps to define a local printer:

1. Physically attach the printer to your computer. Make sure the printer is plugged in and switched on. Make note of what port the printer is connected to (typically, printers are connected through LPT1).

2. Open up the Printers window. This is accessible, as it always has been for Windows, in the Windows Control Panel. Windows 2000 also puts the Printers window directly in the Settings drop-down menu.

3. Double-click the Add Printer icon, as shown here:

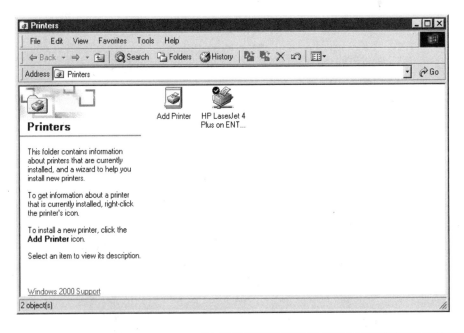

4. The Add Printer Wizard will prompt you to specify whether you're adding a local or network printer, as shown here:

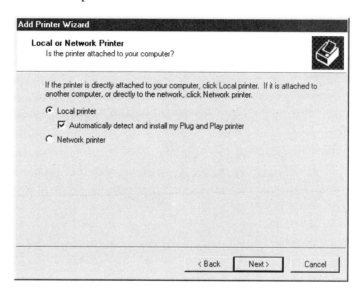

Leave the Local Printer check box selected. Windows will be able to detect virtually all printers manufactured by major makers in the last few years, so, unless you have good reason to suspect otherwise, leave the Automatically Detect And Install My Plug And Play Printer check box selected. Here we've chosen to define a local printer, and allowed Windows to use Plug and Play AutoDetect. Most of the time, AutoDetect works, making your job of configuring printers dramatically easier.

If you choose to skip AutoDetect, you'll be asked to specify a port, as shown here:

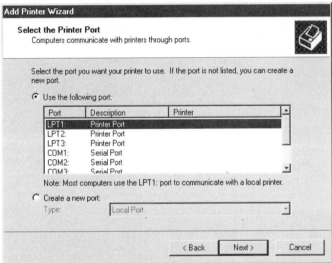

and then select the manufacturer and model, as shown here:

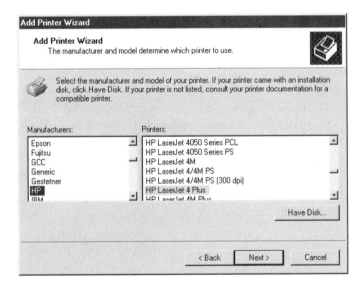

In Windows 2000 Professional, most major drivers are loaded at OS installation. Otherwise, you'll have to supply the driver—the Windows 2000 Professional disk, the disk that came with the printer, or a driver downloaded from the printer manufacturer's site. If you're supplying the driver, click Have Disk and tell it to look in your floppy or hard drive.

If you've told Windows to AutoDetect your printer and it succeeds, you'll see a "Found New Hardware" message, as shown here. Again, for virtually all printers manufactured by major makers, drivers will be included with Windows 2000 Professional.

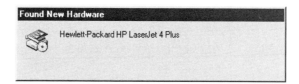

If Windows can't find the driver, or if you told Windows not to auto-detect, you'll have to supply the driver manually. Most likely, the driver will be on the Windows 2000 Professional disk, the printer manufacturer's installation disk, or downloadable from the manufacturer's Web site. Just click Have Disk and point Windows to your floppy or hard drive.

Once you've succeeding in adding a printer, an icon representing that printer will appear in the Printers window.

on the **job**

In the normal course of events, most manufacturers now choose to write their latest drivers for inclusion at the time the Windows 2000 operating system is released. Your chances of finding a driver for a printer that predates the release date are quite good. Microsoft works with literally hundreds of printer manufacturers to make sure that drivers for most of the common printers are included on the distribution disk. That's one reason why the list of supported manufacturers and models is so long in the Add Printer Wizard.

If your printer appeared after the release date of Windows 2000, you might be best served by using the distributed drivers that came with your printer. Over time, chances are that the manufacturer will add that model's driver to the next upgrade of Windows 2000 Professional. If you are having trouble with a printer printing correctly, it is always a good idea to check the manufacturer's Web site to see if an updated driver has been released. A driver on a manufacturer's Web site is likely to be the most up-to-date one that you will be able to find.

For old printers that don't have Windows 2000 drivers, and may not have drivers written, consider using a substitute driver for a similar machine from another vendor. You may also find that a generic driver will allow you to print to a print device, although not all of the features of the printer will be supported.

CertCam 5-2

Defining a Network Printer

Defining a network printer is even easier than defining a local printer. This is because the printer is already defined on another system in the network; that system already knows all the specifications—port, printer type—and already has the printer drivers installed. When you install a network printer, all the information *and* the relevant driver are sent from the network printer's system to your computer.

1. Make sure that the printer you want to connect to is already defined on another network computer.

2. Select Add Printer from the Printers window, as before.

3. At the first prompt, select the Network Printer option, as shown here:

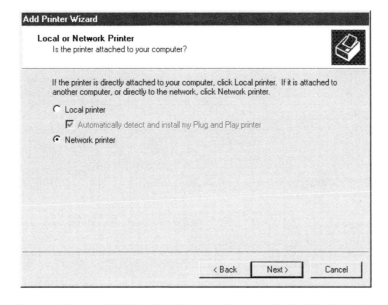

4. You must then specify which printer to install. You can find the printer in Active Directory, if it has an Active Directory. Alternatively, you can simply type in the printer's unique name, in the following format:

*print_server_name**printer_share_name*

Or you can select Type The Printer Name, leave the fill-in box empty, and click Next to browse for your printer, as shown here:

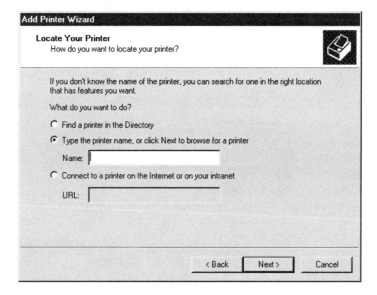

You'd then select the correct network, computer, and printer, as shown here:

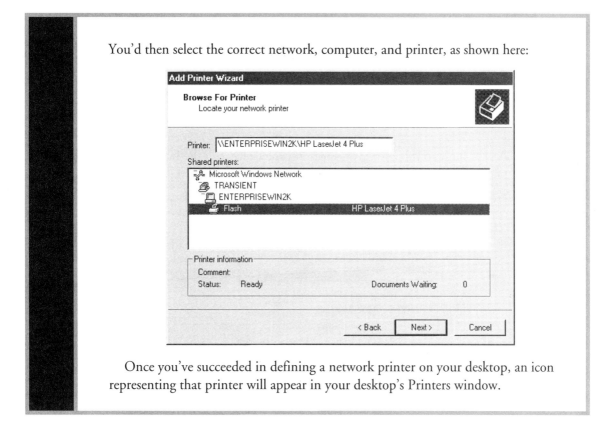

Once you've succeeded in defining a network printer on your desktop, an icon representing that printer will appear in your desktop's Printers window.

CertCam 5-3

Defining an Internet Printer

One of the much-hyped new options in Windows 2000 is the ability for a desktop to print to a properly enabled printer attached to the Internet. (For information on properly enabling a local printer for Internet printing, see the section "Setting Up a Network Printer," later in the chapter.)

1. Find an Internet-enabled printer somewhere on the Internet. There will be a URL associated with this printer. Make a note of this URL.

2. Double-click Add A Printer from the Printers window.

3. Select Network Printers at the first prompt.

4. Select the third option, Internet Printers, and enter the URL, as shown here:

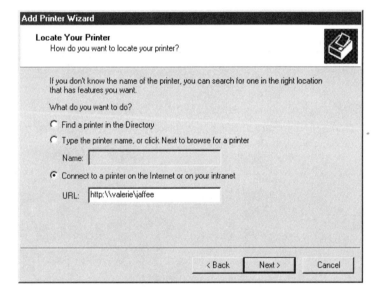

Enter the URL in the following format:

http://*print_server_name*/Printers/*printer_share_name*/.printer

Adding Printers with Active Directory   Microsoft has also added the ability to add a network printer through Active Directory, which occurs almost exactly as adding a network printer does, except that you get AD's searching capabilities, allowing you to search for printers by name, features, and so forth. This is quite useful—you can click Add Printer, specify a local network, and search for a printer that can print high-density color pictures on legal-sized paper. In order to trigger an Active Directory search, just specify that you're adding a network printer, and then select the Entire Directory option in the Find Printers window, shown here:

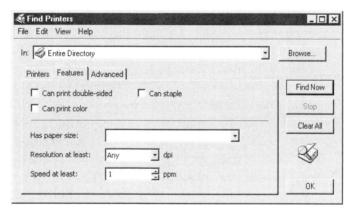

<table>
<tr><td>exam
ⓦatch</td><td>*You can search the Active Directory for printers by name, features, and so forth, at any time by selecting Search For Printers from the Search option in the Start menu.*</td></tr>
</table>

Managing Printers

Printer management in Windows 2000 Professional is deeply coupled with permissions, as set in Active Directory. We'll be covering permissions in more depth in the next section; for right now, what you need to know is that you can always manage local printers, and, if you have been granted permissions in Active Directory, you can manage network printers as fully as if they were local printers.

Setting a Default Printer

From the Printers window, right-click a printer and select Default Printer. This will set this printer as the default printer, and automatically deselect any other printer that previously held this status.

Configuring Printers

To alter the settings on a specific printer, you need to access the printer's Properties menu from your desktop. Open up the Printers window, right-click on the printer you want to configure, and select Properties.

Most of the functionality built into a printer's Properties is fairly intuitive. Some things you should note:

Under the General tab, you'll have control over many of the options concerning how the printer actually prints documents—which paper trays the printer will draw from and how pages appear on each page. Click Printing Preferences at the bottom of the window; you'll get the Printing Preferences window, where you'll have control over elementary printing features. Click Advanced at the bottom of this window, and you'll get the most complete control, through the Advanced options screen, shown in Figure 5-1.

You'll note that you can adjust the same set of options from any office productivity application. From a Microsoft productivity application, like Word 2000, you can access windows that look *precisely* like the Printing Preferences and Advanced Options windows, and which give you control over the same settings. However, when you alter options from within an application, your changes apply only to the particular session you're in. This means if you close your application and reopen the same document, the Printing Preferences will have reset to their default settings. The only way to apply universal, permanent changes—that is, to change the defaults themselves—is through the Printing Preferences window as accessed through the Printers window.

on the job

Altering the timeout settings for a printer is a non-intuitive process. Open the printer's Properties page from the Printers window and go to the Ports tab. Select the port that the printer is connected through and click Configure Port. The timeout setting is here, labeled Transmission Retry.

FIGURE 5-1

The Advanced
options screen

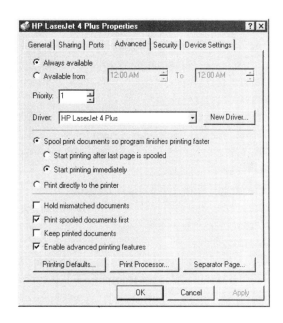

If you find yourself switching settings for a particular application often, you can get around this problem by creating another printer with different settings. Then whenever you want to print with those settings, print to that logical printer. This advice about creating logical printers applies to a whole set of problems you encounter in Windows 2000, such as defining different access privileges to printers, different allowed schedules, and so forth.

Managing Print Jobs

The whole journey through drivers, spoolers, and monitors is invisible for most users. Most of the user's interaction with the printer is through the *print queue*, the list of print jobs either being printed or waiting to be printed.

You can access the print queue in two ways. First, you can double-click the printer in the Printers window; second, whenever there is anything in the printer queue, a printer icon will appear on your taskbar, next to the clock in the Status tray.

If you're printing to a network printer and the printer icon isn't popping up on your taskbar when you're printing, you don't have permission to issue commands to the network printer.

You can interact with the print queue in two ways: by issuing *general* commands to the print queue, affecting all documents in the queue; or by issuing *specific* commands to individual print jobs in the queue.

In order to issue general commands, right-click the printer icon in the Printers window or your taskbar.

In order to issue specific commands, double-click the printer icon. This will open the print queue window, as shown in Figure 5-2. Right-click the print job you want to manage.

You can cancel, pause, and resume all print jobs with a general command, or one print job with a specific command. By selecting the Properties menu from the shortcut menu of either the printer or the print job, you can also change printing preferences—such as print quality and paper sourcing—globally or for one specific print job.

You can also affect the order in which print jobs will be processed. Simply right-click a particular print job and select Properties. On the print job Properties window, shown in Figure 5-3, you can click and drag the Priority slider. Documents with higher priority will be printed first. Unless a print job is underway, you can click and drag that print job up and down in the print order in the print queue dialog box.

Faxing Capabilities

Microsoft has integrated faxing into its printing capabilities. This means that you can send a document as a fax as easily as you can print the document.

We won't go into too much depth for the fax service since almost all of the aspects of the fax service are identical to the printing service (e.g., there is a fax monitor and a fax queue).

FIGURE 5-2

The print queue for a specific printer shows all the print jobs currently printing or pending for a printer

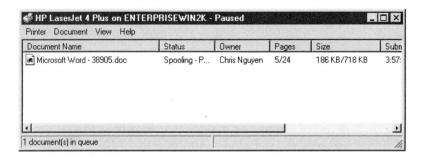

FIGURE 5-3

The print job
Properties menu

In order to set up a fax device like a fax modem, open up Fax from the Control Panel. On the Advanced Options tab, click Add A Fax Printer. Any object capable of sending fax data, like a fax modem, can act as a Fax Printer. Microsoft calls these devices Fax Printers because they show up in the same places as printers and you can send documents to be faxed in the same manner as you send them to be printed.

To fax a document, go through the same steps as you would in printing that document. For example, if you wanted to fax a Word document, you would simply click File, Print. Instead of selecting a conventional printer, you would select a Fax Printer.

You can install Fax Printers, and manipulate Fax Printer properties just as you would with conventional printers. The difference is that when you send a document to be faxed, you go through a Fax Wizard. It will ask you to specify the phone number of the person you want to send the fax to and will also generate a fax cover page.

Setting Up a Network Printer

Initially setting up a local printer as a network printer for other systems is quite easy.

Share a Printer

Here are the steps to follow to allow for a shared printer.

1. Open up the Printers window from the Control Panel or the Settings drop-down menu.

2. Right-click the printer you want to share; select Properties.

3. Click the Sharing tab; select Share As: and enter a share same, which is how the printer will appear on the network:

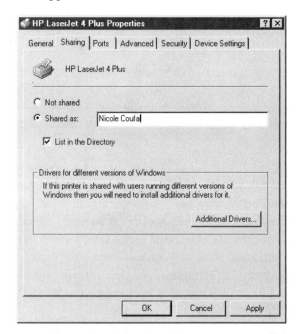

4. Leave List In The Directory selected; this will automatically create an Active Directory object associated with this printer.

5. Add additional drivers. If you're networking your printer in a homogenous Windows 2000 environment, this step is unnecessary. If, however, there are non-Windows 2000 machines in your network, you'll need to load the drivers for those machines. Remember, if another machine tries to contact your system and print using your local printer, it'll need to get the drivers for your particular kind of printer. If that machine isn't a Windows 2000 machine, then it will need different drivers from those loaded onto the Windows 2000 machine. Click Additional Drivers and select all the other sorts of operating systems in your network. Windows will prompt you for disks with these drivers.

exam
ⓦatch

Windows 2000 puts the print drivers in [%system_root%]\ System32\Spool\Drivers, which is shared as Print$. When other computers want to use your local printer as a network printer, they search for the print drivers in \\your_system_name\\Print$.

Using Permissions to Control Access to Printers

Once you share a printer, you must pay attention to the permissions settings for that printer. These govern who can use the printer to print documents and, more importantly, who can change the settings in that printer's Properties and who can interact with that printer's print queue. From Windows 2000 Professional, you can set printer permissions in terms of groups and users as defined in Active Directory through Windows 2000 Server. In order to modify printer permissions, you must have adequate permission yourself. The particular permissions will depend on how Active Directory is set up; with AD's default settings, you can't modify permissions on network printers unless you are an administrator or a member of the Server Operator or Printer Operator group.

To modify permissions for a given printer, right-click that printer in the Printers window and select the Properties command. Click the Security tab; you'll get the Security window, as shown in Figure 5-4. Add and Remove let you add and remove groups and users from the permissions pane.

The Permissions settings in the initial Security dialog box are fairly obvious in function. Allowing a group to Print means that members of that group can print documents on the printer in question. Allowing a group to Manage Printers allows that group access to the Printer Preferences for this printer, and allowing a group to Manage Documents allows that group to interact with this printer's print queue.

Clicking Advanced and selecting the Permissions tab will give you access to a list of all the groups that have any Permission for this printer. When you open up a particular group, you'll be able to set more advanced options (provided you have

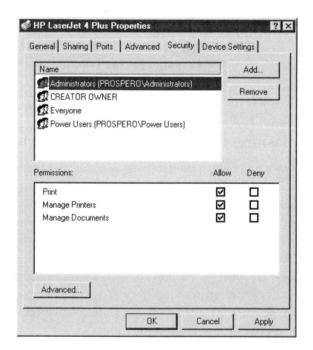

FIGURE 5-4

Security settings of permissions to control who can print to or manage the printer the proper permission), as shown in Figure 5-5. These are the meta-permissions; that is, you can set whether or not a group or user has permission to view and modify permissions, or to take ownership of the printer.

If neither Allow nor Deny is selected for a particular permission, then the group will inherit its permissions status through the Active Directory hierarchy. If the group has no inherited status for this particular permission, Windows will default that group to Deny.

Clicking Advanced and selecting the Auditing tab will allow you to set auditing. You set auditing by group, specifying what sorts of activities you want logged, and whether you want to log successes, failures, or both for each logged activity. How logging proceeds depends on auditing settings.

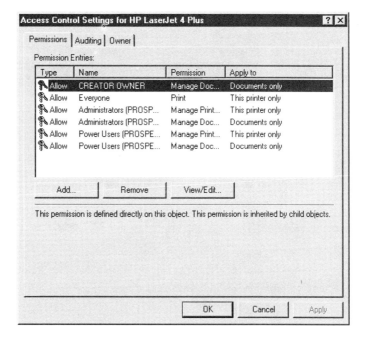

FIGURE 5-5

Advanced security options let you set meta-permissions

SCENARIO & SOLUTION

I plugged in my printer, but I can't print.	Use the Add Printer Wizard, which can be found by going to Start and then Printers. The Add Printer icon opens the wizard.
I upgraded from Windows 95 to Windows 2000; now my printer doesn't work.	You probably need to update the drivers; Windows 95 and Windows 2000 need different drivers to communicate to the same printer. For most major manufacturers, Windows 2000 will automatically update the drivers; but if Microsoft didn't put the new drivers on the Windows 2000 Professional disk, you'll have to hunt them down yourself.
I'm printing a document to a network printer that I need to cancel, but there's no printer icon on my taskbar, and Windows won't let me modify the printer queue.	You don't have permission to manage this printer. You need to grant this permission by joining a group like Print Operators with this permission.
Other Windows 2000 systems are having no problem defining my printer as a network printer, but Windows 98 systems and UNIX systems can't.	You need to load drivers onto your system for all possible systems that will use this printer.

CERTIFICATION OBJECTIVE 5.02

Configuring and Managing File Systems

One of the most critical decisions you can make in the Windows 2000 setup process is that of which file system to use. FAT and its updated brethren, FAT32, are widely used across almost all major operating systems; NTFS lends a lot of power to Windows NT and 2000 systems, with larger maximum partitions, greater efficiency, and greatly increased security capabilities.

Partitioning Basics

When you first get a hard drive that is not specially prepared for Windows 2000 Professional, your computer's BIOS will recognize the drive as unformatted. You must format the disk either in its entirety or in part, which is a process by which

Windows 2000 writes a signature to the boot sector of the disk, and magnetic rings are drawn in a set of successively bigger circles on each of the disks contained in a hard drive. Drives are also marked with lines along various diameters of the disks, creating cylindrical areas of circular tracks called *sectors*.

Sectors are grouped together into *clusters* (also called *allocation units*), which are the smallest logical areas of a disk that can be addressed. Depending upon the number of clusters you designate by varying cluster size, you can raise or lower the effective capacity of the disk, performance, and the amount of fragmentation you typically see. Sectors are designated by the geometry of the disk, and set by the manufacturer—in the U.S., manufacturers typically use 512-byte sectors. Based on that size, an 8-sector cluster would contain 4KB of data. When a file is written to a cluster and that file is smaller than the cluster size, disk space is wasted. Compression schemes often rewrite the data in a continuous fashion to remove empty space.

Clusters can vary in size based on your formatting instructions. Clusters make a disk more granular and offer less overhead for the operating system to manage. Clusters are arranged in circular tracks on your disk, and when it is possible, Windows 2000 attempts to write files in contiguous clusters so that the file can be read in a single pass of the magnetic head. Often, especially as a disk fills, there isn't room to write some files in contiguous clusters, so files get written in multiple locations, or fragmented. A defragmenter or defrag utility can rewrite the disk, putting files together. Windows 2000 contains a Disk Defragmenter in the Computer Management section of the MMC.

Depending upon the capacity of the drive and other factors such as speed, manufacturers may use one or more disks in a disk drive. You are given the opportunity to format a drive, in part or entirely during your installation of Windows 2000 Professional. You can also use the Storage portion of the Computer Management MMC snap-in to format (and partition) portions of a disk after installation.

Once you format a disk or portion of the disk, you can set aside all or part of the formatted space as a *partition*. A partition is a part of your hard drive that is a recognizable volume (or part of a volume) to an operating system. Partitions act like individual hard drives, and are typically assigned a drive letter by the operating system. The Master Boot Record (MBR), which is the first portion of a hard drive, contains the BIOS bootstrap routine, low-level code that directs the loading of the operating system onto the partition that is the active one containing the operating system you wish to boot to. A partition table on the disk contains an index of partitions in the bootstrap routine. Each partition has its own Partition Boot Sector with information about the file system and some bootstrap code on it that helps load the file system.

With Windows 2000, partitions can be combined into volumes (logical volumes) or be volumes by themselves. Volumes in Windows 2000 can now span discontinuous partitions on the same drive, or span two or more drives.

Each partition is formatted in a particular way with its own file system; each partition contains its own method for finding and reading files stored on it. File systems can be created only within a partition. Free space or an unformatted portion of your drive(s) cannot contain a file system. A commonly used file system that was used with Microsoft DOS, Windows 3.1, and Windows 95 is the file allocation table, or FAT file system. A FAT is a table of contents or map that is contained in the first few clusters of a volume and tells the operating system which sectors particular files are located on. Each cluster contains an entry in the FAT telling what it contains and where it's located. FAT16 allows filenames of eight characters, a period, and a three-letter extension. Files in the FAT map are indexed in the directory records. FAT32 retains the basic design of a cluster map and directory indexing from FAT16. The NTFS file system uses a Master File Table (MFT) system, which is an object-oriented hierarchical database.

Both FAT and MFT organize the file system into a hierarchy of filenames called Directories (or folders) using an index. NTFS also supports the indexing of attributes of an MFT database. Files and directories in the MFT appear as records in the database that contain a description of their contents. Entries in an MFT contain more information than those in a FAT and can indexed in more ways than by filename.

You can convert from FAT to FAT32 (see "Convert from One File System to Another," later in the chapter). You can also convert from FAT or FAT32 to NTFS. You cannot convert back from NTFS to FAT; doing so requires reformatting your disk and restoring your data from a backup. You should always back up before conversion in case the conversion fails. To convert between file systems you can go to the Command Prompt and use the CONVERT command. The complete syntax for the CONVERT command may be found in "Convert from One File System to Another" later in this chapter. With the advent of Windows 98, Microsoft had moved its consumer operating system from a 16-bit version of its FAT file system (FAT16, or simply plain FAT) to a 32-bit version of FAT called FAT32. With the Windows 2000 operating system, Microsoft began offering the NTFS5 file system, which is a 64-bit file system. (Remember that initially, Windows 2000 was going to be called Windows NT 5.0, before the marketers took over.) Table 5-1 shows the current state of things with various versions of Windows. R stands for read, W for write, and U stands for unsupported.

FAT32 differs from FAT16 in several significant respects. FAT32 supports larger drive or partition sizes, and smaller file clusters, and has some additional performance optimization features. NTFS supports even larger partitions and drives than FAT32 and small cluster sizes. NTFS goes beyond FAT32 by offering even larger volume sizes, enhanced security features, compression, and logging capabilities. In the next sections, we describe the advantages and disadvantages of using FAT32 versus NTFS on Windows 2000 Professional. Under Windows 2000, a FAT16 file system can grow to 4GB (2^{16} sectors or 64KB theoretically) in size; FAT32 supports 32GB (2^{32} sectors or 2 terabytes—TB, theoretically); and NTFS5 supports 2TB of data (2^{64} sectors or 16 exabytes theoretically). Windows 9x, NT, and 2000 also support the CD-ROM file system, or CDFS. CDFS supports read-only CD-ROM drives and the DVD format. FAT reaches larger allowed sizes by supporting larger cluster sizes. However, once a FAT cluster size exceeds 32KB, it cannot be read by Windows 95 systems; therefore, Windows 9x systems can only access FAT volumes 2GB in size on a Windows 2000 disk.

TABLE 5-1   Disk Partitions and Windows Versions

Windows Version	FAT16	FAT32	NTFS
Windows 3.1	RW	U	U
Windows 95	RW	U	U
Windows 95b	RW	RW	U
Windows 98	RW	RW	U
Windows NT 4.0	RW	U	RW
Windows 2000	RW	RW	RW

FROM THE CLASSROOM

Terminology Distinctions

Many users throw around certain terms, like *disk, drive, volume,* and *partition,* interchangeably. There are actually some fine distinctions.

A *partition* is a chunk of disk space that is under the reign of a single file system; that is, bound by one particular file allocation table.

A *volume* is a chunk of disk space that has been partitioned. "Volume" and "partition" are virtually synonymous.

A *disk* is a physical creature; one individual disk is an actual physical hard drive or floppy disk that you can yank out of the box or drive. In Windows 2000, hard disks are referred to by number—Disk 0, Disk 1, and so on.

A *logical drive* is a logical creature. When I speak of a "drive," I mean a logical drive, not a

hard drive. You can divide a 10GB disk into a single 10GB drive, or two 5GB drives, and so forth. In Windows 2000, drives are referred to by letter—C: drive, D: drive, and so on. When you take a chunk of disk space and partition it, making it into a volume, and assign a drive letter to it, you've made a logical drive.

Previously, *logical drive* was pretty much synonymous with "volume." When you divided a physical disk into lots of volumes, each one had its own drive letter. However, Windows 2000 lets you assign a volume to a folder on another volume, letting a logical drive contain many volumes. That makes it important for us to distinguish between volumes.

—Thi Nguyen

Selecting a File System

Many people are tempted to go straight for NTFS. You should consider carefully whether you are willing to sacrifice certain levels of interoperability for NTFS; remember, you can easily convert a FAT system to NTFS, but going the other way requires reformatting the partition.

FAT

FAT is the original file system; Microsoft adapted it from the UNIX file system way back in the early days of their existence. FAT is highly inefficient spacewise and timewise, and pretty stupid to boot. It also can't deal with partitions larger than 4GB. Keep in mind again that Windows 9*x* systems will only be able to read from 2GB FAT partitions.

FAT was originally conceived back when hard drives were quite small; by this time you're getting into gigabyte hard drives, FAT is using huge clusters. For example, for a partition at 2,048GB, FAT uses clusters that are 65,536 bytes large. Remember that a cluster has to be assigned to one file at a time. That means that, if you have a 10-byte file (be it a tiny .ini file or the tail end of a large file), FAT will use a whole cluster to store it, wasting 65,526 bytes.

FAT also puts the allocation table—the table of contents—at the start of a disk volume. This means that the head must constantly move back to the beginning of the disk volume to consult the allocation table, making FAT quite slow when used for large partitions. FAT also just drops files anywhere, making no attempt to minimize disk fragmentation—that is, to write single files to sectors that are physically close together. Again the drive head is forced to jump around on the disk, slowing disk access.

Finally, FAT is minimally secure. If you can get to the DOS prompt, say by booting up a system with a boot disk, you can have full and unrestricted access to any files stored under FAT.

FAT comes in two varieties, FAT16 and FAT32. The number refers to the allocation scheme—FAT16 uses a 16-bit allocation scheme and FAT32 uses a 32-bit scheme. FAT16 is supported by Windows 95/98, Windows NT, and Windows 2000; FAT 32 is supported by Windows 95/98 and 2000, but not by NT.

NTFS

NTFS stands for New Technology File System, which was created expressly for Windows NT, and now, Windows 2000. NTFS includes a tremendous number of improvements from FAT. This includes intelligent disk writing, a disk logging system to assist in postcrash system recovery, and a powerful and extensible file attribute system.

- **Disk writing**   NTFS pays attention to the physical contiguity of sectors when writing single files. It also places small files near its allocation table (which it calls the Master File Table [MFT]), so the traverse time for the disk head from MFT to file is minimal. In fact, for data smaller than 2KB, NTFS will put the file directly in the MFT itself.

- ■ **Disk logging**   NTFS includes a disk-logging system that stores information critical to the functioning of the file system, for example, name changes and changes to the arrangement of directories and folders. This allows NTFS to go back after a system crash and fix crash-related damage.

- ■ **File attributes**   NTFS has a highly flexible file attribute system. This allows, among other things, permissions setting on files, folders, and associated objects such as printers. All of Windows 2000's permissions setting capabilities simply disappear when you're using FAT. NTFS also allows custom-defined file attributes, which some third-party vendors are already beginning to make use of.

- ■ **More**   NTFS also allows built-in encryption and compression of files, folders, or whole partitions.

exam
ⓦatch

With Windows 2000, you can't both encrypt and compress—it's either one or the other.

Finally, NTFS' designers anticipated rapid technology change. The maximum NTFS partition size is 2 *exabytes*—that is, something like 17 *billion* gigabytes. (If it gives you any idea, one IBM database exec once estimated to us that the world's total paper-and-magnetic-media store probably amounted to about 4 exabytes of data.)

exam
ⓦatch

Windows 2000 integrates all this NTFS functionality right into the shortcut menus and Properties windows for disks, folders, and files. When you right-click a file, folder, or drive, you'll see a Compress or Uncompress selection right there. If you select Properties from the drop-down menu, you'll see a set of tabs, including a Security tab, where you set permissions. Tabs and buttons just magically appear when the object you're addressing is on an NTFS drive. If you can't find the Security tab, or the Compress or Uncompress button, then the object you're addressing is on a FAT drive.

Why Ever Use FAT at All?

Most likely, you'll be using NTFS for your system. Why even think about FAT?

FAT is important in several cases. First, if you're setting up a dual-boot system, many operating systems can't read NTFS. Windows 98, for example, won't be able to read any files on an NTFS partition.

Second, NTFS is terrible for small disk volumes. FAT's overhead problems only start to show their head above 500MB partitions. What's more, NTFS uses a fair amount of space to just set up its basic functionality. This means that NTFS consumes a proportionally high amount of disk space below 500MB, and a proportionally gargantuan amount of disk space below 200MB. Many report that NTFS's efficiency features don't particularly show their head until you're using partitions.

exam
ⓦatch

Microsoft recommends using FAT for partitions 2GB and smaller.

on the
ⓙob

Frequently, the ideal solution is to partition your hard drive space into different logical drives and make one NTFS and another FAT32, with the system files on the NTFS drive. This lets you use the full range of security features for files that need it, while at the same time having a space to put files for full heterogeneous interoperability. But remember that if you have a dual-boot system between an NTFS-enabled system like Windows 2000 Professional and an NTFS-illiterate system like Windows 98, when you boot up in Windows 98, you won't be able to read any of the files on the NTFS drive.

Now that we've gone through the difference between FAT and NTFS, we'll run through a few basic scenarios, deciding which choice is better given a particular situation.

SCENARIO & SOLUTION	
I need to set permissions on my files using Active Directory.	Choose NTFS for your hard drive. This is true for anything dealing with permissions.
My hard drive is 90MB.	Choose FAT for your hard drive. NTFS will waste too much space setting itself up.
My hard drive is 2GB.	You should probably choose NTFS. FAT can handle this, but is inefficient; use FAT only if you have a very good reason, like you double-boot into UNIX.
My hard drive is 40GB, and I want to divide it into two equal partitions.	Choose NTFS for your hard drive. FAT can't handle 20GB partitions.
I need to set permissions for my printers.	Choose NTFS for your hard drive. Windows 2000 handles permissions for printers as file attributes, so you can't set permissions unless your system folders are on an NTFS drive.

Convert from One File System to Another

File systems are initially specified during volume partitioning. You can trigger the partitioning process by typing **FDISK** at the DOS prompt; the partitioning process also triggers when you install Windows 2000. If you've got a fresh hard drive, you'll need to set partitions, assign drive letters to these partitions, and choose a file system for each.

If you have a hard drive that already has some data on it, things get a little more complicated. If you remove a partition, thus removing the file system, you've killed the allocation table for all the files on that partition. Your system will no longer know where to look for each file. All the files on that partition are lost to all but the most radical data recovery operations.

If your hard drive is currently formatted in FAT, you can actually convert from FAT to NTFS. This process changes the file system while leaving files intact and accessible. This is most easily accomplished through an entry at the command line. From the Start menu, open the Accessories menu and select Command Prompt. At the prompt, type

CONVERT [*drive:*] /FS:NTFS [/v]

If convert can't lock the drive—probably because files on that disk are in use—it'll offer to schedule the conversion for the next time the computer restarts. Adding the /v parameter puts CONVERT into verbose mode, displaying many more details of the conversion process.

It's impossible, however, to convert from NTFS to FAT. The only way to get a volume from NTFS to FAT is to back up all the data on the drive, and reformat the drive into NTFS.

CertCam 5-5

EXERCISE 5-5

Changing a Drive from NTFS to FAT

Do the following to reformat a NTFS-formatted drive to a FAT format.

1. Back up all the contents of drive X:.

2. Select Control Panel | Administrative Tools | Computer Management. The Computer Management window is shown here:

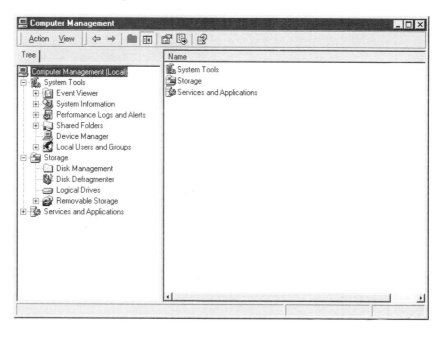

3. You then want to select Disk Management from the Storage folder in the left-hand pane of the Computer Management window. This will open Computer Management's Disk Management pane, as shown here:

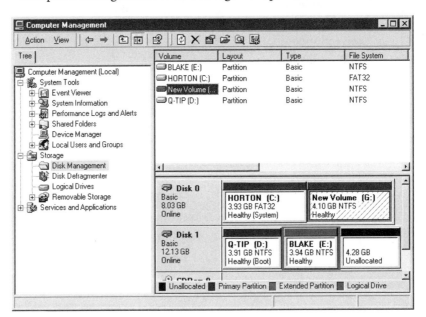

4. Right-click the FAT drive you want to convert, and select Format. When the wizard prompts you for a file system, select NTFS, as shown here:

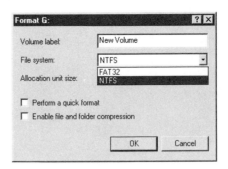

5. Restore the data from the backup to drive X:.

SCENARIO & SOLUTION

My G: drive is in FAT and I want it in NTFS.	Go to the command prompt and type **convert G: /fs:ntfs**.
My G: drive is in NTFS and I want it in FAT.	Back up all the contents of G:. Go to the Disk Manager utility, reformat G: into FAT, and restore the data from the backup.
My entire 4GB hard drive is in FAT. I need it to be half in FAT and half in NTFS.	There is no elegant solution to this scenario. Back up all the data, remove the partition, repartition the drive space into two separate partitions, and format one into FAT and the other into NTFS.

Loving Your Disk Management

Disk Management is where you'll do all your file system configuration and management. You've already seen Disk Management in action in the last section, reformatting a drive into FAT.

exam

ⓦatch *Disk Management, along with a few other tools adjacent to it in Computer Management, covers all the functionality in Windows 2000 that Disk Administrator and the command-line FDISK command did in NT.*

You can do all sorts of things from Disk Manager. Take a look at my system, shown in the Disk Management view in Figure 5-6. You'll see that I have two physical hard drives, known as Disk 0 and Disk 1, which have been partitioned into four logical drives: two logical drives, the C: drive and the G: drive, in Disk 0; and two logical drives, D: and E:, in Disk 1. Each logical drive is also displayed with certain information, including size, file system, health, and a note if the drive contains the system or boot files.

exam

ⓦatch *In Disk Management, physical drives are referred to by number, and logical drives by letter.*

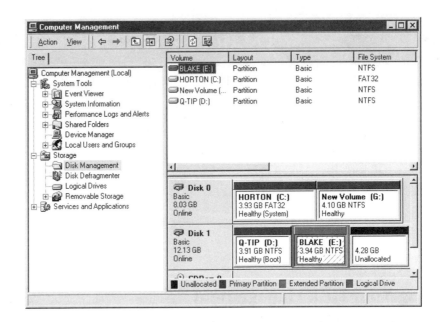

Creating a
partition in the
unallocated space
on Disk 0

You'll notice in Figure 5-6 that I've right-clicked the unallocated space in Disk 0 and selected Create Partition—I'm about to create a fourth logical drive. This is how you interact with Disk Manager. Right-click the image of any logical drive or unallocated space. If you click an unallocated space, you can select Create Partition and partition some or all of the unallocated space. If you right-click a logical drive, you're presented with the option of deleting, reformatting, or reassigning drive letters.

Partitioning

Partitioning is the process that takes unallocated disk space and transforms it into distinct volumes by attaching a file system to the designated disk space. Traditionally, each volume appears as a logical drive.

exam
ⓦatch

You can only partition unallocated space. If a space is already partitioned, you need to delete the partition and create new partitions. This, of course, will destroy any data on the partition.

To partition an unallocated space, right-click that space and select Create Partition. This fires up the Create Partition Wizard.

This wizard will prompt you for some specifications. You'll want to create a primary partition if you're creating the first partition on a disk, and an extended partition for each additional partition on the disk. You'll also choose a size—FAT partitions have an upper bound of 4GB.

You have one additional option if you're creating a primary partition. The wizard will offer to let you "Mount this volume at an empty folder that supports drive paths." At this point, you have to choose an empty, already existing folder on one of your drives. Instead of the new partition appearing as a new drive, it will appear as a folder inside an existing NTFS drive. This is a great new feature, which is part of what Microsoft calls "reparse point technology." It means that you use many physical disks but have only a few drive letters. Let's say we have one 20GB physical disk—Disk 0. You've partitioned it into one NTFS drive—C:. You add another 20GB physical disk—Disk 1. Traditionally, you'd have to partition Disk 1 into another logical drive. However, in Windows 2000, you can partition Disk 1 into a single volume and mount that volume to a folder on C:. That means that you have two physical disks, each 20GB, and *one 40GB logical drive.* Whenever the OS makes a call to that folder, Windows looks on Disk 1.

CERTIFICATION SUMMARY

We've covered two basics of Windows 2000 Professional operation—connecting to print devices, and configuring and managing file systems.

Print devices are pretty simple concepts. Make sure you understand the path from application to printed paper. An application sends a document to be printed as a set of instructions, called a *print job.* Initially, the print job is in the form of a set of calls to the GDI API. These are interpreted by the driver, and then passed to the processor and router, before it ends up in the print queue, held in an application called a *spooler.* At the appropriate time, the spooler sends the print job the print monitor, which communicates with the printer itself. Make sure you understand how to configure the printer. Be sure to remember the ability to publish and search for printers in the Active Directory; Microsoft will likely hit on many of the new AD features in the exam.

File systems are much more theoretical affairs. Make sure you understand what a file system is, and how it acts as the interface between operating system and physical disk. Understand FAT, the problems of FAT—its inefficiencies and its lack of scalability. Make sure you know the features of NTFS, which Microsoft is sure to ask about—its high maximum partition size; its disk logging features; its compression and encryption features; and, most importantly, its ability to contain file attributes, essential to all the permission setting at the heart of Windows 2000 security.

✓ TWO-MINUTE DRILL

Connecting to Local and Network Print Devices

❑ Applications send documents to be printed as a set of calls to the GDI API; they are interpreted by a driver into a form comprehensible to the particular printer.

❑ Since drivers are translators, every pairing of a particular operating system and a particular model of printer demands its own distinct driver.

❑ Print jobs are held in a queue in the *print spooler*, where they are accessible and managed.

❑ Printers, whether local or networked, must be *defined* locally before local applications can print to them.

❑ Windows 2000 allows Internet printers to be defined locally.

❑ Windows 2000 allows networked printers to be located through their Active Directory entries. This lets users search for printers by workgroup; name; and features, such as color printing or automatic stapling.

❑ When system A defines system B's printer as a network printer, system A will download printer drivers from system B. This means that if you're making your printer a network printer, you have to load all the drivers for every system that might define your printer.

Configuring and Managing File Systems

❑ A file system is a way of writing files to a hard drive; a file system knows where a file is located *physically* on the disk.

❑ FAT is the universal file system; every operating system can read a FAT drive.

❑ NTFS is the NT operating system; only Windows NT and 2000 know how to read NTFS.

❑ FAT's maximum partition size is 4GB; NTFS' is 2 *exabytes*—17 billion times larger.

❑ Microsoft recommends FAT for creating partitions 2GB and smaller.

❑ NTFS writes to disk intelligently, reducing drive head travel time.

❑ NTFS contains disk-logging features, which make disk recovery radically better.

❑ NTFS allows compression and encryption of files and folders, though not at the same time.

❑ NTFS allows file attributes such as permissions. Applications can create custom attributes.

❑ All partitioning, formatting, and the like, formerly done from Disk Administrator, is, in Windows 2000, done from the Disk Management pane of the Computer Management window, accessible from the Administrative Tools window in the Control Panel.

SELF TEST

The following questions will help you measure your understanding of the material presented in this chapter. Read all of the choices carefully, as there may be more than one correct answer. Choose all correct answers for each question.

Connecting to Local and Network Print Devices

1. You've shared your local printer as a network printer. You need to

   A. Load drivers individually onto every computer that will define your printer.

   B. Load drivers onto your computer for every computer that will define your printer.

   C. Load drivers onto Active Directory.

   D. Load URLs to driver manufacturer's driver download page onto Active Directory.

2. NTFS is

   A. A file system specifically for servers

   B. A file system specifically for networked computers (clients and servers)

   C. A file system specifically for Microsoft Windows 9.*x*

   D. A file system specifically for Windows NT and 2000

3. If you can't set permissions on a printer, the problem could be

   A. System files aren't on NTFS.

   B. Permissions for printers are turned off in Active Directory.

   C. You don't have permission to set printer permissions.

   D. A and B.

   E. A and C.

   F. All of the above.

4. To cancel a particular print job, you must

   A. Open the print queue, right-click the print-job, and select Cancel.

   B. Open the originating document, find Print Properties, and select Cancel.

   C. Open the Printers window, right-click the printer, and select Cancel All Documents.

   D. Open the Printers window, right-click the printer, select Documents, select the print job, and press DELETE.

5. The correct path from document to printer is

A. Application, monitor, driver, processor, router, spooler, printer

B. Application, driver, processor, router, spooler, monitor, printer

C. Application, router, processor, spooler, monitor, driver, printer

D. Application, spooler, monitor, processor, driver, router, printer

Configuring and Managing File Systems

6. According to Microsoft, you should use FAT for a volume

A. If the volume is 2GB or below

B. If the volume is 4GB or above

C. If the volume is to contain third-party encrypted materials

D. If the volume is on a SCSI hard drive

7. To partition an unallocated space in Windows 2000 Professional, use

A. Partition Management

B. CONVERT

C. Disk Administrator

D. Disk Management

8. To create a double-boot system with Windows 2000 Professional and Windows 98, given that you want to have high security with permissions for half your files, you want to

A. Put all your drives in FAT.

B. Put all your drives in NTFS.

C. Put some drives in FAT and some drives in NTFS, with the secure files on NTFS.

D. Put some drives in FAT and some drives in NTFS, with the secure files on FAT.

9. To change a hard disk from NTFS to FAT, preserving all the files,

A. It's impossible.

B. Type **CONVERT** *drive_letter:*/**ntfs:fat** at the command line.

C. Back up all the files on the disk, reformat all the drives on the disk into FAT, and restore the files.

D. Delete the partition and repartition into FAT.

10. Once you've published a printer in Active Directory, you can

    A. Search for printers via features, etc., when adding a printer.

    B. Search for printers via features, etc., when printing from a productivity application.

    C. Set up your printer as an Internet printer.

    D. Set up your printer as a network printer.

11. NTFS is more efficient than FAT at large volumes for all of the following reasons except

    A. FAT's allocation table stores addresses in a long format.

    B. FAT's clusters grow in direct proportion to the volume, making small files use up lots of disk space.

    C. NTFS writes to disk intelligently, reducing file fragmentation.

    D. NTFS writes to disk intelligently, putting small files near the Master File System.

12. A print spooler is

    A. The part of the printer that holds the ink

    B. The software application that sends the print job to the printer physically

    C. The software application that takes the print job from the driver and sends it to the router

    D. The software application that holds the print job in a queue before sending it to the print monitor

13. To set up your printer as a network printer,

    A. You must publish it in Active Directory.

    B. You must attach it to a server and publish it in Active Directory.

    C. You must define the printer as a network printer on a server.

    D. You must turn on Sharing from the Properties menu.

14. To list a printer in Active Directory, you must

    A. Select Add Printer from the Active Directory management console.

    B. Right-click Properties, select the Active Directory tab, and select Publish.

    C. Right-click Properties, select the Sharing tab, and select List In Directory.

    D. While running the Add Printer Wizard, select the Publish In Active Directory option.

15. There is a print driver

A. For every individual printer a manufacturer makes

B. For every model of printer a manufacturer makes

C. For every pairing of a model of printer and an operating system

D. For every pairing of a model of printer and an application vendor

16. NTFS has all of the following features, which FAT does not, except for

   A. Intelligent disk writing, to reduce drive-head transit times

   B. File attribution, for things such as permissions

   C. File logging, for crash recovery

   D. Simultaneous compression and encryption capability

17. When you're mounting a volume to a folder on your C: drive, you're

   A. Adding space from another physical disk to the existing logical C: drive

   B. Adding all the contents of that volume and copying them to the folder and, therefore, to the C: drive

   C. Creating a new logical drive, with the contents of that folder transferred to the drive

   D. Repartitioning C: into two logical drives, one called C:, the other named as you choose

18. If you can't see the Permissions tab from the Properties drop-down menu of a file,

   A. In Active Directory, you don't have permission to set permissions.

   B. You haven't turned on permissions from the Disk Management pane.

   C. The file is not shared to the network.

   D. The file is not on an NTFS drive.

19. NTFS is bad for small volumes because

   A. NTFS uses very large clusters, creating high inefficiency in small volumes.

   B. NTFS uses a proportionally larger amount of disk space setting up small volumes.

   C. NTFS' intelligent head-drive algorithms consume high processor time.

   D. NTFS' scattered-MFS technique requires that the MFS pieces be gigabytes apart.

20. In order to use a Plug and Play printer directly attached to your desktop, you need to

   A. Plug the printer into your computer; Windows will auto-detect the printer.

   B. Plug the printer into your computer and restart the computer. Windows will auto-detect the printer on startup.

    C. Plug the printer into your computer and run Add Printer from the Printers window.

    D. Plug the printer into your computer and double-click the driver.

21. NTFS disk logging for crash recovery works by

    A. Constantly backing up all live files to a designated storage space

    B. Setting high priority on all automated backups created by applications

    C. Creating a chain of allocation tables, showing the history of file allocation

    D. Storing changes to file system integrity, like name changes, folder and directory movements, and so on

LAB QUESTION

You're configuring a new desktop. The desktop has three hard drives: hard drive 0, which is a 10GB hard disk; hard disk 1, which is a 20GB hard disk; and hard disk 2, which is a 30GB hard disk. You want to turn this into a dual-boot system, bootable into Windows 98 and Windows 2000 Professional. You have a Windows 98 application (call it LittleApp) that you need to run, which takes up about 3GB of space, and a Windows 2000 application (call it BigApp) that you need to run, which takes up 50GB of space. Both of these applications need to be on single logical drives, though their component parts are sprinkled among many folders. Assume that each operating system takes up about 1GB for system files. Detail how you will partition hard drives and assign file systems, and explain why.

SELF TEST ANSWERS

Connecting to Local and Network Print Devices

1. ☑ **B.** When a system tries to define your local printer as a network printer, it will search for drivers on your local system.
   ☒ **A** is incorrect because drivers are automatically loaded to clients when needed in Windows 2000. **C** and **D** are incorrect because Active Directory doesn't contain driver information as part of a printer's description, nor does it contain a URL to a driver's location.

2. ☑ **D.** In fact, NTFS draws its name from Windows NT.
   ☒ **A** is incorrect because NTFS is also used in workstations. **B** is incorrect because you can use NTFS whether your computer is networked or not. **C** is incorrect because NTFS does not run on consumer versions of Windows 9.*x* yet, and certainly not Windows 95.

3. ☑ **E.** The proper file object must be on NTFS for permission setting, and permission settings can only be made by administrators in Group Policy.
   ☒ **B** is incorrect because you generally can't turn off permission settings in Active Directory.

4. ☑ **A.** Canceling on the printer icon from the Printers window.
   ☒ **C** will cancel *all* current print jobs, not just a particular print job. **B** is incorrect because Print Properties contains no such command. The action in **D** will not delete a print job. In fact, it will delete the definition for your logical printer, making that printer and its encapsulated settings unavailable.

5. ☑ **B.** The application sends the document to the driver, which translates it from API calls to printer-specific instructions. It is then sent to the processor, to the router, to the queue in the spooler, and then to the monitor—which actually communicates with the printer.

Configuring and Managing File Systems

6. ☑ **A.** Microsoft recommends FAT for small volumes because NTFS has a high set-up cost in volume consumed, which is quite painful at volumes of 2GB or below.
   ☒ **B** is incorrect, since FAT can't even handle volumes over 4GB. **C** and **D** have nothing to do with file systems.

7. ☑ **D.** The tools for partitioning have been moved to Disk Management inside Computer Management for Windows 2000.

☒   A refers to a tool that doesn't exist, **B** refers to the tool that is used to convert already partitioned FAT volumes to NTFS, and **C** refers to the partitioning tool from Windows NT.

8. ☑   **C.** The FAT drives will allow Windows 98 to have drives to work from, while the NTFS drives provide security through permission usage.
  ☒   FAT is insecure, so **A** and **D** are incorrect. **B** is incorrect because Windows 98 is unable to read NTFS drives.

9. ☑   **C.** Changing a hard disk from NTFS to FAT can only happen by reformatting.
  ☒   **A** is incorrect because it is possible. **B** is incorrect because you can convert from FAT to NTFS, but not the other way around. **D** is incorrect because you'll lose all the files when you delete the partition.

10. ☑   **A.** Microsoft allows you to search for printers while adding a printer.
  ☒   You cannot yet search from an application, as in **B**. While you certainly can set up your printer as an Internet printer or a network printer, you can do this regardless of whether or not the printer is published in AD, so **C** and **D** are incorrect in the context of this question.

11. ☑   **A.** Long format has nothing to do with efficiency; in fact, long formats could be a reason for inefficiency.
  ☒   All of the rest are true and, therefore, incorrect.

12. ☑   **D.** The print spooler is the application component that holds print jobs in the queue.
  ☒   **B** is referring to the print monitor, and **C** is referring to the print processor. **A** is incorrect because the part of the printer that holds the ink is called the cartridge.

13. ☑   **D.** A printer must be shared before other users can connect to it over the network.
  ☒   **A**, this is not necessary to set the printer up as a network printer. **A** and **B** are incorrect, you do not need to publish a printer to the Active Directory. **C** and, in part, **B** are incorrect because you can also print to a print server which is not directly connected to a server.

14. ☑   **C.** Active Directory listing for printers is done in the Sharing tab.
  ☒   None of the other options exist, so **A**, **B**, and **D** are incorrect.

15. ☑   **C.** Drivers translate operating system API calls into printer-specific instructions, so you need one for every printer/OS combination.
  ☒   **A**, **B**, and **D** are incorrect.

16. ☑   **D** is correct. NTFS does not allow concurrent compression and encryption of a folder/file.
  ☒   **A**, **B**, and **C** are incorrect as NTFS has all those features. The question specifically asks which does not.

17. ☑ **A.** Mounting a volume lets you put more than one physical disk into one logical drive. ☒ **B** is incorrect because the contents of the folder remain in their current location. **C** is incorrect because you don't create a new drive with a drive letter when you create a reparse point. **D** is incorrect because there is no repartitioning of the drive, nor do you create a new labeled logical drive in this action.

18. ☑ **D.** NTFS is required for permissions setting. ☒ **A** is incorrect; if you don't have required permission to set permissions on a file, the Permissions tab will be visible, but grayed out. If the file is not shared, as in **C**, you can still set permissions—this is important if a computer has multiple users logging on locally. **B** is incorrect because you don't use the Disk Management pane to turn on permissions. You can do it directly from the desktop, or using Explorer.

19. ☑ **B.** NTFS puts down a heavy footprint to get its file attribute and intelligent disk-writing and logging capability down; this consumes a large amount of disk space, which is proportionally high for small volumes, but almost insignificant at large volumes. ☒ **A** is incorrect because it is FAT that uses large clusters. **C** is incorrect because NTFS has nothing to do with head-drive algorithms. That is a property of your disk drive set by the manufacturer. **D** is incorrect because MFS has no such technique for writing files and tries to write them contiguously whenever possible.

20. ☑ **C.** Windows requires you to run the Add Printer Wizard. ☒ **A** and **B** are incorrect; while Plug and Play allows Windows to know what printer you've plugged in, you still have to run the wizard manually. **D** is incorrect because the printer driver is not exposed in the interface in such a manner.

21. ☑ **D.** NTFS disk logging preserves system integrity at minimum disk cost. ☒ Solution **A** would require lots of storage overhead; NTFS doesn't do that. **B** is incorrect because disk logging is a separate process from backups. **C** is incorrect because disk logging logs file changes, not snapshots of the allocation table.

LAB ANSWER

Here's one way of doing it:

Take disk 1, a 20GB disk. Partition this as one big volume in NTFS, call it drive C:. This gives us a 20GB NTFS logical drive. Establish the folder hierarchy that you need for BigApp. Take disk 2, a 30GB disk. Partition it as one big volume, and mount this to a folder in C:. This gives you a 50GB logical drive, called C:, which is spread across two hard disks. That's enough for BigApp.

Take disk 0, which has 10GB. Partition a 4GB FAT partition; install Windows 98 and LittleApp on this partition.

We're not done yet. We need a place for the system files for Windows 2000 Professional; we need 1GB, and we've got 6. There are a few ways of doing this. We can make another logical drive in NTFS, call it D:, and install Windows 2000 Professional's system files onto that. Or, we could partition that out and mount it onto the C: drive, giving us a 56GB C: drive, and install Windows 2000 Professional's system files onto C:, along with BigApp.

6

Implementing, Managing, and Troubleshooting Disks and Displays

Windows 2000 Professional offers some new features for managing disks and devices. The Plug and Play support, which was not available in Windows NT 4.0, makes it easy for automatic installation of suitable drivers for the devices. A new concept of Basic and Dynamic Disks has also been introduced in Windows 2000. Use of multiple displays is another versatile feature added to the functionality of the operating system.

This chapter covers two major parts of Windows 2000 Professional administration. The first section deals in working with disk devices, and the second part covers display devices. Other removable media—such as tape devices, I 394 Interface, Fiber Channel Interface, and Universal Serial Bus (USB) Interface—are also discussed in this chapter. In the second part of the chapter, we will learn how to manage and troubleshoot display devices using the utilities, wizards, and tools included with Windows 2000 Professional.

CERTIFICATION OBJECTIVE 6.01

Implementing, Managing, and Troubleshooting Disk Devices

With Windows 2000, the device management operations have become a lot easier. The Disk Management tool has been added in the new Computer Management MMC. This replaces the Disk Administrator that was a part of Administrative Tools in Windows NT 4.0. This utility is more powerful than its previous counterpart, and gives us the option of managing and troubleshooting hard drives, partitions, and volumes without restarting the computer. It is even possible to manage disks on remote computers using Disk Management. To access the Computer Management console, right-click the My Computer icon on the desktop. From the drop-down menu that appears, select Manage. This opens the Computer Management console. Figure 6-1 shows the Computer Management console.

Another way to access the Computer Management console is from the Control Panel. From the Start menu, click Start | Settings | Control Panel | Administrative Tools. You will find the Computer Management applet in this window. Double-click it to open the Computer Management console.

The disk management functions are under the Storage snap-in, which is used for common disk management tasks. The common disk management functions include

Computer
Management in
Windows 2000

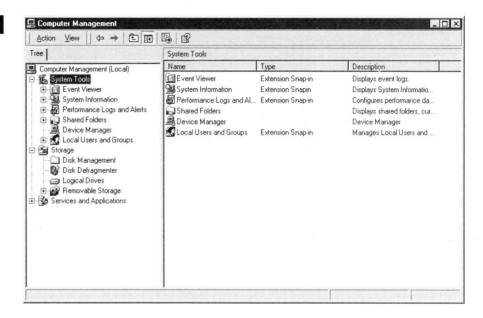

creating, deleting, and formatting disk partitions; and working with basic disks, dynamic disks, and volumes.

Common Disk Management Functions

The Disk Management snap-in of the Computer Management MMC provides a centralized point for performing all disk-related functions. Many of the functions such as working with logical drives and removable storage are also performed within this console. An added feature is that many of the functions can be performed online. This ensures that the computer running Windows 2000 Professional will have fewer power recycles while performing disk- and-device related administrative tasks. This is a welcome improvement from the earlier versions of Windows. The following tasks can be performed using the Disk Management snap-in:

- Managing simple, spanned, and striped volumes
- Adding disks to a computer
- Viewing information
- Remote management of disk devices

Figure 6-2 shows the Storage snap-in of the Computer Management console.

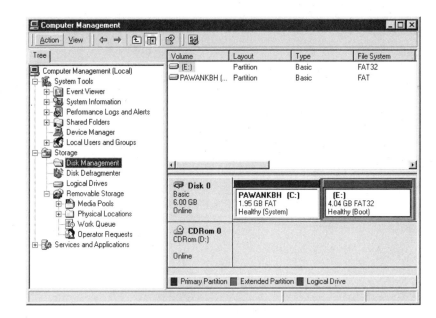

The Storage
snap-in in the
Computer
Management
console

You may notice in Figure 6-2 that Windows 2000 includes a new utility called Disk
Defragmenter. This was not available in Windows NT 4.0. This utility is useful for
analyzing and defragmenting hard drives, and works on both NTFS and FAT volumes.
Although NTFS volumes are less prone to fragmentation as compared to FAT volumes,
the utility is quite useful on large and heavily used disk drives.

Installing, Configuring, and Managing Devices

The Device Manager snap-in under System Tools provides all device management
functions. This provides a single graphical view of the various devices installed in the
computer. This utility is used to install, configure, and troubleshoot hardware devices.
In case some piece of hardware is not functioning properly, this is a perfect place to
locate and find information about the devices, drivers, and resources, and get help in
troubleshooting in case of problems. Figure 6-3 shows the Device Manager.

Any device that is not functioning properly is flagged with a big question mark.
In Figure 6-3, you may notice that a PCI Simple Communications Controller is
shown with a question mark indicating that it is not working. This may be because
the device itself is bad, or an incorrect driver is installed.

FIGURE 6-3

The Device
Manager under
the System Tools
snap-in

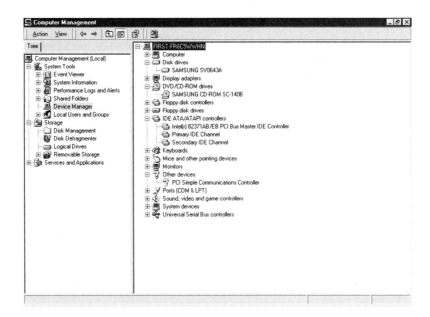

DVD

Digital Versatile Disk (DVD) is supported in Windows 2000 Professional as a storage device and as a movie playback device. When used as a storage device, the DVD-ROM behaves like a large storage medium. Windows 2000 supports Universal Data Format (UDF) as an installable file system. This provides a cost-effective data storage solution for large amounts of data.

When used as a movie playback device, the DVD provides high-quality reproduction of video. DVD support in Windows 2000 includes a DVD-ROM class driver that provides the ability to read data from a DVD-ROM. A DVD movie playback application is provided in Windows 2000 Professional. The WDM stream class driver supports streaming data types, MPEG-2, and AC-3 (Dolby Digital) standards.

CD-ROM

The compact disk read only memory (CD-ROM) has become the choice of storage and distribution medium for all software manufacturers. CD-ROMs have been supported on all platforms of Windows, including Windows 2000. A normal

CD-ROM can store up to 750MB of data. Windows 2000 supports the Compact Disk File System (CDFS) for reading and writing CD-ROM disks, and a large number of CD-ROM disk drivers.

In case you wish to install Windows 2000 Professional on a new computer and you do not have setup disks, you will need an El Torito compatible CD-ROM drive. *El Torito* stands for compatible CD-ROM drives that are bootable.

Monitoring and Configuring Disks

Any free space on an existing disk or a newly added disk needs certain basic operations, such as creating, deleting, and formatting partitions, or creating volumes in order to make it usable by the operating system. If you need to install an operating system or store data on a new disk, you need to initialize it and prepare for further data storage and retrieval operations. Windows 2000 introduces the concept of *basic and dynamic storage*. The various disk management functions in Windows 2000 are as follows:

- Disk initialization
- Creation of partitions on a basic disk
- Creation of volumes on a dynamic disk
- Formatting the disk partition or volume with FAT, FAT32, or NTFS

Before we continue with disk management functions, we need to be familiar with different storage types, partitions, and volumes supported by Windows 2000. The next section describes these concepts in detail.

Basic Disks Versus Dynamic Disks

Windows 2000 supports two types of storage: basic and dynamic. This concept of basic and dynamic disk storage is a new feature in Windows 2000. A disk has to be either basic or dynamic. If a computer has only one hard drive, it can have only one type of storage. You must have a multidisk computer in order to use both basic and dynamic disks.

exam
Ⓦatch

You can have either a basic disk or a dynamic disk if you have only one disk in your computer. For using both types of disks, you need to have more than one disk.

Basic Disks   Basic disks are what we always have been using. This is the traditional industry standard. A basic disk can have primary and extended partitions that make logical drives. The disk is referred to as basic disk when used for traditional basic storage, which is supported by all versions of Microsoft operating systems. For Windows 2000 Professional, it is the default storage type. All disks remain basic disks unless they are converted into dynamic disks using disk management. Basic disks cannot be resized without rebooting the system.

Partition Types   Disk partitions divide the physical hard drive into one or more storage areas used for saving different kinds of data. Two types of partitions can be created on basic disks: *primary* and *extended*. A physical disk can be divided into four primary partitions, or three primary partitions and one extended partition.

One of the primary partitions is set as active and is used for starting up the computer. The operating system boot files are located in this partition. An extended partition is created from free space on a hard disk. You cannot have more than one extended partition on a single disk. It is important to note that the extended partitions are not formatted or assigned drive letters; they contain logical drives.

exam
Watch

Microsoft treats the boot and system partitions in different ways. The active partition containing the startup files is called the "system partition." The partition that contains the operating system specific files is called the "boot partition."

on the
Job

In case you need to dual-boot Windows 2000 with some other operating system, it is recommended that you install the different operating systems on different partitions. You will also need to decide on the file system type on each partition. Windows 2000 supports FAT, FAT32, NTFS4, and NTFS5 file systems. For example, if you have two partitions on your hard drive and wish to make it a dual-boot system, you must take care of the following things:

For dual-booting with Windows 98 or Windows 95 (OSR 2), the primary partition must be FAT16, FAT32, or NFTS. The other partition may be FAT32 or NTFS. However, if you need to access data on a Windows 2000 partition, you must have FAT32 on both partitions.

For dual-booting with MS-DOS, the primary partition must be FAT. You cannot access the NTFS partition while running MS-DOS.

For dual-booting with Windows NT 4.0, you can have NTFS on both partitions, but you will have to install Windows NT service pack 4 for accessing the data on the Windows 2000 NTFS partition.

Adding a Disk to a Computer

As described earlier, the disk management functions are very easy to perform on Windows 2000 computers. In this exercise, we will add a new IDE hard drive to a computer. This will be configured as a secondary drive. Remember that whenever a new hard drive is added to a computer running Windows 2000, it is configured as a basic disk. The following steps will help you understand the process of adding a new disk.

1. Shut down the computer and connect the hard drive to a free connector of the primary IDE cable. Since it will act as a slave drive, you must set the master/slave configuration jumper to the slave position.

2. Start the computer. Log on to the system as an administrator.

3. The disk will be automatically detected if it is a Plug and Play device, and Windows 2000 will configure a suitable driver for it.

4. If the new disk drive is not Plug and Play, the Add New Hardware Wizard will not appear.

5. Right-click the My Computer icon on the desktop, and select Manage. This opens the Computer Management console.

6. From the Action Menu, select Rescan Disks. A new disk will be added to the right-side pane of the console. You may not need to restart your computer.

Dynamic Disks   Dynamic disks or dynamic storage are supported only on systems running Windows 2000. Basic disks can be converted into dynamic disks using Disk Management. The dynamic disk can then be used for creating dynamic volumes. A dynamic volume can consist of a single partition, multiple partitions of a single drive, or multiple partitions of multiple physical hard drives.

Dynamic disks facilitate creation of simple volumes, spanned volumes, and striped volumes. These volumes are called dynamic volumes. It is possible to resize the dynamic volumes without having to reboot the computer; however, there are certain restrictions to this. The reboot becomes necessary when any changes are made to partitions containing the system or boot files.

Requirements for Dynamic Disks and Volumes   There are certain requirements for hard drives to be configured or upgraded as dynamic disks. The following points explain the requirements for dynamic volumes:

- Dynamic volumes need dynamic disks. A basic disk must be upgraded to a dynamic disk before any dynamic volumes can be created.

- The sector size of the disks should not be greater than 512KB. This must be taken care of while formatting the drives.

- Removable media cannot be configured as a dynamic volume.

- The dynamic disk must have a minimum of 1MB free disk space at the end of the drive. If you are using more than one drive as part of a striped set, each drive must have 1MB free at the end.

- If the boot or system partition is a part of a mirrored set, this partition cannot be upgraded to a dynamic disk.

- If you wish to have multiple file systems, you must have multiple volumes. A single volume can have only one type of file system.

- If you have some disks working as a stripe set, each of the disks must first be upgraded to a dynamic disk. This will enable upgrading the stripe set to striped volume.

e x a m
ⓦ a t c h   *Microsoft Windows 2000 does not support dynamic disks or volumes on portable computers or removable media.*

SCENARIO & SOLUTION

Can I upgrade a striped set to striped volume?	Yes. All the drives in the stripe set need to be upgraded to dynamic disks.
Is it possible to upgrade the system or boot partition?	Yes, but you will need to restart the computer.
I have two hard drives that form a mirrored set. Is it possible to upgrade the disks to dynamic disks?	No, mirrored partitions cannot be upgraded to dynamic disks without first breaking the mirrored set.
My notebook has a 6.4GB hard drive. Can I use the dynamic storage features of Windows 2000?	No, dynamic storage is not supported on portable computers.

Converting a Disk from Dynamic to Basic   Converting a dynamic disk back to basic results in loss of all data on the dynamic disk. A dynamic disk can be converted to a basic disk by following the same process in the Disk Management snap-in. In this case, when you right-click on the dynamic disk, select Revert To Basic Disk. You must remove all volumes from the dynamic disk before reverting it to basic.

on the *job*

When I installed Windows 2000 Professional on my home computer, I was very impressed by the idea of having a dynamic disk, and I actually converted my second hard drive from basic to dynamic. In the course of time, I kept on saving some important data on this volume. The other day, one of my friends walked in and wanted to see how conversion from basic to dynamic and vice versa takes place. I immediately opened up the Disk Management snap-in and reverted my dynamic drive to basic.

What do you think? Did I lose all my important data? Theoretically, the answer should be Yes, but my answer is No. This is because I had a backup of my data files. The lesson here is that while doing any such experiments in real life, do not forget to back up your important data.

Monitoring, Configuring, and Troubleshooting Volumes

Management of disk volumes involves many functions, such as the creation of simple or spanned volumes, the creation of striped volumes, and volume maintenance. The Disk Management snap-in of the Computer Management console is the centralized location for performing all disk- and volume-related functions. It is even possible to manage volumes on remote computers running Windows 2000. The volume maintenance utilities in Windows 2000 include checking the disks for errors, back up, disk defragmentation, and online troubleshooting tools.

Volumes

As discussed earlier, volumes can be created only on dynamic disks. Converting a basic disk into a dynamic disk can be accomplished from the Disk Management snap-in of the Computer Management console. Different volumes in a computer allow the user to organize data more efficiently. The following are the types of volumes that can be created on Windows 2000 dynamic disks:

■ **Simple**   A simple volume contains disk space from one physical drive only.

EXERCISE 6-2

Upgrading a Basic Disk to Dynamic Disk

In this exercise, we will upgrade a basic disk to a dynamic disk. To do so, follow these steps:

1. Right-click the My Computer icon on the desktop and select Manage. The Computer Management console window opens.

2. Click the Disk Management snap-in. In the right pane, right-click the basic disk that is to be upgraded.

3. Select the Upgrade To Dynamic Disk menu option. This brings up the Upgrade To Dynamic Disk dialog box. Check that the disk that you wish to upgrade is selected. Click OK.

4. The Disks To Upgrade dialog box appears next. Click Upgrade.

5. A warning dialog box appears saying that you may no longer be able to boot the system using any operating system other than Windows 2000. Click Yes.

6. If the disk selected was a system disk, you are prompted that the system will reboot to complete the upgrade process. Click OK.

7. This restarts the computer. In order to check whether the disk has been upgraded, you may open the Disk Management snap-in and notice that the type of disk has changed from basic to dynamic.

- **Spanned** A spanned volume contains space from more than one hard drive. You may have from 2 to 32 drives on a spanned volume. The operating system writes the data on the disks in a sequential manner until the last of the hard drives is full.

- **Striped** A striped volume contains space from multiple disks and makes it a single logical drive. The data on the participating drives is written simultaneously. This enhances the read-write performance of the system. A striped volume is not fault tolerant—if a single hard drive fails, all the data on the striped volume is lost. The only way to restore the data is to restore it from a tape backup. Again, you can have from 2 to a maximum of 32 drives in a striped volume.

e x a m
ⓦ a t c h

Windows 2000 Professional does not support disk fault tolerance. Striped volumes only improve the read-write performance of a system. Fault-tolerant systems such as disk mirroring (RAID 1) and disk striping with parity (RAID 5) are supported in the Windows 2000 Server operating system.

EXERCISE 6-3

Creating and Formatting a Simple Volume

As noted earlier, a simple volume can have disk space from a single hard drive only. In this exercise, we will create a simple volume and format it using NTFS. You may, however, format a simple volume using any of the file systems FAT, FAT32, or NTFS. The following steps and figures explain the process.

1. Right-click the My Computer icon on the desktop. From the drop-down menu, select Manage.

2. The Computer Management console window appears. Click Disk Management.

3. Right-click the disk on which the volume is to be created. From the menu, select Create Volume. The Create Volume Wizard appears, as shown in the following illustration. Click Next.

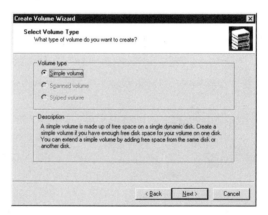

4. The next screen allows you to select which disk you want to use for this volume. You will notice that Select Only One Disk is displayed in this window. You may select the size of the disk. In this exercise, I selected disk 1

and did not change the default size, which was the maximum size for this disk. This is shown here. Click Next.

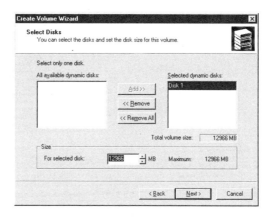

5. In the next window, you may assign the drive letter to the volume. By default, the next available letter is assigned to the volume. Click Next.

6. The Format Volume screen appears. Notice in the following illustration that the default file system is NTFS. You may also choose not to format the volume at this time. Enter a label for the volume. For the purpose of this exercise, we will keep the default label New Volume. Click Next.

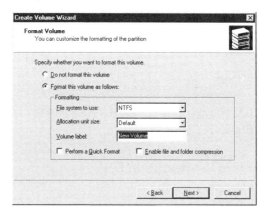

7. This completes the volume creation process. Click Finish to close the wizard.

8. The system starts formatting the newly created volume. This takes a few minutes, depending on the disk capacity. When the formatting is complete, the volume is shown as healthy.

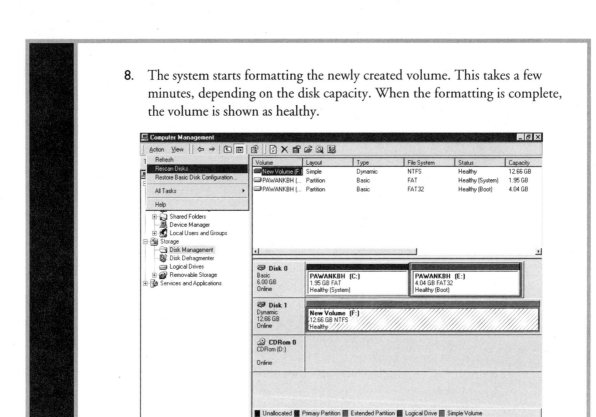

exam

Watch

You must decide well in advance about the file system to use. FAT16 and FAT32 file systems do not offer features such as file compression, encryption, or file-level security.

Volume Properties in Disk Management   Any existing or newly created volumes on Windows 2000 computers have a Properties sheet attached to them. The Properties sheet gives information about the volume and provides tools for administration and maintenance. Volume sharing, security, and quota can be managed using the Properties dialog box. Figure 6-4 shows the Properties sheet of the volume we created in Exercise 6-2.

FIGURE 6-4

Volume
Properties sheet

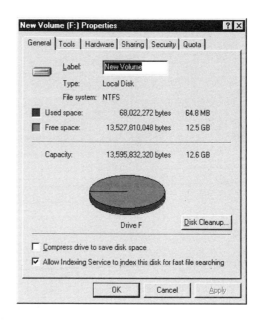

To access and view volume properties in Disk Management, right-click the volume and select Properties. The various tabs in the Properties dialog box are described in the following text.

■ **General** This screen is shown by default and lists label, type, file system used, and free space on the volume. Since the volume is an NTFS volume, you have two other options: Compress Drive To Save Disk Space and Allow Indexing Service To Index This Disk For Fast File Searching. The Indexing Service option is selected by default. You may delete unnecessary files by clicking Disk Cleanup.

■ **Tools** This tab provides tools for error checking, backup, and defragmentation of the volume. Figure 6-5 shows the Tools tab in the volume Properties sheet.

■ **Check Now** This tool is used for checking errors on a volume. When selected, this tool can automatically check for errors on the volume and fix them. You also have the option of scanning and recovery of the bad sectors on the disk.

■ **Backup Now** This utility contains the Backup and Restore Wizards. In addition, an Emergency Repair Disk (ERD) can be created from this

FIGURE 6-5

The Volume
Tools tab

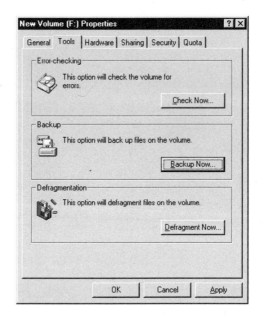

window. The Schedule Jobs tab can be used to run specific jobs at a
predetermined time. Figure 6-6 shows the screen from which the Backup
and Recovery tools can be accessed.

FIGURE 6-6

The Backup and
Recovery Tools
window

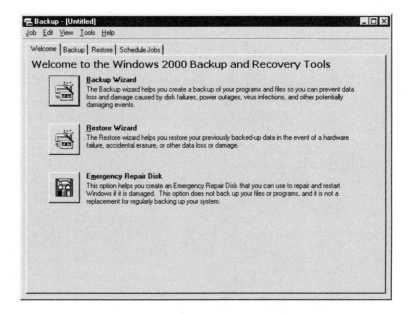

- **Defragment Now**   This tab is used to analyze and defragment volumes (discussed later in this chapter in the section "Disk Defragmentation").

- **Hardware**   This dialog box is used to check properties of the hard drive and provides troubleshooting tools.

- **Sharing**   This tab is used to set parameters and permissions for shared volumes.

- **Security**   Use this tab to set NTFS permissions for the volume. This tab is shown only if the volume is an NTFS volume and is not available for FAT volumes.

- **Quota**   Disk quota on a per-user basis can be set using this tab. This is discussed later in this chapter in the section "Setting Disk Quotas."

Extending a Simple Volume to Create a Spanned Volume   Once created and formatted, adding disk space from other drives can extend the simple volume. This concept is similar to the Volume Set concept in Windows NT 4.0. When extended to anther disk, it becomes a spanned volume; however, the simple volume should have been formatted using NTFS. In order to create a spanned volume, we need to add disk space from at least two hard drives. These drives need to be dynamic disks. The maximum number of disks that can be added to form a spanned volume is 32. Also note that the spanned volume cannot be a part of a striped volume.

Only a simple volume formatted using NTFS can be extended to form a spanned volume. The entire volume is deleted when you delete any part of the spanned volume.

Creating and Formatting a Striped Volume   Striped volumes can be created in Windows 2000 using the same process used to create spanned volumes. Striped volumes enhance the read-write performance of the system, but these volumes do not provide any fault tolerance. The disks or partitions to be used for creating a striped volume must not have any partition information marked and should read as free space. Exercise 6-4 lists the various steps involved in the process.

Basic and Dynamic Storage Terminology   Table 6-1 summarizes the basic and dynamic storage terminologies we have discussed so far.

CertCam 6-4

Creating and Formatting a Striped Volume

To create and format a striped volume, perform the following steps:

1. Open the Computer Management console and click the Disk Management snap-in.
2. Click the first of the drives that will be part of the striped volume.
3. Hold down CTRL while clicking the other drives one by one.
4. From the Action drop-down menu, click Create Striped Volume. You are prompted for the size of the striped volume.
5. Right-click the striped volume and select Format. When prompted, select NTFS as the file system. You have the option of a Quick Format. Leave the check box unselected, because a quick format does not check for the irregularities such as bad sectors in the participating drives.

This completes the creation and formatting of a stripe set.

Setting Disk Quotas

Disk quotas for various volumes can be set on a per-user basis in Windows 2000. This feature is new in Windows 2000 and is available only for NTFS volumes. By

TABLE 6-1	Terms Used for Basic Storage	Terms Used for Dynamic Storage
Terminology of Basic and Dynamic Disks	Partition	Simple volume
	System partition	System volume
	Boot partition	Boot volume
	Active partition	Active volume
	Extended partition	Volume or unallocated space
	Logical drive	Simple volume
	Volume set	Spanned volume
	Stripe set	Striped volume

default, disk quotas are disabled. The following are some conditions that apply to disk quotas:

- Disk quotas can be set on NTFS volumes only.
- Disk quotas are calculated on a per-user basis.
- Disk quotas cannot be set on files and folders.
- Disk quotas set on a volume apply only to that volume.
- The file size calculated is based on the size of the uncompressed files.

The following steps explain how you can set disk quotas.

1. In the Disk Management console, right-click the volume and select Properties.

2. Click the Quota tab. Notice in Figure 6-7 that the Status shows disk quotas as disabled (the traffic light symbol will show red). Select the Enable Quota Management check box to enable disk quotas.

3. Click the radio button Limit Disk Space To and type in the disk space. To set a warning threshold, type in the warning level.

FIGURE 6-7

Setting disk
quotas on NTFS
volumes

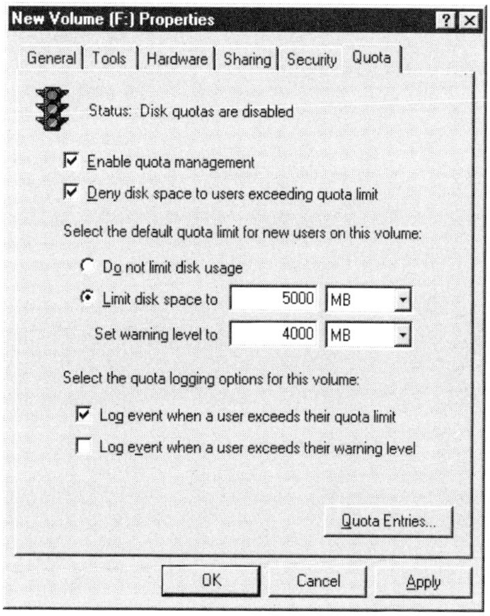

4. In case you wish to log the disk usage activities of users who exceed the warning level or quota level, select the appropriate check boxes.

5. Click Quota Entries to define the users for whom the disk quotas are being set.

exam
ⓦatch

You will not see the Quota tab in the volume Properties sheet in two cases: when the volume is not an NTFS volume, and when you are not logged on as an administrator. Most of the disk management functions discussed in this chapter require you to be a member of the local administrators group.

Disk Defragmentation

Fragmentation refers to uneven spreading of data on noncontiguous disk sectors. This results in degradation of disk read-write performance. The NTFS volumes are less prone to fragmentation than their FAT counterparts, but heavily used, and large drives may become fragmented over a period of time. The Defragmenter utility in Windows 2000 can be used to analyze and defragment installed disks.

The Analysis Display and the Defragmentation Display bands of the Disk Manager give a graphical view of the disk before and after the defragmentation. Exercise 6-5 explains how to defragment a disk.

EXERCISE 6-5

Defragmenting a Disk

Follow these steps to defragment a disk:

1. Right-click the My Computer icon on the desktop and select Manage. This opens the Computer Management console.

2. Click Disk Defragmenter under Storage. From the upper right-hand pane, select the disk you wish to defragment.

3. You are given two options: Analyze and Defragment. Select Defragment. When you select Defragment, the disk analysis is done automatically; then the disk defragmentation process starts:

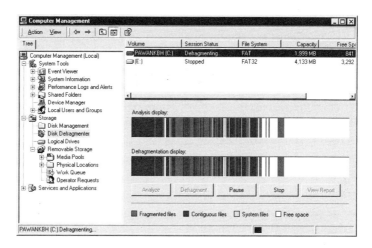

4. While the disk defragmentation is in progress, you may continue with other activities on the computer; but you may find a significant reduction in performance. The process can be paused or stopped at any time.

5. The time taken to complete the defragmentation process depends on the fragmentation factor of the disk. It takes more time for heavily fragmented disks than those with low fragmentation.

6. When the process is over, a dialog box appears, saying that defragmentation is complete:

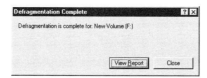

7. Click View Report to view the fragmentation report or Close to close the dialog box.

Usually, the disk defragmentation should be done on a computer when it is not in use. The defragmentation process moves the data in the disk and takes a significant portion of processor time, which may affect other processes or applications running on the computer. Fragmentation may also occur when you delete a large number of files, thereby creating noncontiguous free space on the disk. Defragmentation should be done regularly on heavily used file servers.

In case you are installing some time-sensitive applications, defragment the disk "before" installation. This will create enough contiguous free space for the installation. The installation will be quick and the application will also run efficiently.

Managing Remote Disks

The disk management capabilities of Windows 2000 make it easy to manage hard disks attached to other computers in a Windows 2000 domain. In order to remotely manage disks, you need to be a member of the domain administrators or server operators group. In a workgroup environment, if a Windows 2000 Server does not exist, it is still possible to manage disks on other computers running Windows 2000

SCENARIO & SOLUTION

How do I limit the use of my hard disks for the users of my Windows 2000 Professional computer?	Set disk quotas for each user using the Quota tab of the Volume Properties tab in Disk Management.
My computer was very fast earlier, but now it has become slow. Is there any quick solution to enhance performance?	Yes, use the Disk Defragmenter utility. Fragmentation of the disk degrades performance significantly.
Can I set the quotas for users on my dual-boot computer that has two drives both formatted in FAT32?	No. For setting disk quotas, you must have NTFS volumes.
I have three identical hard drives on my Windows 2000 Professional computer. Can I make a fault-tolerant striped volume?	No. Windows 2000 Professional does not support fault tolerance. Windows 2000 Server supports it.

Professional. The requirement for this is that you must have the same account name and password on all the computers you wish to manage remotely. If this condition is not met, the operation will not be successful. Exercise 6-6 walks you through managing disks on a remote computer.

CertCam 6-6

Managing Disks on a Remote Computer

1. Log on to the computer as administrator. You must have the same username and password on the other computer also.

2. From the Start menu, click Run. Type **MMC**, and then click OK.

3. An empty Management Console window opens. From the Console menu, click Add/Remove Snap-In.

4. In the next window that appears, click Add. From the right-side pane, click Disk Management. Click Add.

5. A dialog box appears, as shown in the following illustration. Click on the Another Computer radio button.

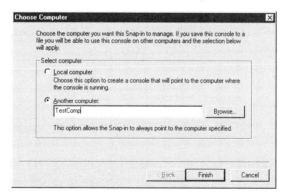

6. Type in the name of the computer. You may also click Browse to select a computer.

7. Click Finish.

EXERCISE 6-6

Troubleshooting Disks and Volumes

The most common problems in disks and volumes arise from any of the following reasons:

- A corrupted or missing Master Boot Record (MBR). If you get a message that the NTLDR file is missing during the system startup, the reason may be that the MBR is corrupt. You may use the Emergency Repair process to repair the startup disk.

- Viruses that replace the MBR and cause the following startup errors:
  - Invalid partition table
  - Missing operating system
  - Error loading operating system

- Boot sector viruses

- Bad cables and connectors

Windows 2000 Professional comes with an antivirus software known as AVBoot. AVBoot can be used to fix the MBR and boot sector viruses. It is located on the Windows 2000 Professional CD-ROM in the \Valueadd\3rdparty\Ca-antiv directory. This antivirus software is able to scan and remove viruses on all of the hard drives in the computer.

You may encounter two types of problems when using volumes in Windows 2000: the volume is displayed as Unknown Volume in the Disk Management console, and the volume is inaccessible.

The reason for these errors is that either the boot sector for the volume is corrupted, or when the volume is an NTFS volume, the permissions may have changed. Another cause of this error is that the Master File Table (MFT) of the volume is corrupt.

exam
ⓦatch

Microsoft does not recommend the use of the Fdisk /MBR command to fix the Master Boot Record of the startup disk.

on the
ⓙob

Viruses in the Master Boot Record can be removed by AVBoot or any third-party antivirus software. Whichever virus cleaner you use, make sure you have the up-to-date virus signatures from the software manufacturer. The AVBoot software is written by Computer Associates. Latest virus signatures for this program can be downloaded from www.cai.com.

Mirroring

Disk mirroring is also known as RAID 1, which stands for Redundant Array of Independent (or Inexpensive) Disks. Mirrored disks essentially consist of two identical hard drives, each containing a replica of the other. RAID 1 is fault tolerant, because if one of the disks fails, the other is still available to keep the system running. This takeover does not happen automatically, but does help in keeping downtime to a minimum. Some basic administrative tasks need to be performed for the changeover.

Mirrored volumes in Windows 2000 can contain any partition, including system and boot partitions. This requires the participating disks to be dynamic disks. Disk mirroring is not supported on computers running the Windows 2000 Professional operating system. It is, however, supported on all versions of Windows 2000 Server.

RAID 5

RAID 5, also known as Stripe Sets with Parity in Windows NT 4.0, is fully fault tolerant. This is called a RAID 5 Volume in Windows 2000 terminology. Parity is a mathematical calculation of a series of even and odd numbers that are used to rebuild data in case one of the drives in the RAID volume fails. Each disk in the set contains parity information. RAID 5 volumes require a minimum of three hard drives and can have a maximum of 32 drives in Windows 2000.

Two types of RAID 5 can be implemented: software based and hardware based. The software-based RAID is inexpensive because there is no need to buy additional RAID hardware. The implementation is provided by the operating system itself, which is often not very efficient, as the processor has to devote a significant amount of time in RAID activities. Another drawback is that software-based RAID 5 volumes cannot have system or boot partitions.

Hardware-based RAID 5 solutions are often preferred by mission-critical businesses. Hardware RAID comes with its own RAID controller cards having their own processors dedicated to RAID functions. These are quite expensive, but are very efficient. This keeps the system processor free from RAID activities and can be utilized for application and data processing. RAID 5 is not supported in Windows 2000 Professional.

Monitoring and Configuring Removable Media

As the name suggests, *removable media* refers to those devices that can be removed from the computer and be used to store and retrieve data as required. These media provide offline storage of data and are instrumental in data recovery in case of disasters. Tape devices were the first such media supported on many old versions of Windows and many other operating systems. Windows 2000 features support for many new technologies such as USB Interface, the Fiber Channel Interface, and the IEEE 1394 Interface. The inclusion of removable storage in Windows 2000 also facilitates cataloging of all removable media.

Tape Devices

Tape devices are the most common type of removable media used in the IT industry. The popular tape drives are Quarter-Inch Cartridge (QIC), Digital Audio Tape (DAT), 8mm cassette, and Digital Linear Tape (DLT). Most of the drives use a SCSI controller interface. Device Manager can be used to configure and troubleshoot the tape devices. Windows 2000 supports many of the commonly used SCSI tape devices and drivers.

IEEE 1394 Interface (Firewire)

The Windows 2000 Professional operating system supports the IEEE 1394 Interface, which is used for storage devices that can handle high-speed data transfer rates. This is a serial protocol that supports data transfer rates ranging from 100 Mbps to 400 Mbps. A maximum of 63 devices can be connected to one IEEE 1394 bus. The bus cable contains two pairs of twisted pair cabling. With Windows 2000 Professional, you can plug any IEEE device to the node on-the-fly. The storage devices are connected using the Serial Bus Protocol-2 (SBP-2).

The IEEE 1394 Interface currently supports the following data transfer rates:

- **S100**   98,304 Mbps
- **S200**   196,608 Mbps
- **S400**   393,216 Mbps

When you plan to connect two computers using the IEEE 1394 bus, make sure you use the correct cable type. Check the documentation that came with the equipment.

Fiber Channel Interface

A Fiber Channel Interface acts as if a network adapter is connected to a fiber channel hub using fiber optic cables. A number of multiple-drive disk arrays known as fiber channel arrays can be connected to the fiber channel hub. This configuration allows formation of large disk volumes that are usually configured as fault-tolerant volumes. In many large-scale corporate companies, such fiber channel arrays are used to hold databases. Windows 2000 supports many popular brands of fiber channel adapters.

USB Interface

The Universal Serial Bus (USB) facilitates the connecting of Plug and Play hardware devices without having to run the setup or restart the computer. All USB devices use the same type of standard connectors, and multiple USB devices can be plugged into a single USB port. This technology also supports hot plugging of devices. The types of USB devices you can connect to your Windows 2000 Professional computer may include keyboards, joysticks, disk drives, CD-ROM drives, modems, network adapters, monitors, printers, and scanners.

The removable storage devices supported by the USB bus are disk drives, CD-ROM drives, and other media. The USB is essentially an external bus to which the devices can be connected without restarting the computer. Up to 127 peripheral devices can be connected to a single USB port. The USB ports and devices can be managed from the Device Manager snap-in of the Computer Management console.

CERTIFICATION OBJECTIVE 6.02

Implementing, Managing, and Troubleshooting Display Devices

This section of the chapter deals with management of display properties such as adding, removing, and configuring display adapters; loading display drivers; and configuring multiple displays. Windows 2000 provides the ability to change any display properties without having to restart the computer. Any user who has rights to load and unload device drivers can perform the display configuration. A new feature, which was not available in earlier versions of Windows NT, is the multiple-display support. This is covered later in this section.

When you right-click the desktop and select Properties, the Display Properties sheet appears. Figure 6-8 shows the Appearance tab.

The Display
Properties
Appearance tab

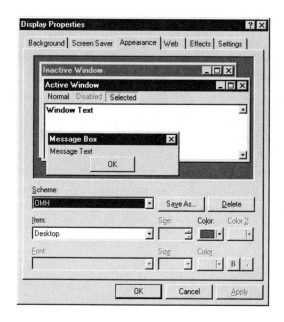

Display device management essentially includes the following tasks:

- Changing the display adapter and driver.

- Setting screen resolution, which can be done without restarting the computer.

- Selecting the color scheme that suits the user's choice.

- Configuring display settings. If there is more than one hardware profile being used, you can configure each of them.

- Configuring multiple monitors.

- Installing, configuring, and troubleshooting video adapters.

Windows 2000 includes advanced display management mechanisms to ensure that you can still access the system if a display driver is misconfigured or corrupted. In this case, you have the option of starting the computer in VGA mode. VGA mode loads the generic display driver. After the system starts up, you can find problems with the installed driver and fix them. This is very similar to Windows NT VGA mode.

Configuring Display Properties

Display properties are shown when we double-click the Display applet in the Control Panel. Another way to access the Display Properties sheet is to right-click the desktop and select Properties. Figure 6-9 shows the Settings tab of this Properties sheet.

You may notice in Figure 6-9 that a Plug and Play monitor is installed on the system. This is followed by the name of the manufacturer and the display adapter model.

The Settings tab provides the following configuration options:

- ■ **Colors**   This tab gives a list of available color depths for the installed display adapter. Select the color depth you wish.

- ■ **Screen Area**   This slide tab allows you to set the resolution for the display adapter.

- ■ **Troubleshooter**   This tab can be used to get help in diagnosing problems with the display.

- ■ **Advanced**   This tab opens the Advanced Properties sheet of the display, which provides some advanced configuration options, as described in the following section.

FIGURE 6-9

Display
Properties
Settings tab

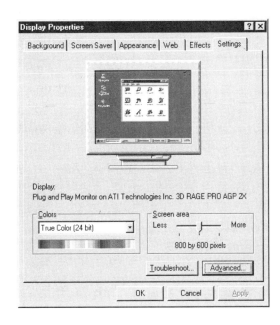

CertCam 6-7

EXERCISE 6-7

Setting the Screen Resolution

This simple exercise gives you an idea of the steps involved in setting the screen resolution.

1. Right-click the free area of the desktop.

2. Select Properties. This opens the Display Properties window.

3. Click the Settings tab.

4. Drag the slide tab under Screen Area to show 800 by 600 pixels, as shown previously in Figure 6-9. If you already have this screen resolution, decrease it to show 600 by 480 pixels—you may change it again.

5. Click Apply. The display changes immediately. A dialog box, as shown in the following illustration, appears, saying that the display settings will return to the previous settings in 15 seconds. You may click Cancel to return to the previous settings.

6. Click Yes to keep the new screen resolution. If you do not make a decision within 15 seconds, the screen area returns to the previous settings. Click OK to close the Display Properties window.

7. In case you changed your screen area from 800 by 600 pixels to 600 by 480 pixels, follow the same procedure to return to your previous settings.

exam
ⓦatch
When the display adapter and its driver are not Plug and Play, you will need to restart the computer.

Advanced Options in Display Settings

Clicking the Advanced tab in the Settings window of Display Properties opens the advanced settings window, as shown in Figure 6-10.

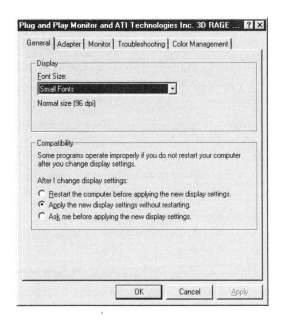

FIGURE 6-10

Advanced settings
options

The following sections describe each of the tabs found in the advanced settings window.

General   This tab provides the option of selecting Small Fonts, Large Fonts, and Other options with which you can select a custom font size. The Compatibility section warns you that some programs may not function properly if the computer is not restarted after changing the display properties. You are allowed to select any of the following options when you change the display settings:

■ Restart the computer before applying the new display settings.

■ Apply the new display settings without restarting. This is selected by default.

■ Ask me before applying the new display settings.

Adapter   The Adapter tab gives the following options:

■ **Adapter Type**   This shows the manufacturer's name and model of the installed display adapter. Clicking Properties displays the device status, resource settings, and information regarding any conflicting devices.

- **Adapter Information**   Provides some advanced information regarding the video chip type, memory size, and so on.
- **List All Modes**   This shows all compatible modes for the installed adapter. You can select the color depth, screen resolution, and screen refresh frequency.

Monitor   The Monitor tab shows the following monitor-related information:

- **Monitor Type**   This shows the information about the manufacturer and model of the installed monitor. You can use the Display troubleshooter to get help in resolving problems.
- **Monitor Settings**   This allows you to set the refresh rate frequency and is applicable to high-resolution display drivers.

Troubleshooting   The Troubleshooting tab allows you to manually increase or decrease the acceleration features of your display hardware so that you are able to diagnose and resolve display problems (Figure 6-11).

Color Management   This tab allows you to choose a color profile for your monitor.

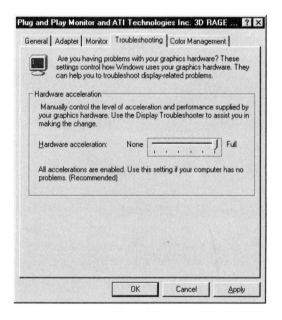

FIGURE 6-11

TheTrouble-shooting tab of the Advanced display options

There are so many display features in Windows 2000 that one gets confused for a while. In practice, if you are not working with any graphics programs, you will seldom need to change any of the display settings. The most commonly accessed display settings are the screen area and the color depth. Some of the advanced options are for use by experienced users only. Use of these options without having proper knowledge may render the display unviewable. If you run into such a problem and cannot view anything on the monitor, just restart the computer in VGA mode. This way, you can check where you were wrong when configuring the display settings.

Configuring Multiple-Display Support

Windows 2000 Professional supports multiple-display configurations, which allows you to spread the desktop across more than one monitor. Up to ten monitors can be attached to a computer. This feature gives you the illusion of a single large monitor. Windows 2000 maintains the desktop coordinates in such a way that even the movement of the mouse can be tracked easily. The display properties—such as appearance, color depth, and resolution—can be adjusted separately for each monitor. In multiple-monitor configurations, the display devices are referred to as *primary* and *secondary* display devices.

Primary and Secondary Display Devices

The display device that is detected by the computer BIOS during system startup is regarded as the primary display device. To find out which of the display devices is the primary device, look for the device that displays the power-on self test (POST) of the computer. The device that remains inactive during the POST is the secondary device.

The computer BIOS selects the primary display device based on the PCI slot number of the adapter. In some computers, you may change the BIOS settings to select the primary display device. Usually, the onboard display device becomes the secondary adapter.

To have a multiple-monitor configuration on a computer running Windows 2000 Professional, the following points must be taken into consideration for secondary devices:

- The maximum number of monitors is ten.
- The secondary monitor must have a Windows 2000–compatible driver.

- The monitors in the multiple-display configuration must use the PCI or AGP device.

- The PCI or AGP device must not use any VGA resources, because these are to be used by the onboard VGA device.

- If there is a video adapter built into the motherboard, it must be used as a VGA device.

Configuring Multiple Displays

In order to have multiple monitors in the computer, each device has to be configured separately. One of the basic requirements is that you must ensure that any secondary display adapter is not using the VGA resources. Exercise 6-8 that follows lists the various steps involved in multiple-monitor configuration. You will need the Windows 2000 Professional CD for this exercise.

EXERCISE 6-8

Adding Multiple Monitors

Perform the following steps to add multiple monitors:

1. Confirm that the primary display adapter is not using any VGA resources.

2. Shut down the computer. Install the additional video adapter in a free PCI slot of the computer motherboard. When you restart the computer, Windows 2000 will detect the adapter automatically.

3. You will be prompted to restart your computer. The video adapter is detected by the operating system, and the Add/Remove Hardware Wizard appears.

4. You are prompted to confirm that a correct adapter has been detected. The wizard asks you to select a driver for the adapter. Click Search. Click Next.

5. When prompted, insert the Windows 2000 Professional CD in the CD-ROM drive. Click OK.

6. The driver files are installed. Click Finish twice to complete the driver installation.

7. Repeat steps 2–6 for each additional device you wish to add.

Configuring Multiple Monitors

1. Right-click the desktop. Select Properties from the drop-down menu.

2. From the Display Properties window, click the Settings tab. You will notice that more than one adapter is listed.

3. Click the monitor number for the primary display device. Select the adapter for this monitor. Choose any color scheme and resolution you wish.

4. Select the monitor number for the secondary display device. Select the adapter for this monitor.

5. Select the check box for Extend My Windows Desktop To This Monitor.

6. Choose any color scheme and resolution you wish for this secondary monitor.

7. Repeat steps 4–6 for each of the additional monitors.

After additional devices are added and the drivers are installed, each will need configuration to become a part of the multiple-monitor system. Exercise 6-9 explains how to configure multiple monitors.

Installing, Configuring, and Troubleshooting a Video Adapter

Most of the computers manufactured today come with an onboard video adapter. Many computers still use a separate video adapter on one of the system PCI slots. If you wish to exchange an older video adapter with a new one for its enhanced features, check with the manufacturer to ensure that the adapter is supported in Windows 2000 Professional and a suitable driver is available. Windows 2000 supports most of the commonly used adapters and drivers. Even then, it's not a bad idea to check the Hardware Compatibility List (HCL), or check with the manufacturer instead of running into installation or configuration problems.

Installing a new PCI Plug and Play video adapter is easy in Windows 2000. Windows 2000 is able to automatically detect Plug and Play adapters. The following steps must be performed for installing a new video adapter.

1. Install the video adapter in one of the free PCI slots of the computer motherboard. Make sure it is seated properly.

2. Switch on the computer. Press F8 while the startup menu options are shown to access the Advanced Boot Options menu.

3. Select Enable VGA Mode. This starts up Windows 2000 using a basic VGA driver.

4. From the Start menu, click Settings | Control Panel. Double-click the Add/Remove Hardware applet. This opens up the Add/Remove Hardware Wizard. Click Next.

5. Select Add/Troubleshoot A Device. Click Next.

6. From the next options list, select Add A New Device. Select the Yes, Search For New Hardware radio button. Click Next.

7. The search for the new video adapter takes awhile. Click Finish. This completes the installation process.

Troubleshooting Video Adapters

Video adapter problems may occur due to any of the following reasons:

- **The video adapter is not supported by Windows 2000.** Check with the adapter manufacturer, or check the Windows 2000 Hardware Compatibility List.

- **You are trying to use a video mode that is not supported by the video driver.** In such a case, try selecting the 640 by 480 screen resolution and 16-bit color depth.

- **You may be using a wrong driver for the adapter.** Check the documentation that accompanied the adapter to find out the correct video driver.

If you have trouble configuring the adapter properties and the screen goes blank after Windows 2000 starts up, reboot the computer using the Last Known Good Configuration.

In many cases, the online troubleshooter is very helpful. To access the Troubleshooter, open the Display Properties windows and select the Settings tab. Click the Troubleshooting tab. This opens the Windows 2000 Troubleshooter Wizard. For advanced troubleshooting, click the Advanced tab from the Settings window. Click the Troubleshooting tab. The troubleshooting window opens. This was shown earlier in Figure 6-11.

on the
()ob

When the display gets misconfigured while trying to set some properties, and you are not able to view the screen properly, you will need to select the Last Known Good Configuration from the Advanced Boot Options menu. This is different from VGA mode, because it starts up Windows 2000 using the configuration that was saved the last time you shut down the computer.

Starting Up in VGA Mode

Often, while installing or configuring a video driver, you run into a problem that renders your display blank after Windows starts loading. This usually happens when the operating system is not able to load a specific video driver. In such a situation when you lose access to the display, Windows 2000 provides you with a tool that can be used to start up the system in basic video mode. You can then either uninstall the troublesome video driver or load another driver that you are sure works.

To enable VGA mode, press the F8 key when Windows 2000 starts up. This way, you can access the Advanced Boot Options menu. Select Enable VGA Mode from the menu and press ENTER. The operating system will disable the bad or corrupted video driver, and start up using the basic VGA driver.

exam
ⓦatch

The procedure for enabling VGA mode is different from Windows NT 4.0, in which you had the option of selecting VGA mode during the main boot options. In Windows 2000, you have to press F8 before the wait time expires, and select Enable VGA mode.

SCENARIO & SOLUTION

I wish to use six monitors to extend the display. Is it possible in Windows 2000 Professional?	Yes. Windows 2000 Professional supports up to ten monitors in a multiple-monitor configuration.
I have two video adapters in my computer. Is there any way to know which one is primary and which one is secondary?	Yes. The adapter attached to the monitor that shows the system BIOS on startup is the primary monitor.
I installed a new updated video driver for my display adapter and restarted the computer. Now the screen is blank. How can I uninstall the new driver?	Start the computer in basic VGA mode. Press F8 to access the Advanced Boot Options menu when the operating system's option menu is shown. Select Enable VGA Mode.

FROM THE CLASSROOM

Understanding Dynamic Disk and Volume Concepts

When you first go through the basic and dynamic disk and volume concepts, it looks a bit confusing. Actually, it is not, if you try to understand one point at a time. The first thing you must understand is the translation of disk terminology as applied in Windows 2000. This chapter discusses the new concepts in detail, but I would like to highlight some additional important points:

■ When you upgrade a disk from basic to dynamic, the Master Boot Record (MBR) hands over the disk data to the Disk Management. This data is contained in the last 1MB of the disk space at the end of the disk.

■ Windows 2000 dynamic disks cannot be read locally by MS-DOS, Windows 95, Windows 98, or any version of Windows NT. However, these are readable when shared.

■ When you upgrade a basic disk partition to a dynamic volume, you cannot extend it for creating spanned volumes. Sometimes these include the system and boot volumes, and it is not possible to extend such volumes.

■ If you have a dynamic volume that was created from unallocated space in a dynamic disk, you cannot install Windows 2000 on it. The reason is that this volume may not be correctly configured in the partition table.

■ When using dynamic volumes, you cannot extend the system and boot volumes. These volumes can also not be part of spanned or striped volumes.

One final word: Dynamic volumes are not supported on laptops. Laptops will not give you an option to upgrade your basic disk to a dynamic disk. In some of the laptops, you may get this option, but don't take any chances. It is not supported or recommended by Microsoft.

—Pawan K. Bhardwaj MCSE, MCP+I, CCNA.

CERTIFICATION SUMMARY

Windows 2000 introduces the concept of basic and dynamic disks, and basic and dynamic volumes. Basic disks are the traditional kind of disks supported by all previous versions of Windows. A new Disk Management snap-in has been added to the Computer Management console that replaces the Disk Administrator in Windows NT 4.0. Newer tools for disk management allow the user to change certain disk configurations without restarting the computer. Windows 2000 Professional supports only simple, spanned, and striped volumes. While it is possible to create and manage volumes in fixed storage devices, removable media such as tape devices is supported for creating basic volumes only.

The Disk Management console is the centralized location for performing all disk-related activities, including managing disks connected to remote computers. Disk quotas on NTFS volumes help the administrator in limiting the disk space used by different users of the computer. The Disk Defragmentation utility is useful in analysis and defragmentation of heavily used hard drives. Disk Management provides tools for disk error checking, data backup, restoration, and creation of an Emergency Repair Disk (ERD). Windows 2000 has additional support for many newer technology storage devices such as DVD-ROMs, the USB Interface, and the IEEE 1394 Interface.

Display devices such as display adapters, drivers, and monitors are managed from the Settings tab of the Display Properties sheet. Windows 2000 can identify most of the popular Plug and Play display adapters and monitors, and automatically installs suitable drivers for them. The display resolution and color depth change can be applied without restarting the computer. The advanced display settings allow the user to troubleshoot some common problems with the display devices. Windows 2000 Professional can also work in a multiple-monitor configuration supporting up to ten monitors, which gives the user an illusion of a large single display. This requires the secondary display devices to be compatible with Windows 2000 and must not use any VGA resources.

When a user has some problems with the display while installing a new video driver and the screen becomes blank, he or she may use the Advanced Boot Options to start the computer in VGA mode. The manual hardware acceleration settings in the Troubleshooting tools also help in diagnosing problems with display adapters.

TWO-MINUTE DRILL

Implementing, Managing, and Troubleshooting Disk Devices

❑ The Disk Manager snap-in of the Computer Management console replaces the Disk Administrator that was a part of Administrative Tools in Windows NT 4.0. It is now possible to perform online disk management.

❑ Disk Management provides tools for creating, configuring, and managing disks and volumes. It also has a disk defragmentation utility.

❑ Windows 2000 supports basic and dynamic disks, and basic and dynamic volumes. Dynamic volumes can exist on dynamic disks only.

❑ A basic disk can be upgraded to a dynamic disk without restarting the computer, if it does not contain any system or boot files. The basic disk must have a 512KB sector size.

❑ If the computer has only a single disk, it can have either a basic disk or a dynamic disk configuration. To have multiple configurations, there must be multiple disks in the computer.

❑ Windows 2000 Professional supports simple, spanned, and striped volumes only. Fault-tolerant mirrored volumes or striped volumes with parity are not supported.

❑ Dynamic volumes are not supported on removable storage media such as tape devices. These are also not supported on portable computers.

❑ In order to manage disks on remote computers in a Windows 2000 workgroup environment, the user must have an identical account name and password on all such computers on which he or she wants to run Disk Management.

Implementing, Managing, and Troubleshooting Display Devices

❑ Display devices are managed from the Settings tab of the Display Properties sheet. It is possible to change a number of display settings without restarting the computer.

❑ Plug and Play video adapters are automatically detected, and Windows 2000 installs suitable drivers.

❑ The Advanced tab of the Settings Properties sheet is used for advanced display configurations, such as updating display drivers and troubleshooting.

❑ The user who wishes to change the display configurations must have sufficient privileges to load and unload device drivers.

❑ Windows 2000 can be configured to have multiple monitors, and up to ten monitors are supported. The secondary display devices must not use any VGA resources.

❑ In order to find out which of the installed display devices is primary and which is secondary, check to see which one is displayed in the BIOS information at startup.

❑ When there is a problem with the display driver and the screen goes blank, VGA mode can be enabled from the Advanced Boot Options menu to load the basic video driver.

SELF TEST

The following questions will help you measure your understanding of the material presented in this chapter. Read all of the choices carefully, as there may be more than one correct answer. Choose all correct answers for each question.

Implementing, Managing, and Troubleshooting Disk Devices

1. Donna's desktop computer has a hard disk that is 13.6GB, and has a sector size of 1024KB, and 12MB of free space available at the end. She is unable to upgrade the disk to dynamic disk. Which of the factors is causing the problem?

   A. Disks can only be upgraded on servers, and Donna's computer is a desktop.

   B. The free space at the end of the disk is too large.

   C. The sector size is too large.

   D. The hard disk is not a basic disk.

2. Which of the following volumes are not supported in Windows 2000 Professional? (Select all that apply.)

   A. Spanned volumes

   B. Striped volumes with parity

   C. Mirrored volumes

   D. Striped volumes

3. What methods can you use to access the Computer Management console in Windows 2000? (Select all that apply.)

   A. Right-click the desktop and selecting Manage.

   B. Run CMC from the Start menu.

   C. Select Control Panel | Administrative Tools | Computer Management.

   D. Right-click the My Computer icon and select Properties.

   E. Right-click the My Computer icon and select Manage.

4. Windows 2000 Disk Management provides a number of utilities for managing disks. Which of the following is not a feature of Disk Management?

   A. Online disk management

   B. Sharing the disks on the Web

C. Remote disk management

D. Disk Administrator utility

5. Which of the following fault-tolerant disk configurations are supported in the Windows 2000 Professional operating system? (Select all that apply.)

A. Disk mirroring

B. Disk striping with parity

C. Striped volumes

D. Spanned volumes

E. None of the above

6. What type of basic disks can be upgraded to dynamic disks without restating the computer?

A. Disks that contain system files

B. Disks that contain boot files

C. Disks that do not contain any system or boot files

D. All kinds of disks

7. You have a dual-boot system running Windows 98 and Windows 2000 Professional, each of which is installed on two separate disk drives. The disk drive C: is 4.3GB, and the disk drive D: is 13.6GB containing Windows 2000 Professional. The computer is shared with your supervisor. Here is what you have to do:

■ **Required result:** Upgrade the disk drive D: into a dynamic volume.

■ **Optional desired results:** You must be able to access the volume while running Windows 98 as well as Windows 2000 Professional. There should be no loss of data during the process. Your supervisor must be able to access the data on your D: drive.

■ **Proposed Solution:** Use the Disk Management in Windows 2000 and upgrade the disk D: to a dynamic disk. Format it using FAT 32 and share it for access by the supervisor.

What results are produced by the proposed solution?

A. The proposed solution produces the required result only.

B. The proposed solution produces the required result and only one of the desired results.

C. The proposed solution produces the required result and only two of the desired results.

D. The proposed solution produces the required result and both of the desired results.

8. Which of the following disks cannot be upgraded to dynamic disks? (Select all that apply.)

    A. Disks on laptop computers

    B. Disks that do not have 1MB free space at the end

    C. Disks that are a part of a striped set

    D. Disks that are a part of a volume set

9. Which antivirus software is included with Microsoft Windows 2000 Professional that can scan and fix problems with the Master Boot Record (MBR)?

    A. Norton AntiVirus

    B. McAffee

    C. AVBoot

    D. Innoculan

Implementing, Managing, and Troubleshooting Display Devices

10. How can you access the Troubleshooting tool for resolving the hardware acceleration problems in a display adapter?

    A. From the Troubleshooting tab of Display Properties

    B. From the Advanced tab of the Display Properties Settings screen

    C. From the Effects tab of the Display Properties screen

    D. From Device Manager | Display Adapters

11. Which of the following methods can be used to access and configure Display Properties? (Select all that apply.)

    A. From the Display applet in the Control Panel

    B. By right-clicking the desktop and selecting Properties

    C. From the Device Manager, selecting Display Properties

    D. From the Device Manager, selecting Display Adapter properties

12. You have just installed a new driver for your video card that is supposed to enhance the screen resolution of the display. However, after restarting your computer, you are not able to view anything on the monitor after the initial Windows 2000 startup screen. How can you resolve the problem?

A. Uninstall the driver using the MS-DOS mode.

B. Start the computer by enabling VGA mode, and unload the driver.

C. Use the Device Manager to uninstall the driver.

D. Call the support engineer.

13. What happens when you start a computer using the Advanced Boot Options and selecting Enable VGA Mode?

A. The faulty display driver is automatically uninstalled.

B. The computer uses the Last Known Good Configuration for the display.

C. The basic VGA display driver is loaded.

D. All of the above.

14. What is the maximum number of secondary monitors that can be connected to a computer running Windows 2000 Professional in order to make it a multiple-monitor system?

A. four

B. seven

C. nine

D. ten

15. You want to increase the screen resolution to 800 by 600 pixels, but are not sure if your video adapter supports it. When you change the resolution and confirm it in the dialog box, the screen becomes unreadable. How can you revert to the old resolution?

A. Shut down the computer immediately and restart in VGA mode.

B. Do nothing. The settings will not be saved.

C. Shut down and restart the computer in Last Known Good Configuration.

D. Switch off the monitor and switch it on again.

16. What can you do to resolve a display problem that arises due to wrong configuration of display properties?

A. Start the computer in VGA mode.

B. Start the computer in Safe mode.

C. Start the computer using Last Known Good Configuration.

D. All of the above.

17. To install four monitors with your computer, you purchase three additional PCI adapters and three more monitors. After installing the adapters and their drivers, you connected the monitors, but the computer is still using only the original monitor. What step should you take to enable the additional monitors?

   A. Configure the display settings to extend display to multiple monitors.

   B. Uninstall additional display drivers, as only one driver is needed for all display adapters.

   C. Change the order of placement of monitors.

   D. All of the above.

18. You installed a new PCI display adapter and restarted the computer. Although the supplier told you that the adapter is Plug and Play, Windows 2000 did not detect it. How can you install the driver for this display adapter that is provided by the supplier?

   A. From the Device Manager, using Add The New Adapter utility.

   B. From the Control Panel, using Add Remove/Hardware.

   C. From the Display Properties window.

   D. You cannot install the adapter because Windows 2000 accepts only onboard adapters.

LAB QUESTION

In this exercise, we will configure a Windows 2000 Professional computer to manage remote hard drives using Disk Management. We are listing some steps to make the process fully operational. You are to check whether any of the given steps are incorrect, or if there are any missing steps.

Current situation: There are four computers running Windows 2000 Professional. The computers are networked in a workgroup environment. The names of the computers are Test1, Test2, Test3, and Test4. Your computer is Test1, and you want to manage disks on the other three computers.

Required Result: Configure Disk Management on Test1 computer to manage remote disks.

Proposed Solution: Perform the following steps:

1. Log on to the Test1 computer as administrator, or as a user having administrative privileges.

2. Make sure that the Test2, Test3, and Test4 computers are alive on the network by double-clicking My Network Places | Entire Network.

3. Click Start | Programs | Administrative Tools | Disk Administrator to open the Microsoft Management Console (MMC).

4. In the MMC, click the Console menu, and select the Add/Remove snap-in. Click Add.

5. Select Disk Administrator from the right-side panel. Click Add.

6. In the next window, select Another Computer and type **Test1**. Click Finish.

7. To add Disk Management snap-ins for the other two computers, repeat steps 3–5. Figure 6-12 shows an MMC with remote disk management snap-ins added for Test1 and Test2 computers.

8. Close all windows. You are ready to manage the disks remotely by using any of the disk management snap-ins.

So, what results do the proposed steps produce? Do you notice any missing or wrong steps?

FIGURE 6-12	

Adding Disk
Management
consoles for
remote
computers

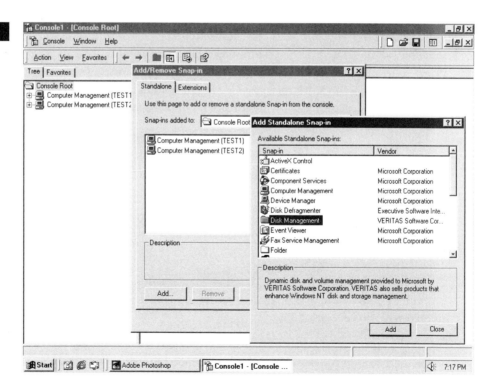

SELF TEST ANSWERS

Implementing, Managing, and Troubleshooting Disk Devices

1. ☑ **C.** This disk cannot be upgraded to a dynamic disk because the maximum sector size on the disk should not exceed 512KB, and the disk in question has a 1024KB sector size.
   ☒ **A** is incorrect because being a desktop should not prevent the disk in the computer from being upgraded. **B** is incorrect because the condition of free disk space at the end of the disk is minimum 1MB. Having more space at the end of the disk is not preventing the upgrade. **D** is incorrect because every disk is a basic disk, unless it is upgraded to a dynamic disk.

2. ☑ **B, C.** Windows 2000 Professional does not support striped volumes with parity (RAID 5) and mirrored volumes (RAID 1). These are fault-tolerance disk systems and are not supported.
   ☒ **A** and **D** are incorrect because these volumes are supported and can be created in Windows 2000 Professional.

3. ☑ **C, E.** The two methods for accessing the Computer Management console are by right-clicking the My Computer icon and selecting Manage, and from the Control Panel, selecting Administrative Tools | Computer Management.
   ☒ **A** is incorrect because there is no such option. **B** is incorrect because this is an invalid command. **D** is an invalid choice, as selecting properties from the My Computer icon shows the computer properties such as identification, network properties, and hardware profiles.

4. ☑ **D.** The Disk Administrator, which was available under Administrative Tools in Windows NT, has been replaced by Disk Management in Windows 2000.
   ☒ **A, B,** and **C** are invalid, as all these utilities are included in Windows 2000 Disk Management.

5. ☑ **E.** Fault tolerance is not supported in the Windows 2000 Professional operating system. It is, however, supported in all versions of Windows 2000 Server.

6. ☑ **C.** Only disks that do not contain any system or boot files can be upgraded to dynamic disks without restarting the computer.
   ☒ **A** and **B** are incorrect because any disk that contains system or boot files will need the computer restarted after the upgrade in order to make the changes effective. This makes **D** an incorrect choice.

7. ☑ **B.** The proposed solution produces the required result and only one of the desired results. The required result is met as the disk gets upgraded to a dynamic disk. The only desired result that is met is that your supervisor will be able to access the disk using its share name. The first desired result is not produced, because if the disk is upgraded to a dynamic volume, it cannot

be accessed locally by any operating system other than Windows 2000. The second desired result is not met because all data on the disk will be lost when you format it using FAT 32.

8. ☑ **A, B.** Upgrading to dynamic disks is not supported on laptop computers. The disks that do not have at least 1MB free at the end can also not be upgraded to dynamic disks, because Disk Management writes the disk data in this part of the disk.
   ☒ **C and D** are incorrect because it is possible to upgrade any disks in the striped set or volume set. This requires you to upgrade all the disks that are part of such sets.

9. ☑ **C.** The AVBoot software is included with Windows 2000 Professional for scanning and fixing problems with the Master Boot Record.
   ☒ **A, B, and D** are incorrect, as none of these antivirus software packages come with Windows 2000 Professional.

Implenting, Managing, and Troubleshooting Display Devices

10. ☑ **B.** This tool can be accessed from the Advanced tab of the Display Properties Settings screen.
    ☒ **A** is incorrect because the Troubleshooting tab in the Display Properties screen opens the general Windows 2000 troubleshooting help. **C** is incorrect because the Effects tab does not have any troubleshooting option for the display adapter. **D** is incorrect because the Display Manager will also open the general troubleshooting help.

11. ☑ **A, B.** Display properties can be configured using the Display applet in the Control Panel, and by right-clicking the desktop and selecting Properties.
    ☒ **C and D** are incorrect because the Device Manager is used to install/uninstall, update, and troubleshoot display drivers. You cannot configure display properties using the Device Manager.

12. ☑ **B.** When a newly installed video driver does not work properly, VGA mode can help resolve the problem. You can uninstall the driver and install a correct driver using VGA mode.
    ☒ **A** is not valid because the driver cannot be uninstalled in MS-DOS mode. **C** is incorrect because the Device Manager is available only when you are able to start the computer in VGA mode. **D** is a last resort option, and is not a good answer for the question.

13. ☑ **C.** Staring a Windows 2000 computer by enabling VGA mode forces the operating system to load a basic VGA driver instead of the installed driver. This mode helps you install a correct video driver when the installed driver is not working properly.
    ☒ **A** is incorrect because the VGA mode does not uninstall the faulty video driver—the faulty video driver has to be replaced manually. **B** is incorrect because the Last Known Good Configuration is used only when you select this option in the Advanced Boot Options menu. **D** is not a valid answer because you have only one correct answer.

14. ☑ **C.** A total of nine additional secondary monitors can be added to a Windows 2000 computer to make it a multiple-monitor system.

    ☒ **A** and **B** are incorrect, because the limit on secondary monitors is nine, and not four or seven. **D** is incorrect because it shows the total number of monitors, including primary and secondary monitors. The question is about the maximum number of secondary monitors.

15. ☑ **B.** Do nothing. If you do not click Yes to make the changes effective immediately after changing the screen resolution, they are not saved, and the screen resolution returns to the previous settings.

    ☒ **A** and **C** are incorrect because you need not restart the computer. **D** is incorrect because switching the monitor off and on will not have any effect on screen resolution.

16. ☑ **C.** When you misconfigure the display properties, it is best to restart the computer in Last Known Good Configuration. This ensures that the configuration that worked previously is used.

    ☒ **A** is not appropriate because the VGA mode is helpful when a newly installed display driver is not working. This mode starts Windows 2000 in basic VGA mode. The installed driver is not used. **B** is incorrect, as Safe mode will still use the wrong display driver. **D** is incorrect because the answers given in **A** and **B** are not good for resolving the problem.

17. ☑ **A.** In order to configure your Windows 2000 computer to use multiple monitors, you must configure Display Properties. In the Settings tab, select each monitor one by one and select the Extend My Desktop Onto This Monitor check box.

    ☒ **B** is incorrect, as each installed adapter needs a suitable driver. **C** is incorrect because changing the placement of monitors will not solve the problem. This will help only if the monitors have been misconfigured. **D** is an invalid choice because only one answer is correct.

18. ☑ **B.** Any new device that is not detected automatically by the Windows 2000 operating system can be added using the Add/Remove Hardware applet, as long as Windows 2000 supports it.

    ☒ **A** is incorrect because there is no such option in Device Manager. You may, however, try again to detect the adapter by right-clicking Display Adapters and selecting Scan For Hardware Changes. **C** is incorrect because you cannot add an adapter using the Display Properties window. **D** is incorrect, as Windows 2000 supports many PCI adapters.

LAB ANSWER

Yes, there are wrong *and* missing steps. The procedure does not specify anywhere that you must have the same username and password on all the computers. Unless you create accounts in Test2, Test3, and Test4, you will not be able to manage the disks on these computers.

   Next, read step 3 carefully. It says that the Disk Administrator will open the MMC. This is wrong—there is no Disk Administrator in Windows 2000. To open MMC, click Start | Run and type **MMC**. Click OK. This will open a blank MMC. You can add snap-ins in this console from the Action menu.

7

Implementing, Managing, and Troubleshooting Hardware Devices and Drivers

W

indows NT users have always had a love/hate relationship with Windows NT. On the one hand, users loved the stability and security that Windows NT provided. On the other hand, hardware configuration was more difficult than under Windows 95/98.

Most hardware devices only came with drivers and support for Windows 95/98. Devices that were supported under Windows NT had to connect via existing bus technology (ISA, PCI, SCSI, and so on), and there was no support for newer technologies such as Universal Serial Bus (USB) and Plug and Play (PnP).

This selective hardware support under Windows NT was intentional. All hardware devices supported under Windows NT had to be on Microsoft's Hardware Compatibility List (HCL), a list of computer models and hardware devices that were tested and approved by Microsoft for use under Windows NT. If a company's peripherals were listed on the HCL, a user had a reasonable guarantee that the hardware and its driver would operate correctly and stably under Windows NT. This also meant that the hardware had NT-specific driver software written for it.

In previous Microsoft operating systems (DOS and Windows 3.*x*, 95, and 98), software applications were permitted by the operating system to communicate directly with the installed hardware. For example, a game program might bypass the operating system and send music or sound effects directly to the sound card. If that program crashed while it was accessing the sound card, any other program or part of the operating system waiting to use that hardware device also crashed. This usually led to the user needing to reboot the computer, resulting in lost time and possibly lost data.

Windows NT changed this model. The NT kernel controlled all access to hardware. This required that programs be rewritten to not attempt to talk directly to the hardware, and that all hardware installed only allowed itself to be controlled by the kernel. If a program crashed while using a hardware device, or if that device became unstable while it was being used, the kernel would isolate the problem program/hardware from the rest of the memory, and would allow the system to continue operating without the need for a system reboot. It is this design that led to the creation of the NT HCL and of the requirement that all supported hardware to be used under NT be on the HCL.

This stability model does not change with Windows 2000. Windows 2000 bridges the gap in hardware support between the convenience and new technology available in Windows 95 and Windows 98 and the stability and hardiness of Windows NT.

Hardware supported under Windows 2000 must appear on the Windows 2000 HCL and have Windows 2000–specific drivers written for it. These drivers will be preinstalled with Windows 2000, available as a download from the hardware vendor's Web site, or included on a CD-ROM or floppy when you purchase a supported device.

on the job

The HCL is an ever-changing list. The devices certified for use under Windows 2000 as of the date of its release are included on the Windows 2000 install media. Any new or updated devices and drivers will be added to the HCL. If you have a new hardware device and it is not listed on the HCL included on the Windows 2000 install media, check to see if it has been added recently to the HCL. The most recent version of the Windows 2000 HCL is always available on Microsoft's Web site at www.microsoft.com/hcl/default.asp.

exam Watch

Some questions on the Microsoft certification exams relating to hardware support may make mention of the HCL. In both the certification tests and the real world, checking the HCL is an important step. Don't get a question wrong by not keeping the HCL in mind!

CERTIFICATION OBJECTIVE 7.01

Implementing, Managing, and Troubleshooting Mobile Computer Hardware

As more organizations discover the productivity enhancements that a community of mobile users can realize, these organizations will need to support more laptops. Traditionally only a necessity for sales personnel or on-the-go executives, laptops weren't a fit for most users.

However, as laptops became faster, more powerful, and as inexpensive as desktop computers, they became more widely used. Laptops still have their own unique support requirements, however, and an organization wishing to provide laptops for their users should ensure that support staff is aware of these unique support needs.

Due to the size of the laptop hardware, it is impossible to use existing bus technologies interchangeably with desktop machines. While laptops will still be able to use the latest computer technology (fastest networks, and latest SCSI and modem technology), that technology needs to be (and is) adapted to buses that laptops use.

For example, an average desktop machine will probably have the hard drive and CD-ROM drive connected via an Integrated Drive Electronics (IDE) or Enhanced IDE (EIDE) controller. Normally, IDE controllers can have two drives per channel; and in order to add a second drive, there must be an open drive bay and a cable to connect the second drive to the controller. If you wanted to make use of faster SCSI drives, you would have to install a SCSI controller in a PCI or ISA slot.

This kind of flexibility is not present in laptop systems. While there may be vendor-specific implementations of ISA, PCI, and IDE technology in a given laptop model, expandability is still an issue. Laptops are designed to be small and portable. Laptop size would be increased by necessity if there were space allocated for standard full-sized PCI slots and a second IDE hard drive. The only way for laptop vendors to provide the same level of expandability and choice of hardware is to support a bus technology designed for mobile hardware.

This is where the Personal Computer Memory Card International Association (PCMCIA) bus comes into play. The PCMCIA bus was designed for laptop use. PCMCIA devices allow for technology available in desktop hardware to be used on laptops. Organizations can use the same Ethernet technology on all computers, whether it is through a PCI network card on a desktop or a PCMCIA network card on a laptop.

Configuration and management of PCMCIA devices are covered later in this section.

Configuring Power Management

Power Management is a set of configuration options that enable your Windows 2000 Professional computer to manage how and when your computer consumes power. Normally, a computer will be plugged into a constant AC power source, but there are many situations for both desktops and laptops in which users will want to manage their power consumption. Power management is configured using the Power Options applet in the Control Panel.

Power Management support under Windows 2000 Professional is divided into two separate power management initiatives supported by the PC industry: Advanced Power Management (APM), and Advanced Configuration and Power Interface (ACPI).

Advanced Power Management (APM)

APM is a legacy power management scheme that is supported by older BIOSes and Windows 95. The design goal of APM was to allow the hardware to be shut down or disabled after a period of inactivity and reenabled if actively needed by the user.

The detection of inactivity was, in most cases, incomplete or nonintuitive under APM. For example, if a user were trying to download a large file over the computer's modem, the APM components under the operating system would detect that neither the mouse nor keyboard was being used. It would then shut down the monitor, spin down the disks, or place the entire computer in a low power consumption mode known as Standby mode. These power-saving tasks would usually also stop the file transfer being performed through the modem.

Advanced Configuration and Power Interface (ACPI)

ACPI is a newer specification jointly developed by Microsoft, Compaq, Toshiba (both computer manufacturers), Intel (processor manufacturer), and Phoenix (BIOS manufacturer). ACPI allows a system that is fully ACPI compliant to not only cleanly power down components when not needed, but also to power the components back up in the event of network or modem activity. For example, a departmental fax server can power down itself after a period of inactivity. Once an incoming fax is detected (by the ringing of the telephone line) or an outgoing fax is requested (by network traffic directed to that server), the fax server can wake up, process the fax, and then reenter its power-saving mode.

ACPI is a management scheme that makes power management part of systems management. ACPI specifications are implemented throughout the entire system, including the hardware, operating system, and application software. For example, ACPI-compliant client PCs can be set to power down after hours when not in use. If a scheduled maintenance task, such as anti-virus software updates or new application installation, is needed after hours, the ACPI computers can wake at a predetermined time, accept the software update, and then power down again. This would not be possible under APM, because once an APM-compliant component is powered down, the only way to reenable it is to move the mouse or keyboard at that computer.

Since part of the specifications for ACPI and APM call for support in the computer's BIOS, you should ensure that some of the options in the computer's CMOS setup program are set for operating system control. Stability issues may result if both the BIOS and Windows 2000 are trying to perform the same power management tasks at the same time. Consult your computer's documentation for information about how to enter the computer's CMOS setup program and how to enable OS control of power management settings.

The choice between APM and ACPI is not made by the user. If your computer's BIOS supports one of the schemes, it will be displayed in the CMOS setup. Newer computers will support ACPI. APM/ACPI support is determined by Windows 2000 Setup. The Setup utility scans the computer's BIOS to determine which scheme is supported. OS support for the detected scheme is installed. After installation is complete, this detection is repeated each time the computer is booted. As part of the Windows 2000 boot process, ntdetect.com checks the BIOS (among other hardware settings) and writes the detected information in the Registry at HKLM/Hardware.

on the **Job**

If APM support is enabled and causes hardware-related problems, they can be fixed by booting into Safe mode (press F8 when rebooting) and deleting the following file: %systemroot%\system32\drivers\ntapm.sys. Problems that may be fixed by this procedure include the system not shutting down properly, problems after resuming, and general system instability when entering a reduced power mode.

Configuring and Managing Card Services

Card Services under Windows 2000 refers to the configuration and management of hardware devices that are designed for the Personal Computer Memory Card International Association (PCMCIA) bus. PCMCIA devices are about the size of a credit card, and are intended to be replacements for devices that connect via the PCI or ISA buses. PCMCIA is a bus technology, and most types of devices that can normally be found for the PCI and ISA buses can also be found for the PCMCIA bus. PCMCIA devices are sometimes referred to as PC Card devices or card devices. There are SCSI cards, network interface cards (NICs), and modems available as PC Card devices.

Part of the PCMCIA specification is tied to the Plug and Play architecture. The software services that allow for PnP on a PC are partially implemented in the PCMCIA

SCENARIO & SOLUTION

How do I determine which power management scheme is being used on my PC?	Go into the CMOS setup of your computer when it is booting up (instructions for doing this will vary according to manufacturer), and if a scheme is supported, it will be displayed on one of these screens.
Can both APM and ACPI be supported on a single system?	Not likely. In most cases, the hardware and BIOS of a computer will only support one of the two power management schemes.
What is the relationship between APM and ACPI?	ACPI is a superset of the features provided by APM. Both provide the same set of functions, but since ACPI is newer technology, it expands on the capabilities of APM.

hardware. Normally, a PC Card modem can be plugged into a system hot, the appropriate drivers are loaded, the modem inserts itself as an available device in the communications stack, and the modem is available for use immediately without a reboot.

Configuring Card Services

Please note that you must be logged on as an administrator or a member of the Administrators group to complete the exercises in this chapter. If your computer is connected to a network, network policy settings may also prevent you from completing this procedure. This exercise walks you through managing and removing a PCMCIA card from a laptop. The PCMCIA card used in this exercise is a 3COM combination modem and NIC card. The screenshots used in this exercise will differ from those you will see unless you have the exact model PCMCIA card.

1. Start the Add/Remove Hardware Wizard by double-clicking that item in the Control Panel. The first screen of the wizard is shown in the following illustration.

2. Click Next. This brings up the next screen of the wizard, shown in the following illustration. On this screen, we can choose to add new hardware, troubleshoot an already installed device, or uninstall/unplug an already installed device. Uninstalling a device will permanently remove it from the

system. Unplugging a device on a bus that supports hot removal of devices (USB, PCMCIA, and so on) temporarily removes it from the system. Since we are going to unplug the PCMCIA modem/network card, select Uninstall/Unplug A Device and click Next.

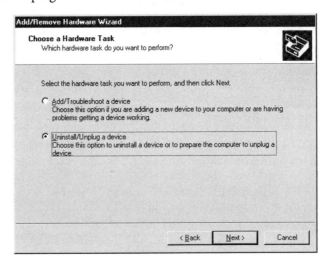

3. On the next screen of the wizard, shown in the following illustration, you are asked to choose between uninstalling (permanent) or unplugging (temporary) a device. Select Unplug/Eject A Device and click Next.

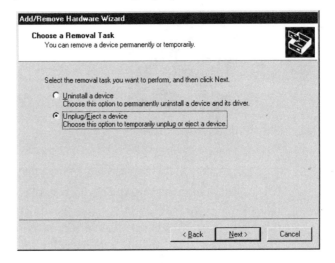

4. The next screen in the following illustration displays all of the devices that can be unplugged from the system. In this example, the only device available for removal is the combination network/modem card installed in the PCMCIA slot. If there were other devices installed on this system that were able to be unplugged or removed while the computer is powered on, they would be displayed here. By default, only the device as listed in the Windows 2000 Device Manager will be displayed on this screen. If you want to see which other devices will also be removed, select the check box marked Show Related Devices.

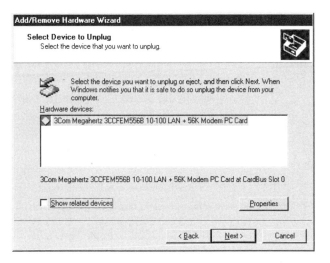

5. The next illustration shows the same information that was displayed in the previous illustration, with related devices also shown. Notice that in this case, the removal of the PCMCIA card will also result in the removal of the Ethernet NIC and modem that would be listed elsewhere in Device Manager. The removal of the modem would also cause the removal of a sound device associated with the modem. This screen lets you see all places in the system where the removal of one device affects the entire system. Since we do want to remove the PCMCIA card (and the NIC and modem), select the top-level device, 3Com Megahertz 3CCFEM556B 10-100 LAN + 56K Modem PC Card, and click Next.

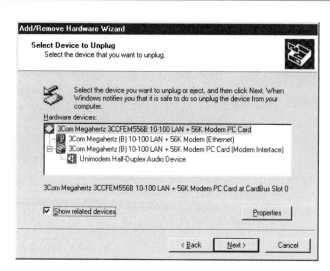

6. The next screen in the wizard (shown in the following illustration) asks you to confirm that removing the selected device is indeed what you wish to do. This screen lists the four devices shown in the previous illustration (a convenient reminder in case you did not choose Show Related Devices in step 5). If you selected the wrong device, you can click Back and choose again. If you decide that you do not wish to remove the selected device, you can click Cancel. For this exercise, click Next to confirm the removal of the displayed devices.

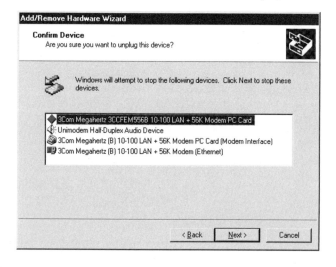

7. The wizard is now completed. The following illustration shows the last screen of the wizard. The screen tells you that the selected device can now be safely removed or unplugged. There is an option that allows you to skip the steps of the wizard and remove devices from the System Tray. Select the check box marked Show Unplug/Eject Icon On The Taskbar, and click Finish.

8. We've just used the Add/Remove Hardware Wizard to remove a PCMCIA card from a Windows 2000 Professional laptop. Continuing in this exercise, we will remove the same PCMCIA card using the icon on the taskbar. Remove the PCMCIA card from the PCMCIA slot. You will notice that any software that requires the networking and modem hardware to work will no longer function.

9. Allow about a minute for the removed PCMCIA card to cool off (it can get pretty hot inside the laptop if it is plugged in for an extended period of time.

10. When the PCMCIA card is cool to the touch, insert it back into the PCMCIA slot. The system will beep, indicating that a card has been inserted. Windows 2000 will automatically detect and load the appropriate drivers for this card. After the drivers are loaded, networking and modem functions will work again.

11. With the PCMCIA started, double-click the Unplug Or Eject Hardware icon on the taskbar. This icon is shown in the following illustration.

12. You should now see the screen shown in the following illustration. Select the hardware device to be unplugged (in this example, it is the same 3Com combo model/network card from earlier in this exercise) and click Stop. Notice that you can also view related devices or cancel the unplugging in the same manner as if you were using the wizard.

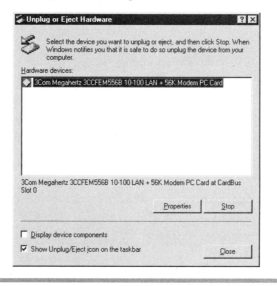

13. You should now see a dialog box similar to that shown in the following illustration. This indicates that the device has been disabled and that it can be removed from the system.

CERTIFICATION OBJECTIVE 7.02

Managing and Troubleshooting the Use and Synchronization of Offline Files

The Offline Files feature in Windows 2000 Professional is a new feature that allows mobile users to keep files stored on a server available to them even if they are not connected to the network. In previous versions of Windows and Windows NT, the Explorer Briefcase was used for this purpose.

The Explorer Briefcase is still supported in Windows 2000, although it is not the recommended way to synchronize files between a laptop and a server.

When using the Briefcase, users had to create a special Briefcase folder on their hard drive (usually stored on their desktop and as part of their profile in *%systemroot%* profiles*username*\\Desktop\\New Briefcase). The user would put into this folder individual files and folders that needed to be available when the computer was not connected to the network. As changes were made to either the local files stored in the Briefcase or the files on the server, a manual synchronization was necessary to merge the changes.

While the ability to keep multiple copies of the same files synchronized via the Briefcase was useful, there were several drawbacks to this approach: The user had to keep track of which files came from which server, and depending on whether the user was connected to the network or not, had to go to two different locations to access the files. The user settings in Microsoft Word, for example, allowed a user to set a default file location that the File Open and Save dialog boxes should use. If a user had to frequently use two locations (file server and local briefcase) to store files, he or she had to either frequently change this setting in Word, or always use the Briefcase copy of the files and perform frequent manual synchronizations.

In most cases, the merging logic used to determine which location to put changes to files was pretty simple. If a file was modified in one location and not in the other (based on the file's timestamp and size), then the *entire* modified file was copied to the other location. If changes were made to both files since the last synchronization, then Briefcase could not determine which copy was more up to date. There were a few exceptions to this (such as Microsoft Excel and Access files, which were able to merge cell- and field-level changes made to both documents); but for the most part, changed files that were shared among multiple users via the Briefcase could not be easily resolved.

The Offline Folders feature in Windows 2000 Professional fixes these problems. Offline Folders still allows users to keep local copies of files stored on a central file server, but it is enabled in a way that allows users not to keep track of whether they are looking at the local or the network copy.

Individual files, folders, mapped network drives, or even Web pages can all be made available offline, and changes made to either copy of the offline item can be synchronized manually or automatically.

on the

()ob *By default, items cached locally as offline files are stored in the root of the computer's boot partition. A utility is provided in the Windows 2000 Professional Resource Kit called Cache Mover (cachemov.exe) that can move this cache to a different location on the hard drive, or even to a different local hard drive. For more information, check the documentation that comes with the Windows 2000 Resource Kit.*

Configuring Offline Files

Offline Files is a client-side enhancement available on computers running Windows 2000. There are no special requirements for the file server whose files are being synchronized. Any file server that supports Server Message Block (SMB)–based file sharing can be used for Offline Files storage, as long as the client computer is running Windows 2000. Examples of supported servers include Windows for Workgroups, Windows NT, and a UNIX-based server running the SAMBA file-sharing software.

Synchronization Manager

The Synchronization Manager is a tool that allows the user to manage from a central location all offline folders and Web pages that have been previously enabled for offline use. We will look at the features of the Synchronization Manager in more detail in Exercise 7-2, which will demonstrate how to configure and use Offline Folders on a computer running Windows 2000 Professional.

CertCam 7-2

Configuring and Using Offline Folders

This exercise walks you through configuring and connecting to Offline Folders from a Windows 2000 Professional computer.

1. First, you must create a share on a network server whose contents will be cached locally by the Offline Folders feature. Create a share called "department" on the server (refer to the documentation appropriate for the server operating system for more details). If you are sharing the directory on a computer running Windows 2000 Server, continue to the next step; otherwise, skip to step 5.

2. If the server sharing the files is running Windows 2000 Server, caching options can be enabled that will increase the performance of the Offline Folders features when accessed from a Windows 2000 Professional computer. When sharing a folder on a Windows 2000 Server computer, additional options appear in the Sharing dialog box, as shown in the following illustration. If you click Caching, you get the screenshot in the next illustration, shown in step 3.

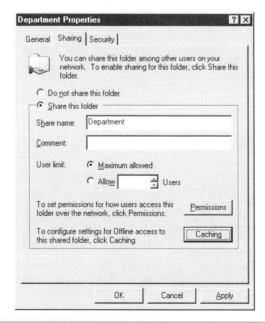

3. In the Caching Settings dialog box, there are three choices for enabling caching of documents, described in the following table. For this exercise, set the caching options to Manual Caching For Documents. The illustration following the table shows the caching settings available to a folder that is shared on a Windows 2000 Server computer.

Cache Setting	Meaning
Automatic Caching For Documents	Any file accessed by a user is automatically made available offline. This does not mean that *all* files in the shared directory are available, only those that have been opened by users. When a file that has not been previously available offline is accessed, it is then made offline. This ensures that only the files that are actually accessed are made available offline.
Automatic Caching For Programs	This setting is intended for caching files that are normally accessed read only, such as a shared network installation of an application. This type of caching reduces network traffic because offline files are opened directly, without accessing the network versions in any way, and generally start and run faster than the network versions. When you use this caching setting, you must restrict permissions on either the share or the files to read-only access.
Manual Caching For Documents	This cache setting provides offline access to only those files that a user specifically (or manually) identifies. This caching option is ideal for a shared network folder containing files that are to be accessed and modified by several people. This is the default option when you set up a shared folder to be used offline.

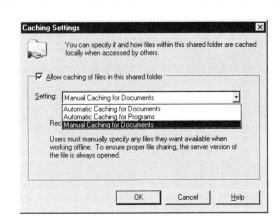

4. Back on your Windows 2000 Professional computer, map a drive to the share you created in step 2. In the following illustration, we mapped the F: drive to the Department share on a Windows 2000 server named Server11.

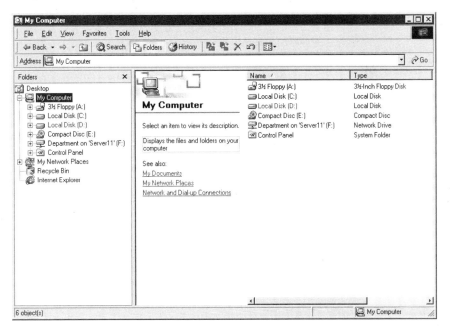

5. Verify that Explorer is set to allow local creation of offline folders by selecting "Folder Options . . . ." under the Tools menu. Select the Offline Files tab. There

are several options that are grayed out, and selecting the check box marked Enable Offline Files enables these options. The following illustration shows these options, which are described in following table.

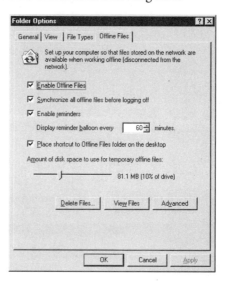

Setting	Description
Synchronize All Offline Files Before Logging Off	Ensures that both the local copy and the server copy of the files are synchronized before logging off the current user.
Enable Reminders	When enabled, tooltip balloons appear in the taskbar to remind the user when the network has been disconnected or reconnected.
Display Reminder Balloon Every *n* Minutes	At the specified interval, the reminder balloon reappears on the taskbar to remind the user of the network's current status.
Place Shortcut To Offline Files Folder On The Desktop	When enabled, it places a shortcut to Offline Files on your desktop. When this shortcut is opened, it displays a list of all files stored locally on your hard drive. Like the Explorer Briefcase, it lists all files (regardless of location) and an overall status of which files are synchronized, and whether the server is available.

Setting	Description
Amount Of Disk Space To Use For Temporary Offline Files	Lets you choose how much space to allocate on the computer's boot partition to storage of offline files. This setting defaults to 10% of the drive.

6. Enable all of the check boxes listed in the table shown in step 3, and then click Advanced. The dialog box shown in the following illustration is displayed. This dialog box allows you to control how the reminders set in the previous dialog box are displayed. Click OK to return to the Folder Options property sheet. Click OK again to apply the Offline Folders settings and close the Folder Options Properties sheet.

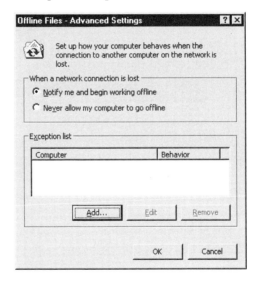

7. In the previous step, we enabled Offline Folders to be used on this Windows 2000 Professional computer, but we haven't yet specified which files and folders are to be available offline. We will do this now. In this exercise, we will make an entire drive available locally, but we can also choose to make just a subfolder or a single file available offline. Right-click the drive letter in Explorer of the drive you mapped in step 5. From the context menu, select Make Available Offline. A wizard will appear to guide you through

the steps. The first screen of the wizard appears in the following illustration. Click Next.

8. The next steps of the wizard ask you to confirm the options chosen in step 7. These options mirror the choices given in the table shown in step 3. Click Next twice to verify these settings.

9. The dialog box shown in the following illustration asks you to choose whether to make only the selected folder available offline, or to make the selected folder and all subfolders underneath it available offline. Keep in mind that if the contents of the entire subdirectory are larger than the space made available locally (refer to the setting made in the table shown in step 3), then files that are less frequently used will be purged in favor of those more frequently used. Click the option marked Yes, Make This Folder And All Its Subfolders Available Offline, and click OK.

10. Windows Explorer then starts copying the contents of the remote folder to the local Offline Files cache. You will see a status box similar to that shown here:

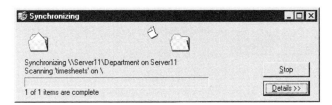

11. When the file copying is complete, Explorer will display all files and folders configured for offline availability with a "roundtrip" overlay in the bottom-left corner of the icon. Notice in the following illustration how the budget and timesheets folders and the Policies.doc file are all marked with the Offline overlay in the bottom-left corner of their icons.

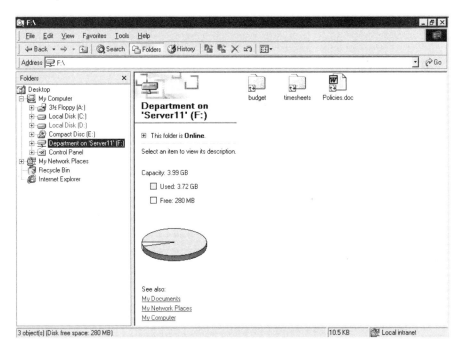

12. Unplug the network cable from the back of your computer. When Windows 2000 detects that the network is no longer available, it will display a balloon

on the taskbar stating that the computer is no longer connected to the network.

13. Open one of the files that has been cached locally and make changes to that file. Save the file to its original location and notice that you can still refer to that folder (or mapped drive) as if the computer were connected to the network.

14. A new icon in the shape of a computer now should appear in the System Tray. Right-click this icon and select Status. The dialog box shown in the following illustration will appear. Notice that for each server whose offline files are stored locally, there is a status line indicating the status of the server (offline or online) and the status of that server's synchronization. In the following illustration, the status line shows that Server11 is not available on the network and that there is one file that needs to be synchronized.

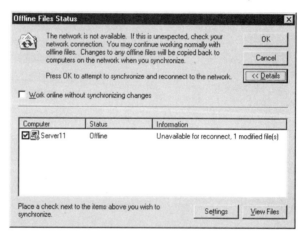

15. Reconnect the network cable to your computer. When Windows 2000 detects that the network is available again, it will display a balloon on the taskbar stating that the computer is again connected to the network. Now we will synchronize the changes made locally to the files on the network.

16. To synchronize individual items, right-click the folder or file whose contents you want to synchronize, and select Synchronize from the context menu. If you want to synchronize all of the locally cached files, regardless of how many servers you are caching, you can use the Synchronization Manager,

shown in the next illustration. Open the Synchronization Manager, located under the Start menu at the following path:

```
Start | Programs | Accessories | Synchronize
```

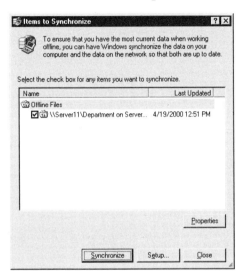

17. The Synchronization Manager shows all items cached locally. Click Synchronize to synchronize all of the items that have been set for offline availability. The following illustration shows the status as local files are synchronized with the server copies.

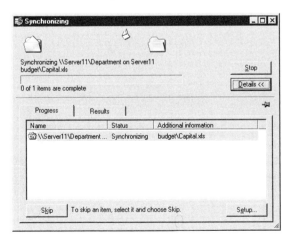

18. When synchronization is complete, the Synchronization Manager shows a summary status screen similar to the next illustration. If any errors occurred, they would be shown here as well.

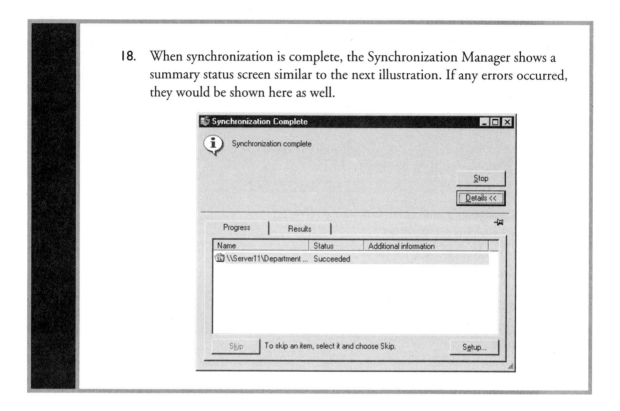

The Synchronization Manager cannot be used to enable Offline Folders or to cache individual items—those tasks can only be performed from Windows Explorer. Once this setup is performed, Synchronization Manager can be used to perform replication of these folders.

In addition to shared directories and files, Web pages and URLs can also be cached locally by adding a site to your Favorites folder, and then selecting to make that page available offline. Once URLs and Web pages are cached locally, they can also be synchronized using the Synchronization Manager.

SCENARIO & SOLUTION

Can I continue to use the Explorer Briefcase?	Absolutely. The preferred method of synchronizing files between two machines is Offline Folders, but the Explorer Briefcase still works and is supported. Keep in mind that you will not get integrated synchronization of files, folders, and Web pages with Briefcase; and if you have multiple Briefcases, you will have to synchronize each of them separately.
Must I connect to a Windows 2000 Server to take advantage of Offline Folders?	No. Since Offline Folders is a client operation, you can locally cache files and folders from any server capable of SMB-based file sharing. These include Windows NT, Windows 98, Windows for Workgroups, and other operating systems. There are certain server-side cache settings that can be made to make the caching more efficient, but the use of Windows 2000 Server is not required.
What types of objects can be cached?	Any file, folder, or Web page that you connect to from Explorer or Internet Explorer can be cached locally.
Once I've set up Offline Folders, what triggers synchronization of those items?	Depending on how the Offline Folders were set up, synchronization can be performed when you log off, when you attach your computer to the network, triggered manually, and according to a set schedule.

CERTIFICATION OBJECTIVE 7.03

Implementing, Managing, and Troubleshooting Input and Output (I/O) Devices

In this section, we will discuss how to configure and troubleshoot input and output devices. Windows 2000 has many improved features for hardware support, and combines the ease of use of Windows 95/98 hardware configuration with the stability of Windows NT.

If you performed an upgrade to Windows 2000 Professional from Windows NT 4.0, all of the hardware that was configured before the upgrade will be installed. If you're installing a hardware device under Windows 2000, you can use the NT 4.0 drivers if they're the only ones available or supported by the manufacturer.

Windows 2000 can also use the same drivers provided for Windows 98 support if those drivers are specifically written for dual Windows 98/Windows 2000 systems. This newer generation of driver support is called the Windows Driver Model (WDM) and is intended to allow hardware manufacturers to write a single driver program that will be supported in both Windows 98 and Windows 2000 (and presumably future versions of these products). Microsoft had previously announced that they would try to merge their consumer line of operating systems (Windows 98 and earlier) with their business operating system (Windows 2000 and Windows NT). The introduction of WDM is one of the first steps in this product merging that will probably take several more years (and product upgrades) to realize.

Windows 95 drivers (referred to as VxD drivers) are not supported under Windows 2000. You must use updated Windows 2000 drivers for that hardware.

To ensure maximum reliability and stability in the hardware devices you configure, you can take advantage of Driver Signing options that are new in Windows 2000. Once a driver and hardware combination has been deemed to be compatible for Windows 2000 and placed on the HCL (see discussion earlier in this chapter for information on the HCL), Microsoft digitally signs the drivers before publishing them. This digital signature ensures that the version of the driver is the exact one that has been tested and approved by Microsoft. The signature is an extra piece of data embedded into the driver software that is derived from an algorithm whose input is the driver code itself. When Windows 2000 tries to install a new driver, it checks for this signature. If the signature is correct, it means that both the signature and the driver have not been altered since their creation at Microsoft. If the signature or the driver program do not match each other, it is assumed that one or both of these pieces of data have been altered and you should not use that driver.

on the
ⓙob

If a hardware device is not listed on the HCL, it does not necessarily mean that it will not work properly on a Windows 2000 system; it only means that it is not certified by Microsoft and will not be supported in case of system failure. If you contact Microsoft Support Services and mention that you are using hardware that is not on the HCL, the first troubleshooting step they will suggest is to replace the failed hardware with a similar device that is found on the HCL.

FIGURE 7-1

Driver Signing
Options

As more companies create and test hardware drivers for Windows 2000, you should expect to see more signed drivers from Microsoft and other hardware vendors. Part of the signature will include a special key available only from that company.

From the System applet in the Control Panel, you can configure support for signed drivers. On the Hardware tab, there is a DRIVER SIGNING . . . button. Clicking this button brings up the dialog box shown in Figure 7-1.

From this screen, you can choose to install all drivers whether or not they are signed, display a warning that a driver is not signed and allow you to choose if you wish to install the driver, or for, maximum security and stability, never allow installation of unsigned drivers.

Microsoft introduced a new Web-based support tool with Windows 98 called Windows Update. This site is enhanced for Windows 2000 and is intended to be the primary source of support for Windows 2000. There is a link to this site under the Start menu and that can be reached at any time at windowsupdate.microsoft.com.

The Windows Update Web site inspects your local configuration and compares that to a database on the Web site. Any new drivers, updates, bug fixes, or security patches are then made available for download in a customized list.

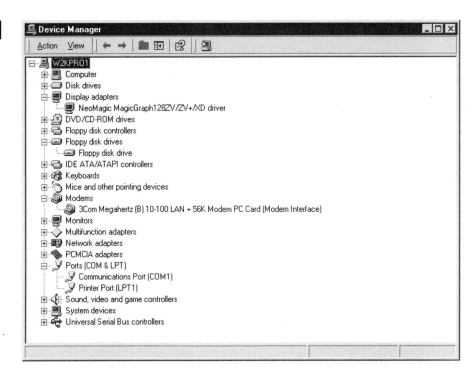

Monitoring, Configuring, and Troubleshooting I/O Devices

The steps required to monitor, configure, and troubleshoot hardware devices is, for the most part, similar, regardless of the type of hardware device in use. Windows 2000 Professional offers a central location to view and change the configuration of installed devices. If you've used Windows 95 and Windows 98, you will recognize the Device Manager. This utility, shown in Figure 7-2, is accessed from the Hardware tab in the System applet in the Control Panel.

The Device Manager is a Microsoft Management Console (MMC) plug-in that organizes its display of hardware according to the type of hardware and the connection in use. Each device has an associated Properties sheet that can be used to view and change that device's hardware configuration.

SCENARIO & SOLUTION

Will older tools such as NT Diagnostics (winmsd.exe) and Server Manager (srvmgr.exe) still work?	Yes. Windows NT tools will still run under Windows 2000, but might not always display the correct information. Differences in how information is stored in the Registry may cause these down-level utilities not to display information correctly. If any information reported by these tools seems strange, verify the information using the Windows 2000 version of the tool.
How about using these utilities across the network? Any caveats?	The same rules apply whether you are looking at the local machine or another machine on the network for which you have the appropriate rights and permissions. Older tools will probably work correctly; but when in doubt, use the updated tools.
What are the ways I can install new hardware?	You can use any of the following methods: Plug and Play, Device Manager, or a vendor-provided setup utility.

FROM THE CLASSROOM

Real World Practice in Preparing for the Exam

You are hopefully using this book to augment other study materials and real-world experience. The lab scenarios presented in this and other books represent only a portion of the possible hardware types you will undoubtedly come across.

After you have studied and worked with Windows 2000 Professional, and before you sit to take the 70-210 exam, you should practice installing and troubleshooting as many different types of hardware devices as you can. The more hardware you become familiar with, the better prepared you will be for the exam.

Keep in mind that hardware configuration is done via the Device Manager, and that areas of the system you may be familiar with from configuring hardware under Windows NT 4.0 have been changed. Some of the Control Panel applets like SCSI Devices, Multimedia Devices, and Modems have been removed completely.

—Erik Sojka, MCSE

Exercise 7-3 walks you through viewing the hardware configuration for a video adapter.

EXERCISE 7-3

Using Device Manager

In this exercise, we will look at verifying a computer's video adapter settings. The steps can be performed on all hardware devices displayed in Device Manager. Keep in mind that the settings for devices on your computer will be different from those shown in the screenshots in this exercise.

1. Open Device Manager by clicking Start | Settings | Control Panel.

2. When Control Panel opens up, double-click the System icon. Click the Hardware tab.

3. Click Device Manager. This will open the Device Manager.

4. Expand the item marked Display Adapters.

5. Right-click the video adapter displayed, and select Properties from the context menu that appears. Note that while in this exercise we will look at a NeoMagic video adapter, you will probably have a different adapter installed on your computer. A Properties sheet similar to the following illustration will appear.

6. Note the information displayed on this tab. This tab shows the Device type, manufacturer, and location (i.e., bus type) of the selected device. If there

were a problem with this device, it would be displayed here. There are no problems with the selected video adapter. Click the Driver tab shown in the following illustration.

7. Note the information displayed on this tab. This tab shows detailed information about the driver in use. There are also buttons that allow you to see more information about the driver, and uninstall or update the driver. Click Driver Details . . . . The resulting dialog box is shown in the following illustration.

8. The preceeding screen shows the files in use by this device. In this example, the NeoMagic video card uses two files, neo20xx.sys and neo20xx.dll. For each file, the version of the file is also listed. This information can help you determine if an update is required. Click OK to return to the Properties sheet. Click the Resources tab. The resulting screen is shown in the following illustration.

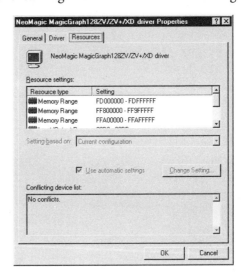

9. Note the information on this screen. The Resource settings section shows the memory ranges and I/O ports in use by the selected device. On the bottom of the screen, it shows which, if any, devices are also attempting to use the same memory ranges or I/O ports. If there is a conflict, you can click Change Settings . . . to modify the memory range and I/O ports to one that isn't being used.

10. Click OK to close the Properties sheet.

11. Close all windows.

The following sections provide overviews of the hardware types listed and troubleshooting tips unique to that device type.

Printers

Printers can be connected to a Windows 2000 machine through the USB port or parallel port, or directly connected to the network. Printers attached to the USB or parallel ports must be located near the computer because of cable length concerns. Printers attached directly to the network on models that support this type of connection can be located anywhere, and can be managed from any machine on the network. If a printer is connected to the network, a single server should manage configuration and spooling for that printer. Printers that are shared on the network to be used by network users can also be published to and searched for via Active Directory.

Printer support in Windows 2000 is improved, with support for newer printer models included on the Windows 2000 Professional CD. Microsoft has tested printer models that have drivers included on the CD and has digitally signed the drivers for these print devices. Updated printer drivers are available at both the manufacturer's Web site and at the Windows Update Web site.

Scanners

Scanners are supported on Windows 2000 Professional through the USB port, SCSI cards, or parallel ports. Advanced features for scanners need to be enabled through a driver provided by the scanner manufacturer.

Mouse

The mouse support installed by Windows 2000 setup will be through the serial port, USB port, or the PS/2 port, depending on how the mouse is installed during setup. Basic support for mice includes two-button mice.

Some mice will have additional buttons or features, such as the Microsoft Intelli-Mouse with the scrolling wheel. For Windows 2000 to take advantage of these advanced features, you will need the drivers supplied with the hardware.

Keyboard

Keyboard support will be provided through the PS/2 port, older AT keyboard port, or the USB port, depending on how the keyboard is attached during setup. The older AT keyboard port will only be found on older machines, and is a 5-pin connector with the pins arrayed in a half circle.

Some keyboards will have additional features, such as additional buttons to control the CD-ROM drive or connect to the Internet. For Windows 2000 to take advantage of these advanced features, you will need the drivers supplied with the hardware.

Smart Card Reader

Smart card technology allows an administrator to store a user's encryption keys in a device other than the local hard drive or on the network. Encryptions keys are a part of a larger Public Key Infrastructure (PKI) that must be in place on your network.

Smart cards come in a variety of types and sizes, but most are similar in size to a credit card. Information is encoded into the card and is read by the card reader (in the form of a magnetic strip or a chip). The card reader can attach to the computer through the parallel port, serial port, USB port, or through the PS/2 port.

Installing, Configuring, and Managing Infrared Data Association (IrDA) Devices

The Infrared Data Association (IrDA) is an industry-sponsored organization founded in 1993 to develop technology that would standardize the use of infrared signals in data communications.

Infrared is a light wave not visible to the eye (it is outside of the visible spectrum), but that can be used to convey digital information in the same way that radio waves in digital cell phones or light pulses in fiber-optic cable are used.

IrDA-compatible devices are usually found in portable and laptop hardware. Two devices that communicate via IrDA can perform wireless network tasks such as printing to an IrDA printer, synchronizing schedules and address books, and exchanging electronic business cards.

Support for IrDA devices must be enabled in the BIOS. Since IrDA technology isn't as widely used as other networking technology, most BIOSes will disable IrDA hardware by default to save those IRQs and memory ranges for other devices. IrDA devices can be configured via the Device Manager.

Installing, Configuring, and Managing USB Devices

Universal Serial Bus (USB) technology is a new generation technology that was designed to address two problems with legacy PC architecture. The first problem was that almost since the first IBM-compatible PCs were introduced, the speed of the serial port hasn't changed. The second problem is that for most power users, there just aren't enough system resources or physical ports to install all of the hardware devices one might have.

USB is a faster serial port technology that imposes no practical limits on the number of devices connected. USB devices connect via a chain, meaning that one USB device connects to the computer, and that device also has a USB port. Subsequent USB devices are added to the chain and to the computer by plugging into the USB port on the outermost device. Additional ports may also be gained by the installation of a USB hub, which splits and repeats the signal among USB devices in a manner similar to an Ethernet hub.

Printers, scanners, mice, joysticks, keyboards, cameras, and disk drives are all technology that has been adapted to take advantage of USB connections. USB devices are installed through Plug and Play (PnP) and can be configured via the Device Manager.

CERTIFICATION OBJECTIVE 7.04

Updating Drivers

After setting up your hardware devices, you may periodically encounter problems or bugs that require updated drivers to fix. Updated drivers may also include code that will enable new features.

CertCam 7-4

EXERCISE 7-4

Updating a Network Card Driver

In this exercise, we will view the properties of a network card, update the drivers, and then verify that the drivers have been updated. The steps here can be applied to any type of hardware, not just network cards.

 1. Open the Device Manager (found on the Hardware tab on the System applet in the Control Panel).

2. In the Device Manager, click the plus icon next to the type of hardware you want to configure. In the following illustration for this exercise, the Network Adapters section is expanded.

3. Right-click the network adapter's icon and select Properties from the context menu that appears. You should get a Properties sheet similar to that shown here:

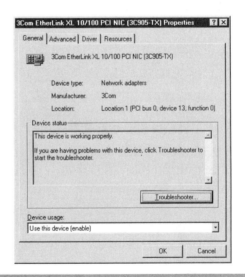

4. Click the Driver tab. This tab shows information about the driver for the device whose properties we are looking at. Look at the driver properties in the following illustration. Notice that for the device in this example, the driver being used does not have information about its version and the driver is not signed by its manufacturer. We are going to update this driver.

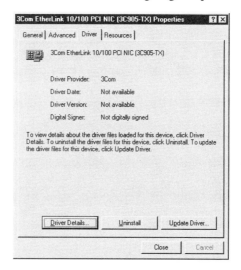

5. Click Update Driver . . . at the bottom of the Properties sheet. A wizard appears whose first screen is shown in the following illustration. Click Next to begin.

6. The next screen of the Upgrade Device Driver Wizard, shown in the following illustration, asks you to choose between searching for an updated driver or selecting a driver from a list of drivers that Windows 2000 already knows about. The latter option will display drivers that are on the Windows 2000 CD or drivers that were previously found if this wizard has been run before. We will explore the former option in this exercise. Select Search For A Suitable Driver For My Device (Recommended), and click Next.

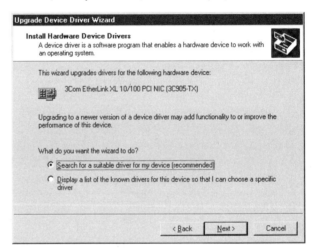

7. You are now asked to choose possible locations where Windows 2000 will look for updated drivers for the device. If you received an updated driver floppy disk from the manufacturer, select Floppy Disk Drives. If the drivers are located on a CD-ROM drive, select CD-ROM Drives. If the drivers are located on a local or remote hard drive, you can specify a path by selecting Specify A Location. If you are connected to the Internet, you can search Microsoft's updated list of drivers located at http://windowsupdate.microsoft.com by selecting Microsoft Windows Update. Select the options shown as follows, and click Next.

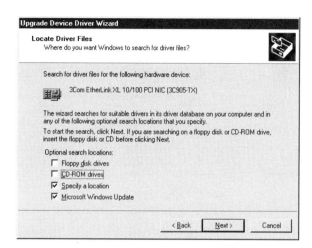

8. The next illustration asks you to specify a path where updated drivers are located. You can either type the full path or click Browse . . . to navigate local and remote folders. Select a local folder and click OK. Don't worry if you specify a folder that does not contain drivers for this exercise. In a production environment, you might have a central server where updated drivers for all supported hardware are stored. The wizard will search all of the specified search locations and report on drivers that are found.

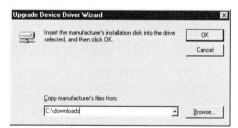

9. Windows 2000 will now search in the locations you specified in step 8 for updated drivers. It will show its progress in a wizard screen similar to that shown in the following illustration. In addition to the locations specified, it

will also search %*systemroot*%\inf, which contains previously loaded drivers and drivers that are included on the Windows 2000 CD.

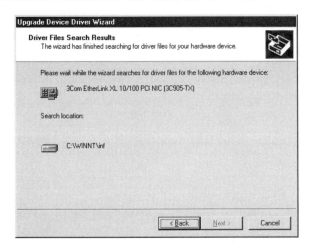

10. When the search is complete, the results are displayed in a dialog box similar to that shown in the following illustration. Select the driver you want to use, and click Next.

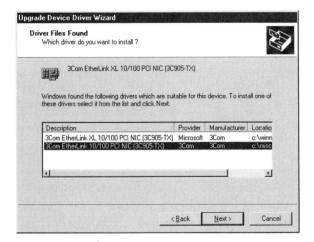

11. If the driver selected does not have a digital signature (described previously), a warning is displayed similar to the following illustration.

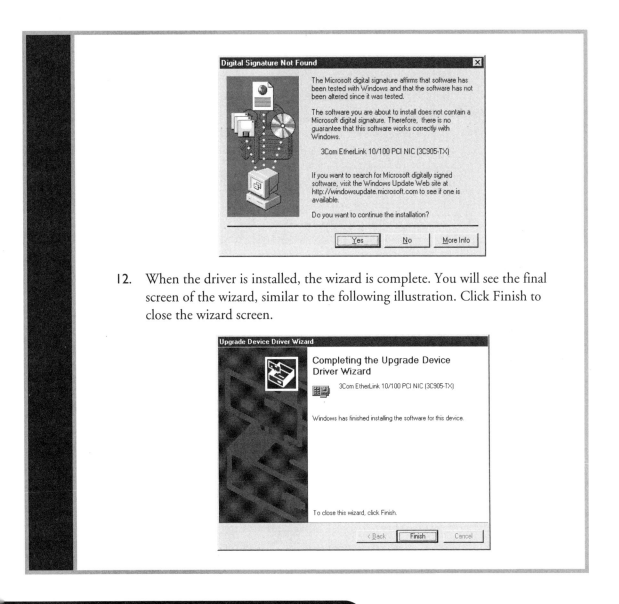

12. When the driver is installed, the wizard is complete. You will see the final screen of the wizard, similar to the following illustration. Click Finish to close the wizard screen.

CERTIFICATION OBJECTIVE 7.05

Monitoring and Configuring Multiple Processing Units

Windows 2000 offers support for using multiple processors. The use of more than one processor improves efficiency and system response time by allowing for multiple tasks to be run separately on the separate processors. For an operating system to be able to make use of multiple processors, it must be able to divide its workload being sent to the processor into manageable slices, and control when and how these slices will be sent to the processor. The ability to divide this workload in this manner is useful even on a system with one processor. An operating system that can do this is said to be a *multitasking* operating system. Multitasking is generally divided into two categories: cooperative and preemptive.

Windows 3.11 employed a scheme called *cooperative multitasking,* which means each application shares the CPU cooperatively with the other applications. Windows 95 introduced *preemptive multitasking,* and Windows 98 supports it as well. Older 16-bit applications are cooperatively multitasked in a virtual machine, but 32-bit applications that were written for Win9*x* are preemptively multitasked. If Microsoft Word and Microsoft Excel (assuming they are the 32-bit versions written for Win9*x*) are both running on a Windows 95 computer, each will take turns running its instructions on the processor, releasing the processor periodically for other applications to use it as well. This system has two major downsides: The first is that there is no hierarchy placed on which programs can use the processor. The operating system itself must also wait its turn to use the processor. The second downside is that since each application must release the processor when it is finished, it is possible (and unfortunately, all too frequent) that an application might crash or freeze; and since it can't release the processor or shut itself down, that one crashed processor will cause the entire system to crash and require a reboot.

Windows NT and Windows 2000 use a different scheme called *preemptive multitasking.* This scheme involves the use of a central portion of the operating system called the *kernel.* The kernel is responsible for scheduling applications to use the processor, and always gets precedence over the other applications. It is able to preempt all other applications. The kernel also is able to remove a program from the processor, either forcing it to wait for another cycle through the processor, or stopping that program completely. By having the kernel control which applications use the processor, the system is more stable. If a program hangs or crashes, the kernel is able to remove it from memory, and the rest of the system is unaffected.

Since the Windows 2000 kernel retains complete control over which applications use the processor, it doesn't matter to the applications being run how many processors there are in a system. This allows Windows 2000 to support multiple CPUs in a single system, and the kernel can tune which applications are run on which CPU for optimum performance.

TABLE 7-1	**Windows 2000 Version**	**Number of Processors Supported**
Processor Support in Windows 2000	Professional	Up to 2
	Server	Up to 4
	Advanced Server	Up to 8
	Datacenter Server	Up to 32

Table 7-1 shows the number of processors supported by each version of Windows 2000.

exam
Ⓦatch
Since Windows 2000 supports only Intel-based processors, beware of questions that refer to non-Intel processors such as Alpha, PPC, or MIPS. Since those processors are not supported under Windows 2000, there is no upgrade path for those processors.

The following exercise demonstrates how you can monitor how Windows 2000 Professional uses multiple processors and how you can set which applications use which processor.

EXERCISE 7-5

Managing Multiple Processors

In this exercise, we will look at how to monitor multiple processors on a Windows 2000 Professional computer. To perform this exercise, you must be running a multiprocessor version of Windows 2000 Professional.

1. Open the Task Manager by pressing CTRL-ALT-DELETE on the keyboard. From the Security dialog box that appears, click Task Manager.

2. The Task Manager appears. Click the Performance tab. The following illustration shows what this tab looks like.

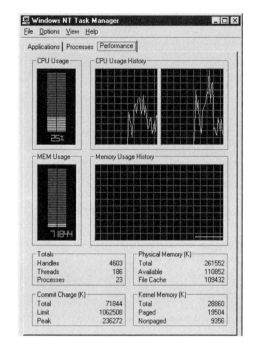

3. Notice the CPU Usage and CPU Usage History graphs. They show current and historical activity for the CPUs installed on the system. The numbers shown represent the percentage of time that the processor is being used. Unless configured otherwise, Windows 2000 will attempt to load balance applications on each of the processors.

4. Click the Processes tab (shown in the following illustration). This tab shows each of the applications and services that are running, and what percentage of the CPU each is using. If the percentage listed for a particular service or application is zero, then it is not actively using the processor. On a system that that isn't heavily taxed, most of the CPU's activity will be used by a special task called the System Idle Process. This is a special null process that still keeps the processor busy if there are no other applications needing to use the processor.

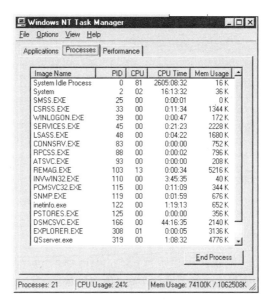

5. Scroll and find an item on this list called spoolsv. This is the Spooler service, a service in Windows 2000 Professional that manages local and network printing. Right-click spoolsv and select Set Affinity . . . from the context menu that appears.

6. Note that Windows 2000 counts the processors starting with CPU0. Select CPU1 (the second processor listed). This will ensure that if the Spooler service needs to use the processor, it will always use CPU1, and be given preference over other applications waiting to use CPU1.

7. Make sure that Always On Top is selected in the Options menu, and drag the taskbar window to the upper-right corner of the screen.

8. Click on the Performance tab.

9. Press Win-E several times. This keyboard shortcut opens up an Explorer window, and opening up several in a short period of time will drive up the utilization of CPU0.

10. On one of the Explorer windows that is now open, expand the Control Panel in the left pane of the window. Click Printers. The right pane of the Explorer window should show all of the installed printers. Select one of these printers and select Properties from the File menu.

11. Click Print Test Page on the Properties box that appears. As the test page is being processed, notice that CPU1 is now active and shows that the Spooler service is only using this processor, since we set its affinity to only use this processor in step 6.

12. Acknowledge the test page printout and close all windows.

on the **job**

Using Task Manager is not always the only way to set an application's affinity. Some higher-end server applications (such as Microsoft SQL Server and Microsoft Internet Information Server) have settings that allow you to further configure performance and processor affinity. Consult the documentation that comes with these products or the vendor's Web site to see if there is a recommended way to tune that product's performance.

CERTIFICATION OBJECTIVE 7.06

Installing, Configuring, and Troubleshooting Network Adapters

Network adapters (also known as network interface cards, or NICs) are an important part of the configuration changes that are new to Windows 2000.

The first thing you will notice when comparing network setup in Windows NT 4.0 to network setup in Windows 2000 is that most if not all of the configuration locations have changed. In Windows NT 4.0, you could add and remove NIC drivers, change a machine's domain membership, configure installed protocols, and change protocol-binding order all from a single Control Panel applet. In Windows 2000, these items have been moved around the system.

NIC card and driver configuration are performed from the Device Manager. Domain membership is managed from the Network Identification tab in the System applet in the Control Panel. Protocols and binding are configured on a per-connection basis from the Network and Dial-Up Connections applet in the Control Panel.

Windows 2000 supports Plug and Play–compliant NICs. A newly discovered NIC will have its drivers automatically loaded, the NIC will automatically be bound to TCP/IP with DHCP, and it will be immediately activated.

Another welcome change from Windows NT 4.0 is that network configuration changes can now be made on the fly. In Windows NT 4.0, most changes to the NIC driver or configuration changes made to the protocol that was bound to that NIC required the entire system to be rebooted. With Windows 2000, you can change domains, register your computer with a new WINS or DNS server, and even change protocol bindings, and the changes take effect immediately.

Protocol bindings refer to the process of mapping which network application will be configured for use with which protocol that will be used for which NIC. On a system with a single NIC, this is usually not an issue, since you would want all installed network applications to work with all installed protocols. It is possible to install multiple NIC cards on a single machine and change the bindings so that only certain applications use certain protocols or be sent certain NIC cards. If two NICs are using the same protocol, they must be configured with different network addresses appropriate for the protocol being used. For example, you might configure a Windows 2000 Professional computer to be a Web server for your company's Web site. It might be configured with two different NICs, both configured for the TCP/IP protocol. One NIC might have an IP address of the internal private network to allow it to be accessed and managed from within the company's network, and the other NIC might have an IP address that would allow it to be accessed by anyone on the Internet.

The order in which protocols are bound will affect the performance of the network. You should always ensure that the primary protocol in use on your network (and hopefully, it's TCP/IP!) is the first protocol listed. Windows NT and Windows 2000 clients will always attempt to use the network using the first protocol in the binding list. If the server or resource isn't available or isn't listening on that protocol, then the next bound protocol on the client is tried. This occurs until either the requested server or resource is found and contacted, or all bound protocols have been tried and failed. If a protocol that is not used is much as the first in the listing, then network performance for that client will be affected. Network sessions initiated by that client will be delayed while requested resources are not found on the first bound protocol.

CERTIFICATION SUMMARY

This chapter introduced you to the improvements in hardware support in Windows 2000 Professional. We discussed some of the changes in the types of hardware supported from Windows NT, and how to configure, monitor, manage, and troubleshoot these hardware devices.

Keep in mind that even though there is a wide array of hardware types, buses, and technologies supported in Windows 2000, the configuration of them will be very similar. You can use the same tools and utilities to manage hardware. These tools include the Device Manager and the Control Panel.

We discussed special hardware considerations, including updating drivers, identifying the number of processors, and managing network interface cards.

✓ TWO-MINUTE DRILL

Implementing, Managing, and Troubleshooting Mobile Computer Hardware

❑ Windows 2000 offers improved hardware support over Windows NT, incorporating all of the hardware improvements supported in Windows 95 and Windows 98.

❑ The power management schemes supported by Windows 2000 are Advanced Power Management (APM) and Advanced Configuration and Power Management (ACPI).

❑ Power Management must be enabled and supported by both the computer's BIOS and the OS in use.

❑ Card Services allow a laptop user to take advantage of the same technology as desktop computers, incorporating them into PCMCIA devices.

Managing and Troubleshooting the Use and Synchronization of Offline Files

❑ Offline File allows a user to locally cache frequently used files, folders, and Web pages that are normally stored on remote servers, and access these files even when the computer is not connected to the network

❑ Changes made to the locally cached copy of the files are synchronized when the computer connects to the network again.

❑ The Synchronization Manager is used to manage offline folders once they have been set up

Implementing, Managing, and Troubleshooting Input and Output (I/O) Devices

❑ The information needed to configure and troubleshoot hardware and I/O devices is contained in the Device Manager.

❑ All hardware requires driver software to enable it to work with the operating system. Hardware intended for use on a Windows 2000 computer must be on the Microsoft Hardware Compatibility List (HCL) and have a Windows 2000–specific driver.

❑ Updated drivers can be provided by the hardware manufacturer or found on the Windows Update Web site.

Updating Drivers

❑ Drivers need to be updated periodically to improve performance and fix bugs.

❑ Driver updates are performed on hardware that is already installed.

❑ Driver updates are performed from the Device Manager.

Monitoring and Configuring Multiple Processing Units

❑ Windows 2000 Professional supports up to two Intel CPUs on a single machine. These two processors work together under the direction of the Windows 2000 kernel to efficiently schedule and run several applications at once.

❑ While the Windows 2000 kernel will load balance between the processors, individual applications can be given preference to run on one processor, and the rest of the system will share the remaining processor.

Installing, Configuring, and Troubleshooting Network Adapters

❑ Network Adapters (also known as network interface cards, or NICs) are used to connect a computer to a network. NIC drivers are configured through the Device Manager.

❑ Windows 2000 supports Plug and Play network adapters, and will configure them automatically.

❑ Configuration changes made to network adapters no longer require a reboot to take effect.

SELF TEST

The following questions will help you measure your understanding of the material presented in this chapter. Read all of the choices carefully, as there may be more than one correct answer. Choose all correct answers for each question.

Implementing, Managing, and Troubleshooting Mobile Computer Hardware

1. How do you determine which power management scheme (APM or ACPI) is supported on a Windows 2000 computer?

   A. View the properties in the Control Panel, Power Management.

   B. Check the BIOS settings in the computer's CMOS utility when booting the computer.

   C. Run PWRCHECK.EXE from the Windows 2000 CD.

   D. Support for both APM and ACPI are installed by default when Windows 2000 is installed.

2. What does ACPI stand for?

   A. Advanced Computer Power Interface

   B. Asynchronous Computer Power Integration

   C. Administrative Computing Promotion Initiative

   D. Advanced Configuration and Power Interface

3. Where is Advanced Power Management configured on a Windows 2000 Professional Computer?

   A. Device Manager

   B. Power Options applet in the Control Panel

   C. Power Manager

   D. Hardware Profiles

Managing and Troubleshooting the Use and Synchronization of Offline Files

4. Which of the following items might be good reasons to enable Offline Folders? (Select all that apply.)

   A. Home Directories

   B. Time and Expense documents created in Microsoft Excel

   C. Intranet pages viewed with Internet Explorer

D. Responses to e-mails that need to be delivered to the appropriate Exchange mailboxes

E. Departmental shares

5. Which utility is used to initially specify which files or folders will be cached locally using the Offline Folders feature of Windows 2000? (Select all that apply.)

A. Windows Explorer

B. Internet Explorer

C. Briefcase

D. Synchronization Manager

Implementing, Managing, and Troubleshooting Input and Output (I/O) Devices

6. Drivers from which operating system are also supported in Windows 2000? (Select all that apply.)

A. Windows 95

B. Windows 98

C. Windows NT 4.0

D. Windows 3.x

E. MS-DOS

7. What steps should be taken to ensure that the hardware in use on your Windows 2000 computer is the most reliable?

A. Ensure that all hardware in use is on the Windows 2000 Hardware Compatibility List (HCL), and then install using the Control Panel.

B. Set Driver Signing options in the Control Panel, System applet to Block, and then use only HCL hardware.

C. Set Driver Signing options in the Control Panel, System applet to Block, use only HCL hardware, and make sure you use signed drivers.

D. Set Driver Signing options in the Control Panel, System applet to Warn, use only HCL hardware, and make sure you use signed drivers.

8. What is the purpose of the Windows Update Web site?

A. Sends marketing and registration information to Microsoft.

B. Allows you to download the latest version of Microsoft Office and other productivity applications.

C. Allows you to keep your system configured correctly by applying the latest bug fixes and driver updates.

D. Allows you to search the Knowledge Base.

9. Which of the following port types does Windows 2000 support for keyboard attachment? (Select all that apply.)

A. Universal Serial Bus

B. SCSI

C. Serial port

D. PS/2 port

Updating Drivers

10. What is the recommended way to verify the version of the driver a particular hardware device is using?

A. Right-click the device in the Control Panel, and then select Properties from the context menu. The driver information will be shown on the first screen.

B. Navigate to the device in the Device Manager, and then right-click the device. Select Properties from the context menu. The driver information will be shown on the first screen that appears.

C. Navigate to the device in the Device Manager, and then right-click the device. Select Properties from the context menu. The driver information will be shown on the Advanced tab.

D. Navigate to the device in the Device Manager, and then right-click the device. Select Properties from the context menu. The driver information will be shown on the Driver tab.

11. When updating a driver, which of the following is *not* a place that can be searched for updated drivers?

A. Windows Update Web site

B. Local CD-ROM drive

C. Hardware manufacturer's Web site

D. Local hard drive

12. What happens when you attempt to upgrade a hardware device's driver to a newer version that is not signed?

   A. Windows 2000 will not allow the unsigned driver to be installed.

   B. It will depend on the settings made for Driver Signing in the Control Panel, System applet.

   C. Windows 2000 does not check driver signatures.

   D. Windows 2000 will give you a choice, asking if you want to proceed with the installation.

Monitoring and Configuring Multiple Processing Units

13. How many processors are supported by Windows 2000 Professional on a new install?

   A. Up to two

   B. Up to four

   C. Up to eight

   D. Only one

14. Which application is used to monitor the real-time usage of each CPU and to set an application's affinity for a certain processor?

   A. Task Manager

   B. Microsoft Management Console

   C. Device Manager

   D. Control Panel, System applet

Installing, Configuring, and Troubleshooting Network Adapters

15. Which of the following tasks will require a reboot?

   A. Changing a computer's IP address

   B. Uninstalling a PCI bus network card

   C. Moving from a workgroup into a domain

   D. Registering with a new WINS server

16. How are bindings configured for network connections?

   A. Bindings are configured centrally in the Device Manager.

   B. Bindings are configured on a per-connection basis in Network And Dial-Up Connections.

C. Bindings are configured in My Network Places.

D. Bindings are configured in Network Neighborhood.

17. When should two NICs be configured with the same network address?

A. Never, network addresses must be unique.

B. All computers should have the same network address because they are all part of the same domain.

C. Only multiple NICs installed in the same computer.

D. Never, because network cards cannot be configured for network addresses.

LAB QUESTION

You are the system administrator for a large software company that is about to release a major upgrade to its flagship product. To better assist the sales force in their sales efforts, the company has decided to outfit all sales personnel with laptops.

Your company has already decided to standardize on Windows 2000 Professional for all user computers, and this decision will make the laptop rollout easier.

The company's sales force will need to demonstrate the software product to prospective customers and keep in constant touch with the home office. Security is a concern for the company, as the sales personnel will be traveling all over the country. If laptop hardware is ever lost or stolen, the company does not want anyone else to be able to sign on to the laptop.

The company's flagship product accesses a database that is too large to be stored on the laptop's hard drives. In addition, there will be updates to the product and the database that need to be applied frequently.

You have been tasked with researching a laptop model that will support all of the sales personnel's needs. You will need to decide which types of hardware to buy, and how to support them.

For this question, you should devise a methodology to determine how you will evaluate hardware, and formalize the criteria that will determine which hardware will be deployed.

SELF TEST ANSWERS

Implementing, Managing, and Troubleshooting Mobile Computer Hardware

1. ☑ **B.** Since power management schemes encompass the entire system (hardware, BIOS, and operating system), the scheme supported by Windows 2000 will be the scheme that is supported by the hardware. To determine which scheme is in use by the computer hardware, view the settings in the BIOS when booting up.

    ☒ **A** is incorrect. Control Panel, Power Management does not display which scheme is in use; it only allows you to change the settings. There is no PWRCHECK.EXE utility, so **C** is incorrect. Since ACPI is a later technology and a superset of the capabilities of APM, it is highly unlikely that both APM and ACPI are installed, so **D** is incorrect.

2. ☑ **D.** ACPI stands for Advanced Configuration and Power Interface, which refers to a set of standards that enable power management on a PC.

    ☒ **A, B,** and **C** are incorrect.

3. ☑ **B.** The Power Options applet in the Control Panel is used to configure power management functions on hardware that supports either the ACPI or APM specification.

    ☒ **A** is incorrect. The Device Manager is a single location that enables you to view the properties and configuration of all of your hardware. Power management is not performed in the Device Manager. **C,** Power Manager, is a nonexistent application. **D,** Hardware Profiles, allows you to select at boot time which drivers and services will be loaded, and is not related to power management.

Managing and Troubleshooting the Use and Synchronization of Offline Files

4. ☑ **A, B, C, E.** All of these items involve data that is stored on a file server or Web server and, therefore, can be cached locally using Offline Folders.

    ☒ **D** is incorrect because Exchange has its own storage and is accessed using a different mechanism from file server or Web server access. While Exchange folders can be cached locally on a user's computer, this is performed within the Exchange client software, and not from Offline Folders.

5. ☑ **A, B.** To configure specific files and folders for offline access, you would use Windows Explorer. To configure specific Web pages or URLs for offline access, you would use Internet Explorer.

☒ **C** is incorrect. The Briefcase is still supported under Windows 2000, but Briefcases do not allow for a central location for all locally cached files. The Briefcase is a separate utility from Offline Folders. **D** is incorrect because the Synchronization Manager is only used to manage synchronization of items that have already been enabled for offline access. New items to be synchronized cannot be added from Synchronization Manager.

Implementing, Managing, and Troubleshooting Input and Output (I/O) Devices

6. ☑ **B, C.** Drivers from Windows 98 that adhere to the Windows Driver Model will also work under Windows 2000. Windows NT 4.0 drivers will also work under Windows 2000, but should be upgraded to Windows 2000 drivers.
☒ **A** is incorrect. Older VxD drivers found in Windows 95 do not work under Windows 2000. **D** and **E** are incorrect because drivers from older 8-bit and 16-bit operating systems are not supported under Windows 2000.

7. ☑ **C.** For maximum reliability, all of the steps described in **C** should be followed. Setting Driver Signing options to Block will ensure that only driver software digitally signed by the hardware manufacturer is installed. Using only HCL hardware and then using signed drivers ensures that only supported hardware is installed.
☒ **A** is incorrect. While you should always use hardware found on the HCL, you should always take the additional step of using signed drivers. **B** is incorrect because it does not include the step of using signed drivers. **D** is incorrect because the Warn option in Driver Signing options will only warn you if you attempt to install a nonsigned driver, but will still allow the installation, possibly causing system failure.

8. ☑ **C.** Windows Update is intended to be the central source for Microsoft to distribute bug fixes and driver updates for Windows 2000. There is a link to the Windows Update site on the Windows 2000 Start menu, and updates can also be found online at the Web site windowsupdate.microsoft.com.
☒ **A** is incorrect because no personal information is sent to Microsoft while you are connected to Windows Update, and even if there were, that is not the primary reason Windows Update was developed. **B** is incorrect because Windows Update only deals with fixes and downloads directly related to Windows 2000, and not other applications. Office users have a similar resource that can be found at officeupdate.microsoft.com, and other applications have pages that can be reached from Microsoft's main Web page at www.microsoft.com. **D** is incorrect because general support information and the Microsoft Knowledge Base can be found at support.microsoft.com. The Knowledge Base is a collection of articles and bug reports that is published by Microsoft. It is intended to be the primary resource library for Microsoft customers to use for support.

9. ☑ **A, D.** USB keyboards are supported by Windows 2000 in addition to more conventional PS/2 keyboards. Also supported are keyboards that connect via the older AT 5-pin keyboard port.
    ☒ **B** is incorrect because Small Computer Serial Interface (SCSI) is a bus technology usually used for hard drives. Keyboards are never attached via SCSI ports. **C** is incorrect. The serial port is usually used for either a mouse or modem, and not the keyboard.

Updating Drivers

10. ☑ **D.** The recommended way to view a device's current driver version is to select it from the Device Manager, view its properties, and then select the Driver tab.
    ☒ **A** is incorrect because hardware devices are not displayed in the Control Panel. **B** is incorrect because the driver information is not shown on the first tab of the device properties (the General tab). You must select the Device tab. **C** is incorrect because it is the Hardware tab and not the Advanced tab that displays hardware information.

11. ☑ **C.** A hardware manufacturer's Web site cannot be directly searched for updated driver files. If updated drivers were available from a manufacturer's Web site, you would have to retrieve them first, and then place them in a location that the Driver Upgrade Wizard can locate.
    ☒ **A, B,** and **D** are all incorrect because they *are* locations that can be searched for updated drivers.

12. ☑ **B.** How Windows 2000 Professional reacts when you attempt to upgrade a device driver with an unsigned version will depend on the settings made in the Driver Signing screen on the Hardware tab found in the System applet in the Control Panel.
    ☒ The choices presented on this screen are the incorrect answers **A, C,** and **D.**

Monitoring and Configuring Multiple Processing Units

13. ☑ **A** is correct. Windows 2000 Professional supports multiprocessor systems of up to two processors. If two processors are detected, Windows 2000 will attempt to balance the system's load between the two processors, guaranteeing optimum performance. This limit of two processors is hard-coded into the Windows 2000 Professional product and cannot be modified. To use more than two processors, you must upgrade to a version of Windows 2000 Server.
    ☒ **B** is incorrect because four is the maximum number of processors supported in Windows 2000 Server. **C** is incorrect because eight is the maximum number of processors supported in Windows 2000 Advanced Server. **D** is incorrect because up to two processors are supported by Windows 2000 Professional.

14. ☑   **A.** Task Manager is used to monitor the performance of each installed CPU using the Performance tab. The Processes tab can be used to control which application(s) is/are given preferred access (or affinity) to certain processors.
☒   **B** is incorrect because the MMC is only an application framework into which a management application can be installed; the MMC has no capability for processor management. **C** is incorrect because the Device Manager is not used for processor management, but for configuration and installation of hardware devices. **D** is incorrect because there is no option in this applet for CPU monitoring or management.

Installing, Configuring, and Troubleshooting Network Adapters

15. ☑   **B** and **C.** Most configuration changes in Windows 2000 networking do not require a reboot to take effect. Normally, uninstalling a network card will not require a reboot of the bus being used (PCMCIA, and so on), and supports live removal or uninstallation of devices. The PCI bus does not support live removal of its devices; so in order to remove a PCI network card (or any PCI device), the system must be rebooted. Moving from a workgroup to a domain also requires a reboot.
☒   **A** and **D** are incorrect because none of those configuration changes require a reboot. These are all software-based changes that can be performed by the operating system, and the network software can be reinitialized without a reboot.

16. ☑   **B.** Bindings are configured separately for each network connection present in the system. Network connections are configured in the Network And Dial-Up Connections applet in the Control Panel.
☒   **A** is incorrect because the hardware configuration for the NIC card is performed in the Device Manager, just like it would be for any other hardware device, but bindings are not configured here. **C** and **D** are incorrect because My Network Places and Network Neighborhood are icons on the desktop that the user can use to browse and navigate available network resources, but cannot configure bindings from these locations. My Network Places is new in Windows 2000, and replaces Network Neighborhood found in Windows 95 and Windows NT 4.0.

17. ☑   **A.** In order for computers to be uniquely identified on the network, each NIC must be configured with a unique address for the protocol being used. Network addresses are configured in the Network And Dial-Up Connections applet in the Control Panel.
☒   **B** is incorrect, since domain membership requires separate configuration from the network card. **C** is incorrect because all NICs require a unique address, even those installed in the same computer. **D** is incorrect because network address is an important parameter in a network card's configuration.

LAB ANSWER

There will be many ways to arrive at an answer to this scenario. The answer presented here is one approach.

First, develop the list of criteria.

Hardware deployed to the sales force must

- Be able to connect to the company's virtual private network (VPN) via the Internet from anywhere in order to allow users to check e-mail and transfer files to and from the home office.

- Be able to connect to an Ethernet network either at a sales demonstration or at the home office.

- Support an external hard drive that will hold the product data for demonstrations.

- Enable the use of smart cards for VPN encryption key storage and secured sign-on to the laptop.

- Make use of the existing bus technology available on laptops.

- Be supported by Windows 2000 Professional and be on the Windows 2000 HCL.

The existing bus technology on laptops is the PCMCIA bus. There may be special laptop versions of PCI and ISA technology, but it will usually be such that it cannot be expanded to include additional devices.

PCMCIA devices include network cards, modems, and SCSI cards. Purchasing one of each of these devices will enable the use of network connections and modem dial-up, and will allow for an external hard drive to be used in presentations. Most laptops only have two PCMCIA slots available, so you would need to either research combination modem and network cards (cards with ports for a network connection and a modem connection, freeing one slot) or train your users how to swap cards out when not in use using Windows 2000's Card Services.

If you decide to use the combination modem/network for the first PCMCPA slot, and a SCSI card for the second PCMCIA slot, you can use the USB port for the smart card device.

With this information, you can now formalize and write up your findings.

8

Monitoring and Optimizing System Performance and Reliability

CERTIFICATION OBJECTIVES

Monitoring your system resources might seem like wasted effort sometimes, but it isn't. By continuously monitoring your system, you can create a baseline for your system. It also allows you to fix problems before they devastate your system, by finding bottlenecks and fixing them before they cause significant problems. The System Monitor and Performance Logs and Alerts can be used to assist in finding bottlenecks. The Disk Defragmenter can be used to keep your hard disks running at optimal performance.

CERTIFICATION OBJECTIVE 8.01

Managing and Troubleshooting Driver Signing

One of the new features in Windows 2000 is Driver Signing. This allows you to verify that Microsoft has certified any drivers you install. By using only certified drivers, you can improve the stability of your computer and improve performance. Microsoft certifies drivers through the Windows Hardware Quality Labs (WHQL) tests, which are comprehensive tests that test for errors and robustness. Once a driver has been certified, the driver package is digitally signed with an encrypted code. The driver package cannot be altered without making the code invalid, so this also allows you to verify the integrity of the driver package. You can verify that the driver package is the same exact package that was tested and has not been altered. All drivers that come with Windows 2000 are digitally signed. Some common devices that use Driver Signing are the keyboard, hard disk controller, sound card, video card, modem, mouse, network card, and printer.

You can configure how Driver Signing behaves when installing drivers. The following list describes the available settings. Warn is the default setting.

- **Ignore**   This setting will allow all drivers to be installed whether or not they are signed, without warning the user.

- **Warn**   This setting will display a warning if a driver being installed is not signed. This will give you the option to choose not to install the driver.

- **Block**   This setting prevents you from installing any drivers that are not signed.

You can verify that existing files on the computer are digitally signed using the File Signature Verification tool and System File Checker (SFC) utility. You can use the File Signature Verification tool to check files to see if they are signed. This utility is run from the command line, and the executable is named **sigverif**. With this tool, you can view the certificates of files that are signed and verify that the files have not been altered. You can also search for signed and unsigned files. Click Advanced to configure this tool. This will allow you to set the search and logging options. Logging data is saved to a filed named Sigverif.txt, which is stored in the SystemRoot folder. The tool logs information about the driver files that are scanned. It logs the name of the file, the date it was modified, its version number, whether it is signed, and the location of the file.

CertCam 8-1

EXERCISE 8-1

Using Driver Signing

Let's look at how to use the File Signature Verification tool and how to configure Driver Signing.

1. From the Start menu, select Run.

2. In the Run dialog box, type **sigverif**, and click OK.

3. This brings up the File Signature Verification tool, as shown in the following illustration.

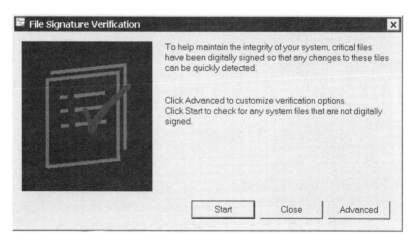

4. Click Advanced. The first tab is for the Search settings. You can choose to search all the system files or look for other files. Leave the default setting as shown in the following illustration.

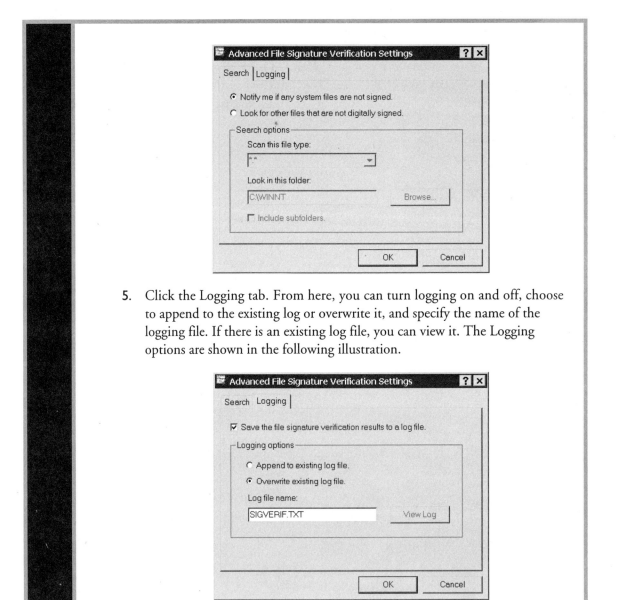

5. Click the Logging tab. From here, you can turn logging on and off, choose to append to the existing log or overwrite it, and specify the name of the logging file. If there is an existing log file, you can view it. The Logging options are shown in the following illustration.

6. Leave the default settings, and click OK.

7. Click Start to scan the system files. When it first starts, it will build a file list. Then a progress bar will show the progress of scanning the files. When it has finished scanning, it will display any files that are not digitally signed. An example is shown in the following illustration.

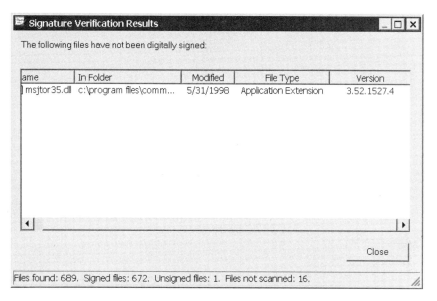

8. Click Close to close the dialog box. Click Close to close the program.

9. Now let's look at configuring Signature Checking. Right-click My Computer and select Properties.

10. Click the Hardware tab, and click Driver Signing . . . . This will allow you to choose the level of signature checking. If you have Administrator privileges, you can make the settings the system default. These options are shown in the following illustration.

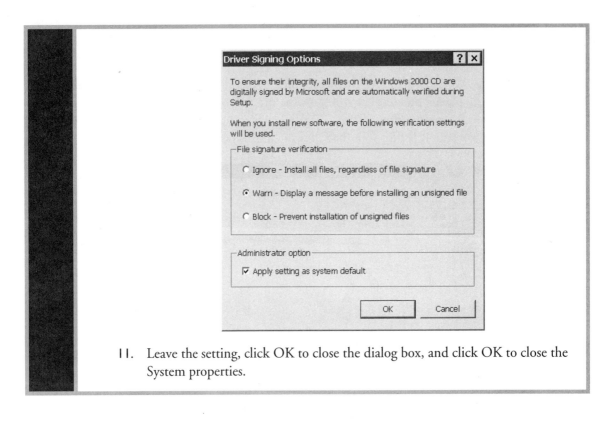

11. Leave the setting, click OK to close the dialog box, and click OK to close the System properties.

SFC (System File Checker) is a command-line utility that can be used to keep track of digital signatures of system files. The name of the executable is Sfc.exe. Following is a list of some of the optional parameters for the SFC utility.

- **scannow**   Will scan all of the system files now
- **scanonce**   Will scan all of the system files one time at the next reboot
- **scanboot**   Will scan all of the system files every time the system is restarted
- **cancel**   Will cancel scanning of the system files
- **quiet**   Will replace all system files that are incorrect versions without prompting the user
- **enable**   Will replace all system files that are incorrect versions, prompting the user for each file

Configuring, Managing, and Troubleshooting the Task Scheduler

The Task Scheduler lets you schedule any program or batch file. This allows you to run maintenance programs such as backups when the computer isn't in use. To start the Task Scheduler, open the Scheduled Tasks icon from the Control Panel.

The Task Scheduler is installed automatically when you install Windows 2000, and is integrated into the operating system.

The Task Scheduler is a graphical user interface to the AT command-line program used in Windows NT. It also adds additional functionality to what was available using the AT command in Windows NT. If you used the AT command in Windows NT, you know that this was a difficult utility to use. Task Scheduler makes scheduling and managing those schedules much easier. When you schedule a program or script to run, it is called a task. You can schedule tasks by date/time, at set intervals, when the computer boots up, when you log on, or to run when the computer is idle. You can have the task automatically deleted when it is no longer scheduled to run. You can have the task stop after running for a specified duration of time. You can set the task to run when idle, and to stop when the computer is being used again. You can even set some power management options. As you can see, there are many options available for a task, which gives you great flexibility.

Each task is saved in a file with a .job extension. By saving the task to a file, you can actually copy the file to another computer so that the task will be run on that computer. This greatly simplifies administration. For example, say you wanted every workstation to perform a backup on Monday, Wednesday, and Friday at midnight. If you had 200 workstations, you wouldn't want to have to configure each one; you can use the .job file to ease this administrative task. When a task is created, the Task Scheduler requires a username and password for a user using Windows 2000 security. This allows you to determine whom the task will run as. This way, a task can perform operations that a normal user may not have permissions for. You can also reset the password for tasks. This is useful if you require your users to change their passwords periodically.

When you transfer a .job file to another computer, the security settings are not stored in the file, so the security settings are not transferred with the file.

When you create a task, permissions are assigned to this task. This allows you to specify who can view, delete, modify, or use tasks. You can set different levels of access for different users; for example, to prevent users from deleting other users' tasks unless they have the delete permission.

You can view the status of a task by selecting the task in the Scheduled Tasks folder. The status will be displayed in the left margin of the folder. Alternately, you can use the Details mode for viewing the folder to see the status information for all of your tasks. It will display the status of the task (running, missed last scheduled run, could not start, or blank if not running), the schedule for the task, and the next time it will run. It will also show the last time the task was run, and who created the task. This can be useful for troubleshooting tasks.

If you are having problems with the Task Scheduler, make sure the Task Scheduler service is running. To see if it is running, from the Scheduled Tasks folder, click the Advanced menu. If it is running, there will be a menu item to Stop Using Task Scheduler. If it is not running, it will say Start Using Task Scheduler. From this menu, there are also options to pause the Task Scheduler service, and to be notified of missed scheduled tasks. You can also set the account used when running the AT service. One of the most important things to check is that your system time and date are correct.

When a task doesn't run correctly, make sure that the system time and date are correct.

Another useful feature for troubleshooting is the log file, which is called SchedLog.txt and is stored in the SystemRoot folder. It records all of the activity for scheduled tasks, including status, why a task stopped, and so forth. To view the log, from the Scheduled Tasks folder on the Advanced menu, click View Log.

If a scheduled task runs for an account that is different from the user who is currently logged on, the task will run invisible to the logged-on user.

You can also view tasks on other computers. You must have administrator privileges on that computer. You can do this by going to My Network Places, finding the computer you want to view the tasks for, and opening the Scheduled Tasks folder on that computer.

CertCam 8-2

Using the Task Scheduler

Let's look at how to use the Task Scheduler to create and edit tasks.

1. To open the Task Scheduler, open the Control Panel by clicking Start | Settings | Control Panel. Then click the Scheduled Tasks icon. This will bring up the Scheduled Tasks folder, which contains an icon to add a scheduled task and icons for any tasks that have been created.

2. Let's add a new task, so click the Add Scheduled Task icon. This will start the Scheduled Task Wizard, as shown in the following illustration.

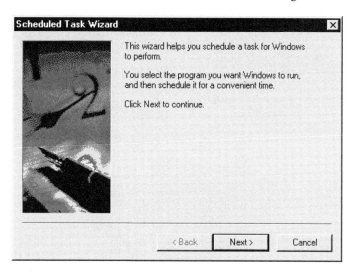

EXERCISE 8-2

3. Click Next to continue. The next dialog box displays a list of available applications. Click Browse if what you are looking for is not displayed. Select the Calculator program, as shown in the following illustration.

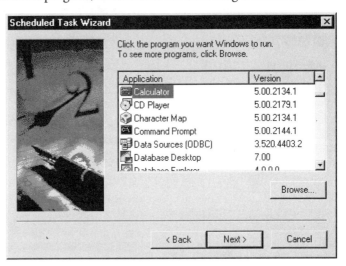

4. Click Next to continue. Now you can choose a name for your task, and choose what type of task to create.

5. Leave the name as the default Calculator. Choose the One Time Only option, as shown in the following illustration.

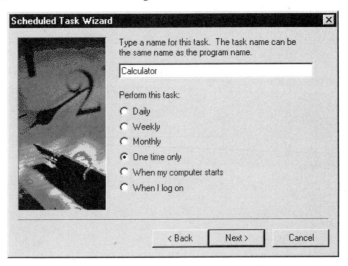

6. Click Next to continue. Now you must choose the date and time to run this task as shown in the following illustration. Enter a date and time to run the task a few minutes after finishing this exercise, so that you can see it work.

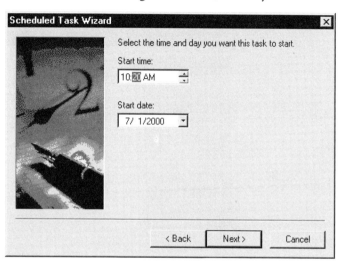

7. Click Next to continue. Now you must enter the username and password for whom the task will run. Your username will be displayed by default. Leave it as it is and enter your password. Your dialog box should look similar to the following illustration.

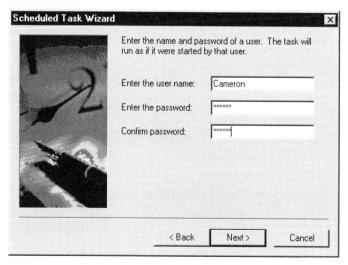

8. Click Next to continue. This dialog box will show your current settings. There is also a check box to allow you to see the advanced settings when you click Finish. Leave this unselected. Your dialog box should look similar to the following illustration.

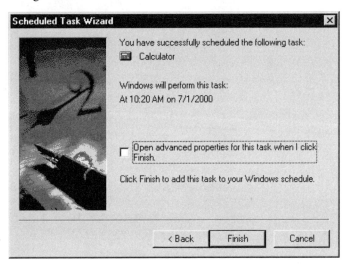

9. Click Finish to create the task. Your task will now appear in the Scheduled Tasks folder, as shown in the following illustration.

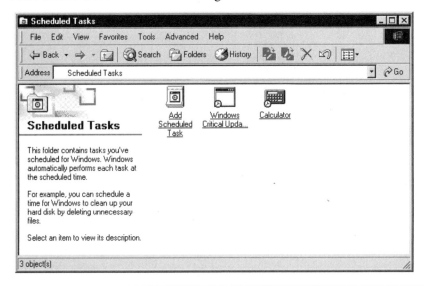

10. You can edit existing tasks. To edit the Calculator task, right-click the Calculator icon and select Properties. This will bring up the Properties dialog box for the task, as shown in the following illustration. Notice that you can change the username and set a new password for the task. There is also a check box to enable and disable the task. If desired, you can add command-line parameters for the task in the Run field.

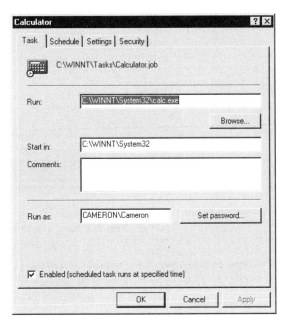

11. Leave the settings as they are, and go to the Schedule tab. Here you can edit the schedule for the task. There is also a check box to show multiple schedules for the task, as shown in the following illustration. You can click Advanced to set interval properties for the task.

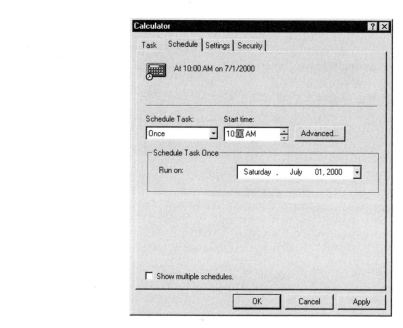

12. Leave the settings as they are, and go to the Settings tab, where you'll find some optional settings. You can have the task automatically deleted when no longer scheduled to run; you can have the task stop after running for a specified duration of time; you can set the task to run when idle and to stop when the computer is being used again; and you can even set some power management options (see the following illustration).

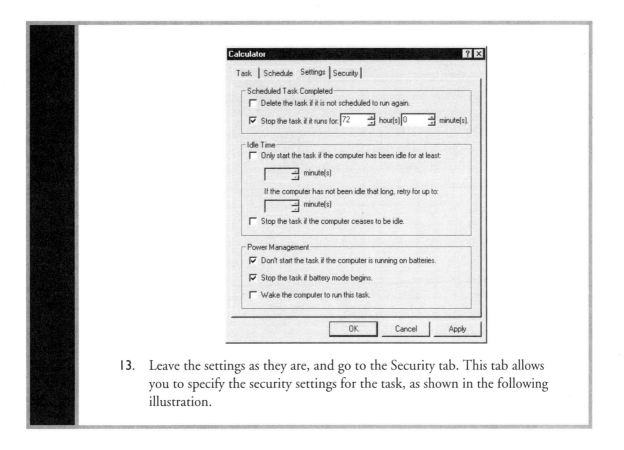

13. Leave the settings as they are, and go to the Security tab. This tab allows you to specify the security settings for the task, as shown in the following illustration.

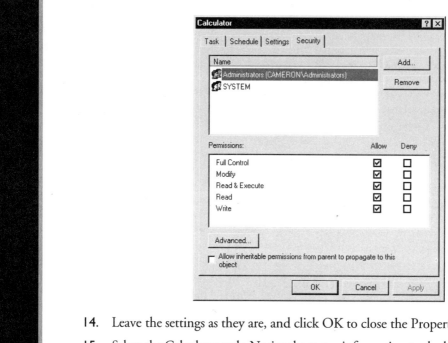

14. Leave the settings as they are, and click OK to close the Properties dialog box.

15. Select the Calculator task. Notice the status information to the left. It displays the schedule, the next time it will run, the last time it was run, the status of the task, and the creator of the task, as shown in the following illustration.

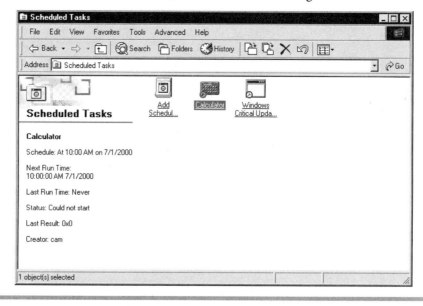

16. Let's make the task run immediately. Right-click the Calculator task and select Run. It will run the Calculator program.

17. Now let's stop the task from running. Right-click the Calculator task and select End Task, or click End Scheduled Task on the File menu. Now let's delete the task. Right-click the Calculator task and select Delete. Notice that the Confirm Delete message asks if you want to delete the Calculator.job file. The task was saved as <task name>.job. Click Yes, and close the Scheduled Tasks folder.

exam
ⓦatch

You should be familiar with all of the Task options available for the exam.

CERTIFICATION OBJECTIVE 8.03

Optimizing and Troubleshooting the Performance of the Windows 2000 Professional Desktop

Part of keeping your Windows 2000 Professional operating at peak performance is monitoring the performance of your computer. In order to understand how your computer is operating, you must establish a baseline. A baseline allows you to know how different aspects of the computer are running when the computer is running at normal levels. By continuously monitoring the computer, you can watch for performance degradation and solve any problems before they impact your network.

Using System Monitor

Part of administering your network includes monitoring the health of your computers. In order for your network to operate efficiently, you need to make sure your computers' performance is good enough to handle the load placed on them by the network. By monitoring the performance of your computers, you can see how the load placed on them affects your computers' resources. You can monitor resource usage to see when upgrades are required. You can also create test environments to see the effects of changes to the network.

One of the tools to aid you in this is System Monitor. System Monitor replaces the Performance Monitor used in Windows NT. System Monitor allows you to collect information about your hardware's performance and network utilization. It also gives you the ability to view this data in many different ways. System Monitor is a snap-in to the Performance console, and is installed automatically with the Performance console. The Performance console is a Microsoft Management Console (MMC), accessed through the Administrative Tools program group.

System Monitor can be used to measure different aspects of a computer's performance. It can be used on your own computer or other computers on the network. System Monitor can collect data for memory usage, processor utilization, network activity, and more. This data can be displayed as a graph, histogram, or report. System Monitor can perform many tasks. It can collect real-time data on different aspects of performance and allow you to view this information. This data can also be saved or printed for viewing later. See Figure 8-1 for an example

FIGURE 8-1	
System Monitor displaying processor utilization	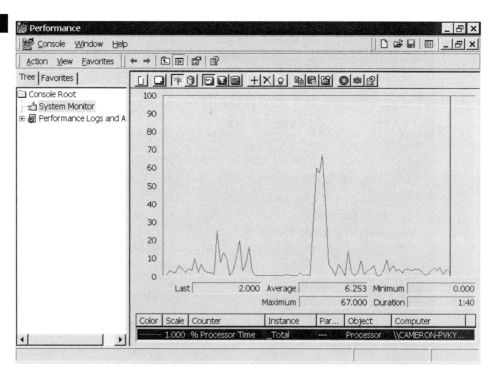

of System Monitor in the Performance console. The example shows processor utilization. The System Monitor is comprised of three basic areas: the graph area, the legend, and the value bar.

The data you can collect in System Monitor is extensive. There are two basic types of items to collect data on: objects and counters. An object is a component of the system such as memory, processor, or hard disk. Performance data is collected from components on your computer. As a component performs different tasks, performance data can be collected about those tasks. An object contains data measuring a component's tasks. Generally, the object is named after the component it is measuring. Counters are the specific data of an object to be measured. Objects can contain many different counters. Objects can also have multiple instances. If there are multiple objects in a computer, then the objects are distinguished by instances. An example would be a computer with multiple processors. You would use instances to differentiate between the objects for each processor. An example of a counter is the counter Available Bytes from the Memory object. See Table 8-1 for a list of the most commonly used objects.

TABLE 8-1	Object	Description
System Monitor Objects	Cache	Measures the disk cache usage
	Memory	Measures memory usage and/or performance of physical and virtual memory
	Objects	Measures miscellaneous data such as events, processes, and threads
	Paging File	Measures page file usage
	Physical Disk	Measures hard disk utilization
	Process	Measures running processes
	Processor	Measures processor usage
	System	Measures overall system performance
	Thread	Measures thread usage

Graph Area

You can view the data that is collected by System Monitor in several ways: as a chart, histogram, or report. By default, the graph view is displayed when you open System Monitor. When you are creating baselines for your systems, you should create the baseline in the report format so that you can easily determine specific values. When configuring a graph, you can choose settings for many attributes. See Figure 8-2 for the toolbar to configure the graph. The toolbar buttons are described in Table 8-2 as they appear from left to right.

TABLE 8-2	Button	Description
	New Counter Set	Removes counters and collected data
System Monitor Toolbar Buttons	Clear Display	Removes all collected data
	View Current Activity	View live data
	View Log File Data	View data saved to a log file
	View Chart	View data in a chart
	View Histogram	View data in a histogram
	View Report	View data in a report
	Add	Add an object counter(s)
	Delete	Delete an object counter(s)
	Highlight	Highlight a counter
	Copy Properties	Copy counter data
	Paste Counter List	Paste counter data
	Properties	View System Monitor properties
	Freeze Display	Stop collecting data
	Update Data	Collect a sample of data
	Help	Help

FIGURE 8-2 System Monitor graph toolbar

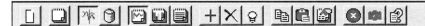

The data that is collected by System Monitor can be updated automatically or on demand. To collect data on demand, stop the data collection by pressing Freeze Display on the toolbar; when you want to collect data, click Update Data on the toolbar. Each time you click Update Data, it will collect one sample of data. The solid red vertical line in the graph is called the timer bar. It moves across the graph as data is collected. The graph can display up to 100 samples at a time.

Some of the attributes that can be set for the graph include background color, text font, and line style in the graph. You can also highlight a particular counter's data. To highlight a selected counter, either press CTRL-H or click Highlight. When the data is highlighted, it is displayed in white.

Value Bar

The value bar is positioned below the graph area. It displays data for the selected counter, such as the last sample value, the average of the counter samples, the maximum and minimum of the samples, and the duration of time the samples have been taken. See Figure 8-3 for an example of the value bar.

FIGURE 8-3   System Monitor value bar

Last	100.000	Average	51.871	Minimum	0.000
		Maximum	100.000	Duration	1:40

Legend

The legend displays information about the counters that are being measured. It is the set of columns at the bottom of System Monitor. The legend displays the following information:

- **Color**   The color the counter is displayed as
- **Scale**   The scale of the counter in the graph
- **Counter**   The counter being measured
- **Instance**   The instance of the object being measured
- **Object**   The object being measured
- **Computer**   The computer that is the counter is being measured on

You can select the counters in the legend. Notice in Figure 8-4 that the %Processor Time counter is selected. The value bar displays information about the counter that is selected. By clicking any of the columns, you can sort the list on that column.

Now that we have talked about System Monitor, let's do an exercise to see how we can use it.

FIGURE 8-4   System Monitor legend

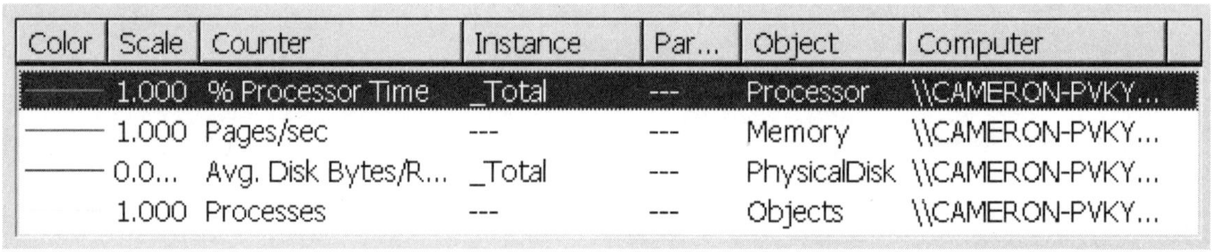

Color	Scale	Counter	Instance	Par...	Object	Computer
	1.000	% Processor Time	_Total	---	Processor	\\CAMERON-PVKY...
	1.000	Pages/sec	---	---	Memory	\\CAMERON-PVKY...
	0.0...	Avg. Disk Bytes/R...	_Total	---	PhysicalDisk	\\CAMERON-PVKY...
	1.000	Processes	---	---	Objects	\\CAMERON-PVKY...

CertCam 8-3

Using System Monitor

1. To start System Monitor from the Start menu, select Start | Programs | Administrative Tools | Performance. This will bring up System Monitor in the Performance console.

2. Now let's add some counters to measure. Click Add, or right-click the graph area and select Add Counters . . . from the context menu.

3. This will bring up the Add Counters dialog box. Select Use Local Computer Counters.

4. From the Performance Object list, select Processor.

5. From the Select Counters From List list, select %Processor Time. Your settings should look like the following illustration.

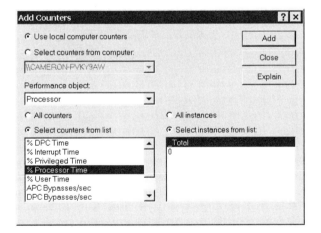

You'll notice that there is a list to choose either the total or per instance on the right side of the dialog box in the previous illustration. What is available depends on the object selected; but in that illustration, the processor object selected. Other than _Total, only 0 is available. That is because there is only one processor available. Windows 2000 Professional supports up to two processors. If you had two processors, 0 and 1 would be available. This would allow you to view the counters for a specific processor rather than the total of both processors.

EXERCISE 8-3

6. Click Add to add the counter.

7. Now let's add another counter. From the Performance Object list, select Memory.

8. From the Select Counters From List list, select Pages/Sec, and click Add. Click Close to exit the dialog box. Your settings should look like the following illustration.

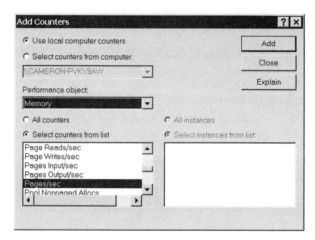

9. Notice the counters have been added to the legend, and data is being displayed in the chart. Let's highlight the %Processor Time counter. In the Legend, select the %Processor Time counter and click Highlight on the toolbar. System Monitor should now show this counter highlighted in white.

10. Let's look at the histogram view. Click View Histogram. Your System Monitor should look similar to the following illustration.

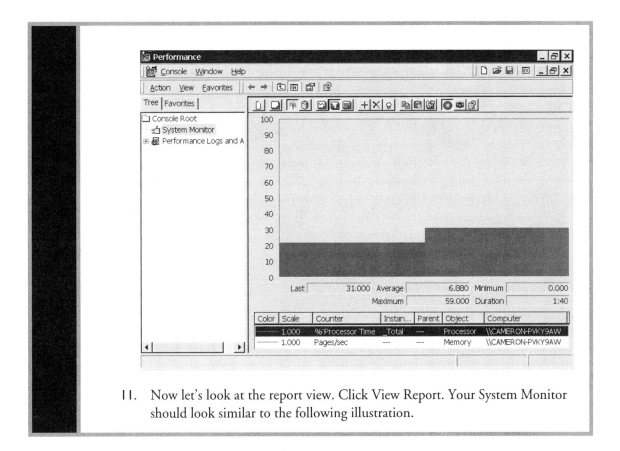

11. Now let's look at the report view. Click View Report. Your System Monitor should look similar to the following illustration.

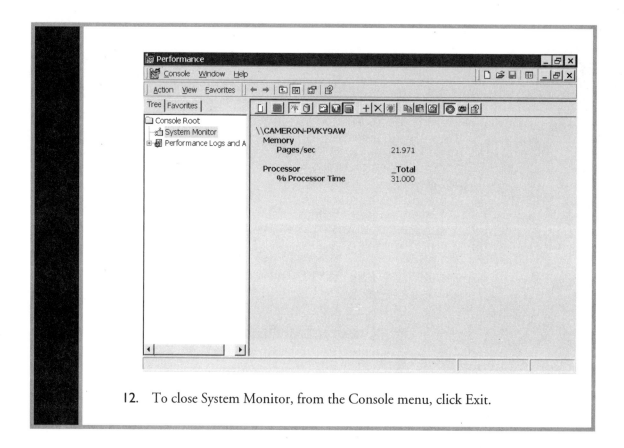

12. To close System Monitor, from the Console menu, click Exit.

Bottlenecks

Now that you have learned how to use System Monitor, what exactly do you use it for? One of the main reasons is finding bottlenecks in your system. A bottleneck is just what it sounds like: A bottle has a neck that restricts the flow from the bottle. A bottleneck in computer terms is also a component of the system as a whole that restricts the system from operating at its peak. When a bottleneck occurs, the component that is a bottleneck will have a high rate of usage, and other components will have low rates of usage. In this section, we will discuss common bottlenecks and how to find and fix them.

Processor Utilization

The most common causes of bottlenecks are the processor, memory, the hard disk, and the network. We will discuss how to measure for bottlenecks in these basic areas. First, let's talk about processor bottlenecks. If your applications perform large or many calculations, they can use a lot of processor time. If your processor cannot fulfill all the requests for processor time, it can become a bottleneck. With System Monitor, you can measure the Processor object's %Processor Time counter. When this counter reaches a sustained level of 80 percent, you will need to fix this problem. This counter will occasional spike to 100 percent. This can occur when applications start up or when certain operations are performed. If you have occasional spikes to 100 percent CPU utilization, this is not a cause for concern. If your processor is a bottleneck, you can either upgrade to a faster processor, or add additional processors to the computer.

Memory Performance

Memory issues are also prevalent bottlenecks. Arguably, memory is the most important component for system performance. Memory can be broken up into physical memory and virtual memory. Physical memory is the actual Random Access Memory (RAM) on the computer. When the physical memory becomes full, the operating system can also use space on the hard disk as virtual memory. When memory becomes full, rather than locking up the computer, the operating system stores unused data on the hard disk in a page file (also called a paging file). It was previously called the swap file in Windows 95 and Windows 98. Data is swapped back and forth between the hard disk and physical memory as needed for running applications. If memory is needed that is in virtual memory, it is swapped back into physical memory.

Memory is a common cause of bottlenecks when your computer doesn't have enough memory for the applications and services that are running. When there isn't enough memory for the applications that are running, pages of memory can be swapped from physical memory to the hard disk and slow the system down. This is also known as paging because *pages* of memory are swapped at a time. Windows 2000 separates memory into 4KB pages to help prevent fragmentation of memory. Swapping can even get bad enough that you can hear your hard disk running constantly.

So, how do we know if memory is running low? The main counters to watch in System Monitor are the Memory object's Available Bytes and Pages/Sec counters. The Available Bytes counter indicates the number of bytes of memory that are currently available for use by applications. When the available memory drops below 4MB, you should add more memory to the computer. The Pages/Sec counter provides the number of pages that were either retrieved from disk or written to disk. When the Pages/Sec counter reaches 20, you should look at your paging activity and consider adding more memory. When a bottleneck occurs in memory, the most common solution is to add more memory. You can also create multiple page files on different hard disks to increase performance. If possible, you can off-load memory-intensive applications to other computers.

Network Performance

Your computers can affect the performance of your network. To analyze your network, you should monitor the resources on the computers and overall network traffic. System Monitor also allows you to monitor network activities. When monitoring network performance of your computer, you should monitor the services provided at each layer of the Open Systems Interconnection (OSI) model. This is a model of breaking networking tasks into layers. Each layer is responsible for a specific set of functionality. There are performance objects available in System Monitor for analyzing network performance. See Table 8-3 for the performance objects at each layer of the OSI model.

TABLE 8-3	OSI Layer	Performance Objects
Performance Objects for Monitoring Network Activities	Application, Presentation, Session	Browser, Server, Redirector, and Server Work Queues for NBT Connection
	Transport	TCP, UDP, NetBEUI for NetBIOS, and AppleTalk
	Network	Network Segment, IP, and NWLink IPX/SPX
	Data Link, Physical	Network Interface

If you suspect that your computer is a bottleneck on the network, start monitoring the objects at the lower layers first. One of the counters you should measure is the %Net Utilization of the Network Segment object. It shows what percentage of your network's capacity it is operating at. On Ethernet networks, the recommended threshold is 30–40 percent. Once it reaches this range, you can start running into problems with collisions. From the Server object, you should monitor the Bytes Total/Sec counter. If the sum of this counter for all computers on the network is close to the maximum throughput of your network, then you should consider segmenting your network. If you have network counters that are above or below normal, the computers' resources could cause this. You should also monitor a computer's memory, processor(s), and hard disk(s).

There are many things you can do to increase network performance. You can segment your network. If you have any protocols that aren't used, you should remove the binding for the protocol or uninstall the protocol entirely. Also, place the most-used protocol first in the binding list. If you have a network adapter that is not being used, remove the binding for the network adapter. If necessary, replace your network adapter with a higher-performance network adapter. For instance, if you have a 16-bit network adapter, replace it with a 32-bit network adapter.

SCENARIO & SOLUTION

I have a computer that I suspect is performing less than expected. What are the common resources that should be analyzed?	When looking for bottlenecks on your computer, you should monitor the processor, memory, hard disks, and network activity.
Which tools can be used to monitor my system resources?	The System Monitor and Task Manager can be used to monitor your system resources.
How do I turn on my hard disk counters?	Use the DiskPerf command-line utility to enable the hard disk counters.

FROM THE CLASSROOM

Bottlenecks and Baselines

Students commonly ask, "why bother with a baseline?" They claim that if a bottleneck occurs, it will be easy to spot. This is often true, but not always. Besides, it would be better to prevent the bottleneck from occurring. Creating a baseline will take some time, but the time will be well worth it in the long run. You can use the System Monitor to measure performance data to create a baseline to compare to over time for the degradation of performance.

In this chapter, and in most classes that are taught, not everything that can be measured by System Monitor can be covered. Only the most important and common counters are discussed. The performance data that can be measured is quite extensive. You should start with these main counters to create your baseline, and continue to monitor them over time. This allows you to see when performance is degrading.

There will be times when a bottleneck is not immediately apparent. There may be times when you need to add some counters to determine the bottleneck. Students normally ask how to find out which ones to use. You can look in the Windows 2000 Resource Kit and in Microsoft TechNet for more detailed information on monitoring your system for bottlenecks.

One last thing to keep in mind is that you don't want to always measure every counter you can think of. Monitoring performance counters takes resources to measure them, and can cause a drain on your system resources. It is best to use a main set of counters for your baseline and normal monitoring, and use other counters when needed.

—*Cameron Wakefield, MCSD, MCP*

Disk Performance

The hard disk can also be a bottleneck. Many different operations are performed using the hard disk. When you boot your computer, the operating system is loaded from the hard disk. The operating system swaps between physical and virtual memory using the hard disk. Also, applications are loaded from the hard disk, and many applications read and write data to the hard disk. The rate at which the hard disk can read and write data can have a large impact on the performance of your computer. You can use System Monitor to determine the performance of your hard disk(s). You can measure your hard disk performance using the PhysicalDisk and the LogicalDisk objects. These objects measure the transfer of data to and from the hard disk. The PhysicalDisk object measures the transfer of data for the entire hard disk.

The LogicalDisk object measures the transfer of data for a logical drive (e.g., C: or D:) or storage volumes. You can use the PhysicalDisk object to determine which hard disk is causing the bottleneck. Then, to narrow the cause of the bottleneck, you can use the LogicalDisk object to determine which, if any, partition is the specific cause of the bottleneck.

Enabling the disk objects can cause a drain on system performance, because the counters interrupt the processor during disk operations. These objects should only be enabled when they are in use. By default, the PhysicalDisk object is enabled and the LogicalDisk object is disabled on Windows 2000 Professional. You can enable and disable these objects using the **diskperf** command. The changes won't take effect until the computer is rebooted. The following is a list of the command-line switches available for DiskPerf.

- **-Y**   Enables all the disk performance counters
- **-YD**   Enables the PhysicalDisk object performance counters
- **-YV**   Enables the LogicalDisk object performance counters
- **-N**   Disables all the disk performance counters
- **-ND**   Disables the PhysicalDisk object performance counters
- **-NV**   Disables the LogicalDisk object performance counters
- **\\Computername**   Allows you to set the counters for remote computers

When measuring the performance of your hard disk, some of the commonly measured counters are %Disk Time, Current Disk Queue Length, Disk Reads/Sec, and Disk Writes/Sec. If the %Disk Time reaches 90 percent or higher, then your hard disk may be a bottleneck. The Disk Reads/Sec and Disk Writes/Sec depend on the hard disk. You should check the transfer rates that are specified by the vendor to ensure that the rates are not higher than the specification. The Current Disk Queue Length should not be more than the number of spindles (most disks have one spindle) on the hard drive plus 2. You should measure this by the average. If your hard disk becomes a bottleneck, you can do several things to alleviate the problem. You can upgrade the hard disk to a higher-speed disk, or add disks on different disk controllers. You can create striped volume sets across different physical disks, which will allow multiple I/O operations to be executed simultaneously. Try to put some of the load on another computer if possible. If a program has heavy disk utilization, you can have that program use a hard disk that is not used by the operating system or other programs. See if the drives are fragmented, and defragment them as needed. You can also consider using RAID.

Increasing the size of the hard disk will not solve a performance bottleneck; it will only help if you are running out of disk space.

Hard disk performance can degrade over time due to fragmentation of files. A file is fragmented when it is not physically stored in contiguous space on the hard disk. This can happen as files grow larger and the contiguous space is already in use by another file. This requires part of the file to be stored elsewhere on the disk. When files become fragmented, it takes additional reads and disk head movements to read/write the fragmented parts of the file. This, of course, means it takes longer to read/write to a file. This also makes the free space fragmented, so when you create a new file, the space allocated can be fragmented if the free space isn't large enough. This is because files are created in the first available free space. As you can guess, this process continues as files are created, deleted, and edited, and it just keeps getting worse.

Disk Defragmenter can help alleviate this problem. Windows NT did not come with a defragmenter tool. This tool is new in Windows 2000. It can move and rearrange files so that they are stored in contiguous space on the hard disk. The task of finding fragmented files and moving them into contiguous space is called *defragmentation.* Disk Defragmenter can analyze your volumes and make a recommendation as to whether you should defragment it. It will also give you a graphical display showing you the fragmented files, contiguous files, system files, and free space. You might be asking, "why not run defragmentation on the volume no matter what?" The reason is that it can literally take hours, depending on several factors. It depends on the size of the volume, the number of files, how bad the fragmentation is, and the amount of free space available. Disk Defragmenter will move all of the files so that the files are stored in contiguous space. It will also move the files to the front of the volume, which will give the added benefit of making the free space contiguous so that all newly created files can also be contiguous. Disk Defragmenter can defragment volumes formatted with FAT, FAT32, and NTFS. Also, you can only run one instance of the Disk Defragmenter program at a time. You must have Administrator privileges to run it.

Disk Defragmenter does not always completely defragment free space; however, it does move it into just a few contiguous areas of the disk, which will still give improved performance. Making the free space one contiguous space would have little added benefit. There are several reasons that would prevent free space from being completely defragmented. The paging file can become fragmented as it grows to meet the virtual memory requirements. The paging file is always opened exclusively by Windows 2000. This means that it cannot be defragmented using Disk Defragmenter. Defragmenting the page file could improve the performance of your computer. The only way to effectively defragment the paging file is to move it to another volume. If possible, Microsoft also recommends placing the paging file on its own volume, which would prevent the paging file from becoming fragmented. This could also increase performance if the volume that contains the paging file is low on free space. However, Microsoft also recommends leaving a small paging file on the boot partitions for recovery purposes. (System and recovery options and configurations are discussed in Chapter 9. On NTFS volumes, Windows 2000 reserves some free space for the master file table (MFT). The MFT stores the information needed by the operating system to retrieve files from the volume. Part of the MFT is stored at the beginning of the volume and cannot be moved. Also, if the volume contains a large number of directories, it can prevent the free space from being defragmented.

exam
ⓦatch
Remember that the paging file cannot be defragmented using Disk Defragmenter; it is locked for exclusive use by Windows 2000. To remove the fragmentation of a paging file, move the paging file to another volume, preferably its own volume without any other data files on it to prevent future fragmentation.

on the
ⓙob
You can often defragment the same drive multiple times to achieve better defragmentation results.

The Disk Defragmenter has three main areas of display. The top area lists the volumes that can be defragmented. The middle volume displays the fragmentation of the volume selected in the upper portion. The bottom portion displays the volume during and after defragmentation. The Disk Defragmenter is shown in Figure 8-5. The display shows fragmented files in red, contiguous files in blue, system files that cannot be moved by Disk Defragmenter in green, and free space in white. After running the defragmenter, you can see the improvement in the fragmentation of the volume by comparing the Analysis display to the Defragmentation display.

FIGURE 8-5

The Disk
Defragmenter
tool

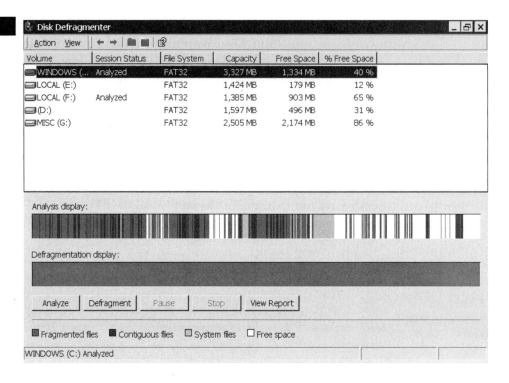

When you analyze a volume, Disk Defragmenter generates a report that gives detailed information about your volume. The top of the report contains information such as volume information, volume fragmentation, file fragmentation statistics, page file fragmentation, and directory fragmentation statistics. The bottom of the report displays information on a file-by-file basis showing the name of the file, its size, and the number of fragments. An Analysis Report is shown in Figure 8-6.

on the
job

You should always analyze your volumes before defragmenting them. This will allow the system to see if defragmentation is needed for the volume.

When should you run Disk Defragmenter? You should create a schedule to run it periodically. The version that comes with Windows 2000 cannot be scheduled to run automatically; it has to be run manually. How often depends on how many file

FIGURE 8-6

Disk
Defragmenter
Analysis Report

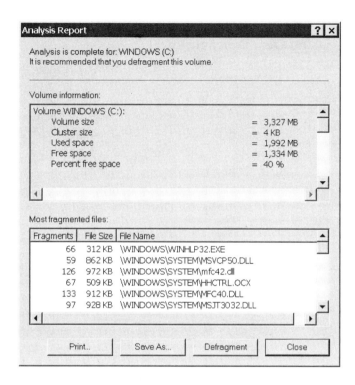

operations are generally performed on your computer. You should run it whenever you delete a large file, or when many files are created or deleted. For general-use workstations, Microsoft recommends defragmenting volumes once a month. Also, since running the defragmenter uses file I/O resources, you should run it during low-volume times. Disk defragmenter places an additional load on the computer and can significantly degrade performance.

exam
⚠atch

You must be logged on with an account that has Administrator privileges to run the Disk Defragmenter.

In the following exercise, we will see how to use the Disk Defragmenter.

Using Disk Defragmenter

1. To start Disk Defragmenter, select Start | Programs | Accessories | System Tools | Disk Defragmenter.

2. When the Disk Defragmenter starts, the Analysis And Defragmentation displays will be blank. Let's see if volume C: needs defragmentation. Select Volume C: and click Analyze. When it has finished, a message box will appear, telling you whether defragmentation is needed. If it is, the message box will be similar to the first illustration that follows. If it isn't, it will be similar to the second illustration.

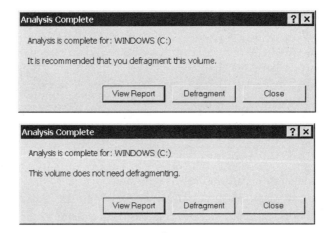

3. Click View Report.

4. Scroll through the top section to see the detailed information for your volume.

5. Click Defragment to start defragmenting the volume. As the defragmentation takes place, you should start seeing the red portion in the Analysis display become blue in the defragmentation display. When it is complete, a message box will appear, as shown in the following illustration.

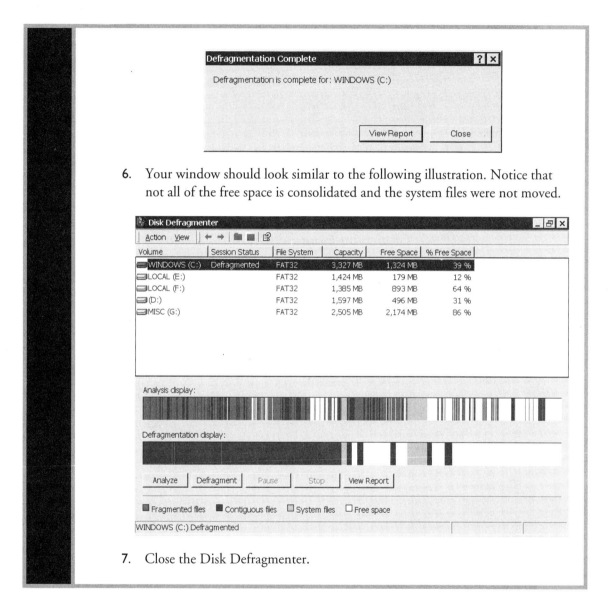

6. Your window should look similar to the following illustration. Notice that not all of the free space is consolidated and the system files were not moved.

7. Close the Disk Defragmenter.

Performance Logs and Alerts

Another useful tool that is preconfigured with the Computer Management MMC is the Performance Logs And Alerts snap-in. It allows you to collect data from the local and remote computers to measure performance. This data can be logged and viewed in System Monitor, or it can be exported to Excel or to a database. This allows you to use the tool of your choice to analyze this data and create reports. You can set thresholds for specified counters, and if any of the thresholds are reached, an alert can be sent to you using the Messenger service.

on the
●job

Since the logging feature runs as a service, data is collected even when there aren't any users logged on.

Performance logging has many features. The data collected is stored in a comma-delimited or tab-delimited format, which allows it to be exported to spreadsheet and database applications for a variety of tasks such as charting and reports. The data can also be viewed as it is collected. You can configure the logging by specifying start and stop times, the name of the log files, and the maximum size of the log. You can start and stop the logging of data manually, or create a schedule for logging. You can even specify a program to automatically run when logging stops. You can also create trace logs. Trace logs track events that occur rather than measuring performance counters. The Performance Logs And Alerts snap-in is shown in Figure 8-7.

You can use the Performance Logs And Alerts snap-in to configure your logging and alerts. You can configure multiple alerts and logs to run simultaneously. When configuring performance counter logs, in the tree on the left side of the Computer Management MMC, select Counter Logs, as shown in Figure 8-8. It displays the name of the log. A sample log file called System Overview is provided by default. It also displays a comment describing the log or alert, the type of log, and the name of the log file.

From the Action menu, you can create logs. When you create a log, the first thing you do is give it a name that is intuitive. Then you can add performance counters to the log; these are the same counters we used in System Monitor. You also specify the

FIGURE 8-7

The Performance
Logs And Alerts
snap-in

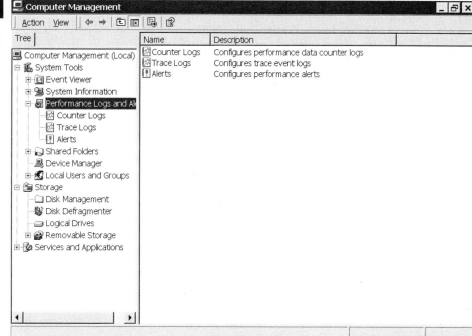

FIGURE 8-8

Viewing
counter logs in
Performance
Logs And Alerts

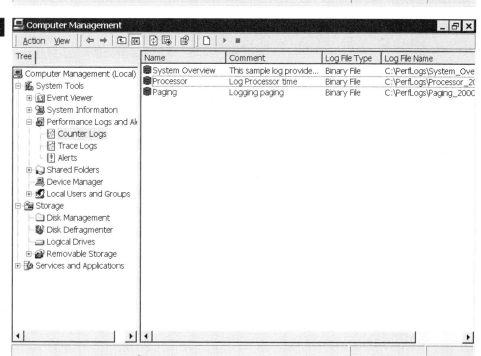

interval at which the data should be collected. By default, it is set to a 15-second interval. Next, you need to configure the log filename. See the following list for parameters you can use to specify the log filename.

- **Location**   Specify the folder in which the log file will be created.
- **File Name**   Type in the base name for the log file. Do not type in the extension.
- **End File Names With**   Allows you to specify the end of the filename. This is added to the filename specified. By default, it uses a six-digit number. You can also choose date/time options.
- **Start Numbering At**   When you choose the numbering scheme for the filename ending, you can specify what the automatic numbering starts with.

After you have configured the log filename, you need to choose the type of log file to create. The log file type can be one of the following:

- **Binary**   This is a counter log file that stores the data in a binary format. It has a .blg extension.
- **binary circular**   This is a counter log file that stores the data in a binary format. When the log reaches a specified size, it starts overwriting the oldest data rather than increasing the size of the file. It has a .blg extension.
- **text-CSV**   This is a counter log file in which the data is stored in a comma-delimited format, which is a common format that can be read by spreadsheet and database applications. It has a .csv extension.
- **text-TSV**   This is a counter log file in which the data is stored in a tab-delimited format, which is a common format that can be read by spreadsheet and database applications. It has a .tsv extension.

- **Circular Trace File**   This is a trace log file. When the log reaches a specified size, it starts overwriting the oldest data rather than increasing the size of the file. It has an .etl extension.

- **Sequential Trace File**   This is a trace log file that saves data until it reaches the maximum size. When the maximum size is reached, it creates a new file. It has an .etl extension.

The next configuration option is the comment. This allows you to enter a description of the log file you are creating. Finally, you select the file size limit. You can either choose the maximum size for the log file allowed by the operating system or disk quotas, or specify a maximum size. For counter logs, you specify the size in kilobytes with a maximum of 2 gigabytes for counter logs. For trace logs, you specify the size in megabytes. When you use the binary circular log type, then you must specify the size of the log.

exam
ⓦatch   *When setting the maximum size of a log file, be careful that it is not larger than the free space on the drive or larger than your disk quota. If the log runs out of disk space, an error will occur.*

You can also schedule logging. To start the log file, you can select to start it manually or specify a time and date. To stop the logging, you can select to stop it manually, after a certain of time, at a specified time, or when the file reaches the specified size limit. When you select the duration or size to stop the logging, you can select the option to start a new log file when the current one is closed. You can also specify a program to be run when the log file is closed. A common use for this is to copy the log file to a remote location for archiving.

Now, let's do an exercise to see how to perform these tasks.

EXERCISE 8-5

Configuring Logs

1. To start the Performance Logs And Alerts, select Start | Programs | Administrative Tools | Performance.

2. In the tree view in the left pane, select Performance Logs And Alerts.

3. Now let's create a new log. In the right pane, select Counter Logs. From the Action menu, select New Log Settings . . .

4. When the New Log Settings dialog box comes up, type **Exercise4** in the Name field.

5. Click OK to bring up the log Properties, as shown in the following illustration.

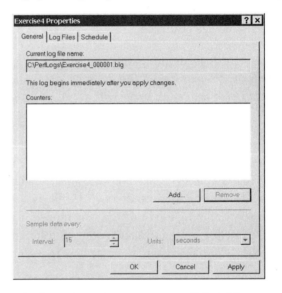

6. From the General tab, in the Counters section, click Add . . . to add a counter to bring up the Select Counters dialog box.

7. Select the Use Local Computer Counters option.

8. In the Performance Objects list, select Processor.

9. In the Select Counters list, select the %Processor Time counter, as shown in the following illustration.

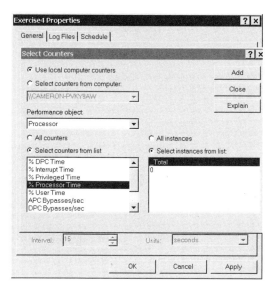

10. Click Add to add the counter.

11. Click Close to close the dialog box.

12. Leave the interval at the default of 15 seconds, and go to the Log Files tab.

13. Leave the default location and filename. In the End File Names With list, select yyyymmddhh. This will add the date and hour to the end of the filename. Notice the example filename, as shown in the following illustration.

14. From the Log File Type List, select Text-CSV.

15. In the comment field, type **This is a log from Exercise 7-4.**

16. Select the Limit Of option and set the size to 500KB. Your settings should look like the following illustration.

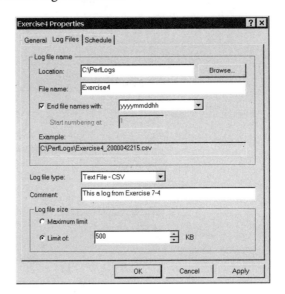

17. Go to the Schedule tab.

18. In the Start Log section, select the At option. For the time, enter **3:26:25 PM**. For the date, use the drop-down calendar to choose **7/1/2000**.

19. In the Stop Log section, choose the When The 500-KB Log File Is Full option.

20. Select the Start A New Log File check box. Your settings should look like the following illustration.

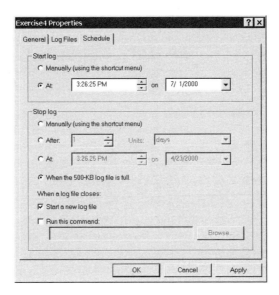

21. Click OK to create the log file.

22. The log file now appears in the right pane, as shown in the following illustration.

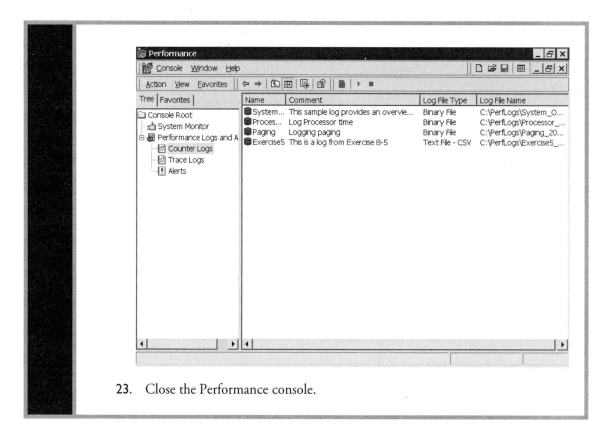

23. Close the Performance console.

Alerts

Alerts allow some action to be performed when a performance counter reaches a particular threshold. A common action is to log the event in the application Event log. You can also send a network message to a specified computer. You can have the alert start a Performance log to start logging when the alert occurs. Finally, you can configure the alert to start a program.

When you create an alert, some of the settings will be similar to creating a log. The first thing you do is give the alert an intuitive name. Then you can enter a comment and choose the counter(s) for the alert. One difference is that you have to set the threshold for the alert. You choose a value and whether you want the alert to occur when the value is over or under the threshold. Then you also specify the interval. The default for alerts is five seconds.

You have some options about what happens when an alert occurs. You can write the alert to the application Event log, send a network message to a specified computer, start a log, and/or run a program. You can also specify the command-line parameters for the program. You have the same basic options for scheduling alerts. You can specify the start and stop options. You can also have the alert start a new scan when it finishes for continuous alert scanning. From the Performance Logs And Alerts console, you can start and stop alerts by right-clicking them and selecting Start or Stop from the context menu.

exam
⍟atch

Make sure you know the settings for configuring logs and alerts. These include sample rates, log file options, and scheduling options.

Application Performance

There are times when you will need to manage the processes that are running on your computer. Sometimes a process will stop responding or it may not be getting enough CPU time. In this section, we will talk about how to deal with these tasks.

As in Windows NT, Windows 2000 has a Task Manager. Task Manager can be used for different tasks. It allows you to monitor applications, processes, and

SCENARIO & SOLUTION

When I ran the Disk Defragmenter, I noticed that the free space was still in several segments. Does this mean that my hard disk will still have a performance hit?	No, having the free space in several contiguous fragments will not have a noticeable performance hit. In fact, there is very little additional benefit from having all of the free space in one contiguous space.
I created a new log file and now my computer is running very slowly. How could this happen?	One common way is setting the sample rate too low. For instance, setting it to less than five seconds can use a significant amount of resources. Try increasing the sample rate until the performance of your computer is at an acceptable level.
I don't want to continuously run logs, but I do want to know when my resources reach certain levels. How can I accomplish this?	You can use alerts. Alerts can be configured to automatically start logs and notify you when a threshold is reached.

different performance statistics. Task Manager has three tabs: Applications, Processes, and Performance, as shown in Figure 8-9. By default, the Task Manager Performance tab will display CPU and memory usage. It also displays the number of handles, threads, and processes running, as well as total KB for physical, kernel, and committed memory. Task Manager can be started by pressing CTRL-ALT-DEL and selecting Task Manager, or pressing CTRL-SHIFT-ESC.

The Applications tab displays all of the applications that are running. From this tab, you can end an application, switch to an application, or start an application. The Processes tab displays all the processes, services, and drivers that are running.

The Processes tab displays the process name, process ID (PID), the percentage of CPU time being used, the elapsed time using the CPU, and memory usage. You can also select other columns to be displayed, as shown in Figure 8-10.

FIGURE 8-9

The Task
Manager

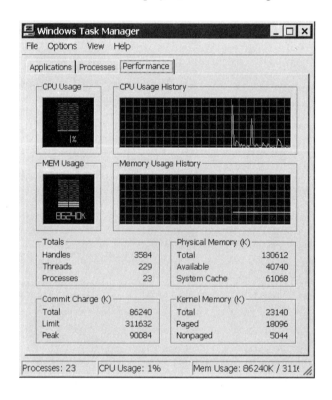

FIGURE 8-10

The Task
Manager
Processes tab
column options

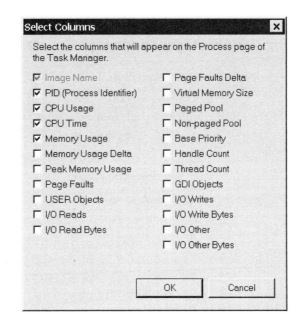

From Task Manager, you can stop applications and processes from running. To stop an application, select the application you want to stop, and click End Task. You can also stop individual processes from running by selecting the process and clicking End Process, or by right-clicking the process and selecting End Process. There is another option to End Process Tree, which will stop all processes related to the process you want to stop, since some applications are comprised of multiple processes. Also, if you have multiple processors on your computer, you can assign a process to a processor(s) by using the Set Affinity command, which is only available on multiple-processor computers. You should be careful using this command, because it will limit the process to only running on those processors. We will look at Task Manager in Exercise 8-6.

on the
job

You cannot stop processes that are critical to running Windows 2000 from Task Manager.

EXERCISE 8-6

Using Task Manager to Manage Processes

1. To start Task Manager, press CTRL-ALT-DEL. Then click Task Manager. You can also press CTRL-SHIFT-ESC to bring up the Task Manager.

2. Go to the Applications tab to see the applications running on your computer. Let's start an application.

3. From the Start button, select Run. Type **winver**, and click OK. Notice that the About Windows application is now running. Now let's stop it.

4. Select the About Windows application in the Task Manager Applications window and click End Task. Notice that it no longer appears in the Applications tab.

5. Now let's end a process. Let's start the winver program again. From the Start button, select Run. Type **winver**, and click OK. Notice that the About Windows application is now running. Now let's stop it.

6. Select the winver.exe process. Notice that it is using little to no CPU time. Also notice that it is using about 912KB of memory. While it is selected, click End Process.

7. To close the Task Manager, select Exit Task Manager from the File menu.

Windows 2000 uses preemptive multitasking in which each process is given a time-slice of processor time. How much processor time a process receives depends on its priority. When processes are started, Windows 2000 gives priorities to processes. There are 32 priorities ranging from 0–31; priority 31 is the highest priority. User applications and noncritical operating system functions use priority levels 0–15.

Critical real-time applications such as the operating system kernel use priority levels 16–31. There are four base process priority levels: Real-Time, High, Normal, and Idle. The priority levels in between these are reserved for thread priority levels that are added to the process' basic priority level. A thread's priority is based on its process' base priority. A thread can be given one of the following priorities: Highest, Above Normal, Normal, Below Normal, and Lowest. A thread's overall priority is determined by adding the thread's priority to the process' base priority (Table 8-4).

You can change the default priority level for a process from the command line or from Task Manager. To change a process' default priority from the command line, use the Start command with one of these switches: /low, /normal, /high, or /realtime. When using the priority switches, the threads will have a default Normal priority. Therefore, the switches will set the program's priority as follows: Real-Time: 24; High: 13; Normal: 8; Low: 4. In Exercise 8-7, we will show you how to use the Start command.

TABLE 8-4   Priority Levels

Thread Priorities	Real-Time	High	Normal	Idle
Highest	26	15	10	6
Above Normal	25	14	9	5
Normal	24	13	8	4
Below Normal	23	12	7	3
Lowest	22	11	6	2
Idle	16	1	1	1

Using the Start Command to Set a Process' Priority

1. From the Start menu, select Programs | Accessories | Calculator.

2. Now let's see what the default priority is. To open the Task Manager, press CTRL-SHIFT-ESC.

3. Go to the Processes tab and find the calc.exe process. Right-click it and select Set Priority. The default priority is Normal, as shown in the following illustration.

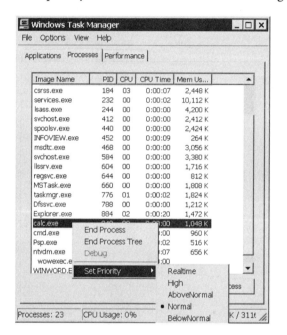

4. Close the Calculator program.

5. Now let's set the priority. From the Start menu, select Programs | Accessories | Command Prompt.

6. At the command prompt, type **start /high calc** to start the Calculator program.

7. Now let's see what the priority level is. Go to the Processes tab of Task Manager and find the calc.exe process. Right-click it and select Set Priority. The priority is now set to High, as shown in the following illustration.

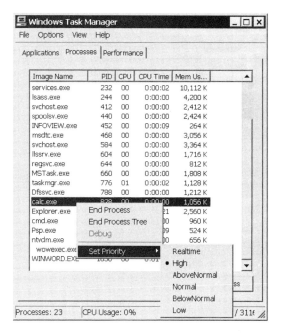

8. Close the Calculator program and the Task Manager.

SCENARIO & SOLUTION

How can I change the default priority level for a program at startup?	You can use the Start command to specify the process base priority using the priority switches.
How can I stop processes from running using Task Manager?	From the Application tab, you can select a process and click End Task to stop it. From the Processes tab, you can right-click a process and select the End Process or End Process Tree option.
How can I change the priority of a running process inside Task Manager?	From the Processes tab of Task Manager, you can right-click a process, select Set Priority, and then select the new priority level from the context menu.

CERTIFICATION OBJECTIVE 8.05

Managing Hardware Profiles

When you have a computer that changes hardware configuration, you don't want to have to keep uninstalling and installing hardware. Changing hardware is common with laptops. When you are in your office, you might be connected to a docking station with your normal monitor, keyboard, and mouse. When you go on the road, you undock the laptop and the configuration of your hardware changes. Windows 2000 Professional uses hardware profiles to manage different hardware configurations. A name is given to each hardware profile, which is used to determine which device drivers to load. Since hardware profile information is stored in the Registry, this allows applications to determine which hardware is available. Windows 2000 will automatically try to determine which hardware profile to use when it boots up. If there are two hardware profiles that are very similar to each other, the user will be prompted to choose which one to load from.

To manage hardware profiles, go to Control Panel | System | Hardware, and click Hardware Profiles. You can create, rename, delete, enable, and disable hardware profiles. You can copy an existing hardware profile to serve as the basis for a new one. Then you can use the Device Manager to enable and disable devices as desired for the hardware profile. During Setup, a hardware profile is created called Profile 1. The profile that the system booted with will be indicated by (Current) next to the name of the profile. The order of the names determines which one is the default. The first one in the list is the default. You can change the order of the profiles.

If there are multiple hardware profiles, you can configure how the system boots up. You can set the number of seconds that Windows 2000 will wait before using the default profile; the default is 30 seconds. If you set the number of seconds to 0, it will always use the default profile. You can also configure the system to wait indefinitely until the user selects a profile.

If you have a portable computer, you can have it automatically detect whether it is connected to a docking station. Windows 2000 queries the BIOS for a Dock ID to determine if it is docked or not. Then it will automatically start with the correct profile.

CertCam 8-8

EXERCISE 8-8

Creating a Hardware Profile

Let's do an exercise to see how to create and manage hardware profiles.

1. From the Control Panel, click the System icon, or right-click the My Computer icon and select Properties. Then go to the Hardware tab.

2. To view the current hardware profiles, click Hardware Profiles. This will bring up the Hardware Profiles dialog box, as shown in the following illustration.

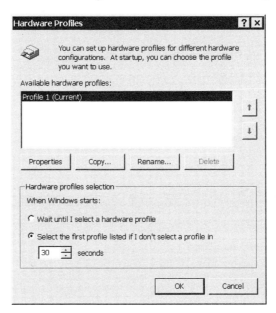

3. To create a new profile, you copy an existing profile as the base. Click Copy.

4. When prompted for a name for the profile, enter **Chapter8**. Notice that Delete is enabled when the Chapter8 profile is selected. This is because you cannot delete the current profile. The profile that the system booted to will be indicated by (Current) next to it.

5. To edit the profile, click Properties. From here you can set properties for portable computers, and check whether this profile is always an option at startup, as shown in the following illustration.

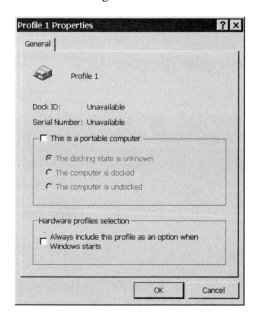

6. Click OK to close the Properties dialog box.

7. Leave the settings as they are, and click OK.

8. Now let's restart the computer with the Chapter8 profile. Click Start and select Shutdown. From the Shutdown Windows dialog box, select Restart, and click OK.

9. When the system restarts and you are prompted to select a hardware profile, choose the Chapter8 profile. Then log on to the computer.

10. From the Control Panel, open the System icon, or right-click the My Computer icon and select Properties. Then go to the Hardware tab and click Hardware Profiles. Notice that the Chapter8 profile is the current profile.

11. Click OK to close the dialog box, and click Device Manager to bring up the Device Manager.

12. Let's disable a device for this profile. If you have a network adapter or dial-up adapter, select it; and from the Action menu, select Properties, or right-click the device and select Properties.

13. At the bottom of the dialog box from the Device Usage drop-down list, select Do Not Use This Device In The Current Hardware Profile (Disable), as shown in the following illustration.

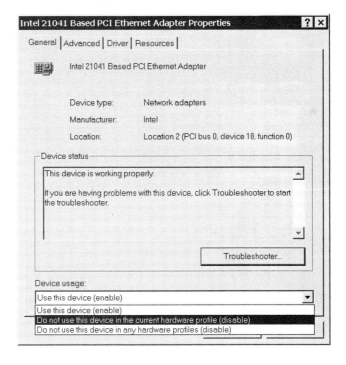

14. Click OK to close the Properties dialog box. Notice that the device now has a Red X through it, as shown in the following illustration.

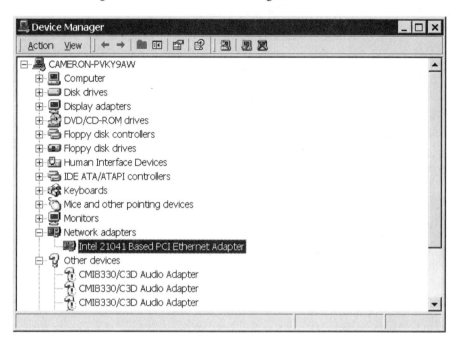

15. Try to connect to the Internet using Internet Explorer. Notice that you get some kind of error, such as "No Internet Connection Available."

16. Let's enable the device. Double-click the device to bring up the Properties dialog box; and from the Device Usage drop-down list, select Use This Device (Enable). Click OK.

17. Try to connect to the Internet using Internet Explorer. Notice that you can now connect again.

18. Let's delete the hardware profile so you won't be prompted to choose a profile every time you boot up. Restart the computer with the original profile. Click Start | Shutdown. From the Shutdown Windows dialog box, select Restart, and click OK.

19. When the system restarts and you are prompted to select a hardware profile, choose the Profile 1 profile. Then log on to the computer.

20. From the Control Panel, open the System icon, or right-click the My Computer icon and select Properties. Then go to the Hardware tab and click Hardware Profiles.

21. Select the Chapter8 profile, and click Delete. When asked to confirm deleting the profile, click Yes.

22. Click OK to close the Hardware Profiles dialog box, and click OK again to close the System Properties.

CERTIFICATION OBJECTIVE 8.06

Recovering Systems and User Data

There will be times when your computer will not boot up properly. When this happens, you need to understand how to solve this problem. There are several ways to fix the problem or restore your computer to its previous state. In this section, we will discuss using the Windows Backup utility, how to use the Safe Mode boot option, the Recovery console tool, and the Windows Startup options.

Windows 2000 Backup and Recovery Tools

The primary defense against losing data should be using backups. Data can be lost due to hard disk failures, power outages, viruses, and so forth. Even if you are using other fault-tolerant techniques, such as RAID, you still need to back up your computer. Windows 2000 comes with the Backup utility to allow you to back up your data. You can back up your operating system, system files, and user data files to another storage media such as tape, floppy, or another hard disk. This allows you to completely restore your computer in the event of a catastrophic failure.

The Backup utility has many options available. It allows you to choose files and folders to back up. You can copy the state of your system, such as the Registry, system files, and boot files. You can also create an Emergency Repair Disk (ERD) that can repair system files if they become corrupt or missing. You can even schedule when the backups occur so that they run at a convenient time when the computer is not in use.

Backup can be used on NTFS and FAT volumes. When data is backed up from an NTFS volume, it should be restored to an NTFS volume. If you restore it to a FAT partition, you could lose data, or features such as permissions or disk quota information. An example of losing data would be if you backed up some encrypted files. Since this feature is not available in FAT, that data would effectively be lost.

There are different types of backups you can perform. Following is a list of the types of backups you can perform using the Backup utility.

- **Normal**   This will back up all files that are selected and mark them as being backed up. This type is also commonly referred to as a full backup.
- **Incremental**   This will back up all files that are selected that have changed since the last normal or incremental backup, and marks them as being backed up.
- **Differential**   This will back up all files that are selected that have changed since the last normal or incremental backup, but does not mark them as backed up.
- **Copy**   This will back up all selected files without marking them as backed up.
- **Daily**   This will back up all selected files that changed the day the backup is performed without marking them as backed up.

So, what are all these types of backups used for? A normal backup will back up all selected files, whether or not they have been changed since the last backup. This will also take longer because all the files are being backed up. This type also marks the file as backed up (this is done by clearing the Archive bit). With this type of backup, you can completely restore the files with this backup alone.

An incremental backup will back up all the files that have changed since the last normal or incremental backup. If you perform regular incremental backups, it will take less time to perform the backups, because you only need to back up the files that have changed since the last incremental backup. However, when you want to restore the files, it will take longer because you will have to restore the files starting with the last normal backup and each incremental backup you have performed since the last normal backup. For example, say you performed a normal backup on Sunday and you perform incremental backups each night of the week. If you needed to perform a restore on Wednesday, you would first have to restore from the normal backup; then restore from the incremental backup from Monday night, and then the incremental backup from Tuesday night. You can see that if you had to restore on Friday, it would take a while, because you would have to restore from so many backups.

A differential backup will also back up all files that have changed since the last normal or incremental backup, but it will not mark the files as backed up. If you use normal and differential backups, it will take longer to perform the backups, because even if a file changed after the normal backup—but not since the last differential backup—it will still back up that file. However, when you want to restore your files, you will only need two backups, the last normal and the last differential backups. This allows you to restore your files faster.

A copy backup will back up all the files without marking them as backed up. This allows you to back up data between normal and incremental backups without affecting them. It is also useful for copying files to another location, or copying files to take home. A daily backup will back up all the files that have changed that day without marking them as backed up.

The actual strategy for backing up your data depends on your business, the importance of your data, and how fast you need to be able to restore your data. A common schedule used for backups is to perform normal backups over the weekend, and perform a differential backup each weeknight. The backup media can also be reused. It takes longer to perform the differential backups, but they can be scheduled to run at night when the computers are not commonly used. However, if you need to restore data during the day when work has to stop to wait for the data to be restored, you will save considerable time restoring from the differential backup rather than the incremental backup.

exam
ⓦatch

Make sure you understand the differences between these types of backups, and when to use them.

Using the Backup Wizard, you can back up files manually or you can schedule backups. When a backup is performed, the data can be saved to a file or to tape. If you save the data to file, it can be saved on a hard disk (including a shared folder on a server), removable disks, or writeable CD-ROM. The backed-up data is saved to a file with an extension of .bkf. When you back up data, you must have the necessary permissions. You can back up the files and folders that are owned by you, and any files that you have the following permissions on: Read, Read And Execute, Modify, or Full Control. Users who are members of the Backup Operators or Administrators group can back up all files.

The Backup Wizard can also back up data from remote computers. You can even perform a single backup from data from multiple computers including the entire network. This can greatly simplify backing up critical data across the network to a single media. However, the Registry and Active Directory can only be backed up on the local computer. If this data needs to be backed up on multiple computers, you will have to perform a local backup on each computer. The Backup program can be started from Start | Programs | Accessories | System Tools | Backup. It has a Backup Wizard and a Restore Wizard. You can also start it by running the **ntbackup** program from the Run dialog box. The Backup program is shown in Figure 8-11.

When you use the Backup Wizard, you will need to decide which files to back up. You will have three choices for files to back up, as shown in the following list. These options are shown in Figure 8-12.

- **Back Up Everything On My Computer**   This option will back up all of the files on the computer.

- **Back Up Selected Files, Drives, Or Network Data**   This option will allow you to select files and folders on the local computer and through My Network Places.

- **Only Back Up The System State Data**   This option will back up critical operating system data such as the Registry, COM+ Class Registration database, and system boot files.

FIGURE 8-11

The Backup program

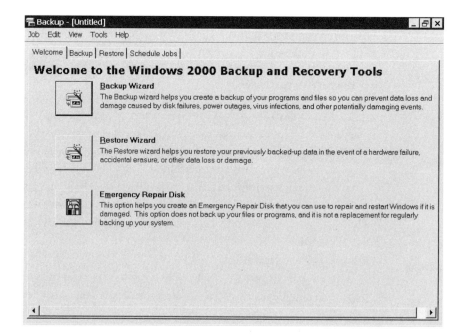

FIGURE 8-12

Selecting files to back up

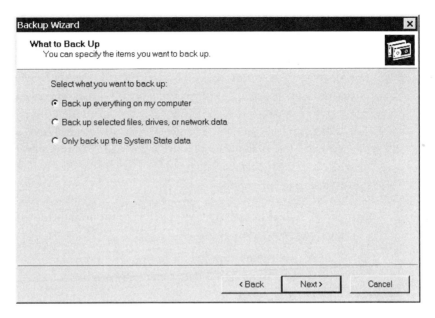

After you choose what data to back up, you will have to choose what media to save the data to, and the tape name or filename. The screen for choosing where to back up the data to is shown in Figure 8-13. If you don't have a tape device on your computer, then the only option that will be available will be to save the data to a file.

FIGURE 8-13

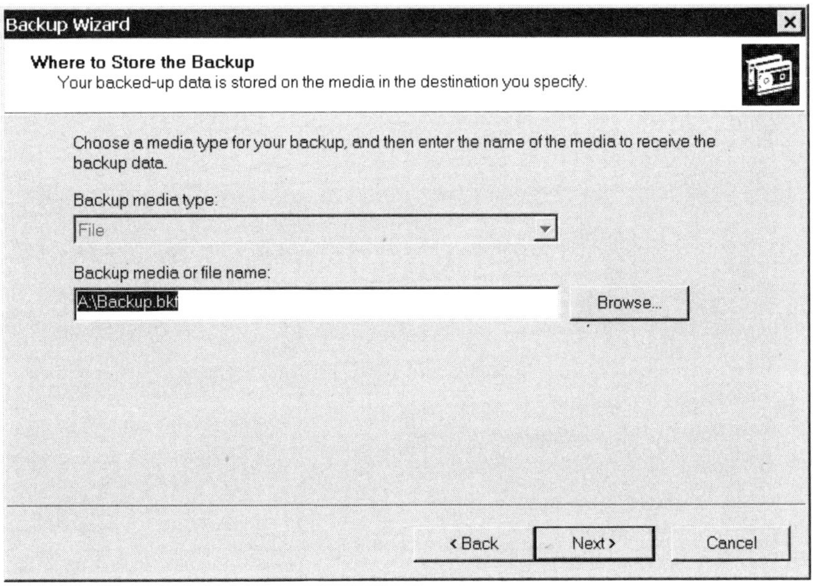

Choosing where to back up the data to

When you want to restore data from a backup, there is a Restore Wizard to guide you through this process. The first step is to choose what data to restore. This screen is shown in Figure 8-14. You can choose to restore an entire backup, or select which files and folders to restore. You can restore files and folders if you have the following permissions: Write, Modify, or Full Control. Users who are members of the Backup Operators or Administrators group can restore all files.

After you have chosen the data to restore, a screen will show you a summary of the settings chosen, as shown in Figure 8-15. Clicking Advanced will allow you to select where to restore the data. The screen to select this option is shown in Figure 8-16. You will have three options:

- **Original Location**   This option will restore the data to the location they were backed up from.

- **Alternate Location**   This option will restore the data to the folder specified, while preserving the folder hierarchy originally backed up from.

- **Single Folder**   This option will restore data to the folder specified without preserving the folder hierarchy. All of the files will be restored to this single directory.

FIGURE 8-14

Choosing data to restore

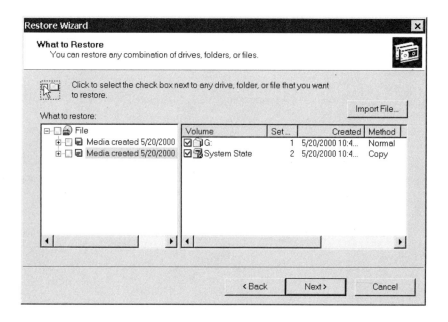

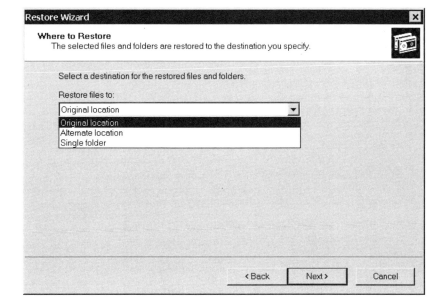

Next, you will have to choose how to handle restoring files when the file already exists. The screen for choosing this option is shown in Figure 8-17. You will have three options from which to choose:

- **Do Not Replace The File On My Disk (Recommended)**   This option will not restore a file if it already exists. It will prevent existing files from being overwritten. This is the default option.

- **Replace The File On Disk Only If It Is Older Than The Backup Copy**   This option will only restore a file if it does not already exist, or if it does exist; it will only overwrite it if the file is older than the file that was backed up.

- **Always Replace The File On My Computer**   This option will always restore a file regardless of whether or not it already exists or how old it is.

Finally, you have some advanced options available. These options allow you to restore permission settings for the files and folders, restore the removable storage database, and restore junction points on the hard disk and the data.

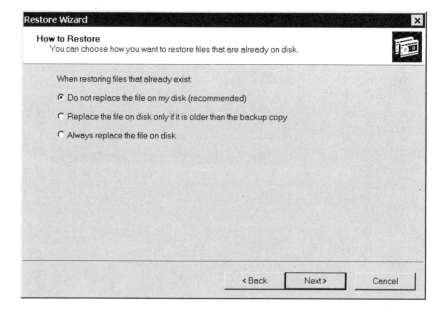

FIGURE 8-17

Choosing how to restore the data

on the

Ⓙ o b *Be sure to periodically test the ability to restore data from a backup. It is very common to hear about people never needing to restore their back ups, and then when they do, they find out they are not able to. This can be caused by tapes going bad or not performing backups correctly.*

Safe Mode

On occasion, Windows 2000 might not be able to start. When this occurs, one of the options available is to start Windows 2000 in Safe Mode. Safe Mode allows you to start Windows 2000 with only the necessary device drivers and services. This includes the mouse, keyboard, CD-ROM, standard VGA video, Event log, and disk controllers. This can help you determine why the computer will not start by allowing you to start Windows 2000 with the minimum devices so you can fix the problem. Once you have started in Safe Mode, you can try to isolate the problem by disabling or deleting services, device drivers, or applications that are started automatically.

Safe Mode is useful in several situations. You should start Windows 2000 in Safe Mode if it stalls or does not work correctly, if your video doesn't work correctly, or if your system all of a sudden becomes very slow.

To start Windows 2000 in Safe Mode, press F8 at the Boot menu while the computer is booting up. This will bring up the Windows 2000 Advanced Options menu. There are several flavors of Safe Mode from which to choose: normal Safe Mode, Safe Mode With Networking, and Safe Mode With Command Prompt. Safe Mode With Networking is the same as normal Safe Mode, except networking services and devices needed to provide network support are also loaded. Safe Mode With Command Prompt is similar to normal Safe Mode, except it only starts with the command prompt.

Recovery Console

Another tool you can use to repair Windows 2000 when it won't start is the Recovery Console, which is a command-line utility that will allow you to access the volumes on your hard disks. However, it does not require the Windows 2000 command prompt to run. This allows it to run when Windows 2000 won't start. It will allow you access to NTFS, FAT, and FAT32 volumes. The Recovery Console allows you to perform very advanced functions, and should be used with caution. It is recommended that only network administrators use this tool. It can be used to manage files and folders, start and stop services, repair the master boot record (MBR), and repair Windows 2000.

The Recovery Console has incorporated some security features to prevent unauthorized access to data, one of which is that you must enter the Administrator password to use it. This prevents someone from using the Recovery Console to access data on the computer without being authorized. You cannot copy files from the hard disk to floppy disks to prevent users from copying data and taking it with them. In order to fix Windows 2000, you are allowed to copy files from a floppy disk, CD-ROM, or another hard disk to a local hard disk. Also, you are only allowed to run commands that are supported by the Recovery Console.

One of the uses for the Recovery Console is to restore the Registry. When you back up the System State, a copy of the Registry is stored in the <SystemRoot>\ Repair\RegBack folder. If you have a corrupt Registry, you can use the Recovery Console to copy the backed-up Registry files over the corrupt Registry files. This will restore the Registry to the state when the System State was backed up. The following is a complete list of the commands that are supported by the Recovery Console.

- **Attrib** This command allows you to set the attributes of files.
- **Batch** This command allows you to run commands in a text file. This allows you to run multiple commands at once.
- **Cd or Chdir** This command allows you to change to a different directory.
- **Chkdsk** This command allows you to run the Check Disk program. It can check and repair volumes.
- **Cls** This command clears the screen.
- **Copy** This command allows you to copy files from one location to another. However, in Recovery Console, wildcards are not allowed.
- **Del or Delete** This command allows you to delete one file. As with the Copy command, wildcards are not allowed.
- **Dir** This command will allow you to view a list of files and subfolders in a folder.
- **Disable** This command allows you to disable a service or driver. You can use the Listsvc command to display a list of services and drivers that you can disable.
- **Diskpart** This command can be used to add and delete partitions.

■ **Enable**   This command allows you to enable a service or driver. You can use the Listsvc command to display a list of services and drivers that you can disable.

■ **Exit**   This command will exit from Recovery Console and restart the computer.

■ **Expand**   This command allows you to expand a compressed file or a file in a CAB file stored on a Windows 2000 CD-ROM. You cannot use wildcards with this command in Recovery Console.

■ **Fixboot**   This command allows you to rewrite the boot sector of a hard disk to repair it.

■ **Fixmbr**   This command allows you to rewrite the master boot record of the startup hard disk to repair it.

■ **Format**   This command allows you to format a volume with FAT, FAT32, or NTFS. NTFS is used by default.

■ **Help**   This command allows you to display the commands available in the Recovery Console.

■ **Listsvc**   This command allows you to display a list of the services and drivers that can be disabled and enabled.

■ **Logon**   This command allows you to list all installations of Windows 2000 and Windows NT. You can choose one of these installations to log on to. You will need to enter the administrator password. If three attempts to log on fail, it will exit from the Recovery Console and restart the computer.

■ **Map**   This command allows you to display a list of information about the drives on the hard disk.

■ **Md or Mkdir**   This command allows you to create a directory. You cannot use wildcards with this command.

■ **More or Type**   This command allows you to display a text file on the screen.

■ **Rd or Rmdir**   This command allows you to delete a directory. You cannot use wildcards with this command.

■ **Ren or Rename**   This command allows you to rename a file or directory. You cannot use wildcards with this command.

■ **Set**   This command allows you to display and set Recovery Console environment values.

■ **Systemroot**   This command allows you to change directory to the <SystemRoot> directory.

The Recovery Console is not installed by default; you must install it manually from the Windows 2000 CD-ROM. To install it, run **winnt32.exe /cmdcons** from the i386 directory on the Windows 2000 CD-ROM. You must have administrator privileges to install it. This will create a directory called Cmdcons in the root of the drive you select. It will also create a file called Cmldr, and create an option on the Boot menu to start the Recovery Console. If your computer will not start, and you do not have the Recovery Console installed on it, you can start the computer from the Windows 2000 CD-ROM or from the Windows 2000 Setup disks, and choose the Recovery Console option.

CertCam 8-9

EXERCISE 8-9

Installing and Using the Recovery Console

Let's do an exercise to see how to install the Recovery Console and how to use it. Prior to starting this exercise, you must be logged on to Windows 2000 with administrator privileges.

1. Insert the Windows 2000 Professional CD-ROM in the CD-ROM drive.

2. Let's install the Recovery Console. From the Start menu, select Run to bring up the Run dialog box.

3. In the Run dialog box, type *X*:\i386\winnt32.exe /cmdcons. Replace *X* with the drive letter for your CD-ROM drive.

4. When the dialog box comes up asking you if you want to install the Recovery Console, click Yes. It will take approximately 7MB of disk space.

5. Setup will copy the files that are required for the Recovery Console. When it is complete, a dialog box will be displayed that will tell you that the Recovery Console has been successfully installed. Click OK.

6. Now restart the computer by clicking the Start menu and selecting Shutdown. Choose Restart and click OK.

7. When the Boot menu appears, select Microsoft Windows 2000 Recovery Console. It may take a few minutes to load.

8. When it has finished loading, you will be prompted to select a Windows 2000 installation. Enter 1, and then press ENTER. (To cancel Recovery Console, you can just press ENTER.)

9. Next, you will be prompted for the Administrator password. Enter the password and press ENTER. Now you will see a command prompt that is defaulted to the SystemRoot folder (e.g., C:\Winnt).

10. Let's use a few commands. Enter **cd . .** , and press ENTER. You should now be at the root of the drive you installed Windows 2000 on (e.g., C:).

11. Let's see a listing of the drivers and services that can be enabled and disabled. Enter **listsvc**, and press ENTER. Press ENTER on your keyboard to scroll one line at a time. To scroll one page at a time, press the SPACEBAR. To quit viewing the list, press ESC.

12. When you have finished, press ESC to exit the list.

13. Now let's see the files and folders. Enter **Dir**, and press ENTER. When you have finished viewing the files and folders, press ESC.

14. To see the mapping of drives to partitions, enter **map**, and press ENTER.

15. To go back to the SystemRoot folder, enter **Systemroot**, and press ENTER.

16. Now exit the Recovery Console by entering **exit** and pressing ENTER.

Windows Startup and Recovery Options

You have some options to control the Boot Loader menu and how system failures are handled. Windows 2000 provides the Startup And Recovery dialog box to choose these options. This dialog box has a System Startup section that allows you to choose which operating system is loaded by default. This is useful when your computer is configured for multiboot. This allows you to automatically load the most commonly used database. You can also choose how long the boot menu is displayed; by default, it is displayed for 30 seconds. You can also choose whether to display the Boot menu.

The Startup And Recovery dialog box also has a System Failure section that determines what Windows 2000 does when you have a system failure. A system failure is when something catastrophic happens that causes all the processes to be stopped. This is also commonly referred to as the "blue screen of death." If a system failure occurs, you can set Windows 2000 to write an event to the System log, have an Administrative alert sent to Administrators, or automatically reboot whenever a system failure occurs. You can also choose some debugging information. You can specify whether a dump file is created, and where to create it. You have four options for the dump file:

- **None**   This option does not create a dump file.

- **Small Memory Dump**   This option only writes the minimum amount of data to the dump file. This will create a 6KB dump file.

■ **Kernel Memory Dump** This option only writes the kernel memory to the dump file. This will create a 50–800MB file, depending on how much RAM you have.

■ **Complete Memory Dump** This option writes the entire system memory to the dump file. This will create a dump file the size of RAM on your computer plus 1MB.

The same dump file is always written to a file called Memory.dmp. If it already exists, it will be overwritten. If you want to save a dump file, you should rename it. In order to create the dump file, there must be a paging file on the system partition, the paging file must be greater than RAM plus 1MB, and you must have enough free disk space for the dump file.

To open the Startup And Recovery dialog box, open the System icon in the Control Panel and in the Advanced tab, click Startup And Recovery. The Startup And Recovery dialog box is shown in Figure 8-18. To set the System Failure options, you must have Administrators privileges.

FIGURE 8-18

The Startup and Recovery settings

CERTIFICATION SUMMARY

In this chapter, we discussed ways to monitor and optimize your computer's resources. Creating a baseline is crucial to determining bottlenecks. A baseline allows you to easily determine which resource has become overburdened by comparing current resources to the baseline. You should monitor your computer's resources continuously. This allows you to monitor for degradation of performance and fix it before it becomes a bottleneck. System Monitor can be used to measure the performance of your computer and even other computers. Some of the common sources of bottlenecks include the processor, memory, hard disk, and the network. You must use the DiskPerf utility to enable and disable the disk counters.

You can manage processes using the Task Manager. You can stop processes and, new in Windows 2000, you can also stop all related processes. This is useful when an application stops responding. If a process is not getting enough CPU time or too much CPU time, you can also change the priority of the process using the Task Manager. You can use the Start command to set the priority of a process.

When a disk volume becomes fragmented, it can affect performance. New to Windows 2000 is the Disk Defragmenter. You can use it to defragment your volumes. When your volumes are defragmented, they will have better performance. You should run the Disk Defragmenter periodically to keep your hard disks running at peak performance.

You can use Performance logs and alerts to monitor performance without continuously logging the data. You can create alerts with thresholds to notify you of meeting the threshold and have it start logging when an alert occurs. You can create logs for specific data and schedule them to save data as desired.

✓ TWO-MINUTE DRILL

Managing and Troubleshooting Driver Signing

❑ You can verify whether drivers have been certified by Microsoft using Driver Signing.

❑ The three settings for driver signing are Ignore, Warn, and Block.

❑ You can see which existing drivers are signed using the System File Checker.

❑ The log file for the System File Checker is called Sigverif.txt.

Configuring, Managing, and Troubleshooting the Task Scheduler

❑ You can use the Task Scheduler to schedule when programs or batch files run.

❑ You can schedule a task by date/time and by interval.

❑ Tasks are stored as a file with the extension .job.

❑ You can set a username and password for the task to run as.

❑ Tasks can be assigned permissions to specify who can manage them.

❑ You can manage tasks on remote computers.

Optimizing and Troubleshooting the Performance of the Windows 2000 Professional Desktop

❑ The MMC has a Performance snap-in that includes System Monitor and Performance Logs And Alerts.

❑ You can use System Monitor to analyze the health of your system.

❑ System Monitor can be used to collect data for memory usage, processor utilization, network activity, and more.

❑ System Monitor can display this data as a graph, histogram, or report.

❑ A bottleneck is a component of the system as a whole that restricts the system from operating at its peak.

❑ To properly administer your computer, you need to monitor the processor, memory, hard disk, and the network for bottlenecks.

❑ Network bottlenecks are sometimes the result of running low on processor and memory resources.

❑ The performance of your hard disk can be degraded due to fragmentation.

❑ Fragmentation is when a file is not stored in contiguous space on the hard disk.

❑ The Disk Defragmenter can remove the fragmentation of your files.

❑ The paging file cannot be defragmented using Disk Defragmenter.

❑ To defragment a paging file, you have to move it to another volume.

❑ You can use the Task Manager to administer and configure processes.

❑ From the Task Manager, you can Start and Stop Processes and Process Trees, as well as set their priorities.

❑ You can assign a process to a processor(s) by using the Set Affinity command.

❑ Process priorities range from 0–31, with 31 being the highest priority.

❑ There are four basic priority levels: Real-Time, High, Normal, and Idle.

❑ You can set a process' priority from the command line using the Start command.

Performance Logs and Alerts

❑ The Performance Logs and Alerts allows you to collect data from the local and remote computers to measure performance. This data can be logged and viewed in System Monitor, or it can be exported to Excel or to a database.

❑ The comment configuration option allows you to enter a description of the log file you are creating.

❑ Alerts allow some action to be performed when a performance counter reaches a particular threshold.

❑ Task Manager allows you to monitor applications, processes, and different performance statistics.

Managing Hardware Profiles

❏ Hardware profiles allow you to have multiple hardware configurations.

❏ Hardware profiles are commonly used for portable computers with docking stations.

❏ You can create new hardware profiles by copying an existing one and then editing it.

❏ You cannot delete the hardware profile that you started Windows 2000 with.

❏ You can use the Device Manager to disable devices in hardware profiles.

Recovering Systems and User Data

❏ You can use the Backup utility to back up files, folders, and the System State.

❏ You can back up to tape or file.

❏ You can schedule backups to run at convenient times.

❏ If you back up a NTFS volume, then it should be restored to an NTFS volume.

❏ You can choose between the following types of backup: Normal, Incremental, Differential, Copy, and Daily.

❏ When you back up to file, it has an extension of .bkf.

❏ You can back up data from remote computers.

❏ You can back up all files if you have Backup Operator or Administrator privileges.

❏ You can restore files to their original locations, an alternate location, or all files to a single folder.

❏ You can specify how to handle restoring files when the file already exists.

❏ Safe Mode allows you to start Windows 2000 with the minimum drivers and services.

❏ Safe Mode can be used to isolate faulty drivers, services, and applications.

❏ You start Safe Mode by pressing F8 at the Boot menu.

❏ The Recovery Console can be used to repair Windows 2000 when your computer won't start.

❏ You must enter the administrator password to use the Recovery Console.

❏ There are many commands available in Recovery Console.

❏ To install the Recovery Console, run winnt32.exe with the Cmdcons switch.

❏ The Startup And Recovery dialog box allows you to choose which operating system is loaded by default, and how long to wait for the user to select an operating system to load.

❏ By default, the Boot menu will be displayed for 30 seconds.

❏ You can specify what debugging information is written.

❏ The dump file options are None, Small Memory Dump, Kernel Memory Dump, and Complete Memory Dump.

❏ The dump file is called Memory.dmp, by default.

SELF TEST

The following questions will help you measure your understanding of the material presented in this chapter. Read all of the choices carefully, as there may be more than one correct answer. Choose all correct answers for each question.

Managing and Troubleshooting Driver Signing

1. You have a computer running Windows 2000 Professional that is used by several users. You want users to be notified if a driver is not signed, so you select the Warn option for Driver Signing. How can you make this setting apply to all users that use the computer? (Select the best answer.)

   A. When you log on as administrator and set it, it automatically applies to all users.

   B. If you have administrator privileges, you can select Apply Setting As System Default.

   C. Have each user sign on and set it to Warn.

   D. You cannot set this for all users. Each user must choose his or her own setting.

2. You want to configure your computer to run the Signature File Checker (SFC) every time the computer is started. Which of the following command-line switches for the SFC utility will do this?

   A. scanalways

   B. scanstart

   C. scanboot

   D. scannow

Configuring, Managing, and Troubleshooting the Task Scheduler

3. Which of the following can be used when scheduling a task with the Task Scheduler? (Select all that apply.)

   A. To run at intervals

   B. When the computer is idle

   C. When the computer boots up

   D. When the computer shuts down

4. You have created a task with the Task Scheduler. You want to copy the task to another computer. What is the extension for task files created by the Task Scheduler?

   A. .tsk

   B. .sch

   C. .run

   D. .job

5. You are having some problems with a task in Task Scheduler. You are troubleshooting the task and decide to look in the Task Scheduler log file. What is the name of the log file?

   A. TaskSched.log

   B. Sched.log

   C. TaskSched.txt

   D. SchedLog.txt

Optimizing and Troubleshooting the Performance of the Windows 2000 Professional Desktop

6. You suspect that one of your computer volumes is becoming a bottleneck in your system. You decide to monitor it in System Monitor, but find that the performance counters for the volume are missing. How can you make the appropriate disk performance objects available?

   A. Reinstall Windows 2000 Professional and select the disk performance components.

   B. Add them using Add/Remove Programs in the Control Panel.

   C. Use the DiskPerf command with the -Y switch.

   D. Use the DiskPerf command with the -N switch.

7. Windows 2000 divides memory into pages of memory to help prevent fragmentation of memory. What is the size of a *page* of memory in Windows 2000?

   A. 1KB

   B. 2KB

   C. 4KB

   D. 8KB

8. You have been using System Monitor to analyze memory usage. One of the counters you are measuring is the Pages/Sec counter. You notice that the value for this counter seems to be stabilizing around 21. What should you do to resolve this problem?

   A. Add more memory.

   B. Increase the size of the pagefile.

   C. Split the pagefile up over several volumes.

   D. Nothing.

9. Some of your users have been complaining that their disk access seems slow. You decide to monitor the hard disk in System Monitor. One of the counters you are measuring is the %Disk Time. What is the threshold for this counter where the hard disk is considered a bottleneck?

   A. 75 percent

   B. 80 percent

   C. 90 percent

   D. 100 percent

10. You have been monitoring the performance of your hard disks and have determined that they are becoming a bottleneck. Which of the following can improve the performance of your hard disks? (Select all that apply.)

   A. Replace them with faster hard disks.

   B. Replace them with larger hard disks.

   C. Put the hard disks on separate drive controllers.

   D. Defragment the volumes on the hard disks.

11. You are using the Disk Defragmenter program to defragment the volumes on your computer. Which of the following file systems can Disk Defragmenter defragment? (Select all that apply.)

   A. FAT

   B. FAT32

   C. HPFS

   D. NTFS

12. You are using Disk Defragmenter to defragment a volume on your computer. You notice that not all of the free space has been consolidated into one contiguous space. Which of the following could be a cause of this? (Select all that apply.)

    A. The pagefile is fragmented.

    B. It would take too long.

    C. Some free space is reserved for the MFT.

    D. There are a large number of directories on the volume.

13. You want to launch a program that is critical to your business needs. You want the program to run with a higher priority than it currently defaults to. What command can you use to set the base priority for your program?

    A. Launch

    B. Run

    C. SetPriority

    D. Start

14. You decide you need to start a program with a priority that is higher than its default priority. You start a process from the command line using the Start command as shown next. What will be the priority level of the clock process?

```
Start /high Clock
```

    A. 8

    B. 10

    C. 13

    D. 15

15. You have been monitoring your processor utilization and have determined that an application is causing a bottleneck. You decide to have the application only run on one of the processors on your computer. What command do you use to specify an application to only run on a specific processor?

    A. Set Processor

    B. Move Application

    C. Set Affinity

    D. Set Application

16. What is the range of priorities a process can be set to, and what is the highest priority?

   A. 1–32, with 1 the highest priority

   B. 1–32, with 32 the highest priority

   C. 0–31, with 1 the highest priority

   D. 0–31, with 31 the highest priority

17. Microsoft Word has stopped responding to mouse and keyboard strokes. You decide to use Task Manager to stop Word from running. Word is a large application that consists of multiple processes. You find the WINWORD.EXE process in the Processes tab of Task Manager. Which of the following commands should you use to stop it before restarting Word?

   A. End Process

   B. Stop Process

   C. End Process Tree

   D. Stop Tree

Performance Logs and Alerts

18. You want to monitor processor and memory utilization on your computer. What utilities can you use to monitor the processor and memory utilization? (Select all that apply.)

   A. Task Manager

   B. System Monitor

   C. Memory And Processor Monitor

   D. System Analyzer

19. How do you start the Task Manager? (Select all that apply.)

   A. By pressing CTRL-ALT-DEL and clicking Task Manager.

   B. By pressing CTRL-SHIFT-ESC.

   C. From the Start menu, select Programs | Administrative Tools | Task Manager.

   D. From the Start menu, select Programs | System Tools | Task Manager.

Managing Hardware Profiles

20. What is the default number of seconds that the hardware profile will wait before automatically using the default profile?

A. 5

B. 10

C. 15

D. 30

Recovering Systems and User Data

21. You are having problems starting your computer. You have determined that the master boot record (MBR) has been damaged. You decide to use the Recovery Console to fix the problem. What command can you use in the Recovery Console to fix the MBR ?

A. mbr

B. mbrfix

C. fixboot

D. fixmbr

22. Your computer is having problems and a dump file was created. You want to save the last dump file so it is not overwritten if another dump file is created. You decide to copy the last one to the server. What is the name of the dump file that you would copy to the server?

A. MemDump.log

B. Memory.dmp

C. Mem.dmp

D. Dump.mem

LAB QUESTION

You have a Windows 2000 Professional computer that appears to be degrading in performance recently. You decide to monitor it to see if there are any bottlenecks. First, you want to just view summary information to get a feel for its overall performance. Then you want to monitor more specific details based on what you found in the summary information. Once you have resolved any problems, you want to set some thresholds for when to start monitoring again, and be notified when any threshold has been reached. What steps should you take to accomplish this?

SELF TEST ANSWERS

Managing and Troubleshooting Driver Signing

1. ☑ **B.** The Driver Signing Options dialog box has a check box called Apply Setting As System Default. If this is selected, then the setting will be used as the default for all users on the computer. You must have administrator privileges to set this option.

    ☒ **A** is incorrect because just selecting an option when logged on as administrator does not set it for other users. **C** is incorrect because even though this would work, **B** is a better answer. Having to coordinate with each user to set the option to Warn is not practical. **D** is incorrect because you can set the default setting for all users.

2. ☑ **C.** The scanboot switch will run SFC every time the computer is started.

    ☒ **A** and **B** are incorrect because these are not valid switches for the SFC program. **D** is incorrect because the scannow switch will only run the SFC time once, immediately.

Configuring, Managing, and Troubleshooting the Task Scheduler

3. ☑ **A, B, C.** You can schedule tasks by date/time, at set intervals, when the computer boots up, when you log on, or to run when the computer is idle.

    ☒ **D** is incorrect because you cannot schedule a task to run when the computer shuts down.

4. ☑ **D.** When the Task Scheduler creates a task, it is saved to a file with the extension .job.

    ☒ **A, B,** and **C** are incorrect because task files have an extension of .job, not .tsk, .sch, or .run.

5. ☑ **D.** The name of the log file for the Task Scheduler is SchedLog.txt.

    ☒ **A, B,** and **C** are incorrect because they are not valid names for the log file.

Optimizing and Troubleshooting the Performance of the Windows 2000 Professional Desktop

6. ☑ **C.** DiskPerf is a command-line utility that is used to turn the hard disk counters on and off. The -Y switch will turn on all of the physical and logical disk counters. You could also use the -YV switch.

    ☒ **A** is incorrect because there isn't an option to select the hard disk performance objects during installation. The PhysicalDisk object is enabled and the LogicalDisk object is disabled by default on Windows 2000 Professional. **B** is incorrect because they cannot be added from Add/Remove Programs in the Control Panel. There isn't an option. **D** is incorrect because the -N switch for the DiskPerf program will disable all of the hard disk performance counters.

7. ☑ C. Windows 2000 uses a 4KB page size for memory.

☒ A, B, and D are incorrect because Windows 2000 uses 4KB pages of memory.

8. ☑ A. When the Pages/Sec counter reaches 20, then memory has become a bottleneck, and this indicates that your system needs more memory.

☒ B and C are incorrect because optimizing your pagefile will not lower the amount of paging being performed; it will just help increase the performance of paging. D is incorrect because when the Pages/Sec counter reaches 20, it is an indication that your memory is a bottleneck and you need to take some corrective action.

9. ☑ C. When the %Disk Time reaches 90 percent, it is considered a bottleneck, and Microsoft recommends taking action to lower this performance counter.

☒ A, B, and D are incorrect because Microsoft considers the hard disk a bottleneck when the %Disk Time reaches 90 percent.

10. ☑ A, C, D. Replacing your existing hard disks with faster hard disks will obviously improve performance. By placing the drives on separate drive controllers, your computer can perform multiple file operations simultaneously, thereby increasing performance. Defragmenting the volumes on your hard disks will also improve performance if they are fragmented.

☒ B is incorrect because replacing a hard disk with a larger one will not improve performance if the hard disk you are replacing it with is not a faster hard disk.

11. ☑ A, B, D. You can use the Disk Defragmenter program on volumes that are formatted with FAT, FAT32, and NTFS.

☒ C is incorrect because the HPFS file system cannot be defragmented with Disk Defragmenter. In fact, the HPFS file system is not even supported within Windows 2000.

12. ☑ A, C, D. If the page file is fragmented, Disk Defragmenter cannot move this file because it is locked by the operating system. If a volume is NTFS, then some free space is reserved at the beginning of the volume for the MFT and cannot be moved. A large number of directories in a volume can also prevent free space from being consolidated.

☒ B is incorrect because Disk Defragmenter does not limit operations by how long it will take; some volumes can take hours to defragment.

13. ☑ D. The Start command can be used to set the process' base priority class from the command line using the priority switches.

☒ A, B, and C are incorrect because Launch, Run, and SetPriority are not valid commands to start programs, much less set the priority of a program. The Run command is no longer available in Windows NT or Windows 2000; it was replaced by the Run menu item on the Start button.

14. ☑   C. If the base priority class is High and the thread's priority class is Normal, then the overall priority is 13.
☒   A is incorrect because an overall priority of 8 would be the case when the process' base priority class was Normal. B is incorrect because an overall priority of 10 would also be the case when the base process priority class is Normal and the thread priority class is Highest. D is incorrect because even though this would be a base process priority class of High, the thread priority class would have to be Highest.

15. ☑   C. If you have multiple processors on your computer, you can assign a process to a processor(s) by using the Set Affinity command. It is only available on multiple-processor computers.
☒   A, B, and D are invalid commands for assigning an application to run on a specific processor.

16. ☑   D. There are 32 priority levels ranging from 0 to 31, with 31 being the highest priority.
☒   A and B are incorrect because process priorities range from 0 to 31, not 1 to 32. C is incorrect because although process priorities do range from 0 to 31, the highest priority is 31, not 0.

17. ☑   C. If an application that contains multiple processes stops responding, you should use the End Process Tree command to stop all of the related processes before restarting the application.
☒   A is incorrect because even though it will stop the WINWORD.EXE process from running, it won't stop the other dependent Word processes from running. This could potentially cause problems when you restart the application. B and D are incorrect because the Task Manager does not have a Stop Process or Stop Tree command.

Performance Logs and Alerts

18. ☑   A, B. The Task Manager can be used to view summary information about processor and memory usage, and the System Monitor can be used to analyze detailed information about the utilization of the processor and memory resources.
☒   C and D are incorrect because Windows 2000 does not have any utilities called Memory And Processor Monitor or System Analyzer.

19. ☑   A, B. You can start the Task Manager by pressing CTRL-ALT-DEL or CTRL-SHIFT-ESC.
☒   C and D are incorrect because there isn't a menu item for the Task Manager under Administrative Tools or System Tools from the Start button.

Managing Hardware Profiles

20. ☑ **D.** By default, the hardware profile menu is set to wait 30 seconds.

☒ **A, B,** and **C** are incorrect because the default is 30 seconds.

Recovering Systems and User Data

21. ☑ **D.** The Recovery Console allows you to use the fixmbr command to repair a corrupt MBR.

☒ **A** and **B** are incorrect because they are not valid commands in the Recovery Console. **C** is incorrect because the fixboot command is used to repair the boot sector, not the MBR.

22. ☑ **B.** The name of the dump file that is created is Memory.dmp. If you don't rename the file or copy it to another directory, the existing file will be overwritten if another dump file is created.

☒ **A, C,** and **D** are incorrect because the name of the dump file is Memory.dmp.

LAB ANSWER

The first step is to monitor summary information to see about the computer's overall performance. You can use the Task Manager's Performance tab to do this. It will graphically display the CPU and memory usage, as well as some other summary statistics. This can sometimes give you some quick insight into what the problem may be or where to start looking.

For more detailed information, you can use System Monitor to measure detailed information about the resources on your computer. When you find a bottleneck, resolve the problem. Then you should monitor the computer some more to ensure that you completely resolved the bottleneck.

Now that the bottleneck has been resolved, you can use the Performance Logs And Alerts. Create some logs for the different resources on your computer. Then create alerts with the thresholds you have determined to use, and have these alerts automatically start the appropriate log and send a message to you that the alert's threshold has been reached.

MICROSOFT CERTIFIED SYSTEMS ENGINEER

9

Configuring and Troubleshooting User Profiles and the Desktop Environment

CERTIFICATION OBJECTIVES

I n this chapter, we'll take a look at how you configure and manage the desktop environment. We'll follow the emphasis of Microsoft's exam, and focus on the *configuration* of the desktop environment—looking not at how a user configures his own desktop environment, but at how an administrator sets up a desktop to allow multiple users to configure their own environment, and conversely, how an administrator denies users configuration control.

In Windows 2000, this occurs largely through manipulation of user profiles and groups. We'll take a glance at group policy and local policy, and also examine Windows 2000 Professional's accessibility services.

CERTIFICATION OBJECTIVE 9.01

Configuring and Managing User Profiles

Let's say I share my computer with this guy named Steve. Steve does everything different from me—he likes to put his taskbar at the top of the screen instead of the bottom. He scatters his icons all over the screen, instead of leaving them in the neat little rows that I like to use. He likes to use Active Desktop to set up a bright, swirling pattern as his wallpaper, which gives me a headache.

Luckily, Steve and I are not forced to struggle over the computer's desktop. Windows 2000 Professional attaches a user profile to each individual account, storing configuration information on a per-user basis. No matter what Steve does to his desktop when he's using my computer, my desktop will always be neat, clean, and simple, as I like it (Figure 9-1).

A user profile consists of desktop settings, like whether or not Auto-Arrange is turned on, or what resolution the display is, or whether menus Scroll or Fade, as well as a desktop image. The user profile actually exists as a folder. If Windows 2000 Professional is installed in drive X:, then for each user, there will be a folder that exists as X:\Documents and Settings*Username.*

Inside this folder are folders representing your various settings—a Favorites folder, a Cookies folder, and a folder labeled Desktop. This folder contains almost all the things that are on your desktop—any files you move to your desktop or any folders you create on your desktop. (Certain icons that appear on your desktop will not appear in this

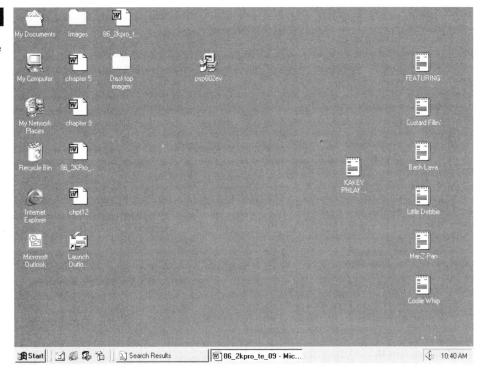

FIGURE 9-1

Here you can see
how my desktop
appears

folder—Recycle Bin, Internet Explorer, and Outlook. Interestingly, shortcuts you place
in the taskbar also do not show up.)

In Figure 9-2, you can see how all the files and folders that appear on the desktop
are contained in the Desktop folder, within my *Username* folder inside Documents
and Settings.

e x a m
Ⓦa t c h

***The exception to the rule is the My Documents folder. The My Documents
folder appears directly in the Username folder, not in the Username\Desktop
folder. A hyperlink resides in the Desktop folder to the My Documents folder.***

A new *Username* and *Username*\Desktop folder is created for each new user, and
the *Username*\Desktop folder is populated with the standard set of shortcuts. Note
that, in the user account process, a new set of shortcut files are *created* and placed
in the new Desktop folder. That means that the Connect To The Internet icon on *my*
desktop represents a different file from the Connect To The Internet icon on *Steve's*

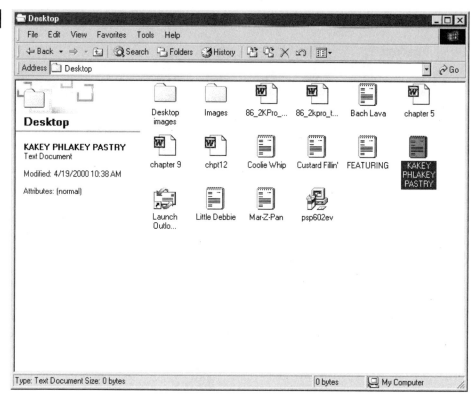

desktop (namely, the one on my desktop is the file X:\Documents and Settings\Chris Nguyen\Desktop\connect.lnk, and the one on his desktop is the file X:\Documents and Settings\Steve Smith\Desktop\connect.lnk). If Steve deletes or modifies his icon, that will do nothing to the Connect To The Internet icon on my desktop. (This does not apply to certain core icons, like My Computer and Recycle Bin, which don't exist as files in the Desktop folder.)

In Figure 9-3, you can see the C:\Documents and Settings\Chris Nguyen folder, attached to my profile. You'll notice that there's a Cookies folder, a Favorites folder, a Desktop folder, and a My Documents folder.

The per-user nature of the desktop also applies to Favorites from Explorer and the Start menu, which exist as *Username*\Favorites and *Username*\Start Menu, respectively.

FIGURE 9-3

The *Username* folder

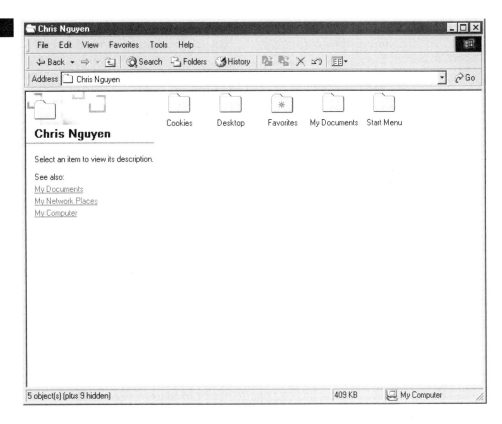

Remember that user profiles keep individual configuration information such as desktop wallpaper, display settings, and a folder for your desktop information. All Windows does is open up what's in your folder Username\Desktop and displays it as your desktop. Anything that you do on your desktop consists of changes to this folder; when someone else logs on, the computer will look up his or her Username\Desktop and access a whole different folder. But if Steve goes into a different folder and starts changing things around, I'll see those changes when I log on. It's not like we're on different computers. In fact, whatever Steve does to his desktop will register for me as a change to the Steve Smith\Desktop folder, which I can visit in Windows Explorer.

on the ① o b

This is why when you drag a file like an executable onto your desktop, it's important to drag it and Create A Shortcut instead of just selecting Move. Create A Shortcut will create a .lnk file in your Desktop folder. If you actually Move the file, then the file will be shifted to your Username\Desktop folder, and thus be very hard to find for any other users who log on to your system and need to use that file. This is also why it's a bad habit to create or move a file that other people need access to on or to your desktop; others will have a tough time finding it. If other people who use your computer need to find that file, create it somewhere else and make a shortcut to it on your desktop.

Adding a User Profile

Everything we're going to do will occur in Users And Passwords. This window is accessible through the Users And Passwords icon in the Control Panel. To interact with Users And Passwords, you must be a member of the Administrators group.

The easiest way to add a new user is by running the Add User Wizard. Simply click Add from the Users And Passwords window.

The more powerful way to add and configure users is to use the Local Users Manager, a snap-in for the Microsoft Management Console. This is accessed simply by clicking the Advanced tab from the Users And Passwords window, and then clicking Advanced and opening up the Users folder. You have a lot more power from the Local Users Manager, so I'll show you how to do everything from there.

CertCam 9-1

EXERCISE 9-1

Adding a User Using Local Users Manager

Follow these steps to add a user using Local Users Manager.

1. Make sure you're logged on with Administrators status. Open Control Panel | Users And Passwords. Click the Advanced tab, which will bring up the Advanced Users And Passwords screen, as shown in the following illustration. Then click Advanced. This will bring up the Local Users And Groups MMC snap-in.

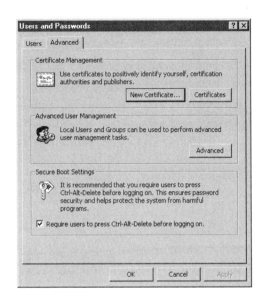

2. Open up the Users folder in the left-hand pane; this will bring up all local users in the right-hand pane, as shown in next illustration. From here, you can get to the Local Users And Groups MMC snap-in by clicking Advanced. This is where you can perform advanced manipulations of your users. Many of the properties available here simply aren't visible through the initial Users And Passwords screen.

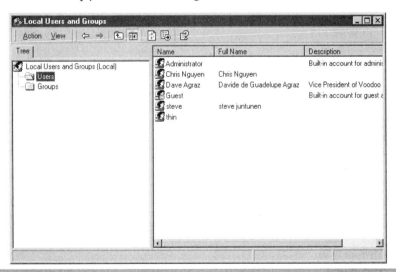

3. Right-click inside the right-hand pane, at an empty space; select New User . . . from the pull-down menu, as shown next. This will start the New User Wizard. The fastest way to start the New User Wizard is by right-clicking somewhere within the right-hand pane, on an empty space. Make sure you don't right-click a name, which will bring up options concerning that particular user.

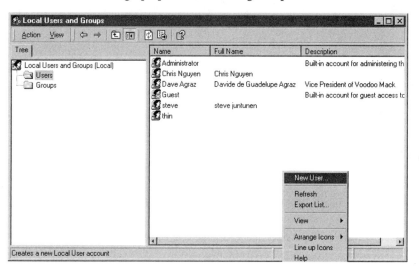

4. Fill in the information that the wizard requests, as shown here. Be sure to specify if you want to force the user to change his or her password, allow the user to change his or her password, or specify that the user's password will never expire. The nice thing about the New User Wizard as accessed from this advanced Local Users And Groups screen is that it doesn't automatically pop you back to the previous window; instead, you get the same New User

Wizard screen again. This is handy for entering lots of new users. Click Close on an empty New User screen when you've finished.

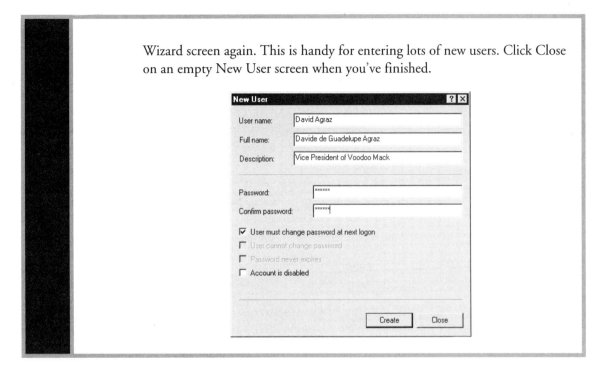

The wizard walks you through inputting all necessary information for a new user account. Click Create when you've finished. Here, we're creating an account for Dave Brown, our new Vice President of Voodoo Mack.

Password Options In Depth

One of the more important decisions you need to make when creating a new user is the option regarding passwords. You can choose from the following:

- **User Must Change Password At Next Logon** This forces the user to set his or her own password, changing the password from what the Administrator has set. When this option is selected, Windows shades out the User Cannot Change Password and Password Never Expires options.

- **User Cannot Change Password** This locks in the password that the Administrator has set. An Administrator can only change the password.

- **Password Never Expires** By default, Windows forces users to change their passwords every 42 days. This option removes the expiration process. This is useful for low-security environments, and for creating user accounts linked to particular applications or automated processes.

- ■ **Account Disabled** This locks the account until the check box is unselected; it prevents anyone using it to log on to the domain.

- ■ **Account Locked Out** This option only appears if Group Policies have been set to allow lockouts, and a user has triggered a lockout. Lockouts are essentially automatic account disablements, triggered by some condition—typically, some number of failures to successfully log on, which can be indicative of an attempted security breach. An Administrator must manually deselect the Account Locked Out check box if, for example, the account's proper user has accidentally triggered the lockout process. If an Administrator wishes to manually lock out a user, he or she must use the Account Disabled function.

See Chapter 12 for more information on passwords and advanced security options available through Group Policy.

exam
Ⓦatch

When you install Windows 2000 Professional, Windows automatically creates three accounts. The first account is your account; its associated username is whatever you tell Windows 2000 Professional your name is. You are assigned Administrator permissions. The second account is the Administrator account, which you specify a password for during the installation process. This is also assigned Administrator permissions. The third account is the Guest account, which requires no password. Initially, Windows creates the Guest account, sets very limited permissions for it, and disables it. In order for people to log on to the system as a Guest, you have to manually enable the Guest account.

Configuring a User Profile

Most of the configurations you as an administrator will make will depend heavily on the security groups defined inside Active Directory at the server level. See Chapter 12 for more on preset groups and creating new groups.

The most elementary move to a user profile is adding that user to a group.

CertCam 9-2

Adding a User to a Group Using Local Users Manager

Let's walk through this exercise of adding a user to a group using Local Users Manager.

1. Now you need to specify advanced properties. Right-click the name of the new user from the Local Users And Groups screen; select Properties.

2. Now select the Member Of tab. This brings up the group membership view, as shown here. We can see that Dave Agraz is only a member of the Users group.

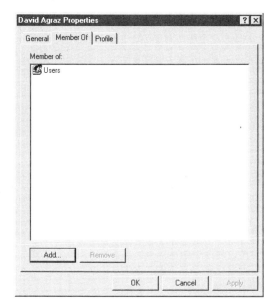

3. Click Add, which will bring up a list of all defined groups. Double-click a group in the top pane to add it to the queue, which is displayed in the bottom pane. When you click OK, the new user will be added to all the groups in the queue. The top pane shows a list of all currently defined groups. Every time you double-click a group, it will be added to the queue, shown at the bottom.

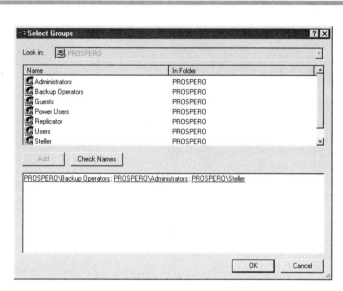

4. After you click on OK, you will return to the Group Membership view, where you'll see that the new user has been added to the groups that you selected, as shown here. We can see that Dave Agraz is now a member of Administrators, Backup Operators, Steller, and Users.

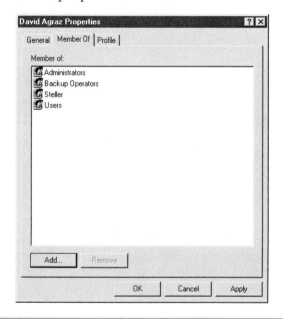

Removing a User from a Group

This exercise walks you through removing a user from a group.

1. From the Local Users And Groups menu, open up Users, and right-click a name. Select Properties, and click the Member Of tab.

2. Select a group by single-left-clicking the group. The group will appear highlighted, as shown here. Click Remove, and the user will be removed from that group.

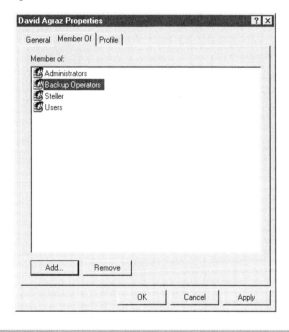

You can see that we've decided that it's unnecessary for Dave Agraz to be part of the Backup Operators Group. We've highlighted Backup Operators; we just need to click Remove.

Alternatively, you can, from the Users And Groups menu, open up Groups, and double-click a group. This will give you a list of members. You can highlight a member and click Remove.

exam
ⓌatcH

Windows refers to an account via a security identification number (SID). This SID is connected to the user profile, the permissions, and so on. The important thing to remember is that the username of an account is merely a property of that account; in other words, the "real name" of an account for Windows 2000 is the SID. That means you can change the username of the account and Windows 2000 won't lose track of things; the account will retain all group memberships, desktop settings, and the like. In fact, it is recommended that you immediately change the username on the Administrator account; that will make it much harder for unwanted visitors to gain Administrator access to your system.

Advanced User Profile Configuration

There are several very powerful account properties for user profile configuration. To access these tools, open a user's Properties, and click the Profile tab. From here, you can modify the profile path, set a logon script, or set a home folder.

All of the manipulations we'll be looking at in this Advanced User Profile Configuration section are not accessible from a Properties window called from the initial Users And Passwords screen. For any of the following tasks, you have to call up Users And Passwords, select the Advanced tab, click Advanced, right-click a user, and select Properties. We'll call this window the Advanced Properties window, even though it appears on your screen labeled Properties.

Local Profile Paths

In the Advanced Properties window, under the Profile tab, there's a fill-in box marked Profile Path:, as shown in Figure 9-4. This tells the operating system where to look for that important folder that stores everything associated with your user profile—the Favorites folder, the Cookies folder, the Desktop folder, and more. If this fill-in box is empty, then Windows defaults to

[*system_drive*]\Documents and Settings*Username*

In Figure 9-4, you can see the Profile tab in the Advanced Properties window. Remember that the Advanced Properties window is accessible by clicking Users And Passwords, Advanced tab, and Advanced; and then, from the Local Users And Groups, right-clicking the desired user.

There are several reasons to change your profile path. You might want the profiles to be on a different disk drive, or in a different folder.

FIGURE 9-4

Advanced
Properties,
Profile tab

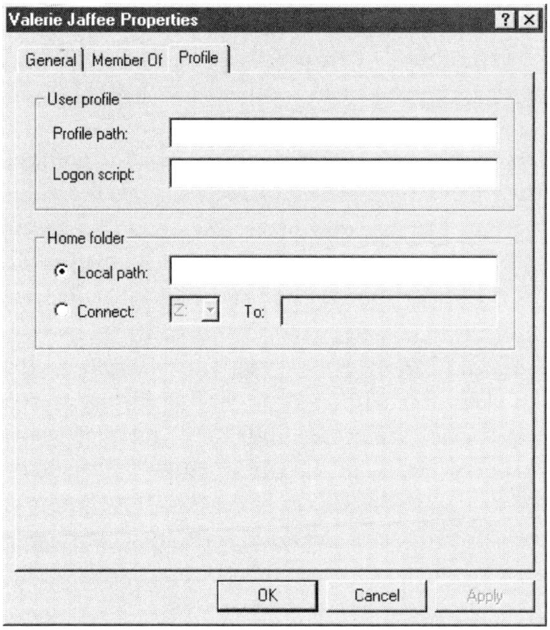

Manipulations for the profile path are very useful when a single user is running several accounts. For example, let's say that, most of the time, you log on as Jane Doe. But, occasionally, you need to log on as Administrator, for whatever reason. By default settings, the Administrator account will have its own desktop and its own Favorites folder, rendering all the configurations that you've set under Jane Doe inaccessible.

You can fix this with the following modification. Let's say you leave the Jane Doe account set to its default profile path; that is, the Profile Path fill-in box is empty for the Jane Doe account. If your system drive is C:, the default profile path would be

C:\Documents and Settings\Jane Doe

Just open up the Administrator Properties menu, click the Profile tab, and type this pathway into the box marked Profile Path. Whenever you open up the Administrator account, Windows will look in the Jane Doe folder and give you the Jane Doe desktop and settings, and so forth.

This is much more effective than going in with Windows Explorer and simply copying the contents of the Jane Doe folder onto the Administrator folder. If you do that, you're simply making a *copy* of the Jane Doe desktop at a single point in time; after that point, any changes made to one account won't propagate to the other account. Whereas, when you set the profile path, you're working on *the very same* desktop, whether you log on as Jane Doe or as Administrator.

on the Job

This local-level profile path manipulation comes in handy more often than you'd think. For example, let's say you sometimes like to log on to your local domain, KAFKA, and sometimes you like to log on to your network domain, PYNCHON. You run the Network Identification Wizard twice. Even if you use the same username, Windows 2000 Professional will establish two different accounts, with the same username, each associated with a different domain. I ran into this problem and had a difficult time figuring out what was going on, since I kept getting different desktops. It wasn't until I looked in Documents And Settings and saw that there were two folders, one named Chris_Nguyen and the other named Chris_Nguyen_Pynchon_001. I simply opened up the Properties on the PYNCHON account and set the profile path to C:\Documents and Settings\Chris_Nguyen, and all was well.

Roaming Profiles

The ability to set profile paths becomes much more valuable once you realize that you can set profiles for network addresses. This allows you to set a single profile, on a server, and point your accounts on many different clients and servers to access a single profile. This creates a "roaming profile," giving you the same desktop and Explorer favorites and display settings no matter what computer you log on from.

The Profile path follows conventional naming conventions, starting with two backslashes, followed by the computer network name, backslash, folder share name, backslash, and profile name.

Login Scripts

In the Advanced Properties window, Profiles tab, below the Profile Path fill-in, is another fill-in window marked Login Script. You can create a login script for a user, normally a batch file (.bat), OS/2 .cmd file, or an executable. Simply enter the pathway and login script name in the fill-in, and Windows will automatically execute this script whenever the user logs on.

Home Folder

Also in the Advanced Properties window, Profiles tab, is a small section labeled Home Folder.

CertCam 9-4

EXERCISE 9-4

Set Up a Roaming Profile

Follow these steps to set up a roaming profile in a workgroup:

1. Open Users And Passwords in the Control Panel.

2. Right-click on one of the users, then click Properties.

3. Click the Profile tab. In the Profile Path text box, type in the box to the user's local profile. Click Apply and then OK.

4. Go to each machine in the workgroup and create a user account with the same name and password as the one on your machine. Enter the same profile path you entered on your machine. Be sure the path is entered as a UNC path.

5. Log on with the user account you created at one of the other machines in the workgroup. Your desktop should appear with the profile settings created on your machine.

By default, when you save a document for the first time, or do a Save As . . ., most applications will save the document to My Documents. When you set a home folder, this becomes the new default save location. This only applies to applications that make the call to Windows for the user's home folder (like all Microsoft's applications). Home folder settings will not affect applications that don't look up the user's home folder setting.

on the Job

You can usually tell which applications are making the call to the Home folder setting. Since the default Home folder setting is My Documents, most apps that default document saving to My Documents are making the call; and most apps that save to some other folder, like a folder within the app's program folder, aren't making the call.

FROM THE CLASSROOM

When to Use a Roaming Profile

Roaming profiles are incredibly useful for a number of reasons. Since your desktop environment data is stored at a network-accessible location, then wherever you go, you'll have the same desktop. If you consistently save your documents to a similarly network-accessible location like My Documents (if you leave the rest of the paths at their default while setting up a roaming profile, My Documents will be network accessible), you'll have your files at your fingertips, at the same place, wherever you may roam.

The downsides are several, though. This flexibility comes at the price of access speed. Every move you make on your desktop has to pass through the network. This may not be a problem for an enterprise with incredibly fast, clear internal pipes—sadly, this is rarely the case. If the local network is heavily congested, then you might get noticeable lag for doing simple things such as moving icons around on your desktop, let alone opening a file. Most of you are familiar now with working with a file over the network—remember that, when you have a roaming profile, everything you do to

your desktop environment is subject to the same advantages and disadvantages of using a network file. This is especially noticeable for those using slow connections. For example, those networking over a telephone line clearly shouldn't use roaming profiles.

More importantly, roaming profiles add to network traffic. If only a few administrators are set to have roaming profiles, this increased traffic is negligible. If, on the other hand, many or all employees have roaming profiles, then the network load is quite sizeable. Remember, every little change to the desktop will have to go over the network.

The lesson? Only give roaming profiles to those who genuinely need them. If a user spends 95 percent of his time at one workstation and 5 percent of his time roaming, and you create a roaming profile for him, remember that he'll still be adding to the network load and experiencing lag for that 95 percent of his time spent at his main workstation. Be judicious—each roaming profile puts a small but discernable, near-constant load on the network.

—Chris Thi Nguyen

You have two options under Home folder: entering something in the Local Path fill-in, or entering something in the Connect fill-in, as shown in Figure 9-5. Strangely enough, you can enter both local paths and network paths after the Local Path fill-in.

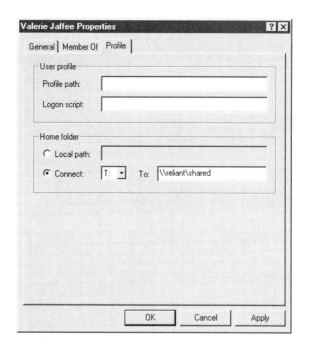

FIGURE 9-5

Home folder

SCENARIO & SOLUTION

I travel between four computers; I want the same desktop on each computer. How can I set this up?	Create a profile on a server; make a note of the folder name and location for that profile. Edit your account Properties at each computer, setting your Profile path to the folder for your profile on the server.
Five people work together extensively. They should put their documents in some place that's easily accessible to all five of them, but they keep forgetting and saving documents to their own My Documents. What's the easiest way to solve this problem?	Create a shared folder on a server. For all five accounts, set the home folder Local Path: to that shared folder. Now, by default, most documents will be saved to the shared folder, which they can all access.
My CEO needs several custom applications to run whenever he boots up. How can I set this up for him?	Create a batch file with command-line calls to all the executables from those custom apps. Enter the batch file into the Login Script: fill-in on the CEO's account Properties Profile tab.

The Connect fill-in performs an additional function: it will set the network path you provide it as the home folder, but also map a local drive onto that folder.

In Figure 9-5, we're doing two things simultaneously with one command: we're setting the folder Shared on the server Reliant as the home folder for user Jane Doe, and we're also mapping the drive T: on Jane Doe's local computer to \\reliant\shared.

Setting up networked home folders can make life much easier for roaming users.

CERTIFICATION OBJECTIVE 9.02

Configuring and Troubleshooting Desktop Settings

In this section, we'll examine the configuration of the desktop environment variables.

There are two forms of configuring the desktop environment. Regular configuration of the desktop involves things like rearranging the Start menu, putting icons in the Quick Start menu, and arranging items on the desktop.

We'll assume you already know how to configure your *own* desktop environment. Instead, we'll focus on how you, as an administrator, can control how much control users have over their own desktop environments.

Getting to Group Policy

You can make all configurational changes from the Group Policy snap-in for the MMC. It's quite easy to access Group Policy from Windows 2000 Server; there are all kinds of links to Group Policy editors, especially from Active Directory. Group Policy is not as integrated into Windows 2000 Professional. All the policy-shaping power is there, but there's no icon for Group Policy in your Control Panel, or anywhere else. There are two ways to access this snap-in. First, you can run gpedit.msc from the Run menu, as in Figure 9-6. Or, you can create an icon for accessing the Group Policy snap-in and put it wherever you like.

Type **gpedit.msc** from the command line, and you'll bring up the Group Policy snap-in.

We've created an MMC with the Local Computer Policy. From here, you can access the Group Policy for your local computer.

FIGURE 9-6

gpedit

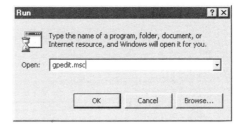

Creating a Group Policy Icon

1. Select Run from the Start menu, and type **mmc /a**. You'll get the MMC Author mode, shown here. The MMC Author mode allows you to custom-create an MMC, populated with whichever snap-ins you want.

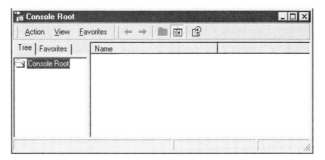

2. From here, select the Console menu and select Add/Remove Snap-In. This brings up the Add/Remove Snap-In window.

3. Click Add. This brings up a menu of snap-ins.

4. Find and double-click Group Policy. Leave the Group Policy Object set to Local Computer, and click Finish. Close the Add/Remove Snap-In window.

5. The Add/Remove Snap-In window should show Local Computer Policy in the queue. Click OK and Windows will add everything in the queue to the snap-in. As shown in the screen following step 6, you can see that we've queued the Local Computer Policy snap-In for addition to the current MMC.

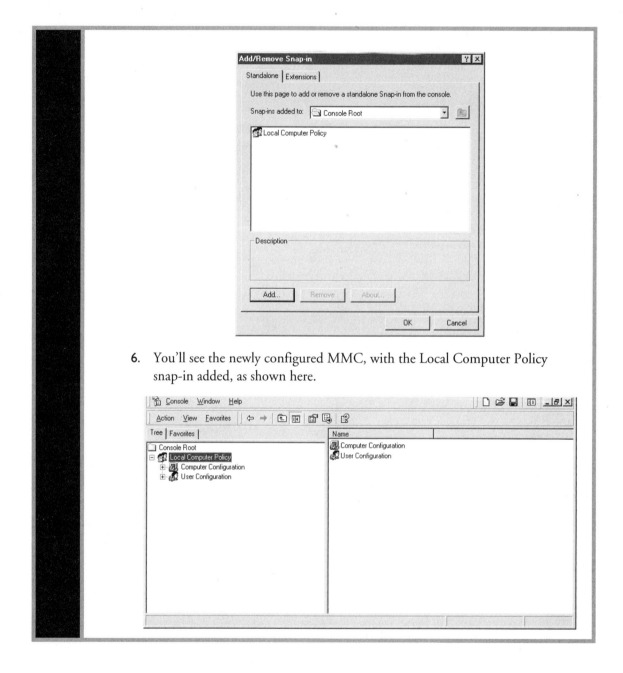

6. You'll see the newly configured MMC, with the Local Computer Policy snap-in added, as shown here.

Select the Console menu and select Save As. Choose a name and a location, and Windows 2000 will put the newly created MMC there.

Once you have access to the Local Computer Policy snap-in, either through a custom-created MMC or through the command-line call, you need to find the relevant templates.

Expand Local Computer Policy from the MMC. Expand User Configuration, and expand Administrative Templates. You'll see all the relevant sections in front of you, as in Figure 9-7.

e x a m
ⓦatch

Group Policy is the general term for all policy settings. Local Computer Policy is the name for the console tree that controls Group Policy for the local computer; another way of referring to the Local Computer Policy snap-in is as the local Group Policy snap-in.

From your local Group Policy snap-in, you'll be able to access various attributes for the desktop environment.

FIGURE 9-7	

Administrative
Templates

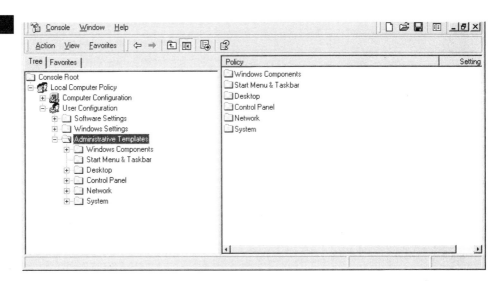

Setting Policy

From the Administrative Templates menu in the local Group Policy snap-in, click Desktop. In the right pane, you'll see a long list of policies. By default, all these policies are turned off, as in Figure 9-8.

Once you select Desktop from Administrative Templates, you will see a variety of policies that you can configure in the right-hand pane.

By double-clicking a policy, you'll bring up that policy's Properties window, as shown in Figure 9-9. The Policy tab lets you enable or disable a policy. Here you can set the policy to Not Configured, Enable, or Disable. The large empty pane in the middle of the Policy window is for configuration information. Since most policies are binary—you either can or can't do something—the configuration pane is empty. You only turn the policy on or off. Certain policies will ask you to set a number or a set of files; relevant buttons and directions will be contained in the configuration pane.

Here you can see the Run Only Allowed Windows Applications Properties box, from Local Computer Policy | User Configuration | Administrative Templates | System. All Policy boxes look the same—Enabled, Disabled, and Not Configured boxes at the top, and a middle section that shows whatever particular configuration information is necessary for the policy in question.

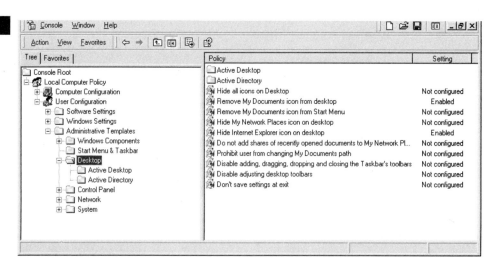

FIGURE 9-8

Desktop Administrative Template

FIGURE 9-9

Policy Properties

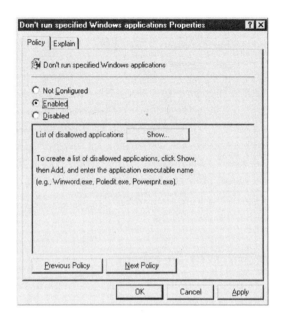

The Explain tab in a policy's Properties window contains a description of what the policy does, as in Figure 9-10.

FIGURE 9-10

Policy Properties, Explain tab

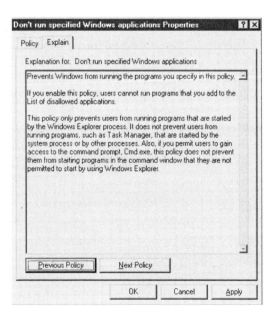

You can see the Don't Run Specified Windows Applications Properties, Explain tab box. This contains Microsoft's summary of this policy's effects.

on the

Job

Everybody trying to configure Local Computer Policy for a Professional machine runs into the same problem. They set the policy—and then nothing happens. Plugging a Windows 2000 Professional machine into the network will not cause the problem; using it to log on to a domain will, however. Local policy is the weakest policy; it is overridden by any policy set at the domain level. In order to set local policy, group policy at all higher hierarchical levels must be in agreement, not set to anything in particular, or turned off. How to manipulate Group Policy in Active Directory, of course, is beyond the scope of this book, and, luckily for you, of this test.

Desktop Environment Settings

There are many policies; we'll run through some important ones, but you should familiarize yourself with the full list.

Everything we're going to be doing to manipulate the desktop environment will be contained in Local Computer Policy | User Configuration | Administrative Templates in your Local Computer Policy MMC snap-in. The two main subfolders of Administrative Templates are the Start Menu & Taskbar folder, which contains policies governing the Start menu and the taskbar; and the Desktop folder, which contains all the policies for everything else on the desktop.

These are *universal changes* to a local computer, which apply to every user.

exam

Watch

Remember, these are policy changes that apply across the board. If a user wants to kill personalized menus, he can do it from the Control Panel, and it will only apply to his own profile. Use the policy settings described in the following sections when you want your changes to apply to anybody who will ever use the computer in question.

Start Menu & Taskbar Settings

Here are some of the more important policies that you can access from Local Computer Policy | User Configuration | Administrative Templates | Start Menu & Taskbar, as shown in Figure 9-11.

In the Local Computer Policy subfolder, you can manipulate policies regarding the Start menu and the taskbar.

FIGURE 9-11

Start Menu &
Taskbar

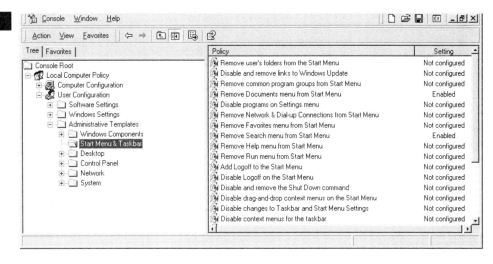

■ **Remove User's Folders From Start Menu**   The Start menu is divided into a user-specific section at the top, and the main section at the bottom. This policy, when activated, hides all folders (not files) in the top, user-specific section. This is useful when redirects are set in the system that replicate user-specific folders in the main section. This policy prevents the same folders from appearing twice.

■ **Disable Programs On Settings Menu**   This kills the programs in the Settings submenu of the Start menu. These include the Control Panel, Network & Dial Up Connections, and Printers. Note that this does not affect the Start Menu & Taskbar Properties item from Settings, which has its own policy.

exam
⒲atch

All the "disable something from the menu" items and the "remove icons from the desktop" policy items don't actually make it impossible for the user to access programs. They still start programs in alternate ways. For example, if you remove the My Documents icon from the desktop, users can still get to their My Documents by navigating Windows Explorer to the correct pathway. If you remove Networks And Dial-Up Access from the Settings submenu, users can still right-click My Network And Dial-Up Properties. And, of course, if users know how, they can run applications through the command-line interface.

■ **Remove X From Start Menu**   X can be Networks & Dial-Up Connections, or the Favorites menu, or the Search menu, or the Help menu, or the Run menu.

While it's hard to imagine why you'd want to disable Search or Help or Favorites (perhaps if you were setting up a kiosk for public use, where you wanted users to be able to run Internet Explorer but nothing else), disabling Run and Networks can be quite useful in securing and idiot-proofing a workstation.

- **Add Logoff To The Start Menu** This policy adds the item Logoff *username* to the Start menu, which makes life a little bit easier for users sharing computers. (It makes logging off slightly faster—the traditional process is to select Shut Down from the Start menu, and select Logoff from the pull-down.)

- **Disable And Remove The Shut Down Command** This policy removes Microsoft's shut-down command. It is useful if you need to use a different tool to shut down your computer, and want to prevent users from triggering the Microsoft shutdown.

- **Disable Changes To Taskbar And Start Menu Settings** This policy prevents users from accessing the Properties window for the taskbar and Start menu, either through the Settings submenu or by right-clicking the taskbar. It is useful for securing and/or idiot-proofing a computer.

on the
Üob

Policies like Disable Changes To Taskbar And Start Menu Settings are especially useful for computers like kiosks, which might have many people logging on under several different accounts, like different Guest accounts. These sorts of policies will keep mischief-makers from wreaking havoc with the settings.

- **Do Not Keep A History Of Recently Opened Documents** This policy kills the functionality of the Documents submenu in the Start menu, which, by default, displays a list of all recently modified documents.

- **Disable Personalized Menus** This policy stops Windows from personalizing menus. When this policy is turned off, Windows will only display frequently called functions on its pull-down menus; the user must hit the expand button at the bottom of each pull-down to show every item.

Desktop Settings

In the Local Computer Policy | User Configuration | Administrative Templates | Desktop subfolder, you'll find many useful policies, as shown in Figure 9-12. Desktop has two subfolders: Active Directory and Active Desktop.

In the Desktop folder, you'll find many policies that allow you to fix or unfix elements of the desktop environment for all users.

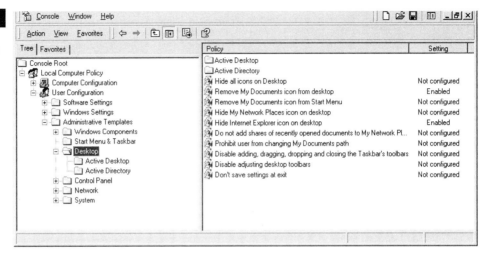

FIGURE 9-12

Desktop policies

- **Hide All Icons On Desktop** This policy kills everything—automatic shortcuts, user-defined shortcuts, documents. All of it. The user can still access things through Run, or the Start menu, or Windows Explorer.

- **Prohibit User From Changing My Documents Path** With this policy disabled, the user can change the pathway by right-clicking My Documents. This prevents the user from doing so, which is quite useful if you've set up multiple users to save to the same place, for cooperative purposes.

- **Disable Adding, Dragging, Dropping And Closing The Taskbar's Toolbars** This policy prevents the user from altering the presence or position of toolbars. The user may not add, dock, move, or close toolbars.

- **Disable Adjusting Desktop Toolbars** This policy prevents the user from changing the length of adjustable toolbars.

- **Don't Save Settings On Exit** When this policy is turned on, things such as which windows are open, and what size and position they're in, are not saved on shutdown or log off. "Settings" is not a super-general term here; even with this policy on, Windows will still remember things like movements of documents onto or off of the desktop.

There are also a bunch of options in the Active Desktop subfolder inside the Desktop folder. These are all pretty intuitive—you can enable, disable, or restrict Active Desktop.

SCENARIO & SOLUTION

You are setting up a kiosk computer. You want the kiosk to look the same for everybody. How would you go about doing this?	Turn on all the "disable" changes and configurations policies.
You want to disallow changes to the toolbars on a computer. What do you need to do?	Turn on the policies Disable Dragging, Dropping, And Closing The Taskbar's Toolbars and Disable Adjusting Desktop Toolbars.
You are setting up a kiosk computer. You want to force everybody who logs on as a Guest to have the same appearance, but allow others to log on with their roaming profiles and get their own configured desktop. What do you need to do to set this up?	Don't touch Local Computer Policy, User Configurations. These make universal changes. Make all your restrictions on the Guest profile.

CERTIFICATION OBJECTIVE 9.03

Configuring and Troubleshooting Accessibility Services

Windows 2000 Professional includes a bunch of accessibility options, designed for variously impaired users. A few of these features—mostly mobility/keyboard type accessibility services—are also useful for any user, in certain situations.

Most of the functionality is accessible from the Accessibility Options window, as shown in Figure 9-13, accessible through the Control Panel.

In the figure you can see the Accessibility Options window, accessed from the Control Panel, on the Keyboard tab. Virtually all accessibility options can be accessed through this window, except for the ones that are very particular applications—Magnifier, Narrator, and the On-Screen Keyboard.

Keyboard Options

You have a few simple options that can make a keyboard much easier to navigate. These are accessible through Accessibility Options, Keyboard tab.

- **StickyKeys** When turned on, StickyKeys makes the SHIFT, TAB, ALT, and CTRL keys act like toggle switches, like the CAPS LOCK key does. Instead of

FIGURE 9-13

Accessibility
Options

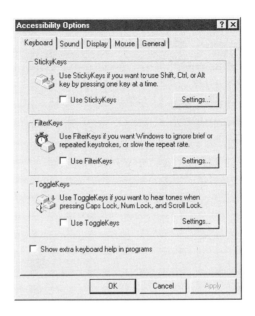

holding SHIFT down and pressing the 1 key to get the exclamation point, for example, you tap SHIFT to toggle SHIFT on, press the 1 key, and then tap SHIFT to toggle SHIFT off. StickyKeys is very useful for mobility impaired users or users lacking the use of some or many fingers. StickyKeys can also be quite useful for every user when using certain applications that demand many ALT or CTRL keys in rapid succession. StickyKeys can be set to turn off as soon as two keys are pressed simultaneously.

- **FilterKeys** When turned on, FilterKeys can filter out certain keystrokes. For those with shaky hands, for example, FilterKeys can filter out very rapidly pressed keystrokes, typical of accidentally double-pressing a key or accidentally pressing two keys at once. This is useful if you find your document full of things like "rthis iss the qway to ggo." FilterKeys is highly customizable.

- **ToggleKeys** When turned on, ToggleKeys will sound out notes whenever SHIFT, CTRL, ALT, or TAB is pressed. This is useful if you find yourself accidentally pressing one of these keys.

Also, under the General tab, you can find the following:

- **SerialKeys** When turned on, SerialKeys will let you use some alternative input device for keyboard input.

CertCam 9-6

EXERCISE 9-6

Turning on StickyKeys

The following exercise demonstrates how to turn on StickyKeys.

1. Open Control Panel | Accessibility Options.

2. Select the Use StickyKeys check box.

3. To configure StickyKeys, click Settings next to the Use StickyKeys box. This opens the Settings For StickyKeys window, which is shown here. Every accessibility option has a different set of settings options. Here you have the options of activating the shortcut, automatically turning StickyKeys off when two keys are depressed simultaneously, and having a sound notification and an onscreen notification when StickyKeys turns on.

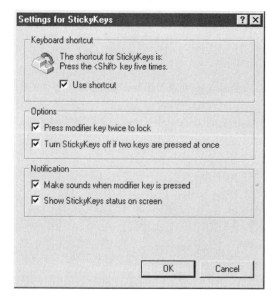

4. Select the Use Shortcut check box. This will allow you to turn on StickyKeys by pressing SHIFT five times.

5. Select the Turn StickyKeys Off If Two Keys Are Pressed At Once, which will automatically turn StickyKeys off when you don't need it.

6. Select both check boxes under Notification. This will make Windows issue a sound when StickyKeys turns on, and leave an onscreen notice when StickyKeys is on.

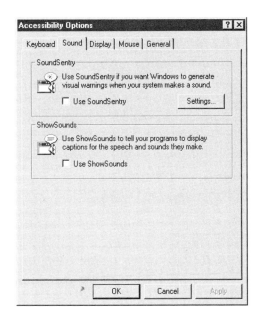

FIGURE 9-14

Accessibility
Sound options

Sound Options

Some useful options for the hearing impaired, or for those who don't have or want sound enabled on their computer, are available through Accessibility Options | Sound tab, as shown in Figure 9-14.

The Sound tab from Accessibility Options gives you access to SoundSentry and ShowSounds.

- **SoundSentry** When turned on, SoundSentry substitutes visual displays for sounds. SoundSentry lets you pick from various substitutes, like pop-up windows and words flashed in the caption bar.

- **ShowSounds** When turned on, ShowSounds tells caption-enabled programs to enter captioning mode. Speech and sounds will be captioned in whatever way the program is set up to caption.

Display Options

One useful option for the vision impaired, or for those whose eyes get tired toward the end of the day, is changing the display. This is available through Accessibility Options | Display tab.

- **HighContrast** HighContrast makes things easier to see and read. Inside the HighContrast Settings box, accessible by clicking Settings, you can choose your HighContrast style. Simple versions include White On Black or Black On White, each of which kills all the background color and makes fonts and icons much easier to see. Inside the Custom pull-down, you can choose lots of particular versions, like very large Black On White, as shown in Figure 9-15, or a simple high-contrast White On Black, as shown in Figure 9-16.

Another approach to allowing access to Windows for the vision impaired is to use the Magnifier and Narrator utilities. To activate either Magnifier or Narrator, go to Start Menu | Programs | Accessories | Accessibility, and then choose the utility.

- **Magnifier** Magnifier opens a window that acts as a magnifying glass, magnifying whatever is around the mouse pointer, as shown in Figure 9-17. You can control the level of magnification. You can see that Magnifier pops a window onto the desktop, magnifying whatever is under the cursor.

- **Narrator** Narrator uses a speech synthesizer to turn whatever you type and whatever appears in the active window into speech.

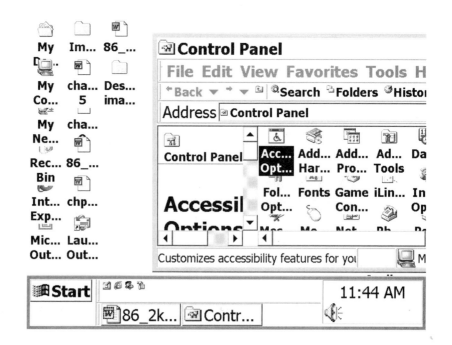

FIGURE 9-15

One HighContrast option

FIGURE 9-16

Another
HighContrast
option

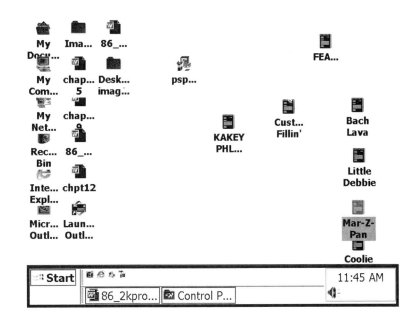

FIGURE 9-17

Magnifier

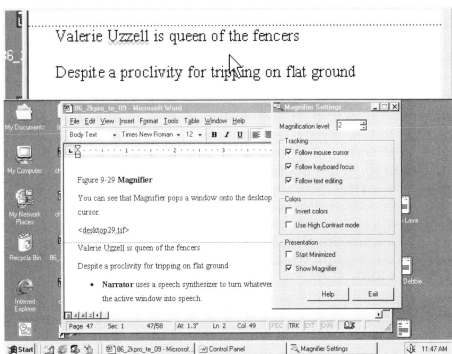

Mouse Options

There is one Mouse option, available through Accessibility Options | Mouse tab:

■ **MouseKeys** MouseKeys allows you to substitute keyboard inputs for mouse handling. This is very useful for those able to type, but unable to grasp a mouse. Normally, MouseKeys allows you to use the numeric keypad to handle the mouse pointer, switching between traditional input and mouse-substitute input by pressing NUM LOCK.

On-Screen Keyboard

For those who are able to handle a mouse, but find it difficult or are unable to use a keyboard, Microsoft offers the On-Screen Keyboard, shown in Figure 9-18. This puts a graphic keyboard on your screen; you type by clicking buttons with your mouse pointer.

Turn on the On-Screen Keyboard from Start Menu | Programs | Accessories | Accessibility | On-Screen Keyboard.

SCENARIO & SOLUTION

A user has shaking hands and has trouble typing. He has trouble holding down keys, and accidentally hits keys repeatedly. How can you adjust his settings to accommodate for this condition?	Turn on FilterKeys, ToggleKeys, and StickyKeys. StickyKeys will relieve the user of having to hold down two keys at once, ToggleKeys will tell the user when he or she has accidentally pressed a critical key, and FilterKeys will filter out many accidentally pressed keys.
A user has trouble seeing words on the screen. What can you do to make it easier for him or her to read?	Play with different display settings. Perhaps changing to a HighContrast mode, especially a large HighContrast mode, will do. Perhaps the user will like using Magnifier. If he or she still cannot see, try using Narrator, which will perform text-to-speech translation.
A user is hearing impaired, and cannot hear noises or speech. What function can you turn on to help the user?	Turn on SoundSentry and ShowSound, which will give visual cues instead of sounds, and trigger captioning in captioning-enabled programs.

FIGURE 9-18

On-Screen
Keyboard

CERTIFICATION SUMMARY

In this chapter, you learned how to configure the desktop environment. Windows 2000 Professional uses user profiles to allow different users to maintain their own distinct desktops on a single physical system. Each profile exists as a folder, by default at X:\Documents and Settings*Username*. You can allow different accounts to access this profile, through manipulations of the Profile path entry, and allow one roaming account, through setting network paths in the Profile path entry.

We also covered basic Group Policy functionality. There are two ways to access the Group Policy Editor—**gpedit.msc** and **mmc /a** commands from the run line. Group Policy lets you set some policies that apply to all users accessing the desktop, and other policies applied by group. Some of these policies allow you to restrict desktop modification, gain permissions, and more. Most policies are simply Enabled or Disabled, and some require a number or other variable to be entered. Group policies set at the local level—Local Computer Policy—are the very weakest, and can be overridden by Group Policy set at any higher level (the domain level, the OU level, and so on).

Finally, you learned about various accessibility services. Certain accessibility features increase visibility, filter bad keystrokes, turn regular keys into toggle keys, sound noises, or allow you to use the keyboard to enter mouse input, or vice versa. Other accessibility features include closed captioning and visual versions of warning noises.

TWO-MINUTE DRILL

Configuring and Managing User Profiles

❑ You must have Administrator status to manipulate Users And Passwords.

❑ Users And Passwords will let you Add and Remove users, change group membership, and manipulate the user profile and home folder.

❑ Group membership is the key to security; what a user can or cannot do depends almost entirely on what groups he is a member of.

❑ The default Profile folder for *Username* exists at

   `[system_drive]:\Documents and Settings\Username`

❑ To create a roaming profile, set all accounts to a profile on a server.

❑ Roaming profiles have profile paths that point to server folders.

❑ You can create a login script for a user, which will run whenever the user logs on.

❑ Your home folder is where many applications will save to by default.

Configuring and Troubleshooting Desktop Settings

❑ Local Computer Policy is a snap-in to Microsoft Management Console.

❑ The fastest way to access Group Policy is to type **gpedit.msc** at the Run prompt.

❑ You can set up a Local Computer Policy icon by typing **mmc /a** at the Run prompt, and then adding the Group Policy snap-in.

❑ Changes made inside Local Computer Policy/User Configuration are all local computerwide—that is, they apply to all users who sit at that computer.

❑ Changes made to policy don't simply change the desktop environment, but set the principles by which users can change their own environments.

❑ Disabling icons and Start menu items through Local Computer Policy only removes the icons; the users can still access these items through Windows Explorer or the command line.

❑ You have tremendous control of the desktop environment, including features like the adjustability and presence of toolbars, the presence of logoff and many other Start menu items, and much more.

❑ Local Computer Policy is the weakest form of policy; it is overridden by policy set at any higher level, like in Active Directory at the server level.

Configuring and Troubleshooting Accessibility Services

❑ StickyKeys, FilterKeys, ToggleKeys, SerialKeys, MouseKeys, and On-Screen Keyboard can be very useful for mobility-impaired users, depending on the type of impairment.

❑ HighContrast, Magnifier, and Narrator are very useful for vision-impaired users.

❑ SoundSentry and ShowSounds are very useful for hearing-impaired users.

❑ All accessibility settings are configurable either through the Accessibility Options pane from the Control Panel, or from the Accessibility menu inside Start Menu | Programs | Accessories.

SELF TEST

The following questions will help you measure your understanding of the material presented in this chapter. Read all of the choices carefully, as there may be more than one correct answer. Choose all correct answers for each question.

Configuring and Managing User Profiles

1. To create a user profile, you must
    A. Create an account for a user.
    B. Create an account for a user and start the Profile Wizard.
    C. Create an account for a user and create a folder for that user in Documents And Settings.
    D. Create an account for a user, create a folder for that user in Documents And Settings, and type that folder and its pathway in the Advanced Properties Profile Path: fill-in.

2. If the system drive is C: and the server is named TRISTAM, the default profile folder for a user named Flannery O'Connor is
    A. C:\Profiles\Flannery O'Connor
    B. \\TRISTAM\Users\Flannery O'Connor
    C. C:\Documents And Settings\Flannery O'Connor
    D. \\TRISTAM\Active Directory\Users And Groups\Users\Flannery O'Connor

3. Jane Doe sets up her login under the network domain SHAH. She then tries to set up another login for herself, in the local domain KIRSCHNER. She discovers that her login to KIRSCHNER gives her a new desktop, not the desktop she has under SHAH. She figures out that her SHAH desktop is saving under Jane Doe\Desktop, and her KIRSCHNER desktop is saving under Jane Doe_KIRSCHNER\Desktop. What can she do to make the desktops look the same, and for changes made to one to propagate to the next?
    A. Copy Jane Doe\Desktop to Jane Doe_KIRSCHNER\Desktop.
    B. Link Jane Doe\Desktop to Jane Doe_KIRSCHNER\Desktop in Windows Explorer.
    C. Log in under KIRSCHNER, and set the Profile Path to Jane Doe\Desktop.
    D. Write a login script to copy Jane Doe\DESKTOP to Jane Doe_KIRSCHNER\Desktop on every login to KIRSCHNER.

4. A roaming profile is
    A. A profile that anybody can use

   B.   The default profile

   C.   A profile for one user who uses multiple computers

   D.   A profile that changes to synchronize with another profile

5. Ginger wants to remove a user from a group. What must she do? (Select all that apply.)

   A.   Open Users And Passwords, select the Groups tab, open the Group, find the User, and click Remove.

   B.   Open Users And Passwords, go to the Advanced Properties menu, open Local Users And Groups, open Groups, find the Group, double-click it, find the user, select the user, and click Remove.

   C.   Open Users And Passwords, go to the Advanced Properties menu, open Local Users And Groups, open Users, double-click the user, click the Member Of tab, select the group, and click Remove.

   D.   Delete the user.

6. The purpose of user profiles is

   A.   To control who has access to files.

   B.   To keep track of who is logged on and where.

   C.   To keep computers secure against unwanted visitors.

   D.   To allow a user to maintain his or her own desktop environment, even if other users are using the same computer.

Configuring and Troubleshooting Desktop Settings

7. How do you access Local Computer Policy? (Select all that apply.)

   A.   Double-click Local Computer Policy in the Control Panel.

   B.   Select Local Computer Policy from Start Menu | Programs | Administrative Tools.

   C.   Run **gpedit.msc.**

   D.   Run **mmc /a** and create a Local Computer Policy console.

8. Local Computer Policy/User Configuration policies apply to whom?

   A.   All users who use the computer

   B.   All groups who have been policy enabled

   C.   Whichever groups have been specified in the policy configuration

   D.   All users but Administrators

9. You are setting up a computer for consultants to use. Some consultants will be coming in and using the computer for a few hours or a day, logging on under the password-less GUEST account. You want these consultants to be able to change their desktop around, but you also want the desktop to return to its original state for each new user. You should

   A. Write a script to copy an "original state" user profile onto the Guest user profile at the end of each day.

   B. Enable all "deny" policies regarding desktop modifications.

   C. Enable the Don't Save Settings On Exit policy.

   D. Enable the Disable Personalized Menus policy.

10. To find out about what a policy listed in the Local Computer Policy snap-in does

    A. Call the Microsoft help line.

    B. Run Help and search under the policy name.

    C. Double-click the policy and select the Explain tab.

    D. Refer to the Microsoft *Local Policy* manual.

11. To disallow certain users from changing their desktops, you should

    A. Change those users' user profiles.

    B. Set policies to prevent desktop changes in Local Computer Policy | User Configuration.

    C. Set policies to prevent desktop changes in the Local Security Policy.

    D. Set policies to prevent desktop changes in Local Computer Policy | User Configuration, set by group.

12. Setting a "disable desktop icons" policy or "disable Start Menu item" policy

    A. Removes the icons and menu items and that is all; the user can still access these items through other means.

    B. Removes all icons and shortcuts; the user can only access functionality through the Run command.

    C. Removes all icons and shortcuts; the user can only access functionality through an administrative force command.

    D. Removes all access to the application in question.

Configuring and Troubleshooting Accessibility Services

13. The On-Screen Keyboard

    A. Lets you use a touch screen with highly visible graphical keys.

    B. Lets you see a picture, onscreen, of what's going on at your actual keyboard.

    C. Lets you use a mouse to type on a graphical keyboard.

    D. Lets you use eye blinks to select letters.

14. StickyKeys lets you

    A. Filter out repeated keystrokes.

    B. Filter out keystrokes very close to one another.

    C. Only enter keys that have been down for some amount of time.

    D. Turn certain keys, like CTRL, SHIFT, and ALT, into toggle keys, letting you turn them on like a CAPS LOCK.

15. SoundSentry lets you

    A. Turn on captioning for caption-enabled programs.

    B. Substitute visual displays for sounds.

    C. Alert you with sounds when Accessibility options have been turned on.

    D. Flash warnings on the screen when someone is speaking to you.

16. MouseKeys is good for

    A. Someone who can't handle a keyboard, but can handle a mouse.

    B. Someone who can't handle a mouse, but can handle a keyboard.

    C. Someone who can't see the On-Screen Keyboard.

    D. Someone who has trouble typing quickly.

17. You turn on Magnifier from

    A. Start Menu | Magnifier.

    B. Start Menu | Programs Accessories | Magnifier.

    C. Control Panel | Accessibility Options | Visual tab | Magnifier.

    D. Control Panel | Accessibility Options | General tab | Magnifier.

18. Ernest has very shaky hands. He has severe trouble typing, frequently pressing two keys simultaneously. What devices will help Ernest?

A. SerialKeys

B. ToggleKeys

C. StickyKeys

D. FilterKeys

LAB QUESTION

You are the IT manager in a small startup. You have a small company, with five users, including yourself. You only want yourself and the CEO to have Administrator status.

Your company has one server and four desktops, all running Windows 2000. You and the CEO roam among all computers, two of the other users have their own desktops, and the last two users share a single desktop. Everybody wants to be able to have easy access to everybody else's documents. Describe how you will set up user profiles and profile paths.

SELF TEST ANSWERS

Configuring and Managing User Profiles

1. ☑ **A.** While everything in D needs to be done in order for a profile to exist and be accessed, Windows 2000 does all of this stuff automatically when you create an account.
   ☒ **B.** You *do* want to create an account for the user, but there is no Profile Wizard for this. C is incorrect; the folder is created automatically during A. D is incorrect; all the latter steps are done automatically during user account creation.

2. ☑ **C.** By default, the profile folder is created *locally*.
   ☒ **A, B,** and **D** are incorrect, and are inside Documents And Settings.

3. ☑ **C.** This will make the desktops under the two logins one and the same.
   ☒ **A** will make the two desktops the same immediately following the copy, but changes will not propagate. **B** is impossible. **D** will make changes made in SHAH propagate to KIRSCHNER, but not vice versa.

4. ☑ **C.** The correct definition of a roaming profile is a profile for one user who uses multiple computers.
   ☒ **A** is incorrect, since a roaming profile is attached to a single user account. **B** is incorrect; the default profile is local. **D** is incorrect; the roaming profile does not synch with anything.

5. ☑ **B, C.** You can remove a user from a group from the Local Users And Groups console either through the user's list of groups, or the group's list of users.
   ☒ **A** is incorrect since users aren't listed under Group. **D** is incorrect, since it destroys the user account.

6. ☑ **D.** User profiles are different desktop environments, even for different users working on the same desktop.
   ☒ **A, B,** and **C** apply to the user *account*. The term "user profile" refers specifically to the set of configurations, settings, and desktop contents associated with each account.

Configuring and Troubleshooting Desktop Settings

7. ☑ **C, D.** Either the runline command or the MMC author mode will get you to Local Computer Policy.
   ☒ **A** and **B** are incorrect, as there is no default icon or menu item associated with Local Computer Policy in Win2K Pro.

8. ☑ **A.** User Configuration policies apply to all users who use the desktop.
☒ **D** is simply wrong. **B** and **C** are incorrect since, while per-group settings can be created in Local Computer Policy | Computer Configuration (as will be explained in Chapter 12) Local Computer Policy | User Configuration policies are computerwide and universal.

9. ☑ **C.** Enabling the Don't Save Settings On Exit policy will cause the desktop connected to the Guest profile to return to the default state at the end of each session.
☒ **A** will not work, since, if multiple users log on to the Guest account in one day, they will see previous users' changes. **B** will prevent any changes to the desktop. **D** will turn off personalized menus, but do nothing else to prevent desktop changes.

10. ☑ **C.** The Explain tab contains an explanation of each policy.
☒ **A** is unnecessary, **B** won't bring the information, and **D** refers to a manual that does not exist.

11. ☑ **A.** Changing by user profile will allow changes to apply to particular users.
☒ **B** is incorrect since it will introduce universal changes. **C** refers to the wrong place, and **D** is impossible.

12. ☑ **A.** The Disable Desktop Icons policy simply removes the shortcuts from the desktop menu. The user can still find the executables through Explorer or the Run command and run them.
☒ **B** is incorrect, since Explorer will function as well as the Run command. **C** refers to a nonexistent command. **D** is incorrect, since the user can still access the items through other means.

Configuring and Troubleshooting Accessibility Services

13. ☑ **C.** The On-Screen Keyboard lets you use your mouse to type on a graphical keyboard.
☒ **A, B,** and **D** are incorrect; they refer to features that don't exist in Windows 2000.

14. ☑ **D.** StickyKeys filters out repeated keystrokes.
☒ **A** and **B** are the functionality of FilterKeys. **C** refers to a nonexistent function.

15. ☑ **B.** SoundSentry substitutes visual displays for sounds.
☒ **A** is the functionality of ShowSounds. **C** and **D** refer to nonexistent functions in Windows 2000.

16. ☑ **B.** MouseKeys translates keystrokes into mouse input, helping those who cannot handle a mouse.
☒ **A** refers to the On-Screen Keyboard, **C** is nonsensical, and **D** refers to a nonexistent accessibility feature.

17. ☑ **B.** Magnifier is one of the few services that are not under Accessibility Options.
⊠ **A** refers to the wrong location. **C** and **D** refer to Accessibility Options, which is where almost all Accessibility Options are found, Magnifier being one of the few exceptions.

18. ☑ **D.** FilterKeys will filter out many mistypes.
⊠ **A** is incorrect, since SerialKeys allows alternative typing devices. **B** is incorrect, since ToggleKeys sounds noises for pressing CTRL, ALT, and SHIFT. **C** is incorrect, since StickyKeys turns CTRL, ALT, and SHIFT into toggle switches, which would probably make things worse for Ernest.

LAB ANSWER

For yourself and the CEO, create accounts on the server. Let's say the server is shared under the name JUDO. Find your and the CEO's account folders, and copy them into a shared folder, call it Roaming Profiles.

Create accounts for each desktop for yourself and the CEO. Go into the Advanced Properties window for both yourself and the CEO, and set the Profile Path: to \\JUDO\Roaming Profiles*Username*, where *Username* is either you or the CEO's username.

For each of the people who have fixed desktops, simply create accounts for them on those desktops.

For the two who are sharing a desktop, simply create two accounts. Since the profile-creation process happens automatically and transparently, each of those two will have their own independent desktops.

Finally, create another shared folder, call it Company Stuff, on JUDO. Go to everybody's account and set the Home folder to \\JUDO\Company Stuff.

Of course, there's an easier way to do all this using Active Directory—but that's for the Server test, not for the Professional test.

MICROSOFT CERTIFIED SYSTEMS ENGINEER

10

Configuring Multilanguage Support and Using Windows Installer

CERTIFICATION OBJECTIVES

10.01	Configuring Support for Multiple Languages or Multiple Locations
10.02	Installing Applications by Using Windows Installer Packages
✓	Two-Minute Drill
Q&A	Self Test

Previous chapters in this book dealt with the physical aspects of deploying and managing a Windows 2000 Professional infrastructure. Important tasks such as the installation and deployment of Windows 2000 Professional, and configuration and management of the installed hardware, were discussed. There are some other issues related to Windows 2000 Professional desktop management that go beyond the deployment and support of the hardware.

This chapter discusses features that will need to be kept in mind when planning your deployment of Windows 2000. If people in your organization are spread out in different countries, then you will need to plan your Windows 2000 deployment to allow those people to communicate regardless of the language they speak. Once your environment has been upgraded to Windows 2000, you will need to plan for installing software and applications in an efficient manner.

Both of these topics are discussed in this chapter.

CERTIFICATION OBJECTIVE 10.01

Configuring Support for Multiple Languages or Multiple Locations

Computers organize things around numbers. Bits and bytes are the building blocks of the data that computers process. Human beings think in a much different manner; we communicate ideas through the construction of sounds, letters, words, and sentences. As computers started to be used for more than speedy numerical computation, there was a need to be able to encode alphabets into numerical codes. Furthermore, there needed to be a standard in place to ensure that data could be transferred between systems. If everyone used a different mapping between letters and numbers, there was no way to reliably and consistently share data among systems.

A very early example of this type of mapping actually predated the invention of the computer. The Morse code was developed for telegraph use in 1838. Each letter of the alphabet and certain punctuation symbols were assigned a unique code. These codes were a combination of two values, the dot and the dash.

This idea of representing human communication constructs with a simple code to facilitate electric representation and transmission has continued over the years and has become a fundamental idea in the invention of computers. Jumping ahead several years, two main standards for representing characters in computers emerged: ASCII and EBCDIC.

ASCII stands for American Standard Code for Information Interchange and uses 7 bits to represent characters. Since ASCII uses 7 bits, there are a total of 128 (2^7) possible characters supported by ASCII, allowing representation of uppercase and lowercase letters, numbers, and punctuation symbols. The ASCII character set is shown in Table 10-1. The ASCII character set was widely used on PCs. Note in the table that for each Decimal value given, there is a corresponding character associated with it. The first 32 ASCII characters (ASCII values 0–31) are control characters used for controlling a terminal session.

EBCDIC stands for "Extended Binary Coded Decimal Interchange Code" and uses 8 bits to represent characters. An 8-bit code leads to 256 (2^8) possible characters, which means that EBCDIC can support lowercase and uppercase letters, numbers, and many symbols and control codes. Table 10-2 shows the EBCDIC character set.

The problem in using a character set like ASCII or EBCDIC is that it isn't as helpful for people who do not use English. These problems are divided into two general categories, based on the language in use.

For non-English languages that are still based on the Roman alphabet, such as French or Spanish, the issue is that these languages use accent symbols to change the sound or meaning of certain letters. These accents should be written as part of the letter, making necessary several additional characters in the character set for the same letter, and increasing the required total number of characters in the character set. For example, in French, a letter E can take one of three accent marks to change the sound of the letter: a grave accent (È), an aigu accent (É), and a circumflex accent (Ê). Expanding the ASCII or EBCDIC character sets to accommodate what amounts to three extra characters will increase the number of characters needed in the set, possibly requiring another less-used character to be removed from the set.

Other non-Roman languages that use completely different alphabets, such as Greek, Arabic, Hebrew, or Chinese, cannot make use of ASCII or EBCDIC. These languages are not based on Roman letters, and some of these languages when written (e.g., Chinese) are not organized around letters at all; each "character" when written represents an entire word or concept. How do you create a usable character set (or even a usable keyboard for that matter) when each written character is one of several thousand words?

TABLE 10-1 ASCII Character Set

Dec	Char	Dec	Char	Dec	Char	Dec	Char
0	NUL	32	SPACE	64	@	96	`
1	SOH	33	!	65	A	97	A
2	STX	34	"	66	B	98	B
3	ETX	35	#	67	C	99	C
4	EOT	36	$	68	D	100	D
5	ENQ	37	%	69	E	101	E
6	ACK	38	&	70	F	102	F
7	BEL	39	'	71	G	103	G
8	BS	40	(	72	H	104	H
9	TAB	41	)	73	I	105	I
10	LF	42	*	74	J	106	J
11	VT	43	+	75	K	107	K
12	FF	44	,	76	L	108	L
13	CR	45	-	77	M	109	M
14	SO	46	.	78	N	110	N
15	SI	47	/	79	O	111	O
16	DLE	48	0	80	P	112	P
17	DC1	49	1	81	Q	113	Q
18	DC2	50	2	82	R	114	R
19	DC3	51	3	83	S	115	S
20	DC4	52	4	84	T	116	T
21	NAK	53	5	85	U	117	U
22	SYN	54	6	86	V	118	V
23	ETB	55	7	87	W	119	W
24	CAN	56	8	88	X	120	X
25	EM	57	9	89	Y	121	Y
26	SUB	58	:	90	Z	122	Z
27	ESC	59	;	91	[	123	{
28	FS	60	<	92	\	124		
29	GS	61	=	93	]	125	}
30	RS	62	>	94	^	126	~
31	US	63	?	95	_	127	DEL

TABLE 10-2   EBCDIC Character Set

Dec	Code	Dec	Code	Dec	Code	Dec	Code	Dec	Code	Dec	Code	Dec	Code	Dec	Code
0	NUL	32		64	space	96	-	128		160		192	{	224	\
1	SOH	33		65		97	/	129	A	161	~	193	A	225	
2	STX	34		66		98		130	B	162	s	194	B	226	S
3	ETX	35		67		99		131	C	163	t	195	C	227	T
4		36		68		100		132	D	164	u	196	D	228	U
5	HT	37	LF	69		101		133	E	165	v	197	E	229	V
6		38	ETB	70		102		134	F	166	w	198	F	230	W
7	DEL	39	ESC	71		103		135	G	167	x	199	G	231	X
8		40		72		104		136	H	168	y	200	H	232	Y
9		41		73		105		137	I	169	z	201	I	233	Z
10		42		74	[	106	|	138		170		202		234	
11	VT	43		75	.	107	,	139		171		203		235	
12	FF	44		76	<	108	%	140		172		204		236	
13	CR	45	ENQ	77	(	109	_	141		173		205		237	
14	SO	46	ACK	78	+	110	>	142		174		206		238	
15	SI	47	BEL	79	|!	111	?	143		175		207		239	
16	DLE	48		80	&	112		144		176		208	}	240	0
17		49		81		113		145	J	177		209	J	241	I
18		50	SYN	82		114		146	K	178		210	K	242	2
19		51		83		115		147	L	179		211	L	243	3
20		52		84		116		148	M	180		212	M	244	4
21		53		85		117		149	N	181		213	N	245	5
22	BS	54		86		118		150	O	182		214	O	246	6
23		55	EOT	87		119		151	P	183		215	P	247	7
24	CAN	56		88		120		152	Q	184		216	Q	248	8
25	EM	57		89		121	'	153	R	185		217	R	249	9
26		58		90	!]	122	:	154		186		218		250	
27		59		91	$	123	#	155		187		219		251	
28	IFS	60		92	*	124	@	156		188		220		252	
29	IGS	61	NAK	93	)	125	'	157		189		221		253	
30	IRS	62		94	;	126	=	158		190		222		254	
31	IUS	63	SUB	95	^	127	"	159		191		223		255	

Computer scientists in these countries have developed standardized ways of representing their languages in computer transferable form (similar to ASCII and EBCDIC in the United States). These standards are all based on the concept of taking each letter, number, symbol, word, or idea, and assigning it a number.

Taking this approach for each language makes it possible for speakers of a certain language to use computers, but does not make it easy for people from two different countries to communicate or share information. To get around this, each speaker might agree to use only one language for communication, or both parties would need software that would display information in both languages, switching character sets when needed.

Unicode (ISO 10646)

A standardized international character set called Unicode was developed to resolve this problem. Unicode is a standard ratified by the International Standard Organization (ISO standard 10646) to allow communication between languages. Instead of supporting multiple separate character sets for each language, Unicode combines characters from all of the world's major languages into a single 16-bit character set, yielding 65,536 (2^{16}) characters. If an operating system uses Unicode instead of ASCII, EBCDIC, or another character set, people can exchange documents created in that operating system with other users of Unicode-based systems. Windows 2000 uses Unicode as its default character set.

There will still be some interoperability problems related to Unicode. Documents that use another character set will still need to be translated into Unicode in order to be read by the user.

on the

Job

It's important to keep in mind that translation used in this context means translating between character sets, and not translating between languages. A Japanese-speaking person who writes an e-mail to her French pen pal will not have her letter automatically translated from Japanese to French. The fact that both the sender and receiver use Unicode means that the recipient will be able to see the message using the same characters and language that the sender intended. It would be up to the French reader to translate the Japanese language in the e-mail into French.

SCENARIO & SOLUTION

What code pages or character sets are supported in Windows 2000?	ASCII is supported for the United States. Localized character sets are supported for localized installations of Windows 2000. Unicode is supported on all versions of Windows 2000 as the default and allows most languages to be used with a single character set.
What is the default character set installed in Windows 2000 Professional?	Unicode is the default character set.
How many characters are found in these character sets?	Unicode uses 2 bytes to store each character (two bytes = 16 bits), so there are 2^{16}, or 65,536, possible characters in Unicode. ASCII is a 7-bit character set and, therefore, only supports 2^7, or 128, different characters.

RTL (Right-to-Left) Orientation API

There are other features in Windows 2000 Professional that allow software developers to create applications for international users. Starting with Visual Basic version 6, Microsoft introduced the Bidirectional Application Programming Interface. This API provides a way for programmers to create dialog boxes in their programs that can automatically format themselves correctly depending on the language. This API is also known as the Right-to-Left API.

In the English language, characters and words are read starting from the left side of the page and moving to the right side of the page. Microsoft's User Interface (UI) guidelines take this idea and extend it to how items in a program are to be displayed. See Figure 10-1 for an example of this. This figure shows one of the Properties sheets used to configure Internet Explorer 5.

The drop-down boxes in the Internet Programs section allow you to choose from the options listed. To the left of each drop-down box is a caption used to describe the setting being made. To a person who reads left to right, this is the natural order to see these settings. If that screen was displayed in a language that read from right to left (such as Hebrew), then the orientation of the caption and drop-down box (both are generically referred to as "controls" in VB parlance) will seem backward.

FIGURE 10-1

Sample dialog box

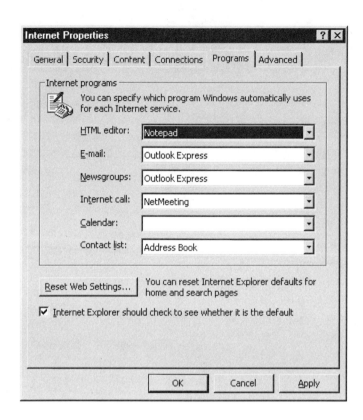

The Bidirectional or RTL API allows a programmer to specify how controls will be oriented on a property sheet or dialog box (both are generically referred to as "forms" in VB parlance), so that the program can be written once and be displayed correctly no matter what language or character set is enabled on the client PC.

So, what does this mean to you as the administrator? Not much initially, unless you also moonlight as a VB programmer! However, if you are tasked with supporting the same application for international users, you'll want to make sure that the developers of the application provide either multiple language versions of the same application, or a single version of the application that can be run in all languages (by writing the application to make use of the RTL API, Unicode, and other topics from this chapter).

Enabling Multiple-Language Support

Support for multiple languages in Windows 2000 Professional falls into two broad categories. The first category makes use of features that allow an end user to interact with applications, dialog boxes, and error messages in that user's native language. The second category deals with ensuring that users in multiple countries speaking multiple languages can use the same network infrastructure and share data without any workstation reconfigurations. As an example, a user in Russia will see menus and dialog boxes in Russian, but will still be able to send an e-mail or a Word document to a colleague in France or China, using that country's language and character set (assuming she knows how to speak and write in French or Chinese!).

MultiLanguage Windows 2000 Professional

Microsoft has released versions of Windows 2000 that allow users to interact with the Windows User Interface (UI) in their native language. If the version of Windows 2000 Professional you are using supports your language, dialog boxes, help files, and application elements will all be displayed in your language. Microsoft has released Windows 2000 versions that will display the UI elements in one of 24 languages. There is also a "MultiLanguage" version that contains the UI for all 24 supported languages in one package. When ordering licenses and media for Windows 2000 Professional, you should request the version localized for the languages you intend to support.

An administrator supporting users in an international organization would install localized versions of Windows 2000 Professional, allowing each user to interact with Windows in his or her native language, and *then* install support for different Locales, allowing each user to interact and share data with other users in other countries.

Locales

A Locale is a set of user preferences relating to a user's language, environment, and cultural settings. These preferences determine how Windows 2000 should display and format information relating to numbers, dates, currencies, and time. The Locales available on a particular Windows 2000 Professional system are determined by what Language Groups are installed.

These settings are different from those found in the MultiLanguage versions of Windows 2000. The MultiLanguage versions of Windows 2000 will display the UI elements in the installed language, but any version of Windows 2000 in any installed language will still be able to save Locale settings to enable communication between users of different languages.

A Language Group is a collection of settings that determine which keyboard layout, font, Input Method Editor (IME), and National Language Support (*.nls) files will be used. It provides all of the necessary files and supporting components that enable a list of available Locales to be generated and chosen from. A particular Language Group must be installed in order to use the corresponding Locale. Language Groups can be installed when Windows 2000 is installed, by clicking Language Options . . . when initiating the install, as shown in Figure 10-2.

When you click Language Options . . . , you are asked to select a primary Language Group and, if desired, one or more additional Language Groups to be installed, as shown in Figure 10-3.

You can also install Language Groups after Windows 2000 Professional has been installed by using the Regional Options applet in the Control Panel. This procedure is covered in Exercise 10-1, later in this section.

FIGURE 10-2

Windows 2000 Professional Setup screen

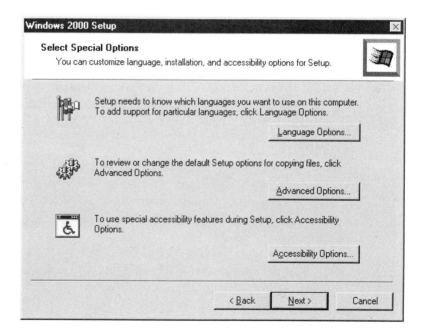

Installing
Language Options

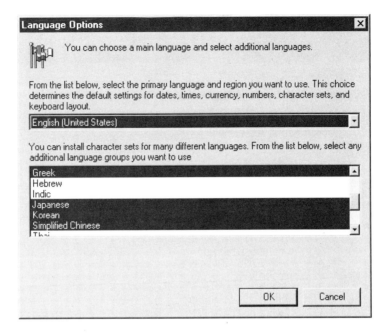

There are some terms introduced in this section that may crop up on the exams: An Input Method Editor (IME) is a software service installed in Windows 2000 Professional that provides common services for inputting text into an application from various sources. Most of the time that source will be the computer's keyboard, but support is built in for speech-to-text software and devices useful for the disabled. The details of the abstraction between how text is input and how the IME converts the text to the Locale's language is transparent to the user and the administrator. National Language Support files have an *.nls extension and contain information on how to provide support for different languages.

Locale settings are divided into three categories: User Locales, Input Locales, and System Locales.

The User Locale is a per-user setting that controls the formatting that will be applied to dates, times, numbers, and currency. When a user is using an application that formats one of these elements (such as Microsoft Excel), the default formatting for the current User Locale will be applied. User Locale settings take effect immediately and do not require a reboot.

FROM THE CLASSROOM

Localized and MultiLanguage Versions

If you take a Microsoft Official Curriculum (MOC) class on Windows 2000 Professional, it will probably be taught using a localized version of Windows 2000 for your country, and will not have the MultiLanguage version installed. You can still do the lab exercises in this chapter and in the MOC course material.

Each localized version (and the MultiLanguage version) of Windows 2000 can still support Locales and Unicode. Therefore, even if you are working with the American English version of Windows 2000, you can still perform the exercises to customize your computer as if you were in Beijing!

—*Erik Sojka, MCSE*

It is important to note that a User Locale is not synonymous with a language. A User Locale contains settings that enable a user to work in a certain area or country, and usually is associated with a language, but not necessarily or exclusively. For example, a user using the Hebrew User Locale will use settings associated regionally with Israel, and not just with the Hebrew language. In addition, England English users will see currency formatted with the British Pound symbol (£), and American English users will see currency formatted with the dollar sign ($)

Input Locales are per-user settings that match an input language with a method to input text. The input language will be one of the installed Language Groups, and the input method will be a configured IME. For example, this flexibility allows a user to use a Greek keyboard to type information in Greek, and use a microphone with speech-to-text software to insert Spanish text into a document. Input Locale settings take effect immediately and do not require a reboot.

System Locales are systemwide settings used to determine which character set and font files will be used on the system. The default System Locale is Unicode based. Changing the System Locale to another language or a non-Unicode language will allow certain localized applications that require a certain language to be present to run. Since this is a systemwide setting, other non-Unicode applications that assume or expect their character set to be present will have display issues when run in another System Locale.

For example, a German user is trying to run a non-Unicode application written for the Japanese language version of Windows 95. This user has to select Japanese as the System Locale to do this. If, at the same time, that user wants to continue to use a non-Unicode German application, certain characters will not be displayed correctly, since they will be using the Japanese character set. System Locale settings require a reboot before they take effect.

Keep the components of the Locales and which Locale they are found in straight. For example, if you are faced with a question dealing with where/how you would set a user's currency settings, look for the answer that deals with User Locales, since that is the only Locale in which that parameter is set.

What settings are contained in User Locales?	User Locale settings control how Windows 2000 formats and displays calendars, dates, times, currency, and numbers. This is set per user and does not require a reboot to take effect.
What settings are contained in Input Locales?	Input Locale settings control how the system maps the language being used to the device used to input text. This is set per user and does not require a reboot to take effect.
What settings are contained in System Locales?	System Locale settings control which fonts, character sets, and code pages will be used to display text in the selected language. This is a per-system setting and requires administrator privileges to change. Changing the System Locale requires a reboot to take effect.

Configuring Multiple-Language Support for All Users

The settings that control which Language Groups are available and which System and User Locales are to be used are stored in the Windows 2000 Registry. As such, they can be controlled and managed via Group Policy.

An administrator can create language-related settings as part of an organization's Group Policy, apply those Group Policies to a user or Organizational Unit, and have them automatically applied when a person logs on to Active Directory.

If users in different locations require the Windows UI to also be displayed in their native language, then a localized version of Windows 2000 Professional should be installed.

Configuring Locale Settings

Locale settings are configured in the Regional Options applet in the Control Panel.
The following exercise demonstrates how to set up location settings.

CertCam 10-1

Configuring Locale Settings

This exercise walks you through installing Language Groups and configuring Locales. Then you will see a simple example of an application using two languages at the same time.

1. To change a locale in Windows 2000 Professional, you must use the Regional Options applet in the Control Panel. Opening this applet yields the display shown here.

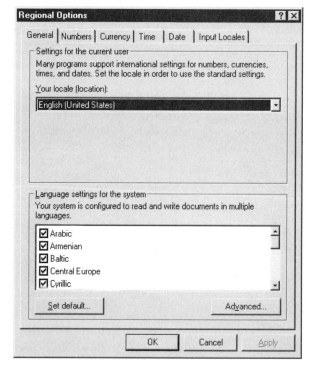

2. The first tab of this dialog box shows that the default Language Group at the top is set to English (United States). Listed at the bottom of the screen are other Language Groups that can be configured or made available. If the

check box next to the Language Group is selected, it is installed and can be enabled. If the check box is not selected, that Language Group is not installed. If it is not already selected, select the check box next to Arabic and click OK. You may be prompted for the Windows 2000 CD to enable the required files to be copied. After the file copy is complete, you will be asked to reboot.

3. After rebooting your computer, log on to your computer again and return to the Regional Options applet in the Control Panel. Change your default Locale to Arabic (Egypt). The dialog box should look similar to one shown here.

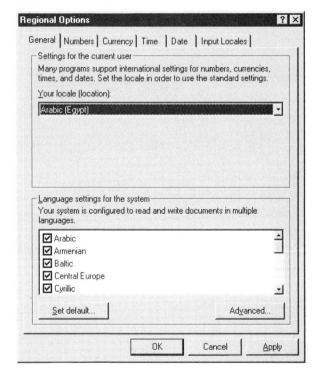

4. Click the Numbers tab. You should see settings similar to ones shown in the following dialog box. The settings here are automatically inherited according

to the Locale set on the General tab. Samples of how numbers will be displayed are shown across the top. If you have a reason to do so, you can change the rules on number formatting using the drop-down boxes, and the changes will be applied to the current User Locale.

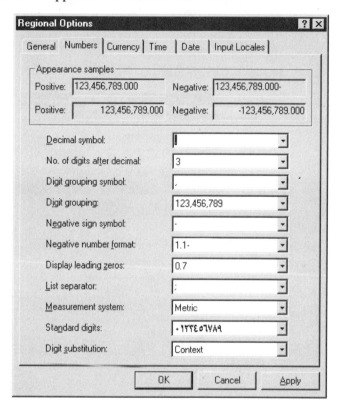

5. Click the Currency tab. You should see settings similar to those shown in the following dialog box. The settings here are automatically inherited according to the Locale set on the General tab. Samples of how currencies

will be displayed are shown across the top. If you have a reason to do so, you can change the rules on currency formatting using the drop-down boxes, and the changes will be applied to the current User Locale. Note that instead of the American dollar symbol ($), the Egyptian Pound symbol is used. Note also that the settings for currency are similar to those for number formatting.

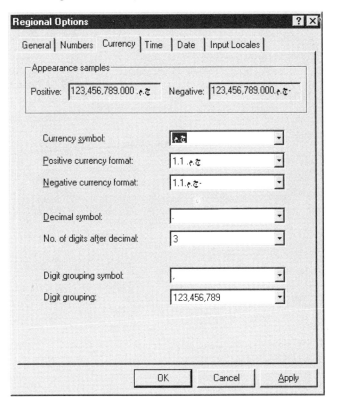

6. Click the Time tab. You should see settings similar to the ones shown in the following dialog box. The settings here are automatically inherited according

to the Locale set on the General tab. Samples of how times will be displayed are shown across the top. Note that since Arabic is a Right-to-Left language, the time sample (and the samples on the other tabs) displays what the time will look like when formatted RTL and LTR.

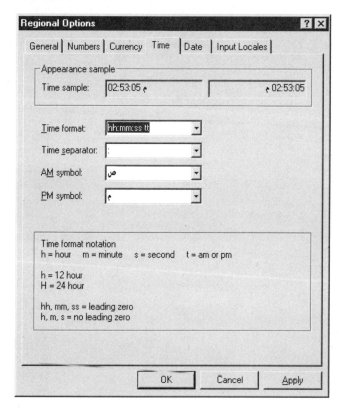

7. Click the Date tab. You should see settings similar to those shown in the following dialog box. The settings here are automatically inherited according to the Locale set on the General tab. Samples of how dates will be displayed are shown across the top. Note that there are options to convert dates between calendar types, as not all countries use the Julian calendar that is

used in the United States and Europe. Note also that when displaying the date from the Julian calendar, the default is to switch the day and the month. 23/05/2000 in this Locale refers to the 23rd day in the 5th month.

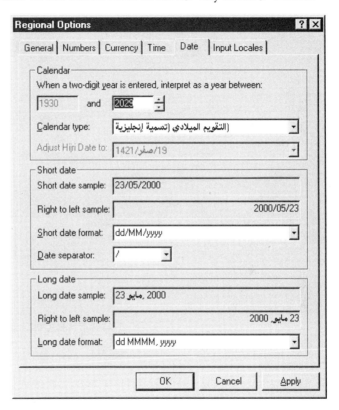

8. Click the Input Locales tab. You should see settings similar to the ones shown in the following dialog box. Across the top of the screen are the mappings of the selected language to the keyboard layout. There are also settings that allow you to specify a keyboard shortcut to be used to switch between configured Input Locales. Select the check the box marked Enable Indicator On Taskbar.

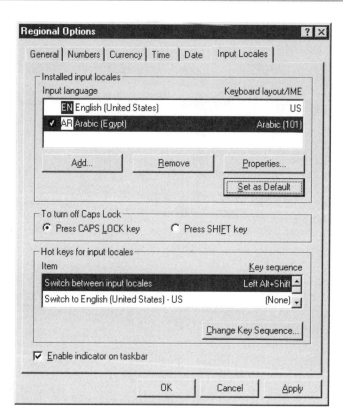

9. Click Add . . . . You should see the following dialog box. If you wanted to add a new Input Locale, you would specify here which keyboard layout or IME should be used.

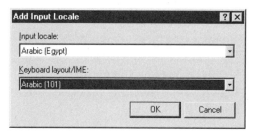

10. Click OK to close the Regional Options dialog box, and apply the settings. We've only made changes to the User and Input Locales, so we do not need

to reboot again. Notice that an icon has been added to the System Tray. The icon is a blue square with a two-letter code indicating which configured Input Locale is currently in use. This icon is here because of the setting made in step 8. Left-click the icon and a context menu appears, similar to that shown in following screen. The triangle indicates the Input Locale currently in use.

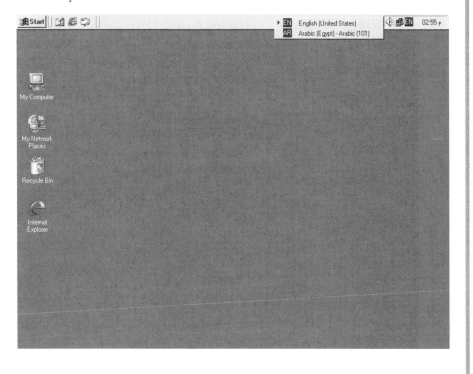

11. Start Notepad (found in the Accessories folder under Start | Programs). Start to type text and notice that as you type, you are able to intersperse text from different languages by changing the Input Locale. The following screen shows a sample document that uses both English and Arabic characters.

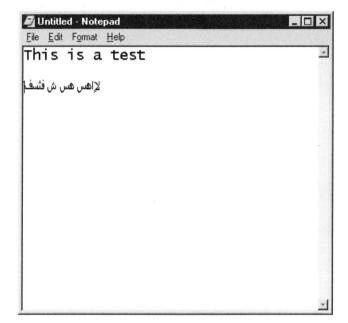

12. Exit Notepad and close all windows.

Avoiding "Illegal" Characters in Computer Names, Account Names, and Passwords

If you are going to be managing Windows 2000 users in a worldwide domain or forest, you will want to take time to carefully plan how your naming convention will be affected by international considerations.

Regardless of the language settings in use, you should always choose names for user and computer accounts that only use letters and numbers. Passwords can be chosen using mixed-case letters, numbers, and symbols. Since these components are stored using Unicode, any language can be used.

You should also ensure your naming convention is still in line with the standards and requirements for other software components. For example, user and computer names stored on an Active Directory DNS server should not contain the underscore (_) character.

To help facilitate central administration, you may want to enforce a policy that user and computer account names are all stored in one language (probably English), regardless of location.

CERTIFICATION OBJECTIVE 10.02

Installing Applications by Using Windows Installer Packages

Whether you are a software vendor or an administrator tasked with installing an application on a workstation, you've been faced with the problem of trying to figure out how to reliably and consistently install software. A piece of software running on Windows 2000 Professional consists of executable files, Dynamically Linked Libraries (DLLs), Registry settings, registered components, and other configuration items. It is the job of a software installer utility to manage and create these settings, allowing a piece of software to run correctly.

At first glance, it seems like it should be simple to configure a utility to copy some files and create some Registry entries—in reality, it's not as simple as it seems. The authors of a software application cannot know what combination of other software, service packs, or hot fixes have been installed on a particular computer. These other configuration changes, and more importantly, the combinations of these changes, can have an effect on how a newly installed application will work.

As an example, there are some application support DLL files that Microsoft provides as part of the Windows 2000 operating system, and a developer may replace or change them as part of an application. (the Visual Basic and Visual C runtime files, msvbrunxx.dll and msvcrtxx.dll, are frequent victims of this "flexibility"). A problem arises if you install an older application on a system that replaces this DLL file. The replaced DLL file might cause other applications that depend on a later version of this file to function incorrectly. Logic would have to be built into the installation utility to try to detect the version of that DLL file in use, and a decision made whether to replace it.

Various third-party software companies, such as InstallShield and Wise, tried to fill this niche by creating a flexible installation utility that handles different situations and makes installation decisions accordingly. The output of these utilities were a couple of script files, a compressed version of the application files, and a wizard-like process to guide the end user in the installation. Windows 2000 Installer packages consist of a single file with an *.msi extension, containing all necessary files, scripts, and logic to complete an application. The MSI file can be copied or e-mailed as a single unit.

Windows Installer technology is updated for Windows 2000 Professional and includes many improved features. A software package created for Windows Installer can roll back a system to its original state if the installation fails for whatever reason. It can prevent applications from overwriting common system files or files created by another application. It can attempt to repair a corrupted installation by keeping a log of what files were installed at the original install date, and replace those files if necessary. It can reliably and completely uninstall an application. It can be scripted to allow the application to be installed automatically without a user's intervention. It can be configured to install only some components of an application to conserve disk space on the client, and those missing components can be automatically installed later if the missing component is needed.

Creating an Installer Package

To create a Windows Installer package, you will first need the application itself. The Installer technology is not intended as a replacement for a programming language or environment such as Microsoft Visual Basic. Installer takes the finished product (the set of compiled *.exe and *.dll files) and provides a way to ensure that those files are copied and registered correctly on the client PC.

As a system administrator, you will probably need to deploy applications to your users. If the application is a newer application (anything created in the last year or so), that software's creators will probably already have an Installer package ready for your use. Giving administrators the ability to deploy an application using Installer technology is one of the requirements for a software application to be able to display the "Designed for Windows 2000" logo. You will probably need to learn to create an Installer package to support and deploy older software that uses a method other than Installer to install itself.

on the
job

If an application does not yet support Installer technology, it might still have some other mechanism to create customized configurable installations. Given the choice between repackaging these applications and using the built-in customization tools, you should deploy an application using the customization tools. An example of this is Internet Explorer. Microsoft has made available an Internet Explorer Administration Kit (IEAK) that allows an administrator to completely customize the installation of IE, including changing the default home page, proxy settings, and so forth. If you need to deploy IE for any reason (IE5 is the latest version of IE at the time of this writing), then you should use the IEAK instead of trying to package an application.

You will also need an application that is capable of creating Installer files. A limited version of WinINSTALL Lite from Veritas Software is included on the Windows 2000 Professional CD in the following location: D:\VALUEADD\ 3RDPARTY\MGMT\WINSTLE (assuming D: is your CD-ROM drive). Other utilities exist that can create Installer-compatible MSI files.

These types of utilities work by taking a snapshot of your system both before and after an application is installed, and creating the Installer package based on the net changes detected. These changes are converted into an Installer script that represents the changes required to repeat the software installation. This script can be edited in the Installer utility to further refine or customize the install process.

on the
job

If your organization already uses Microsoft's Systems Management Server (SMS), the investment in the SMS-based Installer packages is still valid. Microsoft provides an Installer Step-Up utility that will convert SMS packages to Windows 2000 Installer MSI files. At the time of this writing, the step-up utility was in beta testing, and once released, should be available for download from the Microsoft Web site and included in SMS 2.0 SP2.

SCENARIO & SOLUTION	
What types of applications are supported by Installer technology?	All applications support the Installer technology.
What is the process of creating an Installer application installation?	The process involves changes being converted into an installer script. The installer script represents the changes required to repeat the software installation.

Creating a Sample Installer Application

This exercise walks you through creating a sample installer application using an Installer-compatible package creator. The application being installed during this exercise will actually be pretty simple (not to mention useless), but demonstrates the concepts of packaging an application into an MSI file.

1. Install the Veritas Installer Lite software console by running the following file found on the Windows 2000 Professional CD: D:\VALUEADD\ 3RDPARTY\MGMT\WINSTLE\SWIADMLE.MSI (assuming D: is your CD-ROM drive). Note that WinINSTALL is itself distributed as an MSI file. Follow the prompts to install WinINSTALL on your system.

2. Once WinINSTALL is installed, start the software console by selecting Start | Programs | VERITAS Software | VERITAS Software Discover. You will see the following introductory screen.

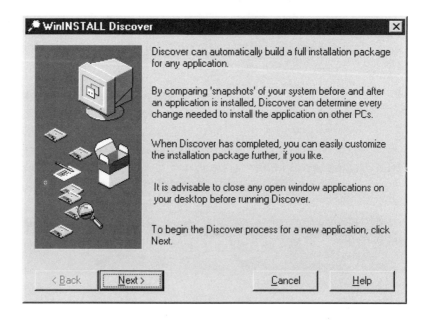

3. Click Next to continue with the wizard. The following screen will appear. From this screen, specify the name of the application (normally along the lines of "Microsoft Excel") and the path where the completed MSI file is to be created. For this example, type **Test Application** and **C:\temp\testapp.msi** in the fields, as shown here. Click Next.

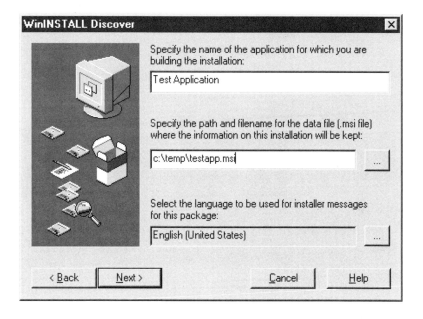

4. The next screen of the wizard is shown in the following illustration. The Discover application needs a temporary location to store its files as it creates the package. Specify a drive with a lot of free space (more than enough to store a copy of the application that you are packaging), and click Next.

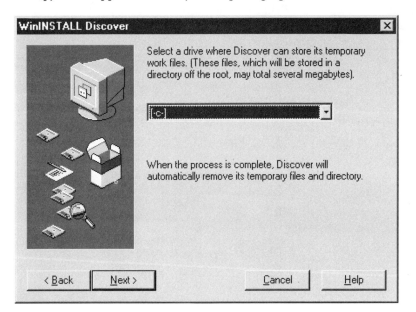

5. During the creation of an Installer package, there will be other activities on the system that may alter files and Registry components unrelated to the application's setup. These changes should not be included and repeated on other machines when the packaged application is installed. Ideally, the

Discover process should be run on a computer that has no third-party software installed and very little customization. If a "clean" computer cannot be found, you can still attempt to create an Installer package, but you will want to limit the places that Discover looks for changes. If your computer has multiple hard disks, some of them can be excluded if the application will not place any files there. The next screen of the wizard, shown here, lets you choose to exclude one or more drives from being scanned. Make sure that the C: drive is included in the Drives To Scan list, and click Next.

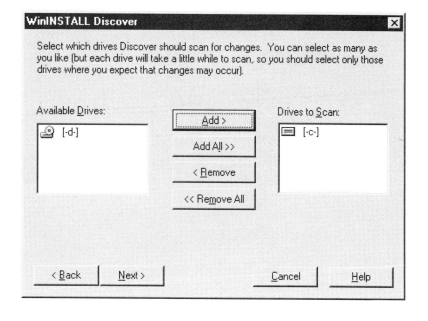

6. In addition to excluding hard drives from scanning, you can choose to exclude certain files and folders from being scanned. The default list shown in the following dialog box should be sufficient for most computers. Note some of the files listed in the Directories And Files To Exclude list. These are files that represent items such as the Virtual Memory swap file, MS Office Fast Find Indexes, and other files and folders that will probably be detected as changed but are unrelated to an application installation. Click Next.

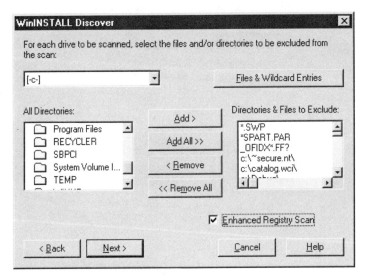

7. WinINSTALL Discover now starts performing the Before scan of the system. This is done to get a snapshot of the system's files, Registry, and INI files before installing the application. You will see a progress box similar to that shown here.

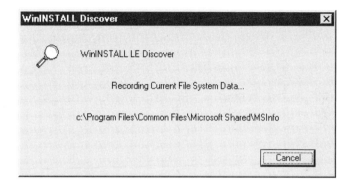

8. When the snapshot is complete, you will see the following dialog box. At this point, you would either click OK to start a vendor-provided install program (if the application being installed does not currently support Installer technology) or Cancel to make manual changes. Click Cancel for this exercise, since we'll be manually creating a simple application.

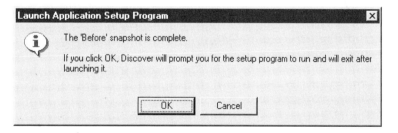

9. Once Discover has exited, create some files and Registry entries that would simulate the types of items that might be created during a real application's installation. In the first screen, shown next, some files and directories have been created under C:\Program Files; and in the second screen, some bogus

Registry entries have been created. These items should be re-created in exactly the same way each time this application is installed.

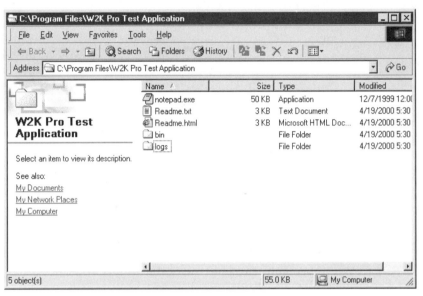

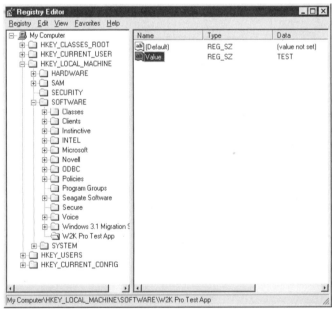

10. Once you have created a few files, directories, and some Registry entries, run the Veritas WinINSTALL Discover program again. When Discover starts up, it should detect that an installation is already in progress and display the following dialog box. From this screen, you have the choice to either run the After scan and complete the installation, or delete all previous settings and start the configuration over. Make sure that Perform The 'After' Snapshot Now is selected, and click Next.

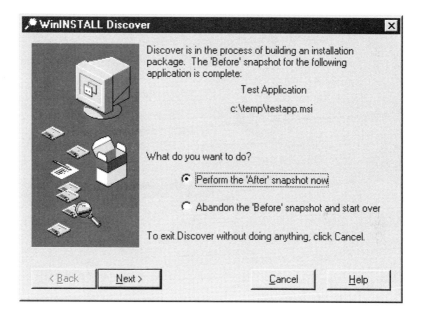

11. Discover now takes another snapshot, showing its progress in a dialog box similar to the one shown here. It is still only checking for changes in the drive, files, and directories that were not excluded in steps 5 and 6.

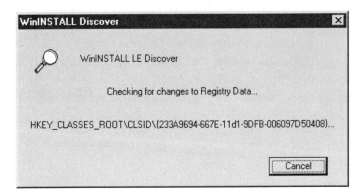

12. Once the After scan is completed, Discover creates the MSI file and reports that the process is completed, as shown here.

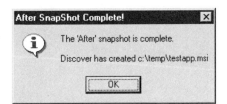

13. Using Explorer, navigate to the location where you told Discover to create the MSI file (c:\temp in this exercise, as shown in the following screen). Note in the illustration to follow that the MSI file has been created, and that there may be other files present in the same directory. The MSI file is the only one needed to re-create the installation on another computer. Right-click the

testapp.msi file and select Edit With WinINSTALL LE from the context menu that appears. Note that there are also options on the context menu to install, uninstall, and repair this application.

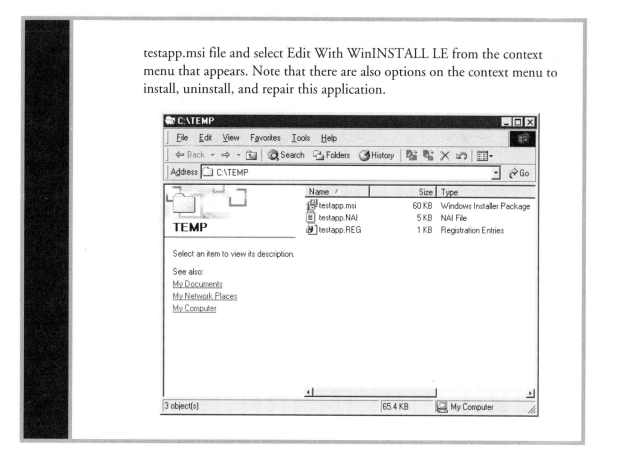

14. Editing the MSI file is done with the other component installed in step 1, the Software Console. The application created in this exercise is shown here. Browse through the items listed and verify that each file, folder, and Registry entry that you manually created is shown in the Editor window.

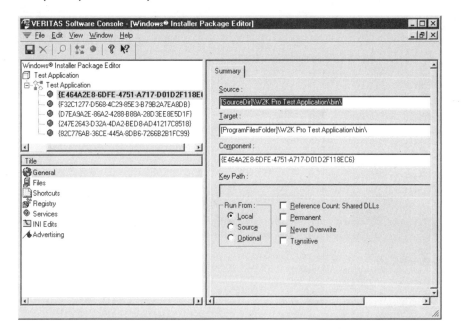

15. The application installed during this exercise was an extremely simple one. The more complicated the application, and the logic required to install the application, the more robust the resulting MSI file needs to be. There are advanced features available in the full version of WinINSTALL and other Installer applications that can help create these more powerful applications. For more information about applications that can create Installer files, see Microsoft's Web site.

16. Exit from the Software Console and close all windows.

Deploying an Installer Package

Once an Installer package is created, it can be deployed to end users in a variety of ways. The easiest way is to make the MSI file available to users through a file server for them to manually install the package (assuming they have the appropriate permissions on their workstation). Once the user receives the MSI file, he or she only has to double-click it in order to install it.

In most cases, an organization that has made the investment in Windows 2000 Professional has also made the investment to deploy Windows 2000 Server and Active Directory. You can take advantage of your Active Directory setup also to assist in deploying software.

Software packages can be made available to users for installation as part of their Active Directory Group Policy Object (GPO). GPOs are collections of settings that allow an administrator to enforce different desktop settings depending on the user account, the groups that users are members of, and where they reside in the Active Directory hierarchy. Software installations are one of these desktop settings.

Software deployed as part of Group Policy can fit into one of the following categories: it can be published to users, assigned to users, or assigned to computers. *Publication* in this context refers to software that is made available to users to install if they choose to do so (optional software), and *assignment* refers to mandatory installation of software. Software assigned or published to a user will be installed under that user's profile wherever that user logs on. Software assigned to a computer is automatically installed on that computer and is available to whoever signs on to that computer.

exam
ⓦatch

While the 70-210 exam focuses mainly on deployment and configuration of Windows 2000 Professional, some basic knowledge of Active Directory and Group Policy concepts is assumed. There are separate exams to certify someone in Active Directory design and implementation. Be sure to read up on these concepts as part of your preparation for 70-210.

CERTIFICATION SUMMARY

In this chapter, we discussed the components and settings that allow an administrator to plan and deploy Windows 2000 to be used in an international organization. The differences between local versions of Windows 2000 Professional and Windows 2000 Locales were also discussed. Local versions of Windows 2000 display the User Interface elements such as menus and dialog boxes in a user's native language, while Locale settings define how applications will process and share data among users who speak different languages.

This chapter also discussed Windows Installer technology. Installer technology allows you to take an application and create a single file that contains the application executables and all logic needed to install that application on any machine. These resulting files can be either directly installed on a client's computer or deployed automatically through integration with Active Directory.

TWO-MINUTE DRILL

Configuring Support for Multiple Languages or Multiple Locations

❑ Windows 2000 Professional can be installed using one of 24 possible localized versions. These localized versions display the User Interface and help files in the local language.

❑ ASCII and EBCDIC are character sets that allow English characters and letters to be displayed in files. Other character sets exist to support other languages.

❑ Unicode is a single-character set that supports characters from most of the world's languages. Applications and documents that use Unicode do not need to switch between character sets to display information in multiple languages.

❑ RTL and other APIs exist to allow developers to create applications that can be displayed correctly in each localized version of Windows 2000. Without these features, a developer would need to create separate programs for each language.

❑ Locales are groups of preferences and settings relating to how a user's local language and customs change how information is formatted. There are three types of Locales: User, Input, and System.

❑ User Locales control how numbers, currency, dates, and times are displayed with regard to the language and country configured.

❑ Input Locales are used to map an input method such as a keyboard or speech-to-text software to an installed language.

❑ System Locales determine which character set and font files will be used.

❑ A Language Group is a collection of all files and configurations required to support a language on Windows 2000. In order to configure a Locale for a particular language or country, the corresponding Language Group must be installed.

Installing Applications by Using Windows Installer Packages

❑ Most Windows applications consist of executable files, Registry settings, and other components that must be installed in certain locations to function correctly.

❑ A software vendor might provide its own utility to create these settings and install an application.

❑ Windows 2000 Installer technology is an updated way to handle these software installations. All required files, settings, and installation logic are contained in a single file with an *.msi extension.

❑ Special applications will be required to help create MSI files. One such utility is included on the Windows 2000 CD.

❑ These applications create the MSI file by looking at a system both before and after an application is installed, and looking at the net changes between the two configurations.

❑ The resulting MSI file can be either installed locally by a user or deployed automatically using Active Directory and Group Policy.

SELF TEST

The following questions will help you measure your understanding of the material presented in this chapter. Read all of the choices carefully, as there may be more than one correct answer. Choose all correct answers for each question.

Configuring Support for Multiple Languages or Multiple Locations

1. Which feature would you use to allow users to see the Windows Graphical User Interface in their native languages? (Select all that apply.)

   A. MultiLanguage version of Windows 2000 Professional

   B. Localized version of Windows 2000 Professional

   C. System Locale

   D. User Locale

2. Which character set is used as part of the default System Locale?

   A. Kanji

   B. ASCII

   C. EBCDIC

   D. Unicode

3. What is the purpose of the Right-to-Left API?

   A. To allow programmers of word processing applications to display text in a document using the correct language

   B. To allow users to share information regardless of the language used

   C. To allow programmers to create applications that will display dialog boxes correctly if a language that reads from right to left is used

   D. To allow an administrator to change character sets

4. Which of the following allow configuration of international or MultiLanguage settings? (Select all that apply.)

   A. Regional Options applet in the Control Panel

   B. System Applet in the Control Panel

   C. Date/Time applet in the Control Panel

   D. Windows 2000 Setup

5. Where are User Locales set?

    A. Control Panel | Users And Passwords

    B. Control Panel | User Locales

    C. Control Panel | Locales

    D. Control Panel | Regional Options

6. Where is the System Locale set? (Select all that apply.)

    A. Control Panel | System

    B. Windows 2000 setup

    C. Control Panel | Locales

    D. Control Panel | Regional Options

7. Where are Input Locales set? (Select all that apply.)

    A. Control Panel | System

    B. Windows 2000 setup

    C. Control Panel | Locales

    D. Control Panel | Regional Options

8. Where can you install Language Groups? (Select all that apply.)

    A. Control Panel | System

    B. Windows 2000 setup

    C. Control Panel | Locales

    D. Control Panel | Regional Options

9. Which of the following are illegal characters for an account name?

    A. e

    B. E

    C. _

    D. É

Installing Applications by Using Windows Installer Packages

10. What extension does an Installer Package use?

    A. *.ins

    B. *.pdf

    C. *.msi

    D. *.mft

11. Which of the following applications might be a candidate for an administrator to repackage before deploying to users?

    A. An application developed by a company's inhouse programming staff

    B. A Windows 2000–certified productivity application

    C. Internet Explorer

    D. Windows 2000 Service Pack

12. Which components are included in an Installer package? (Select all that apply.)

    A. DLL files

    B. Executable programs

    C. Help files

    D. Registry keys

13. Which applications might be used to create an Installer package?

    A. WinINSTALL

    B. SMS Installer

    C. Registry Editor

    D. Explorer

14. Which is a method that might be used to deploy an Installer application?

    A. Send Installer packages via e-mail to users.

    B. Copy Installer packages to a network share.

    C. Assign or Publish the application through Group Policy.

    D. Use Systems Management Server.

15. You have purchased a new utility that you would like to make available to your users if they need it. You have already created the Installer package that performs the installation. Which method would you use to deploy this utility?

   A.   Assign it to all users.

   B.   Publish it to all users.

   C.   Assign it to all computers.

   D.   Publish it to all computers.

16. Where would a user go to install a published Package?

   A.   Control Panel | Regional Options

   B.   Group Policy Management snap-in

   C.   Control Panel | Add/Remove Programs

   D.   Explorer

LAB QUESTION

Your company is about to expand their operations internationally. In addition to the company headquarters in New York, there will soon be offices in London, Paris, Hong Kong, and Moscow.

The company has sent several representatives to oversee the new offices. These representatives all speak the languages of the country in which they will be working, in addition to the languages spoken in the other remote offices. They will need to exchange documents and e-mail with users in the other countries and in the home office. An expansion manager will be frequently visiting each of the new offices. The user in Hong Kong will have a non-Roman keyboard, and the manager will have a microphone and speech-to-text software installed.

You have been asked to plan and deploy the international and multilanguage features of Windows 2000 Professional as appropriate.

How will you plan the deployment? Which features will you deploy to meet the needs of your company? Which features meet which needs?

SELF TEST ANSWERS

Configuring Support for Multiple Languages or Multiple Locations

1. ☑ **A, B.** If you install one of the 24 localized versions of Windows 2000 Professional, then dialog boxes, help files, and menus will be displayed in the installed language. The MultiLanguage version of Windows 2000 Professional contains the files and settings to display the user interface in all 24 supported languages. Using the MultiLanguage version is like having all 24 localized versions installed at once.

☒ **C** is incorrect because the System Locale only determines which fonts and code pages are used. **D** is incorrect because the User Locale determines the formatting of numbers, currency, dates, and times. A localized version of Windows 2000 Professional is required to change the display language of the UI.

2. ☑ **D.** Unicode is a character set that contains the most commonly used letters, numbers, and symbols in most languages, and allows for people to communicate using a single character set.

☒ **A** is incorrect because Kanji is a character set that allows the Chinese and Japanese language to be written. **B** is incorrect because ASCII is an English character set used on earlier PCs. **C** is incorrect because EBCDIC is an English character set used on mainframe computers. These character sets only allow communication in their one configured language, and do not contain provisions for communication in another language.

3. ☑ **C.** The RTL API is one of the features that a programmer can use to create dialog boxes in programs whose controls (check boxes, drop-downs, and so on) will display correctly if either a right-to-left language or a left-to-right language is used.

☒ **A, B,** and **D** are incorrect because these features are a function of the Locale being used, and not a function of the application programming interface being used.

4. ☑ **A, D.** The Regional Options applet in the Control Panel allows you to set User Locales, Input Locales, and install additional Language Groups. Language Groups can also be specified as part of the Windows 2000 setup process.

☒ **B** is incorrect because no options relating to international settings are found in the System applet. **C** is incorrect because the Date/Time applet only allows you to change the value of the system time (assuming you have the appropriate rights), and not how that date and time are displayed or formatted.

5. ☑ **D.** The Regional Options applet in the Control Panel allows you to change the options found in the User Locale, including the formatting of dates, times, currency, and numbers.

☒ **A, B,** and **C** are incorrect. These options either are not found in the Control Panel, or do not contain settings related to User Locales.

6. ☑ **B, D.** The System Locale is a systemwide setting that controls which fonts and character sets are needed for a given language. The availability of a certain language is determined by which Language Groups are installed. Language Groups are installed either as part of the Windows 2000 installation process or after installation in the Regional Options applet in the Control Panel.

   ☒ **A** is incorrect because the System applet contains other systemwide settings such as virtual memory and hardware configuration, but contains no settings related to System Locales. **C** is incorrect, as that option does not exist.

7. ☑ **A, D.** Input Locales are per-user settings that map a language to a method to be used to input characters in that language, usually a keyboard. The hardware device is configured in the Device Manager via Control Panel | System. The mapping between the device and the language is made via Control Panel | Regional Options.

   ☒ **B** is incorrect because Input Locale configuration is not performed from Windows 2000 Setup. **C** is incorrect because that applet does not exist in the Control Panel.

8. ☑ **B, D.** Language Groups are installed either as part of the Windows 2000 setup or after installation via the Regional Options applet in the Control Panel.

   ☒ **A** is incorrect because there are no international or language settings available in the System applet. **C** is incorrect because that applet does not exist in the Control Panel.

9. ☑ **C.** There are no limitations imposed by Locales or languages on the allowable characters of an account name. Other services might have their own limitations; Domain Name Service (DNS), for example, does not allow the underscore character to be used in names.

   ☒ **A, B,** and **D** are incorrect because they are all characters that can be used in account names.

Installing Applications by Using Windows Installer Packages

10. ☑ **C.** An Installer Package can be identified by the *.msi extension at the end of the filename.

    ☒ **A** is incorrect because an INS file is setup information used by older technology used to install software, and is not required for Windows 2000 Installer packages. **B** is incorrect because a PDF file is a Microsoft Systems Management Server package definition file (not to be confused with Adobe's Portable Document Format file!). An SMS PDF file is used to define an SMS-based package, and is not directly compatible with Installer packages. **D** is incorrect because the *.mft file extension is not related to Installer technology.

11. ☑ **A.** Deploying a custom or in-house application is one of the reasons to use a repackager to deploy the application.

☒   **B** and **D** are incorrect, since an application that is certified to be in the Windows 2000 Logo program should already be capable of being deployed as an Installer application. Windows 2000 Service Packs will be available as Installer files. **C** is incorrect because an application that has its own deployment utility, such as the Internet Explorer Administration Kit, should use that utility instead of repackaging.

12.   ☑   **A, B, C, D.** An Installer package contains all of the items needed to install an application on a user's computer. An application might consist of programs, DLLs, Registry settings, and help files, all of which can be packaged into an Installer file.

13.   ☑   **A.** WinINSTALL is one application that can be used to create Installer packages. A limited version of WinINSTALL is included on the Windows 2000 CD, and there are other products available from third-party software companies.
☒   **B** is incorrect because SMS Installer packages are not compatible with Installer packages, but can be converted using a utility found in SMS 2.0 SP2. **C** is incorrect because, while changes to the Registry are part of an application's installation, simply manipulating the Registry is not enough to create an Installer application. **D** is incorrect because Explorer cannot be used to create an Installer package.

14.   ☑   **B, C.** The best choices are B and C. Copying an MSI file to a file share will allow users to install the application when it is convenient to do so. Deploying applications with Group Policy will allow an administrator to control which applications can or should be installed for groups of users.
☒   **A** is incorrect. It is possible to send users small Installer packages through e-mail, but usually e-mail is not intended to be used to transfer large files. **D** is incorrect because even if SMS is deployed in an organization, SMS packages are incompatible with Windows 2000 Installer packages.

15.   ☑   **B.** Publishing an application makes it available for users to install if they choose to do so.
☒   **A** and **C** are incorrect because assigning an application would force it to be installed, and in this case, the utility being installed is optional. **D** is incorrect because applications can only be published to users, not computers.

16.   ☑   **C.** Once an application has been published, a user can install it by going to the Add/Remove Programs applet in the Control Panel.
☒   **A** is incorrect because the Regional Options applet does not have settings for the publication or assignment of applications. **B** is incorrect because administrators use the Group Policy snap-in to publish the application, but users do not use this snap-in to install the application. **D** is incorrect because published applications do not appear in Explorer.

LAB ANSWER

There are many ways to arrive at an answer to this scenario. The answer presented here is one approach.

First, develop the list of criteria:

- Hardware deployed to the sales force must present the Windows User Interface to each user in the appropriate local language.

- The expansion manager should have the UI for all countries installed.

- Per-user and per-computer settings should be made to facilitate written communication between and among the offices and the employees in each country.

Then, match a feature of Windows 2000 to each requirement:

- Deploying the appropriate localized version of Windows 2000 Professional in English, French, Chinese, and Russian will allow each employee working in each country to view the Windows UI in the appropriate language.

- Deploying the MultiLanguage version of Windows 2000 Professional on the manager's computer will allow the manager to choose the language in which his or her UI is displayed.

- Regardless of the language being displayed in the UI, each employee will be able to communicate with other employees using Locales.

- On each computer, install the following Language Groups: English (U.S.), English (U.K.), French (France), Russian, and Chinese. The presence of these Language Groups will allow you to enable various Locales.

- Enable the appropriate User Locale to allow each user to display date, time, numbers, and currency according to his or her country.

- Install the appropriate Input Locale for each user, and ensure that the input device or IME is mapped correctly. Verify that the non-Roman keyboard and the speech-to-text software work correctly, and enable the manager to switch Input Locales quickly by installing the option in the taskbar.

You do not need to do anything extra to set the correct System Locale. The default System Locale is Unicode based, and will allow all users in each country to communicate.

MICROSOFT CERTIFIED SYSTEMS ENGINEER

11

Implementing, Managing, and Troubleshooting Network Protocols and Services

I n the 1960s and 1970s, the use of computers became widespread, and the need for them to communicate with each other became the Mother of Invention. This ability to communicate only fueled the fire even more. Most communication protocols were proprietary to the manufacturer of the computer. The need for different computers to communicate became known as internetworking. The United States Government's Advanced Research Project Agency, or ARPA, funded a number of projects. One of the most significant projects was the technology known as *packet switching*. Packet-switched networks break down data into smaller packets with addresses for the sender and the destination. This enabled routing of these packets, thereby creating the ability to form subnetworks (or subnets). Routers determined how to deliver these packets to the correct destination. ARPA interconnected all their research sites into a network known as ARPANET. This became so successful that many different agencies began working on a standardized set of internetworking protocols—TCP/IP (Transmission Control Protocol/ Internet Protocol) was born! The ARPANET backbone became known as the Internet. The Department of Defense, because of this success, required that all DoD systems connected to wide area networks use TCP/IP as the standard. These standards are developed through the RFC (Request for Comments). You may see these RFCs referenced throughout this chapter, and you would be well advised to explore them to gain greater understanding of the material offered here.

As the Internet grew, the task of managing the millions of computers became more than ARPANET and its offspring NSFNET (National Science Foundation) could handle. Most Internet traffic is now handled by telecommunications companies and Internet Service Providers (ISPs). TCP/IP has become the de facto standard for internetworking communication.

TCP/IP is an industry standard suite of protocols that is the dominant means of communication in Windows 2000. Understanding TCP/IP is integral to Windows 2000.

We will start with an explanation of the Protocol layer, and how it relates to the DoD model. We will also go into how to install TCP/IP and test for connectivity using the various tools that it provides. This suite of protocols is also used to connect to the Internet and other networks using a dial-up connection. In fact, TCP/IP is so widespread that it is used for LAN and WAN communication, as well as the Internet. We will explain how this rich set of protocols enables us to perform many tasks.

Configuring and Troubleshooting the TCP/IP Protocol

Imagine that you are traveling in a country that you have never been to before. It is in a remote part of the world, and you don't speak the language, nor do you know anything about the local customs. You can imagine that communication would be difficult. In fact, the very act of holding out your hand may signify hostility in this strange culture. The point is, you do not know the culture's *protocols*.

TCP/IP is a suite of protocols. It is a set of standards and rules that allow computers to communicate. In order to fully understand how Windows 2000 communicates with other computers, you must have an understanding of TCP/IP.

TCP/IP is defined in four layers:

- **Application**   The Application layer is the top layer in this model. Its function is to provide access to the network for applications that you are running. Two interfaces accomplish this: Winsock and NetBIOS over TCP/IP (NetBT). Examples of these types of applications include Telnet, FTP, and SMTP.

- **Transport (or Host to Host)**   The Transport layer is responsible for providing a reliable exchange of information. It supports multiple simultaneous end-to-end transfers of data. The two protocols at this level are TCP and UDP.

    - **TCP** is a connection-oriented protocol. It is typically used to transfer large amounts of data. It provides a guarantee of delivery, acknowledgments, and proper sequencing of data. A checksum validates the data's integrity.

    - **UDP** is used for small amounts of data. It is connectionless and unreliable. The guaranteed delivery of the packets is the responsibility of the application.

- **Internet (Internetwork)** The Internet layer is where the data is encapsulated. It shields the upper layers from the physical network, providing a "virtual network" view. It also provides routing functions.

  - **IP** (Internet Protocol) is the main protocol at this layer, and provides connectionless packet delivery for all other protocols in the TCP/IP suite. There is no guarantee of delivery or that packets arrive in the proper order; that is the function of higher-layer protocols.

  - **ARP** (Address Resolution Protocol) provides a mapping of IP addresses to MAC sublayer addresses. IP sends a broadcast, and the owner of that address sends back its MAC address.

  - **IGMP** (Internet Group Management Protocol) provides muticasting. Host membership of a group has its information provided to routers by IGMP. Microsoft NetShow is an example of a multicast program.

  - **ICMP** (Internet Control Message Protocol) allows hosts to share status and error messages. PING is a utility that uses ICMP packets.

- **Network Interface** The Network Interface layer is the lowest level of the suite, and is responsible for putting packets onto the wire. It is the interface to the actual network hardware. TCP/IP does not specify any actual protocol here; it can use almost any networking interface: Ethernet, Token Ring, FDDI, ATM, X.25, and others (Table 11-1).

Troubleshooting Tools

Windows 2000 comes with many tools that you can use to help troubleshoot the network and connectivity.

TABLE 11-1 The Four Layers of TCP/IP and Protocols Used

Application	Transport	Internet	Network
Winsock	TCP	IP, ICMP, IGMP, ARP	Ethernet, Token Ring, FDDI
NetBIOS	UDP		WAN (Frame Relay, ATM, Serial Lines)

Ipconfig   Ipconfig is a utility that will show you the IP configuration of a host. Open a command prompt (click Start | Run, type **cmd**, and then click OK). At the command prompt, type **ipconfig /?**. You will be presented with a list of command-line parameters and a short explanation of what they do. The /all parameter will produce a detailed readout of all interfaces. This is a great way to get a quick snapshot of IP information as it is configured on your PC. With this handy tool, you can easily see if something has been configured incorrectly (Figure 11-1).

Ping   Ping is a utility used to test connectivity. It sends an ICMP echo request to a target address or name. Type **ping -?** at a command prompt to see what your command-line options are. A typical scenario in which you would use this tool would be if you were unable to connect to a host on another network. A logical approach would be to first ping the local loopback address, 127.0.0.1. Open a command prompt and type **ping 127.0.0.1**. This is a simple test to see if TCP/IP is installed and working properly (Figure 11-2).

Next, you should ping the IP address assigned to your network card. If this does not work but the previous test did, then you know that your network configuration is wrong.

FIGURE 11-1

Ipconfig display output

```
D:\WINNT\System32\cmd.exe                                                _ □ ×
Microsoft Windows 2000 [Version 5.00.2195]
(C) Copyright 1985-1999 Microsoft Corp.

D:\>ipconfig /all

Windows 2000 IP Configuration

        Host Name . . . . . . . . . . . . : home-vg1ip26xje
        Primary DNS Suffix  . . . . . . . :
        Node Type . . . . . . . . . . . . : Broadcast
        IP Routing Enabled. . . . . . . . : No
        WINS Proxy Enabled. . . . . . . . : No

Ethernet adapter Local Area Connection:

        Connection-specific DNS Suffix  . :
        Description . . . . . . . . . . . : Macronix MX98715 Family Fast Etherne
t Adapter (ACPI)
        Physical Address. . . . . . . . . : 00-80-C6-F7-39-70
        DHCP Enabled. . . . . . . . . . . : Yes
        Autoconfiguration Enabled . . . . : Yes
        IP Address. . . . . . . . . . . . : 24.188.68.30
        Subnet Mask . . . . . . . . . . . : 255.255.255.0
        Default Gateway . . . . . . . . . : 24.188.68.1
        DHCP Server . . . . . . . . . . . : 10.1.0.49
        DNS Servers . . . . . . . . . . . : 167.206.112.4
                                            167.206.112.3
        Lease Obtained. . . . . . . . . . : Saturday, April 01, 2000 8:05:49 AM
        Lease Expires . . . . . . . . . . : Tuesday, April 04, 2000 9:05:49 PM

D:\>
```

FIGURE 11-2

Result of pinging
the loopback
adapter

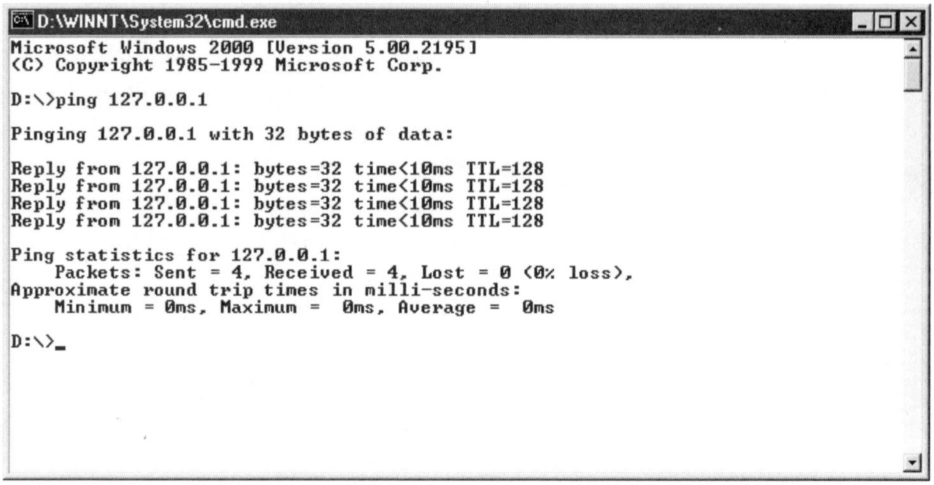

```
D:\WINNT\System32\cmd.exe                                    _ □ ×

Microsoft Windows 2000 [Version 5.00.2195]
(C) Copyright 1985-1999 Microsoft Corp.

D:\>ping 127.0.0.1

Pinging 127.0.0.1 with 32 bytes of data:

Reply from 127.0.0.1: bytes=32 time<10ms TTL=128
Reply from 127.0.0.1: bytes=32 time<10ms TTL=128
Reply from 127.0.0.1: bytes=32 time<10ms TTL=128
Reply from 127.0.0.1: bytes=32 time<10ms TTL=128

Ping statistics for 127.0.0.1:
    Packets: Sent = 4, Received = 4, Lost = 0 (0% loss),
Approximate round trip times in milli-seconds:
    Minimum = 0ms, Maximum =  0ms, Average =  0ms

D:\>_
```

The next step is to ping an address on your local network. If this fails while the previous two tests did not, then you have either an address configuration or a hardware problem. Most likely, you have a cable or hub failure. It is also possible to have a corrupted ARP cache.

If you have passed all these tests so far, you should ping the default gateway address. If this step fails, you could have the wrong gateway address, a possible port failure on the gateway, or the gateway is down or not configured correctly.

Next in line in our troubleshooting scenario is to ping a remote host address. If this is the only step that fails, then you most likely have a misconfigured or malfunctioning gateway, or the subnet mask is incorrect.

You can also try pinging by the name of a host. If you are successful, it will indicate that TCP/IP name resolution is functioning properly.

Tracert   Tracert is used to trace a route from one host to another. It uses the IP TTL field and ICMP error messages to accomplish this. A sample output is shown in Figure 11-3.

Type **tracert** and then press ENTER to see the command-line parameters. You can trace by host name or IP address.

Pathping   A new tool in Windows 2000 is pathping, which is a combination of the ping and tracert tools. Pathping supplies addition information that these tools do not provide. When pathping is first run, you see an output similar to the tracert

FIGURE 11-3

Tracert display
output

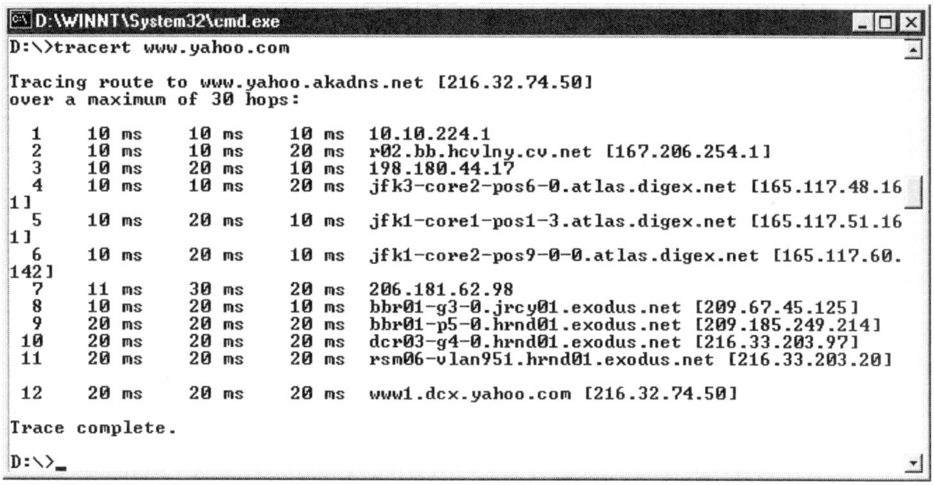

```
D:\WINNT\System32\cmd.exe                                        _ □ ×
D:\>tracert www.yahoo.com

Tracing route to www.yahoo.akadns.net [216.32.74.50]
over a maximum of 30 hops:

  1    10 ms    10 ms    10 ms  10.10.224.1
  2    10 ms    10 ms    20 ms  r02.bb.hcvlny.cv.net [167.206.254.1]
  3    10 ms    20 ms    10 ms  198.180.44.17
  4    10 ms    10 ms    20 ms  jfk3-core2-pos6-0.atlas.digex.net [165.117.48.16
1]
  5    10 ms    20 ms    10 ms  jfk1-core1-pos1-3.atlas.digex.net [165.117.51.16
1]
  6    10 ms    20 ms    10 ms  jfk1-core2-pos9-0-0.atlas.digex.net [165.117.60.
142]
  7    11 ms    30 ms    20 ms  206.181.62.98
  8    10 ms    20 ms    10 ms  bbr01-g3-0.jrcy01.exodus.net [209.67.45.125]
  9    20 ms    20 ms    20 ms  bbr01-p5-0.hrnd01.exodus.net [209.185.249.214]
 10    20 ms    20 ms    20 ms  dcr03-g4-0.hrnd01.exodus.net [216.33.203.97]
 11    20 ms    20 ms    20 ms  rsm06-vlan951.hrnd01.exodus.net [216.33.203.20]

 12    20 ms    20 ms    20 ms  www1.dcx.yahoo.com [216.32.74.50]

Trace complete.

D:\>_
```

command. This is the path that the packets take to reach their destination. Pathping
sends packets to each of these routers and then computes the results based on
returned packets from each hop. At each router, pathping shows the percentage of
packet loss. This is valuable information in determining the weak link that may be
causing problems.

Arp Arp is used for viewing the ARP cache. If two hosts on the same subnet
cannot ping each other, you should try running the **arp** -a command on both
computers. This will tell you if they have the correct MAC address configured
for each other. Type **arp** and press ENTER for a list of command-line parameters
(Figure 11-4).

Route You can use route to view or change the local routing tables. Type **route**
at a command prompt to view all the syntax and command-line parameters. **Print**
will display a list of all the current routes in the host's routing table. **Add** will add
a route, and **delete** will delete a route from the table. When adding a route to the
table, you should use the -p switch to make it persistent. If this switch is not used,
the route will only be in the table until you reboot your computer (Figure 11-5).

Netstat Netstat is a useful tool that can display all connections and protocol
statistics for TCP/IP. Typing **netstat ?** will display the available switches (Figure 11-6).

FIGURE 11-4

Arp display details

```
Command Prompt                                                        _ □ ×
Microsoft Windows 2000 [Version 5.00.2195]
(C) Copyright 1985-1999 Microsoft Corp.

D:\>arp

Displays and modifies the IP-to-Physical address translation tables used by
address resolution protocol (ARP).

ARP -s inet_addr eth_addr [if_addr]
ARP -d inet_addr [if_addr]
ARP -a [inet_addr] [-N if_addr]

   -a              Displays current ARP entries by interrogating the current
                   protocol data.  If inet_addr is specified, the IP and Physical
                   addresses for only the specified computer are displayed.  If
                   more than one network interface uses ARP, entries for each ARP
                   table are displayed.
   -g              Same as -a.
   inet_addr       Specifies an internet address.
   -N if_addr      Displays the ARP entries for the network interface specified
                   by if_addr.
   -d              Deletes the host specified by inet_addr. inet_addr may be
                   wildcarded with * to delete all hosts.
   -s              Adds the host and associates the Internet address inet_addr
                   with the Physical address eth_addr.  The Physical address is
                   given as 6 hexadecimal bytes separated by hyphens. The entry
                   is permanent.
   eth_addr        Specifies a physical address.
   if_addr         If present, this specifies the Internet address of the
                   interface whose address translation table should be modified.
                   If not present, the first applicable interface will be used.
Example:
   > arp -s 157.55.85.212   00-aa-00-62-c6-09   .... Adds a static entry.
   > arp -a                                     .... Displays the arp table.

D:\>_
```

FIGURE 11-5

Route print
display output

```
Command Prompt                                                        _ □ ×
Microsoft Windows 2000 [Version 5.00.2195]
(C) Copyright 1985-1999 Microsoft Corp.

D:\>route print
===========================================================================
Interface List
0x1 ........................... MS TCP Loopback interface
0x2 ...00 80 c6 f7 39 70 ...... PCI Bus Master Adapter
===========================================================================
===========================================================================
Active Routes:
Network Destination        Netmask          Gateway       Interface  Metric
          0.0.0.0          0.0.0.0      24.188.68.1    24.188.68.30       1
      24.188.68.0    255.255.255.0     24.188.68.30    24.188.68.30       1
     24.188.68.30  255.255.255.255      127.0.0.1       127.0.0.1        1
   24.255.255.255  255.255.255.255     24.188.68.30    24.188.68.30       1
        127.0.0.0        255.0.0.0      127.0.0.1       127.0.0.1        1
        224.0.0.0        224.0.0.0     24.188.68.30    24.188.68.30       1
  255.255.255.255  255.255.255.255     24.188.68.30    24.188.68.30       1
Default Gateway:       24.188.68.1
===========================================================================
Persistent Routes:
  None

D:\>
```

FIGURE 11-6

Netstat display
details

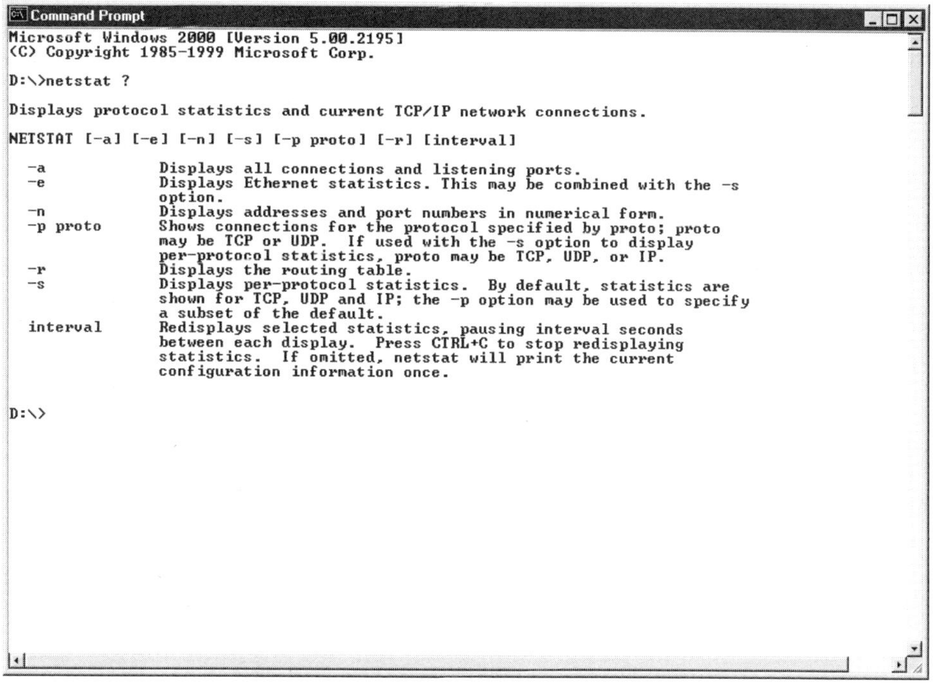

```
Command Prompt                                                    _ □ ×
Microsoft Windows 2000 [Version 5.00.2195]
(C) Copyright 1985-1999 Microsoft Corp.

D:\>netstat ?

Displays protocol statistics and current TCP/IP network connections.

NETSTAT [-a] [-e] [-n] [-s] [-p proto] [-r] [interval]

  -a           Displays all connections and listening ports.
  -e           Displays Ethernet statistics. This may be combined with the -s
               option.
  -n           Displays addresses and port numbers in numerical form.
  -p proto     Shows connections for the protocol specified by proto; proto
               may be TCP or UDP.  If used with the -s option to display
               per-protocol statistics, proto may be TCP, UDP, or IP.
  -r           Displays the routing table.
  -s           Displays per-protocol statistics.  By default, statistics are
               shown for TCP, UDP and IP; the -p option may be used to specify
               a subset of the default.
  interval     Redisplays selected statistics, pausing interval seconds
               between each display.  Press CTRL+C to stop redisplaying
               statistics.  If omitted, netstat will print the current
               configuration information once.


D:\>
```

Nbtstat Nbtstat is used for troubleshooting NetBIOS name resolution problems. You can use this tool to check the state of NetBIOS over TCP/IP connections, display and change the NetBIOS name cache, and list current NetBIOS sessions including statistics. New in Windows 2000 (and NT4 SP5) is the -RR switch. This reregisters all names with a WINS server (Figure 11-7).

Nslookup Nslookup is used for troubleshooting DNS problems. Type **nslookup** and press ENTER at a command prompt. Nslookup will display the currently configured DNS server's name and IP address. It will then return you to a command prompt. If you type **?** at this point, it will display all the switches and options. If you want to find the IP address of a host, just type the host name and press ENTER. You can also enter debug mode by typing **set debug**, or for even more information, type **set d2**. This will make nslookup list all the steps it takes to perform your command (Figure 11-8).

Microsoft Network Monitor Windows 2000 includes a scaled-down version of Network Monitor. The full version is a part of Microsoft's Systems Management

```
Command Prompt                                                                    _ □ ×
Microsoft Windows 2000 [Version 5.00.2195]
(C) Copyright 1985-1999 Microsoft Corp.

D:\>nbtstat

Displays protocol statistics and current TCP/IP connections using NBT
(NetBIOS over TCP/IP).

NBTSTAT [ [-a RemoteName] [-A IP address] [-c] [-n]
        [-r] [-R] [-RR] [-s] [-S] [interval] ]

  -a   (adapter status) Lists the remote machine's name table given its name
  -A   (Adapter status) Lists the remote machine's name table given its
                        IP address.
  -c   (cache)          Lists NBT's cache of remote [machine] names and their IP addresses
  -n   (names)          Lists local NetBIOS names.
  -r   (resolved)       Lists names resolved by broadcast and via WINS
  -R   (Reload)         Purges and reloads the remote cache name table
  -S   (Sessions)       Lists sessions table with the destination IP addresses
  -s   (sessions)       Lists sessions table converting destination IP
                        addresses to computer NETBIOS names.
  -RR  (ReleaseRefresh) Sends Name Release packets to WINs and then, starts Refresh

  RemoteName  Remote host machine name.
  IP address  Dotted decimal representation of the IP address.
  interval    Redisplays selected statistics, pausing interval seconds
              between each display. Press Ctrl+C to stop redisplaying
              statistics.


D:\>
```

```
Command Prompt - nslookup                                                         _ □ ×
Microsoft Windows 2000 [Version 5.00.2195]
(C) Copyright 1985-1999 Microsoft Corp.

D:\>nslookup
Default Server:  caps-he2.optonline.net
Address:  167.206.112.4

> ?
Commands:   (identifiers are shown in uppercase, [] means optional)
NAME            - print info about the host/domain NAME using default server
NAME1 NAME2     - as above, but use NAME2 as server
help or ?       - print info on common commands
set OPTION      - set an option
    all             - print options, current server and host
    [no]debug       - print debugging information
    [no]d2          - print exhaustive debugging information
    [no]defname     - append domain name to each query
    [no]recurse     - ask for recursive answer to query
    [no]search      - use domain search list
    [no]vc          - always use a virtual circuit
    domain=NAME     - set default domain name to NAME
    srchlist=N1[/N2/.../N6] - set domain to N1 and search list to N1,N2, etc.
    root=NAME       - set root server to NAME
    retry=X         - set number of retries to X
    timeout=X       - set initial time-out interval to X seconds
    type=X          - set query type (ex. A,ANY,CNAME,MX,NS,PTR,SOA,SRV)
    querytype=X     - same as type
    class=X         - set query class (ex. IN (Internet), ANY)
    [no]msxfr       - use MS fast zone transfer
    ixfrver=X       - current version to use in IXFR transfer request
server NAME     - set default server to NAME, using current default server
lserver NAME    - set default server to NAME, using initial server
finger [USER]   - finger the optional NAME at the current default host
root            - set current default server to the root
ls [opt] DOMAIN [> FILE] - list addresses in DOMAIN (optional: output to FILE)
    -a              - list canonical names and aliases
    -d              - list all records
    -t TYPE         - list records of the given type (e.g. A,CNAME,MX,NS,PTR etc.)
view FILE           - sort an 'ls' output file and view it with pg
exit            - exit the program

>
```

Server. When a server computer is running Network Monitor, it can attach to other computers running the agent software. This can be done either on the network you are attached to or via dial up. The basic difference between the two versions is that the limited version can only capture packets to and from the computer being traced. These captured packets can be filtered by NIC address, protocol, and patterns.

This tool must be installed on Windows 2000 Server. The Network Monitor Driver is installed on Windows 2000 Professional. Although this is not strictly a utility that is a part of TCP/IP, it is an extremely useful tool that Microsoft provides in Windows 2000 Professional.

To install the Network Monitor Driver, click Start | Settings | Control Panel, and then double-click Network and Dial-Up Connections. In Network And Dial-Up Connections, right-click Local Area Connection, and click Properties. In the Local Area Connection Properties dialog box, click Install. In the Select Network Component Type dialog box, click Protocol, and then click Add. In the Select Network Protocol dialog box, click Network Monitor Driver, and then click OK.

e x a m
Ⓦ a t c h   *Be sure to be familiar with the different switches for each of the TCP/IP tools.*

Configuring a DHCP Client

A client that is configured as a DHCP (Dynamic Host Configuration Protocol) client receives its TCP/IP information automatically from a DHCP server. DHCP is open and standards based, as defined by IETF Requests for Comments (RFCs) 2131 and 2132.

By enabling DHCP on the clients on your network, you can avoid the many problems associated with a manual configuration.

The information that it can automatically receive is

- IP address
- Subnet mask
- Default gateway
- DNS server
- WINS server

The DHCP client upon booting up requests its IP address from a pool of addresses (its scope) defined on the DHCP server. The DHCP server offers its information, and if the client accepts the offer, the DHCP server leases the IP information to the client for a specified period of time.

By enabling DHCP on the clients, you eliminate the need to manually configure each client with its IP address, subnet mask, and default gateway, in addition to any DNS and WINS servers that it needs to know about. This makes your job a lot easier!

You need at least one server configured as a DHCP server. It can be a stand-alone server or a domain controller. For a server to function as a DHCP server, you need it to run the DHCP service. It must also have a static IP address; in other words, it can't be a DHCP client. The DHCP server must also have a scope defined so that the clients can get their IP information from it.

The clients, on the other hand, need to be running Windows 2000, NT 3.51 or later, Windows 95 or later, WFW3.11 with MS TCP/IP-32, MS Network Client v 3 for MS-DOS (with the real-mode TCP/IP driver), or LAN Manager2.2c (2.2c for OS/2 is not supported).

DHCP and APIPA

A new feature in Windows 2000 is that if the DHCP server is not available when the DHCP client boots up, Windows 2000 (and Windows 98) will assign an IP address to itself via Automatic IP Addressing, or APIPA. This is a limited network functionality feature that will assign an address from the 169.254.0.0 to 169.254.255.255 pool with a subnet mask of 255.255.0.0. The client will use this address until it receives information from a DHCP server. It assigns this address to itself via broadcast if no other host responds to the same address. The limited functionality of this feature is such that no other TCP/IP configuration information is assigned besides the IP address. This infers that the only communication available is to the local subnet. Change the IP Autoconfiguration-enabled value to 0 to turn off APIPA. It is REG-WORD data type. The value of 1 (which is the default) will enable it.

exam
ⓦatch

Please note that new features in Windows 2000 are more than fair game as a topic for an exam question. Automatic IP Addressing is more than likely to show up in some form.

DHCP Lease Renewal

If the client attempts to renew a lease that it had previously obtained and is unable to do so, it will ping the default gateway specified in the lease. If it succeeds, it will continue to use the lease assigned. It will also try to renew the lease when half of it expires.

If the ping to the gateway fails, the client assumes it has been moved to a network that does not have DHCP available, and then configures itself. It will also attempt to renew the lease every five minutes.

EXERCISE 11-1

Enabling Windows 2000 to Be a DHCP Client

The actual steps needed to enable Windows 2000 to be a DHCP client are quite simple.

1. Right-click My Network Places and select Properties from the resulting context menu.

2. Right-click the Local Area Connection icon in the Network And Dial-Up Connections window. Click Properties.

3. In the Local Area Connection Properties dialog box, make sure that the check box is selected next to Internet Protocol (TCP/IP). Select this entry and click Properties, as shown in the following dialog box.

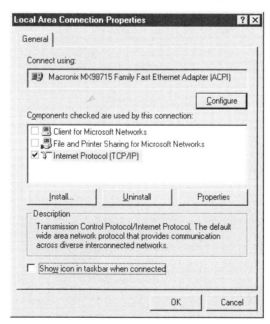

4. On the Internet Protocol (TCP/IP) Properties General tab, make sure that Obtain An IP Address Automatically is enabled, as shown here.

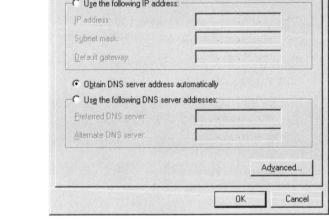

5. Click OK to close the Network And Dial-Up Connections window.

Assigning a Static IP Address

If you are part of a workgroup or do not have a dedicated server that is running a DHCP server, you need to assign a static IP address. It is important to understand how IP addressing and subnetting work. Although the issue of subnetting is not a focus of the Windows 2000 Professional exam, a basic understanding is warranted.

IP Subnetting

Subnetting is, in fact, quite easy when you understand the ground rules. The first thing you have to know how to do is convert from binary (base 2) to decimal (base 10) and back again. I can recommend *Troubleshooting Windows 2000 TCP/IP,* by Debra and Thomas Shinder, for a thorough discussion of this conversion process. In the meantime, you can use the Windows Calculator to do any conversions you may need. You should also know about how addresses are made up of four 8-bit octets. Remember that subnet masking is exactly that: you are masking a portion of the IP address to be used for the network ID, and the remainder for hosts.

You have to know two other things up front:

- What type of address you have been assigned or are working with—Class A, B, or C.
- How many subnets and /or hosts you need.

For the purpose of this discussion, we will assume it is a Class B address. Let's say you need 25 subnets with 500 hosts on each. Okay, let's see if that is possible. Look at Table 11-2 (you will have to memorize this to do this fast!); specifically, look at the Subnets Available row. Which one is the lowest value that will include 25 plus 1 subnets? 30 of course! Your subnet mask for a Class B address is 248, or 255.255.248.0 from the "This is your mask," row. If I asked for 31 subnets, you would have done 31 + 1 = 32, and the next highest is 64, so your subnet would have been 252, or 255.255.252.

We have determined the subnet mask pretty quickly. How many hosts can we have on each of the 25 subnets in our example? Look at the column that has the 248 mask, and note what bit position it is—5, so we have three left for the hosts! Now add that to the 8 bit positions from the last octet, and we have 11 available positions for the hosts (remember, this is a Class B address, so the last two octets are available for hosts and subnets). Now, take 2 to the 11th power and subtract 2. What do you get?

2,4,8,16,32,64,128,256,512,1024,2048!! 2048 less 2 = 2046 hosts per subnet

TABLE 11-2   Addressing and Subnetting table

Bit position	8	7	6	5	4	3	2	1
Power of 2	256	128	64	32	16	8	4	2
High bit sum (reversed); This is your mask.	255	254	252	248	240	224	192	128
Subnets available	254	126	62	30	14	6	2	0
To find network IDs								
Bit position from above	1	2	3	4	5	6	7	8
Pattern key	128	64	32	16	8	4	2	1

Now for the last and best part: What are the valid host IDs? Go to the table, look at the column that has our subnet mask, note the bit position (5), and look at the bottom two rows of our table. What is the pattern key for that bit position—8! Okay, assume we were assigned a Class B IP address of 145.15.0.0. The first group of valid host IDs, using a subnet mask of 255.255.248.0, would use this pattern starting with 8 and increasing in intervals of 8. Therefore, we would get 145.15.8.0, then 145.15.16.0, and then 145.15.24.0, until we ran out at 145.15.248.0, which we can't use because it is all 1's. So then you take the first address we got and add 1 so we get 145.15.8.1. This is the beginning of the range of valid host IDs on a subnet. To get the ending address of the range, take the next address in the pattern-generated addresses (145.15.16.0), subtract 2, and we get 145.15.15.254.

Voilà! We have our range for the first subnet, 145.15.8.1 through 145.15.15.254!!! Repeat this for all subsequent subnets and we get

145.15.16.1 through 145.15.23.254

145.15.24.1 through 145.15.31.254

145.15.32.1 through 145.15.39.254

145.15.40.1 through 145.15.47.254

145.15.48.1 through 145.15.55.254

145.15.56.1 through 145.15.63.254

145.15.64.1 through 145.15.71.254

We continue in this manner until we have reached

145.15.240.1 through 145.15.247.254

exam
⚠atch

Although subnetting is not a stated exam objective, it is assumed that you have a basic knowledge of IP addressing. The material presented here should more than suffice. You should be aware of the default subnet masks and ranges for each class of IP address (Table 11-3). Class D is used for multicasting, and Class E is for experimental use.

Now back to the more hands-on stuff.

	Class	Range of IP Addresses	Default Mask
TABLE 11-3	Class A	1 to 126.*x.y.z*	255.0.0.0
The Default Subnet Masks and Ranges for Each Class of IP	Class B	128 to 191.*x.y.z*	255.255.0.0
	Class C	192 to 223.*x.y.z*	255.255.255.0

Configuring TCP/IP Properties in Windows 2000 Professional

Now that you have your subnets and IP addresses, let's assign them to the Windows 2000 clients.

Go to Start | Settings | Network And Dial-Up Connections, and right-click the connection you want to configure. Click Properties in the resulting dialog box, highlight the Internet Protocol (TCP/IP), and click Properties. You are then presented with the Internet Protocol (TCP/IP) Properties dialog box. It is here that we can configure TCP/IP. Select the Use The Following IP Address radio button. You are now able to enter the IP address assigned to the computer. The subnet mask and default gateway are also entered here. If you are using a DNS server on your network, enter the primary and secondary (Alternate) name servers' IP addresses in the respective fields. When you have finished, click OK (Figure 11-9).

FIGURE 11-9

Internet Protocol (TCP/IP) Properties General tab for static address assignment

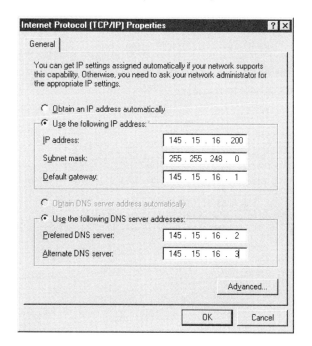

Add IPSec

Internet Protocol Security (IPSec) provides application-transparent authentication and encryption services at the Internetwork layer for communications sent over an IP network. Windows 2000's implementation of IPSec is *policy based.*

To configure an IPSec policy, you must first add the Computer Management, Group Policy, and Certificates snap-ins to the Microsoft Management Console.

CertCam 11-2

Adding a Snap-In to the Microsoft Management Console

EXERCISE 11-2

1. Click Start | Run, and in the Open text box, type **mmc**. Click OK.

2. On the Console menu, click Add/Remove Snap-In.

3. In the Add/Remove Snap-In dialog box, click Add.

4. In the Add Standalone Snap-In dialog box, click Computer Management, and then click Add.

5. Make sure that the Local Computer is selected, and then click Finish.

6. In the Add Standalone Snap-In dialog box, click Group Policy, and then click Add.

7. Make sure that that Local Computer is selected in the Group Policy Object dialog box, and then click Finish.

8. In the Add Standalone Snap-In dialog box, click Certificates, and then click Add.

9. Select Computer Account, and click Next.

10. Verify that Local Computer is selected, and click Finish.

11. Click Close, and then OK.

IPSec Overview   IP Security (IPSec) and TCP/IP filtering are the two basic methods of securing IP packets. IP Security authenticates and can optionally encrypt data at the packet level. TCP/IP filtering controls the incoming data via ports and packet type. One or both of these methods can be configured in Windows 2000. When implemented locally, built-in or custom policies (stored in the Registry) determine the rules for communications with other hosts. Policies can also be distributed via Windows 2000 Server (stored in the Active Directory). You can use one of the built-in security policies if the computers you are configuring are all in the same domain. You must create your own custom policy between computers that are not domain members, because the built-in policies use Kerberos authentication that is provided by a domain controller.

With today's need for data integrity, and the rising amount of network attacks, it is apparent why Microsoft included these methods in Windows2000. A few of the most common attacks include denial-of-service, spoofing, eavesdropping, data modification, and man-in-the-middle. Through data encryption, hashing, digitally signing data, Kerberos, MS-CHAP, access limits, and public keys, to name a few, you can minimize the risk from these types of attacks.

To understand how IPSec works, let's take a scenario in which you are sitting at a computer and you wish to send information to another computer across a network. Before the packets are sent, the IP Security Group Policy settings are checked. The default policies can demand, request, or never request secure communication. When requesting, it is asking for security but still can proceed with unsecured communication if need be. The two computers exchange public keys and then create, locally and independent of each other, a secret key. The originating computer signs the data it wishes to send and can optionally encrypt it. It then sends the packets in the normal way. Routers along the way do not use IPSec; they just pass the data along to its destination host. When this destination host receives the packets, it verifies and decrypts the packets, and sends them on to the proper application. All of this comes at a cost to the performance of your computer. Some manufacturers make network interface cards (NICs) that will handle the extra processing needed, thereby freeing up your computer's CPU.

IPSec and ESP, AH   Encapsulating Security Payload (ESP), which operates at either the Network or Transport layer, is IPSec's standard for encryption and validation. It can encrypt data created from any higher-level layer of the Open Systems Interconnection (OSI) model. When ESP is used at the Transport layer, it inserts an ESP header between the IP and TCP headers. The TCP header and all the data in the packet are encrypted. When ESP is used at the Network layer, the IP address can be obscured. By doing this, data can travel between remote networks, but anyone attempting to watch the traffic will not be able to determine the network's IP address. AH, or Authentication Header, another standard within the IPSec working group, permits the client and the server to validate each other before communication starts. AH and ESP together provide authentication and encryption of IP traffic

Tunnel Mode Versus Transport Mode   ESP Tunnel mode encapsulates and encrypts the entire IP datagram so that we can securely transmit it across public and private internetworks. The IP datagram is encapsulated and then encrypted with ESP. It is then further encapsulated with a plain-text IP header and sent on its way. When it is received at the destination (as it is leaving the tunnel), the plain-text header is processed and discarded. The ESP packet is then authenticated, decrypted, and processed in the normal way. This is most commonly the method used in a VPN, because there are routers and intermediate destination points it must go through before it reaches its final destination. In transport mode, AH and ESP protect the transport header. There are no intermediate destinations that need to process an IP header to send it on its way.

For more information on IPSec, visit the Internet Engineering Task Force (IETF) Web site at www.ietf.org/html.charters/ipsec-charter.html.

Configuring Policies   The best method for configuring IP Security policies is at a domain controller. You are able to set security at many different levels: Domain, Site, Organizational Unit, Computer, User, or Group. For example, a user at a site that has IPSec configured at the Site level will automatically have the policy applied at startup.

Local IPSec policy should be used when you are a member of a domain that does not use IPSec, are a member of an NT network, or are a member of a workgroup. It should also be used when you are connecting to other hosts on an intranet or the Internet.

The three built-in local security policies are

- **Client (respond only)**   This is the lowest security setting. It is used so that the computer can respond to other computers that request secured communications. It can also talk with hosts that do not use IPSec.

- **Server (request security)**   This is a moderate security setting. This setting will request security from a sending host. If the sending host is IPSec enabled, it will establish secure communications. If the sending host is not IPSec enabled, it will proceed with unsecured communication.

- **Secure Server (require security)**   This is the highest security setting. This setting will require that all communications are secured, and will reject unsecured requests. All attempts that the host initiates are secured as well.

Activating a Local IPSec Policy   Go to Start | Settings | Network And Dial-Up Connections. Right-click Local Area Connection, and click Properties. Select Internet Protocol (TCP/IP), and click Properties. Click Advanced and select the Options tab. Select IP Security, and then click Properties. Select the Use This IP Security Policy radio button, and then choose the policy you desire from the drop-down box. Then click OK (Figure 11-10).

IPSec Policy Management   The IPSec Security Management snap-in allows you to perform many tasks, including create local and domain-based IPSec policies, manage IP filter lists, restore default policies, and import and export policies. You

IP Security
dialog box

must add this snap-in to a new or existing Microsoft Management Console. Start a new or existing console and select Console | Add/Remove Snap-In. Click Add in the Standalone dialog box. Select IP Security Management from the Available Standalone Snap-Ins box, and click Add. In the Select Which Computer This Snap-In Will Manage dialog box, select the environment or computer you wish to manage. Click Finish (Figure 11-11).

You can create new policies by selecting the snap-in you just created, and then select Create IP Security Policy from the Actions menu. An IP Security Policy Wizard starts. You must provide the required information:

- An IP policy name and description.

- Activation of the default rule. Additional rules may be added to the default, or you may choose not to activate the default rule.

- Authentication method (Kerberos, Certificate, or a Preshared Key).

TCP/IP Filtering   TCP/IP filtering allows you to specify what type of nontransit IP traffic is to pass through each configured interface. This feature is disabled by default. Nontransit traffic is inbound IP datagrams that are processed by the

FIGURE 11-11

Select Computer environment dialog box

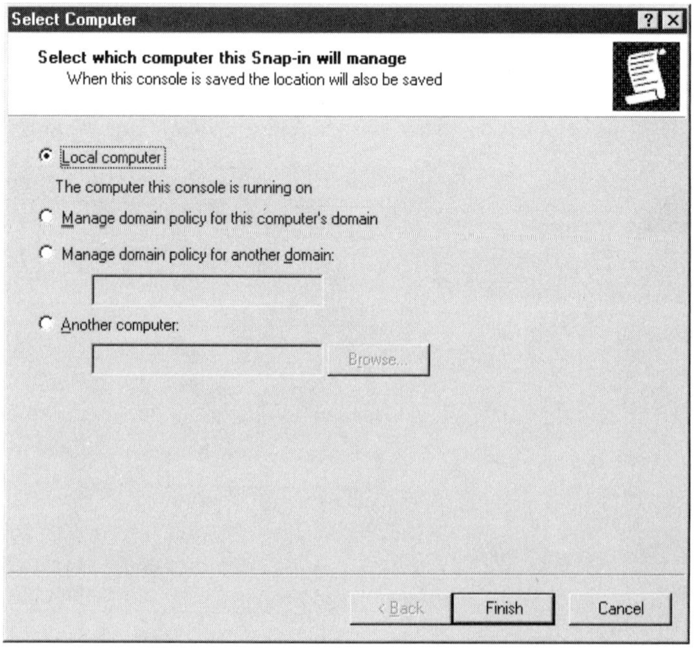

receiving host. This is so because they are addressed to an interface address, subnet broadcast address, or multicast address. You can use TCP/IP filtering to work on both destination UDP and TCP ports, as well as the IP protocol.

To enable TCP/IP filtering, go to Start | Settings | Network And Dial-Up Connections. Right-click the Local Area Connection icon and select Properties. On the General tab, click Internet Protocol (TCP/IP), click Properties, and then click Advanced. Select TCP/IP filtering on the Options tab, and click Properties (Figure 11-12).

Configuring DNS

DNS, or the Domain Name System, is primarily used to translate host names (www.microsoft.com) to IP addresses (207.46.130.45). This process is known as name resolution. It certainly is a lot easier to remember the names rather than all those numbers. Prior to DNS, HOSTS files were responsible for host name resolution. DNS takes an even more important role in Windows 2000 than in previous versions, because the Active Directory is largely based on the hierarchical namespace of DNS. DNS servers are needed on your Windows 2000 network to implement the Active Directory.

on the
Job

Please note that the DNS service is not available on the Windows 2000 Professional CD-ROM. It is distributed via the server products in the Windows 2000 line.

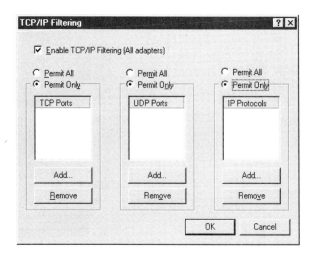

Domain Namespace

Looking at how the Internet namespace is organized will help you understand how a DNS server works. Visually, it looks like any other organizational chart (Figure 11-13).

Root Domain   The Root domain is represented by a space following the trailing dot. It is managed by a few organizations—most notably, Network Solutions, Inc.

Top-Level Domains   Top-level domains are defined with either a two- or three-letter code. Some of the top-level domains are .gov, .com, .org, .net, and two-character country codes such as .uk and .au. These domains can contain hosts as well as other domains called second-level domains.

Second-Level Domains   Second-level domains can contain hosts and other domains called subdomains. To illustrate: Within the .com domain (top level) there exists a second-level domain called Microsoft (microsoft.com). Within this second-level domain, we can have hosts like their Web server www.microsoft.com or subdomains (support.microsoft.com). This subdomain may contain hosts, as well as ftp.support.microsoft.com. Hosts' names refer to specific computers. In a fully qualified domain name (FQDN), the leftmost portion is the host name. Remember that an FQDN includes a period at the end. This represents the root domain.

Zones   Zones are set up to better manage the domain namespace. You can partition the namespace into contiguous logical groupings so that administrative tasks can be assigned to them (Figure 11-14).

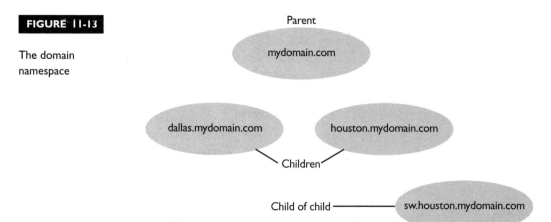

FIGURE 11-13

The domain namespace

FIGURE 11-14

Setting up zones

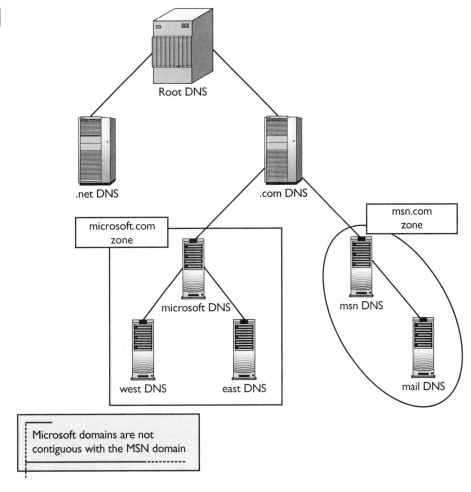

Name Servers   A DNS server that stores its host name to IP mappings for one or more zones in a zone database file is said to have authority for that particular namespace. One server stores the primary zone database files. All changes to this file are made on the server that stores this master file. Every zone must have at least one name server. You can, however (and it is recommended), have more than one DNS name server per zone. In this way, you can perform zone transfers so that additional servers have a copy of the master zone database file. These redundant servers periodically query the server that contains the zone database file for updated information. It will also help speed up response time for remote clients by reducing the load on the server with the primary zone database file.

DNS Name Resolution   When you type a request in your Web browser, you are making a forward lookup query to the closest DNS server to resolve a name (www.microsoft.com) to an IP address. If that local server has resolved the name before, and its TTL (Time To Live) has not expired, it will return the name resolution (TTL is the amount of time an IP mapping can remain in a name server's cache). If it does not know the address, it sends a request to a Root name server. The Root name server will return a referral to the local name server with the address of the .com server. The local name server will then make a request to the .com servers, which will, in turn, send a response with the address of the Microsoft name servers. The local server can then send a request to the Microsoft name servers. Because these servers are authoritative for that portion of the domain namespace, it returns the IP address of www.microsoft.com.

The initial request made by your computer is a recursive query. Recursive queries sent to a DNS server require that the request be responded to with either a successful IP mapping or a failure—it cannot send back a referral to another name server. Typically, a client on a network is a revolver and it makes recursive queries. A name server (Server A) can make recursive queries to another name server (Server B) known as its *forwarder*. A forwarder (Server B, in this example) is a name server configured to handle name resolution for another name server (in this case, Server A).

A name server typically makes an iterative query to another name server. It will accept a referral to another name server and then query that name server. An iterative query can be made by a client. The DNS server returns a pointer to another DNS server where the client can look for itself for name resolution.

Caching   When a name server processes a query, it, in turn, queries other name servers that are authoritative for a portion of the domain namespace. The name server saves these queries in a *cache*. The name server caches this information for an amount of time specified by the server that was authoritative for that zone. This is known as its Time To Live (TTL); the default time is one hour. This cached information is purged when the TTL runs out. The reason for the TTL is so that the information does not become outdated. You might think that maintaining a very short TTL would ensure that the most current information is available, but you must realize that this will increase the load on the name servers.

Reverse Lookup   Normally, we are concerned with mapping names to IP addresses. There are, however, situations that would require a lookup by IP address to name. Because DNS is organized by names, you can imagine how difficult and exhaustive a search it must perform to find a name given only the IP address. There are also applications and troubleshooting tools that rely on the ability to connect to names, not IP addresses. There is a special domain called in-addra.arpa that is used to solve this problem.

Subdomains are named in the reverse order of the IP address. For example, a company that had a range assigned to it of 200.154.20.0 to 200.154.20.255, with a default subnet mask of 255.255.255.0, will represent this range as the 20.154.200.in-addr.arpa domain.

Dynamic DNS (DDNS)   Windows 2000 Server uses DDNS, which automatically registers clients that have their IP addresses dynamically assigned (via DHCP, for example) with a DNS server.

With DNS, if there is a change to the domain, the zone database files must be updated manually on the primary name server. With DDNS, these zone database files are updated automatically.

You can configure a list of servers to perform this update. They can be domain controllers; secondary name servers; or any server performing client registration over the network, such as a DHCP or WINS server.

To perform these updates, a client searches for the primary DNS server and zone that is authoritative for the record to be registered. The client then sends to this server an assertion or prerequisite-only update to see if the registration already exists. If it does not, the client sends the dynamic update to register the record.

If the authoritative zone is multimaster and the initial registration fails, it will attempt to register it with another primary DNS server. If that fails as well, or if there is no other DNS server authoritative for the zone, then the client will attempt to reregister after 5 minutes and then after 10 minutes. If it still fails to register the record, this process, starting with a search for the primary DNS server authoritative for the zone in which the record is to be registered, starts again after 50 minutes of the last attempt.

For more information on Dynamic DNS, refer to RFCs 2136 and 2137.

FROM THE CLASSROOM

Planning a Project

Like everything else, when starting a project, the majority of your work is accomplished in the planning stages. You can easily spend 80 percent of your time on this aspect of the project; in fact, this is where a successful deployment is defined. When setting up DNS servers on your network and its close ties with the Active Directory, you must have a vision of how you want your network architecture to be implemented. Will it be along geographical lines or departmentally? Politics may play a role in how you design your network, as well. Do not cut corners in this stage of a project; it will make or break a successful implementation.

—Paul J. Edwards, MCSE, CCNA

SCENARIO & SOLUTION

What are the four layers used to define the TCP/IP Protocol stack?	Application, Transport, Internet, and Network.
When troubleshooting a network connection problem, which TCP/IP tool should be your first line of defense, and how should it be used?	Use ping to first test the loopback address (127.0.0.1), and then try to ping a computer on your local subnet. The next step would be to ping the default gateway, and, finally, ping the far side of the gateway or router.
What new feature in Windows 2000 dynamically registers host name mappings?	Dynamic DNS.

Connecting to Computers by Using Dial-Up Networking

The Network Connection Wizard can configure all of the protocols and services needed to establish an outbound connection. Whether you are connecting to a private network or to an ISP, the Network Connection Wizard will do the job. To start the wizard, you can open the Network And Dial-Up Connections folder either from the Control Panel (Start | Settings | Control Panel) or directly from the Start menu (Start | Settings | Network And Dial-Up Connections). Double-click Make New Connection. The Network Connection Wizard starts. Click Next to be presented with your choice of network connection type (Figure 11-15).

You can see in Figure 11-15 the different connection options that are available to you from the Network Connection Wizard. We will discuss in this section how to connect to a private network or to an ISP.

FIGURE 11-15

Network
Connection
Wizard

Network Connection Wizard

Network Connection Type
You can choose the type of network connection you want to create, based on your network configuration and your networking needs.

○ **Dial-up to private network**
Connect using my phone line (modem or ISDN).

○ **Dial-up to the Internet**
Connect to the Internet using my phone line (modem or ISDN).

○ **Connect to a private network through the Internet**
Create a Virtual Private Network (VPN) connection or 'tunnel' through the Internet.

○ **Accept incoming connections**
Let other computers connect to mine by phone line, the Internet, or direct cable.

○ **Connect directly to another computer**
Connect using my serial, parallel, or infrared port.

< Back   Next >   Cancel

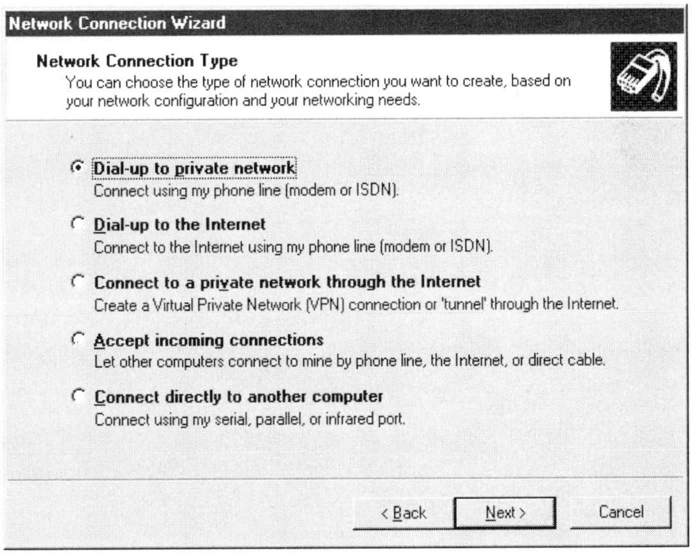

EXERCISE 11-3

Establishing a Dial-Up Connection to a Private Network

1. Right-click My Network Places on your desktop, and choose Properties from the context menu.

2. Double-click Make New Connection. The Make New Connection Wizard starts. Click Next.

3. Select the Dial-Up To Private Network radio button, and click Next.

4. Enter the telephone number of the computer or network you want to dial in to in the resulting dialog box, and click Next.

5. You now have a choice of who can use this connection—For All Users (of this computer) or Only For Myself. Choose the For All Users radio button, and click Next.

6. Type a friendly name for this connection in the dialog box. You may also add a shortcut to your desktop by selecting the Add A Shortcut To My Desktop check box.

7. Click Finish to complete setting up the connection.

Dial-Up To The Internet   To start the Internet Connection Wizard, choose the Dial-Up To The Internet radio button, and click Next. You will be presented with three choices:

- **I want to sign up for a new Internet account. (My telephone line is connected to my modem.)**   This option will allow you to select your ISP and enter billing information, your address, and your e-mail account.

- **I want to transfer my existing Internet account to this computer. (My telephone line is connected to my modem.)**   By choosing this option, you will be prompted for your ISP's telephone number or the modem to which you want to connect. It will ask you for your username and password for the existing account. You will also be prompted to name the connection.

- **I want to set up my Internet connection manually, or I want to connect through a local area network (LAN).**   By choosing this option, you will be able to specify how you connect to the Internet, via LAN or modem, and proxy settings.

Virtual Private Network (VPN) Connection

We will spend a bit more time on the next option and discuss some of the features and protocols used in setting up and using a VPN. By using the PPTP or L2TP protocols, we can access a remote network through the Internet in a secure manner. Lowered cost is a big advantage of using public and private networks to create a network connection. We are using the Internet instead of costly long-distance telephone rates. Security is enhanced because data is encrypted. Only external IP addresses are visible, so your private network addresses are secure. You can run any application that is dependent on TCP/IP, IPX, and NetBEUI.

PPTP

The Point-to-Point Tunneling Protocol (PPTP) allows the Point-to-Point Protocol (PPP) to be tunneled through an IP network. PPTP is an extension of PPP developed by Microsoft, 3Com, US Robotics, Ascend, and EMI Telematics. It allows individuals and corporations to use the Internet as a secure means of communication. *Secure* is the key word here. Packets are encapsulated, and the data is encrypted in a secure manner and then tunneled via a TCP/IP connection.

L2TP

Layer Two Tunneling Protocol (L2TP) is similar in functionality to PPTP, in that its primary purpose is to provide an encrypted tunnel through an untrusted network. Its main difference is that it does not provide the encryption, just the tunneling. Encryption is provided by other technologies such as IPSec. Table 11-4 lists the major differences between the two protocols.

TABLE 11-4		**PPTP**	**L2TP**
The Differences Between PPTP and L2TP	Protocol	IP only	Any packet-oriented, point-to-point protocol—e.g., UDP, Frame Relay, X.25, and ATM
	Header Compression	Not supported (6 bytes overhead)	Supported (4 bytes overhead)
	Tunnel Authentication	Not supported unless used with IPSec	Supported, but can use IPSec for authentication if need be
	Encryption	Supported	Not supported; needs IPSec for encryption capabilities

Connecting to a Virtual Private Network   On the Network Connection Type page of the Network Connection Wizard (shown previously in Figure 11-15), select the Connect To A Private Network Through the Internet radio button. Click Next, and then you have two choices. If you want to establish a connection to your ISP or another network first, then select Automatically Dial This Connection. Select the connection you wish to establish, and click Next. If you do not wish to establish the connection first, click Do Not Dial The Initial Connection, and click Next. You will then be asked to indicate the host name or IP address of the network or computer you wish to connect to. Click Next. If all users of the computer should have the ability to use this connection, click For All Users. If you wish to reserve this connection for yourself, click Only For Myself. Click Next. If you want a shortcut to this connection on your desktop, select Add A Shortcut To My Desktop, and then click Finish.

Remote Access Server

By configuring Windows 2000 to accept incoming connections, you are allowing it to function as a Remote Access Server. Windows 2000 Professional can accept up to three incoming calls (up to one of each of the different types). You can configure these connections via dial-up, VPN, or a direct serial connection. When creating these incoming connections, you are able to choose which users and what protocols are supported. The users must have a local account.

exam
ⓦatch

Windows 2000 Professional will allow up to ten inbound concurrent connections. Windows 2000 Server will accommodate as many as you have Client Access Licenses (CALs) for.

Configuring Incoming Connection to Use TCP/IP

Open Network And Dial-Up Connections (Start | Settings | Network And Dial-Up Connections). Right-click Incoming Connections, and then click Properties. Go to the Networking tab, click Internet Protocol (TCP/IP), and click Properties. To let users have access to the local area network that the dial-up computer is on, make sure you select the Allow Callers To Access My Local Area Network check box.

You now have a choice. To dynamically assign IP addresses, select Assign TCP/IP Addresses Using DHCP. To statically assign an address, select Specify TCP/IP Addresses, and then in From, put in the starting address. In To, type in the ending address. Note that the number of allocated addresses is displayed in Total (Figure 11-16).

FIGURE 11-16

Incoming TCP/IP
Properties
dialog box

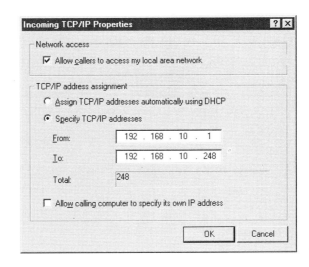

If you need the calling computer to specify an address, select Allow Calling
Computer To Specify Its Own IP Address.

*There is a security risk in allowing remote clients to specify their own TCP/IP
addresses. Someone can impersonate a prior connection and gain access to
your network.*

Allowing and Configuring Inbound Connections and Devices

To configure your Windows 2000 computer in a non-domain environment to accept
inbound connections, you must first start the Network Connection Wizard (Start |
Settings | Network And Dial-Up Connections | Make New Connection). Click Next
when the wizard starts, and then choose the Accept Incoming Connections radio
button on the Network Connection Type dialog box, and click Next. The Devices
For Incoming Connection Page appears. Click the device you want to use to accept
incoming connections on, and choose Properties. You are able to configure port speed,
flow control, compression, and data protocol. The configurable options will depend
on the type of device you are using. The Advanced tab has additional options that you
may want or need to configure; among these are the number of data bits, stop bits, and
the parity.

When you have finished, click OK to close the Properties box, and then click Next.
You are then prompted to either allow or not allow a virtual private connection.
Select your choice, and click Next.

You must now specify what users can access this connection on the next screen (Allowed Users). Select a user and click Properties. Click the Callback tab to set this option.

■ **Do not allow callback.** This option will not enable the Remote Access Server to call the user back after he or she has dialed in.

■ **Allow the caller to set the callback number.** By enabling this option, the remote server will disconnect from the user calling in and call him or her back with a number that the caller specifies. This has the advantage of your remote user not having to pay for the call.

■ **Always use the following callback number.** This is similar to the preceding option, except that it has the enhanced security of dialing a number that has been predetermined. Even if someone breaks in to your system, he or she will not be able to make a connection. Mobile users, on the other hand, would be prevented from connecting, as you will not know the telephone number they will be calling from.

After you have chosen the option that suits your situation, click Next. The Networking Components page appears. Click Internet Protocol TCP/IP, and then click Properties. You are able to configure the protocol's properties here, as discussed previously—that is, to specify TCP/IP addresses or to use a DHCP server to dynamically assign addresses. Click Next, and then Finish.

SLIP

Serial Line Internet Protocol is an older standard that only supports TCP/IP. Like PPP, it is used to encapsulate packets into frames over a serial line. It is less reliable and less secure than PPP. You can only use SLIP to dial out; it will not allow inbound connections.

PPP

The Point-to Point Protocol is a data link protocol that allows TCP/IP, IPX, or NetBEUI packets to be transmitted over a dial-up (serial) connection. Remote access applications from different vendors can interoperate due to this standard set of protocols. It was developed by the IETF in 1991 and has become the de facto standard for most remote access computing. PPP supports several authentication methods, as well as data encryption and compression. It is the basis for L2TP and PPTP when establishing a virtual private network (VPN).

Extensible Authentication Protocol   EAP is a new protocol supported under Windows 2000 that was not supported under Windows NT. It is an extension to the PPP protocol that works with L2TP, PPTP, and dial-up clients. It is a standard mechanism that allows additional authentication schemes to be added. Some of these may be via pubic keys for smart cards and certificates. Token cards and one-time passwords, among others, can be added. This is crucial to establishing a secure VPN. It allows for much stronger authentication methods than others, such as CHAP.

- Generic token cards are physical cards that provide passwords.
- MD5-CHAP is the Message Digest 5 Challenge Handshake Authentication Protocol. Its function is to encrypt usernames and passwords.
- TLS, or Transport Level Security, provides support for smart cards and certificates. A smart card is a physical card that stores a user's private key and certificate.

The greatest feature of EAP is that third-party vendors can write new authentication models.

RADIUS   Remote Authentication Dial-In User Service is a vendor-independent remote user authentication scheme. Windows 2000 can be a RADIUS client and/or server. Because it is extremely difficult to keep user account information current on more than one server, many administrators set up a RADIUS server. The remote access server sends its authentication requests to a central RADIUS server.

BAP   *Multilinking* is the ability to combine multiple physical links into one logical unit. Usually this is done with multiple ISDN lines or modems, so you can achieve greater bandwidth. This was supported in Windows NT; but with the addition of Bandwidth Allocation Protocol and Bandwidth Allocation Control Protocol (BACP) in Windows 2000, we can now dynamically add or drop links based on usage.

BAP can be configured through the use of remote access policies. In this way, you can specify that for a particular group a link be dropped if usage drops below a certain percentage. Different groups can have different policies, which can be a cost savings for companies that have dial-up charges based on bandwidth use.

Configuring and Troubleshooting Internet Connection Sharing

With Internet Connection Sharing, you enable your home or small office network to share a single connection to the Internet. You do not need to install a modem and telephone line at each computer, not to mention setting up separate ISP accounts for each user. Please note that you should not use Internet Connection Sharing on a network that uses static IP addresses, has a Windows 2000 domain controller, or uses other DNS and DHCP servers and gateways. You will lose connectivity to the rest of the network if you do so. ICS sets up a new static IP address for the computer with the physical connection to the Internet, and assigns addresses to the clients that are sharing the connection. It becomes a DHCP allocator for the rest of your network. It does not have the full functionality of a DHCP server.

Configuring ICS

You must be logged on as a member of the Administrators group to configure ICS. You will also need the computer with the physical Internet connection (the gateway) to have two connections: one to the Internet (via dial-up or cable modem with a NIC) and another to the rest of the network via a network adapter (NIC). These connections must be functioning properly before you attempt to enable ICS.

Right-click the Internet connection in the Networking And Dial-Up Connections folder. Choose Properties, and select the Sharing tab. Select the Enable Internet Connection Sharing For This Connection check box. If using a modem and dial-up connection, also select the Enable On-Demand Dialing check box. This will enable other computers that share your connection to initiate a session; otherwise, you will have to be connected first before they can use the connection. Settings allows you to configure network applications and games.

Troubleshooting ICS

Windows 2000 provides you with many tools to help troubleshoot network and dial-up connection problems. Most of the tools previously mentioned in this chapter can be used to provide valuable information in determining the problem.

The Device Manager can show you information on how your hardware is configured. It will show the status of your COM ports, and whether you have a resource conflict. You can also update any device drivers here as well. You can reach the Device Manager by right-clicking My Computer and choosing Properties. Select the Hardware tab, and then click Device Manager.

Here are some common modem problems and their solutions:

- **The modem is not on the HCL.** Check the Hardware Compatibility List at www.microsoft.com/windows2000/upgrade/compat/search/devices.asp.

- **The modem is not connected properly.** Verify all cables and connections. If it is an internal model, make sure it is properly seated in its slot. Make sure the power is on if you are using an external modem.

- **You have dialed the wrong number.** You should also check that any outside line access codes have been configured as well.

- **The telephone line does not support your modem's speed.** Select a lower bps.

- **Call waiting may be disconnecting you.** Configure your modem to disable call waiting

- **Your serial ports have a conflict.** Remember that COM1 and COM3 share IRQ 4. COM2 and COM4 share IRQ 3. You cannot use COM1 and COM3, or COM2 and COM4 together, because they use the same IRQ.

Here are some common problems when your ICS connection is not working:

- **You have shared the wrong LAN adapter.** You must make sure that ICS is configured on the adapter that is connected to the Internet.

- **TCP/IP is not installed on the client computers.** ICS will not work if TCP/IP is not installed on all shared and sharing computers. The client computers should have the following settings—IP Address: Obtain An IP Address Automatically (Through DHCP); DNS Server: Obtain DNS Server Address Automatically; Default Gateways: None Specified.

- **The ICS service may not be started.** Use the Event Viewer to make sure this service has started.

SCENARIO & SOLUTION	
What are some of the features of a virtual private network?	PPTP and L2TP are the protocols we use to access a remote network through the Internet in a secure manner. Lowered cost; enhanced security via data encryption (PPTP only, IPSec is needed for L2TP); and the ability to run any application that is dependent on TCP/IP, IPX, and NetBEUI.
Internet Connection Sharing should not be used in what situations?	When you are part of a domain or are using DHCP.
In what situations can the Device Manager be useful?	The Device Manager can show you information on how your hardware is configured. It will show the status of your COM ports, and whether you have a resource conflict. You can also update any device drivers here as well.

CERTIFICATION OBJECTIVE 11.03

Connecting to Shared Resources on a Microsoft Network

One of the main reasons we become part of a network is to share resources. Sharing the folder that the resource resides in enables this. You can control access to shared folders by limiting the number of simultaneous users, and by configuring which users have access and the type of access they have. You can modify the properties of a folder after it has been shared, stop sharing it, change its name, and change access permissions.

The Administrators and Power Users groups have the ability to share folders. In a Windows 2000 domain, Administrators and Server Operators can share folders on any computer in the domain. Power Users can only share folders on the computer on which their local account or group resides. In a workgroup environment, Administrators and Power Users can share folders on the computers on which their group resides.

exam
ⓦatch *On an NTFS volume, you must have the Read permission on a folder to be able to share it.*

Sharing Folders

Log on with an account that has the ability to share folders. Within Windows Explorer, right-click the folder you wish to share. Choose the Sharing tab from the context menu (Figure 11-17).

Click the Share This Folder radio button. You must have a share name for remote users to be able to connect to it. The default is the name of the folder you shared, but you can call it anything you like. You can put a comment that will describe the contents of the folder. This field is optional, but will be useful when users browse for shared resources. The User Limit specifies how many simultaneous connections you will allow to the share. Windows 2000 Professional will allow ten concurrent connections, while Windows 2000 Server has an unlimited amount.

Clicking Permissions will allow you to apply permissions only to connections made remotely (over the network). The Everyone group has full control by default.

FIGURE 11-17

Folder Properties sheet

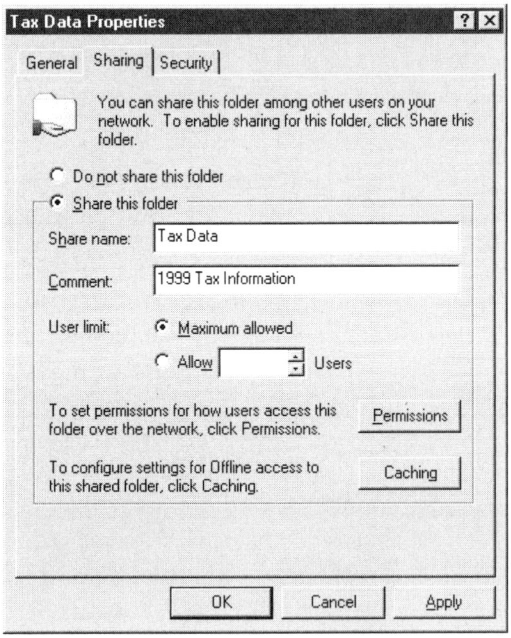

It is wise to remove this group and add groups and users that need access, and only to the level that they need to perform their jobs.

Caching Enabling caching allows users access when they are offline or disconnected from the network. This is especially useful for mobile computer users, as the data will be cached on their hard drive. The default size of this cache is 10 percent, but it can be changed by accessing the Folder Options dialog box from Windows Explorer's Tools menu.

EXERCISE 11-4

Enabling Caching for Offline Folders

1. Make sure you logged on as an Administrator, and start Windows Explorer.

2. Create a folder that you wish to share. For this exercise, we will create the folder C:\CacheTest.

3. Right-click the folder you just created, and click Sharing.

4. The CacheTest Properties dialog box opens with the Sharing tab open.

5. Select the Share This Folder radio button, and then click Caching. The Caching Settings dialog box appears.

6. There are three available settings in the drop-down box to configure how you want the cached folder to perform its function, as shown in the following dialog box.

   - **Manual Caching for Documents** Users connecting to your shared folder must specify any files that they want cached on their local hard drive. This is the default setting.

   - **Automatic Caching for Documents** Only files in the shared folder that are opened by users are automatically cached to their hard drive.

   - **Automatic Caching for Programs** This gives offline access to any shared file that is read, referenced, or run, but not changed. Users will directly access these files without using network bandwidth.

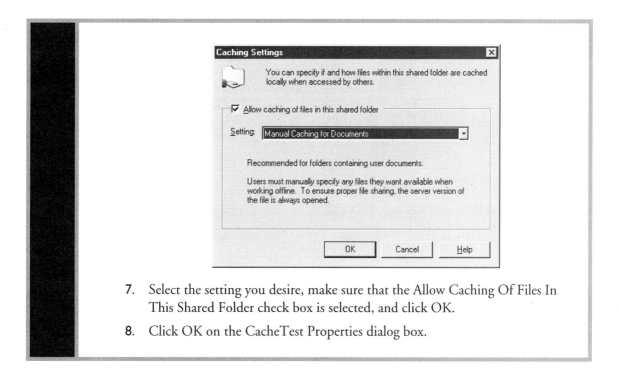

7. Select the setting you desire, make sure that the Allow Caching Of Files In This Shared Folder check box is selected, and click OK.

8. Click OK on the CacheTest Properties dialog box.

Connecting to a Shared Folder   Using the Map Network Drive Wizard, you are able to connect to shared folders on computers across the network.

Right-click the My Network Places icon on your desktop, and click Map Network Drive. The Map Network Drive Wizard starts (Figure 11-18).

In the Folder box, type the UNC path to the shared folder you wish to map to. You can also browse for it by clicking Browse. Assign it a drive letter from the Drive box. If you wish this connection to reconnect automatically when you log on, select the Reconnect At Logon check box. You can connect to a shared folder under another username by clicking Connect Using A Different User Name. You will be prompted to supply the username and password in the Connect As dialog box.

There are other methods to map to a share as well. Double-click My Network Places and browse to the folder you wish to connect to. Double-click the shared folder.

You may also connect via the Run command. Click Start | Run. Type the UNC path to the server on which the folder is located (the syntax is *computer_name*) in the Open box. Double-click the shared folder you wish to connect to.

FIGURE 11-18

The Map
Network Drive
Wizard

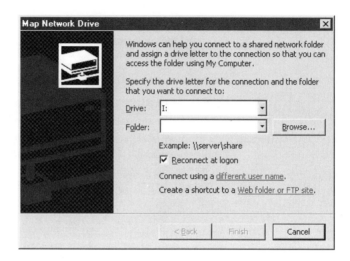

File and Print Sharing for Microsoft Networks

Windows 2000 Professional allows you to share printers across the network. You can also administer them from a central location. The first thing to understand is the terminology that Microsoft uses when referring to printing options. A *printer* is the software interface between the actual print device and the operating system. The *print device* is the actual hardware used to produce a printed document. A *printer port* is again a software interface, but it is the means by which a printer device communicates via a locally attached interface (LPT, COM, or USB). A *print server* is the computer on which the local and network printer interfaces reside. You set up and share printers on a print server. A *printer driver* is the files used to translate print commands into a language the printer can understand.

To set up printing on a Windows 2000 network, you must have at least one computer set up as a print server. That computer can be Windows 2000 Professional, which will allow ten concurrent connections, or Windows 2000 Server, which can handle a large amount of connections. Windows 2000 Server will also support UNIX, NetWare, and Macintosh clients, while Windows 2000 Professional will only support UNIX (besides Windows clients, of course). There must be sufficient disk space to hold the documents before they are printed, and you must have sufficient RAM over and above the Windows OS requirements to ensure adequate performance.

The first step in setting up network or local printing is the same: You must add the printer. Log on as Administrator and go to Start | Settings | Printers.

Double-click Add Printer to start the Add Printer Wizard. Click Next on the splash screen. At this point, you have a choice of installing a Local or Network printer, as shown in Figure 11-19.

Installing a Local Printer

Check the Local Printer radio button if you are adding a printer to the computer that you are sitting at. This will make the computer the print server. If you select Automatically Detect And Install My Plug And Play Printer, Windows 2000 will detect your Plug and Play printer and install it. Click Next. You are then presented with the Select The Printer Port dialog box. You must select the port on the print server that you have attached the print device.

You can also create a new port, but this will be covered when we install a network printer. Click Next and you will be presented with the Add Printer Wizard, which will allow you to select the manufacturer and model of the printer you are installing. If your printer is not listed, you must click Have Disk and supply an appropriate printer driver (from the manufacturer of your printer) for your specific printer. Click Next. You will be prompted in the next dialog box to name the printer. A descriptive name that the users can easily identify is your best choice. If you want this to be the default printer so users don't have to select it every time they print, select the Yes radio button.

FIGURE 11-19

Local Or Network Printer dialog box

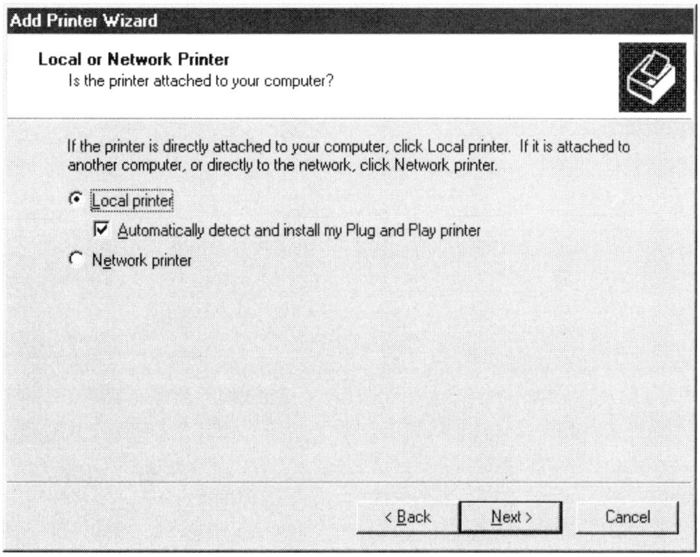

Please note that the first time you add a printer to a print server, it will be selected as the default automatically. Click Next, and then you have the option of sharing the printer. Click the Share As Printer radio button, and name the share. This is the name that will appear when a user browses for printers. The printer name will be shortened to conform to the 8.3 naming convention, so keep that in mind when naming the printer. Click Next and you will be prompted for a location. This is descriptive information so that users can easily determine if the printer fits their needs for the job. Click Next and you will be prompted to print a test page. Select the Yes radio button to print a test page, and click Finish.

Installing a Network Printer

When installing a network-interface printer, the main difference from the procedure in the preceding section is that you must specify additional port and protocol information. It should be noted that networked print connections work much faster than printer cable connections.

Follow the procedure as you did earlier, but when you are presented with the Select The Printer Port dialog box, click the Create A New Port radio button. In the drop-down box, you have a choice of Local Port or Standard TCP/IP Port (Figure 11-20).

FIGURE 11-20

Select The Printer Port page

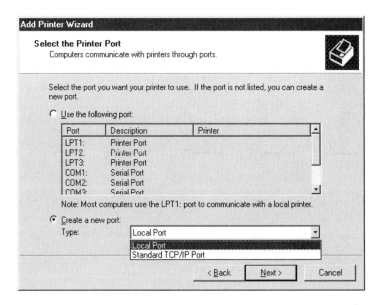

Choose the Standard TCP/IP Port, and click Next. The Add Standard TCP/IP Port Wizard starts. Your print device must be turned on, connected, and configured on a print server. Click Next. The Add Port page appears, and you must fill in the Printer Name (DNS name) or its IP address. If you choose the IP address, the port name is automatically supplied in the form of IP_*IPaddress.* You can enter a friendlier name if you wish. Click Next, and then Finish.

on the
Öob

When connecting to a network print device that is directly connected to the network via an adapter card, such as Hewlett-Packard LaserJet 4Si, you need to install the DLC protocol on the print server for the device.

Configuring Client Computers

If your client is running Windows 2000 and you wish to connect to a shared printer, you must start the Add Printer Wizard. On the Local Or Network Printer page (shown previously in Figure 11-19) select Network Printer and click Next. The Locate Your Printer page appears. Type in the printer name, or click Next to browse for the printer. If you do not know the name or are not sure of the name of the printer you wish to connect to, leave the name blank and click Next. You are then presented with the Browse For Printer page. Locate the printer you want to connect to, select it, and click Next. You will be prompted if you want this to be your default printer. Click Yes if you do, or No if you do not. Look over the Completing The Add Printer Wizard page to make sure your information is correct, and then click Finish.

Printer drivers will be automatically installed on client computers running Windows 2000, Windows NT, Windows 98, and Windows 95. Other Microsoft operating systems need to have printer drivers installed manually. If you use a non-Microsoft operating system, you must install not only the printer drivers, but also the appropriate print services on the print server.

If the client is using NetWare, then File and Print Services for NetWare (FPNW) must be installed on the print server. FPNW is not included with either Windows 2000 Professional or Windows 2000 Server. When using a Macintosh client, Services for Macintosh must be installed, and this service is included with Windows 2000 Server. A UNIX client uses TCP/IP Printing, also known as Line Printer Daemon. It is included with the Windows 2000 Server distribution media.

SCENARIO & SOLUTION

After creating a share, what is the first thing you should do?	The Everyone group has full control by default. It is wise to remove this group, and add groups and users that need access and only to the level that they need to perform their jobs.
What is the Microsoft terminology used when referring to printers?	A *printer* is a software interface, a *print device* is the actual hardware, a *printer port* is a software interface that a printer device communicates with via a locally attached interface (LPT, COM, or USB), and a *print server* is the computer in which the local and network printer interfaces reside.

CERTIFICATION SUMMARY

TCP/IP is fast becoming, if it is not already, the standard in internetworking protocols. It is the main means of communication in a Windows 2000 network. This rich suite of protocols is defined in layers—Application, Transport, Internet, and Network. It includes many troubleshooting tools that make it easier to find and fix problems with your network configuration. In addition, many security enhancements have been added to previous versions of Microsoft's implementation of TCP/IP. The most notable is IPSec. By securing IP packets, it enables the use of a secure virtual private network; and, if implemented locally, it will determine the rules for communications with other hosts.

DNS is used to translate host names (www.microsoft.com) to IP addresses (207.46.130.45), and is the basis for the Active Directory model. Dynamic DNS, which is new to Windows 2000, will dynamically register host name mappings in the DNS database.

Windows 2000 Professional makes it easy to make connections to network, Internet, and intranet resources through its various wizards. This includes the sharing of files, folders, and other resources, which is, after all, the primary function of any network. Windows 2000, with its ease of use for both the user and administrator, make its TCO an attractive benefit.

TWO-MINUTE DRILL

Configuring and Troubleshooting the TCP/IP Protocol

❑ TCP/IP is defined in four layers: Application, Transport, Internet, and Network.

❑ TCP/IP includes many useful tools to aid in troubleshooting. Among them are ping, ipconfig, tracert, pathping, arp, route, nbstat, nslookup, and netstat.

❑ Windows 2000 Professional can obtain its TCP/IP information dynamically via DHCP. The IP address of the client, DNS server, WINS server, subnet mask, and the default gateway can all be automatically configured. DDNS also allows dynamic name registration to a DNS server.

❑ Virtual private networks (VPNs) are a financially prudent way of interconnecting remote clients and networks. The enhanced security enhancements of Windows 2000 (IPSec and EAP) make this an even more viable alternative to other interconnecting technologies.

❑ DNS name resolution is used to map IP addresses to host names. A HOSTS file can be used for the same purpose in smaller networks.

Connecting to Computers by Using Dial-Up Networking

❑ Most network connections can be made through the Network Connection Wizard. You can set up Internet, private networks (LAN or WAN), virtual private networks, incoming connections (RAS), and direct cable connections.

❑ Bandwidth Allocation Protocol (BAP) is new to Windows 2000 and is used to dynamically allocate dial-up resources as needed.

❑ The Extensible Authentication Protocol (EAP) is a standard mechanism that allows you to add additional authentication schemes.

❑ L2TP and PPTP are two protocols that enable the use of virtual private networks (VPNs). Along with IPSec and EAP, it establishes a secure connection to two remote networks.

❑ The encryption and authentication capabilities of PPP (Point-to-Point Protocol) make it a much better choice than SLIP.

Connecting to Shared Resources on a Microsoft Network

❏ New to Windows 2000 is the ability to cache files and folders on your local hard drive. The ability to have folders available for users when they are offline or disconnected from the network is especially useful for mobile users.

❏ Windows 2000 Professional will allow ten concurrent connections, while Windows 2000 Server has an unlimited amount.

❏ Knowing the terms that Microsoft uses to describe the different aspects of printing is integral to understanding its implementation.

❏ When configuring a client computer to connect to a network printer, be aware that printer drivers will automatically be installed on client computers running Windows 2000, Windows NT, Windows 98, and Windows 95. Other Microsoft operating systems need to have printer drivers installed manually. On other clients, you may need to have other services to allow printing.

❏ Caching makes it possible to have folders available for users when they are offline or disconnected from the network. This is especially useful for mobile computer users, as the data will be cached on their hard drives.

SELF TEST

The following questions will help you measure your understanding of the material presented in this chapter. Read all of the choices carefully, as there may be more than one correct answer. Choose all correct answers for each question.

Configuring and Troubleshooting the TCP/IP Protocol

1. NetBEUI is appropriate in which of the following situations?

   A. WAN

   B. Frame Relay

   C. LAN

   D. A routed network

2. What command-line tool would you use on a client machine to find the IP address, subnet mask, and default gateway, and whether they were statically or dynamically assigned?

   A. Arp

   B. Nslookup

   C. Ipconfig

   D. Tracert

   E. Pathping

3. Charlie adds a route using the route command-line tool on his Windows 2000 computer. The next day when he starts his computer, the route is no longer in the routing table. What is the most likely reason that he has lost this information?

   A. He did not add the /persistent switch when he set up the route.

   B. He forgot to specify a default gateway.

   C. He added the route without the /p switch.

   D. Windows 2000 uses dynamic routing, and he will not be able to add a permanent route to the table.

4. Maria wants to change her Windows 2000 computer from obtaining IP information dynamically to one that has static addresses. After doing so, she is no longer able to connect to the Internet or browse the company intranet. What is the most likely cause of the problem?

   A. She used the wrong default gateway address.

   B. Her subnet mask is incorrect.

   C. The DNS address is incorrect.

   D. She is no longer a member of the domain.

5. What will Harriet have to do to enable her DNS servers to register client computers? She is using all Windows 2000 servers, and Windows 2000 clients receive their IP address information via DHCP.

   A. She will have to manually add the clients to the DNS database on the DNS server.

   B. She must assign the DNS server's IP address in the TCP/IP Properties page.

   C. Nothing.

   D. Set a Group Policy that enables Dynamic DNS.

6. The main function of a DNS server is

   A. To assign IP information to a client automatically upon startup

   B. To connect to the Internet

   C. To map IP address to host names

   D. None of the above

7. Samantha has installed an application that requires IP address to host name resolution. The IP address that she needs to connect to is 192.168.20.10 with the default subnet mask of 255.255.255.0. What is the DNS domain entry that will need to be added to the DNS server database.

   A. 192.168.20.in-addr.arpa

   B. 192.168.20.in-arpa.addr

   C. 20.168.192.in-addr.arpa

   D. 10.20.168.192.in-addr.arpa

Connecting to Computers by Using Dial-Up Networking

8. Myrna want to set up a VPN client on her TCP/IP network. Secure authentication and data encryption are required by company policy. How can Myrna meet these requirements?

   A. Set up the VPN via the Network Connection Wizard, and specify PPTP as the protocol to be used.

   B. Set up the VPN via the Network Connection Wizard, and specify L2TP as the protocol to be used.

   C. Set up the VPN via the Network Connection Wizard, and specify PPTP as the protocol to be used. Configure IPSec for tunnel authentication.

   D. Set up the VPN via the Network Connection Wizard, and specify L2TP as the protocol to be used. Configure IPSec for tunnel authentication.

9. The protocol that allows dynamically assigned multilinked bandwidth to occur is

   A. EAP

   B. BAP

   C. VPN

   D. PPTP

10. Which protocol allows third-party vendors develop new authentication schemes?

    A. BAP

    B. EAP

    C. RADIUS

    D. PPTP

    E. L2TP

11. When setting up the Remote Access Service on your Windows 2000 Professional computer, what must you do to enable users to dial in?

    A. Only the Windows 2000 Server products can function as a Remote Access Server.

    B. You must configure it to call the users back on a predefined address or telephone number.

    C. The users must have a local account on the Remote Access Server.

    D. PPTP must be enabled.

Connecting to Shared Resources on a Microsoft Network

12. Which of the following built-in groups have the ability to share files and folders on a Windows 2000 domain? (Select all that apply.)

    A. Power Users

    B. Administrators

    C. Server Operators

    D. Users

13. Which setting should you enable if you want only files in a shared folder that are opened by a user to be automatically cached to his or her hard drive?

    A. Manual Caching For Documents

    B. Automatic Caching For Programs

    C. Automatic Caching For Documents

    D. Automatic Caching For Files And Folders

14. Matt connects to a shared folder via the Run command. Whenever he reboots his machine, he loses the connection. What can he do to make the mapping permanent?

    A. Use the -p parameter after defining the path to the folder.

    B. Select the Reconnect At Logon check box while mapping the drive via the Map Network Drive Wizard.

    C. Enter the path to the computer that contains the share into an LMHOSTS file, and enable LMHOSTS lookup.

    D. Permanent mappings are not available in Windows 2000 Professional.

15. Which of the following client computers will need to have printer drivers manually installed? (Select all that apply.)

    A. Windows 3.1

    B. Windows 95

    C. Windows 98

    D. Windows NT 4.0

    E. Windows 2000

16. Which of the following steps are needed to make your Windows 2000 Professional Computer a print server? (Select all that apply.)

    A. Log on as an Administrator.

    B. Select the Network Printer radio button in the Local Or Network Printer page of the Add Printer Wizard.

    C. Select the Local Printer radio button in the Local Or Network Printer page of the Add Printer Wizard.

    D. In the Select The Printer Port dialog box, you must specify the port that your print device is attached to.

    E. Share the printer.

17. Pete wishes to share a folder on his Windows 2000 Professional workstation that is a part of a domain so that other members of a committee he is heading up will be able to exchange information. When he attempts to share the folder on his computer from a computer in the training room, he is not able to. What could be the reason for this?

    A. He is not a member of the Super Users group.

    B. He cannot share a local folder on his machine because his computer is a member of a domain.

    C. He needs to be given explicit permission to share folders.

    D. He needs to be a member of the Domain Administrators group to be able to share folders remotely.

LAB QUESTION

For this question, you have two networked computers: one is running Windows 2000 Professional, and the other is any of the Windows 2000 family. You have a shared folder or drive to which you can connect. If you only have one computer, you want to share any folder on your computer and use the default permissions (Everyone Group has Full Control). To share a folder, right-click it in Windows Explorer and click the Sharing option on the context menu. Select the Share This folder radio button, and click OK.

What are the steps you should go through to connect to a network drive by using the Map Network Drive Wizard?

SELF TEST ANSWERS

Configuring and Troubleshooting the TCP/IP Protocol

1. ☑ **C.** NetBEUI is a nonroutable protocol and relies on broadcasts to communicate. A small LAN can function quite well under these circumstances.

☒ **A** is incorrect because a WAN is typically a routed environment. Since NetBIOS packets do not have headers to include routing information, NetBEUI would be inappropriate as a transport protocol in a WAN environment. **B** is incorrect because Frame Relay is typically used in a WAN environment, and we just noted that those environments typically are routed. **D** is incorrect for the same reason.

2. ☑ **C.** Ipconfig with the /all switch will give you, among other information, whether DHCP is enabled, the IP address of the DHCP server, the physical address, IP address, default gateway, subnet mask, IP address of the primary and secondary DNS server, and when the DHCP lease was obtained and when it will expire.

☒ **A** is incorrect because ARP is used to obtain information about associations between MAC and IP addresses, and does not provide comprehensive configuration information about the local computer. **B** is incorrect because nslookup does not provide TCP/IP configuration information. Nslookup is used to query DNS zone database files, and is useful in troubleshooting DNS-related problems. **D** is incorrect because tracert is used to evaluate the path of routed messages. Tracert can provide basic information regarding what routers may be responsible for problems when messages fail to reach a destination, or are unreliably reaching a destination network. The pathping utility is similar to tracert, but provides additional information. The pathping command can provide information regarding the tardiness of certain links, as well as information regarding overloaded routers along the path of a message.

3. ☑ **C.** The /p switch will make the route persistent. You may go to a command prompt, type **route?**, and you will get a display of all the parameters and command-line switches that may be used with this tool.

☒ **A** is incorrect because there is no /persistent switch. **B** is incorrect because you can add a static route without specifying a default gateway. **D** is incorrect because even if a machine were configured with a dynamic routing protocol such as RIP or OSPF, you could manually configure static, persistent routes.

4. ☑ **A.** The most likely cause of not being able to connect to Internet resources would be that the host IP address and the default gateway have been configured so they are on different network IDs. When the local host is unable to access its default gateway, it cannot access

resources on any remote network, including the Internet.

☒ **B** is incorrect because while an incorrect subnet mask is possible, there is no indication in the question that the computer has difficulty accessing local resources. Note that the browser service is not a diagnostic tool for TCP/IP, and the inability to browse for network resources is a function of the browser services, and not TCP/IP configuration. **C** is incorrect because the DNS server address is responsible for resolving host names to IP addresses. If the DNS server address is incorrect, the user would not be able to attach to Internet resources by host name, but still would be able to access resources via IP address. **D** is incorrect because domain membership is not a factor in TCP/IP-related configuration problems.

5. ☑ **C.** Windows 2000 now uses Dynamic DNS, where host name to IP address is registered dynamically. In Windows NT 4, a WINS server had to be set up and have DNS configured to use WINS for name resolution for there to be any dynamic registering of computer names.
☒ **A** and **B** are incorrect because of Dynamic DNS. **D** is totally false. Group Policy does not enable DDNS.

6. ☑ **C.** Mappings of IP address to host names are kept in the DNS database.
☒ **A** is incorrect. A DHCP server is used to dynamically assign IP information to a client computer upon boot-up. **B** is incorrect. A DNS server is not used or needed to connect to the Internet. Since **B** is correct, **D** is incorrect.

7. ☑ **C.** Some applications rely on the ability to connect to names, not IP addresses. There is a special domain called in-addra.arpa that is used to solve this problem. These subdomains are named in the reverse order of the IP address.
☒ **A, B,** and **D** are incorrect, as they use the wrong scheme for a reverse lookup domain.

Connecting to Computers by Using Dial-Up Networking

8. ☑ **C.** PPTP needs IPSec for authentication.
☒ **A** is incorrect for the same reason **C** is correct; PPIP needs IPSec for authentication. L2TP needs IPSec for encryption capabilities, and that is not one of the choices; therefore, **B** and **D** are incorrect.

9. ☑ **B.** Bandwidth Allocation Protocol is as its name implies; it will dynamically assign bandwidth as needed.
☒ **A** is the Extensible Authentication Protocol, which allows third-party vendors to develop additional authentication schemes. **C** is a virtual private network that is used for secure communications over the Internet. **D** is the Point-to-Point Protocol, which is one of the protocols used to set up a VPN.

10. ☑   B. The Extensible Authentication Protocol allows third-party vendors to supply new as yet unwritten authentication schemes.
    ☒   A is Bandwidth Allocation Protocol and is incorrect. C is incorrect. RADIUS is an authentication server. D and E are protocols used in a VPN.

11. ☑   C. There must be a valid user account on the RAS server for a remote user to dial in.
    ☒   A is incorrect. Windows 2000 Professional will allow one concurrent connection; however, Windows 2000 Server will allow 256. Although you can configure callback service, it is not required; so B is incorrect. PPTP is a protocol used in virtual private networks and is not applicable to RAS; therefore, D is incorrect.

Connecting to Shared Resources on a Microsoft Network

12. ☑   A, B, and C are the only built-in groups that have the ability to share files and folders. Administrators and Server Operators can remotely do so on any computer in the domain. Power Users can do so on the machine on which the group resides.
    ☒   D is incorrect. The Users group does not have this ability.

13. ☑   C. When Automatic Caching For Documents is selected, only files in the shared folder that are opened by a user are automatically cached to his or her hard drive.
    ☒   A is incorrect because with this option, the user connecting to your shared folder must specify any files that he or she wants cached on the local hard drive. B is incorrect because this option gives offline access to any shared file that is read, referenced, or run, but not changed. D is not an option when enabling caching in Windows 2000.

14. ☑   B. To enable a permanent mapping of a drive through subsequent reboots you must select the Reconnect At Logon check box when mapping the drive.
    ☒   A is incorrect, as this is used to create a persistent route in the routing table when using the route command-line tool. C is totally false. Permanent mappings are indeed available in Windows 2000, so D is also incorrect.

15. ☑   A. Windows 3.1 is the only operating system in the list that needs to have printer drivers manually installed.
    ☒   B, C, D, and E all have the correct drivers installed automatically upon first connecting to the networked printer. This assumes that the drivers are available on the server where the printer is installed.

16. ☑ A, C, D, and E are correct. You must be logged on as an Administrator and add the printer as a Local printer. You then choose the port it is attached to and share the printer. You must also install the proper printer drivers when prompted.

☒ B is incorrect. By choosing the Network Printer radio button, you will be connecting to a networked printer, not setting up a print server.

17. ☑ D. He must be a member of the Domain Administrators group or the Servers Operators group to share folders remotely.

☒ A, B, and C are all incorrect and invalid statements as to the possible reasons why he is unable to share the folder.

LAB ANSWER

First off, right-click My Network Places, and then click Map Network Drive from the context menu.

In the resulting dialog box, type *//computername/sharename*, where *computername* is the name of the computer on which the share resides, and *sharename* is the name of the folder or drive you have just shared.

In the Drive box, select Q (or any unused drive letter).

Note that if you want to have this connection mapped every time you boot, make sure the Reconnect At Logon check box is selected.

Click Finish.

When you open Windows Explorer, you should see an icon for the drive or folder you just mapped to as a network cable attached to a drive. If not, go to View | Refresh in Windows Explorer. You can explore this drive like any other local drive. An interesting aspect of this is that if you use a local drive to map to when you browse the mapped drive, you are connecting "remotely"; that is, all share permissions apply just as if you were connecting over the network.

12

Implementing, Monitoring, and Troubleshooting Security and User Accounts

Part of the promise of Windows 2000 is of a much more highly secure environment, with highly manageable security features. This chapter focuses on two major improvements in Windows 2000 Professional regarding security. First, we'll take a look at Windows 2000 Professional's policy-based security system. By editing local Group Policy, you can limit users' activities, assign and remove rights by groups, change password policy and other account policy, and start logging your users' activities.

Second, there's the EFS encryption system, a transparent, built-in encryption system that users can access directly from Windows Explorer, encrypting and decrypting with a few clicks inside a file's or folder's Properties dialog box. EFS is designed to keep a file inaccessible to all users but the user who originally encrypted the file. However, in case the user loses his or her private key, Windows allows designated encryption recovery agents to decrypt any file.

CERTIFICATION OBJECTIVE 12.01

Implementing, Configuring, Managing, and Troubleshooting Local Group Policy

Group Policy is one of the essences of the Windows 2000 lifestyle. A group policy controls who can do what. Traditionally, group policy allows directory objects to perform certain actions. At domain-level security, group policy can act on objects such as servers, organizational sites, and so forth. However, at the local level, group policy acts pretty much exclusively on users and groups. Some modifications to group policy, such as modifications to account and audit polices, affect all users; other modifications to group policy affect only certain users depending on whether the user is a member of the proper group. (We call the latter sort of group policy *group-oriented group policy*.)

One way to understand group-oriented group policy is to note that, when you create a new group, there is no Properties button on the group. You can't just right-click the group and start assigning powers and restrictions. Instead, you must modify group-oriented group policy objects, choosing for each policy whether or not to enable that policy for a given group.

Combined with Active Directory in Windows 2000 Server, group policy is a powerful tool toward creating an integrated, hierarchical policy-based security infrastructure for an enterprise. For our limited Windows 2000 Professional-based discussion, Active Directory will not come into play. However, a limited version of Group Policy implemented at a local level in Windows 2000 Professional allows for a fair amount of control over security issues.

There's a lot of meat to Group Policy. We won't be able to cover every single policy, or even policy type, available to you in Group Policy Editor. However, we will take an in-depth look at those parts of Group Policy that concern security. Microsoft is emphasizing the security-related portions of Group Policy in the test.

exam
ⓦatch

Group Policy can be applied at the local, site, domain, or OU level.

- *Local Computer Policy* is the set of Group Policy settings for a local computer.
- A *Group Policy Object* is any single set of settings. A Group Policy Object exists as a document.

Start the Group Policy Editor

The Group Policy Editor application is a snap-in for the Microsoft Management Console (MMC). You modify Local Computer Policy from the Group Policy Editor. For some reason, Microsoft thought it prudent not to include an icon or menu item *anywhere* in Windows 2000 Professional for conveniently accessing the full Group Policy Editor. (There is a Local Security Policy icon in Control Panel | Administrative Tools, which gives you a limited version of Local Computer Policy, with only the contents of Local Computer Policy/Computer Configuration/Windows Settings/ Security Settings.) There are two ways you can access the full Editor.

Accessing the Group Policy Editor via the Command Line

This is one quick way to get to Group Policy Editor.

1. Open Run . . . from the Start menu.

2. Type **gpedit.msc**, as shown in the following dialog box.

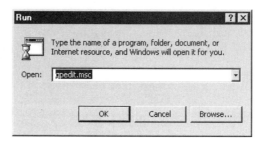

3. You will get the Group Policy MMC snap-in, as shown here. The Group Policy snap-in is divided into two main areas: Computer Configuration and User Configuration.

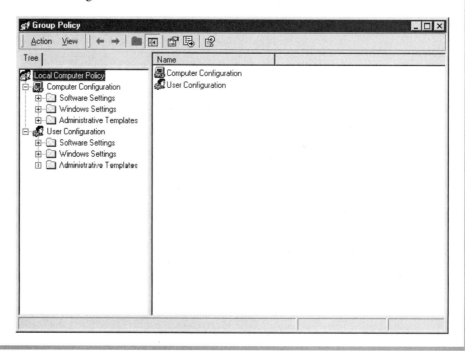

If you find this method of accessing the Group Policy snap-in cumbersome, you can create your own custom-made console, with icon, for Local Computer Policy.

on the ! Job

Why, some of you might ask, go to all the trouble of custom-creating a console when you can just create an icon with a shortcut to a Run GPEDIT.MSC command? Well, the answer is simple: Custom-created consoles are quite flexible; you can keep adding and removing snap-ins as needed. That means that if you're working a lot with the Group Policy and the Local Users And Groups console, you can just open up your custom-made Local Computer Policy and click Console, Add/Remove Snap-In, and add the Local Users And Groups snap-in. This gives you a single console with all the different functions you need, expandable and contactable as needed. This is why MMC snap-ins are actually snap-ins—you can pop in whatever modules you need at any particular moment.

The custom-made Local Computer Policy console is precisely the same as the GPEDIT.MSC Group Policy console, except for the fact that, in the custom-made console, there's a folder at the root called *Console Root* that you have to open to get to the Local Computer Policy object.

Inside the Local Computer Policy object are two subfolders. The first is called Computer Configuration, and the second is called User Configuration. Most of what we will discuss in this chapter will occur in Computer Configuration—more exactly, in Computer Configuration, Windows Settings, Security Settings, as shown in Figure 12-1.

FIGURE 12-1

Security Settings subfolder

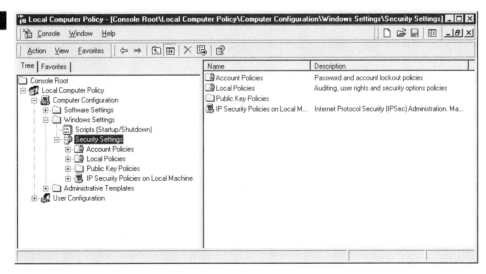

User Configuration options are covered in depth in Chapter 9.

Account Security Policies

When we talk about account policy, we're mostly talking about logging in. Account policy refers to policies concerning passwords and account lockouts. Inside the Security Settings folder is the Account Policies, which contains two subfolders: the Password Policy folder and the Account Lockout Policy folder.

Password Policy

The default settings for Password Policy allow insecure passwords—with no minimum password length and no password complexity requirement, users can set their passwords as things like "cat" and "a" and "password." You can issue as many memos as you like, begging your users to select complex, random or semi-random passwords, but many will still insist on making their passwords easy to remember, and thus easy for an intruder to guess or generate.

There are two solutions. First, administrators can either create the passwords themselves or ask the system to generate random passwords. This is done from User Properties. Second, administrators can ask users to generate their own passwords, but, through Password Policy settings, disallow simplistic passwords.

In the Password Policy folder, found in Local Computer Policy | Computer Configuration | Windows Settings | Security Settings | Account Policies, you'll see several policies regarding password security, as shown in Figure 12-2. Here you can modify the minimum and maximum password age, minimum password length, and several other features.

One important policy is the Passwords Must Meet Complexity Requirement policy. If this policy is enabled, Windows 2000 will not allow a user or administrator to set a simple password. The complexity requirement forces passwords to jumble letters and digits, and disallows words and simple deviations from words.

Another important policy is the Maximum Password Age. This sets the expiration date for a password, forcing users to change their password periodically.

FIGURE 12-2

Password Policy

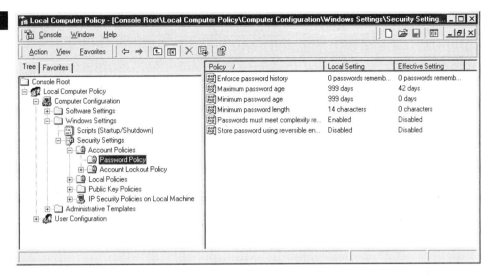

EXERCISE 12-2

Forcing More Secure Passwords

Following this exercise, an administrator can force users to select more secure passwords.

1. Open the Group Policy Editor, as in Exercise 12-1.

2. Open the Password Policy folder, found in Local Computer Policy | Computer Configuration | Windows Settings | Security Settings | Account Policies.

3. Double-click Passwords Must Meet The Complexity Requirement policy in the right-hand pane. This brings up a Local Security Policy Setting dialog box, as shown here. Most Local Security Policy Setting dialog boxes are this simple; your only options are to enable or disable the policy.

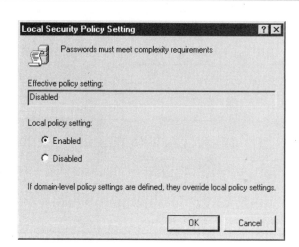

4. Click the Enable option, and click OK.

5. Back at the Password Policy folder, double-click the Minimum Password Length policy. This will bring up another Local Security Policy Setting dialog box, as shown in the following illustration. Note that this box has a number to specify. For most policies like this, you disable the policy by entering **0**, and enable the policy by entering some number. In this case, the number you enter specifies the minimum number of characters in a password.

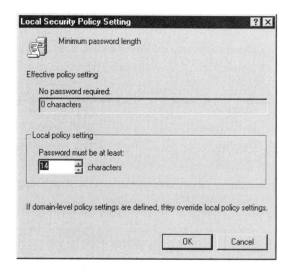

6. Click the Password Must Be At Least: and enter **10**. Passwords must now be at least ten characters long. Click OK.

7. Back at the Password Policy folder, double-click Maximum Password Age.

8. In the Passwords Expire In box, enter **30**. This forces users to change their password every 30 days. Click OK.

The most important thing to remember is that domain-level policies override local policies. This means that if any of these policies are set in Active Directory at the domain level, then any modifications you make to these policies in Local Computer Policy will be ineffective when logged on to the domain. This is why, in any MMC display for Local Computer Policy, like the one in Figure 12-3, each policy is shown with two settings: Local Setting and Effective Setting. Local Setting shows what you've set the policy to locally, and Effective Setting shows what your local computer is actually doing. If changes in Local Setting propagate to Effective Setting, then your policy changes are taking hold. If changes in Local Setting don't propagate, as you'll see if you look closely at Figure 12-3, then those policies have been set at a higher level—the domain level, the site level, or the organizational unit (OU) level.

FIGURE 12-3

Higher-level settings override local settings

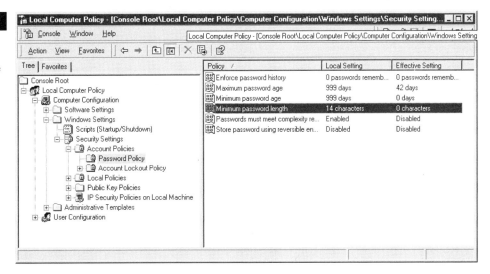

exam
🅦atch

Domain-level settings override local settings. Site-level settings override local settings. Organizational unit–level settings override local settings. Any group policy set anywhere in the hierarchy that's higher than the Local Computer Policy level will override group policy settings made in Local Computer Policy, and everywhere is higher than Local Computer Policy (except, of course, group policy set to Local Computer Policy on a different computer). We can't emphasize this enough. Remember this if you remember nothing else: Local group policy settings are the weakest possible settings. Just repeat that to yourself every night before you go to bed.

Account Lockout Policy

The Account Lockout Policy folder, also found in Local Computer Policy | Computer Configuration | Windows Settings | Security Settings | Account Policies, has only three policies, as shown in Figure 12-4. Account Lockout Policy is very simple. If you have an account lockout policy, then if someone tries to log on to a single account and fails X number of times in Y minutes, the account locks out. Once the account is locked out, no one can log on to that account, even with the proper password, for Z minutes. There are three policies in this folder, one each for each of the variables X, Y, and Z.

Set Account Lockout Duration to specify, in minutes, how long a lockout lasts. Set Account Lockout Threshold to specify the number of times someone must fail

FIGURE 12-4	
Account Lockout Policy	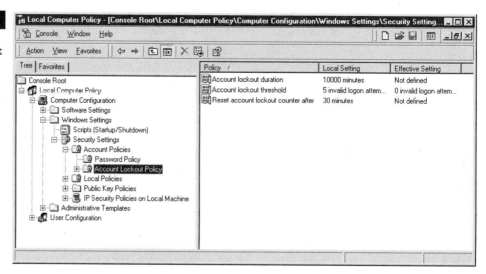

to supply the correct password for an account, and set Reset Account Lockout Counter After to specify the number of minutes in which those failures must occur, in order for the account to lock out.

All three policies must be set for account lockouts to occur.

on the **Job**

Once an account is locked out, there are two ways to unlock it. First, the user can wait out the lockout duration. If this duration is set to some very high number, or if the user needs access immediately, then an administrator can unlock the account manually. This happens by accessing that user's properties from Local Users And Groups or Active Directory. There will be an Account Locked Out option that will appear, selected, once the account locks out. The administrator simply deselects this option, and the account unlocks.

Audit Policy

Setting Audit Policy allows administrators to log user activity. The Audit Policy folder, located in Local Computer Policy | Computer Configuration | Windows Settings | Security Settings | Local Policies, contains a number of auditing policies, as shown in Figure 12-5. Each specifies some type of activity; for example, you can Audit Logon Events or Audit Directory Service Access. When auditing is turned on for a set of events, occurrences of those events are recorded in the Security Log.

FIGURE 12-5

Audit Policy

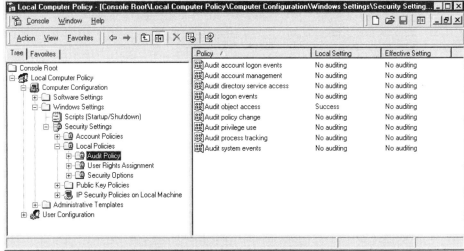

You can access the Security Log by opening Start menu | Programs | Administrative Tools, and running Event Viewer. Once Event Viewer is up, click Security Log in the left-hand pane.

When you double-click an audit policy, you'll get a Local Security Policy Setting box. All such audit policy boxes have two check boxes: one for Successes, and one for Failures. This is how you specify what to audit. For example, if we open the Audit Account Logon Events and select Failures, Windows will log only failed logon attempts. Similarly, if we select Successes, Windows will log only successful logon attempts. It is very important to note that you can select *both* boxes, and have Windows log both successes and failures.

Important audit policies include

- **Audit Account Logon Events** Logs attempts and/or failures of users to log on to accounts.

- **Audit Object Access** Logs attempts and/or failures of users to gain access to specified files, folders, and printers.

- **Audit Policy Change** Logs attempts and/or failures of users to change policy.

- **Audit Account Management** Logs attempts and/or failures of users to change properties associated with user accounts.

Audit Object Access is a special audit policy. It allows you to specify particular files and folders to be audited. Once you've turned Audit Object Access on, you have to specify which particular objects you want logged.

CertCam 12-3

Auditing Access to a Folder

This exercise shows you how to log successful accesses to a folder.

1. Open the Local Computer Policy Editor.

2. Open the Audit Policy folder, inside Local Computer Policy | Computer Configuration | Windows Settings | Security Settings | Local Policies.

3. Double-click Audit Object Access in the right-hand pane. This brings up the Local Security Policy Setting dialog box.

4. Check the Successes box. This will audit every person who successfully accesses all specified objects. Click OK.

5. Now we need to specify the object(s) to be audited. In this case, let's audit all attempts to access the Config folder inside the WINNT folder. Open My Computer, open the drive that has your system files, and open WINNT.

6. Right-click the Config folder and select Properties from the pull-down menu.

7. Click the Security tab, and Advanced. This will bring up the Access Control Settings For Config dialog box, as shown in the following illustration.

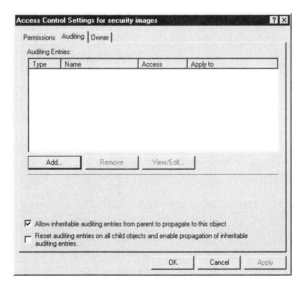

8. Click Add. This brings up the Select User, Computer, Or Group screen, with a list of all local users, computers, and groups, as shown here. In this screen, you specify a directory object whose activities you want to audit.

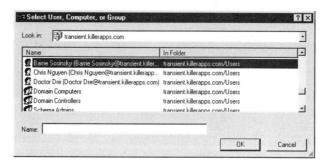

9. Select a directory object (user, computer, or group) and click OK.

10. This brings up the Auditing Entry For Config screen, which allows you to specify exactly what sorts of actions you want to audit for this directory object and this file or folder. We've chosen to audit the Administrator's failures to Traverse Folder/Execute File, failures to List Folder/Read Data, and successes to Read Attributes and Read Extended Attributes, as shown in following dialog box. Click OK. You're auditing!

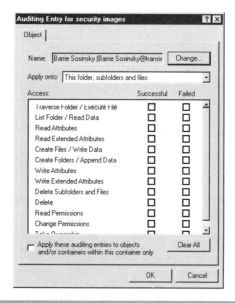

SCENARIO & SOLUTION	
I want to see who logs on to this computer. How can I do this?	Open up Audit Policy, Audit Account Logon Events, and select Successes.
I want to see if anybody without access is trying to change policy. How can I find this out?	Open up Audit Policy, Audit Policy Changes, and select Failures.
I keep changing the local settings and they don't take effect. What am I doing wrong?	Domain-level policy settings are overriding local settings. Change or remove policy settings at the domain level.

exam
Watch
Microsoft cautions administrators to select auditing carefully, since the size of the Security Log is limited. Auditing also consumes computing resources and slows performance.

User Rights Assignment

User Rights Assignment is the most interesting part of policy setting. It is in the User Rights Assignment folder, found in Local Computer Policy | Computer Configuration | Windows Settings | Security Settings | Local Policies, that you set policies *by group*, as shown in Figure 12-6. Since User Rights Assignment lets you set policies by group, you'll see a list of the groups that a policy is enabled for under Local Setting and Effective Setting.

User Rights assignment is fairly elementary. Simply double-click the User Right in question. This will bring up a Local Security Policy Setting, as shown in Figure 12-7. You can select or deselect any of the listed groups—the right is given to any selected group. To add a group to the list, click Add.

exam
Watch
Some rights are actually negative rights. For example, granting a user the "Deny logon locally" right kills that user's ability to log on locally.

Here are some of the key user rights:

- **Access This Computer From The Network**   Allows users to access resources on this computer from the network. By default, this is assigned to Everyone.

- **Take Ownership Of Files Or Other Objects**   Allows users to take ownership of a file, which then allows the user to change permissions. Users

FIGURE 12-6

User Rights
Assignment

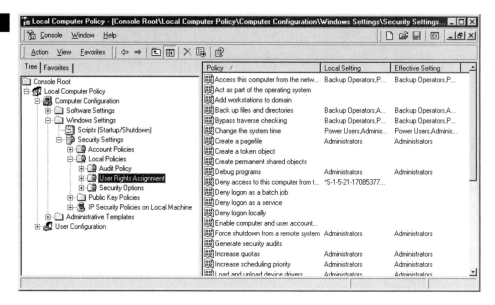

with this right can take ownership of resources that they have been denied
control over, making this a very powerful right. This is discussed in more
detail in the upcoming "From the Classroom."

FIGURE 12-7

User Right policy
setting

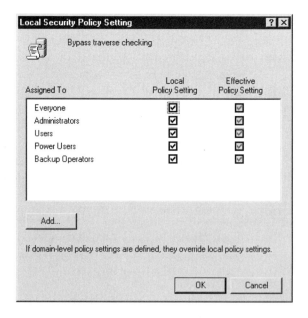

■ **Act As Part Of The Operating System** This gives a user the right to issue commands to Windows 2000 Professional that carry the same authority as a message that Windows 2000 Professional sends itself. *This is the most powerful user right possible.* Traditionally, this is only assigned to the highest-level administrator group, since it essentially gives members of the group the same power as the operating system.

FROM THE CLASSROOM

File Ownership and Permissions

The notion of ownership is pretty tricky. Originally, the person who creates a file, folder, or other object has ownership of it. The owner has full control over permissions.

If you have been granted Full Control over a file or folder, then you can change permissions. If you don't have Full Control, but you either have been granted the ability to take ownership specifically for this file, or have the Take Ownership Of Files Or Other Objects right, you can take ownership and then give yourself Full Control. In other words, *ownership overrides permissions.* While taking ownership doesn't immediately give you permission to access, taking ownership gives you the power to give yourself permission to access. This is why the Take Ownership . . . right is such a powerful right; it essentially gives users the right to access *all* files and folders, no matter what the permissions set on them.

To take ownership of an object, right-click the object, click Properties, click the Security tab, click Advanced, click the Owner tab, highlight your username, and click OK.

However, ownership is logged. You can't *give* ownership; you can only take it or give other people permission to take it. This means that if, say, an administrator takes ownership of a file that he doesn't have permission to view, he can't transfer ownership back to the original owner. If the rightful owner, or anyone who knows what's up, looks at the Owner tab, he or she can see that ownership has been transferred to the administrator.

This means that, while a member of the administrator account (or any account with the Take Ownership right) can gain access to anything, even a file that he or she has been explicitly denied access to, he or she can't *secretly* gain access to something that he or she has been denied access to. To override the permissions by taking ownership, a user will leave a visible footprint.

—Chris Thi Nguyen

Group Policy Configuration

Most of Group Policy involves policies concerning how users interact with the rest of the operating system environment. Of course, Group Policy itself is configurable, too. You configure Group Policy not by accessing some separate set of Group Policy Properties, but rather by dealing with a particular subset of Group Policy that specifically concerns itself.

Almost all of the options controlling the Group Policy are contained in the Group Policy subfolder, within Local Computer Policy | Computer Configuration | Administrative Templates | System, as shown in Figure 12-8.

FIGURE 12-8	

Meta-Group Policy

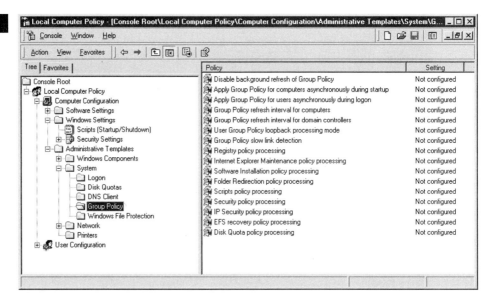

Some important Group Policies are as follows:

- **Group Policy Refresh Interval For Computers** This policy controls how frequently Group Policy propagates throughout the system. If you have a long refresh interval, then Group Policy changes will take a while to propagate. This means that you can, for example, remove a group from some powerful user right, and, for the length of time between your policy change and the next refresh, that group still has that user right.

- **Disable Background Refresh Of Group Policy** If this policy is on, Group Policy will not refresh while a computer is running.

exam
ⓦatch
If you need to propagate a Group Policy change immediately, you can force an immediate Group Policy refresh. From the Start menu, click Run. Type secedit /refreshpolicy MACHINE_POLICY and click OK.

SCENARIO & SOLUTION

I am making frequent changes to Group Policy, and want those changes to take effect quickly. How do I do this?	Set the Group Policy Refresh Rate to a very small interval.
Group Policy is not very important in my environment, and the refresh occupies a lot of machine time. What should I do to minimize processor time taken by refreshes?	Either set the Group Policy Refresh Rate to a very large interval, or select Disable Background Refresh.
I made a change to an important Group Policy. How do I make that change take effect immediately?	From the command line, type **secedit/ refreshpolicy MACHINE_POLICY**.

CERTIFICATION OBJECTIVE 12.02

Encrypting Data on a Hard Disk by Using EFS

Files on NTFS-formatted drives can be encrypted with Windows 2000's integrated encryption.

There are a few key things to understand about encryption through EFS:

- Encryption depends on NTFS.

- NTFS's two big file features—encryption and compression—are not simultaneously applicable. You can encrypt a file or compress it, but not both.

- Access to encrypted files is slower than access to unencrypted files.

- Encryption is intended to make a file accessible only to the user who encrypted it. There's no easy way to encrypt a file for two regular users to access it.

- Encryption is transparent to the user who has access. The user doesn't have to do anything to unencrypt the file before reading it—he just double-clicks the icon and the file opens, as usual. To users without access, the file will not open, or will open as garbage.

- EFS uses a public key/private key encryption scheme.

- EFS comes with a built-in recovery scheme. Certain users are designated as Encryption Recovery Agents. If a user loses his private key or certificate, a designated Encryption Recovery Agent can decrypt the file.

When you encrypt a file, EFS randomly generates a specific EFS encryption key. This key is used to encrypt the file, and will eventually be used to decrypt the file.

This EFS key, however, needs to be secured. Once the EFS key is used to encrypt the file, the key itself is protected by being encrypted within the user's public key. To unlock the public key, you need your private key. Thus, in order to decrypt a file, you have to have access to your private key to get at the EFS key.

Your private key is stored on your workstation. This means that you can only gain access to the file when you have authenticatable access to your private key.

exam
ⓦatch

Private key/public key encryption schemes are asymmetric encryption schemes. This means that the key that is used to encrypt a file is different from the key that is used to decrypt the file. The key randomly generated by EFS at encryption works on a symmetric encryption scheme—the same key is used to decrypt the file. So EFS works, in the end, by double-encryption—first a symmetric encryption with a single key, and then an asymmetric encryption of that single key with the public/private key system.

CertCam 12-4

EXERCISE 12-4

Encrypting an Object

1. Right-click an object (this can be from Windows Explorer, your desktop, and so on) that is located on an NTFS partition. Select Properties, select the General tab, and click Advanced.

2. This brings up the Advanced Attributes dialog box. Select the Encrypt Contents To Secure Data check box, as shown in the following dialog box.

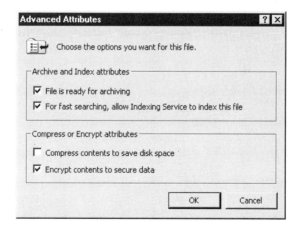

3. Click OK. This will bring up a number of options. If you're encrypting a file, you will be prompted to specify whether you want to encrypt the folder that the file is in. If you're encrypting a folder, you will be prompted to specify whether you want to encrypt just the folder, or all the contents of the folder.

4. When you select your option and click OK to get out, Windows will encrypt the object. (If the folder is compressed, when you select the Encrypt check box, the Compress check box will automatically deselect itself.)

<table>
<tr><td>

EXERCISE 12-5

</td><td>

Decrypting an Object as the Originally Encrypting User

Decrypting permanently unencrypts a file or file, letting everybody have access.

1. You must be the user who originally encrypted the object.

2. Right-click an object (this can be from Windows Explorer, your desktop, and so on). Select Properties, select the General tab, and click Advanced.

3. Deselect the Encrypt Contents To Secure Data box, click OK.

4. If you're decrypting a folder, you'll get the same dialog box as shown in Exercise 12-4, asking you whether you want to decrypt just the folder, or all its contents.

</td></tr>
</table>

exam
ⓦatch
When you encrypt a folder, Windows 2000 doesn't actually encrypt the folder itself. Rather, it simply puts a mark on the folder, telling Windows to encrypt any files added to the folder.

on the
ⓙob
If you can't see the Advanced button, then the object is not on an NTFS drive. You can't encrypt or compress on a non-NTFS partition.

Moving Your Private Key

There are two ways to take your private key with you, giving you access to your encrypted files as you move from workstation to workstation. You do this by exporting and importing your certificate with its private key.

The first way is to set up a roaming profile. The private key will be accessible through the roaming profile.

The second way is to take your private key with you on a floppy disk. To do this, you need to *export* and *import* your certificate. To do this, you need to use the Certificates MMC snap-in. To gain access to the Certificates MMC snap-in, Select Run from the Start menu, and type **mmc /a**. At the Console menu, select Add/Remove Snap-In. This brings up the Add/Remove Snap-In window.

Click Add. This brings up a menu of snap-ins; choose Certificates. At step 5, instead of choosing Local Computer, choose My User Certificates. (You can also add the Certificates snap-in to your custom-made Local Computer Policy console by opening the custom-made console, clicking Console, selecting Add/Remove snap-in, and adding the Certificates snap-in.) You then need to export your certificate.

Exporting Your Private Key

Exporting your private key to a new computer will let you access your old encrypted files from that new computer.

1. Open the Certificates MMC snap-in.

2. Open Certificates | Current User folder. (If you can't see this, you need to add another Certificate MMC snap-in, and select My User Certificates, as described earlier.)

3. Open the Personal folder, and then the Certificates folder. This will reveal your certificate in the left-hand pane, as shown next. (In this screen, we've added the Certificates MMC snap-in to our custom-made Local Computer Policy snap-in, and drilled down to the Personal | Certificates folder.)

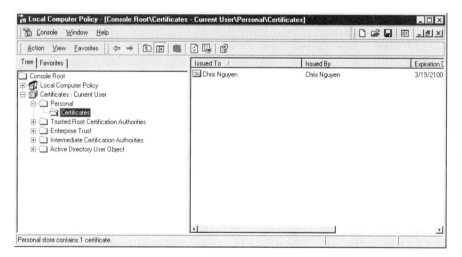

4. Single-click the certificate, highlighting it.

5. Click the Action menu, expand All Tasks, and select Export . . . This will begin the Export Certificate Wizard.

6. You need to tell the wizard to send your private key along with your certificate. At the first prompt, highlight Yes, Export The Private Key to export your private key with your certificate.

7. If you're moving to another Windows 2000 or NT4 SP4 system, leave Enable Strong Protection selected; otherwise, deselect it.

8. Specify a password. You'll need this password to import the certificate.

9. Windows will now save your certificate with private key to a file. Click Browse to specify the location to save the certificate to, and enter a filename. Your exported certificate will be saved as a Personal Information Exchange .pfx file.

10. Copy this file to a floppy disk. Put the disk in your pocket. You are now carrying your private key.

You'll need to transfer this file to the new workstation where you need access to the encrypted files. The import process is almost identical to the export process.

CertCam 12-7

EXERCISE 12-7

Import the Private Key

Importing a private key to a new computer will allow you to access and decrypt your encrypted files from that new computer.

1. Get to or create a Certificates (Current User) MMC snap-in at the new computer.

2. Open Certificates (Current User), Personal.

3. Inside the Personal folder is a Certificates folder. Right-click the Certificates folder, expand the All Tasks item, and choose Import . . . .

4. This will run the Import Certificate Wizard. You will be asked to locate the file with the exported private key and certificate that you created in Exercise 12-6 and to supply the password that you specified in that same exercise.

5. This will import the private key, allowing you access to encrypted files from the new computer.

Recovery Agents

Things can happen to private keys—they can get deleted, or lost in disk crashes, or erased in formats. If a user loses his private key, then he also loses access to encrypted files and folders. There is nothing a normal user can do on his own to regain access to encrypted files and folders once his public key is lost.

Windows 2000, however, comes with a built-in recovery system. You can designate certain users to be recovery agents. Recovery agents can decrypt files without needing the original encryptor's private key or randomly generated EFS key. To be a recovery agent, you need to be assigned a special recovery agent certificate.

To add a recovery agent, you need to be an Administrator, and you need to know the location of the certificate of the user who is to be a recovery agent. If you are part of an Active Directory system, then speak to your network administrator about the location of the certificate. To gain access to a certificate locally, you need to create a concrete instance of the certificate as a .cer file. To do this, follow Exercise 12-6, steps 1–5. At step 6, choose No, Do Not Export Private Key. At step 7, make sure you're exporting not as a .pfx, but as a .cer. Save this .cer to a location, and remember where that location is.

Recovery agents can simply decrypt files, as demonstrated in Exercise 12-5.

Adding a Recovery Agent

With this exercise, you can add recovery agents who can decrypt files, even if the associated public key is unavailable.

1. Open the Group Policy Editor from Exercise 12-1.

2. Open Local Computer Policy | Computer Configuration | Windows Settings | Security Settings | Public Key Policies | Encrypted Data Recovery Agents, as shown in the following screen.

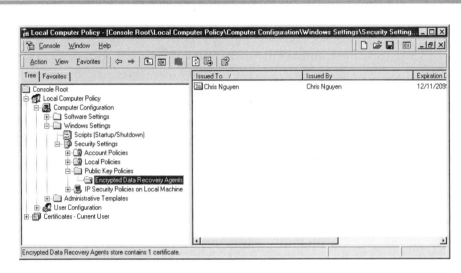

3. Right-click the Encrypted Data Recovery Agent folder. Select Add.

4. This will run the Add Recovery Agent Wizard.

5. You'll need to locate the certificate. If you're searching in Active Directory, click Browse Directory. To gain access to a certificate locally, you need to create a concrete instance of the certificate as a .cer file.

6. Finish the wizard. The user whose certificate you selected will be added as a recovery agent.

SCENARIO & SOLUTION

You want no one else to access your file but you. What should you do to the file?	Encrypt the file.
You want to be able to access your encrypted file wherever you go, without bothering with importing and exporting certificates. What should you do?	Set up a roaming profile. Your private key will be stored on the network.
You have lost your private key and need access to an encrypted file. How do you decrypt the file?	Send the file to an encryption recovery agent, or, assign yourself status as an encryption recovery agent.

Disabling EFS

To prevent anybody from encrypting data on a computer system, simply remove all Encryption Recovery Agents. Windows will not allow encryption unless there are certificated recovery agents.

Simply open Local Computer Policy | Computer Configuration | Windows Settings | Security Settings | Public Key Policies | Encrypted Data Recovery Agents, and delete every listed agent.

The Cipher Command

The Cipher command is a powerful runline command for encrypting and decrypting data.

To execute Cipher, from the Start menu, click Run and type the following:

cipher [/e| /d] [/s:*dir*] [/a][/i] [/f] [/q] [/h] [*pathname* [. . .]]

The variables do the following:

- ■ /e Encrypts the specified file.
- ■ /d Decrypts the specified file.
- ■ /s: *dir* Performs the selected operation on all folders and subfolders within the specified directory *dir*.
- ■ /a Performs the selected operation on all files with the specified name.
- ■ /i Continues the selected operation even if errors occur.
- ■ /f Forces encryption, even if the files are already encrypted.
- ■ /q Minimizes reporting during the encryption process.
- ■ /h Performs the selected operation on hidden files.

CERTIFICATION OBJECTIVE 12.03

Implementing, Configuring, Managing, and Troubleshooting Local User Accounts

Users and groups are important because they allow an administrator the ability to limit the ability of users and groups to perform certain actions by assigning them rights and permissions. On Member Servers you can create and manage local users and groups using Computer Management Users And Groups. A local user or group is an account that can be granted permissions and rights on the computer on which it was created. Local Users And Groups is not available on domain controllers, as Active Directory is used to manage users and groups on domain controllers.

Creating and Managing User Accounts

Windows 2000 creates some users by default on a Member Server: the Administrator account and the Guest account (which is disabled by default). User Accounts that you create can have usernames that contain up to 20 uppercase or lowercase characters, excluding the following; " / \ [ ] : ; | = + * ? < >. A username cannot consist solely of periods or spaces, and cannot be the same as any other user or group name on the computer being administered. When creating a User Account, you will also need to assign the user a password, which the user will by default be prompted to change the first time he or she logs on to the system. Windows 2000 passwords can be up to 127 characters long, but Windows 98 and Windows 95 support only 14-character passwords; so if you are working in a mixed environment, you will want to keep that in mind. Exercise 12-9 shows you how to add a new user.

EXERCISE 12-9

Adding a New User

Perform the following steps in adding a new user:

1. Click Start | Programs | Administrative Tools | Computer Management. Open Local Users And Groups.

2. In the left pane, highlight the Users folder.

3. From the Action menu, select New User.

4. Give the user a username based on your organization's conventions. It is common to use the first initial and last name of the user. You should also give the user a description, so that you and future administrators will be able to easily identify the user. You will also need to give the user a password. Note that the user will be prompted to change this password the first time

he or she logs on. You may also disable the account at this screen if it is not needed immediately. The following dialog box shows the New User window.

5. Click Create, and then click Close. Note that in the following screen, the new user appears in the list of users.

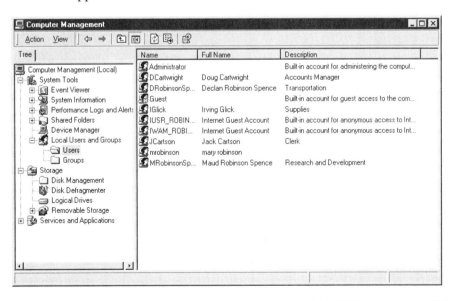

6. Now you can manage the new user account by double-clicking the new user in the right pane. Note that there are now four tabs associated with the properties of the user account.

7. Click the Member Of tab. Note that, by default, the user is only a member of the Users Group. Click Add.

8. From the top pane of the Select Groups Windows, highlight Backup Operators and click Add. Note that the Backup Operators group now appears in the lower pane and is associated with the computer on which it was created: Robinson. Click OK.

The Profile tab is used to map the user to the location of the profile, to give the user a login script, and to map the user to the home directory. In the Profile Path you would enter the location in which you want the user's profile to be stored. This profile can be stored locally or on another server. Figure 12-9 shows the Properties windows for the user.

FIGURE 12-9

The User
Properties
window

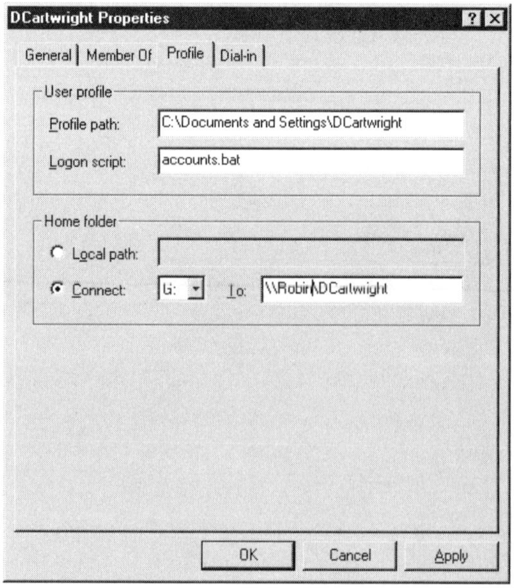

DCartwright Properties	? X

General | Member Of | Profile | Dial-in |

User profile

Profile path: `C:\Documents and Settings\DCartwright`

Logon script: `accounts.bat`

Home folder

○ Local path: [   ]

● Connect: `G:` ▾ To: `\\Robin\DCartwright`

[OK] [Cancel] [Apply]

If a user complains that it is taking an extremely long time to log on to his or her computer, check the size of the profile. Each time a user logs on to a machine, the entire profile is downloaded to that particular machine. If the user has a large amount of data stored in the profile, this download will obviously take longer.

The Login Script will map the user to whatever network drives you choose as the administrator. This is written as a batch file using the Net Use command.

The user's home folder is generally a place where users are allowed to keep their own data. In many organizations, the only people with rights to this folder are the user and the administrator. If the folder is kept locally, use Local Path to enter its location. If the user's folder is kept on another server, connect it as a mapped drive using the *servername\sharename* convention.

The Dial-In tab is used to give the user permissions for a dial-in account to your network.

Creating users on a domain controller is a process very similar to creating them on a Member Server, except that the operations are performed in Start | Programs | Administrative Tools | Active Directory Users And Computers.

Creating and Managing Computer Accounts

A computer account is an account that is created by a domain administrator and uniquely identifies the computer on the domain. The newly created account is used so that a computer may be brought into a Windows 2000 domain.

In order to create a new computer account, you must be logged on as a member of the Domain Admins Group.

Exercise 12-10 shows you how to add a computer to your domain.

In order to manage tasks such as disk management or services on the computer you have added, highlight the computer, and choose Manage from the Action menu.

Creating and Managing Local Groups

On a Member Server, a local group is one that is granted rights and permissions for that computer. If the computer participates in a domain, user accounts and global

CertCam 12-10

EXERCISE 12-10

Adding a Computer to the Domain

1. Log on as a member of the Domain Admins Group.

2. Open the Active Directory Users And Computers snap-in.

3. From the Action menu, choose New, and then choose Computer. The New Object – Computer window will open.

4. From the New Object – Computer window, add the name of the new computer. Note that you can also add pre-Windows 2000 computers to your domain. The following dialog box shows a computer named Scott being added to the domain.

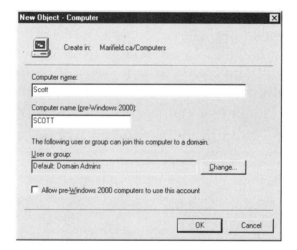

5. When you have entered the name of the computer, click OK.

groups from the domain can also be granted rights and permissions. Like local users, local groups are created in the Local Users And Groups portion of Computer Management in the Administrative Tools. By selecting Groups from the console tree, you can select New Group from the Action menu. You will give the group a name and click Add to add members to your group. Figure 12-10 shows the members of the group Researchers.

on the

!

() ob

A local group name cannot be the same as any other group name or username on the computer being administered.

A user who belongs to a group has all the rights and privileges assigned to that group. If a user is assigned to more than one group, then the user has all the rights and permissions granted to every group to which he or she belongs. If a user is a member of two groups the user will have the least-restrictive access provided by his or her group membership.

Windows 2000 provides several groups for you. By default, the following groups are placed in the built-in folders for Active Directory Users And Computers: Account Operators, Administrators, Back-Up Operators, Guests, Printer Operators, Replicator, Server Operators, and Users.

FIGURE 12-10

Group members

CERTIFICATION OBJECTIVE 12.04

Creating and Managing User Authentication

User profiles are collections of data and folders that are used to configure the desktop settings, applications settings, and personal data for each user. Thus, when multiple users share a computer, each can have a unique desktop and connection when logging on. This also provides consistency for each user. Desktop settings incorporate things like mapped network connections, files in My Documents, icons on the desktop, wallpaper, and Start menu items. As illustrated in Figure 12-11, profiles are defined on the Profile tab for each user's properties. This is where you assign a path to the user's profile.

There are three types of user profiles:

- **Local profiles** Local user profiles are kept on one local computer hard drive. When users initially log on to a computer, a Local profile is created for them in the \%*systemdrive*%\Documents And Settings\<*username*> folder (for example, C:\Winnt\Documents And Settings\gsimard). When users log off the computer,

FIGURE 12-11

The user
Properties
dialog box.
This is where
you enter the
user profile path.

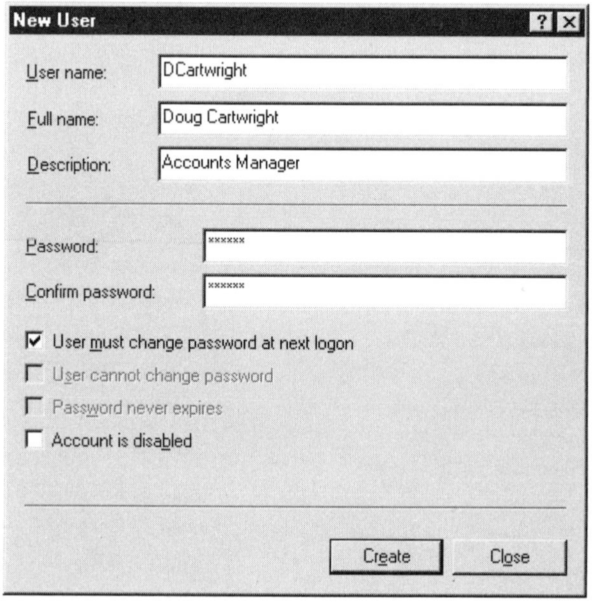

the changes that they made while they were logged on will be saved to their Local profile on that client computer. This way, subsequent logons to that computer will bring up their personal settings. When users log on to a different computer, they will not receive these settings, as they are local to the computer in which they made the changes. Therefore, each user who logs on to that computer receives individual desktop settings. Local profiles are ideal for users who only use one computer. For users who require access to multiple computers, the Roaming profile would be the better choice.

exam
ⓦatch

Remember that local profiles are always stored on the local computer. They are created in the \%systemdrive%\Documents And Settings\<username> folder on the local computer by default.

■ **Nonmandatory Roaming profiles** Roaming user profiles are stored on the network file server, and are the perfect solution for users who have access to multiple computers. This way, their profile is accessible no matter where they log on in the domain. When users log on to a computer within their domain, their Roaming profile will be copied from the network server to the client computer, and the settings will be applied to the computer while they are logged on. Subsequent logons will compare the Roaming profile files to the Local profile files. The file server then copies only any files that have been altered since the user last logged on locally, significantly decreasing the time required to log on. When the user logs off, any changes that the user made on the local computer will be copied back to the profile on the network file server. If a user attempts to log on to a computer with a Nonmandatory Roaming user profile, and the profile is not available, the user can still log on. A user who has logged on to the particular computer previously receives a locally cached copy of the Roaming profile. Unfortunately, none of the changes that the user makes to the local Roaming profile will be saved if the file server is still unavailable when the user logs off. The changes will be saved back to the file server if it is back online by the time the user logs off. If the user has never logged on to the computer before and the file server is unavailable, the computer gives the user a temporary profile created from the workstation's default user profile. The temporary file is then stored in the \%*systemroot*%\Documents And Settings\Temp directory. As soon as the user logs off, the Temp directory is deleted, and none of the changes are saved to the profile.

■ **Mandatory Roaming profiles** Mandatory user profiles are Roaming profiles that cannot be changed by the user. They are usually created to define desktop configuration settings for groups of users in order to simplify administration and support. Users can make changes to their desktop settings while they are logged on, but these changes will not be saved to the profile, as Mandatory profiles are read only. The next time they log on, their desktop will be set back to the original Mandatory profile settings. The downside to Mandatory user profiles is that a user who tried to log on when the Mandatory Roaming profile was not available would not be permitted to log on at all. The user would receive an error message, and would not be allowed to log on until the profile could be loaded. You can have a different Mandatory Roaming profile for each user, for each group of users, or for all users. If you assign a Roaming profile to groups of users or all users, make sure that they are Mandatory. This is because more than one user uses it; you don't want any of them to make changes to it, because this would change the profile that everyone else receives.

exam
⍟atch

To make a Nonmandatory Roaming profile Mandatory, a hidden file called ntuser.dat in the user profile must be renamed to ntuser.man.

SCENARIO & SOLUTION

What are the three profile types?	Local user profiles, Roaming user profiles and Mandatory Roaming user profiles.
What kind of profiles are stored on file servers?	Roaming user profiles and Mandatory Roaming user profiles.
Where are Local profiles stored?	On the local computer.
What happens if a user tries to log on and the user's Mandatory Roaming profile is unavailable?	They will not be permitted to log on.

on the
job

Mandatory Roaming user profiles are very handy to use from the help desk support perspective. The user support staff will be able to determine the causes of user problems more quickly, as they will see any changes to the profile immediately. They can also be used to lock down users' systems so that they are limited in the "damage" that they can do (for example, installing unauthorized gaming software that conflicts with existing work-related software).

EXERCISE 12-11

Switching Between a Local Profile and a Roaming Profile

To switch between a Local profile and a Roaming profile on a particular computer, simply follow these steps:

1. Access the System Properties for the computer and click the User Profiles tab. The following dialog box shows the User Profiles tab of System properties.

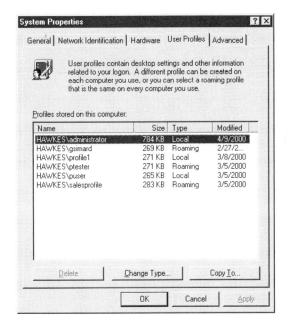

2. Select the user that you would like to change the profile type for, and then click Change Type.

3. Select the profile type (Roaming or Local) that you would like the user to have.

4. Click OK twice to accept the changes you have made. Shown here is the Change Profile Type dialog box.

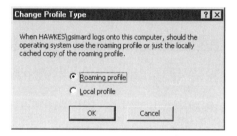

All new profiles are a copy of the default user profile. You can have them modified initially by an administrator, or allow the users to log on and make changes. Note that this works only if you are a member of the Administrator's group. To copy a user profile, go into the System Properties and choose the User Profiles tab. Next, select the profile that you would like to copy and click Copy To. In the Copy To dialog box, you can either type in or click Browse to look for the profile that you would like to copy to (for example, \\hawkes\profiles\gsimard). Figure 12-12 shows the Copy To dialog box. You also need to change the Permitted To Use user to the person whose profile you are copying to. Simply click Change, find the user or group that you want to have access to the profile, and click OK. Click OK two more times to complete the profile copy.

FIGURE 12-12

The Copy To dialog box. Be sure to give the appropriate permissions to the user to whom you are copying the profile.

User profiles include the My Documents folder, which Windows 2000 automatically creates on the desktop where users can store their personal files. The My Documents folder is the default location for File Open and File Save As commands. Users can change their profiles by doing things such as adding an icon to the desktop, changing a screensaver, making a new network connection, or adding a file to the My Document folder. These settings are then saved back to the profile on the server. The next time the user logs on, the profile changes are there.

You can create a customized Roaming user profile to give specialized profiles to users, depending on which department they are in. You can then add or remove any applications, shortcuts, and connections according to what each department requires. Customized Roaming user profiles are also helpful for troubleshooting and for technical support. They make technical support easier, as the technical support staff would know what programs and exact shortcuts should be there, so they will notice any deviations immediately. To create a customized Roaming user profile, set up a desktop environment and connections for a user as a template. Once you have the template profile set up, you can copy the template profile to the user's Roaming profile location. Note: Windows 2000 does not support the use of encryption with Roaming user profiles.

exam Watch

When you use Roaming user profiles with Terminal Services clients, the profiles are not replicated to the server until the user logs off.

CERTIFICATION SUMMARY

We've learned many important security features for Windows 2000 Professional in this chapter.

First, we've learned how to handle security features through Group Policy. In Windows 2000 Professional, you can make alterations to Local Computer Policy, setting user rights by group, starting audits, setting password and account lockout policy, and allowing and disallowing many different actions by users. However, Local Computer Policy is the weakest of all policy levels, being overridden by policy set at the domain level, site level, or organizational unit level in a domain environment.

We've also learned how to use EFS, the built-in encryption system that comes with NTFS. EFS encryption works on a public key/private key system. This means that only the encrypting user can view the encrypted files, and this user must bring his private key with him wherever he goes, if he wants to continue reading encrypted files. Only designated encryption recovery agents can decrypt files with a private key.

TWO-MINUTE DRILL

Implementing, Configuring, Managing, and Troubleshooting Local Group Policy

❑ Group Policy settings alter users' rights, abilities, and powers.

❑ The Group Policy Editor is an MMC snap-in, accessible through the GPEDIT.MSC command or through a custom-made MMC.

❑ Audit Policy sets auditing, which allows you to record activity to the Security Log.

❑ Password Policy can force users to create harder-to-guess passwords, and to change these passwords more often.

❑ Account Lockout Policy sets the circumstances under which an account will lock out, refusing access even to the proper password, and sets the length of time a lockout lasts.

❑ Higher-level settings to Group Policy override local settings.

❑ In a domain environment, every level is higher than the local level.

❑ Group Policy changes don't take effect immediately; they take effect at the next refresh.

Encrypting Data on a Hard Disk by Using EFS

❑ EFS is built-in encryption that is available on NTFS.

❑ You can either encrypt or compress, but not both.

❑ Encrypted files are only accessible to the encrypting user.

❑ Encrypted files can only be decrypted by the encrypting user, or a designated encryption recovery agent.

❑ You can take your private key with you by creating a Roaming profile.

❏ You can take your private key with you by exporting your certificate with a private key.

❏ You can encrypt and decrypt from the command line, using the Cipher command.

❏ When you encrypt a folder, Windows simply marks the folder and automatically encrypts any files placed inside the folder.

Implementing, Configuring, Managing, and Troubleshooting Local User Accounts

❏ New Users are created in Computer Management, Users, And Groups.

❏ You have to be a member of the Domain Admins Group to create a computer account in a domain.

❏ Users get all the rights and permissions granted to them by their group membership.

Creating and Managing User Authentication

❏ Local user profiles are used to save any personal desktop settings made by a user on a particular computer, and are stored locally on that computer.

❏ Roaming user profiles are used to save a user's settings to be used on any computer in the domain. These profiles are stored on a network file server.

❏ Mandatory profiles are read-only Roaming profiles.

❏ Default user profiles can be created as a basis for users' settings.

❏ Ntuser.dat in the user profile must be renamed to ntuser.man to make a Nonmandatory Roaming profile Mandatory.

SELF TEST

The following questions will help you measure your understanding of the material presented in this chapter. Read all of the choices carefully, as there may be more than one correct answer. Choose all correct answers for each question.

Implementing, Configuring, Managing, and Troubleshooting Local Group Policy

1. The lowest authority level of Group Policy is
   A. Domain level
   B. Site level
   C. Organizational unit level
   D. Local level

2. To make Group Policy refresh every day on your computer
   A. Force a manual refresh every morning.
   B. Set the policy Group Policy Refresh Interval For Computers to one day.
   C. Enable the policy Disable Background Refresh of Group Policy.
   D. In Group Policy Properties, set Refresh Interval to 1 day.

3. User Rights
   A. Are set universally, applying to all users.
   B. Are set for all users in the Group that the Group Policy is tuned toward.
   C. Are set for all groups that are specified for that User Right.
   D. Are set for all users who are User Right Enabled.

4. You must take ownership to
   A. Delete a file.
   B. Change permission on a file.
   C. Change permissions on a file that you don't have permission to change permissions for.
   D. Transfer ownership to another.

5. In the right-hand pane of the Group Policy Editor MMC snap-in, the policy that is actually operational is shown under the column
   A. Local Setting

    B. Domain Setting

    C. Current Setting

    D. Effective Setting

6. Roger is trying to set minimum password length to 10 characters. He opens the Group Policy Editor, opens Local Computer Policy, opens up the Minimum Password Age policy, enters the number **10**, and clicks OK. He finds, however, that users are still able to enter short passwords. What went wrong?

    A. Roger is not an administrator.

    B. Roger does not have permission to change password policy.

    C. Higher-level Group Policy overrode Local Group Policy.

    D. The Password Policy general policy is disabled.

7. To disable a policy that has no Disable button in its Local Security Policy Setting dialog box, such as Minimum Password Length,

    A. Enter **0** as the value.

    B. Highlight the policy in the MMC, and press DELETE.

    C. Right-click the policy from the MMC, and select Disable.

    D. Right-click the policy from the MMC, select Properties, and deselect Configured.

8. Many users in Rich's company use very simple passwords, such as "password" and "mypassword." Rich has tried to get these users to use more complex passwords, but they keep forgetting to. What should Rich do to force these users to use harder-to-guess, non-meaningful passwords?

    A. Enable the Passwords Must Meet Password Complexity Requirement policy.

    B. Enable the Passwords Must Be Digits Only policy.

    C. Disable the Allow Recognizable Password policy.

    D. Set the Minimum Password Length policy to 10 characters.

9. To audit an object

    A. From Security Log, select Add, Object, and select the object.

    B. Turn on Audit Object Access, and, from the object's Properties menu, turn on auditing.

    C. From Security Log, select Audit, and from the Group Policy Editor, add the object to the auditing list.

D. Turn on Audit Object Access, and, from the Audit Object Access Local Security Policy Settings dialog box, click Add and select the object.

10. To access full Group Policy Editor (choose all that apply),

A. Run GPEDIT.MSC.

B. Select the Group Policy Editor from Start | Settings Control Panel | Administrative Tools.

C. Run MMC /A and add the Group Policy snap-in.

D. Select the Group Policy Editor from Start | Programs | Administrative Tools.

11. Audited events appear in

A. Event Viewer, Audit Log.

B. Event Viewer, Security Log.

C. The file specified in Audit Policy, Save Log To policy.

D. The file specified in Control Panel | Local Security Policy | Audit Wizard.

12. Mark suspects that another administrator is forcing access to his private files and changing them. Mark's private files are set to allow only him to read the files. When he checks the permissions, he sees that they are still set to his access only. What should he then check?

A. Security Log, to see who has accessed the file.

B. Event Viewer, to see who could have changed permissions.

C. Look at the current owner since ownership cannot be given back.

D. Group Policy, to see if anyone has changed permission.

13. An encryption recovery agent

A. Can recover your private key if you lose it

B. Can decrypt your encrypted files if you lose your private key

C. Can recover your randomly generated EFS key if you lose your private key

D. Can turn off encryption of any system

14. What is the best way to access a file that you've encrypted, assuming that you have access to your private key?

A. Open the file as usual.

B. Right-click the file, open the General tab, select Advanced, and deselect Encrypt Data.

C. Run the cipher /d on the file.

D. Pass the file to an encryption recovery agent.

15. To export your private key, you must

   A. Run the Private Key Export Wizard from Local Security Policy MMC.

   B. Copy the private key from your user profile folder.

   C. Run the Certificate Export Wizard from the Certificate MMC.

   D. Copy the private key from the WINNT\Security folder.

16. Who can decrypt an encrypted file? (Select all that apply.)

   A. Encrypting user

   B. Administrator

   C. Encryption recovery agent

   D. User designated by encrypting user

Encrypting Data on a Hard Disk by Using EFS

17. EFS randomly generates a key when it encrypts a file or folder. It then

   A. Throws away this key

   B. Encrypts this key in the encrypting user's public key

   C. Encrypts this key in the encrypting user's private key

   D. Stores this key in Active Directory

18. How do you encrypt a file with EFS? (Select all that apply.)

   A. You must be enabled to encrypt in Active Directory.

   B. The file must be on an NTFS drive.

   C. The file must be in an encrypted folder.

   D. The file must not be compressed by the Win2K's built-in NTFS compression.

19. Son House is a designated recovery agent. One of the employees, Sleater Kinney, has lost her private key. Ms. Kinney sends her encrypted files to House. What does House need to do to decrypt the files?

   A. Get Kinney's certificate and re-create the private key.

   B. Decrypt the file with Recovery Manager.

   C. Simply decrypt the file as a user would decrypt his or her own file.

    D. Nothing—decryption is impossible without the private key.

20. The Encrypt Contents To Secure Data check box for File X is located in

    A. Windows Explorer | Tools | Options | Encrypt | Browse | File X

    B. Windows Explorer | File X Properties | Security tab | File Properties button

    C. Windows Explorer | Tools | NTFS Properties

    D. Windows Explorer | File X Properties | General tab| Advanced button

21. The exported certificate with private key is stored as a

    A. .txt file

    B. .cer file

    C. .pfx file

    D. .pki file

22. To designate someone as a recovery agent without Active Directory, you need to know

    A. Her password

    B. The location of her .pfx

    C. The location of her .cer

    D. Nothing but her username

Implementing, Configuring, Managing, and Troubleshooting Local User Accounts

23. In order to create a computer account in a domain, you must be logged on as a member of which group? (Select all that apply.)

    A. Domain Admins

    B. Administrators

    C. Domain Users

    D. Backup Operators

24. Several users from the Accounting department will be working on a project with users from the Programming department. They need to share documents with each other, but don't want other users from the rest of the Accounting or Programming departments to have access to them. How can you facilitate this? (Select all that apply.)

A. In the Local Users And Groups section of Computer Management, create a group with those users as members. Give that group rights to the data they need to access, and deny access to all other users.

B. In Active Directory, create a group with the users in it who need access to the files.

C. Create a single logon for all the users who need access to the data to use. Tell all those working on the project the username and password.

D. In the Group Policy snap-in, give the users who need it rights to the folders.

25. A user complains to you that it is taking a long time to log on each morning. You check the size of his profile on the server and find that it is 30MB. What can you do to speed up the user's logon time? (Select all that apply.)

A. Put the profile on the user's local machine.

B. Move the user's profile to another server.

C. Have the user keep some data in a personal folder on the server rather than in the profile.

D. Delete the user's profile.

26. What are some examples of login rights? (Select all that apply.)

A. Log On As A Service

B. Shut Down The System

C. Generate Security Audits

D. Log On Locally

27. Which utility would you use to create new User Accounts?

A. User Manager For Domains

B. Computer Management Users And Groups

C. Account Manager

D. System Information

28. Which of the following are types of User Profiles? (Select all that apply.)

A. Mandatory user profiles

B. Local user profiles

C. Primary user profiles

D. Group user profiles

Creating and Managing User Authentication

29. What kinds of profiles are stored on a file server?

    A. Local user profiles

    B. Mandatory and Nonmandatory Roaming user profiles

    C. Local and Roaming user profiles

    D. Mandatory Roaming profiles and Local user profiles

30. What is the difference between a Roaming user profile and a Local user profile?

    A. A Local profile is stored on a user's computer, and a Roaming user profile is stored on a file server.

    B. A Local user profile can be stored on a user's computer or a file server, and a Roaming user profile is stored on a file server.

    C. A Local user profile is stored on a file server, and a Roaming user profile is stored on a user's computer.

    D. A Local user profile is stored on a user's computer, and a Roaming user profile can be stored on a user's computer or on a file server.

31. A user logs on and makes the following changes. Which changes will be saved to the user's Roaming profile? (Select all that apply.)

    A. Network printer connections

    B. Bookmarks that the user placed in the Windows 2000 Help system

    C. Shortcuts that the user created on the desktop

    D. User-definable settings in Windows Explorer

32. You run a company that offers computer help desk support. Which of the following profile types would aid in client help desk support?

    A. Have users use Local profiles.

    B. Have users use Mandatory Roaming profiles.

    C. Have users use Roaming profiles.

    D. Have users use group profiles.

33. Your Art department users require the same computer settings no matter where they log on. What can you do to simplify this process? (Select all that apply.)

A. Set the users up with identical Local profiles.

B. Set up Local and Roaming user profiles for each user.

C. Set up a Mandatory profile for the users in the Art department.

D. Assign a customized Roaming user profile.

LAB QUESTION

Someone has been accessing and modifying the accounting files contained in C:\Accounting. You want to catch who's doing it. Explain the audit policy you will set.

SELF TEST ANSWERS

Implementing, Configuring, Managing, and Troubleshooting Local Group Policy

1. ☑ **D.** Any Group Policy settings made at any of the other levels will override locally set Group Policy.
   ☒ **A, B,** and **C** are incorrect as they are higher levels of authority than Group Policy.

2. ☑ **B.** Setting the policy Group Policy Refresh Interval For Computers to 1 day is guaranteed and automatic.
   ☒ **A, C,** and **D** are incorrect. **A** would technically have the same effect, but it's not the most efficient way of doing things. **C** will have the opposite effect, and **D** is impossible.

3. ☑ **C.** While many other policies are set universally, User Rights in particular are set to apply to groups that are specified in each User Right.
   ☒ **A** is incorrect as it's not for all users, but for all groups specified for that User Right. **B** and **D** refer to functionality that is nonexistent.

4. ☑ **C.** You can change permissions on a file that you don't have permission to change permissions for.
   ☒ **A** is incorrect as you need not take ownership to delete a file. **B** is incorrect; without ownership, you will need permission to do so. **D** is impossible; you can only take permission, not give it.

5. ☑ **D.** While Domain settings do override Local settings, so do Site settings and OU settings. The highest-level setting is always shown under the Effective Setting column.
   ☒ **A, B,** and **C** are incorrect as the policy that is actually operational isn't shown under these columns.

6. ☑ **C.** Local Group Policy is the lowest level of Policy; any Group Policy set at OU, domain, or workgroup level overrides it.
   ☒ **A** is incorrect, since you can have permission to change policies even if you're not an administrator. **B** is incorrect, since if you didn't have permission, you wouldn't be able to open policies and change numbers. **D** refers to a nonexistent policy.

7. ☑ **A.** Entering **0** will disable a policy that has no Disable button in its Local Security Policy Setting dialog box
   ☒ **B** does nothing, and **C** and **D** are impossible.

8. ☑ **A.** Enable the Passwords Must Meet Password Complexity Requirement policy.
☒ **B** and **C** refer to nonexistent policies, and **D** does not accomplish the goal of removing *simple* passwords—you could still enter long, meaningful passwords.

9. ☑ **B.** You must turn on the Audit Object Access policy, and then go to the individual object in Windows Explorer.
☒ **A, C,** and **D** are incorrect as they instruct you through the wrong series of steps to audit an object.

10. ☑ **A, C.** To access the Group Policy Editor you must either run GPEDIT.MSC or Run MMC /A and add the Group Policy snap-in.
☒ There is no icon or menu item as in **B** or **D** (although you could create one using the methods of **C**). While there is a Local Security Policy icon in Administrative Tools, as in **B**, it only gives you access to a very limited Group Policy Editor—only the parts contained in Local Computer Policy | Computer Configuration | Windows Settings | Security Settings.

11. ☑ **B.** Event Viewer, Security Log.
☒ **A, C,** and **D** do not exist.

12. ☑ **C.** If another administrator has taken ownership, that administrator can give himself permission and then remove those permissions. However, the ownership taken will remain recorded.
☒ **A** is incorrect, since the file is not necessarily already audited. **B** is incorrect, since Event Viewer doesn't log this kind of activity. **D** is incorrect, since permission changing of particular files is not recorded in Group Policy.

13. ☑ **B.** No one can recover a private key or a randomly generated EFS key—their irreproducibility is part of the security of the system.
☒ **A, C,** and **D** are incorrect.

14. ☑ **A.** Reading encrypted files is transparent to the right user.
☒ **B** and **C** will decrypt the file permanently; if you just want to *access* the file, then you just open it. While **D** would actually work, it is extremely inefficient—encryption recovery agents are only necessary when you've lost your private key.

15. ☑ **C.** You export the private key only as part of the certificate; you can't export the private key on its own.
☒ **A, B,** and **D** are incorrect as you need not follow these instruction to export your private key.

16. ☑ **A, C.** Frequently, administrators are assigned status as encryption recovery agents, but this is not always the case. Only the original encrypting user and encryption recovery agents can decrypt a file or folder.

    ☒ **B and D.** B is incorrect for the reasons stated above, and D is incorrect as only the Encrypting user him- or herself can decrypt the file.

Encrypting Data on a Hard Disk by Using EFS

17. ☑ **B.** EFS encrypts the key using the user's public key. The private key is necessary to decrypt the public key and gain access to the randomly generated key, but the randomly generated key is actually put inside the public key.

    ☒ **A, C, and D** do not accurately describe what occurs after EFS randomly generates a key when it encrypts a file or folder.

18. ☑ **B, D.** The file must be on an NTFS drive, and the file must not be compressed by the Win2K's built-in NTFS compression.

    ☒ Anybody can encrypt, so **A** is incorrect. **C** is incorrect because encrypted files can exist in unencrypted folders.

19. ☑ **C.** The recovery agent's certificate allows someone to decrypt all files; this decryption is transparent.

    ☒ **A** is impossible. **B** refers to Recovery Manager, which does not exist. **D** is simply wrong; decryption is possible without the private key—by all recovery agents.

20. ☑ **D.** Interestingly, the encrypt feature is under the General tab, not the Security tab, as in **B**.

    ☒ **A, B, and C** are not the location of the Encrypt Contents To Secure Data check box.

21. ☑ **C.** Exporting a certificate without a private key generates a .cer; with a private key, you get a .pfx.

    ☒ **A, B, and D** are incorrect as it is stored as a .pfx file.

22. ☑ **C.** You need the straight certificate file of the .cer, not the private key containing the .pfx file, to designate someone as a recovery agent.

    ☒ **A, B, and D** are incorrect.

Implementing, Configuring, Managing, and Troubleshooting Local User Accounts

23. ☑ **A.** Domain Admins is the only group with rights to add computers to the domain as a whole.

☒　**B** is incorrect, because the Administrators Group is allowed access only to add new user or group accounts to a local machine. **C** is incorrect, because the only way a Domain User would be able to add a computer account to a domain would be if this user were also a member of the Domain Admins Group. **D** is incorrect, because Backup Operators are not permitted to perform this role.

24.　☑　**A.** Creating a group with the users who are members of the new team is a good way to keep things well organized, rather than giving all the individual users special access to the data. Local Users And Groups is where this would be done. You also need to give that group access to the data, and make sure the rest of the users don't have access to the data.
☒　**B** is partially correct, if the files reside on a server in an Active Directory domain. However, you also need to give that group rights to the data they need to access, and deny access to all other users. **C** would work, but it is not a very secure policy to give a large number of users a single logon name and password to use, as this is information that could easily be passed on to those who shouldn't have access. It also makes it easier on users to only have to remember one username and password. Finally, you would also need to give that single user account access to the data, and deny access to other user accounts. **D** is incorrect, as the Group Policy snap-in is not used for creating users and groups; it is used for creating security policies, among other things.

25.　☑　**A, C.** If the user's profile is on the local machine, the user will no longer have to download it each morning. The only stipulation would be that you are probably not backing up the user's machine, so the data may be prone to being lost. Also, by having users keep data in a personal directory on the server rather than in their profile, you eliminate the downloading time.
☒　**B** is incorrect, because by moving the data to another server, you do not solve the problem of the length of time it takes to download the profile. **D** is incorrect, because you may not want to be around when the user comes in and finds that you have deleted all the information the user has stored in his or her profile, including Internet Favorites and any data stored on the user's desktops, both part of the profile.

26.　☑　**A, D.** Both Logon As A Service and Logon Locally are considered user rights that are Logon rights. **B**, Shut Down The System, is also considered a Privilege.
☒　**C** is incorrect, because Generate Security Audits is considered a Privilege User right.

27.　☑　**B.** Computer Management Users And Groups would be used to create new User Accounts.
☒　**A** is incorrect, because this is the place where, in Windows NT 4.0 Server, users accounts were created; this is one of the changes made in Windows 2000 Server. **C** is also incorrect,

because there is no Account Manager in Windows 2000 Server, nor is there a **D**, System Information.

28. ☑   **A, B.** Mandatory user profiles and Local user profiles are two of the three types of user profiles. Roaming user profiles is the third type.
     ☒   **C** and **D** are incorrect, because Group user profiles and Primary user profiles are not profile types.

Creating and Managing User Authentication

29. ☑   **B.** All Roaming user profiles (whether Mandatory or Nonmandatory) are kept on a file server. This way, users can log on to any computer in the domain and receive their profile settings.
     ☒   **A, C,** and **D** are incorrect, because Local user profiles are stored on the local computer, not on a file server. A user who uses Local profiles needs to make changes to each computer that he or she logs on to, as the profile setting changes will not apply to any other computer than the one the user made the changes on.

30. ☑   **A.** Local profiles are always stored on the user's local machine, and Roaming user profiles are always stored on a file server. When using a Roaming user profile, a user can log on to any computer in the network and still receive the same profile. Local user profiles must be created on each machine that a user logs on to.
     ☒   **B, C,** and **D** are all incorrect, because Local user profiles are stored on the local user computer, and Roaming user profiles are stored on the file server.

31. ☑   **A, B, C,** and **D** are correct, as long as you haven't set any policies to prohibit users from doing any of them.

32. ☑   **B.** Mandatory Roaming profiles do not save users' changes back to the server. If a user deletes a printer connection or an icon, the help desk support staff would be able to figure that out immediately, as it would be different from the regular profile. They can simply ask the user to log off and log back on to return the user's desktop to the way it should be.
     ☒   **A, C,** and **D** are incorrect, because they would not aid your help desk staff in supporting the users. Local profiles would be different on every computer that a client logs on to, which might cause confusion. Roaming profiles that are not Mandatory can be changed and saved back to the server; therefore, the help desk staff will not be able to gauge what is wrong by what they have on their desktop, and so on, as every user's desktop is different. There is no such thing as group profiles, so they would not aid help desk support.

33. ☑ C, D. C is the ideal solution, because Mandatory profiles will ensure that the users always have access to the same data. **D** is also correct, because a customized Roaming user profile would set up all Art department users with the same settings. With customized Roaming user profiles, users can change their desktop settings, and those settings are saved to the file server. Therefore, they are not as easy to troubleshoot as Mandatory profiles, as the users can alter the customized settings you defined.

☒ **A** is incorrect, because configuring identical Local profiles is a lot of work, and they apply only to the one local computer. A user who changes computers will no longer have the same Local profile. **B** is incorrect, because users cannot have both Local and Roaming user profiles.

LAB ANSWER

You need to figure out who is accessing the accounting folders, and whether or not that person is internal (or has access to internal passwords) or external, and hacking in.

First, turn on Audit Object Access. Go to the C:\Accounting folder, and turn on auditing for the folder and all the folder contents. Log all successful and unsuccessful attempts to read or modify the files.

Compare this list to the list of who ought to be reading or modifying these files. You should be able to figure out which account is being used to access these files.

Now you need to figure out if the intruder is internal or is hacking in. One way to do this is to force a password change for the account, and then turn on Audit Account Logon Events, and turn on both Successes and Failures. A high number of Failures associated with the account(s) being used to access the files normally indicates an automated hack attack.

If the account still continues to access the files, with no interruption after the forced password change, then the intruder is either the actual user who is supposed to be associated with the account, or someone with access to that user's password.

MCSE

MICROSOFT CERTIFIED SYSTEMS ENGINEER

A

About the CD

T he CD-ROM accompanying this book contains the CertTrainer software. CertTrainer comes complete with ExamSim, Skill Assessment tests, CertCam movie clips, the e-book (electronic version of the book), and Drive Time. CertTrainer is easy to install on any Windows 98/NT/2000 computer and must be installed to access these features. You may, however, browse the e-book directly from the CD without installing it.

Installing CertTrainer

If your computer CD-ROM drive is configured to autorun, the CD-ROM will automatically start up upon inserting the disk. From the opening screen, you may either browse the e-book or install CertTrainer by pressing the Install Now button. This will begin the installation process and create a program group named CertTrainer. To run CertTrainer, Use Start | Programs | CERTTRAINER.

System Requirements

CertTrainer requires Windows 98 or higher, Internet Explorer 4.0 or above, and 600MB of hard disk space for full installation.

CertTrainer

CertTrainer provides a complete review of each exam objective, organized by chapter. You should read each objective summary and make certain that you understand it before proceeding to the SkillAssessor. If you still need more practice on the concepts for any objective, use the In Depth button to link to the corresponding section from the Study Guide or use the CertCam button to view a short AVI clip illustrating various exercises from within the chapter.

Once you have completed the review(s) and feel comfortable with the material, launch the SkillAssessor quiz to test your grasp of each objective. Once you complete the quiz, you will be presented with your score for that chapter.

ExamSim

As its name implies, ExamSim provides you with a simulation of the actual exam. The number of questions, the type of questions, and the time allowed are intended to be an accurate representation of the exam environment. You will see the following screen when you are ready to begin ExamSim:

When you launch ExamSim, a digital clock display will appear in the upper-left corner of your screen. The clock will continue to count down to zero, unless you choose to end the exam before the time expires.

There are three types of questions on the exam:

- **Multiple choice**   These questions have a single correct answer that you indicate by selecting the appropriate check box.

- **Multiple-multiple choice**   These questions require more than one correct answer. Indicate each correct answer by selecting the appropriate check boxes.

- **Simulations**   These questions simulate actual Windows 2000 menus and dialog boxes. After reading the question, you are required to select the appropriate settings to most accurately meet the objectives for that question.

Saving Scores as Cookies

Your ExamSim score is stored as a browser cookie. If you've configured your browser to accept cookies, your score will be stored in a file named History.

If your browser is not configured to accept cookies, you cannot permanently save your scores. If you delete this History cookie, the scores will be deleted permanently.

E-Book

The entire contents of the Study Guide are provided in HTML form, as shown in the following screen. Although the files are optimized for Internet Explorer, they can also be viewed with other browsers, including Netscape.

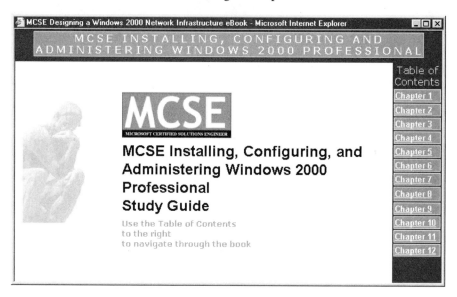

CertCam

CertCam AVI clips provide detailed examples of key certification objectives. These clips walk you step-by-step through various system configurations and are narrated by Thomas Shinder, M.D., MCSE, MCT. You can access the clips directly from the CertCam table of contents (shown in the following screen) or through the CertTrainer objectives.

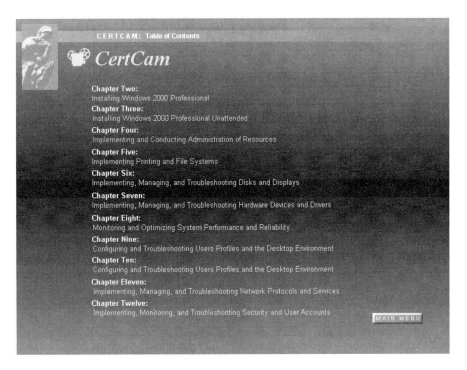

The CertCam AVI clips are recorded and produced using TechSmith's Camtasia Producer. Since AVI clips can be very large, ExamSim uses TechSmith's special AVI Codec to compress the clips. The file named tsccvid.dll is copied to your Windows\System folder when you install CertTrainer. If the AVI clip runs with audio but no video, you may need to reinstall the file from the CD-ROM. Browse to the bin folder, and run TSCC.EXE.

DriveTime

DriveTime audio tracks will automatically play when you insert the CD-ROM into a standard CD-ROM player, such as the one in your car or stereo. There is one track for each chapter. These tracks provide your with certification summaries for each chapter and are the perfect way to study while commuting.

Help

A help file is provided through a help button on the main ExamSim Gold screen in the lower-right corner.

Upgrading

A button is provided on the main ExamSim screen for upgrades. This button will take you to www.syngress.com, where you can download any available upgrades.

B

About the
Web Site

At Access.Globalknowledge, the premier online information source for IT professionals (http://access.globalknowledge.com), you'll enter a Global Knowledge information portal designed to inform, educate, and update visitors on issues regarding IT and IT education.

Get *What* You Want *When* You Want It

At the Access.Globalknowledge site, you can

- Choose personalized technology articles related to your interests. Access a news article, a review, or a tutorial, customized to what you want to see, regularly throughout the week.

- Continue your education, in between Global courses, by taking advantage of chat sessions with other users or instructors. Get the tips, tricks, and advice that you need today!

- Make your point in the Access.Globalknowledge community by participating in threaded discussion groups related to technologies and certification.

- Get instant course information at your fingertips. Customized course calendars show you the courses you want, and when and where you want them.

- Obtain the resources you need with online tools, trivia, skills assessment, and more!

All this and more is available now on the Web at http://access.globalknowledge.com. Visit today!

Glossary

ACPI   *See* Advanced Configuration and Power Interface

Active Directory   The Active Directory is implemented on Windows 2000 domain controllers, and the directory can be accessed from Windows 2000 Professional as an Active Directory client. The Active Directory arranges objects—including computer information, user and group information, shared folders, printers, and other resources—in a hierarchical structure, in which domains can be joined into trees (groups of domains that share a contiguous namespace). Trees can be joined into forests (groups of domain trees that share a common schema, configuration, and global catalog).

Active Directory Service   This service provides the means for locating the Remote Installation Service (RIS) servers and the client computers on the network. The RIS server must have access to the Active Directory.

Administration   The word *administer* is generally used as a synonym for *manage,* which in turn means to exert control. One of the many enhancements to Windows 2000—both the Professional and Server incarnations—is the ability Microsoft has given administrators to apply the degree of control desired, in a flexible and granular manner.

Add Printer Wizard   All clients running a version of the Windows operating system (Windows 2000, Windows NT, Windows 98, and Windows 95) can use the Add Printer Wizard to create a printer entry on the client. This Add Printer Wizard can create and share a printer on a print server. The Windows 2000 version of the Add Printer Wizard has more options than the wizard in other versions of Windows, but many of the same methods can be used to get the printer set up on the client.

Advanced Configuration and Power Interface (ACPI)   ACPI combines Plug and Play (PnP) capability with Power Management, and places these functions under complete control of the operating system.

Advanced Power Management (APM)   An Intel/Microsoft application programming interface (API) allowing programs indicate their requirements for power to regulate the speed of components.

Alerts   Alerts allow some action to be performed when a performance counter reaches a particular threshold. A common action is to log the event in the application event log. You can also send a network message to a specified computer. You can have the alert start a performance log to start logging when the alert occurs. Finally, you can configure the alert to start a program.

Analysis   Analysis is the process of comparison, contrast, diagnosis, diagramming, discrimination, and/or drawing conclusions.

Answer file   An answer file is a file containing the information you would normally have to key in during the setup process. Answer files help automate the installation process as all the queries presented to you during installation are answered by the answer files. With careful planning, you can prepare answers that eliminate the possibility of incorrect answers typed in by the person performing the installation, thus reducing the chances of setup failure. You can use the Setup Manager wizard to create a customized answer file. This technique minimizes the chances of committing syntax-related errors while manually creating or editing the sample answer files.

APIPA   *See* Automatic Private Internet Protocol Addressing.

APM   *See* Advanced Power Management.

AppleTalk   The AppleTalk protocol suite was developed by Apple Computer for use in its Macintosh line of personal computers. AppleTalk is a local area networking system that was developed by Apple Computer, Inc. AppleTalk networks can run over a variety of networks that include Ethernet, FDDI, and Token Ring, as well as Apple's proprietary media system LocalTalk. Macintosh computers are very popular in the education and art industries, so familiarity with the way they communicate using their native protocol is very useful.

AppleTalk printing device   Another type of remote printer is the AppleTalk printing device. Like a Transmission Control Protocol/Internet Protocol (TCP/IP) printer, an AppleTalk printer can be connected directly to an AppleTalk network or shared across the network through an AppleShare print server. Like the TCP/IP printers, a large number of modern, high-capacity PostScript printers can be configured to communicate with an AppleTalk network, as well as a TCP/IP network. In fact, many Hewlett-Packard LaserJet printers have JetDirect cards that will speak TCP/IP and AppleTalk at the same time.

Application (software)   A program designed to perform a specific function directly for the user or for another application program. Examples of applications would be, for example, word processors, database programs, graphics/drawing programs, Web browsers, e-mail programs.

Application Service Provider (ASP)   ASPs are companies that manage applications and provide organizations with application hosting services. Analysts expect the ASP market will be a six billion-dollar industry by the year 2001. The application-hosting model offers organizations the option of outsourcing application support and maintenance.

ASP   *See* Application Service Provider.

Auditing   Windows 2000 gives the ability to audit security-related events, track access to objects and use of user rights, and detect attempted and successful access (authorized and unauthorized) to the network. Auditing is not enabled by default, but once enabled, a security log is generated that provides information in regard to specific activities performed on the computer.

Automatic Private Internet Protocol Addressing (APIPA)   APIPA, or Automatic Client Configuration, is a new feature initially available in Windows 98. The feature has been extended to Windows 2000 and allows Dynamic Host Control Protocol (DHCP) client computers to self-configure their IP addressing information in the event a DHCP server is not available when the computer issues a DHCPDISCOVER message. It also allows self-configuration when it senses that it has been moved from a previous network via Windows 2000 media sensing capabilities.

Backup Domain Controller (BDC)   A backup file or copy of the Primary Domain Controller (PDC). Periodically, the BDC is synchronized with the PDC.

Backup logs   Windows Backup generates a backup log file for every backup job. These files are the best place to review the backup process in case some problem is encountered by the program. The backup log is a text file that records all the events during the backup process.

Basic Input/Output System (BIOS)   A set of programs encoded in ROM on IBM PC-compatible computers programs handle startup operations such as Power On Self Test (POST) and low-level control for hardware such as disk drives, keyboards, and so on.

BDC   *See* Backup Domain Controller.

BIOS   *See* Basic Input/Output System.

Boot   The process of loading an operating system into the computer's memory (RAM) so those applications can be run on it.

Boot ROM   A boot ROM is a chip on the network adapter that helps the computer boot from the network. Such a computer need not have a previously installed operating system. The BIOS of the computer that has a PXE-based boot ROM must be configured to boot from the network. Windows 2000 Server RIS supports PXE ROM versions 99 or later.

Bottleneck   A bottleneck in computer terms is also a component of the system as a whole that restricts the system from operating at its peak. When a bottleneck occurs, the component that is a bottleneck will have a high rate of usage and other components will have a low rate of usage. A lack of memory is a common cause of bottleneck when your computer doesn't have enough memory for the applications and services that are running.

CA   *See* Certificate Authority.

CAL   *See* Client Access License.

CAPI   *See* CryptoAPI.

Centralized model   This model consolidates administrative control of group policies. A single team of administrators is responsible for managing all Group Policy Objects (GPOs), no matter where they are. This is usually applied by giving all the top-level Organizational Unit (OU) administrators full control to all GPOs, no matter where they are located. They give each second-level OU administrator Read permission only to each GPO. You can also decentralize other resources or keep all resources centralized, depending on the environment.

Certificate Authority (CA)   An authority/organization that produces digital certificates with its available public key. A Certificate Authority (CA) is a public key certificate issuer (for example, VeriSign). To use a public key certificate, you must trust the issuer (CA). This means that you have faith in the CA's authentication policies. The CA is used for doing things such as authorizing certification authenticity, revoking expired certificates, and responding to certification requests. Windows 2000 offers an alternative to a third-party CA. You can become a CA within your own Intranet. Thus you can manage your own certificates rather than relying on a third-party Certification Authority.

Certificate service   Provides security and authentication support, including secure e-mail, Web-based authentication, and smart card authentication.

Change Permission   You can use this permission to allow users the ability to change permissions on files and folders without giving them the Full Control permission. You can use this permission to give a user or group access to modify permissions on file or folder objects without giving them the ability to have complete control over the object.

Cipher command   The cipher command is another way to encrypt and decrypt data. You can use it from the command line, and it has many switches, so that you can define exactly what you want to have done. The Cipher.exe command syntax is simply CIPHER, followed by the switches that you would like to use, followed by the path and directory/file name. The most common switches are the /E switch (encrypts the specified directories) and the /D switch (decrypts the specified directories). You can also use wildcards with the cipher command. For example, C:\>cipher /e /s *win* will encrypt all files and folders with "win" in the name and all files within them.

CIW   *See* Client Installation Wizard.

Client Access License (CAL)   The CAL allows clients to access the Windows 2000's network services, shared folders, and printers. There are two types of CAL modes: Per Seat and Per Server. It important to understand the difference between the two modes: Per Seat and Per Server. When you use the Per Seat mode, each computer that accesses the server must have a CAL. The Per Server mode requires a CAL for each connection to the server. This is a subtle but significant difference. In addition, the CAL allows clients to access the Windows 2000 Server's network services, shared folders, and printers. The licensing modes are the same as under Windows NT 4.0.

Client Installation Wizard (CIW)   When a client computer boots using either the Remote Boot Disk or the PXE-based Boot ROM, it tries to establish a connection to the Remote Installation Service (RIS) server. If the RIS server is preconfigured to service the RIS clients, it helps the client get an Internet Protocol (IP) address from the Dynamic Host Control Protocol (DHCP) service. The CIW is then downloaded from the RIS server. This wizard has four installation options. The options that are presented to the user depend on the group policy set in the Active Directory. A user may get all four options, or may not get any of the options starting an automatic setup.

Cloning   *See* Disk imaging/cloning.

Comprehension   The process of distinguishing between situations, discussing, estimation, explaining, indicating, paraphrasing, and giving examples.

Computer account   A computer account is an account that is created by a domain administrator and uniquely identifies the computer on the domain. A newly created account is used so that a computer may be brought into a Windows 2000 Domain.

Configuration   Configuration of an operating system involves specifying settings that will govern how the system behaves.

Container Object   Container objects can contain other objects. A special type of container object you can create in the Active Directory is the Organizational Unit (OU).

Containers   Containers are used to describe any group of related items, whether they are objects, containers, domains, or an entire network.

Control Panel Accessibility Options   These are options are which include StickyKeys, FilterKeys, ToggleKeys, SoundSentry, ShowSounds, High Contrast, MouseKeys, and SerialKeys.

Cooperative multitasking   An environment in which an application relinquishes its use of the computer's Central Processing Unit (CPU) so that another application can use the CPU.

Copy backup   This type of backup simply copies the selected files. It neither looks for any markers set on the files nor does it clear them. The Copy backup does not affect the other Incremental or Differential backup jobs and can be performed along with the other types of backup jobs.

Counter logs   Counter logs are maintained in a similar fashion as they were in Windows NT 4.0, but the procedure for configuring the Counter logs is a bit different. Trace logs are much easier to configure in Windows 2000 because you now can set them up from the console, rather than having to edit the registry as you had to do in Windows NT 4.0.

CryptoAPI (CAPI)   CryptoAPI (CAPI) architecture is a collection of tasks that permit applications to sign or encrypt data digitally while providing security for the user's private key data.

Daily backup   This type of backup does not use any markers to back up selected files and folders. The files that have changed during the day are backed up every day at a specified time. This backup will not affect other backup schedules.

Data backup   A backup and disaster protection plan is an essential part of a network administrator's duties. Windows 2000 provides a built-in Backup utility used to back up data to tape or file, or to create an Emergency Repair Disk (ERD). An ERD can be used to repair a computer with damaged system files.

Data compression   Windows 2000 offers the capability of compressing data on a file-level basis, so long as the files and folders are located on an NT File System (NTFS) formatted partition or volume. Compression saves disk space; however, NTFS compression cannot be used in conjunction with file encryption.

Data Link Control (DLC)   DLC is a nonroutable protocol used for connecting to IBM mainframes and some network-connected laser printers.

Debugging Mode   This is the most advanced startup option of all. To use this option you will need to connect another computer to the problematic computer through a serial cable. With proper configuration, the debug information is sent to the second computer.

Decentralized model   This model is appropriate for companies that rely on delegated levels of administration. They decentralize the management of Group Policy Objects (GPOs), which distributes the workload to a number of domains. To apply this model, simply give all Organizational Unit (OU) administrators full control of their respective GPOs.

Dedicated server   A dedicated printer server is a Windows 2000 server whose only role is to provide printing services. The server does not provide directory space for users other than storage for spooled print jobs. It does not provide authentication services, does not host database services, does not act as a Domain Name System (DNS) server, and so on. A dedicated print server can host several hundred printers and print queues, however. Though it may not be obvious, the printing process does have an impact on the performance of the server providing the printing services. An environment with a large number of printers or print jobs should strongly consider using at least one dedicated print server.

Defragmentation The task of finding fragmented files and moving them into contiguous space is called defragmentation.

Deny permissions Unlike the Allow permission, the Deny permission overrides all other permissions set for a file or folder. If a user is a member of one group with a Deny Write permission for a folder and is a member of another group with a Allow Full Control permission, the user will be unable to perform any of the Write permission tasks allows because it has been denied. The Deny permission should be used with extreme caution, as it can actually lock out all users, even administrators, from a file or folder. The proper way to remove a permission from a user or group on a file or folder is to uncheck the Allow permission for that user or group, not to check the Deny permission.

Dfs *See* Distributed File System.

DHCP *See* Dynamic Host Control Protocol.

Differential backup The Differential backup checks and performs a backup of only those files that are marked. It does not clear the markers after the backup, which means that any consecutive differential backups will backup the marked files again. When you need to restore from a differential backup, you will need the most current full backup and the differential backup performed after that.

Digital Subscriber Line (DSL) There are many variants of digital subscriber line (xDSL). All versions utilize the existing copper loop between a home and the local telco's Central Office (CO). Doing so allows them to be deployed rapidly and inexpensively. However, all DSL variants suffer from attenuation, and speeds drop as the loop length increases. Asymmetrical DSL (ADSL) and Symmetrical DSL (SDSL) may be deployed only within 17,500 feet of a CO, and Integrated Services Digital Network emulation over DSL (IDSL) will work only up to 30,500 feet. All DSL variants use Asynchronous Transfer Mode (ATM) as the data-link layer.

Direct Memory Access (DMA) DMA is a microprocessor capable of transferring data between memory units without the aid of the Central Processing Unit (CPU). Occasionally, built-in circuitry can do this same function.

Directory   A directory is a database that contains information about objects and their attributes.

Directory service   The directory service is the component that organizes the objects into a logical and accessible structure, and provides for a means of searching and locating objects within the directory. The directory service includes the entire directory and the method of storing it on the network.

Directory Services Restore Mode   This startup mode is available on Windows 2000 Server domain controller computers only. This mode can be used to restore the SYSVOL directory and Active Directory on the domain controller.

Discover   A Dynamic Host Control Protocol (DHCP) client begins the lease process with a DHCPDISCOVER message. The client broadcasts this message after loading a minimal Transmission Control Protocol/Internet Protocol (TCP/IP) environment. The client does not know the address of the DHCP server, so it sends the message using a TCP/IP broadcast, with 0.0.0.0 as the source address and 255.255.255.255 as the destination address. The DHCPDISCOVER message contains the clients network hardware address, its computer name, a list of DHCP options the client supports, and a message ID that will be used in all messages between the client and server to identify the particular request.

Disk compression   This compression allows you to compress folders, subfolders, and files to increase the amount of file storage, but slow down access to the files.

Disk Defragmenter   Disk Defragmenter can analyze your volumes and make a recommendation as to whether or not you should defragment it. It will also give you a graphical display showing you the fragmented files, contiguous files, system files and free space. Disk Defragmenter does not always completely defragment free space; instead, it often moves it into just a few contiguous areas of the disk, which will still improve performance. Making the free space one contiguous space would have little added benefit.

Disk imaging/cloning   The deployment of a new operating system is one of the most challenging and time-consuming tasks that a network administrator has to perform. The disk duplication methods are particularly useful when you need to deploy Windows 2000 Professional on a large number of computers. This is also known as disk imaging or cloning. These tools make the rollout fast and easy.

Disk quota   Windows 2000 comes with a disk quota feature that allows you to control users' disk consumption on a per user/per partition basis. To begin setting disk quotas for your users, right-click any partition in either Windows Explorer or the My Computer object. Click Properties and then click the Quota tab. Also, a disk quota allows you to limit the amount of disk space used by each user.

Distributed File System (Dfs)   The Windows 2000 Distributed File System provides you a method to centralize the organization of the shared resources on your network. In the past, shared resources were most often accessed via the Network Neighborhood applet, and users would have to wade through a number of domains and servers in order to access the shared folder or printer that they sought. Network users also had to remember where the obscure bit of information was stored, including both a cryptic server name and share name. The Distributed File System (Dfs) allows you to simplify the organization of your network resources by placing them in central shares accessed via a single server. Also, the Dfs allows you to create a central share point for shared resources located through the organization on a number of different servers.

Distribution Server   This is a server on which the Windows 2000 installation files reside. When you install the operating system over the network, the client machine does not need a CD-ROM drive. The first requirement for network installation is a distribution server that contains the installation files. The distribution server can be any computer on the network to which the clients have access.

DLC   *See* Data Link Control.

DMA   *See* Direct Memory Access.

DNS   *See* Domain Name System.

Domain   A collection of connected areas. Routing domains provide full connectivity to all end systems within them. Also, a domain is a collection of accounts and network resources that are grouped together using a single domain name and security boundary.

Domain controller   Domain controllers validate logons, participate in replication of logon scripts and policies, and synchronize the user account database. This means that domain controllers have an extra amount of work to perform. Since the Terminal Server already requires such heavy resources, it is not a good idea to burden a Terminal Server with the extra work of being a domain controller. Also, all user accounts, permissions, and other network details are all stored in a centralized database on the domain controllers.

Domain Local Groups   Domain Local Groups are used for granting access rights to resources such as file systems or printers that are located on any computer in the domain where common access permissions are required. The advantage of Domain Local Groups being used to protect resources in that a member of the Domain Local Group can come from both inside the same domain and from outside as well.

Domain Name System (DNS)   Because the actual unique Internet Protocol (IP) address of a web server is in the form of a number difficult for humans to work with, text labels separated by dots (domain names) are used instead. DNS is responsible for mapping these domain names to the actual Internet Protocol (IP) numbers in a process called resolution. Sometimes called a Domain Name Server.

Domain restructure   Domain restructure, or domain consolidation, is the method of changing the structure of your domains. Restructuring your domains can allow you to take advantage of the new features of Windows 2000, such as greater scalability. Windows 2000 does not have the same limitation as the Security Accounts Manager (SAM) account database in Windows NT. Without this limitation, you can merge domains into one larger domain. Using Windows 2000 Organizational Units (OUs), you have finer granularity in delegating administrative tasks.

Domain tree   A domain tree is a hierarchical collection of the child and parent domains within a network. The domains in a domain tree have contiguous namespaces. Domain trees in a domain forest do not share common security rights, but can access one another through the global catalog.

Driver signing   One of the most frustrating things about Windows operating systems is that any software vendors can overwrite critical system level files with their own versions. Sometimes the vendor's version of a system level file is buggy or flawed, and it prevents the operating system from functioning correctly, or in the worst case, prevents it from starting at all. Windows 2000 uses a procedure called Driver Signing that allows the operating system to recognize functional, high-quality files approved by Microsoft. With this seal of approval, you should be confident that installing applications containing signed files will not disable your computer. Windows 98 was the first Microsoft operating system to use digital signatures, but Windows 2000 marks the first Microsoft operating system based on NT technology to do this.

DSL   *See* Digital Subscriber Line.

Dynamic disks   Dynamic disks introduce conceptual as well as technical changes from traditional basic disk structure. Partitions are now called volumes, and these can be created or changed without losing existing data on the disk. Recall that when using basic disks, you must first create primary partitions (up to a maximum of four), then extended partitions (a maximum of one) with logical drives. Dynamic disks allow you to create volume after volume, with no limit on the number or type that can exist on a single disk; you are limited only by the capacity of the disk itself.

Dynamic Host Configuration Protocol (DHCP)   A software utility that is designed to assign Internet Protocol (IP) addresses to clients and their stations logging onto a Transmission Control Protocol/Internet Protocol (TCP/IP) and eliminates manual IP address assignments.

EAP   *See* Extensible Authentication Protocol.

EFS   *See* Encrypting File System.

Encrypting File System (EFS)   Unlike Windows NT 4.0, Windows 2000 provides the Encrypting File System (EFS), which allows you to encrypt and decrypt data on a file-by-file basis without the need for third-party software, as long as it is stored on an NTFS formatted partition or volume. EFS is based on public key cryptography.

Encryption   Scrambling of data so as to be unreadable; therefore, an unauthorized person cannot decipher the data.

Ethernet   A networking protocol and shared media (or switched) Local Area Network (LAN) access method linking up to 1K nodes in a bus topology.

Evaluation   Evaluation is the process of assessing, summarizing, weighing, deciding, and applying standards.

Extended partitions   Although extended partitions cannot be used to host operating systems, they can store other types of data and provide an excellent way to create more drives above the four-partition limit. Extended partitions do not represent one drive; rather, they can be subdivided into as many logical drives as there are letters in the alphabet. Therefore, one extended partition can contain several logical drives, each of which appears as a separate drive letter to the user.

Extensible Authentication Protocol (EAP)   EAP allows the administrator to "plug in" different authentication security providers outside of those included with Windows 2000. EAP allows your organization to take advantage of new authentication technologies including "smart card" logon and Certificate-based authentication.

FAT   *See* File Allocation Table.

Fault tolerance   Fault tolerance is high-system availability with enough resources to accommodate unexpected failure. Fault tolerance is also the design of a computer to maintain its system's performance when some internal hardware problems occur. This is done through the use of backup systems.

FEK   *See* File Encryption Key.

File Allocation Table (FAT)   A FAT is an area on a disk that indicates the arrangement of files in the sectors. Because of the multiuser nature of Terminal Server, it is strongly recommended that the NTFS file system be used rather than the FAT file system. FAT does not offer file and directory security, whereas with NTFS, you can limit access to subdirectories and files to certain users or groups of users.

File Allocation Table 16 (FAT16)   The earlier version of the FAT file system implemented in MS-DOS is known as FAT16, to differentiate it from the improved FAT32.

File Allocation Table 32 (FAT32)   FAT32 is the default file system for Windows 95 OSR2 and Windows 98. The FAT32 file system was first implemented in Windows 95 OSR2, and was supported by Windows 98 and now Windows 2000. While FAT16 cannot support partitions larger than 4GB in Windows 2000, FAT32 can support partitions up to 2TB (Terabytes) in size. However, for performance reasons, the creation of FAT32 partitions is limited to 32GB in Windows 2000. The second major benefit of FAT32 in comparison to FAT16 is that it supports a significantly smaller cluster size—as low as 4K for partitions up to 8GB. This results in more efficient use of disk space, with a 15 to 30 percent utilization improvement in comparison to FAT16.

File Encryption Key (FEK)   A random key called a file encryption key (FEK) is used to encrypt each file and is then itself encrypted using the user's public key. At least two FEKs are created for every encrypted file. One FEK is created with the user's public key, and one is created with the public key of each recovery agent. There could be more than one recovery agent certificate used to encrypt each file, resulting in more than two FEKs. The user's public key can decrypt FEKs created with the public key.

File Transfer Protocol (FTP)   Transfers files to and from a computer running an FTP server service (sometimes called a *daemon*).

FireWire   Also known as IEEE 1394. An Apple/Texas Instruments high-speed serial bus allowing up to 63 devices to connect; this bus supports hot swapping and isochronous data transfer.

Forest   A forest is a grouping of one or more domain trees that do not share a common namespace but do share a common schema, configuration, and global catalog; in fact, it forms a noncontiguous (or discontiguous) namespace. The users in one tree do not have global access to resources in other trees, but trusts can be created that allow users to access resources in another tree.

Forward Lookup Query   A forward lookup query occurs when a computer needs to get the Internet Protocol (IP) address for a computer with an Internet name. The local computer sends a query to a local Domain Name System (DNS) name server, which resolves the name or passes the request on to another server for resolution.

FQDN   *See* Fully Qualified Domain Name.

FTP   *See* File Transfer Protocol.

Fully Qualified Domain Name (FQDN)   A full site name of a system rather than just its host name. The FQDN of each child domain is made up of the combination of its own name and the FQDN of the parent domain. The FQDN includes the host name and the domain membership of that computer.

Gateway   In networking, gateway refers to a router or a computer functioning as one, the "way out" of the network or subnet, to get to another network. You also use gateways for software that connects a system using one protocol to a system using a different protocol, such as the Systems Network Architecture (SNA) software (allows a Local Area Network (LAN) to connect to an IBM mainframe). You can also use Gateway Services for NetWare used to provide a way for Microsoft clients to go through a Windows NT or Windows 2000 server to access files on a Novell file server.

Global Groups   Global Groups are used for combining users who share a common access profile based on job function or business role. Typically organizations use Global Groups for all groups in which membership is expected to change frequently. These groups can have as members only user accounts defined in the same domain as the Global Group.

Globally Unique IDentifier (GUID)   The Globally Unique IDentifier (GUID) is a unique numerical identification created at the time the object is created. An analogy would be a person's social security number, which is assigned once and never changes, even if the person changes his or her name, or moves.

GPC *See* Group Policy Container.

GPO *See* Group Policy Object.

GPT *See* Group Policy Template.

Graphical User Interface (GUI) An overall and consistent system for the interactive and visual program that interacts (or interfaces) with the user. GUI can involve pull-down menus, dialog boxes, on-screen graphics, and a variety of icons.

Group Policy Group Policy provides for change management and desktop control on the Windows 2000 platform. You are familiar with the control you had in Windows NT 4.0 using System Policies. Group Policy is similar to System Policies but allows you a much higher level of granular configuration management over your network. Some of the confusion comes from the change of names applied to different groups in Windows 2000. You can apply Group Policy to sites, domains, and organizational units. Each of these represents a group of objects, so Group Policy is applied to the group of objects contained in each of these entities. Group Policy cannot be directly applied to Security Groups that are similar to the groups you are used to working with in Windows NT 4.0. However, by using Group Policy Filtering, you can successfully apply Group Policy to individual Security Groups.

Group Policy Container (GPC) The Active Directory object Group Policy Containers (GPCs) store the information for the Folder Redirection snap-in and the Software Deployment snap-in. GPCs do not apply to local group policies. They contain component lists and status information, which indicate whether Group Policy Objects (GPOs) are enabled or disabled. They also contain version information, which ensures that the information is synchronized with the Group Policy Template (GPT) information. GPCs also contain the class store in which GPO group policy extensions have settings.

Group Policy Object (GPO) After you create a group policy, it is stored in a Group Policy Object (GPO) and applied to the site, domain, or Organizational Unit

(OU). GPOs are used to keep the group policy information; essentially, a GPO is a collection of policies. You can apply single or multiple GPOs to each site, domain or OU. Group policies are not inherited across domains, and users must have Read permission for the GPO that you want to have applied to them. This way, you can filter the scope of GPOs by adjusting who has read access to each GPO.

Group Policy Template (GPT)   The subset of folders created on each domain controller that store Group Policy Object (GPO) information for specific GPOs are called Group Policy Templates (GPTs). GPTs are stored in the SysVol (System Volume) folder, on the domain controller. GPTs store data for Software Policies, Scripts, Desktop File and Folder Management, Software Deployment, and Security settings. GPTs can be defined in computer or user configurations. Consequently, they take effect either when the computer starts or when the user logs on.

GUI   *See* Graphical User Interface.

GUID   *See* Globally Unique IDentifier.

HAL   *See* Hardware Abstraction Layer.

Hardware Abstraction Layer (HAL)   The Windows NT's translation layer existing between the hardware, kernel, and input/output (I/O) system.

Hardware Compatibility List (HCL)   The Hardware Compatibility List is published by Microsoft for each of its operating systems, and is updated on a monthly basis. There is a copy of the HCL on the Windows 2000 Professional CD, located in the Support folder and named Hcl.txt.

Hardware profile   A hardware profile is a set of instructions that tells your computer how to boot the system properly, based on the setup of your hardware. Hardware profiles are most commonly used with laptops. This is because laptops are frequently used in at least two different settings: stand-alone and in a docking station on a network. For example, when the laptop is being used at a docking station, it requires a network adapter. However, when the laptop is used away from the network, it does not. The hardware profile dialog manages these configuration changes. If a profile is created for each situation, the user will automatically be presented these choices on Windows startup.

HCL   *See* Hardware Compatibility List.

HKEY_CLASSES_ROOT   Contains information used for software configuration and object linking and embedding (OLE), as well as file association information.

HKEY_CURRENT_CONFIG   Holds data about the current hardware profile that is in use.

HKEY_CURRENT_USER   Has information about the user who is currently logged on.

HKEY_LOCAL_MACHINE   Stores information about the hardware, software, system devices, and security information for the local computer.

HKEY_USERS   Holds information and settings for the environments of all users of the computer.

HTML   *See* HyperText Markup Language.

HTTP   *See* HyperText Transfer Protocol.

HyperText Markup Language (HTML)   The format used to create documents viewed on the World Wide Web (WWW) by the use of tags (codes) embedded within the text.

HyperText Transfer Protocol (HTTP)   HTTP is an Internet standard supporting World Wide Web (WWW) exchanges. By creating the definitions of Universal Resource Locators (URLs) and their retrieval usage throughout the Internet.

IAS   *See* Internet Authentication Services.

ICS   *See* Internet Connection Sharing.

IDE   *See* Integrated Drive Electronics.

IIS   *See* Internet Information Service.

Incremental backup   This backup process is similar to the Differential backup, but it clears the markers from the selected files after the process. Because it clears the markers, an incremental backup will not back up any files that have not changed since the last incremental backup. This type of backup is fast during the backup but is very slow while restoring the files. You will need the last full backup and all of the subsequent incremental backups to fully restore data. The positive side of this backup type is that it is fast and consumes very little media space.

Indexing service   Provides indexing functions for documents stored on disk, allowing users to search for specific document text or properties.

Industry Standard Architecture (ISA)   A PC's expansion bus used for peripherals plug-in boards.

Integrated Drive Electronics (IDE) drive   An IDE drive is a hard disk drive for processors containing most controller circuitry within the drive. IDE drives combine Enhanced System Device Interface (ESDI) speed with Small Computer System Interface (SCSI) hard drive interface intelligence.

Integrated Services Digital Network (ISDN)   Integrated Services indicates the provider offers voice and data services over the same medium. Digital Network is a reminder that ISDN was born out of the digital nature of the intercarrier and intracarrier networks. ISDN runs across the same copper wiring that carries regular telephone service. Before attenuation and noise cause the signal to be unintelligible, an ISDN circuit can run a maximum of 18,000 feet. A repeater doubles this distance to 36,000 feet.

Internet Authentication Services (IAS)   IAS performs authentication, authorization, and accounting of dial-up and Virtual Private Networking (VPN) users. IAS supports the Remote Access Dial-In User Service (RADIUS) protocol.

Internet Connection Sharing (ICS)   ICS can be thought of as a less robust version of Network Address Translation (NAT lite). ICS uses the same address translation technology. ICS is a simpler version of NAT useful for connecting a few computers on a small Local Area Network (LAN) to the Internet or useful for a remote server through a single phone line and account.

Internet Information Service (IIS)   Windows NT Web browser software that supports Secure Sockets Layer (SSL) security protocol from Netscape. IIS provides support for Web site creation, configuration, and management, along with Network News Transfer Protocol (NNTP), File Transfer Protocol (FTP), and Simple Mail Transfer Protocol (SMTP).

Internet Packet eXchange (IPX)   Novell NetWare's built-in networking protocol for Local Area Network (LAN) communication derived from the Xerox Network System protocol. IPX moves data between a server and/or workstation programs from different network nodes. Sometimes called an Internetnetwork Packet eXchange.

Internet Protocol Security (IPSec)   IPSec is a new feature included in Windows 2000 and provides for encryption of data as it travels between two computers, protecting it from modification and interpretation if anyone were to see it on the network.

Internet Service Provider (ISP)   The organization allowing users to connect to its computers and then to the Internet. ISPs provider the software to connect and sometimes a portal site and/or internal browsing capability.

Interrupt ReQuest (IRQ)   An electronic signal that is sent to the computer's processor requiring the processor's attention. Also, a computer instruction designed to interrupt a program for an Input/Output (I/O).

IPSec   *See* Internet Protocol Security.

IPX   *See* Internet Packet eXchange.

IRQ *See* Interrupt ReQuest.

ISA *See* Industry Standard Architecture.

ISDN *See* Integrated Services Digital Network.

ISP *See* Internet Service Provider.

Kerberos Kerberos guards against username and password safety vulnerability by using tickets (temporary electronic credentials) to authenticate. Tickets have a limited life span and can be used in place of usernames and passwords (if the software supports this). Kerberos encrypts the password into the ticket. It uses a trusted server called the Key Distribution Center (KDC) to handle authentication requests. Kerberos speeds up network processes by integrating security and rights across network domains and also eliminates workstations' need to authenticate themselves repeatedly at every domain they access. Kerberos security also makes maneuvering around networks using multiple platforms such as UNIX or NetWare easier.

Knowledge Knowledge is the very lowest level of learning. It is, of course, important that a network administrator have this knowledge. Knowledge involves the processes of defining, location, recall, recognition, stating, matching, labeling, and identification.

L2TP *See* Layer-Two Tunneling Protocol.

Last Known Good Configuration This mode starts the system using the configuration that was saved in the registry during the last system shutdown. This startup option is useful when you have changed some configuration parameters and the system fails to boot. When you use this mode to start the system, all changes that were made after the last successful logon are lost. Use this option when you suspect that some incorrect configuration changes are causing the system startup failure. This mode does not help if any of the installed drivers have been corrupted or any driver files are deleted by mistake.

Layer Two Tunneling Protocol (L2TP)   L2TP offers better security through the use of IPSec and creates Virtual Private Networks (VPNs). Windows 2000 uses L2TP to provide tunneling services over Internet Protocol Security (IPSec)-based communications. L2TP tunnels can be set up to traverse data across intervening networks that are not part of the VPN being created. L2TP is used to send information across intervening and nonsecure networks.

LDAP   *See* Lightweight Directory Access Protocol.

Legend   The legend displays information about the counters that are being measured. It is the set of columns at the bottom of System Monitor.

Lightweight Directory Access Protocol (LDAP)   A simplified Directory Access Protocol (DAP) accessing a computer's directory listing. LDAP is able to access to X.500 directories.

Line Printer Daemon (LPD)   LPD is the server process that advertises printer queues and accepts incoming print submissions, which are then routed to the print device.

Line Printer Remote (LPR)   LPR is a process that spools a print job to a remote print spool that is advertised by the Line Printer Daemon (LPD).

Local policy   A group policy stored locally on a Windows 2000 member server or a Windows 2000 professional computer is called a local policy. The local policy is used to set up the configuration settings for each computer and for each user. Local policies are stored in the \%*systemroot*%\system32\grouppolicy folder on the local computer. Local policies include the auditing policy, user rights and privilege assignment, and various security options.

Local printer   A print device that is directly attached, via a parallel or serial cable, to the computer that is providing the printing services. For a Windows 2000 Professional workstation, a local printer is one that is connected to the workstation. For a Windows 2000 Server, a local printer is one that is connected to the server. Drivers for the print device must reside on the computer that connects to the printer.

Local user profiles (local profiles)   Local user profiles are kept on one local computer hard drive. When a user initially logs on to a computer, a local profile is created for them in the \%*systemdrive*%\Documents And Settings\<*username*> folder. When users log off the computer, the changes that they made while they were logged on will be saved to their local profile on that client computer. This way, subsequent logons to that computer will bring up their personal settings. When users log on to a different computer, they will not receive these settings, as they are local to the computer in which they made the changes. Therefore, each user that logs on to that computer receives individual desktop settings. Local profiles are ideal for users who only use one computer. For users that require access to multiple computers, the Roaming profile would be the better choice.

LogicalDisk object   The LogicalDisk object measures the transfer of data for a logical drive (for example, C: or D:) or storage volumes. You can use the PhysicalDisk object to determine which hard disk is causing the bottleneck. Then, to narrow the cause of the bottleneck, you can use the LogicalDisk object to determine which, if any, partition is the specific cause of the bottleneck. By default, the PhysicalDisk object is enabled and the LogicalDisk object is disabled on Windows 2000 Server.

LPD   *See* Line Printer Daemon.

LPR   *See* Line Printer Remote.

Mandatory roaming profiles   Mandatory roaming profiles are mandatory user profiles the user cannot change. They are usually created to define desktop configuration settings for groups of users in order to simplify administration and support. Users can make changes to their desktop settings while they are logged on, but these changes will not be saved to the profile, as Mandatory profiles are read-only. The next time they log on, their desktop will be set back to the original Mandatory profile settings.

Master File Table (MFT)   The MFT stores the information needed by the operating system to retrieve files from the volume. Part of the MFT is stored at the beginning of the volume and cannot be moved. Also, if the volume contains a large number of directories, it can prevent the free space from being defragmented.

Master image After configuring one computer with the operating system and all the applications, SysPrep is run to create an image of the hard disk. This computer serves as the master or model computer that will have the complete setup of the operating system, application software, and any service packs. This hard disk image is the master image and is copied to a CD or put on a network share for distribution to many computers. Any third-party disk-imaging tool can then be used to replicate the image to other identical computers.

MCSE *See* Microsoft Certified Systems Engineer.

Message queuing service Provides a communication infrastructure and a development tool for creating distributed messaging applications. Such applications can communicate across heterogeneous networks and with computers that might be offline. Message queuing provides guaranteed message delivery, efficient routing, security, transactional support, and priority-based messaging.

MFT *See* Master File Table.

Microsoft Certified Systems Engineer (MCSE) An engineer who is a technical specialist in advanced Microsoft products, specifically NT Server and NT Workstation.

Microsoft Management Console (MMC) The MMC provides a standardized interface for using administrative tools and utilities. The management applications contained in an MMC are called Snap-ins, and custom MMCs hold the Snap-ins required to perform specific tasks. Custom consoles can be saved as files with the .msc file extension. The MMC was first introduced with NT Option Pack. Using the MMC leverages the familiarity you have with the other snap-ins available within MMC, such as SQL Server 7 and Internet Information Server 4. With the MMC, all your administrative tasks can be done in one place.

Mini-Setup Wizard The purpose of this wizard is to add some user-specific parameters on the destination computer. These parameters include: end-user license agreement (EULA); product key (serial number); username, company name, and administrator password; network configuration; domain or workgroup name; and, date and time zone selection.

Mirror set   In a mirror set, all data on a selected partition or drive are automatically duplicated onto another physical disk. The main purpose of a mirror set is to provide fault tolerance in the event of missing or corrupt data. If one disk fails or contains corrupt files, the data is simply retrieved and rebuilt from the other disk.

Mirrored volume   Like basic disks, dynamic disks can also be mirrored, and are called mirrored volumes. A continuous and automatic backup of all data in a mirrored volume is saved to a separate disk to provide fault tolerance in the event of a disk failure or corrupt file. Note that you cannot mirror a spanned or striped volume.

Mirroring   Also called RAID 1. RAID 1 consists of two drives that are identical matches, or mirrors, of each other. If one drive fails, you have another drive to boot up and keep the server going.

Mixed Mode   When in Mixed Mode, the domain still uses master replication with a Windows 2000 DC. The Windows NT Backup Domain Controllers (BDCs) replicate from the Windows 2000 server, as did the Windows NT Primary Domain Controller (PDC). When you are operating in Mixed Mode, some Windows 2000 functionality will not be available. You will not be able to use group nesting or transitive trusts. Mixed Mode is the default mode.

MMC   *See* Microsoft Management Console.

NAT   *See* Network Address Translation.

Native Mode   Native Mode allows only Windows 2000 domain controllers to operate in the domain. When all domain controllers for the domain are upgraded to Windows 2000 Server, you can switch to Native Mode. This allows you to use transitive trusts and the group-nesting features of Windows 2000. When switching to Native Mode, ensure that you no longer need to operate in Mixed Mode, because you cannot switch back to Mixed Mode once you are in Native Mode.

NDS   *See* NetWare Directory Service.

NetBEUI   *See* NETwork Basic Input/Output System Extended User Interface.

736 Glossary

NetBIOS   *See* Network Basic Input/Output System.

NetWare Directory Service (NDS)   NDS (created by Novell) has a hierarchical information database allowing the user to log on to a network with NDS capable of calculating the user's access rights.

Network   Two or more computers connected together by cable or wireless media for the purpose of sharing data, hardware peripherals, and other resources.

Network Address Translation (NAT)   With NAT, you can allow internal users to have access to important external resources while still preventing unauthorized access from the outside world.

Network Basic Input/Output System (NetBIOS)   A program in Microsoft's operating system that links personal computers to a Local Area Network (LAN).

NETwork Basic Input/Output System Extended User Interface (NetBEUI)   The transport layer for the Disk Operating System (DOS) networking protocol called Network Basic Input/Output System (NetBIOS).

Network Interface Card (NIC)   A board with encoding and decoding circuitry and a receptacle for a network cable connection that, bypassing the serial ports and operating through the internal bus, allows computers to be connected at higher speeds to media for communications between stations.

Network printer   A print device that has a built-in network interface or connects directly to a dedicated network interface. Both workstations and servers can be configured to print directly to the network printer, and the network printer controls its own printer queue, determining which jobs from which clients will print in which order. Printing clients have no direct control over the printer queue and cannot see other print jobs being submitted to the printer. Administration of a network printer is difficult. Drivers for the print device must reside on the computer that connects to the printer.

NIC *See* Network Interface Card.

Nondedicated server A nondedicated print server is a Windows 2000 server that hosts printing services in addition to other services. A domain controller, database server, or Domain Name System (DNS) server can provide printing services as well, but should be used only for a smaller number of printers or for printers that are not heavily used. Anyone setting up a nondedicated print server should monitor the performance of the printing process and the other tasks running on the server and be prepared to modify the server configuration if the performance drops below acceptable levels.

Nonmandatory Roaming profiles Roaming user profiles are stored on the network file server and are the perfect solution for users who have access to multiple computers. This way their profile is accessible no matter where they log on in the domain. When users log on to a computer within their domain, their roaming profile will be copied from the network server to the client computer and the settings will be applied to the computer while they are logged on. Subsequent logins will compare the roaming profile files to the local profile files. The file server then copies only any files that have been altered since the user last logged on locally, significantly decreasing the time required to log on. When the user logs off, any changes that the user made on the local computer will be copied back to the profile on the network file server.

Normal backup This is the most common type and is also known as a full backup. The Normal backup operation backs up all files and folders that are selected irrespective of the archive attributes of the files. This provides the easiest way to restore the files and folders but is expensive in terms of the time it takes to complete the backup job and the storage space it consumes. The restore process from a Normal backup is less complex because you do not have to use multiple tape sets to completely restore data.

NT File System (NTFS) The NT File System (with file names up to 255 characters) is a system created to aid the computer and its components recover from hard disk crashes.

NTFS *See* NT File System.

NWLink IPX/SPX/NetBIOS Compatible Transport Protocol (NWLink)   Microsoft's implementation of Novell's Internet Packet eXchange/Sequenced Packet eXchange (IPX/SPX) protocol stack, required for connecting to NetWare servers prior to version 5. NWLink can also be used on small networks that use only Windows 2000 and other Microsoft client software. NWLink is a Network Driver Interface Specification (NDIS) compliant, native 32-bit protocol. The NWLink protocol supports Windows sockets and NetBIOS.

ODBC   *See* Open DataBase Connectivity.

Offer   After the Dynamic Host Control Protocol (DHCP) server receives the DHCPDISCOVER message, it looks at the request to see if the client configuration request is valid. If so, it sends back a DHCPOFFER message with the client's network hardware address, an IP address, a subnet mask, the length of time the lease is valid, and the IP address of the server that provided the DHCP information. This message is also a Transmission Control Protocol/Internet Protocol (TCP/IP) broadcast, as the client does not yet have an Internet Protocol (IP) address. The server then reserves the address it sent to the client so that it is not offered to another client making a request. If there are more than one DHCP servers on the network, all servers respond to the DHCPDISCOVER message with a DHCPOFFER message.

Open DataBase Connectivity (ODBC)   A database programming interface that allows applications a way to access network databases.

Open Systems Interconnection (OSI) model   This is a model of breaking networking tasks into layers. Each layer is responsible for a specific set of functionality. There are performance objects available in System Monitor for analyzing network performance.

Organizational Units (OUs)   OUs in Windows 2000 are objects that are containers for other objects, such as users, groups, or other organizational units. Objects cannot be placed in another domain's OUs. The whole purpose of an OU is to have a hierarchical structure to organize your network objects. You can assign a group policy to an OU. Generally, the OU will follow a structure from your company. It may be a location, if you have multiple locations. It can even be a department-level organization. Also, OUs are units used to organize objects within a domain. These objects can include user accounts, groups, computers, printers, and even other OUs. The hierarchy of OUs is independent of other domains.

OSI *See* Open Systems Interconnection.

OU *See* Organizational Unit.

Paging When enough memory is not available for the running applications, pages of memory can be swapped from physical memory to the hard disk too much and slow the system down. This is also known as paging because pages of memory are swapped at a time. Windows 2000 separates memory into 4KB pages of memory to help prevent fragmentation of memory. Swapping can even get bad enough that you can hear your hard disk running constantly.

Paging file A file on the hard disk (or spanning multiple disks) that stores some of the program code that is normally in the computer's RAM. This is called virtual memory, and allows the programs to function as if the computer had more memory than is physically installed.

Password policy A password policy regulates how your users must establish and manage their passwords. This includes password complexity requirements and how often passwords must change. There are several settings that can be used to implement a successful password policy. You can enforce password uniqueness so those users cannot simply switch back and forth between a few easy to remember passwords. This can be set to low, medium, or high security. With low security, the system remembers the user's last 1–8 passwords (it is your choice as administrator to decide how many); with medium, it remembers the last 9–16 passwords; with high, it remembers the last 17–24 passwords.

PCMCIA *See* Personal Computer Memory Card Interface Adapter.

PDC *See* Primary Domain Controller.

Peer-to-peer network   A workgroup is also referred to as a peer-to-peer network, because all the computers connected together and communicating with one another are created equal. That is, there is no central computer that manages security and controls access to the network.

Performance logging   Performance logging has many features. The data collected are stored in a comma-delimited or tab-delimited format, which allows for exportation to spreadsheet and database applications for a variety of tasks such as charting and reports. The data can also be viewed as collected. You can configure the logging by specifying start and stop times, the name of the log files and the maximum size of the log. You can start and stop the logging of data manually or create a schedule for logging. You can even specify a program to run automatically when logging stops. You can also create trace logs. Trace logs track events that occur rather than measuring performance counters.

Permissions Inheritance   By default, all permissions set for a folder are inherited by the files in the folder, the subfolders in the folder, and the contents of the subfolders. When the permissions on a folder are viewed in the Security tab of the file or folder Permissions window, inherited permissions are indicated with a gray check box.

Personal Computer Memory Card Interface Adapter (PCMCIA)   An interface standard for plug-in cards for portable computers; devices meeting the standard (for example, fax cards, modems) are theoretically interchangeable.

Physical memory   Physical memory is the actual Random Access Memory (RAM) on the computer. When the physical memory becomes full, the operating system can also use space on the hard disk as virtual memory. When memory becomes full, rather than locking up the computer, the operating system stores unused data on the hard disk in a page file (also called paging or swap file). Data are swapped back and forth between the hard disk and physical memory as needed for running applications. If memory is needed that is in virtual memory, it is swapped back into physical memory.

PhysicalDisk object   The PhysicalDisk object measures the transfer of data for the entire hard disk. You can use the PhysicalDisk object to determine which hard disk is causing the bottleneck. By default, the PhysicalDisk object is enabled and the LogicalDisk object is disabled on Windows 2000 Server.

Plug and Play (PnP)   A standard requiring add-in hardware to carry the software to configure itself in a given way supported by Microsoft Windows 95. Plug and Play can make peripheral configuration software, jumper settings, and Dual In-line Package (DIP) switches unnecessary. PnP allows the operating system to load device drivers automatically and assign system resources dynamically to computer components and peripherals. Windows 2000 moves away from this older technology with its use of Kernel-mode and User-mode PnP architecture. PnP autodetects, configures, and installs the necessary drivers in order to minimize user interaction with hardware configuration. Users no longer have to tinker with IRQ and I/O settings.

PnP   *See* Plug and Play.

Point-to-Point Protocol (PPP)   A serial communication protocol most commonly used to connect a personal computer to an Internet Service Provider (ISP). PPP is the successor to Serial Line Internet Protocol (SLIP) and may be used over both synchronous and asynchronous circuits. Also, PPP is a full-duplex, connectionless protocol that supports many different types of links. The advantages of PPP made it de facto standard for dial-up connections.

Point-to-Point Tunneling Protocol (PPTP)   One of two standards for dial-up telephone connection of computers to the Internet, with better data negotiation, compression, and error corrections than the other Serial Line Internet Protocol (SLIP), but costing more to transmit data and unnecessary when both sending and receiving modems can handle some of the procedures.

Policy inheritance   Group policies have an order of inheritance in which the policies are applied. Local policies are applied first, then group policies are applied to the site, then the domain, and finally the Organizational Unit (OU). Policies applied first are overwritten by policies applied later. Therefore, group policies applied to a site overwrite the local policies and so on. When there are multiple Group Policy Objects (GPOs) for a site, domain, or OU, the order in which they appear in the Properties list applies. This policy inheritance order works well for small companies, but a more complex inheritance strategy may be essential for larger corporations.

Ports   A channel of a device that can support single point-to-point connections is known as a port. Devices can be single port, as in a modem.

Power options   Power options are dependent on the particular hardware. Power options include Standby and Hibernation modes. Standby mode turns off the monitor and hard disks to save power. Hibernation mode turns off the monitor and disks, saves everything in memory to disk, turns off the computer, and then restores the desktop to the state in which you left it when the computer is turned on.

PPP   *See* Point-to-Point Protocol.

PPTP   *See* Point-to-Point Tunneling Protocol.

Preboot eXecution Environment (PXE)   The PXE is a new Dynamic Host Control Protocol (DHCP)-based technology used to help client computers boot from the network. The Windows 2000 Remote Installation Service (RIS) uses the PXE technology along with the existing Transmission Control Protocol/Internet Protocol (TCP/IP) network infrastructure to implement the RIS-based deployment of Windows 2000 Professional. The client computer that has the PXE-based ROM uses its Basic Input/Output System (BIOS) to contact an existing RIS server and get an Internet Protocol (IP) address from the DHCP server running on the network. The RIS server then initializes the installation process on the client computer.

Preemptive multitasking   An environment in which timesharing controls the programs in use by exploiting a scheduled time usage of the computer's Central Processing Unit (CPU).

Primary Domain Controller (PDC)   Performs NT security management for its local domain. The PDC is periodically synchronized to its copy, the Backup Domain Controller (BDC). Only one PDC can exist in a domain. In an NT 4.0 single domain model, any user having a valid domain user account and password in the user accounts database of the PDC has the ability to log onto any computer that is a member of the domain, including MetaFrame servers.

Primary Domain Name System (DNS) Server   The Primary DNS server maintains the master copy of the DNS database for the zone. This copy of the database is the only one that can be modified, and any changes made to its database are distributed to secondary servers in the zone during a zone transfer process. The server can cache resolution requests locally so a lookup query does not have to be sent across the network for a duplicate request. The primary server contains the address mappings for the Internet root DNS servers. Primary servers can also act as secondary servers for other zones.

Primary partitions   Primary partitions are typically used to create bootable drives. Each primary partition represents one drive letter, up to a maximum of four on a single hard disk. One primary partition must be marked as active in order to boot the system, and most operating systems must be loaded on a primary partition to work.

Print device   The hardware that actually does the printing. A print device is one of two types as defined in Windows 2000: local or network-interface. A local print device connects directly to the print server with a serial or parallel interface. A network-interface print device connects to the printer across the network and must have its own network interface or be connected to an external network adapter.

Print driver   A software program used by Windows 2000 and other computer programs to connect with printers and plotters. It translates information sent to it into commands that the print device can understand.

Print server   A print server is a computer that manages printing on the network. A print server can be a dedicated computer hosting multiple printers, or it can run as one of many processes on a nondedicated computer.

Printer permissions   Printer permissions are established through the Security tab in the printer's Properties dialog. The security settings for printer objects are similar to the security settings for folder shares.

Protocols Protocols are sets of rules that computers use to communicate with one another. Protocols usually work together in stacks, so called because in a layered networking model, they operate at different layers or levels. These protocols govern the logic, formatting, and timing of information exchange between layers.

Publishing resources Resources, such as folders and printers, which are available to be shared on the network, can be published to the Active Directory. The resources are published to the directory and can be located by users, who can query the directory based on the resource's properties (for example, to locate all color printers).

PXE *See* Preboot eXecution Environment.

Quality of Service (QoS) Admission Control Admission control allows you to control how applications are allotted network bandwidth. You can give important applications more bandwidth, less important applications less bandwidth.

RAID *See* Redundant Array of Inexpensive Disks.

RAS *See* Remote Access Service.

RDP *See* Remote Desktop Protocol.

Recovery agent The recovery agent restores the encrypted file on a secure computer with its private recovery keys. The agent decrypts it using the cipher command line and then returns the plain text file to the user. The recovery agent goes to the computer with the encrypted file, loads the recovery certificate and private key, and performs the recovery. It is not as safe as the first option because the recovery agent's private key may remain on the user's computer.

Recovery Console The Recovery Console is a new command-line interpreter program feature in Windows 2000 that helps in system maintenance activities and resolving system problems. This program is separate from the Windows 2000 command prompt.

Redundant Array of Inexpensive Disks (RAID)   Although mirroring and duplexing are forms of RAID, most people think of RAID as involving more than two drives. The most common form of RAID is RAID-5, which is the striping of data across three or more drives, providing fault tolerance if one drive fails. For the best disk performance, consider using a SCSI RAID (Redundant Array of Independent Disks) controller. RAID controllers automatically place data on multiple disk drives and can increase disk performance. Using the software implementation of RAID provided by NT would increase performance if designed properly, but the best performance is always realized through hardware RAID controllers.

Redundant Array of Inexpensive Disks 5 (RAID-5) Volume   A RAID-5 volume on a dynamic drive provides disk striping with parity, and is similar to a basic stripe set with parity. This disk configuration provides both increased storage capacity and fault tolerance. Data in a dynamic RAID-5 volume are interleaved across three or more disks (up to 32 disks), and parity information is included to rebuild lost data in the event of an individual disk failure. Like a spanned or striped volume, a RAID-5 volume cannot be mirrored.

Registry   The Registry is the hierarchical database that stores operating system and application configuration information. It was used in Windows 9x and NT and replaced much of the functionality of the old initialization, system, and command files used in the early versions of Windows (.ini, .sys, and .com extensions). The registry is also a Microsoft Windows program allowing the user to choose options for configuration and applications to set them; it replaces confusing text-based INI files.

Remote   The word "remote" can take on a number of different meanings, depending on the context. In the case of an individual computer, the computer you are sitting in front of is sometimes referred to as being "local," while any other computer is considered "remote." In this context, any machine but your own is considered a remote computer. In discussions related to network configuration and design, "remote" may refer to segments and machines that are on the far side of a router. In this context, all machines on your physical segment are considered local and machines located on other physical segments are referred to as remote.

Remote Access Policy   Remote access policies allow you to create demand-dial connections to use specific authentication and encryption methods. In Windows NT versions 3.5*x* and Windows NT 4.0, authorization was much simpler. The administrator simply granted dial-in permission to the user. The callback options were configured on a per-user basis.

Remote Access Service (RAS)   Remote Access Service is a built-in feature of the Microsoft NT operating system. It allows users to dial establish a connection to an NT network over a standard phone line. Remote Access allows users to access files on a network or transfer files from a remote PC, over a Dial-Up Networking connection. The performance of transferring files over a dial-up connection is very similar to the performance you would get if you were downloading a file from the Internet.

Remote Desktop Protocol (RDP)   Remote Desktop Protocol (RDP) is the application protocol between the client and the server. It informs the server of the keystrokes and mouse movement of the client and returns to the client the Windows 2000 graphical display from the server. RDP is a multichannel, standard protocol that provides various levels of compression so that it can adapt to different connection speeds and encryption levels from 40 to 128 bit. Transmission Control Protocol/Internet Protocol (TCP/IP) carries the messages, and RDP is the language in which the messages are written. Both are needed to use Microsoft's implementation of Terminal Services.

Remote Installation Preparation (RIPrep)   RIPrep is a disk duplication tool included with Windows 2000 Server. It is an ideal tool for creating images of fully prepared client computers. These images are the customized images made from the base operating system, local installation of applications such as Microsoft Office, and customized configurations.

Remote Installation Preparation (RIPrep) Wizard   The RIPrep wizard enables the network administrator to distribute to a large number of client computers a standard desktop configuration that includes the operating system and the applications. This not only helps in maintaining a uniform standard across the enterprise, but also cuts the costs and time involved in a large-scale rollout of Windows 2000 Professional.

Remote Installation Service (RIS)   The RIS, part of Windows 2000 Server, allows client computers to install Windows 2000 Professional from a Windows 2000 Server with the service installed. The Remote Installation Services (RIS) facilitates installation of Windows 2000 Professional remotely on a large number of computers with similar or dissimilar hardware configurations. This not only reduces the installation time but also helps keep deployment costs low. Also, the Windows 2000 Remote Installation Services allow you a way to create an image of Windows 2000 Professional you can use to install Windows 2000 Professional on your network client systems. This image actually consists of the installation files from the Windows 2000 Professional CD-ROM.

Remote local printer   A print device connected directly to a print server but accessed by another print server or by workstations. The queue for the print device exists on the server, and the print server controls job priority, print order, and queue administration. Client computers submit print jobs to the server and can observe the queue to monitor the printing process on the server. Drivers for the print device are loaded onto the client computer from the print server.

Remote network printer   A network printer connected to a print server that is accessed by client workstations or other print servers. Like the remote local printer, the printer queue is controlled by the print server, meaning that the client computers submit their print jobs to the print server, rather than to the print device directly. This allows for server administration and monitoring of the printer queues. Drivers for the print device are loaded onto the client computers from the print server.

Request   After the client receives the DHCPOFFER message and accepts the Internet Protocol (IP) address, it sends a DHCPREQUEST message out to all Dynamic Host Control Protocol (DHCP) servers indicating that it has accepted an offer. The message contains the IP address of the DHCP server that made the accepted offer, and all other DHCP servers release the addresses they had offered back into their available address pool.

Reverse lookup query   A reverse lookup query resolves an Internet Protocol (IP) address to a Domain Name System (DNS) name, and can be used for a variety of reasons. The process is different, though, because it makes use of a special domain called in-addr.arpa. This domain is also hierarchical, but is based on IP addresses and not names. The subdomains are organized by the *reverse* order of the IP address. For instance, the domain 16.254.169.in-addr.arpa contains the addresses in the 169.254.16.* range; the 120.129.in-addr.arpa domain contains the addresses for the 129.120.*.* range.

RIPrep   *See* Remote Installation Preparation.

Rollback strategy   As with any upgrade, problems can sometimes require going back to the previous state. This possibility also applies to upgrading your domain to Windows 2000. You need to create a plan to roll back your network to its previous state if the upgrade to Windows 2000 fails. When upgrading the domain controllers, do not upgrade the Backup Domain Controller (BDC) that has the current directory database. Make sure the BDC is synchronized with the Primary Domain Controller (PDC), and then take it offline. Leave the BDC as is until the upgrade is successful. If you run into problems during the upgrade, you can bring the BDC back online, promote it to the PDC, and recover the Windows NT state. If this process is successful, you can upgrade the BDC to Windows 2000.

Routing and Remote Access (RRAS)   Within Windows NT, a software routing and remote access capability combining packet filtering, Open Shortest Path First (OSPF) support, and so on.

RRAS   *See* Routing and Remote Access.

Safe Mode   Safe Mode starts Windows 2000 using only some basic files and device drivers. These devices include monitor, keyboard, mouse, basic VGA video, CD-ROM, and mass storage devices. The system starts only those system services that are necessary to load the operating system. Networking is not started in this mode. The Windows background screen is black in this mode, and the screen resolution is 640 by 480 pixels with 16 colors.

Safe Mode with Command Prompt   This option starts the operating system in a safe mode using some basic files only. The Windows 2000 command prompt is shown instead of the usual Windows desktop.

Safe Mode with Networking This mode is similar to the Safe Mode, but networking devices, drivers, and protocols are loaded. You may choose this mode when you are sure that the problem in the system is not due to any networking component.

SAM *See* Security Accounts Manager.

Scripted method This method for Windows 2000 Professional installation uses an answer file to specify various configuration parameters. This is used to eliminate user interaction during installation, thereby automating the installation process. Answers to most of the questions asked by the setup process are specified in the answer file. Besides this, the scripted method can be used for clean installations and upgrades.

SCSI *See* Small Computer System Interface.

Secondary Domain Name System (DNS) Server Secondary DNS servers provide fault tolerance and load balancing for DNS zones. A secondary server contains a read-only copy of the zone database that it receives from the primary server during a zone transfer. A secondary server will respond to a DNS request if the primary server fails to respond because of an error or a heavy load. Since secondary servers can resolve DNS queries, they are also considered authoritative within a domain, and can help with load balancing on the network. Secondary servers can be placed in remote locations on the network and configured to respond to DNS queries from local computers, potentially reducing query traffic across longer network distances. While there can be only one primary server in a zone, multiple secondary servers can be set up for redundancy and load balancing.

Security Accounts Manager (SAM) The Security Accounts Manager (SAM) is the portion of the Windows NT Server registry that stores user account information and group membership. Attributes that are specific to Terminal Server can be added to user accounts. This adds a small amount of information to each user's entry in the domain's SAM.

Security Groups The Windows 2000 Security Groups allow you to assign the same security permissions to large numbers of users in one operation. This ensures consistent security permissions across all members of a group. Using Security Groups to assign permissions means the access control on 'resources remains fairly static and easy to control and audit. Users who need access are added or removed from the appropriate security groups as needed, and the access control lists change infrequently.

Security Templates   Windows 2000 comes with several predefined Security Templates. These templates address several security scenarios. Security Templates come in two basic categories: Default and Incremental. The Default or Basic templates are applied by the operating system when a clean install has been performed. They are not applied if an upgrade installation has been done. The incremental templates should be applied after the Basic Security Templates have been applied. There are four types of incremental templates: Compatible, Secure, High Secure, and Dedicated Domain Controller.

Segment   In discussions of Transmission Control Protocol/Internet Protocol (TCP/IP), segment often refers to the group of computers located on one side of a router, or sometimes a group of computers within the same collision domain. In TCP/IP terminology, segment can also be used to describe the chunk of data sent by TCP over the network (roughly equivalent to the usage of "packet" or "frame").

Sequenced Packet eXchange (SPX)   The communications protocol (from NetWare) used to control network message transport.

Server   The word "server" can take on a variety of different meanings. A server can be a physical computer. Such as "Check out that server over in the Accounting Department." A server can also represent a particular software package. For example, Microsoft Exchange 2000 is a mail and groupware server application. Often server applications are just referred to as "servers," as in "Check out what the problem is with the mail server." The term "server" is also used to refer to any computer that is currently sharing its resources on the network. In this context, all computers, whether Windows 3x or Windows 2000, can be servers on a network.

Service pack   A service pack typically contains bug fixes, security fixes, systems administration tools, drivers, and additional components. Microsoft recommends installing the latest service packs as they are released. In addition, as a new feature in Windows 2000, you do not have to reinstall components after installing a service pack, as you did with Windows NT. You can also see what service pack is currently installed on a computer by running the WINVER utility program. WINVER brings up the About Windows dialog box. It displays the version of Windows and the version of the service pack you are running.

Setup Manager   The Setup Manager is the best tool to use when you have no idea of the answer file syntax or when you do not want to get into the time-consuming task of creating or modifying the sample answer file. When you choose to use the Setup Manager for unattended installations, you need to do a lot of planning beforehand. It is understood that you will not be using Setup Manager for automating installations on one or two computers; that would be a waste of effort. Setup Manager is useful for mass deployments only.

SETUPACT.LOG   The Action log file contains details about the files that are copied during setup.

SETUPAPI.LOG   This log file contains details about the device driver files that were copied during setup. This log can be used to facilitate troubleshooting device installations. The file contains errors and warnings, along with a time stamp for each issue.

SETUPCL.EXE   The function of the SETUPCL.EXE file is to run the Mini-Setup wizard and to regenerate the security IDs on the master and destination computers. The Mini-Setup Wizard starts on the master computer when it is booted for the first time after running SysPrep.

SETUPERR.LOG   The Error log file contains details about errors that occurred during setup.

SETUPLOG.TXT   This log file contains additional information about the device driver files that were copied during setup.

Shared folders   Sharing folders so that other users can access their contents across the network is easy in Windows 2000, as easy as right-clicking the folder name in

Windows Explorer, selecting the Sharing tab, and choosing Share This Folder. An entire drive and all the folders on that drive can be shared in the same way.

Shared folders permissions   As only folders, not files, can be shared, shared folder permissions are a small subset of standard NT File System (NTFS) permissions for a folder. However, securing access to a folder through share permissions can be more restrictive or more liberal than standard NTFS folder permissions. Shared folder permissions are applied in the same manner as NTFS permissions.

Shared printers   The process for sharing a printer attached to your local computer is similar to that for sharing a folder or drive. If the users who will access your printer will do so from machines that don't run the Windows 2000 operating system, you will need to install drivers for the other operating system(s).

Shared resource   A shared resource is a device, data, or program that is made available to network users. This can include folders, files, printers, and even Internet connections.

Simple volume   A simple volume is a volume created on a dynamic disk that is not fault tolerant, and includes space from only one physical disk. A simple volume is just that—it is a single volume that does not span more than one physical disk, and does not provide improved drive performance, extra capacity, or fault tolerance. One physical disk can contain a single, large simple volume, or several smaller ones. Each simple volume is assigned a separate drive letter. The number of simple volumes on a disk is limited only by the capacity of the disk and the number of available letters in the alphabet.

Single-Instance-Store (SIS) volume   When you have more than one image on the Remote Installation Service (RIS) server, each holding Windows 2000 Professional files, there will be duplicate copies of hundreds of files. This may consume a significant hard drive space on the RIS server. To overcome this problem, Microsoft introduced a new feature called the Single-Instance-Store, which helps in deleting all the duplicate files, thus saving on hard drive space.

SIS   *See* Single-Instance-Store volume.

Site Server Internet Locator Server (ILS) Service   This service supports Internet Protocol (IP) telephony applications. Publishes IP multicast conferences on a network, and can also publish user IP address mappings for H.323 IP telephony. Telephony applications, such as NetMeeting and Phone Dialer in Windows Accessories, use Site Server ILS Service to display user names and conferences with published addresses. Site Server ILS Service depends on Internet Information Services (IIS).

Small Computer System Interface (SCSI)   A complete expansion bus interface that accepts such devices as a hard disk, CD-ROM, disk drivers, printers, or scanners.

SMP   *See* Symmetric Multiprocessing.

SMS   *See* Systems Management Server.

SNA   *See* Systems Network Architecture.

Spanned volume   A spanned volume is similar to a volume set in NT 4.0. It contains space from multiple disks (up to 32), and provides a way to combine small "chunks" of disk space into one unit, seen by the operating system as a single volume. It is not fault tolerant. When a dynamic volume includes the space on more than one physical hard drive, it is called a spanned volume. Spanned volumes can be used to increase drive capacity, or to make use of the leftover space on up to 32 existing disks. Like those in a basic storage volume set, the portions of a spanned volume are all linked together and share a single drive letter.

SPX   *See* Sequenced Packet eXchange.

Stack   A data structure in which the first items inserted are the last ones removed, unlike control structure programs that use the Last In First Out (LIFO) structure.

Static Internet Protocol (IP) address   A static IP address allows users to use a domain name that can be translated into an IP address. The static IP address allows the server to always have the same IP address, so the domain name always translates to the correct IP address. If the address was assigned dynamically and occasionally changed, users might not be able to access the server across the Internet using the domain name.

Stripe set   The term "striping" refers to the interleaving of data across separate physical disks. Each file is broken into small blocks, and each block is evenly and alternately saved to the disks in the stripe set. In a two-disk stripe set, the first block of data is saved to the first disk, the second block is saved to the second disk, and the third block is saved to the first disk, and so on. The two disks are treated as a single drive, and are given a single drive letter.

Stripe set with parity   A stripe set with parity requires at least three hard disks, and provides both increased storage capacity and fault tolerance. In a stripe set with parity, data is interleaved across three or more disks, and includes parity (error checking) information about the data. As long as only one disk in the set fails, the parity information can be used to reconstruct the lost data. If the parity information itself is lost, it can be reconstructed from the original data.

Striped volume   Like a stripe set in NT 4.0, a striped volume is the dynamic storage equivalent of a basic stripe set and combines free space from up to 32 physical disks into one volume by writing data across the disks in stripes. This increases performance but does not provide fault tolerance. A striped volume improves drive performance and increases drive capacity. Because each data block is written only once, striped volumes do not provide fault tolerance.

Striping   Striping is when the data are striped across the drives, along with parity information. The parity information is based on a mathematical formula that comes up with the parity based on the data on the other drives.

Subnetting   Using several data paths to reduce traffic on a network and avoid problems if a single path should fail; usually configured as a dedicated Ethernet subnetwork between two systems based on two Network Interface Cards (NICs).

Symmetric Multiprocessing (SMP)   SMP is a system in which all processors are treated as equals, and any thread can be run on any available processor. Windows 2000 also supports processor affinity, in which a process or thread can specify which set of processors it should run on. Application Programming Interfaces (APIs) must be defined in the application.

Synthesis   The process of design, formulation, integration, prediction, proposal, generalization, and showing relationships.

SYSPREP.INF   SYSPREP.INF is an answer file. When you want to automate the Mini-Setup wizard by providing predetermined answers to all setup questions, you must use this file. This file needs to be placed in the %Systemroot%\Sysprep folder or on a floppy disk. When the Mini-Setup wizard is run on the computer on which the image is being distributed, it takes answers from the SYSPREP.INF file without prompting the user for any input.

System Monitor   The System Monitor is part of this Administrative Tools utility, and allows you to collect and view data about current memory usage, disk, processor utilization, network activity, and other system activity. The System Monitor replaces the Performance Monitor used in Windows NT. System Monitor allows you to collect information about your hardware's performance, as well as network utilization. System Monitor can be used to measure different aspects of a computer's performance. It can be used on your own computer or other computers on the network.

System Preparation (SysPrep)   SysPrep provides an excellent means of saving installation time and reducing installation costs. SysPrep is the best tool to copy the image of a computer to other computers that have identical hardware configurations. It is also helpful in standardizing the desktop environment throughout the organization. Since one SysPrep image cannot be used on computers with identical hardware and software applications, you can create multiple images when you have more than one standard. It is still the best option where the number of computers is in hundreds or thousands, and you wish to implement uniform policies in the organization.

System policy   Group policies have mostly replace system policies, since group policies extend the functionality of system policies. A few situations still exist in which system policies are valuable. The system policy editor is used to provide user and computer configuration settings in the Windows NT registry database. The system policy editor is still used for the management of Windows 9x and Windows NT server and workstations and stand-alone computers using Windows 2000.

Systems Management Server (SMS)   This Windows NT software analyzes and monitors network usage and various network functions.

Systems Network Architecture (SNA)   Systems Network Architecture (SNA) was developed by IBM in the mainframe computer era (1974, to be precise) as a way of getting its various products to communicate with each other for distributed processing. SNA is a line of products designed to make other products cooperate. In your career of designing network solutions, you should expect to run into SNA from time to time because many of the bigger companies (such as, banks, healthcare institutions, government offices) bought IBM equipment and will be reluctant to part with their investment. SNA is a proprietary protocol that runs over SDLC exclusively, although it may be transported within other protocols, such as X.25 and Token Ring. It is designed as a hierarchy and consists of a collection of machines called nodes.

Take Ownership Permission   This permission can be given to allow a user to take ownership of a file or folder object. Every file and folder on an NT File System (NTFS) drive has an owner, usually the account that created the object. However, there are times when ownership of a file needs to be changed, perhaps because of a change in team membership or a set of new responsibilities for a user.

Task-based model   This model is appropriate for companies in which administrative duties are functionally divided. This means that this model divides the management of Group Policy Objects (GPOs) by certain tasks. To apply this model, the administrators that handle security-related tasks will also be responsible for managing all policy objects that affect security. The second set of administrators that normally deploy the companies' business applications will be responsible for all the GPOs that affect installation and maintenance.

TCP/IP   *See* Transmission Control Protocol/Internet Protocol.

Terminal Services   In application server mode, Terminal Services provides the ability to run client applications on the server, while "thin client" software acts as a terminal emulator on the client. Each user sees an individual session, displayed as a Windows 2000 desktop. The server manages each session, independent of any other client session. If you install Terminal Services as an application server, you must also install Terminal Services Licensing (not necessarily on the same computer). However, temporary licenses can be issued for clients that allow you to use Terminal servers for up to 90 days. In remote administration mode, you can use Terminal Services to log on remotely and manage Windows 2000 systems from virtually anywhere on your network (instead of being limited to working locally on a server). Remote administration mode allows for two concurrent connections from a given server and minimizes impact on server performance. Remote administration mode does not require you to install Terminal Services Licensing.

TFTP   *See* Trivial File Transfer Protocol.

Token Ring   A Local Area Network (LAN) specification that was developed by IBM in the 1980s for PC-based networks and classified by the (Institute of Electrical and Electronics Engineers) IEEE as 802.5. It specifies a star topology physically and a ring topology logically. It runs at either 4Mbps or 16Mbps, but all nodes on the ring must run at the same speed.

Transmission Control Protocol/Internet Protocol (TCP/IP)   A set of communications standards created by the U.S. Department of Defense (DoD) in the 1970s that has now become an accepted way to connect different types of computers in networks because the standards now support so many programs.

Trees   Trees are hierarchical groups of domains that share a contiguous namespace. This hierarchy allows global sharing of resources among domains in the tree. All the domains in a tree share information and resources with a single directory, and there is only one directory per tree. However, each domain manages its own subset of the directory that contains the user accounts for that domain. So, when a user logs into a domain, the user has global access to all resources that are part of the tree, providing the user has the proper permissions.

Trivial File Transfer Protocol (TFTP)   A simplified of the File Transfer Protocol (FTP), associated with the Transmission Control Protocol/Internet Protocol (TCP/IP) family, that does not provide password protection or a user directory.

Trust   The users in one tree do not have global access to resources in other trees, but trusts can be created that allow users to access resources in another tree. A trust allows all the trees to share resources and have common administrative functions. Such sharing capability allows the trees to operate independently of each other, with separate namespaces, yet still be able to communicate and share resources through trusts.

Trust relationship   A trust relationship is a connection between domains in which users who have accounts in and log on to one domain can then access resources in other domains, provided they have proper access permissions.

UDF   *See* Unique Database File.

UDP   *See* User Datagram Protocol.

Unattended method   The unattended method for Windows 2000 Server installation uses the answer file to specify various configuration parameters. This method eliminates user interaction during installation, thereby automating the installation process and reducing the chances of input errors. Answers to most of the questions asked by the setup process are specified in the answer file. In addition, the scripted method can be used for clean installations and upgrades.

UNATTEND.TXT file   The creation of customized UNATTEND.TXT answer files is the simplest form of providing answers to setup queries and unattended installation of Windows 2000. This can either be done using the Setup Manager or by editing the sample UNATTEND.TXT file using Notepad or the MS-DOS text editor. The UNATTEND.TXT file does not provide any means of creating an image of the computer.

UNATTEND.UDF   This file is the Uniqueness Database File, which provides customized settings for each computer using the automated installation.

UNC   *See* Universal Naming Convention.

UNICODE   UNICODE is a 16-bit character encoding standard developed by the Unicode Consortium between 1988 and 1991 that uses two bytes to represent each character and enables almost all of the written languages of the world to be represented using a single character set.

Uninterruptible Power Supply (UPS)   A battery that can supply power to a computer system if the power fails. It charges while the computer is on and, if the power fails, provides power for a certain amount of time allowing the user to shut down the computer properly to preserve data.

Unique Database File (UDF)   When you use the WINNT32.EXE command with the /unattend option, you can also specify a Unique Database File (UDF), which has a .udb extension. This file forces Setup to use certain values from the UDF file, thus overriding the values given in the answer file. This is particularly useful when you want to specify multiple users during the setup.

Universal Groups   Universal Groups are used in larger, multidomain organizations, in which there is a need to grant access to similar groups of accounts defined in multiple domains. It is better to use Global Groups as members of Universal Groups to reduce overall replication traffic from changes to Universal Group membership. Users can be added and removed from the corresponding Global Groups with their account domains, and a small number of Global Groups are the direct members of the Universal Group. Universal Groups are used only in multiple domain trees or forests. A Windows 2000 domain must be in native mode to use Universal Groups.

Universal Naming Convention (UNC)   A UNC is an identification standard of servers and other network resources.

Universal Serial Bus (USB)   A low-speed hardware interface (supports MPEG video) with a maximum bandwidth up to 1.5MB per second.

UPS   *See* Uninterruptible Power Supply.

USB *See* Universal Serial Bus.

User account The information that defines a particular user on a network, which includes the username, password, group memberships, and rights and permissions assigned to the user.

User Datagram Protocol (UDP) A Transmission Control Protocol/Internet Protocol (TCP/IP) normally bundled with an Internet Protocol (IP) layer software that describes how messages received reached application programs within the destination computer.

Value bar The value bar is positioned below the graph area. It displays data for the selected sample, the last sample value, the average of the counter samples, the maximum and minimum of the samples, and the duration of time the samples have been taken over.

Virtual Private Networking (VPN) VPNs reduce service costs and long distance/usage fees, lighten infrastructure investments, and simplify Wide Area Network (WAN) operations over time. To determine just how cost-effective a VPN solution could be in connecting remote offices, use the VPN Calculator located on Cisco's Web site at www.cisco.com.

Volume set The term "volume" indicates a single drive letter. One physical hard disk can contain several volumes, one for each primary partition or logical drive. However, the opposite is also true. You can create a single volume that spans more than one physical disk. This is a good option when you require a volume that exceeds the capacity of a single physical disk. You can also create a volume set when you want to make use of leftover space on several disks by piecing them together as one volume.

VPN *See* Virtual Private Networking.

WDM *See* Windows32 Drive Model.

Windows 3x   Windows 3 changed everything. It was a 16-bit operating system with a user interface that resembled the look and feel of IBM's (at that time not yet released) OS/2, with 3D buttons and the ability to run multiple programs simultaneously, using a method called cooperative multitasking. Windows 3 also provided virtual memory, the ability to use hard disk space to "fool" the applications into behaving as if they had more RAM than was physically installed in the machine.

Windows 9x   In August of 1995, Microsoft released its long-awaited upgrade of Windows, Windows 95. For the first time, Windows could be installed on a machine that didn't already have MS-DOS installed. Many improvements were made: the new 32-bit functionality (although still retaining some 16-bit code for backward compatibility); preemptive multitasking (a more efficient way to run multiple programs in which the operating system controls use of the processor and the crash of one application does not bring down the others that are currently running); and support for filenames longer than the DOS-based eight-character limit.

Windows 2000   Microsoft's latest incarnation of the corporate operating system was originally called NT 5, but the name was changed to Windows 2000 between the second and third beta versions—perhaps to underscore the fact that this is truly a *new* version of the operating system, not merely an upgrade to NT.

Windows 2000 Control Panel   The Control Panel in Windows 2000 functions similarly to the Control Panel in Windows 9x and NT, except that "under the hood" there are now two locations that information is stored, which is modified by the Control Panel applets. The Control Panel in previous operating systems was a graphical interface for editing Registry information.

Windows Backup   Windows Backup is a built-in Backup and Restore utility, which has many more features than the backup tool provided in Windows NT 4.0. It supports all five types of backup: Normal, Copy, Differential, Incremental, and Daily. Windows Backup allows you to perform the backup operation manually, or you may schedule it to run at a later time in unattended mode. Included with the operating system, it is a tool that is flexible and easy to use.

Windows Internet Name Service (WINS) WINS provides name resolution for clients running Windows NT and earlier versions of Microsoft operating systems. With name resolution, users can access servers by name, instead of having to use Internet Protocol (IP) addresses that are difficult to recognize and remember. WINS is used to map NetBIOS computer names to IP addresses. This allows users to access other computers on the network by computer name. WINS servers should be assigned a static IP address, which allows clients to be able to find the WINS servers. Clients cannot find a WINS server by name because they need to know where the WINS server is in order to translate the name into an IP address.

Windows Internet Name Service (WINS) Name Registration Each WINS client has one or more WINS servers identified in the network configuration on the computer, either through static assignment or through DHCP configuration. When the client boots and connects to the network, it registers its name and IP address with the WINS server by sending a registration request directly to the server. This is not a broadcast message, since the client has the address of the server. If the server is available and the name is not already registered, the server responds with a successful registration message, which contains the amount of time the name will be registered to the client, the Time To Live (TTL). Then the server stores the name and address combination in its local database.

Windows Internet Name Service (WINS) Name Release When a WINS client shuts down properly, it will send a name release request to the WINS server. This releases the name from the WINS server's database so that another client can use the name if necessary. The release request contains the WINS name and address of the client. If the server cannot find the name, it sends a negative release response to the client. If the server finds the matching name and address in its database, it releases the name and marks the record as inactive. If the name is found but the address does not match, the server ignores the request.

Windows Internet Name Service (WINS) Name Renewal As with Dynamic Host Control Protocol (DHCP), WINS name registrations are temporary and must be renewed to continue to be valid. The client will attempt to renew its registration when half (50 percent) of the Time To Live (TTL) has elapsed. If the WINS server does not respond, the client repeatedly attempts to renew its lease at ten-minute intervals for an hour. If the client still receives no response, it restarts the process with the secondary WINS server, if one is defined. The client will continue attempting to renew its lease in this manner until it receives a response from a server. At that time, the server sends a new TTL to the client, and the process starts over.

Windows Internet Name Service (WINS) Proxy agent   A WINS Proxy agent is similar to a Dynamic Host Control Protocol (DHCP) Relay Agent. It listens for requests for non-WINS network clients and redirects those requests to a WINS server. A WINS proxy operates in two modes.

Windows Internet Name Service (WINS) Snap-in   With the snap-in, you can view the active WINS entries under the Active Registrations folder. In addition, you can supply static mappings for non-WINS clients on the network through the snap-in. To configure a static mapping, select the Active Registrations folder and the select New Static Mapping from the Action menu. Once a static mapping is entered into the WINS database, it cannot be edited. If you need to make changes to a static mapping, you must be delete and recreate the entry.

Windows NT   The NT kernel (the core or nucleus of the operating system, which provides basic services for all other parts of the operating system) is built on a completely different architecture from consumer Windows. In fact, NT was based on the 32-bit preemptive multitasking operating system that originated as a joint project of Microsoft and IBM before their parting of the ways, OS/2. NT provided the stability and security features that the "other Windows" lacked, albeit at a price, and not only a monetary one; NT was much pickier in terms of hardware support, did not run all of the programs that ran on Windows 9x (especially DOS programs that accessed the hardware directly), and required more resources, especially memory, to run properly.

Windows32 Driver Model (WDM)   The Win32 Driver Model (WDM) provides a standard for device drivers that will work across Windows platforms (specifically Windows 98 and 2000), so that you can use the same drivers with the consumer and business versions of the Windows operating system.

WINNT.EXE program   The WINNT.EXE program is used for network installations that use an MS-DOS network client. The WINNT32.EXE program is used to customize the process for upgrading existing installations. The WINNT32.EXE program is used for installing Windows 2000 from a computer that is currently running Windows 95/98 or Windows NT.

WINS *See* Windows Internet Name Service.

Workgroup A workgroup is a logical grouping of resources on a network. It is generally used in peer-to-peer networks. This means that each computer is responsible for access to its resources. Each computer has its own account database and is administered separately. Security is not shared between computers, and administration is more difficult than in a centralized domain.

Zones of authority The Domain Name System (DNS) name space is divided into zones, and each zone must have one name server that is the authority for the name mapping for the zone. Depending on the size of the name space, a zone may be subdivided into multiple zones, each with its own authority, or there may be a single authority for the entire zone. For instance, a small company with only 200–300 computers could have one DNS server handle the entire namespace.

INDEX

B

T

U

Z

Custom Corporate Network Training

Train on Cutting Edge Technology   We can bring the best in skill-based training to your facility to create a real-world hands-on training experience. Global Knowledge has invested millions of dollars in network hardware and software to train our students on the same equipment they will work with on the job. Our relationships with vendors allow us to incorporate the latest equipment and platforms into your on-site labs.

Maximize Your Training Budget   Global Knowledge provides experienced instructors, comprehensive course materials, and all the networking equipment needed to deliver high quality training. You provide the students; we provide the knowledge.

Avoid Travel Expenses   On-site courses allow you to schedule technical training at your convenience, saving time, expense, and the opportunity cost of travel away from the workplace.

Discuss Confidential Topics   Private on-site training permits the open discussion of sensitive issues such as security, access, and network design. We can work with your existing network's proprietary files while demonstrating the latest technologies.

Customize Course Content   Global Knowledge can tailor your courses to include the technologies and the topics which have the greatest impact on your business. We can complement your internal training efforts or provide a total solution to your training needs.

Corporate Pass   The Corporate Pass Discount Program rewards our best network training customers with preferred pricing on public courses, discounts on multimedia training packages, and an array of career planning services.

Global Knowledge Training Lifecycle   Supporting the Dynamic and Specialized Training Requirements of Information Technology Professionals

- Define Profile
- Assess Skills
- Design Training

- Deliver Training
- Test Knowledge

- Update Profile
- Use New Skills

College Credit Recommendation Program   The American Council on Education's CREDIT program recommends 53 Global Knowledge courses for college credit. Now our network training can help you earn your college degree while you learn the technical skills needed for your job. When you attend an ACE-certified Global Knowledge course and pass the associated exam, you earn college credit recommendations for that course. Global Knowledge can establish a transcript record for you with ACE, which you can use to gain credit at a college or as a written record of your professional training that you can attach to your resume.

Registration Information

COURSE FEE: The fee covers course tuition, refreshments, and all course materials. Any parking expenses that may be incurred are not included. Payment or government training form must be received six business days prior to the course date. We will also accept Visa/MasterCard and American Express. For non-U.S. credit card users, charges will be in U.S. funds and will be converted by your credit card company. Checks drawn on Canadian banks in Canadian funds are acceptable.

COURSE SCHEDULE: Registration is at 8:00 a.m. on the first day. The program begins at 8:30 a.m. and concludes at 4:30 p.m. each day.

CANCELLATION POLICY: Cancellation and full refund will be allowed if written cancellation is received in our office at least six business days prior to the course start date. Registrants who do not attend the course or do not cancel more than six business days in advance are responsible for the full registration fee; you may transfer to a later date provided the course fee has been paid in full. Substitutions may be made at any time. If Global Knowledge must cancel a course for any reason, liability is limited to the registration fee only.

GLOBAL KNOWLEDGE: Global Knowledge programs are developed and presented by industry professionals with "real-world" experience. Designed to help professionals meet today's interconnectivity and interoperability challenges, most of our programs feature hands-on labs that incorporate state-of-the-art communication components and equipment.

ON-SITE TEAM TRAINING: Bring Global Knowledge's powerful training programs to your company. At Global Knowledge, we will custom design courses to meet your specific network requirements. Call 1 (919) 461-8686 for more information.

YOUR GUARANTEE: Global Knowledge believes its courses offer the best possible training in this field. If during the first day you are not satisfied and wish to withdraw from the course, simply notify the instructor, return all course materials, and receive a 100% refund.

REGISTRATION INFORMATION:

Course title _____

Course location _____ Course date _____

Name/title _____ Company _____

Name/title _____ Company _____

Name/title _____ Company _____

Address _____ Telephone _____ Fax _____

City _____ State/Province _____ Zip/Postal Code _____

Credit card _____ Card # _____ Expiration date _____

Signature _____

In the US:

CALL: 1 (888) 762-4442

FAX: 1 (919) 469-7070

VISIT OUR WEBSITE:

www.globalknowledge.com

MAIL CHECK AND THIS FORM TO:

Global Knowledge

Suite 200

114 Edinburgh South

P.O. Box 1187

Cary, NC 27512

In Canada:

CALL: 1 (800) 465-2226

FAX: 1 (613) 567-3899

VISIT OUR WEBSITE:

www.globalknowledge.com.ca

MAIL CHECK AND THIS FORM TO:

Global Knowledge

Suite 1601

393 University Ave.

Toronto, ON M5G 1E6